JOURNAL OF THE NORTH-CHINA BRANCH OF THE ROYAL ASIATIC SOCIETY

皇家亚洲文会北华支会会刊

（1858—1948）

导论·索引·附录

上海图书馆 编

上海科学技术文献出版社

图书在版编目（CIP）数据

皇家亚洲文会北华支会会刊（1858-1948）：导论·索引·附录／上海图书馆编．—上海：上海科学技术文献出版社，2013.5
ISBN 978-7-5439-5808-1

Ⅰ．①皇… Ⅱ．①上… Ⅲ．①中国学—期刊—汇编—中国—近代 Ⅳ．①K207.8-55

中国版本图书馆 CIP 数据核字（2013）第 072006 号

责任编辑：邹西礼　倪文君　张靖伟
封面设计：何　旸

皇家亚洲文会北华支会会刊（1858-1948）：导论·索引·附录
上海图书馆　编
出版发行：上海科学技术文献出版社
地　　址：上海市长乐路746号
邮政编码：200040
经　　销：全国新华书店
印　　刷：常熟市人民印刷厂
开　　本：889×1194　1/16
印　　张：33
字　　数：802 000
版　　次：2013年5月第1版　2013年5月第1次印刷
书　　号：ISBN 978-7-5439-5808-1
定　　价：480.00元
http://www.sstlp.com

《徐家汇藏书楼西文文献丛刊》编委会

主　任　吴建中

委　员　周德明　黄显功　吴建明　王仁芳　赵　炬　邹西礼

《皇家亚洲文会北华支会会刊》编委会

主　编　吴建中　周德明

顾　问　周振鹤　熊月之

编　委　黄显功　王仁芳　王　毅

整　理（以姓氏笔画为序）

　　　　王仁芳　王　毅　包　中　单　雪　徐锦华

序

熊月之

中国与欧洲，虽然文明历史都很悠久，但相隔遥远，13世纪以前，交通不便，联系不多，了解不深。13世纪末14世纪初，意大利人马可·波罗的游记问世，书中对于中国种种奇妙的描述，诸如美丽繁华的城市、花香扑鼻的果园、华美廉价的丝绸、笔墨难摹的珍宝、发达的工商、辉煌的宫殿，空前拓展了欧洲人的心灵空间，激起了欧洲人对中国无限的遐思妙想。马可·波罗其人是否到过中国，学术界尚有争议，但其游记的广泛影响则毋庸置疑。15世纪末到16世纪上半叶，地理大发现与东西方航线开辟，东西两半球被联系在一起。此后，西人络绎东来，从利玛窦、汤若望到马礼逊、郭实腊，传教、殖民、经商，对于东方的了解与研究也逐步开展。各种关于中国的游记、通信、字典、译作与论著陆续出版，亚洲学会等机构也在巴黎、伦敦等处成立，并出版了《亚洲学刊》等专门性刊物，对中国的了解逐渐从传闻、游记发展为对历史、地理、语言文字、风俗民情的研究。鸦片战争以后，中国开放广州、厦门、福州、宁波与上海作为通商口岸，日后又陆续开放沿海、沿江、沿边几十处口岸，西方人得以进入中国沿海、沿江及广阔内地，在这些地方居住、经商、行医、办学、传教，与众多中国人有直接的接触，对中国社会有更为广泛与深入的了解。

随着来华欧美人数的日益增多，对中国研究兴趣的日趋浓厚，在华欧美人成立了专门性研究机构，出版了专门性刊物。亚洲文会及其会刊，就是其中最为著名的一种。

亚洲文会全称是"皇家亚洲文会北华支会"，前身为"上海文理学会"，1857年9月26日在上海成立，会长为裨治文，成员有艾约瑟、雒魏林、汉璧礼等人，以调查、研究中国及其周围国家现状与历史为宗旨。1859年，上海文理学会加入大不列颠及爱尔兰皇家亚细亚学会，改名"皇家亚洲文会北华支会"，简称亚洲文会。文会会所设在上海英租界下圆明园路，1872年建成，为上下两层楼房，设有图书馆、演讲厅等。1928年，会所因过于破败而拆除。1933年，新会所在原址落成，六层楼房，设有演讲厅、图书馆、生物标本陈列室、文物古董陈列室、美术片陈列室等。

亚洲文会之所以在上海成立，因为其时上海为来华欧美人集聚的中心地。据统计，1859年，上海有外侨408名，广州有127名，厦门有45名，福州有57名，宁波有49名，上海外侨人数远远超过其他四个通商口岸外侨人数总和。以后，上海租界不断扩大，外侨人数不断增多（最多时超过15万），上海对外侨的吸引力、影响力也远远超过其他通商口岸。之所以名为"北华支会",盖其时欧美人以香港为在华活动中心地,视香港以北之中国皆为北华。英人在上海所办的一份很有名的报纸,即名为"北华捷报"。此外,还在1847年,驻留香港的英国人组建中国亚洲学会,同年加入大不列颠及爱尔兰皇家亚细亚学会,名为"皇家亚洲学会中国支会",后此成立的上海同类组织,也就不可能使用"中国支会"的名称了。

亚洲文会历时首尾95年。其间,1861年至1863年,因会长裨治文生病,一些骨干成员离开上海,文会活动停止。1941年至1945年,因日军占领上海,英美等国侨民或离开上海,或被日军关进集中营,文会活动也被迫停止。1949年前夕,文会将一部分图书、文物运出中国,1952年5月19日正式关闭。扣除停止活动的年份,亚洲文会实际活动87年。

亚洲文会会员分名誉会员、终生会员、通讯会员与普通会员四种,不同时期会员人数多少不等,历年累计会员有3000多名,来自世界各国,分布在中国各地。身份可考者1000多人,内以英国籍最多,近500人,占会员总数将近一半;其次为美国籍,100多人;其余德国、法国、俄国、日本、加拿大、瑞典、瑞士、比利时等国,多者六七十人,少者三五人。会员身份形形色色,有传教士、外交官、海关职员、大学教授、商人、报人、法官、律师与学者。中国也有一些学者参与其中,确切可考者61人,如江亢虎、胡适、蔡元培等,多为有西学背景者。历任会长有30多人,多为外侨中著名人士,包括外国驻沪领事、海关人员、传教士与知名学者。

亚洲文会的活动,主要有:设立图书馆、博物院,举办例会与年会,举行演讲,出版会报,出版书籍,开展对于中国国情的调查,包括黄河新河道、各地溺婴陋俗、孝的内涵、企业合伙、农村土地使用情况、各省度量衡、内地交通、中国地质、气象、水文、矿藏、动植物、货币等诸多方面。

发行《会刊》是亚洲文会中心工作之一。第1期会刊于1858年6月出版,最后一卷出版于1948年,每年一卷,有时是两年一卷,总共出版75卷。《会刊》先后由上海北华捷报馆、望益纸馆、高福洋行等处印刷,由别发洋行销售,定价不同时期高低不一,少者一元,多者六七元。《会刊》主要是向会员免费赠送,也向社会发行,发行量多的时候有千份左右。

《会刊》内容在不同时期有不同侧重面,栏目有文章、书评、调查报告、问题释疑、亚洲文会年度报告、会议记录、读者来信等,内有一半以上的内容在文会演讲过。19世纪《会刊》内容绝大多数来自演讲,20世纪初年以后,因会员增多,文会影响扩大,《会刊》外来稿件增多,使用演讲以外稿件的比例大为增加。中国学者王国维、胡适、伍连德、竺可桢等均有文章刊载其中。

《会刊》总共发表633篇文章,791篇书评,17篇调查报告,34篇汉学文摘,163则问题释疑。所载文章,历史学、地学、生物学、文学方面数量较多。其中,不少成果有较高学术价值,比如:德国穆林德的《直隶的脊椎动物及中国动物命名法》,被当时中国科学界誉为"虽非巨著,要为名作"。俄国贝勒的《先辈欧人对中国植物的研究》,获近代欧洲汉学最高奖"儒莲奖",被学术界认为是"遥遥领先于同时代同类的研究,并且被公认为后来研究的奠基石"。德国佛尔克的《王充与柏拉图论死亡与永生》,开启了将王充与柏拉图哲学比较的先河。德国费理饬的《东亚气候》、英国苏阿德的《中国博物学》、英国海德生的《长江三角洲的成长》、俄国钢和泰的《玄奘及其现代研究》、德国夏德的《古代陶瓷:中世纪中国工商业研究》,均为近代中国同类研究的先导性成果。《会刊》所载一些文章因为有特别的价值,发表后曾以单行本另行出版,如贝勒的《中亚与西亚中古时代之史地考》(1876)、《先辈欧人对中国植物的研究》(1881)、《中国植物志》(1891),慕阿德的《中国乐器及其他发声器之目录》(1908),福开森的《中国历代瓷器》(1932)等。20世纪20年代,欧美人士曾评出40种对于"理解和认识中国最有帮助的英文书籍",其中就有《会刊》在内。

历史进入21世纪以后,随着中国国际地位的提升,重估中国文化价值成为国际上一个引人注目的议题,汉学研究已经成为国际学术界一大重要领域,历史上的汉学研究成果也更加受到人们的关注与重视。亚洲文会是以近代在华外国侨民为主体的著名汉学研究机构,在近一个世纪的历程中,对于中国的自然、历史、文化与社会等方面,都做出了相当丰富的很有价值的研究,影响广泛。作为反映亚洲文会研究成果重要部分的《会刊》,现在存世已经十分稀少,查阅不易,上海图书馆将其影印出版,供学术界研究使用,很有必要。

对于亚洲文会与《会刊》内容,学术界已有很好的研究。本书附录所收王毅博士的论著《皇家亚洲文会北华支会研究》,对学会与《会刊》作了相当细致的研究,对《会刊》的文章有具体的梳理,附有学会演讲题目与会员名录,很有参考价值。本序言的素材、数据均来自该书。读者在查阅《会刊》时,不妨同时参考王毅的著作,作为渡河津梁,一定会收到事半功倍之效。

2012年10月30日

整 理 说 明

《皇家亚洲文会北华支会会刊》(以下简称《会刊》)是近代外侨在上海创办的一份汉学期刊。该刊自1858年出版第一期，至1948年停刊，历时近百年，共出版75卷[1]。本书系对该刊的全文影印。全书共35册，第一册为导论索引卷，其余34册为原刊之影印。本次整理使用的底本均为上海图书馆徐家汇藏书楼所藏《会刊》，其中大部分为初刊本，少数为重印本。[2]

本书导论由中原工学院王毅副教授撰写，该文对《会刊》的出版概况、编纂者和编纂宗旨、具体内容以及资料价值等进行了完整详尽的梳理，读者可据此获悉《会刊》的基本情况。当然，如果想要更深入地了解《会刊》及其发行机构皇家亚洲文会北华支会，导论的介绍可能尚嫌简略。王毅曾于2005年出版其专著《皇家亚洲文会北中国支会研究》，该书利用了大量的中外文献、档案和相关的汉学期刊，通过对资料的分析与梳理，系统地介绍了该机构的来龙去脉，论述了其组织机构的沿革、作用及其日常活动，分析了文会会员在中国进行的调查活动及其在中西文化交流过程中的地位与作用，并附有相关文献整理资料，是目前唯一可见的一部研究亚洲文会的学术专著。此次影印出版《会刊》，特将该书作为附录收入本书第一册中[3]，以供读者参阅。

此外，为便读者查阅和检索，我们还制作了详细的分卷目录以及索引。以下就目录和索引的编制方式作以说明：

分卷细目详列各卷文章篇目及主要栏目，共分5栏，分别为题名、中译题名、责任者、责任者中文名以及页码。其中题名为原刊题名，若原刊目录题名与正文题名不同，以正文为准；中译题名系整理者所译；责任者指该篇文章的责任人，或为著者，或为译者，或为编者；责任者中文名系整理者查阅各类工具书和相关文献后所得，有若干中文名者则选取其中一种，查阅不到中文名者，则付之阙如；页码由两部分组成，连接符号前指册数，后为页码，如2-20，即指第二册第20页。为简洁起见，题名中的 North-China Branch of the Royal Asiatic Society 一律缩写为 NCBRAS，JNCBRAS 则指 Journal of the North-China Branch of the Royal Asiatic Society，即《会刊》。此外，分卷目录中不再详列各栏目的子目，而仅列出栏目总名，如"新书评

---

[1] 其中两卷为老刊(Old Series，简称 O. S.)，即 1858－1860 年间发行的两卷四期《会刊》；73 卷为新刊(New Series，简称 N. S.)，即1864年复刊后发行的全部《会刊》。

[2] 由于会刊在重印时或会加入一些重印当时的内容，因此偶有较早年份的会刊附有较晚年份会员名录等附件的现象出现。

[3] 在将该书收入本书之前，王毅已对其做了全面的修订。

介"、"释疑"、"年会纪要"、"年度报告"等,至于相关细目,有兴趣的读者可在索引中进行检索。

索引分为两部分,第一部分为篇目索引,第二部分为作者索引。

篇目索引由论文、书评、释疑、杂记和札记、讣告和悼文、大事记、会务七部分组成。

论文部分由原刊的主体部分,即不列于任何栏目下的研究文章、调查报告等组成。

书评部分除收录原刊"新书评介"栏目中所有书评外,也将原列于论文或其他栏目下的书评一并纳入。

"释疑"部分为原刊"Notes and Queries"栏目下的所有内容。

杂记和札记部分则收录了原刊"Miscellaneous"、"Items"、"Literary"、"Sinological Notes"等栏目中除书评以外的内容。[1]

讣告和悼文部分收有原刊所载之汉学家及文会重要会员的讣告或悼文。

"大事记"为《会刊》早期所设专栏,虽然10卷之后便再无此栏目,但因其内容较为独立,故仍单列为一个部分。

"会务"部分则较为复杂。作为一份由公共文化机构出版发行的刊物,会务纪要构成了该刊一个相当重要的组成部分,因此,整理者据原刊相关内容整理出了9个子目,分别为"年报"、"年会纪要"、"会议纪要"、"会员名录"、"规章"、"演说和致辞"、"图书目录"、"其他重要目录"以及"通信"。"会务"部分出现的专称,若不特别说明,均指文会下设机构,如图书馆即文会图书馆,博物院即文会博物院等等。

由于各栏目性质不同,在编排索引时,论文、书评、释疑、杂记和札记、讣告和悼文这5个部分分别按照题名字顺排序[2],大事记及会务则按照时间顺序排序。

与分卷细目不同,篇目索引中并未列出责任者中文名一栏,因索引第二部分即为"作者索引",读者可以方便地通过该索引查阅到会刊所有文章责任者的中文名及其作品在本书中的对应页码。

最后需要说明的是,《会刊》文章的作者绝大多数为近代西方人士,其立场观点往往带有历史的或地域的局限,尤其在涉及中国的历史、外交、疆域、民族和宗教时,某些措辞或提法或有不当、片面之处。尽管如此,出于完整呈现历史文献原貌的考虑,此次整理仍对《会刊》进行了全文影印,请读者在阅读利用时对上述问题予以注意并研判是非。

---

[1] "释疑"和"杂记和札记"中,原刊栏目下有小标题者,按小标题分列;无小标题者,则仍仅列栏目名称。

[2] 在编制索引的过程中,为使排序更加清晰准确,整理者对篇目题名进行了统一规范,即将题名起始部分不作为排列依据的前置词移到了题尾。

目 录

第一册

序 …………………………………………………………………………………… 1
整理说明 …………………………………………………………………………… 1
导论 ………………………………………………………………………………… 1
分卷细目 …………………………………………………………………………… 23
索引 ………………………………………………………………………………… 75
　篇目索引 ………………………………………………………………………… 77
　作者索引 ………………………………………………………………………… 177
附录：亚洲文会北华支会研究（王毅）………………………………………… 195

第二册

O. S. VOL. I No. I(1858) …………………………………………………………… 1
O. S. VOL. I No. II(1859) ………………………………………………………… 157
O. S. VOL. I No. III(1859) ………………………………………………………… 291
O. S. VOL. II No. I(1860) ………………………………………………………… 399

第三册

N. S. VOL. I(1864) ………………………………………………………………… 1
N. S. VOL. II(1865) ………………………………………………………………… 215
N. S. VOL. III(1866) ……………………………………………………………… 431

第四册

N. S. VOL. IV(1867) ……………………………………………………………… 1
N. S. VOL. V(1868) ……………………………………………………………… 273

第五册

N. S. VOL. VI(1869－1870) ……………………………………………………… 1

N. S. VOL. VII(1871－1872) ··· 225

第六册

N. S. VOL. VIII(1873) ·· 1
N. S. VOL. IX(1874) ·· 207

第七册

N. S. VOL. X(1875) ·· 1

第八册

N. S. VOL. XI(1876) ·· 1
N. S. VOL. XII(1877) ··· 207

第九册

N. S. VOL. XIII(1878) ··· 1
N. S. VOL. XIV(1879) ··· 179
N. S. VOL. XV(1880) ·· 265

第十册

N. S. VOL. XVI(1881) ··· 1
N. S. VOL. XVII(1882) ·· 305

第十一册

N. S. VOL. XVIII(1883) ··· 1
N. S. VOL. XIX(1884) ··· 243
N. S. VOL. XX(1885) ·· 439

第十二册

N. S. VOL. XXI(1886) ··· 1
N. S. VOL. XXII(1887) ·· 379

第十三册

N. S. VOL. XXIII(1888) ··· 1
N. S. VOL. XXIV(1889－1890) ·· 349

第十四册

N. S. VOL. XXV(1890－1891) ··· 1

第十五册

    N. S. VOL. XXVI(1891－1892) ·· 1

第十六册

    N. S. VOL. XXVII(1892－1893) ·· 1
    N. S. VOL. XXVIII(1893－1894) ··· 291

第十七册

    N. S. VOL. XXIX（1894－1895） ··· 1

第十八册

    N. S. VOL. XXX(1895－1896)·· 1
    N. S. VOL. XXXI(1896－1897) ·· 291
    N. S. VOL. XXXII(1897－1898) ·· 521

第十九册

    N. S. VOL. XXXIII(1899－1900) ··· 1
    N. S. VOL. XXXIV(1901－1902) ·· 381
    N. S. VOL. XXXV(1903－1904) ··· 531

第二十册

    N. S. VOL. XXXVI(1905) ··· 1
    N. S. VOL. XXXVII(1906) ··· 183
    N. S. VOL. XXXVIII(1907) ··· 435

第二十一册

    N. S. VOL. XXXIX(1908) ··· 1
    N. S. VOL. XL(1909) ·· 253
    N. S. VOL. XLI(1910) ·· 439

第二十二册

    N. S. VOL. XLII(1911) ··· 1
    N. S. VOL. XLIII(1912) ·· 289

第二十三册

    N. S. VOL. XLIV(1913) ··· 1
    N. S. VOL. XLV(1914) ·· 277
    N. S. VOL. XLVI(1915) ·· 517

第二十四册
- N. S. VOL. XLVII(1916) ············ 1
- N. S. VOL. XLVIII(1917) ············ 213

第二十五册
- N. S. VOL. XLIX(1918) ············ 1
- N. S. VOL. L (1919) ············ 243

第二十六册
- N. S. VOL. LI(1920) ············ 1
- N. S. VOL. LII(1921) ············ 247

第二十七册
- N. S. VOL. LIII(1922) ············ 1
- N. S. VOL. LIV(1923) ············ 339

第二十八册
- N. S. VOL. LV(1924) ············ 1
- N. S. VOL. LVI(1925) ············ 385

第二十九册
- N. S. VOL. LVII(1926) ············ 1
- N. S. VOL. LVIII(1927) ············ 275

第三十册
- N. S. VOL. LIX(1928) ············ 1

第三十一册
- N. S. VOL. LX(1929) ············ 1
- N. S. VOL. LXI(1930) ············ 199

第三十二册
- N. S. VOL. LXII(1931) ············ 1
- N. S. VOL. LXIII(1932) ············ 269

第三十三册
- N. S. VOL. LXIV(1933) ············ 1
- N. S. VOL. LXV(1934) ············ 237
- N. S. VOL. LXVI(1935) ············ 517

第三十四册
- N. S. VOL. LXVII(1936) ··· 1
- N. S. VOL. LXVIII(1937) ·· 295
- N. S. VOL. LXIX(1938) ·· 429

第三十五册
- N. S. VOL. LXX(1939) ·· 1
- N. S. VOL. LXXI(1940) ·· 167
- N. S. VOL. LXXII(1946) ·· 351
- N. S. VOL. LXXIII(1948) ·· 471

导　论

王　毅

1857年9月24日,在上海的英美外侨裨治文(E. C. Bridgman)、艾约瑟(J. Edkins)、卫三畏(S. W. Williams)、汉璧礼(Hanbury)、立德(Reid)等18人聚集到一起,讨论研究认识中国的重要性。经商议,决定成立一个学会,命名为"上海文理学会"(Shanghai Literary and Scientific Society),以调查中华帝国及其周围国家。同年10月17日,在该会成立大会上,首任会长裨治文提出要创办一份期刊,以发表成员将来的研究成果。[1] 1858年6月该会会刊——《上海文理学会会刊》(Journal of the Shanghai Literary and Scientific Society)诞生。

1858年9月21日,"上海文理学会"加盟"大不列颠及爱尔兰皇家亚洲文会"(Royal Asiatic Society of Great Britain and Ireland),成为其支会,并更名为"皇家亚洲文会北华支会"(The North-China Branch of The Royal Asiatic Society),简称"亚洲文会"(R. A. S.)[2],随后会刊亦更名为《皇家亚洲文会北华支会会刊》(Journal of The North-China Branch of The Royal Asiatic Society,缩略语为"JNCBRAS")。该刊发行至1948年,成为近代中国境内发行时间最长的西文期刊。[3] 在其重印之际,现就该刊之历史、内容及其资料价值作一介绍。

出版概况

一、会刊的出版历程

《皇家亚洲文会北华支会会刊》之出版历程颇为曲折,可谓"两次易名、三度中断",这主要是由会刊之母体——亚洲文会——的发展历程造成的。

所谓"两次易名",指的是会刊之名的变化。

首次易名:从《上海文理学会会刊》到《皇家亚洲文会北华支会会刊》。

上文已述,1858年"上海文理学会"加盟"大不列颠及爱尔兰皇家亚洲文会"后,学会及其会刊随之易名。1859年5月,该会出版的第2号会刊即以《皇家亚洲文会北华支会会刊》为名,并在前言中说明了更名的缘由:"上海文理学会的命名是暂时的。现在加入了英国皇家学会,关系变了,所以会刊的名字也要变成'皇家亚洲文会北华支会会刊'"[4]。

从《上海文理学会会刊》到《皇家亚洲学会北华支会会刊》,尽管会刊名字变了,但前后的继

---

[1] Bridgman, Rev. E. C. D. D., Inaugural Address, JNCBRAS, O. S. No. I, June, 1858, P13.
[2] 关于亚洲文会之历史,参见本书附录《皇家亚洲文会北华支会研究》。
[3] 根据1959年出版的《全国西文期刊联合目录》,该刊是近代中国境内出版时间最长的西文期刊。
[4] Preface, JNCBRAS, O. S. No. II. May, 1859.

承关系未变。1859年5月出版的会刊封面标注的是"No. II",且起始页码也与第一号相衔接。

二次易名:1884—1905年,一度更名为《皇家亚洲文会中国支会会刊》。

1882年9月24日,亚洲文会理事会修订该会章程,把该会名称由此前的"皇家亚洲文会北华支会"更改为"皇家亚洲文会中国支会"。[1]虽然章程没有规定会刊之名也要更改,但1884年第19卷会刊的刊名已经没有"北部"(North)一词,变成了《皇家亚洲文会中国支会会刊》(Journal of The China Branch of The Royal Asiatic Society),直至1905年的第36卷。1906年,该刊刊名再次恢复为"皇家亚洲文会北华支会会刊"。关于这次易名,笔者尚未见到相关说明。

所谓"三度中断",指的是该刊在其出版历程中的3次停刊现象。

首度停刊:1861—1864年

1861年11月,裨治文病逝,加之艾约瑟北上、伟烈亚力回国,核心成员的离去,导致亚洲文会停止活动。[2]同年,会刊亦停止发行。

这次停刊使得该刊初期(1858—1860)只发行了4期,分别出版于1858年6月、1859年5月、1859年12月和1860年9月,其中最后一期封面标注有"第2卷第1号"字样。目前,这两卷四册的会刊已存世不多,从1959年出版的《全国西文期刊联合目录》看,国内也只有国家图书馆、中国科学院图书馆、北京大学图书馆、上海图书馆等几处藏有,而且所收藏的估计也多是后来的重印本,真正的第一版就更少了。

1864年3月1日,在金斯密、伟烈亚力及英国驻上海领事巴夏礼等人的努力下,亚洲文会得以重建,并确立了文会的三个目标:(1)调查研究中国及其邻近国家各项事情;(2)出版会刊;(3)建立一个图书馆和博物院。[3]同年12月1日,会刊重新出版。复刊后,该刊变为定期出版物,连续发行达77年之久。

再度停刊:1942—1945年

1941年7月,日军占领上海英美租界,外侨纷纷离沪,亚洲文会停止活动。本该于1942年年初出版的会刊亦被迫中断。

1946年秋天,亚洲文会恢复活动,同年12月出版了第72卷《会刊》,刊登的半数文章系1941年后积压的旧稿。

第三次停刊:1948年

尽管1946年亚洲文会恢复了活动,会刊亦复刊,但因租界的消亡、工部局的不复存在,亚洲文会丧失了来自"官方"的资助。缺少活动经费,会刊之出版再度受挫,1947年就没有如期出版会刊。1948年,亚洲文会与尚贤堂合作出版了纪念福开森的专号(第73卷)后,因财力原因,第三次停办会刊。

幸运的是,2010年《皇家亚洲文会北华支会会刊》再次复刊[4];现在,以往的会刊也得以

---

[1] Report of the Council of the China Branch of the Royal Asiatic Society, JNCBRAS, Vol. XVII, 1882, Pxiii.
[2] The Royal Asiatic Society, North-China Herald, Vol. XII, No. 586, 19th October, 1861.
[3] The North-China Branch of the Royal Asiatic Society, North-China Herald, 12th Mar., 1864.
[4] 新刊第74卷见:Journal of the Royal Asiatic Society China in Shanghai, Vol. 74, No. 1, Apr., 2010, China Economic Review Publishing (HK) Ltd. for Earnshaw Books.

影印再版。

二、会刊的演变

伴随着出版之艰难历程，该刊经历了由季刊变成年刊、从"老刊"走向"新刊"、由号变为卷、由分册本走向整卷本的复杂演变历程。

1857年10月17日，裨治文在上海文理学会创建大会上说："要办一份刊物，季刊。"但因稿源有限，未能如期出版，1858年6月出版第1号后，1859年5月才出版第2号会刊。所以，1858年9月25日，亚洲文会理事会决定"下次出版会刊，删去封面上的'季刊'（Quarterly）一词"，变为不定期出版。1864年始，该刊才以年刊发行。

1864年复刊后，新出版的会刊封面上印有"新刊"（New Series）一词，同年的会务记录中将1858－1860年间发行的会刊称为"老刊"（Old Series），以示二者的区别。尽管如此，新老之间传承关系十分明显。1864年新刊第1号首页页码是第129页，与1860年的老刊第2卷第1号末页页码第128页相衔接。

在会刊序号上，1864年的新刊以"第1号"标注。1882年改"号"为"卷"，当年会刊标注为"新刊第17卷"。"新刊"共计发行73卷，加上1860年前的2卷旧刊，《皇家亚洲文会北华支会会刊》共计发行了75卷。

刊名、卷号、出版周期的数度变化，加之语言隔阂，造成近代以来国人对该刊认识不清，相关介绍均十分简略，关于该刊存世时间的记载错误百出，中文译名也是五花八门。

1927年，戈公振在其《中国报学史》上首次介绍该刊：

> 发刊于1858年，为伟烈亚力所编辑，其中梅雅士（W. F. Mayer）之《华人发明火药史》、笪伟德（Abbe Armond David）之《中国博物志》、布润珠（E. Bretschueider）之《马可·波罗事略》、鲍乃迪（Archimandrite Palladius）之《中国古时代亚洲中部地志》等篇，均极有价值。[1]

戈氏作此介绍时，该刊尚未终结，故未谈及停刊时间。尽管如此，上引寥寥数语竟被后来之人全袭。从20世纪30年代的《上海通志馆期刊》到90年代郭卫东主编的《外国在华文化机构综录》与马光仁主编的《上海新闻史》等有关文献中，对于该刊的介绍几乎一字未变地沿袭戈氏之语。其他少数学者论及该刊时，往往把自己见到的最后一卷视为该刊的终结版，所以，张海林认为该刊终结于1907年，叶再生提出"一直出版到1917年"，李建中认为到1941年，美国堪萨斯大学的马克梦提出了1946年。[2] 2002年，笔者经过详细查阅后才确认该刊终结于1948年的第73卷。

就中文译名而言，先后有陈潜的"大亚细亚上海支会会报"、傅振伦的"英国亚洲文会华北支会会报"、戈公振的"皇家亚洲文会北中国分会会报"、胡道静的"皇家亚洲文会北中国支会会报"、莫东寅的"皇家亚洲学会华北分会会报"、方汉奇的"皇家亚细亚文会北中国分会会报"、叶再生的"皇家亚洲协会华北分会学报"、张海林的"上海亚洲文会会

---

[1] 戈公振：《中国报学史》，《民国丛书》第二编，第49册，上海书店1990年版，第86－87页。

[2] 李建中：《亚洲文会北中国支会图书馆》，《图书馆杂志》1983年9月；马克梦：《十九世纪西方人眼中的中国》，载王小盾编《扬州大学中国文化研究所汇刊》（第一辑），江苏古籍出版社1998年版，第379页。

刊"、马光仁的"皇家亚洲文会北华支会会刊"等多种译名。[1]而当时在华的外国学者,如日本的小竹文夫、石田干之助,英国的贝德士等人,则将该刊分别译为"英国亚细亚学会北支那支会会报"、"皇家亚洲学会华北分会会刊"、"皇家亚洲学会北华分会学报",[2]可谓五花八门!

如果从19世纪后半期外侨在上海创办的新闻报刊之中文名字看,此刊名当译为"皇家亚洲文会北华支会会刊"。原因如下:(1)"亚洲文会"是该机构自身的中文译名。[3](2)1858年"上海文理学会"加盟"大不列颠及爱尔兰皇家亚洲文会"时,香港有一个雷同机构——"皇家亚洲文会中国支会"(The China Branch of the Royal Asiatic Society),故胡道静先生解释为"所以名为北中国支会者,系立于香港的地位观之,上海居于北方故也",[4]可谓正确!但是由此而把该会及其会刊之名直译为"北中国支会"则略显僵硬,因为当时西文报章上之"North China"一词之中文译名已有先例,即"北华",最为突出的就是当时同城发行的著名西文报纸《北华捷报》(North China Herald)。较之"北中国","北华"二字显然更为精准。(3)以往对于该刊的介绍,多把其说成"学报"、"会报",主要系当时从新闻出版的角度视之,今天观之,作为一个学术性较强的文化机构出版的杂志,"会刊"则更为合适些,故本次重印该刊,中文译名取《皇家亚洲文会北华支会会刊》。

三、会刊之发行

1858—1860年间的四册会刊,由《北华捷报》馆承印并帮助销售,也曾在望益纸馆(Carvalho, A. H. de)与高福洋行(Crawford & Co.)印刷销售。1864年后的新刊一直由别发洋行(Kelly & Walsh, Ltd.)负责发行,在上海、香港、横滨、新加坡等地设有销售点。此外,在伦敦、巴黎、莱比锡、法兰克福等地,由当地经销商负责发行。

新刊1—19卷(1864—1884)每册高21.5cm,宽14.5cm,封面除了会刊名称外,还有发行和印刷公司的名字,英文字母采用罗马体,相对简朴。从第20卷起,每册变为高24cm,宽15.5cm,印刷比较精美,封面四周印有方格,边框内左上角有一条喷火的飞龙,下面为艺术体的英文名字及卷号、年份,底部附有上海、伦敦、巴黎、莱比锡、法兰克福等处的发行代办单位。42卷起封面又和以前一样简朴,1928年后目录成为封面主要内容。

会刊定期发行,基本上每年一卷。稿源多时,就先分册出版,然后再出版一整卷,最多时一年曾出6分册;稿源少时,两年出一卷。自1905年,每年定期出版一卷。每卷页码不一,要视内容而定,但纸张都很好,时隔百余年仍触手如新。早年会刊每册售价壹元墨洋,后来增至2—3元,较厚的5元;1906年后,每卷均在6元大洋左右,30年代法币改革后,价格均翻一倍,达到每卷10元。

---

[1] 参见陈潜:《西人译中国书籍及在中国发行之报章》,《东方杂志》第五年第九期;傅振伦:《中国博物馆史略》,《东方杂志》第十一卷第十五号;戈公振:《中国报学史》,第86页;胡道静:《历史上以上海为研究对象的学术团体》,《档案与史学》1989年第2期;叶再生主编:《中国近现代出版通史》(第1卷),北京华文出版社2002年版,第158页;莫东寅:《汉学发达史》,大象出版社2006年版,第95页;方汉奇:《中国新闻事业编年史》,载《新闻研究资料》(第三辑)1981年;张海林:《上海亚洲文会述论》,《南京大学学报》1996年第1期;马光仁:《上海新闻史》,复旦大学出版社1996年版,第21页。

[2] 小竹文夫:《上海の英国亚西亚学会北支那支会图书馆》,见东亚同文书院支那研究部:《支那研究》第十九号[昭和四年(1930年)五月发行];石田干之助:《欧米人に於けろ支那研究》,创元社刊行,昭和十七年,第105页。贝德士编:《西文东方学报论文举要》,金陵大学中国文化研究所印行,民国二十二年,第5页。《上海通志馆期刊·上海的定期刊物》第一卷第三期,民国二十二年十二月,第867页。

[3] 见本书附录《皇家亚洲文会北华支会研究》。

[4] 胡道静:《上海博物院史略》,见《上海研究资料续集》,上海书店1993年版,第393页。

1885年理事会设定了会刊的主要阅读对象:"在数以千计的科研机构成员中传阅,在东方学、地理学及所有国家的科研机构中出现,还有我们的公共阅览室。"[1]所以,除了免费寄送各个会员外,会刊主要用于与国内外的学术机构交换刊物,其余才向社会销售。通过对历年亚洲文会会员数量及会刊销售金额两项数据的考察,大致可推算出一些年份会刊的发行量。1870—1890年,会刊的年发行量在300份以上,其中"1883年印制了468份(不包含每位作者的20份抽印本),1884年印制了500份"[2]。但在社会上售出的很少,这一时期最高的年销售量也不过是150份左右。[3]根据1877年《北华捷报》之报道:"1876年,150份期刊分发至各个会员及学术机构,当年会刊销售收入是304.61洋"[4],按每卷2元计,销售量也不过150份。而更多的年份销售量都在50份以下,其中1875年的销售量不足15份。[5]这些数据说明早期会刊销售不畅,有时还会滞存很多。[6]

1890年后,发行逐渐改观,除了发放给会员外,平均每年还能售出100份左右。1901年后突破150份。[7]这一时期年度会员数量在300人左右,所以每年会刊的出版总量也在500份以上。其中1903—1904年会刊出版700份,至少400份售至社会。[8]1906—1907年的会刊"销售收益非常悦人,分册本的全部份数在一个月内全部售完"[9]。1921年销售达1643元,占据亚洲文会全年收入的1/3,当年会刊出版量当有900份左右,销售量在200份左右。[10]

20世纪30年代,随着会员数量和交换机构的增加,加之社会上对会刊有更多的需求,会刊出版量有较大增加。1934年发行497份,交换105份。日益增加的会员(该年度达到670名)和交换机构(117个),使得到1935年"发行量必须从800份提高到1100份"[11]。这一时期,亚洲文会为了改善财务状况,还不断重印过刊,向社会公开出售以获利。1939年时,1909年前出版的会刊全部售罄,成为绝版。[12]需要指出的是,这一时期发行量增大,但主要还是分发给会员,从每年的会刊销售额看,当时能够在社会上卖出的也不过在100份左右。[13]因此,这一时期的年发行量也不会超过1500份。

---

[1] Proceeding, JNCBRAS, VoL. XX, 1885, P298.
[2] Report of the Council for the year 1884, JNCBRAS, Vol. XIX, 1884, Piii.
[3] 1869年会员总数182个,会费收入当有555洋;会刊销售总额677.50元墨洋。当年会刊价格1元,故当年会刊销售量在130份左右,再加上赠给会员的数量,全年发行量至少在310份。参见Report of the Council for 1869, JNCBRAS, Vol. VI, 1869–1870, Piv.
[4] North China Herald, 24th Jan., 1878.
[5] 本年度会刊销售26.93墨洋,单价2元。参见Report of the Council for the year 1875, JNCBRAS, Vol. X, 1875, Pix.
[6] 如1917年在别发洋行的仓库中发现了以往的全套会刊。参见Proceedings, JNCBRAS, Vol. XLIX, 1918, Px.
[7] 历年会刊销售金额是:1889年145.54两;1890年103.10两;1892年136.56两;1893年219.33两;1895年124.04两;1897年221.04两;1899年190.20两;1901年191.28两;1903年255.3洋;1904年408.34两;1905年285洋。这一时期银两与大洋的平均兑换比率是1∶1.37,会刊售价2元。
[8] Proceedings, JNCBRAS, Vol. XXXVI, 1905, P162.
[9] Proceedings, JNCBRAS, Vol. XXXVIII, 1907, P266.
[10] 按照每册售价5元计,销售量有300份。此外1921年会员数量达532,交换机构100家,所以估算有900份。Proceedings, JNCBRAS, Vol. XXXVI, 1921, Pvii.
[11] Proceedings, JNCBRAS, Vol. LXVII, 1936, Pix.
[12] Proceedings, JNCBRAS, Vol. LXX, 1939, Pvii.
[13] 这一时期会刊销售收入分别是:1933年920.48元;1936年1243元,1938年845元;1940年最多,为2393.63元,而当时会刊价格是7—10元。

编纂者与编纂宗旨

一、编纂者

出版会刊是亚洲文会的活动目标之一,也被视为其心脏,所以亚洲文会理事会十分重视会刊之编纂工作,设有专门的编辑委员会。

1909年前,会刊没有留下具体的编纂者之姓名。"会务记录"显示,编辑委员会成员主要由会长、副会长、秘书及理事会其他成员组成。尽管曾任亚洲文会图书管理员的高第(H. Cordier)后来回忆"亚洲文会的很多会长都是学者",理应参与编辑工作,但是从会长的任职时间及个人履历可以看出,多数不具备参与编辑会刊的条件。如巴夏礼(Sir Harry Smith Parkes),身为驻华公使,动辄到日本、香港出访,常常缺席例会,不可能参与编辑;而汉璧礼(T. Hanbury)、福勃士(F. B. Forbes)身为商人,生意已使得他们很早就放弃了汉学研究,恐难胜任会刊之编纂工作。古德温(C. W. Goodwin)在埃及学、希腊学和盎格鲁撒克逊学方面颇有声望,但在上海,他的学问及学术地位罕为人知,不可能参与汉学期刊之编辑。[1] 因此,会刊之编辑当是长期服务于亚洲文会、且具有汉学研究背景之人士。查阅1858–1909年历年理事会成员名单,可大体推断出1858–1908年间会刊的几个实际编纂者。

裨治文:首位来华的美国传教士,亚洲文会首任会长。1859年3月他提出会刊要"涉猎各项主题"的编纂方略,说明他当属早期的主要编纂者。

伟烈亚力:亚洲文会创建者之一,著名汉学家,先后任该会秘书、副会长、理事。根据曾与他共事的亚洲文会理事会成员高第的回忆,"伟烈亚力是早期会刊的真正编辑"[2]。

艾约瑟:亚洲文会创建者之一,汉学家,自1857年开始直至1905年去世,艾约瑟一直都活跃在亚洲文会,先后任秘书、副会长、理事。会务记录显示,秘书负责宣读会议讨论的稿件及来稿的接受,所以,艾约瑟当参与实际的编辑工作。

金斯密:1864年加入亚洲文会,先后任次理事、副会长、会长、财务、博物馆馆长等职。1910年,亚洲文会秘书福开森在纪念金斯密的贡献时提出"他是会刊的编辑"[3]。

夏德:1877年加入亚洲文会,1883–1887年任副会长、会长。作为一名著名的东方学家,夏德在亚洲文会会刊上还参与了关于中亚史地问题的论战,并曾经向公众呼吁供稿。

自1910年始,每卷会刊目录前均注明本卷会刊之编辑姓名,此后会刊的编辑者依次为:福开森(J. C. Ferguson)、莫安仁(Evan Morgan)、库寿龄(Samuel Couling)、苏阿德(A. de. C. Sowerby)、益乐(Esson M. Gale)、伊博恩(Bernard E. Read)。

1932年,莫安仁在亚洲文会年会上赞扬历届会刊编辑,称他们"多为饱学之士"[4],此话不虚。裨治文、伟烈亚力、艾约瑟、金斯密、夏德都是19世纪中后期的著名汉学家。1910年后的六位编辑,也都称得上是博学之士。

福开森是著名的文物古董收藏家,并在中国艺术、青铜器等方面都有不凡的研究。库寿龄

---

[1] Proceedings, JNCBRAS, Vol. XXXV, 1903–1904, Pxvi.
[2] Proceedings, JNCBRAS, Vol. XXXV, 1903–1904, Pxviii.
[3] Proceedings, JNCBRAS, Vol. XLI, 1910, P137.
[4] Proceedings, JNCBRAS, Vol. LXIII, 1932, Pix.

则以《中国百科全书》(Encyclopaedia Sinica)获取"儒莲奖",二人不必赘言。其他四位也都是学有所长的专家,且在汉学领域也有比较突出的贡献。

莫安仁:1906年到达上海,广学会成员,亚洲文会会长。自1911年先后担任了9卷会刊之编辑。1928年被威尔士大学授予神学博士学位。[1] 在华期间,以编译"汉语新名词"著称,而他对《淮南子》的译注,更是令当时的西方汉学界震惊,由此登入了汉学家之列。[2]

苏阿德:又名苏柯仁,是著名的博物学家。亚洲文会会长,并多年担任亚洲文会博物馆馆长,1928－1937年间曾担任4卷会刊之编辑。苏阿德先后撰写了《中国博物志》、《中国珍稀动物》等论著。在汉学方面,苏阿德由博物学延伸至中国民俗与文化的研究,先后在会刊上发表了《中国艺术中的动物》、《中国古墓中陶俑》、《中国动物主题神话》等论文,把"自己广博的博物学知识和民俗历史结合在一起,正确地解释了中国老百姓习俗背后的文化渊源"[3],曾被学者评价为"对中国文化做出了很有价值的贡献"[4]。而他撰写的旅行日记——《穿越陕甘》(Through Shen-Kan, 1912)、《一个博物学家在中国的记录》(A Naturalist's Note Book in China)等著作,也都是20世纪西方人认识中国的重要参考书,一经出版,即销售一空,1946年时已成绝版。[5]

盖乐:1933－1936年担任会刊之编辑。莱顿大学毕业的博士,曾任加利福尼亚大学东方语言系主任,后在上海中国盐税管理处任外文秘书,退休后到东北大学任政治科学教授。在汉学方面,他最早翻译了《盐铁论》。[6]

伊博恩:博士,北京协和医学院教授,后任职于上海雷氏德医学院。1938－1946年担任会刊编辑。长年致力于对中医药的研究,并对中药中的动物做了文化分析,由此进入汉学的阵营中。

二、编纂宗旨

会刊之编纂宗旨实际上也是亚洲文会的宗旨,即"调查研究中华帝国及其周围各项事情"。会刊首篇文章,也是裨治文在该会成立大会上的就职演说,比较详尽地阐述了亚洲文会的宗旨、目标、任务与发展方向。[7]

> 文学和科学是仅次于真教的最贵重、最崇高、最光亮的人类之饰品。在文学与科学的领域中,一些重大的成就却是在没有上帝启示的真知下实现的。……在这个古老的帝国,由于缺乏神的感召,他们的文学与科学成就,尽管比近邻的民族及同类要高,但总体上看,仍然低于基督教国家。
>
> 大洪水之后,人类为上帝建造了一个祭坛,从那里开始向东方迁移,最终抵达这块遥远的地域,并在这里点燃了文明之火。如果承认这些,那么这个帝国的创建者们就是来自西方早期国家的后裔。在某种程度上,洪水之后的知识,无论是文学还是科学,中西双方

---

[1] Obituary, JNCBRAS, Vol. LXXII, 1946, P78.
[2] Reviews of Recent Books, JNCBRAS, Vol. LXVI, 1935, P83.
[3] Proceedings, JNCBRAS, VOL. LXX, 1939, Pviii.
[4] Reviews of Recent Books, JNCBRAS, VoL. LXXI, 1940, P99, 100.
[5] Sowerby, A. de C., Zoological Exploration in China, JNCBRAS, VoL. LXII, 1946, P22.
[6] Review of Recent Books, JNCBRAS, Vol. LXII, 1932, P203.
[7] Bridgman, Rev. E. C. D. D., Inaugural Address, JNCBRAS, O. S. No. I, June, 1858, pp1-13.

一定拥有相似之处。

在中国的文学与科学成果中……无论是历史、哲学，还是科学，都存在着缺乏神的智慧、忠实可信的学问、真正的逻辑……这里有荒诞的宗教和伦理学说，荒谬的物理学和抽象论，错误的国内和国际政策，所有这一切都被误称的"科学"粘合在一起。这些谬论一定要被推翻、戳穿，也注定会在真知和正当理由前消失、让道。

现在，本机构将要在一些领域开展调查研究工作。对于科学和博学之士来说，在中国，有大量的课题可以做。他可以从事地理学的调查，随着帝国的开放，广阔的幅员将会催促旅行者们穿越其平原、河流，攀登其山巅，并描绘之。在海岸测绘方面，中国海、台湾周围、琉球、日本、满洲海岸等地仍有大量的工作要做。

博物学家们将会非常高兴地记录岩石、丘陵和山谷，鸟类、兽类和鱼类，以及每一种树木、灌木、鲜花。博物学的三大门类，矿物、植物和动物，这里有成千上万的对象可供研究。……奥森伯格、雅裨理、福钧等人已经采集到了一些灿烂的标本，向西方世界告知全能的神在这个东方帝国境内做的工是多么丰富和绚丽！但是，西方所知的不到一半，甚至不及千分之一。

他也可以从事深入地表下之研究，挖掘永存的山脉，寻早古老的岩石，把这些证据与它们的创造者——上帝之力和智慧——联系起来，给《圣经》的忠实以确凿的证据。

他也可以努力去解决更为微妙的流体问题，发现关于飓风的规则，探讨巨轮航行的原理。

或许民族学的研究，应该优先于上述一些科目。……东亚部落与太平洋北部、东部岛屿上的族群来自哪里？

中国政治制度中的继承法则，他的立法、行政与司法制度，选官制度，竞争性的考试制度，税收制度，他在治理与统治间是如何平衡的？他对周围国家的政策是什么？尤其是在当前国内外处于重大变革的时代，任何课题都没有上述题目显得迫切。

作为一个文学与科学学会，我们将会责无旁贷地去探究：目前在这里出现的、似乎有加速趋势的民族间的较量，究竟仅仅是武力的角逐，还是智力的较量？被授权去和中国政府高官谈判的外国官员们在与这个帝国的主要有才智之人进行交涉时，在多大程度上做好了准备？……目前，由于对中国政治机制的无知，导致我们在与中国政府交往时变得十分无能。尽管我们拥有武力，但是与他们打交道时必须要审慎和有技巧，唯此，才能在最后获得尽可能大的成果。

必须研究他们的语言，无论多么艰难，都要展开，并掌握之，在这场战争中没有退伍令。……对于中国的文献学而言，我们进入了一个真正巨大、且每一个分支都十分重要的领域。古今经典文献、历史、诗歌、以及中国人的政治手稿，都比其他民族的同类文献要复杂得多！整理他们的法律和法规，许多延续朝代的统计数字，关于宗教、教育、音乐、医技方面的卷宗，以及其他类似的工作等，都是上海文理学会成员们需要较早和仔细关注的内容。

随着学会科研活动的推进，为了提升我们自己在文学和科学方面的贡献，需要一个刊物，每季出版。

裨治文的发言反映出19世纪中叶前后西方人迫切想要了解中国的两个原因：第一、中国，这个非基督教国家为何能在文学与科学方面取得如此伟大的成就？没有真教指引的中华民族，为何具有人类的一切智知特征？这一点，对于传教士，乃至在基督教文化背景下成长的其他西方人，都是难于理解的，因此，他们迫切想了解中国的历史，以究其因。第二、基于殖民侵略，尤其是为正在进行中的第二次鸦片战争服务，来华西人急切想了解中国的资源、语言、政治制度等各项事情。

根据亚洲文会图书馆馆长爱司克夫人（F. Ayscough）与高第两人的回忆，1843年租界形成后，寓沪外侨感觉，无论茶、丝及曼彻斯特的货物在商业上多么重要，都无法满足精神上的需求，因为他们对周围环境一片茫然。随着时间的发展，他们决定通过学习和努力来改变这种状态。[1] 1857年，以裨治文为首的英美侨民遂建立了上海文理学会，并创办会刊，调查研究中国各项事情。

为什么是裨治文，而不是别人，创建这样的一个机构和期刊，并确立这样一个"无所不包"的研究对象？这要追溯两份与裨治文均有密切关系的英文期刊——《中国丛报》（*Chinese Repository*, 1832–1851）与《皇家亚洲文会中国支会纪要》（*Transactions of the China Branch of the Royal Asiatic Society*, 1847–1859）

1830年，裨治文抵达广州，"从抵达中国的那一刻起，裨治文就深信，一名基督传教士在为他所面临的责任做准备时，最可靠的方法就是获取服务所在领地的知识。这不仅包括了解该国的地理和人口等基本信息，还包括熟悉社会各阶层日常生活的实际知识"[2]。所以两年后裨治文在广州创办了《中国丛报》，该报宗旨"评介关于中国的外文书籍，观察这些书籍内容的变化过程；调查中国的气候、矿藏、河流、动植物、物产、商情；关于社会关系方面，注意中国人的道德素质、教育制度、妇女地位、宗教情况等"[3]。由于种种原因，《中国丛报》于1851年停刊，这令裨治文十分伤悲，近乎是"他生命中的一个亮点的熄灭"，从此，"裨治文生命中便一直有一个未竟之梦",[4] 即再创办一份类似的期刊。

《中国丛报》停刊前后，1847年在香港的英国外侨德庇时（Sir John Francis Davis）、史丹顿（Rev. V. Stanton）、梅莎（W. T. Mercer）等人成立了一个"中国亚洲学会"（The Asiatic Society of China），旨在"调查研究中国之艺术、科学、文学、天然产物"[5]。同年该会加入"大不列颠及爱尔兰皇家亚洲文会"，成为其支会，遂改称为"皇家亚洲文会中国支会"（The China Branch of the Royal Asiatic Society）（简称香港支会）。裨治文是该会的通讯会员。虽然香港支会能够继续《中国丛报》的办刊风格，但是该会多数资深成员住在香港，而在香港以外的会员很难参加该会的定期会议和活动。[6] 这令裨治文感到颇为遗憾！

鉴于《中国丛报》的停刊与香港支会的不便，1853年再次抵达上海的裨治文努力实现余生的一个夙愿——让《中国丛报》能够以某种形式再次出现，并采纳香港支会的形式，于是创建了

---

[1] [法]高第著，马军译：《对英国近代汉学家伟烈亚力的回忆》，《中国史研究动态》1998年第5期。Notes and Queries, JNCBRAS, Vol. XLVII, 1916, P156.

[2] [美]雷孜智著，尹文娟译：《千禧年的感召：美国第一位来华新教传教士裨治文传》，广西师范大学出版社2008年版，第267页。

[3] Introduction, The Chinese Repository, May, 1832, pp2–3.

[4] [美]雷孜智著，尹文娟译：《千禧年的感召：美国第一位来华新教传教士裨治文传》，第322–323页。

[5] Asiatic Society of China, Chinese Repository, Vol. XVI, Feb., 1847, pp93.

[6] [美]雷孜智著，尹文娟译：《千禧年的感召：美国第一位来华新教传教士裨治文传》，第322–323页。

上海文理学会,并发行会刊,即后来的《皇家亚洲文会北华支会会刊》。

早期《皇家亚洲文会北华支会会刊》与《中国丛报》十分相似。在栏目上,与《中国丛报》的"新闻杂俎"一样,每期也设有"最近中国大事记"的专栏,对中国近期发生的重要事做一个总结,其中不少信息摘自各种报刊和中国人发行的刊物。[1] 在内容上,《中国丛报》的内容涉及31个主题,有传教、语言、文献、政治制度、中英战争、商贸、鸦片、圣经、博物学、旅行及东南亚各国事情,这些也都是亚洲文会会刊继续刊登的内容。艾约瑟后来就回忆"通过邀请裨治文先生担任我们的主席,我们把在上海的文学和科学研究工作与其在广州28年的传教生涯和在《中国丛报》工作中所取得的成就,联系在了一起"[2]。

根据高第的《西人论中国书目》中摘录的香港支会会刊——《皇家亚洲文会中国支会纪要》——之目录,可以看出该刊涉及了中国的土地、温泉、哲学、铜钱、矿井、罗盘、沿海岛屿、《大学》译注、中国的继承法、古汉语之发音、《洗冤录》译注、中国的人口、中国的宝塔、道教、暹罗、广州的公审、林则徐、上海发现的汉蒙碑刻、最近日本朝鲜之现象、客家人之寺庙、中国的鸦片、中国的水车、新安城等多方面的内容。[3] 这些题目很多也都是后来亚洲文会继续研究的对象。所以后任亚洲文会秘书的艾约瑟说:"我们学会是基于亚洲文会香港支会创建者的理念建立的,那就是对这个国家进行研究的强烈愿望——欧洲对于亚洲这个大的帝国知之甚少。"[4]

尽管上述两刊与"北华支会会刊"颇有渊源,风格也雷同,但后者宗旨更加宽泛:在内容上,要求涉猎各项事情;在深度上,不仅仅是"了解"、"调查",而且要"研究"!

三、编纂方针

亚洲文会对会刊要求很严,无论来稿是否演讲,都必须经过理事会一致投票,通过后才予刊登。选文章的依据就是亚洲文会的宗旨,在实际编纂过程中形成了四个原则。

第一、内容必须是关于中国及周围地区之知识。

查阅亚洲文会"历次演讲目录"与"会刊目录"[5],会发现文章能否被刊登,关键是其是否提供了关于中国的知识。1865年4月3日三顺(T. Sampson)演讲了《西印度群岛贩卖苦力》,因内容与中国关系不大,故被抛弃而难以面世。1897年3月3日考克斯(R. H. Cox)演讲了《X光射线》一文,虽然在秘书艾约瑟眼中对于了解"当代科学颇具价值"[6],但因非中国之信息,亦未被发表。而1923-1946年在华的商人、旅行家斐士(E. S. Fisher)一人就在会刊上发表了5篇作品,其中3篇是未演讲过的作品:《紫禁城太庙》、《热河》与《喇嘛教的圣舞》。

第二、会刊要涉猎各项课题。

1859年3月裨治文提出"我们可以在大量来稿中精选优稿。我们的目标是涉猎各种课题,并特别关注与我们目前在东方所在地区相关的问题"[7]。因此,涉猎各项课题也成为编纂该刊的一个重要方针。会刊的第1号很好地体现了裨治文的"涉猎各种课题"之承诺,尼克逊船长的《飓风之规律》属于气象方面的观测,伟烈亚力的《大清钱币》是对当时中国社会经济生

---

[1] [美]雷孜智著,尹文娟译:《千禧年的感召:美国第一位来华新教传教士裨治文传》,第325页。
[2] Proceedings, JNCBRAS, Vol. XXXV, 1903-1904, Pii.
[3] 高第:《西人论中国书目》(第4册),北京文典阁书庄,民国27年影印,第2401-2402页。
[4] Preceedings, JNCBRAS, VoL. XXXV, 1903-1904, Pvi.
[5] 见本书附录《皇家亚洲文会北华支会研究》。
[6] Proceedings, JNCBRAS, Vol. XXXV, 1903-1904, Pii.
[7] North China Herald, 3rd, Mar., 1859. 转引自(美)雷孜智著,尹文娟译:《千禧年的感召:美国第一位来华新教传教士裨治文传》,第327页。

活的调查,玛高温的《东亚民族学论稿》是对中国及周边民族习俗的探究,艾约瑟的《〈壹输卢迦论〉译稿与注释》是对中国古代典籍的整理,福德的《日本下田与函馆游记》是对刚刚开埠的日本之描述,《中国大事记》是对当时中外局势的描述和有关资料的搜集,每一篇都是开幕词提出的研究课题。会刊第2号进一步扩展了专业领域,涉及音乐、文献整理、地磁学、博物学、气象学、地理测绘等学科。

自始至终,"涉及多项主题"这个原则一直未变,每一卷各篇文章所讨论的主题都不一样,而全部会刊上的所有文章之主题,彼此重合的也少之又少。这样的编纂原则,较之于那些有着具体研讨对象的各类专业期刊而言,《皇家亚洲文会北华支会会刊》向西方世界传播的中国知识,其内容量无疑是最大的。因此,早在1883年,《北华捷报》就高度评价会刊"是《中国丛报》之后最有利于西方人了解中国的刊物"[1]。1923年,在外侨民调中显示,会刊也被视为是最能帮助西方了解中国的两份西文期刊之一。[2]

第三、会刊要具有一定的实用性。

会刊也一直努力向西方人提供比较实用的中国之信息。1866年会刊前言明确提出:"亚洲文会的具体目标是获取亚洲资源的有用信息。"[3]1887年,会长夏德向公众呼吁:

> 我们真诚欢迎投稿,尤其是关于植物、动物、矿藏等方面内容的文章,或者是商业生活,如中国人的商业行规,那些没有明文规定而在实践中又颇具效用的制度、原则等法律内容。如果有一系列关于商业方面的文章,那么在亚洲文会的资助者眼中,会刊的价值会极大提高。[4]

在实用性原则的指导下,会刊的很多文章都有着相对具体的所指。学习语言,便于外交谈判;调查黄河及长江,目的在商贸;论及哲学,在于掌握中国政治运作过程。1868年刊载了爱莲斯的《黄河新河道考察报告》,该文直接解决了当时地理学和商业问题,使得西方人了解到黄河下游已丧失航运能力。倭尔特的《长江航路指南:从吴淞到汉口》向侨民提供了该段长江的航行方位和具体信息。艾约瑟的《古代长江入海口》为当时黄浦江之疏浚工程提供历史借鉴。[5]1893年刊发的《中国之内陆交通》,目的是为将来列强在华修建铁路做准备。1900年班德瑞的《可能的改革与不可能的改革》为的是"便于在华外人更自由地进行商业贸易"[6]。相反,有些文章即便有知识价值,但实用性不高,也被编辑弃之不用。如1887年有不少来稿,因"难以引起听众兴趣,也难以引起讨论",故放弃之。[7]

正如后来研究近代西方中国观的马森所言:"亚洲文会会刊是知识界的刊物,尽管刊登了有关中国文明方面的许多材料,但具有实用性的资料还是占据首位。"[8]

第四、学术质量也是编纂者们时刻注意的一个方向。

---

[1] Literature in China, North China Herald, 12th, Dec., 1868.
[2] L. Newton Hayes: The Most Helpful Books on China, The Chinese Recoreder, Vol. LVI, 1925, P302.
[3] Preface, JNCBRAS, Vol. III, 1866.
[4] Preceedings, JNCBRAS, VoL. XXII, 1887, pp117-118.
[5] Report of the Council for the year 1874, JNCBRAS, Vol. IX, 1874, Pxxvi.
[6] Frederick Sarmuel Augustus Bourne, Possible and Impossible Reforms, JNCBRAS, Vol. XXXIII, 1899-1900, P10.
[7] Report of the Council for the year 1887, JNCBRAS, VoL. XXII, 1887, P292.
[8] [美]M. G. 马森著,杨德山译:《西方的中华帝国观》,时事出版社1999年版,第75页。

会刊之学术质量,直接关系到亚洲文会的兴亡。亚洲文会的资金主要来自会员会费,每个会员则能够免费获取一份会刊。1880年代,一册会刊的出版成本是普通会员会费的1/5,[1]会刊之质量直接影响会费之收入,编纂者千方百计要保持会刊的质量,是为了能够吸引尽可能多的会员,而其会员多数又是具有较高文化素养的在华侨民,所以,会刊必须要具有一定的学术性。

因此,在编纂过程中,对于一些质量较高的论文,无论作者是否是会员,文章是否参加了演讲,编辑们都会予以录用。正如编者所言:"如果有较高的科学价值,不论是否演讲,抑或直接投稿,都可在会刊上发表。"[2]1858年,倭尔特的《长江航路指南:从吴淞到汉口》一文其实就是航行日志,但因能向侨民提供长江沿岸的新情况,虽属投稿,亦能发表。而首任会长裨治文于1858年1月19日演讲的《宁波雪窦山之地理及最近旅行情况》一文,因属草创,对于雪窦山的情况并无一个相对清楚的认识[3],所以被弃而不用。1884年刊登的第一篇文章是由英国领事嘉托玛(C.T Gardner)撰写的《湖北宜昌地区的动物、化石、矿物与植物物产》,该文因有很多汉字,不适宜演讲,但因其价值重大,依然被刊登。1911年3月7日,文显理演讲了自己在蒙古沙漠的旅行经历,虽然故事生动,有出版成书的前景,但因仅是草稿,同样未被刊发。[4]相反,1914年,叶长清在西藏及黄河口的游记,因内容新颖,"大大不同于以往的文章"[5],虽未参加演讲,仍受到编辑的赏识,并在同一期中刊发了他的两篇作品。

遇上质量较高的论文,理事会也会隆重推出。如贝勒(E. Bretschneider)的《先辈欧人对中国植物的研究》、《中国植物志》等皇皇巨著,因价值巨大,理事会不惜挤压许多他人之文章,不顾因延期而遭的许多抱怨之言,仍坚持全文专版发行。[6]后来此文获得汉学最高奖——"儒莲奖"。

学术性原则使得该刊吸引一批学者之供稿。浏览会刊文章之作者,会发现半数以上是近代著名的汉学家,或一些领域内的专家,如裨治文、伟烈亚力、卫三畏、艾约瑟、贝勒、翟理思、郁和、夏德、费理饬、杨格非、丁韪良、慕稼谷、韦廉臣、庄延龄、立德、何天爵、花之安、白挨底、巴尔福、鲍乃迪、卜士礼、玛高温、方法敛、毛里逊、梅辉立、慕阿德、穆麟德、佛尔克、卫贤、福森、钢和泰、高延、福威勒、柔克义、叶长清、晏文士、金斯密、库寿龄、李提摩太、祁天锡、裴必胜、师克勤、苏阿德、谭微道、瓦特斯、德拉图什,等等。此外也有会外人士的来稿,作者也多是相关领域的著名学者,其中还有10余位中国籍学者,他们是王国维、胡适、蔡元培、伍连德、丁文江、竺可桢、郑德坤、李绍昌、林语堂、张星烺、林同济、朱元鼎、姚善友等。

学术性的原则也使得《皇家亚洲文会北华支会会刊》在学术界、尤其在汉学界,一直享有崇高声誉,不仅欧美150余家学术机构都积极收藏该刊,在中国,1928年后很多大学及科研单位也纷纷订阅。[7]石田干之助、贝德士、莫东寅以及《史学杂志》的编辑等学者在介绍近代汉学

---

[1] 按:1883年会刊印制了468份(不包含作者的20份抽印本),印制费用482元,故单册成本在1元左右,售价是2元;会员会费5元。Report of the Council for the year 1884, JNCBRAS, Vol. XIX, 1884, Piii.

[2] Proceedings, JNCBRAS, Vol. LXV, 1934, Pxxiv.

[3] 从当时的谈话记录看,该篇文章只是描述了外国人考察雪窦山的大致情况,且考察尚在继续。在笔者看来,裨治文的这篇演讲稿无法向听众提供相对清晰的雪窦山知识,所以未被刊发。见 North China Herald, Vol. III, No. 391, 23th Jan., 1858, P. 102.

[4] The Lecture on Mongolia, JNCBRAS, Vol. XLIII, 1916, P120.

[5] Proceedings, JNCBRAS, Vol. XLV, 1914, Pviii.

[6] 按:贝勒之文涉及大量汉字,排版校对都需要大量时间,不得不延期。Proceeding, JNCBRAS, Vol. XXXI, 1899, P194.

[7] Proceedings, JNCBRAS, Vol. LIX, 1928, Pvii.

杂志时,也均提及该刊。

四、编纂方针的变化

尽管会刊坚持亚洲文会之宗旨,但是在长达91年的发行历史中,因时代及学术环境的变化,20世纪后会刊之编纂方针和风格还是发生了一些变化。

20世纪初全球汉学研究发生了重大变化,开始进入各个专业领域的精深研究时代。各国纷纷成立专业性的汉学研究组织,开设中国语言学校和课程,出版各类专业型的学术期刊。汉学研究已经由此前的文献整理、信息搜集、语言学习转变到对具体问题的学术研究层面上,正如会刊编辑福开森在1910年时所言:"人们正在向其所熟悉的中国问题的各个分支进行深入研究,而不再是对中国文献做泛泛研究。"[1]

与此同时,各类专业的汉学研究期刊,如欧洲的《通报》、《东亚杂志》(*Ostasiatische Zeitschrift*),北京的《华裔学志》和《中国社会及政治学报》等期刊,纷纷吸引了20世纪初高水平学者之研究成果,如著名汉学家沙畹,其研究成果常常刊载于《通报》,却不见于会刊。

20世纪初汉学研究态势的变化对《皇家亚洲文会北华支会会刊》产生了很大冲击。会刊本是一个业余汉学家的学术摇篮,19世纪会刊的撰稿人主要是来华的传教士、外交官、海关人员,他们都是身居侨居地的业余汉学家,如伦敦会的伟烈亚力、艾约瑟,海关的夏德、马士(H. B. Morse),外交官卫三畏、谢立山(Alexander Hosie)等。这批业余汉学家在19世纪末已相继谢世,之后,在华侨民中能够在传教、工作之余从事汉学研究的人很少了,1912年莫安仁说:"目前人们为生活而奔波,能够专门做学问的时间已经很少了。"[2]1915年,编辑库寿龄感慨:"今年的会刊编辑工作比去年困难,在这个时代,每一个人似乎都很忙,并且,我也没有充足的材料。"[3]尽管还有少数业余从事对华研究之人,但他们更多热衷于对当时中国社会的关注,而不是对中国古代历史文明的探究。

传统汉学家相继谢世、新的专业汉学期刊分割市场的局面,直接导致会刊高质量稿源的减少。1909年,编辑坦言:"会刊文章没有以往三四年出版之文章有趣或有价值。"[4]该年会刊正文只有108页,是以往正常年份的一半。而稿源的减少,又直接影响到会刊的质量和销售。因此,编辑必须要使会刊受到学者及社会的欢迎。

1912年理事会决定将会刊的编辑工作从"理事会秘书常务工作中剥离,由专门的编辑负责,同时期刊趋向大众化,可读性强的方针受到一致赞同"。根据编辑莫安仁的报告,当年会刊是在一些对中国感兴趣之人的协助下完成编辑的,莫安仁认为"这些参与之人都期望会刊的内容既能吸引学者,也能吸引普通大众。论文变得短小,讨论各类有趣的问题"。而李提摩太听说会刊编辑方针改变后十分高兴,认为"以往亚洲文会并不受人欢迎,很难使普通大众接近",无疑说明,李提摩太极力要求会刊能够成为普通大众的阅读物。[5]1914年,编辑库寿龄明确提出:"会刊不仅要有汉学家和远东问题学者感兴趣的内容,它也必须在多数会员眼中显得有价值。必须既满足学者,也要满足读者的口味,要一视同仁。编辑希望将来的会刊中能够有普

---

[1] Preceedings, JNCBRAS, Vol. XLII, 1911, pp256-257.
[2] Proceedings, JNCBRAS, Vol. XLIII, 1912, P189.
[3] Proceedings, JNCBRAS, Vol. XLVI, 1915, Pix.
[4] Proceedings, JNCBRAS, Vol. XL, 1909, P130.
[5] Proceedings, JNCBRAS, Vol. XLIII, 1912, P190, 195.

通读者认为值得阅读的内容。"[1]

编辑方针的变更,效果比较突出,社会对会刊的兴趣日益增高。1913年来稿很多,编辑库寿龄高兴地说不再担忧稿源,并声明不可能刊登所有的来稿。[2]这一年会员费用收入突增,达1400元,占据年度收入的1/3之强!20世纪30年代每期会刊刊登的文章都在10篇左右,而19世纪也不过才7篇左右。1933—1936年会刊上的29篇论文分别来自以下国家:英国5篇、中国8篇、美国10篇、日本2篇、德国2篇、法国1篇、瑞典1篇。[3]稿件内容也呈现多样化,来自各个领域和各个地区的学者和考察者都向会刊投稿。

编辑方针的变更,也使得会刊的风格发生改变。在内容上,每期都有一篇与当时社会生活联系紧密的文章,保持刊登深入中国内陆的旅行游记之类的文章,这些游记文章题目广泛,内容丰富、信息量大,给读者以更多的关于中国的知识,如1912年会刊首篇文章是慕阿德(Moule, A. C.)的《泰山》,此篇文入选是因其"为当今旅游泰山提供了指南"[4]。在篇幅上,由以前的长篇大论,逐渐演变为短小精悍的小文章。20世纪会刊刊载的文章篇幅很少有超过50页的,而在19世纪常见100页以上的文章。在版式上,增加了关于中国百姓日常生活之图片、插图以吸引读者。如1938年刊登的《商代动物驯养与祭祀》一文就有27幅插图。此外,多设栏目,尽量满足所有阶层之口味。结果"会刊十分受到社会欢迎,已不仅仅局限于学术圈内了"[5],也成为普通大众的休闲用书,其销量得以增加,会刊实现了自负盈亏。

但会刊毕竟还是有一个学术性的原则,所以在走向通俗化的同时,也一直努力保持其一定的学术含量。在面临专业学术期刊竞争的环境下,会刊另辟蹊径,刊载了不少中国博物学方面的学术文章,借此维持其在学术界的地位。1919年,编辑们在组稿时就"抛弃了备用的讨论中国人思想的论文"[6],而采用的主要是自然科学的文章,13篇文章中博物学有6篇,其中《中国的农学、植物学和动物学》一文主要是拉丁文科学名词,比较枯燥,连编辑自己都感觉"令人生畏",但是依然能够被刊发,因为"商人及其他人会接受","对于学术和商业来说,这些都是重要的"。[7]1922年的会刊16篇文章中,11篇是科技文章。1937年,编辑苏阿德甚至将会刊称为"纯正的科技期刊"。[8]尽管如此,每期会刊依然还是有传统的汉学研究论文。1930年刊登的是1928年牛津大学东方学大会之7篇论文专辑,讨论的全部是传统汉学中的历史、哲学、语言、考古等方面的主题。1933年会刊上的11篇不同类型的文章"都是公认的远东问题研究专家之作,文章专业分布:历史3、考古1、哲学1、地理1、建筑1、文献1、目录学1、文学1。[9] 即便是博物学文章,也有不少研究中国民俗之文章,如苏阿德对中国动物象征意义的考察、伊博恩对中医文化的论述等,这类文章亦受到汉学界的好评。此外,1933年会刊增设"汉学札记"栏目,评述《通报》、《中国戏剧》(法文)、《艺术》等汉学期刊上的论文及国际汉学研究动态与国际东方学消息,向学术界传递了最新的研究动态。

---

[1] Proceedings, JNCBRAS, Vol. XLV, 1914, Pvii.
[2] Proceedings, JNCBRAS, Vol. XLIV, 1913, P210.
[3] Proceedings, JNCBRAS, Vol. LXVI, 1935, Pviii.
[4] Proceedings, JNCBRAS, Vol. XLIII, 1912, P195.
[5] 谭维理:《1830—1920年美国人之汉学研究》,《清华学报》(台湾)新二卷第二期(1961年),第266页。
[6] Proceedings, JNCBRAS, Vol. L, 1919, Pxi.
[7] Proceedings, JNCBRAS, Vol. L, 1919, Pxi.
[8] Proceedings, JNCBRAS, Vol. LXVIII, 1937, Px.
[9] Preceedings, JNCBRAS, Vol. LXV, 1934, Pxxv.

正是这种在学术与通俗间平衡的编辑方略,使得该刊在20世纪初汉学专业期刊林立的年代还能有一席之地,一直受到学界之重视,被视为汉学界的重要学术期刊,全世界的科学机构也都纷纷与亚洲文会交换各自的期刊。

内　　容

亚洲文会章程规定,会刊内容包括数篇在文会例会上宣读的文章、理事会和会计的年度总结报告及其他与理事会相关的内容。[1] 据此,每卷会刊均都包含三部分内容:会务纪要、正文、会员名录。

一、会务纪要

亚洲文会历年的活动记录,主要是年度总结报告,含会长之发言、财务之状况、图书馆与博物馆相关活动信息。有些年份还刊载了当年例会的详细记录,如1891年5月11日的例会记录长达13页,系玛高温演讲的《中国的驴、猫和羊可能来自外国》一文之内容。1889年12月20日之会务纪要全文刊登了花之安演讲的《汉字所反映的史前中国》之内容,及卫三畏、金斯密、艾约瑟等人就该文的讨论,其中金斯密一人的发言就长达8页。[2] 会务纪要对于了解亚洲文会之历史十分重要。

二、会员名录

会员是亚洲文会的重要组成部分,所以该会十分重视会员之信息。早年会员名录列在年度报告中,自1886年,每卷会刊都专列当年会员之名录,含会员之姓名、身份、联系地址、当选时间、会员类别等信息。笔者曾就所有的会员名录予以统计,初步显示有3100余名。会员名录不仅有助于深入了解亚洲文会,而且也能透视出近代在华外侨之社会文化生活,以及他们在近代中西文化交流中的贡献。

三、正文

会刊的正文部分,以栏目计,共有633篇文章、791篇书评、229个释疑、杂俎类短文、55个汉学家及会员之讣告、14年的中国大事记、34个图书馆新进书目,此外还有10余封读者来信,2份亚洲文会图书馆藏书目录。

1. 文章

每卷会刊都有关于中国及东亚之调查研究文章(Article),多则10余篇,少则1篇,此类文章总计有633篇。由于会刊的编辑原则是"涉猎各个课题",所以,在类别上,既有窄而专的研究型论文,也有宽而泛的普及型述论;既有调查报告,也有游记散文。所论述的具体对象,空间上覆盖全中国,时间上贯穿古今。所涉及的领域则有地理、历史、民俗、动物、植物、哲学、语言、宗教、法律、音乐、考古、医药、化学、物理、工程、地磁、地质、绘画、商业贸易、政府交通、社会经济、科学总论、图书馆学、人类学、政治学、文献学、星象学、碑刻、货币、陶瓷等30余个学科。

其中历史学方面的文章最多,近200篇,所讨论的内容涵盖面很广。既有对中国历史的综论,也有对某个阶段的专史做深入分析。有对大禹、周文王、刘邦、项羽、郭子仪、王安石、康熙、

---

[1] Report of the Council for the year 1874, JNCBRAS, Vol. IX, 1874, Pxx.
[2] Preceedings, JNCBRAS, Vol. XXIV, 1890, pp240-251.

骆秉章及明清来华传教士等历史人物的评介,有对漳州、南京、绍兴、和林、西安等古代都城的研究,有对中国外交政策的梳理,有对中外文化交流的研究等内容。

其中讨论较多的还是关于中国古代历史及文明,这方面的研究都围绕着一个主题——中国的历史与文明与西方是否有关?这个主题其实也是裨治文在开幕词中的发问,根源还是来自基督教文化的思考——中国取得如此辉煌的文学与科学成就,是否来自神的大能?是否在大洪水之后,闪族的后代来到了中国及东亚地区?循此,学者们纷纷展开了对中国古代历史文明的探究,并延伸至对中西文化交流的研究,成为近代中国学术史上一个热点。金斯密的《〈书经〉中关于周朝神秘起源的记载》与花之安的《史前中国》都探究了神话时代的中国社会形态,以说明神的后裔是否在华有痕迹;梅辉立的《火药和火器在中国人中的引介和使用》旨在考察火药是否由中国传向了西方。希姆利(Himly)的《中国棋类游戏》通过分析中国象棋与欧洲象棋的异同,来寻找西方可能影响中国的证据;艾约瑟的《古代中国对希腊和罗马的了解》提出欧洲的思想和希腊的艺术是通过亚历山大对中亚、西亚的侵掠所开辟的道路传入到中国的;夏德的《大秦在哪里?》、金斯密的《中国古代"月氐"和"羌"族考》、贝勒的《中亚与西亚中古时代之史地考》、林仰山(Drake,F. S.)的《中国西北通道》等论文都旨在寻求早期中西交往的历史痕迹。部分学者还从动物的分布与迁徙来寻找古代中国和西方的关系,如苏阿德的《中国的珍稀动物》与史莱德(David Sjölander)的《中亚盘羊的分布及习性》等。

地理和游记类文章是会刊正文的第二大内容,计有百篇左右。但是严格意义上的地理学论文很少,主要还是西人在华的旅行游记。这些逐日记录的游记详载了旅行者眼中的中国,内容包罗万象,含地理环境、物产、气候、交通、动植物、民俗等各个方面的内容。笔者仔细阅读后认为,这些游记与19世纪末欧洲出版的在华游记之畅销书,内容上有着本质的区别:会刊上游记文章之作者是探求知识,而不是寻求新奇;旨在传播真知,而不是扩大"传说",恪守了会刊的原则——提供实用的信息,比较客观地记录了近代中国的社会现状及风土人情。如1868年伟烈亚力的《湖北、四川和陕西三省旅行记》,与其说是游记,不如说是对长江河谷的学术考察。作者记录了从汉口到成都长江两岸所有聚落的名称及方位,以及沿途的地质地貌、建筑与习俗、商贸与矿藏、民族与人口等信息,套用人类学的术语,可以说是一部长江河谷的"民族志",而其罗列的四川省百余种物产的名录更令外侨看重,《北华捷报》建议读者将此记载与《商务指南》(Chamber of Commerce Report)做比较阅读。[1] 1923年斐士的《从太原府经五台山至蒙古边境纪行》一文,记录了峡谷风情、官员交涉、官方大楼、旅馆环境、五台风景、邮政方式、山西名产、佛教寺庙、蒙古大汗、迎客方式、驼队旅途、民间故事、河流地貌、大同街景、归绥物产、当地工业、旅程时间等等各类信息,[2] 简直是一幅民国时期晋北、蒙南的全景式画卷。由于这些游记反映了一个比较真实的中国,因此会刊成为近代西方知识界了解中国的一个重要信息来源,如《柏林地理学会》(Geographical Society of Berlin)上经常发表文章对西方游客在中国各地的探索结果作介绍,这些资料通常引自会刊。[3]

博物学论文是会刊正文的第三大内容。博物学是亚洲文会的重要调查研究对象之一,亚洲文会还设有博物馆,所以会刊上有不少关于中国博物学方面的文献,其中不乏名篇之作。植

---

[1] Review, North China Herald, 19th, Aug., 1869.
[2] Fischer, Emil Sigmund, Modern Travel from Tai Yuan Fu via Mount Wu Tai to the Mongolian Frontier. JNCBRAS, Vol. LIV, 1923, P81.
[3] [美]M. G. 马森著,杨德山译:《西方的中华帝国观》,第76页。

物学方面,如贝勒的《先辈欧人对中国植物的研究》;动物学方面有生物学家祁天锡的成名作《长江下游河滩鸟类名录》[1]、福威勒(Fauvel, A. A.)的《中国的短吻鳄》等,后者确认了扬子鳄这一物种,具有重要的学术价值。博物学理论方面,有谭微道的《华西和华北博物志》、苏阿德的《中国博物志》,两文都是关于中国博物学的奠基之作;地质学方面有金斯密的《地质学和历史学的交汇领域》,该文就古代东亚地质变迁与人类历史之间的关系进行了理论分析,从古代中外民族交往、中亚历史地理、历史气候变迁、动植物分布等方面阐释了中国文献对于研究地质变迁的重要性。这些博物学论文向西方世界诉说着一个拥有科学知识的中国,促进了西方人对中国这一领域的认识。

在其他多个领域,会刊也有不少重要的文章。天文学有伟烈亚力的《中国典籍中关于日月食的记录》、谢立山的《公元前28年至公元1617年在中国观测到的太阳黑子及太阳阴影》;气象学有费理饬(Fritsche, H. P. H.)的《东亚气候》、莫耶(Raymond T. Moyer)的《中国北方的干旱》、叶长清的《青藏高原边境高海拔气温观测记录》;民俗学有苏阿德的《中国动物主题神话》、陶然士的《四川的丧葬习俗》;宗教方面有卫理的《清朝的国教》、钢和泰的《玄奘及其现代研究》、翟理斯的《〈历代神仙通鉴〉中的基督》、毕士勃的《古代中国之土地崇拜》、季理斐的《河南犹太人》、梅益盛的《中国回教徒》;语言学有穆麟德的《比较语言学的局限》、庄延龄的《汉语方言比较研究》;碑铭学有丁韪良的《开封府的犹太教纪念碑》、卜士礼的《周朝石鼓》、贾礼士对朝鲜《大清皇帝功德碑》的解释[2];哲学方面有佛尔克的《王充与柏拉图论死亡与永生》与《中国之辩士》,及卜道成(J. P. Bruce)的《宋代哲学中的有神论》;政治学有童克圣(L. Tomkinson)的《中国人历史上的战争与和平观》、修中诚(E. R. Hughes)的《公元前三四世纪时的中国政治理想主义者和现实主义者》、班德瑞的《可能的改革与不可能的改革》;人类学有史禄国的《关于中国北方人的人类学研究》、葛学溥(Daniel H. Kulp)的《中国人体测量学:浙江与广东的研究》、法磊斯的《鱼皮鞑靼》、陶然士的《羌族的宗教信仰》;商贸方面有马士的《中国货币考》、玛高温的《中国行会制度》、益乐的《〈盐铁论〉选译》;文学有司登得《中国的抒情诗》、爱司克夫人的《中文诗及其内涵》;艺术方面有慕阿德(A. C. Moule)的《中国的乐器》;农业有西蒙的《中国农业物产图》;手工业有夏德的《古代陶瓷:中世纪中国工商业研究》、古庇的《华北白酒酿制》;医学有贝勒的《中国植物志》、伊博恩的、《中药中的龙》等中医系列研究论文,与当时伍连德、王吉民形成了中医药的研究阵地。[3]

正文中还有一些颇有价值的学术综述,如赖德烈的《西方学者中国历史研究成果综述》、史禄国的《通古斯文献研究综述》、苏阿德的《中国北部哺乳动物研究近况》、罗炳吉的《中国法律研究文献介绍》、盖乐的《东北亚研究的汉语文献》、来会理的《近十年之中国文学》、福开森的《罗振玉论著综述》、瓦特斯的《〈妙法莲华经〉述评》等,在当时,该类文章为相关研究奠定了基础,受到学界的重视,曾被多次引用和转载,如今也是我们了解相关学术史的重要文献。

由于亚洲文会以调查研究为主,所以正文中有各类对华调查报告十余篇。这些调查报告含有明确的考察目标、详细的考察过程、规范的书写内容,因其科学性较高,刊发之后一直受到中外学界的注意。如1868年《黄河新河道考察报告》,系1867年9月24日到11月20日间爱

---

[1] 王志稼:《祁天锡博士事略》,《科学》24卷1期(1940年1月),第70页。
[2] 关于此碑刻拓片的价值,参见程龙:《三田渡碑的一段学术史》,《读书》,2011年第4期。
[3] Preceedings, JNCBRAS, Vol. LXVII, 1936, Pix.

莲斯(Mr. Elias)在江苏、河南、山东三省对1855年铜瓦厢决口后黄河新河道的变迁情况做的考察记录,该文绘制了清晰的黄河新河道图,对于黄河新河道的水文特征、航运能力、河道沿岸的商业贸易、山东境内的物产情况均做了详细的记录。由于考察报告科学价值大,爱莲斯因此获得了英国皇家地理学会金奖。[1] 1913年祁天锡与慕维德(Lacy I. Moffett)撰写的《长江下游河滩鸟类名录》,闻名世界生物学界。[2] 其他调查报告还有:1885年的《何为孝顺?》、《中国溺婴的盛行》、《中国戏剧调查》,1886年的《用汉语传播西方知识的正反效果》,1887年的《中国合伙企业中成员的责任与义务》,1888年的《中国佃制及农民状况报告》、《钱塘江潮涌》,1889年的《中国货币和度量衡》,1893－1894年的《中国之内陆交通》等。

2. 杂纂、"释疑"与"汉学札记"

会刊正文部分还有一些短小的杂俎类文章。1864年新刊第一卷始就刊登有此类文章,主要是一些未被刊登的文章之简介,或对某些文章内容之增补。1885年,会刊模仿《远东释疑》杂志设"释疑"(Notes and Queries)栏目,主要介绍一些汉学界的信息,或者是一些学术争议,如1885年的《意大利汉学》一文谈到了意大利传教士的功绩。[3] 1886年刊登了夏德与啊查理关于大秦国的学术争议。[4]

1934年,"释疑"为"汉学札记"所代替,主要评述有关汉学期刊上的文章,介绍国际汉学动态及东方学消息。[5] 如1933年对《通报》、《远东博物院汇刊》等汉学杂志上的文章之驳斥,1935年刊载的美国汉学研究论文索引。这些文章多数都比较有趣,颇有学术价值。

3. "新书评介"

会刊中另一大内容是"新书评介"栏目。最初会刊并无此专栏,1880年代由于缺乏资金,亚洲文会图书馆无力购买图书,遂倡议社会捐赠,呼吁作者或者出版商向亚洲文会捐赠图书,凡捐赠的图书,会刊都予评介,以示感谢。由于亚洲文会图书馆旨在收藏关于中国的各类西文图书,所以被评介的图书几乎都是近代出版的各类西文汉学书籍。

1882年会刊上已有书评文章,但19世纪晚期比较少,只有15篇。自1900年,每年刊载的"新书评介"有30篇左右,截至1948年,共计有783篇书评,评介了787部书,其中专论中国的有730部。评论者多数是相关领域内的专家,甚至是著名的汉学家,点评精彩而到位。有些书评本身就是很好的学术论文,如第66卷(1935年)刊登美国建筑师茂非(Murphy, H. K.)的《评麻伦的〈清代皇家园林史〉》一文被认为是"当年最精彩的书评,读起来像一篇论文"[6]。这些书评材料侧面反映了近代西方汉学的发展概况。

4. 大事记内容

1858－1875年,每册会刊还设有专栏"最近中国大事记",摘录中外报刊中的一些新闻,主要内容是有三:当年中外交往中的重要大事,如第二次鸦片战争谈判的细节;中国的内政和动乱,如辛酉政变与太平天国运动;各国在华的科学考察活动,如李希霍芬来华之介绍。这些消息很受侨民欢迎,《北华捷报》曾予以好评:"对于热衷于远东事务的学者来说,其价值可谓不

---

[1] The North-China Branch of the Royal Asiatic Society, North-China Herald, 30th, Oct., 1873, P361.
[2] 王志稼:《祁天锡博士事略》,《科学》24卷1期(1940年1月),第70页。
[3] Italian contributions to Sinology, North-China Herld, 13th, Jan., 1886.
[4] 该文被朱杰勤先生全部翻译成中文,见(德)夏德著,朱杰勤译:《大秦国全录》,商务印书馆1964年版,第141-155页。
[5] Preceedings, JNCBRAS, Vol. LXV, 1934, Pxxv.
[6] Our Book Table, Chinese Recorder, Vol. LXVII, 1926, P111.

菲,对于普通读者也是非常有趣的。"[1]

5. 学者之讣告

会刊正文中还有65位著名汉学家及重要会员的讣告,内容含逝者生平、履历及学术成果。这些讣告中,不仅有翟理思、沙畹、夏德、劳费尔、鲍润生、傅兰雅、马士等一流汉学家的小传,而且可以见到一些二流汉学家之信息,如立德、韦廉臣、维维安·邓德、谢立山、庄延龄、柔克义、莫安仁、法磊斯、任修本、卫斐列、阿理文、欧特曼、梅尔思等人的工作与学术经历。

会刊之资料价值

会刊创刊号前言提出:"希望通过对华的调查研究为西方汉学提供令人满意的成果。"[2]已有的汉学史论著中都会提到《皇家亚洲文会北华支会会刊》,并认为其是近代国际汉学的重要园地之一。[3] 1933年贝德士从19种西文东方学报中一一精选出那些"材料丰富、解释精当、观念准确,且能引起研究中国文化各方面之兴趣,中国学者可参考之中国问题之论文",共计281篇,其中来自会刊的有55篇,数量仅次于《通报》的66篇,位居第二。[4] 1936年《史学消息》辟专栏介绍世界汉学有关杂志,高度评价会刊,称赞其"在许多方面都有佳作和珍贵资料。百余年间,对中国有价值之探讨数见不鲜",并对1936－1937年会刊上之论文一一做了提要。[5]

笔者曾著专文论述了会刊在近代汉学史上的地位与影响,概括为三:(1)会刊是近代西方汉学研究的前沿阵地之一,刊登了一些近代西方汉学的最新研究成果,推动了近代西方汉学之发展,是西方认识中国的重要刊物。(2)会刊为那些后来成为汉学家的早期在华外交官、传教士、部分商人提供了学习交流的外部环境,促成他们进入了汉学的研究领域。(3)会刊的学术价值要予以客观评价。就汉学研究而言,因为会刊文章类型多样化,内容无所不包,导致精深考证型的研究文章较少,而通俗性的游记文章占了一定的篇幅,所以当《通报》(T'oung Pao)、《华裔学志》(Monumenta Serica)、《哈佛亚洲研究》(Journal of Asiatic Studies)等专业类汉学研究学术期刊出现后,该刊在汉学界的地位就降低了。[6]

虽然该刊在汉学史及各专业学者眼中不是顶尖的学术期刊,但是该刊的资料价值丝毫不比任何一份期刊低,甚至要高很多,因为会刊的综合性、多样性所带来的信息量之大,是任何一份期刊都难以企及的,所以留下了颇具研究价值的资料。

实际上,会刊之资料价值很早就受到中外学者的关注。1885年的《中国戏剧调查》刊出后,《教务杂志》就曾予以好评,认为该文"大大有助于比较文学的研究"[7]。1915年韦伯在论

---

[1] The North-China Stunday News, 19th, Jan., 1930, P11.
[2] Preface, JNCBRAS, O. S. No. I, June, 1858.
[3] 见莫东寅:《汉学发达史》,上海书店1989年;方豪:《中西交通史》,岳麓书社1987年版;袁同礼:《西方论述中国文献目录:续高第〈中国书目〉》(China in Western Literature: a continuation of Cordier'a Bibliotheca Sinica, Yuan Tung-li, Cordier, Henri. Far Eastern Publications, Yale University, 1958);(日)石田干之助:《欧米人に於けろ支那研究》,东京创元社昭和十七年(1942年);(美)谭维理:《1830－1920年美国之汉学研究》,《清华学报》新二卷第二期(1962);高第:《西方汉学研究:1895－1898》(Les Etudes Chinoises 1895－1898)。
[4] 贝德士:《西文东方学报论文举要》,金陵大学中国文化研究所印行,民国二十二年。
[5] 《西洋汉学论文提要》,《史学消息》,第一卷第一期,第10页。
[6] 王毅:《〈皇家亚洲文会北中国支会会报〉之汉学价值》,《汉学研究通讯》2008年8月。
[7] Editoral Notes and Missionary News, Chinese Recorder, Vol. XVII, 1886, P243.

述中国古代农业制度时,因得不到《中国佃制及农民生活状况报告》一文而感到遗憾![1]

一些专业领域的文献索引也常常把会刊列为重要的参考文献。1928年袁同礼编的《中国音乐书举要》一文就收录了会刊中的两篇音乐文章。[2] 1936年杨遵仪编的《中国地质文献目录》也收录了会刊上发表的地质学学论文。[3] 1960年中国科学院地理研究所编的《中国地貌学文献目录1855-1958》收录了9篇会刊文章,至于被各个领域研究引用的文章就更多了。

会刊中的部分文章,因资料价值重大,20世纪50年代就被中国学者翻译成中文以便研究者利用。如1886年会刊上的玛高温之《中国的行会制度》一文成为《中国工商行会史料集》的开篇之作。[4] 1911年会刊中的《卫三畏日记》,因记录作者参加第二次鸦片战争中的见闻,受到中国史学会的重视而被选译入《第二次鸦片战争史料集》。[5]而1888年的《中国佃制及农民生活状况报告》一文则被章有义、李文治编纂的《中国近代农业史资料》全部翻译收录,遗憾的是,编译者受时代局限,从阶级斗争角度出发,人为拆分调查报告内容,分别编入地主与佃农的各个章节中,[6]割裂了原文的应有之义,以至后世学人即便见到资料出处,也难体会该篇调查报告原有之面目。

尽管如此,会刊中依然有大量的资料有待发掘和整理。在此重印之即,笔者不揣浅薄,以自己对会刊内容之阅读体会,略谈其一些资料价值,以说明重印之必要。

一、就近代西方汉学史研究而言,会刊是任何一个角度都绕不过的。正如《新中国评论》之评价:"任何一个致力于中国研究的学者都不能忽视会刊,因为它提供了许多有趣可读的文章。"[7]

90余年的"会务纪要"几乎完整地保存了近代西方汉学史,尤其是侨居地汉学之发展历程,有大量可资利用的学术信息。如1893年5月16日的例会记录全文刊登了艾约瑟的《国际东方学会议概要》,该文详细介绍了1892年在伦敦举办的东方学大会的情况,尤其是阐述了当时东方学研究的五大热点问题,对于考察历届东方学大会颇具参考意义。1885年的"释疑"栏目中介绍了"北京东方学会"(Peking Oriental Society)这一重要汉学机构的筹建过程及其与亚洲文会之间的关系。1936年的会务纪要提及了庚子赔款对汉学研究的资助。而会员讣告及会员名录也提供了一些汉学家的学术信息。如在对司登得的介绍中,不仅说明他对汉语之研究来自威妥玛的帮助和鼓励,而且提到其撰写的《北京方言词典》是十分畅销的书。"书评"内容及图书馆馆藏目录,则更加细腻地展现了近代西方汉学的发展状况。

二、就新闻史研究而言,这份近代中国境内发行时间最长的英文期刊,本身就是值得研究的对象。会刊记录了自身的发行历史,而且也能帮助我们了解近代上海西文报刊的一些侧影,如亚洲文会财务报表详细列出了历年的广告费用,这份序列完整的数字,无疑有助于了解近代上海西文报刊之广告经营。此外,会刊上早年的《最近中国大事记》对于研究19世纪中期之中

---

[1] [德]韦伯著,康乐、简惠美译:《韦伯作品集·中国的宗教》(V),广西师范大学出版社2004年版,第112页。
[2] 袁同礼:《中国音乐书举要》,《中华图书馆协会会报》1928年第3卷第4期。
[3] 杨遵仪编:《中国地质文献目录》,国立北平研究院总办事处出版课印行,民国二十四年。
[4] 彭泽益主编:《中国工商行会史料集》,中华书局1995年版,第2-51页。
[5] 中国史学会主编《第二次鸦片战争史》(六),上海人民出版社1979年版,第140-144、150-151、156-163、166-170、174、187-188、206-209、215-216、220-229页。
[6] 见李文治、章有义:《中国近代农业史资料》,生活·读书·新知三联书店1957年版,第42-61、57-62、193-198、216-217、229-230、284-292、462、648-672、680-690页。
[7] Recent Literature, The New China Review, Oct., 1919, P543.

国新闻史来说,亦是重要资料。

三、就中西文化交流史研究而言,会刊也是最佳的研究载体之一。1931年,工部局总董贝尔(Mr. Brean)在亚洲文会新楼奠基仪式上说:"亚洲文会是在华外侨研究东方文化的中心,也是东西方学者沟通的中心。"[1]而会刊则记录了亚洲文会近乎完整的历史。会刊也是西方人认识了解中国的重要窗口,阅读会刊能发现近代文化交流的一些具体的细节和生动的场景。如1928年6月28日亚洲文会选举胡适为理事会成员。1938年的《广州东印度公司商行的语言学生》一文则回顾了鸦片战争前夕,广州、澳门地区外国人学习汉语的情况。

四、就科技史研究而言,会刊有着大量珍贵的资料可资利用。亚洲文会博物馆的活动情况和标本信息显示了近代西方人在华采集动植物及矿物标本的途径,以及鉴定与科学命名的方法。如地质学标本就是由洋务运动时在华的工程师提供的,而亚洲文会则常常把标本送到英美相关机构去鉴定。一些文章保存了近代中国境内一些科学活动的具体过程,如郇和的《台湾纪行》详细描述了他在台湾发现鸟类标本的过程;晏文士的《中国三万英里行》记录的则是中国境内的首次地磁学科考行程;高第的《安南东京近事记》一文中叙述了1866年法国人在湄公河及云南地区科考的原因、过程和目标。1858年的"中国大事记"中详述了李希霍芬入华后的具体情况;劳费尔的讣告中介绍了19世纪末20世纪初远东四大探险活动。苏阿德的《中国博物志》一文,留下了关于近代西人在华采集动物物种的信息。

更为重要的是,会刊上还有各类原始观测数据及资料,如1859年5-12月烟台每日之气压、温度、风力、晴雨等观测数据,1874-1875年徐家汇天文台的各项观测数据,1876年俄国天文台绘制的当年东亚季风洋流图,1919年祁天锡撰写的《苏州及其周边地区动植物初探》,1922年艾勒斯(J. Hers)撰写的《豫北植物汉语名称》等,都是相关领域研究的重要资料。

五、就历史地理研究而言,1857年倭尔特对长江下游的详细勘测记录,可以帮助我们更为精准地理解近代长江河道的变迁。1894年的《中国之内陆交通》详述了村镇之间的交通线路与距离,无疑是研究近代交通地理的极好资料。1926年谢立山夫人撰写的《一张制作中的中国地图》则提供了中国近代地图制作的重要信息。

六、就书籍史及阅读史研究而言,会刊也留下了大量可资利用的材料。会务纪要中不乏关于近代汉学书籍的出版与发行信息,如学界均认为《中国丛报》对于西方人了解中国颇有价值,但是高第指出1885年亚洲文会重印《中国丛报》价值并不大,相反,应出版专门介绍中国各方面的小册子,每种8-10页即可,因为人们很难有时间阅读大部头著作。[2]而"书评栏目"更是提供了大量的书籍史资料,每篇书评几乎都涵盖了书的主要内容、学术价值、是否受到欢迎,部分书评还会提及作者信息,同类主题的学术背景,部分读者的阅读体会以及出版发行情况。阅读这些书评,可以了解到部分汉学著作在当时的受欢迎程度,以及各个出版商之间的差异化竞争策略。这些不仅对于书籍史、阅读史来说是极好的材料,而且也为研究别发洋行、商务印书馆等近代著名的出版机构提供了相关素材。

七、就文学研究而言,会刊上有一些最早被翻译成英文的中国诗歌,如爱司克夫人对杜甫诗歌的翻译。而百余篇游记所塑造的中国形象,更是比较文学所应关注的研究对象。

---

[1] Preceedings, JNCBRAS, Vol. LXIII, 1932, Pi.
[2] Report of the Council for the year 1874, JNCBRAS, Vol. IX, 1874, Px.

八、就上海史研究而言，会刊更是不可忽视的资料。亚洲文会设在上海，其图书馆、博物馆、会刊都是近代上海文化生活中的重要组成部分。会刊还留下了近代上海的社会史资料，如财务报告中的历年房租及工人工资，侨民对于上海气候、乡间民俗、华资银行的记载等内容，1939年还专门出版了号外《上海的食用鱼》，这些对于了解近代上海的社会经济史都是不可缺的资料。所以，胡道静先生也把亚洲文会称为"以上海为研究对象的团体"[1]。

以上只是笔者的一些阅读体会，实际上，每一个学科都可在《皇家亚洲文会北华支会会刊》中找到可资利用的资料。相信会刊之重印，必然会推动各个学科与领域的相关研究。

---

[1] 胡道静：《历史上以上海为研究对象的学术团体》，《档案与史学》1989年第2期。

分卷细目

题　　名	中译题名	责任者	责任者中文名	页码
O. S. VOL. I No. I(1858)				
Inaugural Address	裨治文就职演说	Bridgman, Elijah Coleman	裨治文	2-11
On Cyclones, or the Law of Storms	飓风之规律	Nicolson, F. W.		2-27
Coins of the Ta-Ts'ing, or Present Dynasty of China	大清货币	Wylie, Alexander	伟烈亚力	2-54
Contribution to the Ethnology of Eastern Asia	东亚民族学论稿	Macgowan, Daniel John	玛高温	2-113
A Buddhist Shastra, Translated from the Chinese: with an analysis and notes	《壹输卢迦论》译稿与注释	Edkins, Joseph	艾约瑟	2-117
Visit to Simoda and Hakodadi in Japan	日本下田与函馆游记	Foote, A. H.		2-139
Record of Occurrences in China	中国大事记			2-148
O. S. VOL. I No. II(1859)				
Narrative of a Visit to the Island of Formosa	台湾纪行	Swinhoe, Robert	郇和	2-167
Notices of the Character and Writings of Meh Tsï	墨子述略	Edkins, Joseph	艾约瑟	2-187
Chinese Bibliography	中国的文献学	Macgowan, Daniel John	玛高温	2-192
On the Musical Notation of the Chinese	中国的乐谱	Syle, Edward W.	帅福守	2-198
Lecture on Japan	关于日本的演讲	Williams, Samuel Wells	卫三畏	2-214
On the Study of the Natural Science in Japan	自然科学学习在日本	Meerdervoort, Johannes Lijdius Catharinus Pompe van		2-245
Memorandum on the Present State of Some of the Magnetic Elements in China and Places Adjacent	中国及周边地区地磁纪要	Shadwell, C. B.		2-256
Notes on Some New Species of Birds Found on the Island of Formosa	台湾岛上新发现的鸟类	Swinhoe, Robert	郇和	2-259
Sailing Directions for the Yang-tsze Kiang, from Woosung to Hankow	长江航路指南：从吴淞到汉口	Ward, John	倭尔特	2-265
Thermometrical Observations, Taken During a Passage from Nagasaki to Shanghai	长崎到上海沿途温度记录	Fedorovitch, J.		2-281
Record of Occurrences in China	中国大事记			2-282

(续表)

题 名	中译题名	责任者	责任者中文名	页码
O. S. VOL. I No. III(1859)				
Sketches of the Miáu-tsze	苗族概述	Bridgman, Elijah Coleman	裨治文	2-301
The Small Chinese Lark	中国的云雀	Swinhoe, Robert	郇和	2-327
On the Banishment of Criminals in China	中国的流刑	Macgowan, Daniel John	玛高温	2-332
Cotton in China	中国的棉花	Robertson, D. B.	罗伯逊	2-339
A Sketch of Tauist Mythology in its Modern Form	道教神话的现代形式概述	Edkins, Joseph	艾约瑟	2-345
Narrative of the American Embassy to Peking	美国使团北京纪行	Williams, Samuel Wells	卫三畏	2-350
Meteorological Tables, from Observations in Japan	日本气象观测表	Fedorovitch, J.		2-381
Record of Occurrences	中国大事记			2-384
O. S. VOL. II No. I(1860)				
A Sketch of the Life of Confucious	孔子的生平	Edkins, Joseph	艾约瑟	2-409
The Ethics of the Chinese, with Special Reference to the Doctrines of Human Nature and Sin	中国人的伦理观：关于人性和罪的信条	Griffith, John	杨格非	2-428
On the Cosmical Phenomena in the Neighborhood of Shanghai, during the Past Thirteen Centuries	过去13个世纪上海周边地区观测到的特异自然现象	Macgowan, Daniel John	玛高温	2-453
On the Ancient Mouths of the Yang-tsï Kiang	古代长江入海口	Edkins, Joseph	艾约瑟	2-485
Dissection of a Japanese Criminal	解剖一名日本死囚	Meerdervoort, Johannes Lijdius Catharinus Pompe van		2-493
Notes on the Mineral Resources in Japan &c.	日本的矿藏及其他	Shock, W. H.		2-500
Supplemental Memorandum on the Present State of the Magnetic Elements in China and Places Adjacent	中国及周边地区地磁学纪要补充	Shadwell, C. B.		2-503
Temperature of Hakodadi, from Observations Taken at the English Consulate, from October 1858 to September 1859	1858年10月至1859年9月函馆气温记录	Courtney, Charles		2-504
Winds and Weather at Chefoo, during Seven Months of the Year 1859	1859年7个月中芝罘（烟台）的风与气候	Ward, John	倭尔特	2-505
Record of Occurrences	中国大事记			2-513

(续表)

题　　名	中译题名	责任者	责任者中文名	页码
N. S. VOL. I(1864)				
Notes on the City of Yedo, the Capital of Japan	日本首都江户	Lindau, Rudolph	林道	3-7
Notes on Some of the Physical Causes which Modify Climate	影响气候的物理因素	Henderson, James	韩德森	3-20
Narrative of an Overland Trip, Through Hunan, from Canton to Hankow	陆上行纪：从广州经湖南至汉口	Dickson, W.	迪克森	3-37
The Overland Journey from St. Petersburg to Pekin	陆上之旅：从圣彼得堡到北京	Wylie, Alexander	伟烈亚力	3-53
The Medicine and Medical Practice of the Chinese	中医和中药	Henderson, James	韩德森	3-73
The Sea-board of Russian Manchuria	俄占外东北（外满洲）的海岸线	Canny, J. M.	甘霓仁	3-122
Retrospect of Events in the North of China during the Years 1861-1864	1861—1864年华北大事记	Jamieson, R. A.	詹美生	3-161
Miscellaneous	杂记			3-185
Summary of Proceedings	1864年会议纪要			3-198
Report for the Year 1864	1864年度报告			3-201
List of Members (Corrected to March 10th, 1865)	会员名录（更新至1865年3月10日）			3-208
Rules of the NCBRAS, Passed at the Annual Meeting of the Society Held Jan. 10th 1865	亚洲文会北华支华章程（1865年1月10日年会上通过）			3-211
N. S. VOL. II(1865)				
Notes on the Geology of the Great Plain	大平原地质简论	Lamprey, Dr.	兰普雷	3-221
A Sketch of the Geology of a Portion of Quang-tung Province	广东省局部地质概述	Kingsmill, Thomas William	金斯密	3-241
Neau-show: Birds and Beasts (of Formosa)	台湾鸟兽（译自《台湾府志》）	Swinhoe, Robert	郇和	3-261
Sei Yo Ki-Bun, or *Annals of the Western Ocean*	西洋纪闻	Brown, S. R.	勃朗	3-275
Sorgo, or Northern Chinese Sugar Cane	中国北方的甜高粱	Collins, Varnum D.	葛林德	3-307
A Visit to the Agricultural Mongols	访蒙古农耕区	Edkins, Joseph	艾约瑟	3-321
The Hieroglyphic Character of the Chinese Written Language	中国书法——草书	Jamieson, R. A.	詹美生	3-335
The Remains of Ancient Kambodia	高棉遗迹	Bastion, Dr.	巴斯琴	3-347

(续表)

题　名	中译题名	责任者	责任者中文名	页码
Retrospect of Events in China and Japan during the Year 1865	1865年中国和日本大事记	Kingsmill, Thomas William	金斯密	3-357
Miscellaneous	杂记			3-393
Summary of Proceedings	1865年会议纪要			3-404
Report for the Year 1865	1865年度报告			3-411
List of Members, 1865	1865年会员名录			3-421

N. S. VOL. III(1866)

题　名	中译题名	责任者	责任者中文名	页码
Report for the Year 1866	1866年度报告			3-437
List of Members, 1866	1866年会员名录			3-446
Notes of a Journey from Peking to Chefoo via Grand Canal, Yen-Chow-Foo, etc.	北京出发经大运河、兖州府等至芝罘之旅	Williamson, A.	韦廉臣	3-451
Account of an Overland Journey from Peking to Shanghai, Made in Feburary and March 1866	1866年2、3月间北京至上海的陆上之旅	Martin, William Alexander Parsos	丁韪良	3-476
Sei Yo Ki-Bun (*Annals of the Western Ocean*)	西洋纪闻(续)	Brown, S. R.	勃朗	3-490
Description of the Great Examination Hall at Canton	广东贡院	Keer, J. G.	寇尔	3-513
Notes on the Opinions of the Chinese with Regard to Eclipses	中国人对月食的看法	Wylie, Alexander	伟烈亚力	3-523
On Some Wild Silkworms of China	中国野生蚕蛹	McCartee, D. B.	麦嘉缔	3-527
Political Intercourse between China and Lewchew	中国与琉球的政治关系	Williams, Samuel Wells	卫三畏	3-533
Notes on Some Outlying Coal-fields in the South-eastern Provinces of China	中国东南省份偏远地区的煤田	Kingsmill, Thomas William	金斯密	3-546
A Short Sketch of the Chinese Game of chess	中国象棋	Hollingworth, H. G.	荷魏尔	3-559
Retrospect of Events in the North of China during the Year 1866	1866年华北大事记	Butcher, H.	布彻	3-565
Supplementary Notes to the Intercourse between China and Lewchew	中国与琉球关系的补充说明			3-571

N. S. VOL. IV(1867)

题　名	中译题名	责任者	责任者中文名	页码
Sketch of a Journey from Canton to Hankow Through the Provinces of Kwangtung, Kwangsi, and Hunan, with Geological Notes	从广州出发穿越广东、广西、湖南到达汉口之旅(附地质笔记)	Bickmore, Albert S.	贝克莫尔	4-7
Translation of Inscription on Tablet at Hang Chow, Recording the Changing the T'ien Chu Tang (Roman Catholic Church) into the T'ien Hao Kung	杭州《天主堂改为天后宫碑记》英译	Gardner, Christopher T.	嘉托玛	4-27

(续表)

题 名	中译题名	责任者	责任者中文名	页码
Notes on the North of China, it's Productions and Communications	华北记略：物产与交通	Williamson, A.	韦廉臣	4-39
Notes on the Productions, Chiefly Mineral of Shan-tung	山东物产（以矿产为主）	Williamson, A.	韦廉臣	4-70
Entomology of Shanghai	上海的昆虫	Pryer, W. B.	朴贲懿	4-80
Notes on a Portion of the Old Bed of the Yellow River and the Water Supply of the Grand Canal	黄河古河床及大运河水源供给	Elias, Ney	爱莲斯	4-86
Eclipses Recorded in Chinese Works	中国典籍中关于日月食的记录	Wylie, Alexander	伟烈亚力	4-93
Chinese Chronological Tables	中国历史年表	Mayers, William Frederick	梅辉立	4-165
The Christianity of Hung Tsiu Tsuen, a Review of Taeping Books	洪秀全之基督教：评太平天国发行的神学书籍	Forrest, Robert James	富礼赐	4-193
Carte Agricole Générale de l'Empire Chinois, Texte Préface, Légende et Répertoire	中国农业物产图	Simon, G. Eug.	西蒙	4-215
Chinese Notions about Pigeons and Doves	中国人关于鸽子的看法	Werner, Edward Theodore Chalmers	倭讷	4-231
The Bituminous Coal Mines West of Peking	北京西部的烟煤矿	Edkins, Joseph	艾约瑟	4-249
Retrospect of Events in China and Japan during the Year 1867	1867年中国和日本大事记	Kingsmill, Thomas William	金斯密	4-257
Miscellaneous	杂记			4-272
N. S. VOL. V(1868)				
Note sur les Petites Société d'Argent en Chine	中国小型钱庄概要	Simon, G. Eug.	西蒙	4-279
Notes on the Coal Fields and General Geology of the Neighbourhood of Nagasaki	长崎周边的煤田及地质概述	Kingsmill, Thomas William	金斯密	4-302
Notions of the Ancient Chinese Respecting Music	古代中国人的音乐观念	Jenkins, B.	秦右	4-308
Some Remarks on Recent Elevations in China and Japan	关于近期中国和日本陆地上升的解释	Bickmore, Albert S.	贝克莫尔	4-336
Notions of Lok'Ping Cheung, Late Governor General of Sze Chuen	前四川总督骆秉章	Preston, C. F.	丕思业	4-345
The Tablet of Yü	大禹碑	Medhurst, W. H.	麦华陀	4-356
Note sur Quelques unes des Recherches que l'on Pourrait Faire en Chine et au Japon au Point de vue de la Geologie et de la Paléontologie	中国和日本古生物学和地质学研究刍议	Simon, G. Eug.	西蒙	4-365

(续表)

题　　名	中译题名	责任者	责任者中文名	页码
Itinerary of a Journey Through the Provinces of Hoo-pih, Sze-chuen and Shen-se	湖北、四川和陕西三省旅行记	Wylie, Alexander	伟烈亚力	4－431
Report of an Exploration of the New Course of the Yellow River	黄河新河道考察报告	Elias, Ney	爱莲斯	4－537
Retrospect of Events in China and Japan during the Year 1868	1868年中国和日本大事记			4－558

N. S. VOL. VI (1869－1870)

题　　名	中译题名	责任者	责任者中文名	页码
Report for the Year 1869	1869年度报告			5－7
List of Members, 1869	1869年会员名录			5－11
Report for the Year 1870	1870年度报告			5－15
List of Members, 1870	1870年会员名录			5－19
Notes on the Shantung Province, being a Journey from Chefoo to Tsiuhsien, the City of Mencius	山东纪略：从芝罘（烟台）到邹县之旅	Markham, John.	马安	5－23
On Wen-ch'ang, the God of Literature, his History and Worship	文昌星的由来及文昌崇拜	Mayers, William Frederick	梅辉立	5－53
The Fabulous Source of the Hoang-ho	黄河源头	Eitel, E. J.	艾德	5－67
Sur les Institutions de Crédit en Chine	中国银行机构	Simon, G. Eug.	西蒙	5－75
On the Introduction and Use of Gunpowder and Firearms among the Chinese	火药和火器在中国人中的引介和使用	Mayers, William Frederick	梅辉立	5－95
The Chinese Game of Chess as Compared with that Practised by Western Nations	中国棋类游戏	Himly, K.	希姆利	5－127
Note on the Chihkiang Miautsz	浙江苗族	Macgowan, Daniel John	玛高温	5－145
Notes on the Provincial Examination of Chekeang of 1870, with a Version of One of the Essays	浙江1870年乡试（附范文一篇）	Moule, G. E.	慕稼谷	5－151
Chinese Chemical Manufactures	中国化工制造	Smith, F. Porter.	师维善	5－161
Journal of a Mission to Lewchew in 1801	1801年使琉球记	Williams, Samuel Wells	卫三畏	5－171
Translation of the Inscription upon a Stone Tablet Commemmorating the Repairs upon the Ch'eng Hwang Miau or Temple of the Tutelary Deity of the City	郑板桥《重修城隍庙碑记》英译	McCartee, D. B.	麦嘉缔	5－195
Retrospect of events in China and Japan During the years 1869 and 1870	1869－1870年中国和日本大事记			5－201

N. S. VOL. VII (1871－1872)

题　　名	中译题名	责任者	责任者中文名	页码
Report for the Year 1872	1872年度报告			5－231

(续表)

题　名	中译题名	责任者	责任者中文名	页码
List of Members, 1871-1872	1871-1872年会员名录			5-236
A Historical and Statistical Sketch of the Island of Hainan	海南简史	Mayers, William Frederick	梅辉立	5-241
The Aborigines of Hainan	海南土著居民	Swinhoe, Robert	郇和	5-265
Narrative of an Exploring Visit to Hainan	海南探险记	Swinhoe, Robert	郇和	5-281
Chinese Lyrics	中国的抒情诗	Stent, George Carter	司登得	5-333
The Mythical Origin of the Chow or Djow Dynasty, as Set Forth in the Shoo-king	《书经》中关于周朝神秘起源的记载	Kingsmill, Thomas William	金斯密	5-377
The Obligations of China to Europe in the Matter of Physical Science Acknowledged by Eminent Chinese	中华先驱从欧人那里引进自然科学知识	Moule, G. E.	慕稼谷	5-387
The Life and Works of Han Yu or Han Wen-kung	韩愈生平及作品	Werner, Edward Theodore Chalmers	倭讷	5-405
Chinese Legends	中国的(民间)传说	Stent, George Carter	司登得	5-423
The Antiquities of Cambodia	柬埔寨古迹	Thompson, J.	汤顺	5-437
Quelques Renseignements sur l'Histoire Naturelle de la Chine Septentrionale et Occidentale	华西和华北博物志	David, Armand.	谭微道	5-445
Chinese Use of Shad in Consumption and Iodine Plants in Scrofula	中国人用鲥鱼治痨病、用碘酒治淋巴疾病的方法	Macgowan, Daniel John	玛高温	5-475
On the "Mutton Wine" of the Mongols and Analogous Preparations of the Chinese	蒙古的烤羊肉和酒	Macgowan, Daniel John	玛高温	5-477
Retrospect of Events in China &c. During the Years 1871 and 1872	1871-1872年中国大事记			5-481
Meteorological Observations for 1872	1872年气象观测			5-491
N. S. VOL. VIII(1873)				
Report for the Year 1873	1873年度报告			6-7
List of Members, 1873	1873年会员名录			6-15
Recollections of China Prior to 1840	在华往事(1840年前)	Williams, Samuel Wells	卫三畏	6-19
The Legend of Wên Wang, Founder of the Dynasty of the Chows in China	关于周朝建立者周文王的传说	Kingsmill, Thomas William	金斯密	6-41
Extracts from the History of Shang-hai	上海史摘要	Schmidt, C.	史密德	6-49
Chinese Fox-myths	中国神狐故事	Werner, Edward Theodore Chalmers	倭讷	6-63

(续表)

题　名	中译题名	责任者	责任者中文名	页码
Brief Account of the French Expedition of 1866 into Indo-China	法国1866年远征印度支那概要	Viguier, S. A.	威基谒	6-85
A Visit to the City of Confucius	孔子家乡曲阜之旅	Edkins, Joseph	艾约瑟	6-97
Short Notes on Chinese Instruments of Music	中国乐器简介	Dennys, N. B.	丹尼斯	6-111
The Stone Drums of the Chou Dynasty	周朝石鼓	Bushell, S. W.	卜士礼	6-151
Retrospect of Events in China for the Year 1873	1873年中国大事记			6-199

N. S. VOL. IX(1874)

题　名	中译题名	责任者	责任者中文名	页码
Report for the Year 1874	1874年度报告			6-213
Rules of the NCBRAS	亚洲文会北华支会章程			6-229
List of Members, 1874	1874年会员名录			6-233
Introduction. Presidents Address, Delivered Feb. 19th, 1874	亚洲文会北华支会会长1874年2月19日致辞			6-237
Notes on Col. Yule's Edition of Marco Polo's "Quinsay"	亨利·裕尔版《马可波罗游记》中的"行在"	Moule, G. E.	慕稼谷	6-247
Legends of the Ancient Mazdayaçnian Prophets, and the Story of Zoroaster	古代胡腊玛教先知的传说和琐罗亚斯德的故事	Camajee, D. N.	卡姆杰	6-271
The Aborigines of Northern Formosa	台湾北部的土著居民	Taintor, E. C.	廷得尔	6-299
Notes on the Miao-fa-lien-hua-ching, a Buddhist Sutra in Chinese	《妙法莲华经》述评	Werner, Edward Theodore Chalmers	倭讷	6-335
Narrative of Recent Events in Tong-King	安南东京近事记	Cordier, Henri	高第	6-361
Notes on Chinese Toxicology	中国毒物学	Macgowan, Daniel John	玛高温	6-419
Retrospect of Events in China and Japan for the Year 1874	1874年中国和日本大事记	Thomas, James.	唐默思	6-429
A Classified Index to the Articles Printed in the JNCBRAS, from the Foundation of the Society to the 31th of Dec., 1874	亚洲文会北华支会自创立至1874年12月31日止所刊文章分类索引			6-447

N. S. VOL. X(1875)

题　名	中译题名	责任者	责任者中文名	页码
Report for the Year 1875	1875年度报告			7-9
List of Members, 1875	1875年会员名录			7-18
Elucidations of Marco Polo's Travels in North-China, Drawn from Chinese Sources	用中国文献释马可波罗中国北部之游	Palladius, Archimandrite.	鲍乃迪	7-21

(续表)

题　名	中译题名	责任者	责任者中文名	页码
Notes Made on a Tour Through Shan-Hsi and Shen-Hsi	陕西和山西旅行记	Holcombe, C.	何天爵	7-75
Short Notes on the Identification of the Yuè-ti and Kiang Tribes of Ancient Chinese History	中国古代"月底"和"羌"族考	Kingsmill, Thomas William	金斯密	7-91
Notices of the Mediaeval Geography and History of Central and Western Asia	中亚与西亚中古时代之史地考	Bretschneider, E.	贝勒	7-95
Retrospect of Events in China for the Year 1875	1875年中国大事记	Little, Archibald J.	立德	7-329
List of the Principal Tea Districts in China and Notes on the Names Applied to the Various Kinds of Black and Green Tea	中国主要产茶区及红茶、绿茶名录			7-347
Observatoire Météorologique et Magnétique des Pères de la Compagnie de Jesus, à Zi-Ka-Wei	徐家汇天文台1874年9月至1875年8月天气与地磁公报			7-363
N. S. VOL. XI (1876)				
Report for the Year 1876	1876年度报告			8-7
List of Members, 1876	1876年会员名录			8-20
Inaugural Address by the President, Delivered on the 20th of Feb., 1877. —The Border Lands of Geology and History	地质学和历史学的交汇领域（亚洲文会会长1877年2月20日就职演说）	Kingsmill, Thomas William	金斯密	8-23
Fort Zelandia, and the Dutch Occupation of Formosa	热兰遮城及荷兰对台湾的殖民	Hobson, H. E.	好博逊	8-55
The Vertebrata of the Province of Chihli with Notes on Chinese Zoological Nomenclature	直隶的脊椎动物及中国动物命名法	Mollendorff, O. F. von.	穆林德	8-63
On the Style of Chinese Epistolary Composition	中国书信格式	Martin, William Alexander Parsos	丁韪良	8-135
On Chinese Names for Boats and Boat Gear with Remarks on the Chinese Use of the Mariner's Compass	船、舵之中文名及指南针的应用	Edkins, Joseph	艾约瑟	8-145
Chinese Eunuchs	中国的宦官	Stent, George Carter	司登得	8-165
N. S. VOL. XII (1877)				
List of Members, 1877	1877会员名录			8-213
On the Stone Figures at Chinese Tombs and the Offering of Living Sacrifices	中国墓地中的石像和活祭品	Mayers, William Frederick	梅辉立	8-217
The Comparative Study of Chinese Dialects	汉语方言比较研究	Parker, Edward Harper	庄延龄	8-235

(续表)

题　名	中译题名	责任者	责任者中文名	页码
Droughts in China, A. D. 620 to 1643	公元620年至1643年中国的旱灾	Hosie, Alex.	谢立山	8-267
Sunspots and Sun-shadows Observed in China, B. C. 28 – A. D. 1617	公元前28年至公元1617年在中国观测到的太阳黑子及太阳阴影	Hosie, Alex.	谢立山	8-307
The Ancient Language and Cult of the Chows	周朝的语言和文化	Kingsmill, Thomas William	金斯密	8-313
The Climate of Eastern Asia	东亚气候	Fritsche, H.	费理饬	8-347

N. S. VOL. XIII(1878)

题名	中译题名	责任者	责任者中文名	页码
Report for the Year 1878	1878年度报告			9-7
List of Members, 1878	1878年会员名录			9-9
Address to the Members of the NCBRAS, delivered at Shanghai, 3rd Feb., 1879	亚洲文会北华支会会长1879年2月3日的演讲	Kingsmill, Thomas William	金斯密	9-25
Alligators in China	中国短吻鳄	Fauvel, A. A.	福威勒	9-39
Periodical Change of Terrestrial Magnetism	地磁周期变化	Schulze, F. W.	舒尔兹	9-81
The Family Law of the Chinese, and its Comparative Relations with that of Other Nations	中国人之家法及其与他国家法之比较	Möllendorff, P. G. von.	穆麟德	9-145
The Story of the Emperor Shun	舜帝的传说	Kingsmill, Thomas William	金斯密	9-169

N. S. VOL. XIV(1879)

题名	中译题名	责任者	责任者中文名	页码
Report for the Year 1879	1879年度报告			9-185
List of Members (May, 1880)	会员名录(更新至1880年5月)			9-187
The Intercourse of China with Central and Western Asia in the 2nd Century B. C.	公元前2世纪中国与中亚西亚各国的交往	Kingsmill, Thomas William	金斯密	9-201
Rock Inscriptions at the North Side of Yentai Hill	雁荡山北麓的石刻	Rhein, J.	来因	9-231
Siamese Coinage	暹罗货币	Haas, Joseph.	夏士	9-235

N. S. VOL. XV(1880)

题名	中译题名	责任者	责任者中文名	页码
Report for the Year 1880	1880年度报告			9-269
List of Members (July, 1881)	会员名录(更新至1881年7月)			9-272

(续表)

题　　名	中译题名	责任者	责任者中文名	页码
Early European Researches into the Flora of China	先辈欧人对中国植物的研究	Bretschneider, E.	贝勒	9-313
Coins of the Present Dynasty of China	大清钱币	Bushell, S. W.	卜士礼	9-507
The "Naturalistic" Philosophy of China	中国的自然主义哲学	Balfour, Frederic Henry	巴尔福	9-621

N. S. VOL. XVI(1881)

题　　名	中译题名	责任者	责任者中文名	页码
Notes on the Hydrology of the Yang-tse, the Yellow River, and the Pei-ho	长江、黄河和白河的水文	Guppy, H. B.	古庇	10-7
Some Notes on the Geology of Takow, Formosa	台湾打狗地质记录	Guppy, H. B.	古庇	10-19
Botanicon Sinicum (Part I)	中国植物志(一)	Bretschneider, E.	贝勒	10-24
The Climate of Shanghai	上海的气候	Dechevrens, M.	能恩斯	10-237
Miscellaneous—List of Ferns Found in the Valley of the River Min, Foochow	杂记：福州闽江河谷发现的几种蕨类植物			10-257
Report for the Year 1881	1881年度报告			10-259
List of Members (April 1882)	会员名录(更新至1882年4月)			10-266

N. S. VOL. XVII(1882)

题　　名	中译题名	责任者	责任者中文名	页码
Notes on Chinese Composition	汉语修辞	Giles, Herbert Allen	翟理思	10-311
Notes on the Geology of the Neighbourhood of Nagasaki	长崎及其周边地质概况	Guppy, H. B.	古庇	10-333
Notes on the South Coast of Saghalien	库页岛南岸旅行记	Anderson, C.	安德森	10-345
Annam and its Minor Currency	安南及其钱币	Toda, Ed.	多达	10-351
The Hoppo-book of 1753	1753年的河伯书(粤海关报告)	Hirth, F.	夏德	10-531
Bibliography: Chinesische Grammatik mit Ausschluss des Niederen Stiles und der Heutigen Umgangs-sprache	嘎伯冷兹的《汉语语法》			10-547

N. S. VOL. XVIII(1883)

题　　名	中译题名	责任者	责任者中文名	页码
Report for the Year 1883	1883年度报告			11-7
What Did the Ancient Chinese Know of the Greeks and Romans	古代中国对希腊和罗马的了解	Edkins, Joseph	艾约瑟	11-37
Corea	法译《朝鲜志》摘要	Scherzer, F.	师克勤	11-61
Researches into the Geology of Formosa	台湾地质研究	Kleinwachter, George	康发达	11-73

(续表)

题　　名	中译题名	责任者	责任者中文名	页码
Fragmens d'un Voyage dans l'Interieur de la Chine	中国内陆游记	Imbault-Huart, Camille	于雅乐	11-91
Some Notes of a Trip to Corea, in July and August, 1883	1883年朝鲜旅行记	Morrison, G. James	毛里逊	11-185
Notes on Some Dikes at the Nouth of the Nankow Pass	南口关岩层小析	Guppy, H. B.	古庇	11-203
Samshu-brewing in North China	华北白酒酿制	Guppy, H. B.	古庇	11-207
Notes on Szechuen and the Yangtse Valley	四川及长江峡谷小记	Little, Archibald J.	立德	11-209
List of Members (Corrected up to 30th September 1884)	会员名录（更新至1884年9月30日）			11-229
Revised Rules of the NCBRAS (Instituted 24th September 1857)	亚洲文会北华支会章程（1857年9月24日修订）			11-234
Rules for the Issue of Books from the Library of the NCBRAS	亚洲文会北华支会图书馆借书条例			11-240

N. S. VOL. XIX（1884）

题　　名	中译题名	责任者	责任者中文名	页码
Report for the Year 1884	1884年度报告			11-249
Animal, Fossil, Mineral and Vegetable Products. Cousular District of Ichang in the Province of Hupeh, China	湖北宜昌地区动物、化石、矿物与植物物产	Gardner, C. T.	嘉托玛	11-259
A Journey in Chêkiang	浙江行记	Parker, Edward Harper	庄延龄	11-285
A Journey in Fukien	福建行记	Parker, Edward Harper	庄延龄	11-312
A Journey from Foochow to Wênchow Through Central Fukien	福州至温州旅行记	Parker, Edward Harper	庄延龄	11-333
A Buddhist Sheet-tract	一张佛教画	Moule, G. E.	慕稼谷	11-352
Trade Routes to Western China	华西商路	Hosie, Alex.	谢立山	11-361
Un Poëte Chinios du XVIIIe Siècle, Yüan Tseu-ts'ai, sa Vie et ses Oeuvres	诗人袁枚生平及其著作	Imbault-Huart, Camille	于雅乐	11-379
The Sêrica of Ptolemy and its Inhabitants	托勒密笔下的"秦国"及其居民	Kingsmill, Thomas William	金斯密	11-421

N. S. VOL. XX（1885）

题　　名	中译题名	责任者	责任者中文名	页码
The Hung-lou-mêng: Commonly Called "The Dream of the Red Chamber"	《红楼梦》简介	Giles, Herbert Allen	翟理思	11-447
The Prevalance of Infanticide in China	中国溺婴的盛行			11-471

(续表)

题　　名	中译题名	责任者	责任者中文名	页码
Notes and Queries	释疑			11-497
In Memoriam	悼文			11-504
Items	杂录			11-509
Literature	文献书目			11-510
The Mystery of Ta-ts'in [Review of Dr. Hirth's *China and the Roman Orient*]	大秦之谜：评夏德《中国和罗马人的东方》	Playfair, G. M. H.	白挨底	11-515
How Snow Inspired Verse, and A Rash Order Made the Flowers Bloom	《镜花缘》第四回英译	T., C. B.		11-527
Notes and Queries	释疑			11-533
In Memoriam	悼文			11-545
Literature Items	杂录			11-547
List of Members (Corrected up to 1st October 1885)	会员名录（更新至1885年10月1日）			11-552
What is Filial Piety?	何为孝顺？			11-561
Is China a Conservative Country?	中国是个保守的国度么？	Moromastix		11-591
Sinology in Italy	意大利汉学	Nocentini, Ludovico	诺琴蒂尼	11-601
Western Appliances in the Chinese Printing Industry	中国印刷业中的西方设备	Hirth, F.	夏德	11-609
Notes and Queries	释疑			11-624
Chinese Theatricals and Theatrical Plots: The Beating of a Golden Branch	中国戏剧调查：打金枝	Balfour, Frederic Henry	巴尔福	11-639
Chinese Theatricals and Theatrical Plots: The Widow no Widow	中国戏剧调查：寡妇上坟	Playfair, G. M. H.	白挨底	11-640
Chinese Theatricals and Theatrical Plots: Tattooing	中国戏剧调查：刺字	Edkins, Joseph	艾约瑟	11-641
Chinese Theatricals and Theatrical Plots: The Three Suspicions	中国戏剧调查：三疑	Giles, Herbert Allen	翟理思	11-643
Chinese Theatricals and Theatrical Plots: The Sheepfold	中国戏剧调查：牧羊圈	Allen, Herbert J.	啊查理	11-644
Chinese Theatricals and Theatrical Plots: A Dutiful and Unselfish Heart	中国戏剧调查：孝廉心	Brewitt-Taylor, C. H.	邓罗	11-646
Chinese Theatricals and Theatrical Plots: The Miser	中国戏剧调查：看财奴	Rhein, J.	来因	11-646
Chinese Theatricals and Theatrical Plots: The Two Soles, or Becoming an Acotr from Love	中国戏剧调查：比目鱼	Imbault-Huart, Camille.	于雅乐	11-647

(续表)

题　名	中译题名	责任者	责任者中文名	页码
Chinese Theatricals and Theatrical Plots: Imperial Troubles Settled	中国戏剧调查：定王难	Macgowan, Daniel John	玛高温	11-649
The Seaports of India and Ceylon. Part I	《瀛涯胜览》所载印度与锡兰的海港（一）	Phillips, George	费笠子	11-655
Some Additions to my *Chinese Grammar*	《汉语语法》补遗	Gabelentz, Georg Von der	嘎伯冷兹	11-673
Bibliography: List of Books and Papers on China, Published Since 1st January, 1884	中国专题书籍与论文目录（1884年1月后出版）	Hirth, F.	夏德	11-681
Notes and Queries	释疑			11-721
In Memoriam	悼文			11-733
Notices on New Books and Literary Notes	新书通告与文献札记			11-735
Proceedings	会议纪要			11-738
Report for the Year 1885	1885年度报告			11-740
List of Members, Having Joined from 1st October 1885	会员名录（1885年10月1日后加入的）			11-761
N. S. VOL. XXI（1886）				
The Advisability, or The Reverse, of Endeavouring to Convey Western Knowledge to the Chinese Through the Medium of Their Own Language	用汉语传播西方知识的正反效果			12-9
Histrionic Notes	戏曲演技札记	Macgowan, Daniel John	玛高温	12-30
Seaports of India and Ceylon. Part II	《瀛涯胜览》所载印度与锡兰的海港（二）	Phillips, George	费笠子	12-38
Roadside Religion in Manchuria	满洲的"路神"信仰	Macintyre, John	马钦泰	12-51
Alphabetical List of the Dynastic and Reign-Titles	中国王朝世系表	Playfair, G. M. H.	白挨底	12-75
Where was Ta-Ts'in?	大秦在哪里？	Allen, Herbert J.	啊查理	12-97
Reply to Mr. H. J. Allen's Paper "Where was Ta-Ts'in?"	答啊查理"大秦在哪里？"	Hirth, F.	夏德	12-106
Notes and Queries	释疑			12-113
Literary Notes	文献笔记			12-121
Proceedings	会议纪要			12-131
Chinese Guilds or Chambers of Commerce and Trades Unions	中国的行会制度	Macgowan, Daniel John	玛高温	12-141
Is Confucius a Myth?	孔子是虚构的吗？	Allen, Herbert J.	啊查理	12-201

(续表)

题　名	中译题名	责任者	责任者中文名	页码
Philological Importance of Geographical Terms in the *Shi-Ki*	《史记》中地理名词的语言学意义	Edkins, Joseph	艾约瑟	12-207
Ta-Ts'in and Dependent States	大秦及其属国	Allen, Herbert J.	啊查理	12-212
Reply to Mr. H. J. Allen's Paper *Ta-Ts'in and Dependent States*	《大秦及其属国》回应	Hirth, F.	夏德	12-217
Chinese Equivalents of the Letter "R" in Foreign Names	外国名称中字母"R"的中文对应词	Hirth, F.	夏德	12-222
Notes and Queries	释疑			12-232
Literary Notes	文献札记			12-241
Correspondence	通信			12-245
Proceedings	会议纪要			12-249
The Family Names	百家姓	Giles, Herbert Allen	翟理思	12-263
Manchu Relations with Tibet, or Si-Tsang	满洲与西藏的关系	Parker, Edward Harper	庄延龄	12-297
In Memoriam	悼文			12-313
Notices on New Books and Literary Notes	新书通告与文献札记			12-322
Proceedings of the Annual General Meeting, 1887	1887年年会纪要			12-334
Report for the Year 1886	1886年度报告			12-340
List of Members, 1886	1886年会员名录			12-371
N. S. VOL. XXII(1887)				
The Military Organization of China Prior to 1842	中国1842年前之军事组织(节选自魏源《圣武记》)	Parker, E. H.	庄延龄	12-385
Notes on the Mineral Resources of Eastern Shantung	山东东部的矿产资源	Becher, H. M.		12-406
Chinese Partnerships: Liability of the Individual Members	中国合伙企业成员的责任和义务			12-423
Notes on the Early History of the Salt Monopoly in China	中国早期盐业垄断史	Hirth, F.	夏德	12-437
The Salt Revenue of China	中国之盐税	Parker, Edward Harper	庄延龄	12-451
Remarks on the Production of Salt in China	中国盐业述评	Carles, W. R.; Zwehtkoff, P.	贾礼士	12-465
Names of the Sovereigns of the Old Corean States, and Chronological Table of the Present Dynasty	古代朝鲜君主名号及现王朝年表	Nocentini, Ludovico	诺琴蒂尼	12-474

(续表)

题　　名	中译题名	责任者	责任者中文名	页码
Notes and Queries	释疑			12-484
Literary Notes	文献札记			12-490
Correspondence	通信			12-497
Proceedings	会议纪要			12-500
Ancient Porcelain: A Study in Chinese Mediaeval Industry and Trade	古代陶瓷：中世纪中国工商业研究	Hirth, F.	夏德	12-513
The Chinese Oriental College	中国之东方学会——四夷馆	Hirth, F.	夏德	12-587
Notes and Queries	释疑			12-608
Literary Notes	文献札记			12-490
Chinese Names of Plants	植物汉语名称	Henry, Augustine	韩尔礼	12-617
Proceedings	会议纪要			12-669
Proceedings of the Annual General Meeting, 1888	1888年年会纪要			12-672
Report for the Year 1887	1887年度报告			12-674
List of Members (Corrected to 1st August 1888)	会员名录（更新至1888年8月1日）			12-705

N. S. VOL. XXIII(1888)

题　　名	中译题名	责任者	责任者中文名	页码
A Corean Monument to Manchu Clemency	朝鲜大清皇帝功德碑	Carles, W. R.	贾礼士	13-7
A Guide to True Vacuity	元阳子真空直指	Moule, G. E.	慕稼谷	13-15
Changchow, the Capital of Fuhkien in Mongol Times	元时福建省会漳州	Phillips, George	费笠子	13-29
The Porcelain Pagoda of Nanking	南京大报恩寺琉璃塔	Hobson, H. E.	好博逊	13-37
Notes and Queries	释疑			13-45
Proceedings	会议纪要			13-48
Appendix	附录			13-55
Tenure of Land in China and the Condition of the Rural Population	中国佃制及农民状况报告	Jamieson, George	哲美森	13-65
Proceedings	会议纪要			13-183
The Bore of the Tsien-tang Kiang (Hang-Chau Bay)	钱塘江涌潮	Moore, Osborne		13-195
Chinese Chess	中国象棋	Volpicelli, Z.	武尔披齐	13-260
Notes and Queries	释疑			13-298
Proceedings	会议纪要			13-300

(续表)

题　　名	中译题名	责任者	责任者中文名	页码
Procedings of the Annual General Meeting，1889	1889年年会纪要			13-302
Report for the Year 1888	1888年度报告			13-304
List of Members（Corrected to 31st August 1889）	会员名录（更新至1889年8月31日）			13-341

N. S. VOL. XXIV（1889－1890）

题　　名	中译题名	责任者	责任者中文名	页码
Essay on Manchu Literature	论满洲文献	Möllendorff, P. G. von	穆麟德	13-357
Currency and Measures in China	中国的货币与度量衡			13-402
Correspondence：The Preservation of the Nestorian Tablet and Other Ancient Monuments at Si-an-fu	关于西安景教碑与其他古迹保护的通信	Hughes, P. J.；Brandt, M. Von	许士；巴兰德	13-492
Literary Note	文献札记			13-496
Prehistoric China	史前中国	Faber, Ernst	花之安	13-497
Obituary	讣告			13-577
An Expounder of Dark Sayings：Review of Gile's Translation of *Chuang-tzǔ*	评翟理思译《庄子》	Playfair, G. M. H.	白挨底	13-580
Proceedings	会议纪要			13-590
Chinese Architecture	中国的建筑	Edkins, Joseph	艾约瑟	13-609
Notes on the Nestorians in China	中国景教徒纪略	Parker, Edward Harper	庄延龄	13-645
The Tent Theory of Chinese Architecture	中国建筑中的"帐幕理论"	Fries, S. Ritter Von	费习孟	13-659
Note on the Comparative Longevity of Males and Females in Japan	日本男女的相对长寿	Hallifax, T. E.		13-663
Proceedings	会议纪要			13-665
Proceedings of the Annual General Meeting，1889－1890	1889－1890年年会纪要			13-672
Report for the Year 1889－1890	1889－1890年度报告			13-675
Obituary	讣告			13-696
List of Members（Corrected to 20th October 1890）	会员名录（更新至1890年10月20日）			13-699

N. S. VOL. XXV（1890－1891）

题　　名	中译题名	责任者	责任者中文名	页码
Botanicon Sinicum（Part II）	中国植物志（二）	Bretschneider, E.	贝勒	14-9
Proceedings	会议纪要			14-479

(续表)

题　名	中译题名	责任者	责任者中文名	页码
List of Members (Corrected to December 20th, 1892)	会员名录(更新至1892年12月20日)			14-512

N. S. VOL. XXVI(1891-1892)

题　名	中译题名	责任者	责任者中文名	页码
The Fish-skin Tartars	鱼皮鞑靼	Fraser, E. H.	法磊斯	15-9
A Comparative Table of the Ancient Lunar Asterisms	古代月亮星群及时辰对照表	Kingsmill, Thomas William	金斯密	15-52
Wei-ch'i	围棋	Volpicelli, Z.	武尔披齐	15-88
Militant Spirit of the Buddhist Clergy in China	中国佛教僧侣的尚武精神	Groot, J. J. M. de	高延	15-116
Notes and Queries	释疑			15-129
Proceedings	会议纪要			15-137
Minutes of the Annual General Meeting, 1890-1891	1890-1891年年会纪要			15-149
Report of the Council for the Year 1890-1891	1890-1891年度报告			15-182
Proceedings	会议纪要			15-190
Report for the Year 1892	1892年度报告			15-224
List of Members (Corrected to October 31st 1893)	会员名录(更新至1893年10月31日)			15-246
A Classified Index to the Articles. Printed in the JNCBRAS: from the Foundation of the Society, 1858, to the end of 1893	文会会刊自1858年创立至1893年底所刊文章分类索引	Haas, Joseph	夏士	15-254
Catalogue of the Library of the NCBRAS (Including the Library of Alex. Wylie, Esq.)	文会图书馆目录(包括伟烈亚力图书馆所藏)			15-307

N. S. VOL. XXVII(1892-1893)

题　名	中译题名	责任者	责任者中文名	页码
The Salt Administration of Ssǔch'uan	四川盐务管理	Rosthorn, Arthur von	罗士恒	16-11
Early Portuguese Commerce and Settlements in China	早期在华的葡萄牙人之商业及其殖民地	Volpicelli, Z.	武尔披齐	16-43
The Coinage of Corea	朝鲜货币	Gardner, C. T.	嘉托玛	16-81
The Family Law of the Chinese	中国人的家法	Möllendorff, P. G. von	穆麟德	16-141
Report for the Year 1892-1893	1892-1893年度报告			16-201
Proceedings	会议纪要			16-208
Report for the Year 1893-1894	1893-1894年度报告			16-226
Proceedings	会议纪要			16-256

(续表)

题　名	中译题名	责任者	责任者中文名	页码
Synopsis of *How to Awaken Faith in the Mahayana School*	马鸣菩萨《大乘起信论》纲要	Richard, Timothy	李提摩太	16-273
N. S. VOL. XXVIII (1893－1894)				
List of Members (Corrected to March 31st, 1897)	会员名录(更新至 1897 年 3 月 31 日)			16-295
Inland Communications in China	中国之内陆交通			16-311
Stray Notes on Corean History and Literature	朝鲜历史与文献散论	Scott, James	萨允格	16-528
The Yü-li, or Precious Records	《玉历》英译	Clarke, Geo. W.	花国香	16-547
N. S. VOL. XXIX (1894－1895)				
Botanicon Sinicum (Part III)	中国植物志(三)	Bretschneider, E.	贝勒	17-13
N. S. VOL. XXX (1895－1896)				
Le Voyage de l'Ambassade Hollandaise de 1656 a Travers la Province de Canton	1656 年荷兰使团广东行记	Imbault-Huart, Camille	于雅乐	18-9
The Financial Capacity of China	中国之财政能力	Parker, Edward Harper	庄延龄	18-82
Chinese Revenue	中国之税收	Parker, Edward Harper	庄延龄	18-114
The Hsi Hsia Dynasty of Tangut: Their Money and Peculiar Script	西夏的货币及其独特文字	Bushell, S. W.	卜士礼	18-154
A Manchu Ukase	大清告示一则	Fraser, F. A.	富美基	18-175
Notes and Queries	释疑			18-191
Correspondence	通信			18-196
List of Additions to the Catalogue of the Library of the NCBRAS	文会图书馆目录补遗			18-201
N. S. VOL. XXXI (1896－1897)				
Inscriptions de L'Orkhon	鄂尔浑河碑铭	Parker, Edward Harper	庄延龄	18-305
Wang-Chung and Plato on Death and Immortality	王充与柏拉图论死亡与永生	Forke, A.	佛尔克	18-344
The Chinese System of Family Relationship and Its Aryan Affinities	中国之家庭制度及其与雅利安人的联系	Kingsmill, Thomas William	金斯密	18-365
Scarcity of Copper Cash and the Rise in Prices	铜钱稀缺与物价上涨			18-377
On the Limitations of Comparative Philology	比较语言学的局限	Möllendorff, P. G. von	穆麟德	18-385

(续表)

题　　名	中译题名	责任者	责任者中文名	页码
The Grand Canal of China	中国之大运河	Carles, W. R.	贾礼士	18-406
Report for the Year 1894-1895	1894-1895 年度报告			18-425
Proceedings	会议纪要			18-432
Report for the Year 1896-1897	1896-1897 年度报告			18-467
Proceedings	会议纪要			18-474
Report for the Year 1897-1898	1897-1898 年度报告			18-501
Report for the Year 1898-1899	1898-1899 年度报告			18-505
Notes on the *Taoteh King*	《道德经》注释	Kingsmill, Thomas William	金斯密	18-514

N. S. VOL. XXXII(1897-1898)

题　　名	中译题名	责任者	责任者中文名	页码
The Chinese Calendar: Its Origin, History and Connections	中国历法的起源、历史及联系	Kingsmill, Thomas William	金斯密	18-529
The Office of District Magistrate in China	中国之县官	Brenan, Byron	璧利南	18-564
On the Chinese Coins and Small Porcelain Bottles Found in Egypt	埃及发现的中国钱币和小瓷瓶	Rondot, Natalis		18-594
Sealing and Whaling in the Northern Pacific	北太平洋捕猎海豹与鲸	Brass, E.		18-607

N. S. VOL. XXXIII(1899-1900)

题　　名	中译题名	责任者	责任者中文名	页码
Possible and Impossible Reforms	可能的改革与不可能的改革	Bourne, Frederick Samuel Augustus	班德瑞	19-9
Some Popular Religious Literature of the Chinese	中国广为流传的宗教文学作品	Williams, E. T., Mrs.	卫理夫人	19-19
Additional Coins of the Present Dynasty	大清货币补遗	Bushell, S. W.	卜士礼	19-38
Siün King, the Philosopher, and his Relations with Contemporary Schools of Thought	哲学家荀子及其与当代思想流派的关系	Edkins, Joseph	艾约瑟	19-54
Review: *The Heart of Asia: a History of Russian Turkestan and the Central Asian Khanates from the Earliest Times*	《亚洲腹地：俄罗斯突厥斯坦及中亚汗国史》书评			19-64
Proceedings	会议纪要			19-75
Report for the Year 1899-1900	1899-1900 年度报告			19-87
Social Life of the Miao Tsĭ	苗族的社会生活	Betts, Geo. Edgar		19-97
Irrigation of the Ch'eng-tu Plain	成都平原的灌溉系统	Vale, Joshua	斐焕章	19-118
Notes on the Ting-Chi, or Half-Yearly Sacrifice to Confucius	文庙丁祭评述	Moule, G. E.	慕稼谷	19-133
The Philippine Chinese Labour Question	菲律宾华人劳工问题	Mencarini, Juan	绵嘉义	19-182

(续表)

题　　名	中译题名	责任者	责任者中文名	页码
Tableau Chronologique de la Dynastie Mandchoue-Chinoise Ta-Ts'ing	清朝帝王世系表	Hoang, Pierre; Tobar, Jérôme	黄汝梅；管宜穆	19-210
Mencius and Some Other Reformers of China	孟子及其他中国改革者	Macklin, W. E.	马林	19-265
The Ancient City of Shaohing	古代绍兴城	Walshe, W. Gilbert	华立熙	19-290
Review: China, Her History, Diplomacy and Commerce from the Earliest Times to the Present Day	《中国从古至今的历史、外交和商业》书评			19-313
Review: Mythologie des Buddhismus in Tibet und der Mongolei	《西藏与蒙古的佛教神话》书评	Forke, A.	佛尔克	19-324
Obituary	讣告			19-329
Proceedings	会议纪要			19-337
Report for the Year 1900-1901	1900-1901年度报告			19-359
List of Members (Corrected to December 31st, 1901)	会员名录（更新至1901年12月31日）			19-371
N. S. VOL. XXXIV(1901-1902)				
The Chinese Sophists	中国之辩士	Forke, A.	佛尔克	19-389
Shanghai Folk-lore	上海民俗（一）	Box, Ernest	包克私	19-489
Dr. F. Hirth and the Hiung Nu: Review of Hirth's Ueber Wolga-Hunnen und Hiung-nu	夏德与匈奴：评夏德《伏尔加河的匈人和匈奴人》	Kingsmill, Thomas William	金斯密	19-524
N. S. VOL. XXXV(1903-1904)				
Kwo Tsï Yi, an Eminent Military Commander of the Tang Dynasty	郭子仪——唐朝的杰出军事将领	Edkins, Joseph	艾约瑟	19-537
Standard Weights and Measures of the Ch'in Dynasty	秦朝标准度量衡	Chalfant, Frank Herring	方法敛	19-557
Some Chinese Funeral Customs	若干中国丧葬礼仪	Walshe, W. Gilbert	华立熙	19-564
Wang An-shih	王安石	Ferguson, John Calvin	福开森	19-603
The Mantses and the Golden Chersonese	蛮子与黄金半岛（牂牁地区）	Kingsmill, Thomas William	金斯密	19-614
Proceedings	会议纪要			19-641
Proceedings of the Annual General Meeting, 1903-1904	1903-1904年年会纪要			19-663
N. S. VOL. XXXVI(1905)				
Notes of a Journey Overland from Szemao to Rangoon	从思茅至仰光纪行	Carey, Fred. W.	甘福履	20-9

(续表)

题　　名	中译题名	责任者	责任者中文名	页码
Irrigation of the Ch'eng-tu Plain and beyond	再论成都平原的灌溉系统	Vale, Joshua	斐焕章	20-44
Journey to Sungp'an	松潘行记	Watson, W. C. Haines	花荪	20-59
The History of the Loochoo Islands	琉球群岛的历史	Leavenworth, Charles S.		20-111
Java	爪哇	Mencarini, Juan	绵嘉义	20-128
Shanghai Folk-lore	上海民俗（二）	Box, Ernest	包克私	20-138
In Memoriam: Rev. Joseph Edins, D. D.	艾约瑟悼文			20-165
Proceedings of the Annual General Meeting, 1905	1905年年会纪要			20-168
List of Societies, Public Institutions, etc. Exchanging Publications with the Society	与亚洲文会北华支会交换图书的社团及公共机构名录			20-177

N. S. VOL. XXXVII (1906)

题　　名	中译题名	责任者	责任者中文名	页码
The Jewish Monument at Kaifengfu	开封府的犹太教纪念碑	Martin, William Alexander Parsos	丁韪良	20-191
Ancient Tibet and its Frontagers	古代西藏及其前沿地带	Kingsmill, Thomas William	金斯密	20-211
Notes on Chinese Banking System in Shanghai	上海华资银行体系	Ferguson, John Calvin	福开森	20-245
Notes on Chinese Law and Practice Preceding Revision	修订前的中国法律及其实施	Alabaster, Ernest	阿拉巴德	20-273
Chinese Children's Games	中国儿童游戏	Headland, Isaac Taylor	何德兰	20-340
Notes and Queries	释疑			20-375
Literary Notes	新书评介			20-392
Recent Books on China	中国专题出版物书讯			20-406
In Memorian	悼文			20-408
Proceedings of the Annual General Meeting, 1906	1906年年会纪要			20-412
List of Members (Correceted to June 30th, 1906)	会员名录（更新至1906年6月30日）			20-426

N. S. VOL. XXXVIII (1907)

题　　名	中译题名	责任者	责任者中文名	页码
Currency in China	中国货币考	Morse, Hosea Ballou	马士	20-443

（续表）

题　　名	中译题名	责任者	责任者中文名	页码
Witchcraft in the Chinese Penal Code	中国刑法中的巫术	Williams, Edward Thomas	卫理	20-513
Contribution to the Nomenclature of Chinese Plants	中国植物命名法论稿	Faber, Ernst	花之安	20-549
The Two Zodiacs (Solar and Lunar), Their Origin and Connections: A Study in the Earlist Dawn of Civilisation	一项关于文明起源之研究——两个黄道带：太阳和月亮，它们的起源及联系	Kingsmill, Thomas William	金斯密	20-617
Notes and Queries	释疑			20-668
Literary Notes	新书评介			20-679
A Classified List of the Articles Printed in the JNCBRAS from 1892 to 1907	1892年至1907年文会会刊总目			20-710
Recent Books on China and the Far East	中国和远东专题出版物书讯			20-715
Proceedings of the Annual General Meeting, 1907	1907年年会纪要			20-717
List of Members (Correceted to June 30th, 1907)	会员名录（更新至1907年6月30日）			20-725

N. S. VOL. XXXIX(1908)

题　　名	中译题名	责任者	责任者中文名	页码
A List of the Musical and Other Sounding Producing Instruments of the Chinese	中国乐器及其他发声器之目录	Moule, Arthur Christopher	慕阿德	21-11
Notes and Queries	释疑			21-199
Literary Notes	新书评介			21-215
Recent Books on China and the Far East	中国和远东专题出版物书讯			21-241
List of Members (Corrected to June 30th, 1908)	会员名录（更新至1908年6月30日）			21-243

N. S. VOL. XL(1909)

题　　名	中译题名	责任者	责任者中文名	页码
Archaeological Survey of the Environs of China's Ancient Capitals	中国诸古都郊区考古调查	Alexeieff, V.	阿莱克塞夫	21-261
The Principles of Chinese Law and Equity	中国成文法与衡平法的原则	Parker, Edward Harper	庄延龄	21-270
The Ascent of Mt. Morrison	攀登玉山山脉	Arnold, Julean Herbert	安立德	21-304
The Collection of Birds in the Shanghai Museum	亚洲文会博物院藏鸟类标本	Touche, J. D. D. de la	德拉图什	21-359
Notes and Queries	释疑			21-398

(续表)

题　　名	中译题名	责任者	责任者中文名	页码
Literary Notes	新书评介			21-406
Recent Books on China and the Far East	中国和远东专题出版物书讯			21-418
Proceedings of the Annual General Meeting, 1909	1909年年会纪要			21-419
List of Members(Corrected to June 30th, 1909)	会员名录(更新至1909年6月30日)			21-429
N. S. VOL. XLI(1910)				
The Confucian Reformers in Japan, in the 18th Century	18世纪日本的儒家改革者	Hall, J. C.	贺若贤	21-447
The Music of China	中国的音乐	Kingsmill, Thomas William	金斯密	21-472
Burial Customs in Sz-chuen	四川的丧葬习俗	Torrance, Thomas	陶然士	21-507
The Christian Mounment at Hsi-an Fu	西安府的大秦景教碑	Moule, Arthur Christopher	慕阿德	21-548
In Memoriam	悼文			21-604
Notes and Queries	释疑			21-607
Literary Notes	新书评介			21-610
Recent Books on China	中国专题出版物书讯			21-623
Proceedings of the Annual General Meeting, 1910	1910年年会纪要			21-624
List of Members (Corrected to August 1, 1910)	会员名录(更新至1910年8月1日)			21-631
N. S. VOL. XLII(1911)				
The Journal of S. Wells Williams, LL. D.	卫三畏日记	Williams, Frederick Wells	卫斐列	22-15
In Memorian	悼文			22-247
Literary Notes	新书评介			22-248
Books Contributed to the Library	图书馆受赠图书目录			22-261
Recent Books and Re-publications on China	中国专题出版物及再版书书讯			22-262
Recent Accessions to the Library	图书馆新增图书目录			22-264
Proceedings of the Annual General Meeting, 1911	1911年年会纪要			22-269
List of Members (Revised to October 1, 1911)	会员名录(更新至1911年10月1日)			22-279

(续表)

题　名	中译题名	责任者	责任者中文名	页码
N. S. VOL. XLIII(1912)				
T'ai Shan	泰山	Moule, Arthur Christopher	慕阿德	22-299
Notes on Chinese Archery	射箭在中国	Du Bois-Reymond,C.	谛部	22-348
Three Sites in Hunan Connected with the Classical Legendary History of China	湖南境内的三处上古史迹	Warren, Gilbert G.	任修本	22-360
Chinese Art Metal Work	中国的金属艺术品	Stanley, Arthur	史笪来	22-383
The Great Summer Festival of China as Observed in Foochow: A Study in Popular Religion	福州夏至节气仪式：民间信仰研究	Hodous, Lewis.	何乐益	22-403
In Memorian	悼文			22-415
Literary Notes	新书评介			22-419
Notes and Queries	释疑			22-452
Books Presented to the Library	图书馆受赠图书目录			22-455
Recent Accessions to the Library	图书馆新增图书目录			22-457
In Memorian	悼文			22-460
China Monuments	中国的纪念碑	McCormick, Frederick		22-463
Proceedings of the Annual General Meeting, 1912	1912年年会纪要			22-525
List of Articles Contributed to the JNCBRAS	会刊论文分类索引	Ayscough, Florence Wheelock	爱司克夫人	22-537
List of Members of the NCBRAS (Revised to September 30, 1912)	会员名录（更新至1912年9月30日）			22-553
N. S. VOL. XLIV(1913)				
One of the World's Literary Masterpieces: Introduction to a Great Chinese Epic or Religious Allegory by Ch'iu Ch'ang Ch'un	世界文学杰作《长春真人西游记》介绍	Richard, Timothy	李提摩太	23-9
The State Religion of China During the Manchu Dynasty	清朝的国教	Williams, Edward Thomas	卫理	23-21
A Study in the Life and Philosophy of Wang Yang Ming	王阳明的生平及其哲学思想	Henke, Frederick G.		23-72
Chinese Embroidery and Other Art Textile Work	中国刺绣及其他艺术纺织品	Stanley, Arthur	史笪来	23-93
Mongolia After the Genghizides and Before the Manchus	明朝时的蒙古	Parker, Edward Harper	庄延龄	23-114

(续表)

题 名	中译题名	责任者	责任者中文名	页码
Omei San: The Sacred Moutain of West China	华西圣山峨眉山	Shields, E. T.		23-140
Check List of Birds of the Lower Yangtze Valley from Hankow to the Sea	长江下游河滩鸟类名录	Moffett, Lacy I. & Gee, N. Gist	慕维德、祁天锡	23-151
Obituary	讣告			23-192
Literary Notes	新书评介			23-193
Notes and Queries	释疑			23-241
Books Presented to the Library	图书馆受赠图书目录			23-249
Recent Accessions to the Library	图书馆新增图书目录			23-252
Proceedings of the Annual General Meeting, 1913	1913年年会纪要			23-257
List of Members (Revised to June 5, 1913)	会员名录（更新至1913年6月5日）			23-265

N. S. VOL. XLV(1914)

题 名	中译题名	责任者	责任者中文名	页码
Proceedings of the Annual General Meeting, 1914	1914年年会纪要			23-285
On the Sources of Chinese Taoism	中国道教源头考	Wilhelm, Richard	卫礼贤	23-295
"Ink Remains", by An I-chou	安仪周书《墨缘录观》墨迹	Ferguson, John Calvin	福开森	23-307
The Collection of Chinese Reptiles in the Shanghai Museum	亚洲文会博物院藏中国爬行动物标本	Stanley, Arthur	史笪来	23-315
Through the Land of Deep Corrosions: from Batang to Menkong	穿越荒漠：从巴塘河到湄公河	Edgar, J. Huston	叶长清	23-326
The Great Weal: or a Christmas Journey to Huangho Mouth	大伤痕：圣诞节黄河入海口之行	Edgar, J. Huston	叶长清	23-340
Notes on Temperatures in High Altitudes on the Tibetan Border	青藏高原边境高海拔气温观测记录	Edgar, J. Huston	叶长清	23-353
The Oracle-bones from Honan	河南甲骨	Couling, Samuel	库寿龄	23-363
Chinese Wooding Caving	中国木雕	Stanley, Arthur	史笪来	23-376
A Chinese Sun-dial	中国日晷	Du Bois-Reymond, C.	谛部	23-401
Reminiscences of a Chinese Viceroy's Secretary	总督秘书的回忆录：《张文襄公府纪闻》节译（一）	Ardsheal (pseud.)		23-409
A Bibliographical Introduction to the Study of Chinese Law	中国法律研究文献介绍	Lobinger, Charles Sumner	罗炳吉	23-428
A Table of the Emperors of the Yüan Dynasty	元代皇帝年表	Moule, Arthur Christopher	慕阿德	23-442

(续表)

题 名	中译题名	责任者	责任者中文名	页码
Reviews of Recent Books	新书评介			23-443
Notes and Queries	释疑			23-489
Books Presented to the Library (May 31st, 1913 – May, 1914)	图书馆1913年5月31日至1914年5月受赠图书目录			23-495
Additions to the Library (May 1913 – May 1914)	图书馆1913年5月至1914年5月新增图书目录			23-498
List of Members, 1914	1914年会员名录			23-503
N. S. VOL. XLVI(1915)				
Proceedings of the Annual General Meeting, 1915	1915年年会纪要			23-525
Putoshan: A Draught at the Well-springs of Chinese Buddhist Art	普陀山：中国佛教艺术探源	Stanley, Arthur	史笪来	23-537
Notices of Christianity in China: Extracted from Marco Polo	《马可波罗游记》中中国基督教史料评介	Moule, Arthur Christopher	慕阿德	23-571
The Tone-accents of Two Chinese Dialects	中国两种方言的声调	Bradley, Cornelius Beach		23-590
Chinese Pagodas	中国的塔	Couling, Samuel	库寿龄	23-597
The Ch'ing Ming Festival	清明节	Hodous, Lewis	何乐益	23-610
Reminiscences of a Chinese Viceroy's Secretary	总督秘书的回忆录：《张文襄公府纪闻》节译(二)	Ardsheal (pseud.)		23-613
The Wu Pan Tablet	武斑碑	Warren, Gilbert G.	任修本	23-629
On a Large Meteorite Which Fell in the Sea near Video, Chusan Archipelago, on the 13th February, 1915	舟山列岛1915年2月13日坠落的大陨石	Tyler, William Ferdinand	戴理尔	23-653
William Woodville Rockhill	柔克义悼文	Hinckley, F. E.		23-669
Reviews of Recent Books	新书评介			23-672
Notes and Queries	释疑			23-705
Books Presented to the Library	图书馆受赠图书目录			23-707
Additions to the Library (June 1914 – June 1915)	图书馆1914年6月至1915年6月新增图书目录			23-710
Books Added to the Library by Exchange of Publications	图书馆交换所得图书目录			23-715
List of Exchanges	与图书馆交换图书的机构名录			23-717

(续表)

题 名	中译题名	责任者	责任者中文名	页码
List of Members, 1915	1915年会员名录			23-719

N. S. VOL. XLVII(1916)

题 名	中译题名	责任者	责任者中文名	页码
Proceedings of the Annual General Meeting, 1916	1916年年会纪要			24-9
Early Chinese Bronzes	早期中国青铜器	Ferguson, John Calvin	福开森	24-21
M. Chavannes' Edition of Ssŭ-man Ch'ien	沙畹译注的《史记》	Warren, Gilbert G.	任修本	24-42
Notes on the Flora of the W. Ssŭch'uan Mountains	川西山区植物笔记	Ward, Francis Kingdon		24-69
Freshwater Sponges from the T'ai Hu (Great Lake) of the Kiangsu Province, China	太湖的淡水海绵	Annandale, N.		24-79
Recent Research upon the Mammalia of Northern China	中国北部哺乳动物研究近况	Sowerby, Arthur de Carle	苏阿德	24-83
Two New Species of Chinese Snakes	中国新发现的两个蛇类品种	Stanley, Arthur	史笪来	24-113
Some Notes on the History and Folk Lore of Old Shanghai	老上海历史与风俗笔记	Parker, Alvin Pierson	潘慎文	24-117
A Survey of the Work by Western Students of Chinese History	西方学者中国历史研究成果综述	Latourette, Kenneth Scott	赖德烈	24-135
Chinese State Papers from the Boxer Days: Translated from the Chinese	义和团运动期间清朝政府的官方文件	Parker, Edward Harper	庄延龄	24-147
Reviews of Recent Books	新书评介			24-168
Notes and Queries	释疑			24-188
List of Books on China Recently Published	中国专题出版物书讯			24-194
Additions to the Library	图书馆1916年新增图书目录			24-196
Books Presented to the Library	图书馆受赠图书目录			24-196
Additions to the Library (July 1915-June 1916)	图书馆1915年7月至1916年5月新增图书目录			24-198
Books Added to the Library by Exchange of Publications	图书馆交换所得图书目录			24-200
List of Members, 1916	1916年会员名录			24-201

N. S. VOL. XLVIII(1917)

题 名	中译题名	责任者	责任者中文名	页码
Proceedings of the Annual General Meeting, 1917	1917年年会纪要			24-221

(续表)

题名	中译题名	责任者	责任者中文名	页码
The Vows of Amida: A Comparative Study	《阿弥陀经》版本比较研究	Inglis, J. W.	英雅各	24-231
The Nestorian Share in Buddhist Translation	景教徒参与佛经翻译事迹考	Inglis, J. W.	英雅各	24-242
Magical Practice in China	中国的巫术实践	Chatley, Herbert	查得利	24-246
The Dragon	说龙	Hodous, Lewis	何乐益	24-261
The Country and Some Customs of the Szechwan Mantze	四川边陲地区的农村习俗	Edgar, J. Huston	叶长清	24-274
Shrines of History: Peak of the East—T'sai Shan	历史胜迹：东岳泰山	Ayscough, Florence Wheelock	爱司克夫人	24-291
Land Birds and Others Met with at Sea off the Coast of China in 1915	中国沿海地区1915年所见鸟类	Laver, H. E.		24-305
The Method of Making Ink Rubbings	拓印的方法	Stanley, Arthur	史笪来	24-319
Stone Implements on the Upper Yangtze and Min Rivers	长江上游及岷江流域发现的石器	Edgar, J. Huston	叶长清	24-321
The G. E. Morrison Library	莫理循图书馆	Couling, Samuel	库寿龄	24-326
The Kinship of the English and Chinese Languages	汉语和英语的近似特征	Lanning, George	蓝宁	24-329
Introduction to the *Buddhist Library of Huen Chwang*	《雁塔圣教序》译文	Couling, Samuel	库寿龄	24-353
Coins of the Republic of China	民国的铸币	Ros, Giuseppe	罗斯	24-356
Recent Discoveries in Ancient Chinese Sculpture	最近发现的中国古代雕塑	Segalen, Victor		24-407
Four Example of Chinese Bronze Statuary	中国青铜雕像四范例	Ferguson, John Calvin	福开森	24-433
The Religious Element in the *Tso Chuan*	《左传》中的宗教元素	Wright, Harrison King	励德厚	24-445
Reviews of Recent Books	新书评介			24-463
Notes and Queries	释疑			24-509
Additions to the Library (July 1916 – June 1917)	图书馆1916年7月至1917年6月新增图书目录			24-522
List of Members, 1917	1917年会员名录			24-527
N. S. VOL. XLIX(1918)				
Proceedings of the Annual General Meeting, 1918	1918年年会纪要			25-11
River Problems in China	中国河流问题	Chatley, Herbert	查得利	25-19

(续表)

题　名	中译题名	责任者	责任者中文名	页码
Some Notes on Land-birds, Including Also General Remarks on the Birds Observed at Sea on the Coast of China in 1916	陆禽，包括中国沿海地区1916年所见鸟类	Laver, H. E.		25-31
Animistic Elements in Moslem Prayer	穆斯林祷告中的泛灵论元素	Zwemer, Samuel Marinus	知味墨	25-56
The Eight Immortals of Taoist Religion	道教中的八仙	Ling, Peter C.	凌爱国	25-71
A Chapter of Folklore	民俗记			25-94
The Kite Festival in Foochow	福州重阳节的风筝民俗	Hodous, Lewis	何乐益	25-94
On a Method of Divination Practised at Foochow	福州的"打童"民俗	Harding, H. L.	哈尔定	25-100
Notes on the Tu T'ing Hui Held at Chinking on the 31st May, 1917	1917年5月31日浙江的都天会	Ottewill, H. A.	奥泰蔚	25-104
The Domestic Altar	家神	Hutson, James	哈司顿	25-111
Ku K'ai-chi's Scroll in the British Museum	大英博物馆藏顾恺之绘《女史箴图》	Ferguson, John Calvin	福开森	25-119
The Theistic Import of the Sung Philosiphy	宋代哲学中的有神论	Bruce, Joseph Percy	卜道成	25-129
A Case of Ritualism	祭祀仪式的个案研究	Morgan, Evan	莫安仁	25-146
Chinese Puzzledom	中国之迷局	Kliene, Charles	葛麟瑞	25-162
Reviews of Recent Books	新书评介			25-178
Notes and Queries	释疑			25-218
Additions to the Library (July 1917 – June 1918)	图书馆1917年7月至1918年6月新增图书目录			25-226
List of Members, 1918	1918年会员名录			25-229
N. S. VOL. L(1919)				
Proceedings of the Annual General Meeting, 1919	1919年年会纪要			25-253
Thirty Thousand Miles in China	中国三万英里行	Edmunds, Charle Keyser	晏文士	25-263
Chinese Metaphorical Zoology	汉语修辞中的动物学	Williams, Charles Alfred Speed	威立师	25-291
The Early Malays and Their Neighbours	早期马来人及其周边文化	Lobinger, Charles Sumner	罗炳吉	25-301
Notes on the Agriculture, Botany and the Zoology of China	中国的农学、植物学和动物学（一）	Skvortzow, B. W.		25-315
The Land of Peach Bloom	《桃花源记》译文及短评	Kliene, Charles	葛麟瑞	25-384

(续表)

题　名	中译题名	责任者	责任者中文名	页码
Recent Books by a Chinese Scholar	罗振玉著作综述	Ferguson, John Calvin	福开森	25－398
Chemical Industry in Kwangtung Province	广东的化学工业	Yan-tsz Chiu		25－409
A List of the Birds in the Museum of the Anglo-Chinese College of Foochow	福州英华书院博物院鸟类标本目录	Kellogg, Claude R.	克立鸽	25－420
Formosa	台湾	Old Cathay [pseud.]		25－434
The Attractions of Entomond	昆虫学的魅力	Moore, Alfred	穆信诚	25－438
A Beginning of the Study of the Flora and Fauna of Soochow and Vicinity	苏州及其周边地区动植物初探	Gee, Nathaniel Gist	祁天锡	25－446
Notes on Kansu	甘肃概说	King, George E.	金文宽	25－461
An Exhibition of Pictures by a Russian Artist	俄国艺术家的画展	Howell, E. B.	好威乐	25－465
Reviews of Recent Books	新书评介			25－469
Notes and Queries	释疑			25－514
Additions to the Library (July 1918 － June 1919)	图书馆1918年7月至1919年6月新增图书目录			25－515
Obituary	讣告			25－519
List of Members, 1919	1919年会员名录			25－527

N. S. VOL. LI(1920)

Proceedings of the Annual General Meeting, 1920	1920年年会纪要			26－9
The Relation of Chinese and Siamese	中国与暹罗关系	Dodd, W. Clifton	铎德	26－21
Greek and Chinese Art Ideals	希腊和中国的艺术思想	Stanley, Arthur	史笪来	26－35
Destiny, Fate	宿命论	Morgan, Evan	莫安仁	26－47
China's Petrified Sun-rays	中国的化石能源	Chatley, Herbert	查得利	26－67
Chinese Ideas of Antiques	中国人的古董观	Huston, James	哈司顿	26－73
Names and Nicknames of the Shanghai Settlements	上海租界的地名和别名	Lanning, George	蓝宁	26－103
Chinese Poetry and Its Connotations	中文诗及其内涵	Ayscough, Florence Wheelock	爱司克夫人	
Notes on the Agriculture, Botany and the Zoology of China	中国的农学、植物学和动物学(二)	Skvortzow, B. W.		26－157
A Chinese Life of Modhammed	一个回教徒的中式生活	Mason, Isaac	梅益盛	26－181
Reviews of Recent Books	新书评介			26－203

(续表)

题　　名	中译题名	责任者	责任者中文名	页码
Notes and Queries	释疑			26-226
Additions to the Library (July 1919-June 1920)	图书馆1919年7月至1920年6月新增图书目录			26-229
List of Members, 1920	1920年会员名录			26-232

N. S. VOL. LII(1921)

题　　名	中译题名	责任者	责任者中文名	页码
Proceedings of the Annual General Meeting, 1921	1921年年会纪要			26-255
The Operations and Manifestations of the Tao Exemplified in History or the Tao Confirmed by History	历史上"道"的作用及其表现形式	Morgan, Evan	莫安仁	26-263
The Hainanese Miao	海南的苗族	Moninger, M. M.	孟言嘉	26-302
Notes on the Symbolism of the Purple Forbidden City	紫禁城的象征主义	Ayscough, Florence Wheelock	爱司克夫人	26-313
Notes on the Agriculture, Botany and the Zoology of China	中国的农学、植物学和动物学(三)	Skvortzow, B. W.		26-341
Exogamy in China	中国的异族通婚	Wilkinson, Hiram Parhes	威金生	26-374
Lampaçao, a Mystery of the Far East	浪白窜:远东的不解之谜	Morse, Hosea Ballou	马士	26-399
The Marriage Maker	媒婆	Kliene, Charles	葛麟瑞	26-401
The Highways and Byways of Kweichow	贵州的大道与小径	Kemp, Emily Georgiana	葛安布	26-418
Christ in the "Li Tai Shen Hsien T'ung Chien"	《历代神仙通鉴》中的基督	Werner, Edward Theodore Chalmers	倭讷	26-448
A Trip to Hua Kang	人日游花埭[汉诗英译]	Fletcher, William John Bainbridge	佛来遮	26-454
The Song of a Skirt	贫女[汉诗英译]	Fletcher, William John Bainbridge	佛来遮	26-455
Reviews of Recent Books	新书评介			26-456
Notes and Queries	释疑			26-492
Additions to the Library (July 1920-June 1921)	图书馆1920年7月至1921年6月新增图书目录			26-496
List of Members, 1921	1921年会员名录			26-499

(续表)

题　名	中译题名	责任者	责任者中文名	页码
N. S. VOL. LIII(1922)				
Proceedings of the Annual General Meeting, 1922	1922年年会纪要			27－9
The Natural History of China	中国博物学	Sowerby, Arthur de Carle	苏阿德	27－17
The Growth of the Yangtze Delta	长江三角洲的成长	Heidenstam, H. von	海德生	27－39
The Shuh Country	蜀地(一)	Hutson, James	哈司顿	27－71
Notes on Names of Non-Chinese Tribes in Western Szechwan	川西少数名族的称谓	Edgar, J. Huston	叶长清	27－95
Fir-flower Tablets	《松花笺》评赏	Ferguson, John Calvin	福开森	27－104
Lan-tsih	兰芝[《孔雀东南飞》英译]	Hudson, Elfrida		27－118
Ling Yin Monastry Poem	宋之问灵隐寺诗文考	Gaunt, T.	恭多马	27－127
Some Geological Notes on the Coal and Iron Ore Deposits in the Carboniferous Sediments of Central Shansi	山西中部石炭纪沉积物中的煤铁蕴藏	Norin, E.		27－129
Chinese Names of Plants: A Preliminary List of the Trees and Shrubs of North Honan	豫北植物汉语名称	Hers, Joseph	艾勒斯	27－139
Oribatoidea Sinensi I	中华甲螨名录(一)	Jacot, Arthur Paul	贾珂	27－152
The Distribution and Habits of the Argali Sheep of Central Asia	中亚盘羊的分布及习性	Sjolander, David		27－165
Plants from Peitaiho	北戴河的植物	Cowdry, N. H.		27－192
Notes on the Agriculture, Botany and the Zoology of China	中国的农学、植物学和动物学(四)	Skvortzow, B. W.		27－223
A Partial Bibliography of Chinese Birds	中国鸟类相关文献管窥	Riley, J. H. & Richmond, C. W.		27－230
Christ in the "Li Tai Shen Hsien T'ung Chien"	《历代神仙通鉴》中的基督	Giles, Herbert Allen	翟理思	27－272
Records of the Geological Committee of the Russian Far East	俄国远东地理学会报告	Ancell, B. L.	韩忾明	27－281
Obituaries	讣告			27－283
Notes and Queries	释疑			27－318
Additions to the Library (July 1921 - June 1922)	图书馆1921年7月至1922年6月新增图书目录			27－320
List of Members, 1922	1922年会员名录			27－323

(续表)

题　名	中译题名	责任者	责任者中文名	页码
N. S. VOL. LIV(1923)				
Proceedings of the Annual General Meeting, 1923	1923年年会纪要			27-347
A Snowstorm	《风雪》[汉诗英译]	Budd, Charles	卜德	27-357
Chu-goh Leang and the Arrows	诸葛亮与《草船借箭》[京剧英译]	Jamieson, C. A.	陈国将	27-359
The Drought	《云汉》[汉诗英译]	Hudson, Elfrida		27-369
Then-and Now	《今昔》[汉诗英译]	Hudson, Elfrida		27-370
A Night in Mountains	《宿天竺寺》[汉诗英译]	Hudson, Elfrida		27-371
Hsüan-Tsang and Modern Research	玄奘及其现代研究	Stael-Holstein, Baron Alexander von	钢和泰	27-372
The Shuh Country	蜀地（二）	Huston, James	哈司顿	27-381
Culture, the Basis of Chinese Art	文化：中国艺术之基	Ferguson, John Calvin	福开森	27-411
Science in Old China	中国古代科技	Chatley, Herbert	查得利	27-421
Modern Travel from Tai Yuan Fu via Mount Wu Tai to the Mongolian Frontier.	从太原府经五台山至蒙古边境纪行	Fischer, Emil Sigmund	斐士	27-439
A Page from Ancient Chinese History: The Story of Kou Tsien—King of Yueh	中国古代史一页：越王勾践	Darroch, John	窦乐安	27-476
Preliminary Notes on the Literary Background of "The Great River"	关于"大河"文献的初步注解	Ayscough, Florence Wheelock	爱司克夫人	27-491
The Religion of The Ch'iang	羌族的宗教信仰	Torrance, Thomas	陶然士	27-520
Oribatoidea Sinensis II	中华甲螨名录（二）	Jacot, Arthur Paul	贾珂	27-538
Bishop Della Chiesa and the Story of his Lost Grave	伊大仁主教和他失踪坟墓的故事	Heeren, John J.	奚尔恩	27-552
Some Similarities in Chinese and Ancient Egyptian Culture	中国和古埃及文化的相似之处	Kliene, Charles	葛麟瑞	27-574
A Partial Bibliography of Chinese Birds	中国鸟类相关文献管窥（补遗）	Riley, J. H. & Richmond, C. W.		27-599
How Tonnage was Measured in Ancient China	古代中国衡量船只吨位的方法	Morgan, Evan	莫安仁	27-601
The Taoist Superman	道教真人	Morgan, Evan	莫安仁	27-603
General Theory of Shamanism among the Tungus	通古斯的萨满教通论	Shirokogoroff, Sergei Mikhailovich	史禄国	27-620
Chinese Composite Deities	中国的复合神	Werner, Edward Theodore Chalmers	倭讷	27-624
Reviews of Recent Books	新书评介			27-642

(续表)

题　　名	中译题名	责任者	责任者中文名	页码
Notes and Queries	释疑			27-665
Additions to the Library (July 1922 - June 1923)	图书馆1922年7月至1923年6月新增图书目录			27-668
List of Members, 1923	1923年会员名录			27-671
N. S. VOL. LV(1924)				
Proceedings of the Annual General Meeting, 1924	1924年年会纪要			28-11
Who are the Northern Chinese?	关于中国北方人的人类学研究	Shirokogoroff, Sergei Mikhailovich	史禄国	28-21
Southern Migration of the Sung Dynasty	宋朝的南渡	Ferguson, John Calvin	福开森	28-34
Was Chu Hsi a Materialist?	朱熹是唯物论者吗？	Warren, Gilbert G.	任修本	28-48
The Dead Hand in China	中国不散的阴魂	Chatley, Herbert	查得利	28-65
The Origin and History of the Irrigation Work of the Chengtu Plain	成都平原水利工程的起源和历史	Torrance, Thomas	陶然士	28-80
The History of Shuh	蜀志	Torrance, Thomas	陶然士	28-86
Oribatoidea Sinensis III	中华甲螨名录（三）	Jacot, Arthur Paul	贾珂	28-98
The Gods of the Chinese	中国之神佛	Hayes, L. Newton	海士	28-106
Sramana-Shaman: Etymology of the Word "Shaman"	沙门-萨满："萨满"一词的语源	Mironov, N. D.		28-133
Cult of the Ch'êng Huang Lao Yeh	城隍老爷崇拜	Ayscough, Florence Wheelock	爱司克夫人	28-159
List of the Birds of Chihli Province	直隶鸟类目录	Wilder, Geo. D.	万卓志	28-184
Reviews of Recent Books	新书评介			28-272
Critical Bibliographical Notes-Study of the Tungus languages	通古斯语研究文献综述	Shirokogoroff, Sergei Mikhailovich	史禄国	28-293
Additions to the Library (July 1923 - June 1924)	图书馆1923年7月至1924年6月新增图书目录			28-302
List of Members, 1924	1924年会员名单			28-305
Index to the JNCBRAS from Vol. I to Vol. LIV	《亚洲文会会刊》第1卷至第54卷索引			28-323
N. S. VOL. LVI(1925)				
Obituary Notices	讣告			28-393
Proceedings of the Annual General Meeting, 1925	1925年年会纪要			28-397

(续表)

题　名	中译题名	责任者	责任者中文名	页码
Some Observations on China's International Relations	中国国际关系观察	MacNair, Harley Farnsworth	宓亨利	28-405
An Edict of Ch'in Shih Huang	秦诏版	Qin Shi Huang	嬴政	28-434
The Teaching of Micius	墨子学说	Pott, Francis Lister Hawks	卜舫济	28-436
The Life and Times of Confucius	孔子生平及其时代	Dovey, J. Whitsed	杜明德	28-455
The Springs of Tsinanfu	济南的泉水	Barbour, George B.	巴博尔	28-478
Shantung Foraminifera	山东有孔虫类	Jacot, Arthur Paul	贾珂	28-486
The Burial-place of Genghis Khan	成吉思汗埋葬地	Werner, Edward Theodore Chalmers	倭讷	28-492
Some New Light on the Life and Times of Bishop Della Chiesa	意大利天主教士康和之生平	Heeren, John J.	奚尔恩	28-503
Stories in Chinese Paintings	中国绘画中的故事（一）	Ferguson, John Calvin	福开森	28-526
Rebuttal Notes on Chinese Religion and Dynastic Tombs	关于中国宗教和皇陵的辩驳	Werner, Edward Theodore Chalmers	倭讷	28-550
Critical Review of Chalfant's Notes upon the "Shuo Wen"	方法敛注《说文》评述	Gillis, I. V.	义理寿	28-569
Notes on Chinese Mohammedan Literature	中国回教书籍解题	Mason, Isaac	梅益盛	28-592
Reviews of Recent Books	新书评介			28-640
Additions to the Library (July 1924 – June 1925)	图书馆1924年7月至1925年6月新增图书目录			28-657
Presentations to the Library (July 1924 – June 1925)	图书馆1924年7月至1925年6月受赠图书目录			28-658
List of Members, 1925	1925年会员名单			28-661

N. S. VOL. LVII(1926)

题　名	中译题名	责任者	责任者中文名	页码
Obituary Notices	讣告			29-9
Proceedings of the Annual General Meeting, 1926	1926年年会纪要			29-17
Flood and Famine in North China	中国北方的洪涝和饥荒	Turner, F. B.	德辅廊	29-25
A Map of China in the Making	一张制作中的中国地图	Hosie, Lady	谢福芸	29-45
The Tibetan and His Environment: an Interpretation	藏民及其生存环境	Edgar, J. Huston	叶长清	29-54
A League of Nations in Ancient China	中国古代的弥兵运动	Morgan, Evan	莫安仁	29-76

(续表)

题 名	中译题名	责任者	责任者中文名	页码
General Survey of Standard Chinese Histories	中国历史要览	Ferguson, John Calvin	福开森	29-83
Yen Hsi Chai: a 17th Century Philosopher	颜习斋:17世纪的中国哲人	Freeman, Mansfield	费孟福	29-96
Li Siu-cheng, the Chung Wang or "Faithful Prince"	忠王李秀成	Teesadale, J. H.	天赐德	29-118
Chinese Fresh Water Sponges	中国淡水海绵	Gee, Nathaniel Gist	祈天锡	29-136
The Chinese Cat	中国的猫	Torrance, Thomas	陶然士	29-139
Northern Tungus Migrations in the Far East	北通古斯族在远东之迁徙	Shirokogoroff, Sergei Mikhailovich	史禄国	29-149
Corrections and Additions to the List of the Birds of Chihli Province	直隶鸟类目录补正	Wilder, Geo. D.	万卓志	29-210
A Postscript on Tomb-destruction	关于皇陵被毁的备注说明	Werner, Edward Theodore Chalmers	倭讷	29-223
Some Notes on the Remains of a Phallic Shrine in Japan	日本的一处生殖崇拜遗迹			29-229
Reviews of Recent Books	新书评介			29-231
Additions to the Library (July 1925 – June 1926)	图书馆1925年7月至1926年6月新增图书目录			29-255
Presentations to the Library (July 1925 – June 1926)	图书馆1925年7月至1926年6月受赠图书目录			29-257
List of Members, 1926	1926年会员名单			29-258
N. S. VOL. LVIII(1927)				
Obituary Notices	讣告			29-283
Proceedings of the Annual General Meeting, 1927	1927年年会会议录			29-287
The Siege of Saianfu and the Murder of Achmach Bailo	阿合马事件(《马可波罗游记》两章相关内容)	Moule, Arthur Christopher	慕阿德	29-297
Political Parties of the Northern Sung Dynasty	北宋朋党	Ferguson, John Calvin	福开森	29-332
Mei Lan-fang (the Man and his Art)	梅兰芳其人其艺	Leung, George Kin.	梁社乾	29-355
The Motives of Chinese Art	中国的艺术主旨	Abraham, R. D.	亚伯拉罕	29-370
Little Lu-fu	陌上桑	Hudson, Elfrida		29-382
Looking at a Painting by Wang-Tzu (a T'ang Poem)	杜甫题王宰《戏题画山水图歌》	Hudson, Elfrida		29-386
The Genus Gueldenstaedtia (leguminoseae)	米口袋属(豆科)	Jacot, Arthur Paul	贾珂	29-389

(续表)

题　名	中译题名	责任者	责任者中文名	页码
Chou-kung; the Duke of Chou	周公	Morgan, Evan	莫安仁	29-430
Some Contributions to the Anthropology of the Buriats	布里亚特人人类学论稿	Kojeuroff, George P.		29-446
The Patriarch Lü, Reputed Founder of the the Chin Tan Chiao	金丹教创建者吕洞宾	Couling, C. E.		29-470
Reviews of Recent Books	新书评介			29-486
Additions to the Library (July 1926 – June 1927)	图书馆1926年7月至1927年6月新增图书目录			29-544
Presentations to the Library (July 1926 – June 1927)	图书馆1926年7月至1927年6月受赠图书目录			29-546
List of Members, 1927	1927年会员名单			29-548

N. S. VOL. LIX(1928)

题　名	中译题名	责任者	责任者中文名	页码
Obituary	讣告			30-9
Proceedings of the Annual General Meeting, 1928	1928年年会纪要			30-11
Three Score Years and Ten: the Seventieth Anniversary of the NCBRAS	亚洲文会北华支会七十周年纪念	Mason, Isaac	梅益盛	30-19
The Jews of Honan	河南犹太人	MacGillivray, Donald	季理斐	30-42
Shapes of Porcelain Vessels	瓷器的形状	Ferguson, John Calvin	福开森	30-70
The Great Wall of China	中国长城	Hayes, L. Newton.	海士	30-105
The Ch'ing Dynasty Criticism of Sung Politico-philosophy	清代对宋代理学的批判	Freeman, Mansfield	费孟福	30-130
Chinese Foot-measures of the Past Nineteen Centuries	中国过去19个世纪的量具	Wang, Kuo-wei.	王国维	30-165
A German Translation of the *Hsi Hsiang Chi*	《西厢记》德语版概述	Meerkerk, M. E. R. F.		30-182
The Place of Music in the Platonic and Confucian Systems of Moral Education	柏拉图和孔子道德教育体系中音乐的地位	Phelps, D. L.	费尔璞	30-186
The Origin and Growth of Deserts and the Encroachment of the Desert on North-China	沙漠的起源和发展及华北的沙漠化	Englaender, A. L.	恩格莱德	30-204
Early Christianity in Japan	日本早期基督教	White, Laura M.	亮乐月	30-227
The Origin of the Chinese Priesthood	中国神职起源	Werner, Edward Theodore Chalmers	倭讷	30-246

(续表)

题 名	中译题名	责任者	责任者中文名	页码
Contributions from the Herbarium of the Shantung Christian University	齐鲁大学植物标本室报告	Jacot, Arhtur Paul	贾珂	30-258
Wang Mang, the Socialist Emperor of Nineteen Centuries Ago	王莽	Hu, Shih.	胡适	30-276
K'ü Yüan, His Life and Poems	屈原生平及其诗歌	Biallas, Franz Xavier	鲍润生	30-289
The Kite's Message	《风筝误》(节译)	Hudson, Elfrida		30-312
The Murder of Achmach Bailo	阿合马被杀案	Moule, Arthur Christopher	慕阿德	30-314
Reviews of Recent Books	新书评介			30-317
Additions to the Library (July 1927-June 1928)	图书馆1927年7月至1928年6月新增图书目录			30-399
Presentations to the Library (July 1927-June 1928)	图书馆1927年7月至1928年6月受赠图书目录			30-401
List of Members, 1928	1928年会员名单			30-404
N. S. VOL. LX(1929)				
Obituary	讣告			31-9
Proceedings of the Annual General Meeting, 1929	1929年年会纪要			31-13
Some Types of Chinese Historical Thought	中国人的几种历史观	Chang, Hsin-hai	张歆海	31-21
The Establishment of Confucianism as a State Religion During the Han Dynasty	汉代儒家思想统治地位的确立	Hu, Shih	胡适	31-40
The Mohammedans of China, When and How, They First Come	中国回教徒:他们首次入华之时间和方式	Mason, Isaac	梅益盛	31-62
Did Ancient Chinese Culture Come from Egypt	中华文明源于埃及吗?	Chatley, Herbert	查得利	31-99
Gold in China: in its Historical Practical and Financial Aspects	中国的黄金:历史、应用及财政功能	Kann, E.	耿爱德	31-104
Some Notes on Asia's Ice Age	亚洲冰川纪释疑	Englaender, A. L.	恩格莱德	31-121
Did Manichaeism Influence Lamaism?	摩尼教影响了喇嘛教吗?	Edgar, J. Huston	叶长清	31-135
A List of Plant Names Included in the Cowdry Chihli Flora not Recorded in the Index Florae Sinensis and its Two Supplements	Cowdry《直录植物志》中的植物名录(Forbes和Hemsley的《中国植物志》及其两份补充目录所未载者)。	Liu, J. C.	柳中兴	31-140

(续表)

题　名	中译题名	责任者	责任者中文名	页码
List of Legible Inscriptions on Stones in the Foreign Cemetery on Double Island, Swatow, 1922	汕头双岛西人墓地1922年石刻目录	Talbot, R. M.	铎博赍	31-147
The George Eumorfopoulos Collection: Catalogue of the Chinese and Corean Bronzes, Sculpture, Jades, Jewellery and Miscellaneous Objects, by W. Perceval Yetts	颜慈编《颜氏集古录》	Morgan, Evan	莫安仁	31-149
Reviews of Recent Books	新书评介			31-156
Additions to the Library	图书馆1929年新增图书目录			31-178
List of Members, 1929	1929年会员名单			31-181

N. S. VOL. LXI(1930)

题　名	中译题名	责任者	责任者中文名	页码
Obituary	讣告			31-209
Proceedings of the Annual General Meeting, 1930	1930年年会纪要			31-211
The Light Thrown on Ancient Chinese History by Recent Archaeological Discoveries	考古新发现对古代中国历史的昭示	Buxton, Dudley		31-219
Some Points on the History of Science in China	中国科技史之管见:以数学为主	Vacca, Giovanni		31-232
A Journey to the Tung Ling	东陵行记	Fischer, Emil Sigmund	斐士	31-242
Stories in Chinese Paintings, II	中国绘画中的故事(二)	Ferguson, John Calvin	福开森	31-266
Language and New Thought	语言与新思想	Morgan, Evan	莫安仁	31-287
Can Chinese Writing be Simplified?	汉字可以简化么?	Chatley, Herbert	查得利	31-302
The Book of Changes and Genesis	《易经》及其起源	Wells, H. R.		31-307
Kingship in China	中国之王权	Soothill, W. E.	苏慧廉	31-318
The I Wei	《易纬》	Bruce, Percy	步如旭	31-326
The Philosopher Yang Hsiung	哲学家扬雄	Forke, A.	佛尔克	31-334
The Symbolism of the Forbidden City, Peking	紫禁城的象征意义	Ayscough, Florence Wheelock	爱司克夫人	31-337
Contributions from the Herbarium of the Shantung Christian University (Continued)	齐鲁大学植物标本室报告(续)	Jacot, Arthur Paul	贾柯	31-353
Why the Sinologue Should Study Manchu	汉学家为何应学满文	Hauer, Erich		31-386
Chinese Poems: A Song of Autumn Winds	汉诗选译:《秋风辞》	Budd, Charles	卜德	31-395

(续表)

题名	中译题名	责任者	责任者中文名	页码
Chinese Poems: A Snowstorm	汉诗选译:《风雪》	Budd, Charles	卜德	31-396
Chinese Poems: The South Bank of the Brook	汉诗选译:《南溪》	Budd, Charles	卜德	31-398
Reviews of Recent Books	新书评介			31-399
Presentations to the Library (July 1929 - June 1930)	图书馆1929年7月至1930年6月受赠书目			31-430
List of Members, 1930	1930年会员名录			31-433
N. S. VOL. LXII(1931)				
Obituary	讣告			32-9
Proceedings of the Annual General Meeting, 1931	1931年年会纪要			32-11
Early Days of Western Medicine in China	西医传入中国的早期阶段	Wu, Lien-Teh	伍连德	32-21
Climatic Changes During Historic Time in China	中国历史时期的气候变化	Chu, Coching	竺可桢	32-52
Bamboos in China	中国之竹	Porterfield, W. M.	包达甫	32-61
Preliminary Notes on the Natural History of Nanking	南京博物志初探	Ping, C.	平文谦	32-79
The History of The Days of the Week	一周七日的历史	Chatley, Herbert	查得利	32-105
Contributions from the Herbarium of the Shantung Christian University (Continued)	齐鲁大学植物标本室报告(再续)	Jacot, Arthur Paul	贾柯	32-116
Chinese Pottery and Porcelain: an Appreciation	中国陶瓷器鉴赏	Abraham, R. D.	亚伯拉罕	32-131
Chinese-Moslem Chronology	中国之伊斯兰纪年	Mason, Isaac	梅益盛	32-143
The Indian Frontier	印度边界	Haward, Edwin	何立德	32-146
The Chinese Nation and the Doctrine of the Golden Mean	中华民族与中庸之道	Tsai, Yuen-pei	蔡元培	32-157
The Western Transcription of Chinese	汉语西式标音	Gardner, Charles S.		32-163
Confucianism, Democracy and Nationalism	儒家思想、民主政体与民族主义	Lu, Yen-Ying		32-174
The Cosmic Spirit	宇宙观	Morgan, Evan	莫安仁	32-179
The Asiatic Origin of South American Man	南美人的亚洲起源	Gapanovich, J. J.	噶邦福	32-198
Passing of the R. A. S. Old Premises at Shanghai	亚洲文会旧会所暂停使用	Mason, Isaac	梅益盛	32-225
Reviews of Recent Books	新书评介			32-229

(续表)

题　　名	中译题名	责任者	责任者中文名	页码
Presentations and Additions to the Library（July 1930 – June 1931）	图书馆 1930 年 7 月至 1931 年 6 月受赠及新增图书目录			32－248
List of Members，1931	1931 年会员名录			32－251
N. S. VOL. LXIII（1932）				
The New Building of the Royal Asiatic Society	亚洲文会新大楼			32－277
Proceedings of the Annual General Meeting，1932	1932 年年会纪要			32－282
Porcelains of Successive Dynasties	中国历代瓷器	Ferguson, John Calvin	福开森	32－293
A Poet-Monk of Modern China	当代中国的一个寺僧	Johnston, Reginald Fleming	庄士敦	32－306
The Hsü-t'ing Mi-shi-so Sutra, or *Jesus-Messiah-Sutra*	《喜听迷诈所经》英译	Saeki, P. Y.	佐伯好郎	32－323
Political Idealists and Realists of China of the Fourth and Third Centuries B. C.	公元前三、四世纪时的中国政治理想主义者和现实主义者	Hughes, E. R.	修中诚	32－340
The Aridity of North China	中国北方的干旱	Moyer, Raymond T.	穆懿尔	32－359
Stories in Chinese Paintings，III	中国绘画中的故事（三）	Ferguson, John Calvin	福开森	32－383
Chinese Anthropometrics: Studies in Chekiang and Kwangtung	中国人体测量学：浙江与广东的研究	Kulp II, Daniel H.	葛学溥	32－402
A Research Museum in Far Eastern Antiquities	瑞典远东文物博物馆	Murphy, Dagny Carter	美斐	32－420
Studies in Conduct and Character	行为与性格研究	Morgan, Evan	莫安仁	32－430
List of Articles Which Have Appeared in the JNCBRAS, 1912 – 1931	文会会刊 1912 – 1931 年所刊论文目录	Woo, Z. T.; Chao, T. Y.	吴氏；赵氏	32－453
Reviews of Recent Books	新书评介			32－465
Notes and Queries	释疑			32－515
Presentations and Additions to the Library（June 1931 – May 1932）	图书馆 1931 年 6 月至 1932 年 5 月受赠及新增图书目录			32－524
List of Members，1932	1932 年会员名录			32－529
N. S. VOL. LXIV（1933）				
Proceedings of the Annual General Meeting，1933	1933 年年会纪要			33－9

(续表)

题　名	中译题名	责任者	责任者中文名	页码
Early Chinese Travellers and Their Successors	早期中国之旅行家及其后继者	Wu, Lien-Teh	伍连德	33-29
The Worship of Earth in Ancient China	古代中国之土地崇拜	Bishop, Carl Whitney	毕士勃	33-52
Lo-yang as the National Capital	古都洛阳	Ferguson, John Calvin	福开森	33-72
The Philosophy of Tai Tung-yüan	戴震的哲学思想	Freeman, Mansfield	费孟福	33-80
T'ai Miao: A Description of the Supreme Hall of Sacrifices of the Forbidden City	紫禁城太庙	Fischer, Emil Sigmund	斐士	33-102
Further Notes on the History of the Days of the Week	一周七日的历史再论	Chatley, Herbert	查得利	33-107
The Translation of the Fragments of the Nestorian Writings in China	中国景教文献英译（《一神论》、《世尊布施论》）	Saeki, P. Y.	佐伯好郎	33-117
The Origin of Loess	黄土的起源	Penniston, John B.		33-136
Some Chinese Sources for the Study of Northeastern Asia	东北亚研究的汉语文献	Gale, Esson Mcdowell	盖乐	33-142
The Travels of Emperor Mu	《穆天子传》英译（一）	Cheng, Te-k'un	郑德坤	33-154
Notes sur les Alphabets Lü du Yün-nan et les Denominations Ethniques Donnees aux T'ay	云南字母音律及民族名称资料	Rispaud, Jean		33-173
Reviews of Recent Books	新书评介			33-183
Sinological Notes	汉学札记			33-205
Presentations and Additions to the Library (June 1932 - April 1933)	图书馆1932年6月至1933年4月受赠及新增图书目录			33-213
List of MembersS, 1933	1933年会员名录			33-217
N. S. VOL. LXV(1934)				
The Reopening of the Shanghai Museum (R. A. S.)	亚洲文会北华支会博物院重新开放	Ferguson, John Calvin	福开森	33-247
The History of the Shanghai Museum (R. A. S.)	亚洲文会北华支会博物院史	Sowerby, Arthur de Carle	苏阿德	33-249
Proceedings of the Annual General Meeting, 1934	1934年年会纪要			33-257
The Beginnings of the Human Race	人类的起源	Grabau, A. W.	葛利普	33-285
Painters Among Catholic Missionaries and Their Helpers in Peking	北京天主教传教士中的画家及其助手	Ferguson, John Calvin	福开森	33-307

(续表)

题　名	中译题名	责任者	责任者中文名	页码
The Cycles of Cathay	六十甲子——中国古代历法	Chatley, Herbert	查得利	33-330
Bamboo and Bamboo Painting	竹与竹画	Teng, Kuei	藤圭	33-349
The Past Decade in Chinese Literature	近十年之中国文学	Lyon, David Willard	来会理	33-358
Discoursed on Salt and Iron (Yen T'ieh Lun: Chaps. XX-XXVIII)	《盐铁论》选译	Gale, Esson Mcdowell	盖乐	33-369
The Translation of the Nestorian Writings in China	中国景教文献英译（《世尊布施论》续）	Saeki, P. Y.	佐伯好郎	33-407
The Travels of Emperor Mu (Continued from Vol. LXIV, P. 142)	《穆天子传》英译（二）	Cheng, Te-k'un	郑德坤	33-424
The Prajna-Paramita Hridaya Sutra	《般若波罗密多心经》英译	Lee, Shao-chang	李绍昌	33-446
Reviews of Recent Books	新书评介			33-450
Sinological Notes	汉学札记			33-485
Summaries of Lectures Delivered Before the Society 1933-1934	亚洲文会北华支会1933-1934年间演讲概要			33-496
Obituary	讣告			33-504
Presentations and Additions to the Library, 1934	图书馆1934年受赠及新增图书目录			33-508

N. S. VOL. LXVI（1935）

题　名	中译题名	责任者	责任者中文名	页码
Proceedings of the Annual General Meeting, 1935	1935年年会纪要			33-527
The Worship of Lei Tsu, Patron Saint of Silk Workers	嫘祖崇拜	Williams, Edward Thomas	卫理	33-547
How the Chinese Look upon the Art of Painting	中国人如何看待绘画艺术	Sirén, Osvald	喜仁龙	33-561
The Technique and Spirit of Chinese Poetry	中国诗歌的技巧及其精神	Lin, Yu-tang	林语堂	33-577
China's North-West Passage: a Chapter in its Opening	中国西北通道：开拓篇	Drake, F. S.	林仰山	33-588
The Word "One" in Chinese Poetry	中国诗歌中的"一"字	Lin, Tung-chi	林同济	33-598
Men and Matters in the Land of the Yellow Earth	黄土地带的居民和物产	Andrew, G. Findlay	安献令	33-604
Inscriptions on Bronzes	青铜器铭文	Ferguson, John Calvin	福开森	33-612
Eclipses during the First Fifty Years of the Earlier Han Dynasty	西汉前五十年的日月食	Dubs, Homer Hasenpflug	德效骞	33-621

(续表)

题 名	中译题名	责任者	责任者中文名	页码
Reviews of Recent Books	新书评介			33-631
Sinological Notes	汉学札记			33-662
Summaries of Lectures Delivered Before the Society 1934-1935	亚洲文会北华支会1934-1935年间演讲概要			33-679
Obituary	讣告			33-690
Presentations and Additions to the Library, 1935	图书馆1935年受赠及新增图书目录			33-698
List of Members, 1935	1935年会员名录			33-708

N. S. VOL. LXVII(1936)

题 名	中译题名	责任者	责任者中文名	页码
Proceedings of the Annual General Meeting, 1936	1936年年会会议录			34-11
The Six Horses of T'ang T'ai Tsung	昭陵六骏	Ferguson, John Calvin	福开森	34-29
T'ai Chi Shan Yuan—The Chinese Astrological Theory of Creation	太极上元——中国天文学的宇宙论	Chatley, Herbert	查得利	34-41
The Inscribed Bones of Shang	殷商甲骨	Gibson, Harry E.	裘必胜	34-49
Agricultural Rites in the Religion of Old China	中国古代的农业祭仪	Williams, Edward Thomas	卫理	34-61
On the Building History of the Pao Shu T'a, Hangchow	杭州保俶塔的历史	Prip-Møller, Johannes	艾术华	34-86
Han Kao-Tsu and Hsiang Yü	汉高祖与项羽	Dubs, Homer Hasenpflug	德效骞	34-98
Old Problems Concerning the Nestorian Monument in China Re-examined in the Light of Newly Discovered Facts	大秦景教碑相关老问题的新发现	Saeki, P. Y.	佐伯好郎	34-123
The Chinese Attitude to Peace and War in Pre-Confucian Times	前孔子时代中国人的战争与和平观	Brown, Margaret Helen	薄玉珍	34-142
Geophysical Prospecting for Gold, Metallic Ores and Petroleum and its Possible Application in China	中国黄金和其他金属矿藏及石油勘探和开采的可能	Nyström, Erik T.	新常富	34-173
China's North-West Passage: The Struggle for the Tarim Basin in the Later Han Dynasty	中国西北通道:东汉在塔里木盆地的经营	Drake, F. S.	林仰山	34-189
Sang Huang-Yang, Economist of the Early Han	西汉经济学家桑弘羊	Ch'en, S. C.		34-202
Reviews of Recent Books	新书评介			34-213
Sinological Notes	汉学札记			34-242

(续表)

题　名	中译题名	责任者	责任者中文名	页码
Obituary	讣告			34-256
Presentations and Additions to the Library (June 1935 – May 1936)	图书馆1935年6月至1936年5月受赠及新增图书目录			34-257
List of Members, 1936	1936年会员名录			34-269

N. S. VOL. LXVIII(1937)

题　名	中译题名	责任者	责任者中文名	页码
Proceedings of the Annual General Meeting, 1937	1937年年会纪要			34-305
Animals in Chinese Art (Pressidential Address)	中国艺术中的动物（会长演讲）	Sowerby, Arthur de Carle	苏阿德	34-329
Music and Musical Instruments of Shang	商代的音乐和乐器	Gibson, Harry E.	裘必胜	34-336
Some Observations on the Agriculture of Inner Mongolia	内蒙古农业观察	Moyer, Raymond T.	穆懿尔	34-351
Korean Interference with Chinese Historical Records	朝鲜对中国历史编纂的抵触	Goodrich, Luther Carrington	傅路德	34-367
Chekiang Highways	《浙江公路》	Gale, Esson Mcdowell	盖乐	34-375
Reviews of Recent Books	新书评介			34-379
Sinological Note	汉学札记			34-407
Correspondence	通信			34-420
Personal Notes	通告			34-423
Presentations and Additions to the Library (June 1936 to May 1937)	图书馆1936年6月至1937年5月受赠及新增图书目录			34-424

N. S. VOL. LXIX(1938)

题　名	中译题名	责任者	责任者中文名	页码
Proceedings of the Annual General Meeting, 1938	1938年年会纪要			34-437
President Address	会长致辞	Sowerby, Arthur de Carle	苏阿德	34-455
Pottery Tomb Figures of Ancient China (President Address)	中国古墓中的陶俑（会长演讲）	Sowerby, Arthur de Carle	苏阿德	34-455
Domesticated Animals of Shang and Their Sacrifice	商代动物驯养与祭祀	Gibson, Harry E.	裘必胜	34-467
Times and Manners in the Age of the Emperor K'ang Hsi	康熙时代与当时的风尚	Morgan, Evan	莫安仁	34-481
The Language Students of the East India Company's Canton Factory	广州东印度公司商行的语言学生	Stifler, Susan Reed		34-504

(续表)

题名	中译题名	责任者	责任者中文名	页码
The Influence of Liquids upon the Dissolution of the Initial Consonant Groups in the Indo-Sinic Family	流音对中印语族辅音群消失的影响	Wen, Yu	闻宥	34-541
Reviews of Recent Books	新书评介			34-550
Sinological Note	汉学札记			34-569
Presentations and Additions to the Library (June 1937 to December 1938)	图书馆1937年6月至1938年12月受赠及新增图书目录			34-571
List of Members, 1938	1938年会员名录			34-577

N. S. VOL. LXX(1939)

题名	中译题名	责任者	责任者中文名	页码
Proceedings of the Annual General Meeting, 1939	1939年年会纪要			35-9
President Address	会长致辞	Sowerby, Arthur de Carle	苏阿德	35-45
Some Chinese Animal Myths and Legends	中国动物主题神话	Sowerby, Arthur de Carle	苏阿德	35-47
The Dragon in Chinese Medicine	中药中的龙	Read, Bernard Emms	伊博恩	35-71
Sacrifices in Ancient China	古代中国的祭仪	Morgan, Evan	莫安仁	35-86
The Evolution of Chinese Characters Beginning from Shang Pictographs	商代甲骨文以降汉字的演变	Gibson, Harry E.	裘必胜	35-93
Worshipping Imperial Ancestors in Peking	北京的皇家祭祖仪式	Williams, Edward Thomas	卫理	35-102
Reviews of Recent Books	新书评介			35-122
Obituary Notice	讣告			35-137
Presentations and Additions to the Library (January to December, 1939)	图书馆1939年受赠及新增图书目录			35-138
List of Members, 1939	1939年会员名录			35-145

N. S. VOL. LXXI(1940)

题名	中译题名	责任者	责任者中文名	页码
Proceedings of the Annual General Meeting, 1940	1940年年会纪要			35-175
Presidential Address	会长致辞	Sowerby, Arthur de Carle	苏阿德	35-193
Some Remarkable Animals of China	中国珍稀动物	Sowerby, Arthur de Carle	苏阿德	35-195

(续表)

题　名	中译题名	责任者	责任者中文名	页码
Insects Used in Chinese Medicine	昆虫在中药中的使用	Read, Bernard Emms	伊博恩	35-218
The Use of Cowries as Money During the Shang and Chou Periods	商周时代的贝壳货币	Gibson, Harry E.	裘必胜	35-231
An Inscribed Pottery Vessel of the Chow Dynasty (Fighting States Period 481-225 B. C.)	战国陶器铭文	Drake, F. S.	林仰山	35-246
Chinese Historical Attitude to Peace and War	中国历史上的战争与和平观	Tomkinson, L.	童克圣	35-256
The Chin Shan Tsui Temple: Peitaiho	北戴河秦山寺	Dunlap, Eva Wyman		35-269
Bits of Old Soochow	古代苏州散记	Poston, Divid Gray		35-276
Jehol	热河	Fischer, Emil Sigmund	斐士	35-286
Reviews of Recent Books	新书评介			35-302
Chinese Libraries	亚洲文会北华支会图书馆中文书目信息			35-317
Obituary	讣告			35-319
Sinological Notes	汉学札记			35-320
Presentations and Additions to the Library (January to December, 1940)	图书馆1940年受赠及新增图书目录			35-323
Perodicals Received by the Library (January to December, 1940)	图书馆1940年所收期刊目录			35-326
List of Members, 1940	1940年会员名录			35-328

N. S. VOL. LXXII(1946)

题　名	中译题名	责任者	责任者中文名	页码
Proceedings of the Annual General Meeting, 1946	1946年年会纪要			35-361
Decorations of Chinese Bronzes	中国青铜装饰品	Ferguson, John Calvin	福开森	35-369
Ching Te Chen Porcelain City of Emperors	中国瓷都景德镇	Beath, Sterling S.		35-375
Interpretations of Chinese History	中国的历史诠释学	Roberts, Donald	罗道纳	35-383
Zoological Exploration in China	中国动物学探险	Sowerby, Arthur de Carle	苏阿德	35-389
The Saced Lamaist Dances	喇嘛教的圣舞	Fischer, Emil Sigmund	斐士	35-400
Criminal Law in Ancient Chia	古代中国刑法	Ruffé, M. d'Auxion de		35-412
The Chinese Shadow Play	中国皮影戏	Ankerson, W. A.	安克生	35-420

(续表)

题　　名	中译题名	责任者	责任者中文名	页码
A Descriptive and Bibliographical Catalogue of the European Books Printed Before 1800 in the Library of the R. A. S.	亚洲文会北华支会图书馆藏1800年前出版欧洲文献书目提要	Schwarz, Kurt L.		35-429
Reviews of Recent Books	新书评介			35-438
Obituary	讣告			35-452
Library Report	亚洲文会北华支会图书馆报告			35-453
Presentations and Additions to the Library (January to December, 1941)	图书馆1941年受赠及新增图书目录			35-454
Presentations and Additions to the Library (September 1945 to December 1946)	图书馆1945年9月至1946年12月受赠及新增图书目录			35-457
N. S. VOL. LXXIII (1948)				
Proceedings of the Annual General Meeting, 1948	1948年年会纪要			35-479
Preface	编者按			35-481
A Tribute to Dr. John C. Ferguson	悼念福开森	Ly, J. Usang	李	35-483
A Missonary Contribution to Chinese Nationalism	传教士对中国民族主义的贡献	Francis, John de	德范克	35-493
Butterfly Hunting in Pi Hu, S. Chekiang	在浙江碧湖捕捉蝴蝶	House, I. E.		35-527
The Cosmolohical and Anthropological Philosophy of Tung Chung-shu	董仲舒的天人观	Yao, Shan yu	姚善友	35-532
The Cause Which Induced the Monk I-szu, the Nestorian Archbishop of Ch'ang an, to Come to China and the Exact Date of his Arrival	景教主教伊斯来华原因及时间考	Chang, Hsing-lang	张星烺	35-561
Some Notes on the Blue Turkish Tongue	突厥语笔记	Gillett, Michael Cavenagh	支乐德	35-581
A Descriptive and Bibliographical Catalogue of the European Books Printed Before 1900 in the Library of the R. A. S.	亚洲文会北华支会图书馆藏1900年前出版欧洲文献书目提要	Schwarz, Kurt L.		35-605
Reviews of Recent Books	新书评介			35-612
Presentations and Additions to the Library (January to December, 1948)	图书馆1948年受赠及新增图书目录			35-628

索引

篇目索引

论 文

题 名	中译题名	责任者	卷期	页码
A				
Aborigines of Hainan, The	海南土著居民	Swinhoe, Robert	VOL. VII	5-265
Aborigines of Northern Formosa, The	台湾北部的土著居民	Taintor, E. C.	VOL. IX	6-299
Account of an Overland Journey from Peking to Shanghai, Made in Febrary and March 1866	1866年2、3月间北京至上海的陆上之旅	Martin, William Alexander Parsos	VOL. III	3-476
Additional Coins of the Present Dynasty	大清货币补遗	Bushell, S. W.	VOL. XXXIII	19-38
Advisability, or The Reverse, of Endeavouring to Convey Western Knowledge to the Chinese Through the Medium of Their Own Language, The	用汉语传播西方知识的正反效果		VOL. XXI	12-9
Agricultural Rites in the Religion of Old China	中国古代的农业祭仪	Williams, Edward Thomas	VOL. LXVII	34-61
Alligators in China	中国的短吻鳄	Fauvel, A. A.	VOL. XIII	9-39
Alphabetical List of the Dynastic and Reign-Titles	中国王朝世系表	Playfair, G. M. H.	VOL. XXI	12-75
Ancient City of Shaohing, The	古代绍兴城	Walshe, W. Gilbert	VOL. XXXIII	19-290
Ancient Language and Cult of the Chows, The	周朝的语言和文化	Kingsmill, Thomas William	VOL. XII	8-313
Ancient Porcelain: A Study in Chinese Mediaeval Industry and Trade	古代陶瓷：中世纪中国工商业研究	Hirth, F.	VOL. XXII	12-513
Ancient Tibet and its Frontagers	古代西藏及其前沿地带	Kingsmill, Thomas William	VOL. XXXVII	20-211
Animal, Fossil, Mineral and Vegetable Products. Consular District of Ichang in the Province of Hupeh, China	湖北宜昌地区动物、化石、矿物与植物物产	Gardner, C. T.	VOL. XIX	11-259
Animals in Chinese Art (Presidential Address)	中国艺术中的动物（会长演讲）	Sowerby, Arthur de Carle	VOL. LXVIII	34-329
Animistic Elements in Moslem Prayer	穆斯林祷告中的泛灵论元素	Zwemer, Samuel Marinus	VOL. XLIX	25-56
Annam and its Minor Currency	安南及其钱币	Toda, Ed.	VOL. XVII	10-351
Antiquities of Cambodia, The	柬埔寨古迹	Thompson, J.	VOL. VII	5-437

(续表)

题　名	中译题名	责任者	卷期	页码
Archaeological Survey of the Environs of China's Ancient Capitals	中国诸古都郊区考古调查	Alexeieff, V.	VOL. XL	21-261
Aridity of North China, The	中国北方的干旱	Moyer, Raymond T.	VOL. LXIII	32-359
Ascent of Mt. Morrison, The	攀登玉山山脉	Arnold, Julean Herbert	VOL. XL	21-304
Asiatic Origin of South American Man, The	南美人的亚洲起源	Gapanovich, J. J.	VOL. LXII	32-198
Attractions of Entomond, The	昆虫学的魅力	Moore, Alfred	VOL. L	25-438

B

题　名	中译题名	责任者	卷期	页码
Bamboo and Bamboo Painting	竹与竹画	Teng, Kuei	VOL. LXV	33-349
Bamboos in China	中国之竹	Porterfield, W. M.	VOL. LXII	32-61
Beginning of the Study of the Flora and Fauna of Soochow and Vicinity, A	苏州及其周边地区动植物初探	Gee, Nathaniel Gist	VOL. L	25-446
Beginnings of the Human Race, The	人类的起源	Grabau, A. W.	VOL. LXV	33-285
Bibliographical Introduction to the Study of Chinese Law, A	中国法律研究文献介绍	Lobinger, Charles Sumner	VOL. XLV	23-428
Bibliography: Chinesische Grammatik mit Ausschluss des Niederen Stiles und der Heutigen Umgangs-sprache	嘎伯冷兹的《汉语语法》		VOL. XVII	10-547
Bishop Della Chiesa and the Story of his Lost Grave	伊大仁主教和他失踪坟墓的故事	Heeren, John J.	VOL. LIV	27-552
Bits of Old Soochow	古代苏州散记	Poston, Divid Gray	VOL. LXXI	35-276
Bituminous Coal Mines West of Peking, The	北京西面的沥青煤田	Edkins, Joseph	VOL. IV	4-249
Book of Changes and Genesis, The	《易经》及其起源	Wells, H. R.	VOL. LXI	31-307
Bore of the Tsien-tang Kiang (Hang-Chau Bay), The	钱塘江涌潮	Moore, Osborne	VOL. XXIII	13-195
Botanicon Sinicum (Part I)	中国植物志（一）	Bretschneider, E.	VOL. XVI	10-24
Botanicon Sinicum (Part II)	中国植物志（二）	Bretschneider, E.	VOL. XXV	14-9
Botanicon Sinicum (Part III)	中国植物志（三）	Bretschneider, E.	VOL. XXIX	17-13
Brief Account of the French Expedition of 1866 into Indo-China	法国1866年远征印度支那概要	Viguier, S. A.	VOL. VIII	6-85
Buddhist Shastra, Translated from the Chinese: with an analysis and notes, A	《壹输卢迦论》译稿与注释	Edkins, Joseph	O. S. VOL. I No. I	2-117
Buddhist Sheet-tract, A	一张佛教画	Moule, G. E.	VOL. XIX	11-352
Burial Customs in Sz-chuen	四川的丧葬习俗	Torrance, Thomas	VOL. XLI	21-507

(续表)

题　名	中译题名	责任者	卷期	页码
Burial-place of Genghis Khan, The	成吉思汗埋葬地	Werner, Edward Theodore Chalmers	VOL. LVI	28-492
Butterfly Hunting in Pi Hu, S. Chekiang	在浙江碧湖捕捉蝴蝶	House, I. E.	VOL. LXXIII	35-527
C				
Can Chinese Writing be Simplified?	汉字可以简化么？	Chatley, Herbert	VOL. LXI	31-302
Carte Agricole Générale de l'Empire Chinois, Texte Préface, Légende et Répertoire	中国农业物产图	Simon, G. Eug.	VOL. IV	4-215
Case of Ritualism, A	祭祀仪式的个案研究	Morgan, Evan	VOL. XLIX	25-146
Cause Which Induced the Monk I-szu, the Nestorian Archbishop of Ch'ang an, to Come to China and the Exact Date of his Arrival, The	景教主教伊斯来华原因及时间考	Chang, Hsing-lang	VOL. LXXIII	35-561
Changchow, the Capital of Fuhkien in Mongol Times	元时福建省会漳州	Phillips, George	VOL. XXIII	13-29
Chapter of Folklore, A	民俗记		VOL. XLIX	25-94
Check List of Birds of the Lower Yangtze Valley from Hankow to the Sea	长江下游河滩鸟类名录	Moffett, Lacy I. & Gee, N. Gist	VOL. XLIV	23-151
Chemical Industry in Kwangtung Province	广东的化学工业	Yan-tsz Chiu	VOL. L	25-409
Chin Shan Tsui Temple: Peitaiho, The	北戴河秦山寺	Dunlap, Eva Wyman	VOL. LXXI	35-269
China Monuments	中国的纪念碑	McCormick, Frederick	VOL. XLIII	22-463
China's North-West Passage: A Chapter in its Opening	中国西北通道：开拓篇	Drake, F. S.	VOL. LXVI	33-588
China's North-West Passage: The Struggle for the Tarim Basin in the Later Han Dynasty	中国西北通道：后汉在塔里木盆地的经营	Drake, F. S.	VOL. LXVII	34-189
China's Petrified Sun-rays	中国的化石能源	Chatley, Herbert	VOL. LI	26-67
Chinese Anthropometrics: Studies in Chekiang and Kwangtung	中国人体测量学：浙江与广东的研究	Kulp II, Daniel H.	VOL. LXIII	32-402
Chinese Architecture	中国的建筑	Edkins, Joseph	VOL. XXIV	13-609
Chinese Art Metal Work	中国的金属艺术品	Stanley, Arthur	VOL. XLIII	22-383
Chinese Attitude to Peace and War in Pre-Confucian Times, The	前孔子时代中国人的战争与和平观	Brown, Margaret Helen	VOL. LXVII	34-142

(续表)

题 名	中译题名	责任者	卷期	页码
Chinese Bibliography	中国的文献学	Macgowan, Daniel John	O. S. VOL. I No. II	2-192
Chinese Calendar: Its Origin, History and Connections, The	中国历法的起源、历史及联系	Kingsmill, Thomas William	VOL. XXXII	18-529
Chinese Cat, The	中国的猫	Torrance, Thomas	VOL. LVII	29-139
Chinese Chemical Manufactures	中国化工制造	Smith, F. Porter.	VOL. VI	5-161
Chinese Chess	中国象棋	Volpicelli, Z.	VOL. XXIII	13-260
Chinese Children's Games	中国儿童游戏	Headland, Isaac Taylor	VOL. XXXVII	20-340
Chinese Chronological Tables	中国历史年表	Mayers, William Frederick	VOL. IV	4-165
Chinese Composite Deities	中国的复合神	Werner, Edward Theodore Chalmers	VOL. LIV	27-624
Chinese Embroidery and Other Art Textile Work	中国刺绣及其他艺术纺织品	Stanley, Arthur	VOL. XLIV	23-93
Chinese Equivalents of the Letter "R" in Foreign Names	外国名称中字母"R"的中文对应词	Hirth, F.	VOL. XXI	12-222
Chinese Eunuchs	中国的宦官	Stent, George Carter	VOL. XI	8-165
Chinese Foot-measures of the Past Nineteen Centuries	中国过去19个世纪的量具	Wang, Kuo-wei.	VOL. LIX	30-165
Chinese Fox-myths	中国神狐故事	Werner, Edward Theodore Chalmers	VOL. VIII	6-63
Chinese Fresh Water Sponges	中国淡水海绵	Gee, Nathaniel Gist	VOL. LVII	29-136
Chinese Game of Chess as Compared with that Practised by Western Nations, The	中国棋类游戏	Himly, K.	VOL. VI	5-127
Chinese Guilds or Chambers of Commerce and Trades Unions	中国的行会制度	Macgowan, Daniel John	VOL. XXI	12-141
Chinese Historical Attitude to Peace and War	中国历史上的战争与和平观	Tomkinson, L.	VOL. LXXI	35-256
Chinese Ideas of Antiques	中国人的古董观	Huston, James	VOL. LI	26-73
Chinese Legends	中国的（民间）传说	Stent, George Carter	VOL. VII	5-423
Chinese Life of Modhammed, A	一个回教徒的中式生活	Mason, Isaac	VOL. LI	26-181
Chinese Lyrics	中国的抒情诗	Stent, George Carter	VOL. VII	5-333

(续表)

题 名	中译题名	责任者	卷期	页码
Chinese Metaphorical Zoology	汉语修辞中的动物学	Williams, Charles Alfred Speed	VOL. L	25-291
Chinese-Moslem Chronology	中国之伊斯兰纪年	Mason, Isaac	VOL. LXII	32-143
Chinese Names of Plants	植物汉语名称	Henry, Augustine	VOL. XXII	12-617
Chinese Names of Plants: A Preliminary List of the Trees and Shrubs of North Honan	豫北植物汉语名称	Hers, Joseph	VOL. LIII	27-139
Chinese Nation and the Doctrine of the Golden Mean, The	中华民族与中庸之道	Tsai, Yuen-pei	VOL. LXII	32-157
Chinese Notions about Pigeons and Doves	中国人关于鸽子的看法	Werner, Edward Theodore Chalmers	VOL. IV	4-231
Chinese Oriental College, The	中国之东方学会——四夷馆	Hirth, F.	VOL. XXII	12-587
Chinese Pagodas	中国的塔	Couling, Samuel	VOL. XLVI	23-597
Chinese Partnerships: Liability of the Individual Members	中国合伙企业成员的责任和义务		VOL. XXII	12-423
Chinese Poems: *A Snowstorm*	汉诗选译:《风雪》	Budd, Charles	VOL. LXI	31-396
Chinese Poems: *A Song of Autumn Winds*	汉诗选译:《秋风辞》	Budd, Charles	VOL. LXI	31-395
Chinese Poems: *The South Bank of the Brook*	汉诗选译:《南溪》	Budd, Charles	VOL. LXI	31-398
Chinese Poetry and Its Connotations	中文诗及其内涵	Ayscough, Florence Wheelock	VOL. LI	26-121
Chinese Pottery and Porcelain: an Appreciation	中国陶瓷器鉴赏	Abraham, R. D.	VOL. LXII	32-131
Chinese Puzzledom	中国之迷局	Kliene, Charles	VOL. XLIX	25-162
Chinese Revenue	中国之税收	Parker, Edward Harper	VOL. XXX	18-114
Chinese Shadow Play, The	中国皮影戏	Ankerson, W. A.	VOL. LXXII	35-420
Chinese Sophists, The	中国之辩士	Forke, A.	VOL. XXXIV	19-389
Chinese State Papers from the Boxer Days: Translated from the Chinese	义和团运动期间清朝政府的官方文件	Parker, Edward Harper	VOL. XLVII	24-147
Chinese Sun-dial, A	中国日晷	Du Bois-Reymond, C.	VOL. XLV	23-401
Chinese System of Family Relationship and Its Aryan Affinities, The	中国之家庭制度与及其与雅利安人的联系	Kingsmill, Thomas William	VOL. XXXI	18-365
Chinese Theatricals and Theatrical Plots: A Dutiful and Unselfish Heart	中国戏剧调查:孝廉心	Brewitt-Taylor, C. H.	VOL. XX	11-646

(续表)

题　名	中译题名	责任者	卷期	页码
Chinese Theatricals and Theatrical Plots: Imperial Troubles Settled	中国戏剧调查：定王难	Macgowan, Daniel John	VOL. XX	11－649
Chinese Theatricals and Theatrical Plots: Tattooing	中国戏剧调查：刺字	Edkins, Joseph	VOL. XX	11－641
Chinese Theatricals and Theatrical Plots: The Beating of a Golden Branch	中国戏剧调查：打金枝	Balfour, Frederic Henry	VOL. XX	11－639
Chinese Theatricals and Theatrical Plots: The Miser	中国戏剧调查：看财奴	Rhein, J.	VOL. XX	11－646
Chinese Theatricals and Theatrical Plots: The Sheepfold	中国戏剧调查：牧羊圈	Allen, Herbert J.	VOL. XX	11－644
Chinese Theatricals and Theatrical Plots: The Three Suspicions	中国戏剧调查：三疑	Giles, Herbert Allen	VOL. XX	11－643
Chinese Theatricals and Theatrical Plots: The Two Soles, or Becoming an Acotr from Love	中国戏剧调查：比目鱼	Imbault-Huart, Camille	VOL. XX	11－647
Chinese Theatricals and Theatrical Plots: The Widow no Widow	中国戏剧调查：寡妇上坟	Playfair, G. M. H.	VOL. XX	11－640
Chinese Use of Shad in Consumption and Iodine Plants in Scrofula	中国人用鲥鱼治痨病、用碘酒治淋巴疾病的方法	Macgowan, Daniel John	VOL. VII	5－475
Chinese Wooding Caving	中国木雕	Stanley, Arthur	VOL. XLV	23－376
Ch'ing Dynasty Criticism of Sung Politico-philosophy, The	清代对宋代理学的批判	Freeman, Mansfield	VOL. LIX	30－130
Ch'ing Ming Festival, The	清明节	Hodous, Lewis	VOL. XLVI	23－610
Ching Te Chen Porcelain City of Emperors	中国瓷都景德镇	Beath, Sterling S.	VOL. LXXII	35－375
Chou-kung; the Duke of Chou	周公	Morgan, Evan	VOL. LVIII	29－430
Christ in the "Li Tai Shen Hsien T'ung Chien"	《历代神仙通鉴》中的基督	Werner, Edward Theodore Chalmers	VOL. LII	26－448
Christ in the "Li Tai Shen Hsien T'ung Chien"	《历代神仙通鉴》中的基督	Giles, Herbert Allen	VOL. LIII	27－272
Christian Mounment at Hsi-an Fu, The	西安府的大秦景教碑	Moule, Arthur Christopher	VOL. XLI	21－548
Christianity of Hung Tsiu Tsuen, a Review of Taeping Books, The	洪秀全之基督教：评太平天国发行的神学书籍	Forrest, Robert James	VOL. IV	4－193
Chu-goh Leang and the Arrows	诸葛亮与《草船借箭》[京剧英译]	Jamieson, C. A.	VOL. LIV	27－359
Climate of Eastern Asia, The	东亚气候	Fritsche, H.	VOL. XII	8－347
Climate of Shanghai, The	上海的气候	Dechevrens, M.	VOL. XVI	10－237

(续表)

题　　名	中译题名	责任者	卷期	页码
Climatic Changes During Historic Time in China	中国历史时期的气候变化	Chu, Coching	VOL. LXII	32-52
Coinage of Corea, The	朝鲜货币	Gardner, C. T.	VOL. XXVII	16-81
Coins of the Present Dynasty of China	大清钱币	Bushell, S. W.	VOL. XV	9-507
Coins of the Republic of China	民国的铸币	Ros, Giuseppe	VOL. XLVIII	24-356
Coins of the Ta-Ts'ing, or Present Dynasty of China	大清货币	Wylie, Alexander	O. S. VOL. I No. I	2-54
Collection of Birds in the Shanghai Museum, The	亚洲文会博物院藏鸟类标本	Touche, J. D. D. de la	VOL. XL	21-359
Collection of Chinese Reptiles in the Shanghai Museum, The	亚洲文会博物院藏中国爬行动物标本	Stanley, Arthur	VOL. XLV	23-315
Comparative Study of Chinese Dialects, The	汉语方言比较研究	Parker, Edward Harper	VOL. XII	8-235
Comparative Table of the Ancient Lunar Asterisms, A	古代月亮星群及时辰对照表	Kingsmill, Thomas William	VOL. XXVI	15-52
Confucian Reformers in Japan, in the 18th Century, The	18世纪日本的儒家改革者	Hall, J. C.	VOL. XLI	21-447
Confucianism, Democracy and Nationalism	儒家思想、民主政体与民族主义	Lu, Yen-Ying	VOL. LXII	32-174
Contribution to the Ethnology of Eastern Asia	东亚民族学论稿	Macgowan, Daniel John	O. S. VOL. I No. I	2-113
Contribution to the Nomenclature of Chinese Plants	中国植物命名法论稿	Faber, Ernst	VOL. XXXVIII	20-549
Contributions from the Herbarium of the Shantung Christian University	齐鲁大学植物标本室报告	Jacot, Arhtur Paul.	VOL. LIX	30-258
Contributions from the Herbarium of the Shantung Christian University (Continued)	齐鲁大学植物标本室报告(续)	Jacot, Arthur Paul	VOL. LXI	31-353
Contributions from the Herbarium of the Shantung Christian University (Continued)	齐鲁大学植物标本室报告(再续)	Jacot, Arthur Paul	VOL. LXII	32-116
Corea	法译《朝鲜志》摘要	Scherzer, F.	VOL. XVIII	11-61
Corean Monument to Manchu Clemency, A	朝鲜大清皇帝功德碑	Carles, W. R.	VOL. XXIII	13-7
Corrections and Additions to the List of the Birds of Chihli Province	直隶鸟类目录补正	Wilder, Geo. D.	VOL. LVII	29-210
Cosmic Spirit, The	宇宙观	Morgan, Evan	VOL. LXII	32-179
Cosmolohical and Anthropological Philosophy of Tung Chung-shu, The	董仲舒的天人观	Yao, Shan yu	VOL. LXXIII	35-532

(续表)

题　　名	中译题名	责任者	卷期	页码
Cotton in China	中国的棉花	Robertson, D. B.	O. S. VOL. I No. III	2-339
Country and Some Customs of the Szechwan Mantze, The	四川边陲地区的农村习俗	Edgar, J. Huston	VOL. XLVIII	24-274
Criminal Law in Ancient Chia	古代中国刑法	Ruffé, M. d'Auxion de	VOL. LXXII	35-412
Critical Bibliographical Notes-Study of the Tungus Languages	通古斯语研究文献综述	Shirokogoroff, Sergei Mikhailovich	VOL. LV	28-293
Critical Review of Chalfant's Notes upon the "Shuo Wen"	方法敇注《说文》评述	Gillis, I. V.	VOL. LVI	28-569
Cult of the Ch'êng Huang Lao Yeh	城隍老爷崇拜	Ayscough, Florence Wheelock	VOL. LV	28-159
Culture, the Basis of Chinese Art	文化：中国艺术之基	Ferguson, John Calvin	VOL. LIV	27-411
Currency and Measures in China	中国的货币与度量衡		VOL. XXIV	13-402
Currency in China	中国货币考	Morse, Hosea Ballou	VOL. XXXVIII	20-443
Cycles of Cathay, The	六十甲子——中国古代历法	Chatley, Herbert	VOL. LXV	33-330

D

题　　名	中译题名	责任者	卷期	页码
Dead Hand in China, The	中国不散的阴魂	Chatley, Herbert	VOL. LV	28-65
Decorations of Chinese Bronzes	中国青铜装饰品	Ferguson, John Calvin	VOL. LXXII	35-369
Description of the Great Examination Hall at Canton	广东贡院	Keer, J. G.	VOL. III	3-513
Destiny, Fate	宿命论	Morgan, Evan	VOL. LI	26-47
Did Ancient Chinese Culture Come from Egypt	中华文明源于埃及吗？	Chatley, Herbert	VOL. LX	31-99
Did Manichaeism Influence Lamaism	摩尼教影响了喇嘛教吗？	Edgar, J. Huston	VOL. LX	31-135
Discoursed on Salt and Iron (Yen T'ieh Lun: Chaps. XX-XXVIII)	《盐铁论》选译	Gale, Esson Mcdowell	VOL. LXV	33-369
Dissection of a Japanese Criminal	解剖一名日本死囚	Meerdervoort, Johannes Lijdius Catharinus Pompe van	O. S. VOL. II No. I	2-493
Distribution and Habits of the Argali Sheep of Central Asia, The	中亚盘羊的分布及习性	Sjolander, David	VOL. LIII	27-165

(续表)

题　名	中译题名	责任者	卷期	页码
Domestic Altar, The	家神	Hutson, James	VOL. XLIX	25-111
Domesticated Animals of Shang and Their Sacrifice	商代动物驯养与祭祀	Gibson, Harry E.	VOL. LXIX	34-467
Dragon, The	说龙	Hodous, Lewis	VOL. XLVIII	24-261
Dragon in Chinese Medicine, The	中药中的龙	Read, Bernard Emms	VOL. LXX	35-71
Drought, The	《云汉》[汉诗英译]	Hudson, Elfrida	VOL. LIV	27-369
Droughts in China, A. D. 620 to 1643	公元620年至1643年中国的旱灾	Hosie, Alex.	VOL. XII	8-267

E

Early Chinese Bronzes	早期中国青铜器	Ferguson, John Calvin	VOL. XLVII	24-21
Early Chinese Travellers and Their Successors	早期中国之旅行家及其后继者	Wu, Lien-Teh	VOL. LXIV	33-29
Early Christianity in Japan	日本早期基督教	White, Laura M.	VOL. LIX	30-227
Early Days of Western Medicine in China	西医传入中国的早期阶段	Wu, Lien-Teh	VOL. LXII	32-21
Early European Researches into the Flora of China	先辈欧人对中国植物的研究	Bretschneider, E.	VOL. XV	9-313
Early Malays and Their Neighbours, The	早期马来人及其周边文化	Lobinger, Charles Sumner	VOL. L	25-301
Early Portuguese Commerce and Settlements in China	早期在华的葡萄牙人之商业及其殖民地	Volpicelli, Z.	VOL. XXVII	16-43
Eclipses during the First Fifty Years of the Earlier Han Dynasty	西汉前五十年的日月食	Dubs, Homer Hasenpflug	VOL. LXVI	33-621
Eclipses Recorded in Chinese Works	中国典籍中关于日月食的记录	Wylie, Alexander	VOL. IV	4-93
Edict of Ch'in Shih Huang, An	秦诏版	Qin Shi Huang	VOL. LVI	28-434
Eight Immortals of Taoist Religion, The	道教中的八仙	Ling, Peter C.	VOL. XLIX	25-71
Elucidations of Marco Polo's Travels in North-China, Drawn from Chinese Sources	用中国文献释马可波罗中国北部之游	Palladius, Archimandrite.	VOL. X	7-21
Entomology of Shanghai	上海的昆虫	Pryer, W. B.	VOL. IV	4-80
Essay on Manchu Literature	论满洲文献	Möllendorff, P. G. von	VOL. XXIV	13-357
Establishment of Confucianism as a State Religion During the Han Dynasty, The	汉代儒家思想统治地位的确立	Hu, Shih	VOL. LX	31-40

(续表)

题　名	中译题名	责任者	卷期	页码
Ethics of the Chinese, with Special Reference to the Doctrines of Human Nature and Sin, The	中国人的伦理观：关于人性和罪的信条	Griffith, John	O. S. VOL. II No. I	2-428
Evolution of Chinese Characters Beginning from Shang Pictographs, The	商代甲骨文以降汉字的演变	Gibson, Harry E.	VOL. LXX	35-93
Exhibition of Pictures by a Russian Artist, An	俄国艺术家的画展	Howell, E. B.	VOL. L	25-465
Exogamy in China	中国的异族通婚	Wilkinson, Hiram Parhes	VOL. LII	26-374
Extracts from the History of Shang-hai	上海史摘要	Schmidt, C.	VOL. VIII	6-49

F

题名	中译题名	责任者	卷期	页码
Fabulous Source of the Hoang-ho, The	黄河源头	Eitel, E. J.	VOL. VI	5-67
Family Law of the Chinese, The	中国人的家法	Möllendorff, P. G. von	VOL. XXVII	16-141
Family Law of the Chinese, and its Comparative Relations with That of Other Nations, The	中国人之家法及其与他国家法之比较	Möllendorff, P. G. von.	VOL. XIII	9-145
Family Names, The	百家姓	Giles, Herbert Allen	VOL. XXI	12-263
Financial Capacity of China, The	中国之财政能力	Parker, Edward Harper	VOL. XXX	18-82
Fir-flower Tablets	《松花笺》评赏	Ferguson, John Calvin	VOL. LIII	27-104
Fish-skin Tartars, The	鱼皮鞑靼	Fraser, E. H.	VOL. XXVI	15-9
Flood and Famine in North China	中国北方的洪涝和饥荒	Turner, F. B.	VOL. LVII	29-25
Formosa	台湾	Old Cathay [pseud.]	VOL. L	25-434
Fort Zelandia, and the Dutch Occupation of Formosa	热兰遮城及荷兰对台湾的殖民	Hobson, H. E.	VOL. XI	8-55
Four Example of Chinese Bronze Statuary	中国青铜雕像四范例	Ferguson, John Calvin	VOL. XLVIII	24-433
Fragmens d'un Voyage dans l'Interieur de la Chine	中国内陆游记	Imbault-Huart, Camille	VOL. XVIII	11-91
Freshwater Sponges from the T'ai Hu (Great Lake) of the Kiangsu Province, China	太湖的淡水海绵	Annandale, N.	VOL. XLVII	24-79
Further Notes on the History of the Days of the Week	一周七日的历史	Chatley, Herbert	VOL. LXIV	33-107

(续表)

题　名	中译题名	责任者	卷期	页码
G				
G. E. Morrison Library, The	莫理循图书馆	Couling, Samuel	VOL. XLVIII	24-326
General Survey of Standard Chinese Histories	中国历史要览	Ferguson, John Calvin	VOL. LVII	29-83
General Theory of Shamanism among the Tungus	通古斯的萨满教通论	Shirokogoroff, Sergei Mikhailovich	VOL. LIV	27-620
Genus Gueldenstaedtia（leguminoseae）, The	米口袋属（豆科）	Jacot, Arthur Paul	VOL. LVIII	29-389
Geophysical Prospecting for Gold, Metallic Ores and Petroleum and its Possible Application in China	中国黄金和其他金属矿藏及石油勘探和开采的可能	Nyström, Erik T.	VOL. LXVII	34-173
German Translation of the *Hsi Hsiang Chi*, A	《西厢记》德语版概述	Meerkerk, M. E. R. F.	VOL. LIX	30-182
Gods of the Chinese, The	中国之神佛	Hayes, L. Newton.	VOL. LV	28-106
Gold in China: in its Historical, Practical and Financial Aspects	中国的黄金：历史、应用及财政功能	Kann, E.	VOL. LX	31-104
Grand Canal of China, The	中国之大运河	Carles, W. R.	VOL. XXXI	18-406
Great Summer Festival of China as Observed in Foochow: A Study in Popular Religion, The	福州夏至节气仪式：民间信仰研究	Hodous, Lewis.	VOL. XLIII	22-403
Great Wall of China, The	中国长城	Hayes, L. Newton.	VOL. LIX	30-105
Great Weal: or a Christmas Journey to Huangho Mouth, The	大伤痕：圣诞节黄河入海口之行	Edgar, J. Huston	VOL. XLV	23-340
Greek and Chinese Art Ideals	希腊和中国的艺术思想	Stanley, Arthur	VOL. LI	26-35
Growth of the Yangtze Delta, The	长江三角洲的成长	Heidenstam, H. von	VOL. LIII	27-39
Guide to True Vacuity, A	元阳子真空直指	Moule, G. E.	VOL. XXIII	13-15
H				
Hainanese Miao, The	海南的苗族	Moninger, M. M.	VOL. LII	26-302
Han Kao-Tsu and Hsiang Yü	汉高祖与项羽	Dubs, Homer Hasenpflug	VOL. LXVII	34-98
Hieroglyphic Character of the Chinese Written Language, The	中国书法——草书	Jamieson, R. A.	VOL. II	3-335

(续表)

题　　名	中译题名	责任者	卷期	页码
Highways and Byways of Kweichow, The	贵州的大道与小径	Kemp, Emily Georgiana	VOL. LII	26－418
Historical and Statistical Sketch of the Island of Hainan, A	海南简史	Mayers, William Frederick	VOL. VII	5－241
History of Shuh, The	蜀志	Torrance, Thomas	VOL. LV	28－86
History of the Days of the Week, The	一周七日的历史	Chatley, Herbert	VOL. LXII	32－105
History of the Loochoo Islands, The	琉球群岛的历史	Leavenworth, Charles S.	VOL. XXXVI	20－111
Histrionic Notes	戏曲演技札记	Macgowan, Daniel John	VOL. XXI	12－30
Hoppo-book of 1753, The	1753年的河伯书（粤海关报告）	Hirth, F.	VOL. XVII	10－531
How Snow Inspired Verse, and a Rash Order Made the Flowers Bloom	《镜花缘》第四回英译	T., C. B	VOL. XX	11－527
How the Chinese Look upon the Art of Painting	中国人如何看待绘画艺术	Sirén, Osvald	VOL. LXVI	33－561
How Tonnage was Measured in Ancient China	古代中国衡量船只吨位的方法	Morgan, Evan	VOL. LIV	27－601
Hsi Hsia Dynasty of Tangut: Their Money and Peculiar Script, The	西夏的货币及其独特文字	Bushell, S. W.	VOL. XXX	18－154
Hsüan-Tsang and Modern Research	玄奘及其现代研究	Stael-Holstein, Baron Alexander von	VOL. LIV	27－372
Hsü-t'ing Mi-shi-so Sutra, or, *Jesus-Messiah-Sutra*, The	《喜听迷诈所经》英译	Saeki, P. Y.	VOL. LXIII	32－323
Hung-lou-mêng: Commonly Called "The Dream of the Red Chamber", The	《红楼梦》简介	Giles, Herbert Allen	VOL. XX	11－447

I

题　　名	中译题名	责任者	卷期	页码
I Wei, The	《易纬》	Bruce, Percy	VOL. LXI	31－326
Inaugural Address	裨治文就职演说	Bridgman, Elijah Coleman	O. S. VOL. I No. I	2－11
Inaugural Address by the President, Delivered on the 20th of Feb., 1877.— The Border Lands of Geology and History	地质学和历史学的交汇领域（亚洲文会会长1877年2月20日就职演说）	Kingsmill, Thomas William	VOL. XI	8－23
Indian Frontier, The	印度边界	Haward, Edwin	VOL. LXII	32－146
Influence of Liquids upon the Dissolution of the Initial Consonant Groups in the Indo-Sinic Family, The	流音对中印语族辅音群消失的影响	Wen, Yu	VOL. LXIX	34－541

(续表)

题　名	中译题名	责任者	卷期	页码
Ink Remains, by An I-chou	安仪周书《墨缘录观》墨迹	Ferguson, John Calvin	VOL. XLV	23-307
Inland Communications in China	中国之内陆交通		VOL. XXVIII	16-311
Inscribed Bones of Shang, The	殷商甲骨	Gibson, Harry E.	VOL. LXVII	34-49
Inscribed Pottery Vessel of the Chow Dynasty, An	战国陶器铭文	Drake, F. S.	VOL. LXXI	35-246
Inscriptions de L'Orkhon	鄂尔浑河碑铭	Parker, Edward Harper	VOL. XXXI	18-305
Inscriptions on Bronzes	青铜器铭文	Ferguson, John Calvin	VOL. LXVI	33-612
Insects Used in Chinese Medicine	昆虫在中药中的使用	Read, Bernard Emms	VOL. LXXI	35-218
Intercourse of China with Central and Western Asia in the 2nd Century B. C., The	公元前2世纪中国与中亚西亚各国的交往	Kingsmill, Thomas William	VOL. XIV	9-201
Interpretations of Chinese History.	中国的历史诠释学	Roberts, Donald	VOL. LXXII	35-383
Introduction to *The Buddhist Library of Huen Chwang*	《雁塔圣教序碑》译文	Couling, Samuel	VOL. XLVIII	24-353
Irrigation of the Ch'eng-tu Plain	成都平原的灌溉系统	Vale, Joshua	VOL. XXXIII	19-118
Irrigation of the Ch'eng-tu Plain and beyond	再论成都平原的系统灌溉	Vale, Joshua	VOL. XXXVI	20-44
Is China a Conservative Country?	中国是个保守的国度么？	Moromastix	VOL. XX	11-591
Is Confucius a Myth?	孔子是虚构的吗？	Allen, Herbert J.	VOL. XXI	12-201
Itinerary of a Journey Through the Provinces of Hoo-pih, Sze-chuen and Shen-se	湖北、四川和陕西三省旅行记	Wylie, Alexander	VOL. V	4-431

J

Java	爪哇	Mencarini, Juan	VOL. XXXVI	20-128
Jehol	热河	Fischer, Emil Sigmund	VOL. LXXI	35-286
Jewish Monument at Kaifengfu, The	开封府的犹太教纪念碑	Martin, William Alexander Parsos	VOL. XXXVII	20-191
Jews of Honan, The	河南犹太人	MacGillivray, Donald	VOL. LIX	30-42
Journal of a Mission to Lewchew in 1801	1801年使琉球记	Williams, Samuel Wells	VOL. VI	5-171
Journal of S. Wells Williams, LL. D., The	卫三畏日记	Williams, Frederick Wells	VOL. XLII	22-15

(续表)

题　名	中译题名	责任者	卷期	页码
Journey from Foochow to Wênchow Through Central Fukien, A	福州至温州旅行记	Parker, Edward Harper	VOL. XIX	11－333
Journey in Chêkiang, A	浙江行记	Parker, Edward Harper	VOL. XIX	11－285
Journey in Fukien, A	福建行记	Parker, Edward Harper	VOL. XIX	11－312
Journey to Sungp'an	松潘行记	Watson, W. C. Haines	VOL. XXXVI	20－59
Journey to the Tung Ling, A	东陵行记	Fischer, Emil Sigmund	VOL. LXI	31－242

K

题　名	中译题名	责任者	卷期	页码
Kingship in China	中国之王权	Soothill, W. E.	VOL. LXI	31－318
Kinship of the English and Chinese Languages, The	汉语和英语的近似特征	Lanning, George	VOL. XLVIII	24－329
Kite Festival in Foochow, The	福州重阳节的风筝民俗	Hodous, Lewis	VOL. XLIX	25－94
Kite's Message, The	《风筝误》(节译)	Hudson, Elfrida	VOL. LIX	30－312
Korean Interference with Chinese Historical Records	朝鲜对中国历史编纂的抵触	Goodrich, Luther Carrington	VOL. LXVIII	34－367
Ku K'ai-chi's Scroll in the British Museum	大英博物馆藏顾恺之绘《女史箴图》	Ferguson, John Calvin	VOL. XLIX	25－119
K'ü Yüan, His Life and Poems	屈原生平及其诗歌	Biallas, Franz Xavier	VOL. LIX	30－289
Kwo Tsï Yi, an Eminent Military Commander of the Tang Dynasty	郭子仪——唐朝的杰出军事将领	Edkins, Joseph	VOL. XXXV	19－537

L

题　名	中译题名	责任者	卷期	页码
Lampaçao, a Mystery of the Far East	浪白窑:远东的不解之谜	Morse, Hosea Ballou	VOL. LII	26－399
Land Birds and Others Met with at Sea off the Coast of China in 1915.	中国沿海地区1915年所见鸟类	Laver, H. E.	VOL. XLVIII	24－305
Land of Peach Bloom, The	《桃花源记》译文及短评	Kliene, Charles	VOL. L	25－384
Language and New Thought	语言与新思想	Morgan, Evan	VOL. LXI	31－287
Language Students of the East India Company's Canton Factory, The	广州东印度公司商行的语言学生	Stifler, Susan Reed	VOL. LXIX	34－504
Lan-tsih	兰芝[《孔雀东南飞》英译]	Hudson, Elfrida	VOL. LIII	27－118

(续表)

题　　名	中译题名	责任者	卷期	页码
League of Nations in Ancient China, A	中国古代的弥兵运动	Morgan, Evan	VOL. LVII	29-76
Lecture on Japan.	关于日本的演讲	Williams, Samuel Wells	O. S. VOL. I No. II	2-214
Legend of Wên Wang, Founder of the Dynasty of the Chows in China, The	关于周朝建立者周文王的传说	Kingsmill, Thomas William	VOL. VIII	6-41
Legends of the Ancient Mazdayaçnian Prophets, and the Story of Zoroaster	古代胡腊玛教先知的传说和琐罗亚斯德的故事	Camajee, D. N.	VOL. IX	6-271
Li Siu-cheng, the Chung Wang or "Faithful Prince"	忠王李秀成	Teesadale, J. H.	VOL. LVII	29-118
Life and Times of Confucius, The	孔子生平及其时代	Dovey, J. Whitsed.	VOL. LVI	28-455
Life and Works of Han Yu or Han Wen-kung, The	韩愈生平及作品	Werner, Edward Theodore Chalmers	VOL. VII	5-405
Light Thrown on Ancient Chinese History by Recent Archaeological Discoveries, The	考古新发现对古代中国历史的昭示	Buxton, Dudley	VOL. LXI	31-219
Ling Yin Monastry Poem	宋之问灵隐寺诗文考	Gaunt, T.	VOL. LIII	27-127
List of Legible Inscriptions on Stones in the Foreign Cemetery on Double Island, Swatow, 1922	汕头双岛西人墓地1922年石刻目录	Talbot, R. M.	VOL. LX	31-147
List of Plant Names Included in the Cowdry Chihli Flora not Recorded in the Index Florae Sinensis and its Two Supplements, A	Cowdry《直隶植物志》中的植物名录（Forbes和Hemsley的《中国植物志》及其两份补充目录所未载者）	Liu, J. C.	VOL. LX	31-140
List of the Birds in the Museum of the Anglo-Chinese College of Foochow, A	福州英华书院博物院鸟类标本目录	Kellogg, Claude R.	VOL. L	25-420
List of the Birds of Chihli Province	直隶鸟类目录	Wilder, Geo. D.	VOL. LV	28-184
List of the Musical and Other Sounding Producing Instruments of the Chinese	中国乐器及其他发声器之目录	Moule, Arthur Christopher	VOL. XXXIX	21-11
List of the Principal Tea Districts in China and Notes on the Names Applied to the Various Kinds of Black and Green Tea	中国主要产茶区及红茶、绿茶名录		VOL. X	7-347
Little Lu-fu	陌上桑	Hudson, Elfrida	VOL. LVIII	29-382
Looking at a Painting by Wang-Tzu (a T'ang Poem).	杜甫题王宰《戏题画山水图歌》	Hudson, Elfrida	VOL. LVIII	29-386

题　　名	中译题名	责任者	卷期	页码
Lo-yang as the National Capital	古都洛阳	Ferguson, John Calvin	VOL. LXIV	33－72

M

题　　名	中译题名	责任者	卷期	页码
M. Chavannes' Edition of Ssǔ-man Ch'ien.	沙畹译注的《史记》	Warren, Gilbert G.	VOL. XLVII	24－42
Magical Practice in China	中国的巫术实践	Chatley, Herbert	VOL. XLVIII	24－246
Manchu Relations with Tibet, or Si-Tsang	满洲与西藏的关系	Parker, Edward Harper	VOL. XXI	12－297
Manchu Ukase, A	大清告示一则	Fraser, F. A.	VOL. XXX	18－175
Mantses and the Golden Chersonese, The	蛮子与黄金半岛（牂牁地区）	Kingsmill, Thomas William	VOL. XXXV	19－614
Map of China in the Making, A	一张制作中的中国地图	Hosie, Lady.	VOL. LVII	29－45
Marriage Maker, The	媒婆	Kliene, Charles	VOL. LII	26－401
Medicine and Medical Practice of the Chinese, The	中医和中药	Henderson, James	VOL. I	3－73
Mei Lan-fang (the Man and his Art)	梅兰芳其人其艺	Leung, George Kin.	VOL. LVIII	29－355
Memorandum on the Present State of Some of the Magnetic Elements in China and Places Adjacent	中国及周边地区地磁纪要	Shadwell, C. B.	O. S. VOL. I No. II	2－256
Men and Matters in the Land of the Yellow Earth	黄土地带的居民和物产	Andrew, G. Findlay	VOL. LXVI	33－604
Mencius and Some Other Reformers of China	孟子及其他中国改革者	Macklin, W. E.	VOL. XXXIII	19－265
Meteorological Observations for 1872.	1872 年气象观测		VOL. VII	5－491
Meteorological Tables, from Observations in Japan.	日本气象观测表	Fedorovitch, J.	O. S. VOL. I No. III	2－381
Method of Making Ink Rubbings, The	拓印的方法	Stanley, Arthur	VOL. XLVIII	24－319
Militant Spirit of the Buddhist Clergy in China	中国佛教僧侣的尚武精神	Groot, J. J. M. de	VOL. XXVI	15－116
Military Organization of China Prior to 1842, The	中国 1842 年前之军事组织（节选自魏源《圣武记》）	Parker, Edward Harper	VOL. XXII	12－385
Missonary Contribution to Chinese Nationalism, A	传教士对中国民族主义的贡献	Francis, John de	VOL. LXXIII	35－493
Modern Travel from Tai Yuan Fu via Mount Wu Tai to the Mongolian Frontier.	从太原府经五台山至蒙古边境纪行	Fischer, Emil Sigmund	VOL. LIV	27－439

(续表)

题名	中译题名	责任者	卷期	页码
Mohammedans of China, When and How, They Fist Come	中国回教徒:他们首次入华之时间和方式	Mason, Isaac	VOL. LX	31-62
Mongolia After the Genghizides and Before the Manchus	明朝时的蒙古	Parker, Edward Harper	VOL. XLIV	23-114
Motives of Chinese Art, The	中国的艺术主旨	Abraham, R. D.	VOL. LVIII	29-370
Murder of Achmach Bailo, The	阿合马被杀案	Moule, Arthur Christopher	VOL. LIX	30-314
Music and Musical Instruments of Shang	商代的音乐和乐器	Gibson, Harry E.	VOL. LXVIII	34-336
Music of China, The	中国的音乐	Kingsmill, Thomas William	VOL. XLI	21-472
Mystery of Ta-ts'in [Review of Dr. Hirth's *China and the Roman Orient*], The	大秦之谜:评夏德《中国和罗马人的东方》	Playfair, G. M. H.	VOL. XX	11-515
Mythical Origin of the Chow or Djow Dynasty, as Set Forth in the *Shooking*, The	《书经》中关于周朝神秘起源的记载	Kingsmill, Thomas William	VOL. VII	5-377

N

Names and Nicknames of the Shanghai Settlements	上海租界的地名和别名	Lanning, George	VOL. LI	26-103
Names of the Sovereigns of the Old Corean States, and Chronological Table of the Present Dynasty	古代朝鲜君主名号及现王朝年表	Nocentini, Ludovico	VOL. XXII	12-474
Narrative of a Visit to the Island of Formosa	台湾纪行	Swinhoe, Robert	O. S. VOL. I No. II	2-167
Narrative of an Exploring Visit to Hainan	海南探险记	Swinhoe, Robert	VOL. VII	5-281
Narrative of an Overland Trip, Through Hunan, from Canton to Hankow	陆上行纪:从广州经湖南至汉口	Dickson, W.	VOL. I	3-37
Narrative of Recent Events in Tong-King	安南东京近事记	Cordier, Henri	VOL. IX	6-361
Narrative of the American Embassy to Peking	美国使团北京纪行	Williams, Samuel Wells	O. S. VOL. I No. III	2-350
Natural History of China, The	中国博物学	Sowerby, Arthur de Carle	VOL. LIII	27-17
Naturalistic Philosophy of China, The	中国的自然主义哲学	Balfour, Frederic Henry	VOL. XV	9-621
Neau-show: Birds and Beasts (of Formosa)	台湾鸟兽(译自《台湾府志》)	Swinhoe, Robert	VOL. II	3-261

(续表)

题　　名	中译题名	责任者	卷期	页码
Nestorian Share in Buddhist Translation, The	景教徒参与佛经翻译事迹考	Inglis, J. W.	VOL. XLVIII	24－242
Night in Mountains, A	《宿天竺寺》[汉诗英译]	Hudson, Elfrida	VOL. LIV	27－371
Northern Tungus Migrations in the Far East	北通古斯族在远东之迁徙	Shirokogoroff, Sergei Mikhailovich	VOL. LVII	29－149
Note on the Chihkiang Miautsz	浙江苗族	Macgowan, Daniel John	VOL. VI	5－145
Note on the Comparative Longevity of Males and Females in Japan	日本男女的相对长寿	Hallifax, T. E.	VOL. XXIV	13－663
Note sur les Petites Société d'Argent en Chine	中国小型钱庄概要	Simon, G. Eug.	VOL. V	4－279
Note sur Quelques unes des Recherches que l'on Pourrait Faire en Chine et au Japon au Point de vue de la Geologie et de la Paléontologie	中国和日本古生物学和地质学研究刍议	Simon, G. Eug.	VOL. V	4－365
Notes Made on a Tour Through Shan-Hsi and Shen-Hsi	陕西和山西旅行记	Holcombe, C.	VOL. X	7－75
Notes of a Journey from Peking to Chefoo via Grand Canal, Yen-Chow-Foo, etc.	北京出发经大运河、兖州府等至芝罘之旅	Williamson, A.	VOL. III	3－451
Notes of a Journey Overland from Szemao to Rangoon	从思茅至仰光纪行	Carey, Fred. W.	VOL. XXXVI	20－9
Notes on a Portion of the Old Bed of the Yellow River and the Water Supply of the Grand Canal	黄河古河床及大运河水源供给	Elias, Ney	VOL. IV	4－86
Notes on Chinese Archery	射箭在中国	Du Bois-Reymond, C.	VOL. XLIII	22－348
Notes on Chinese Banking System in Shanghai	上海华资银行体系	Ferguson, John Calvin	VOL. XXXVII	20－245
Notes on Chinese Composition	汉语修辞	Giles, Herbert Allen	VOL. XVII	10－311
Notes on Chinese Law and Practice Preceding Revision	修订前的中国法律及其实施	Alabaster, Ernest	VOL. XXXVII	20－273
Notes on Chinese Mohammedan Literature	中国回教书籍解题	Mason, Isaac	VOL. LVI	28－592
Notes on Chinese Toxicology	中国毒物学	Macgowan, Daniel John	VOL. IX	6－419
Notes on Col. Yule's Edition of Marco Polo's "Quinsay"	亨利·裕尔版《马可波罗游记》中的"行在"	Moule, G. E.	VOL. IX	6－247

(续表)

题 名	中译题名	责任者	卷期	页码
Notes on Kansu	甘肃概说	King, George E.	VOL. L	25-461
Notes on Names of Non-Chinese Tribes in Western Szechwan	川西少数名族的称谓	Edgar, J. Huston	VOL. LIII	27-95
Notes on Some Dikes at the Nouth of the Nankow Pass	南口关岩层小析	Guppy, H. B.	VOL. XVIII	11-203
Notes on Some New Species of Birds Found on the Island of Formosa	台湾岛上新发现的鸟类	Swinhoe, Robert	O. S. VOL. I No. II	2-259
Notes on Some of the Physical Causes which Modify Climate	影响气候的物理因素	Henderson, James	VOL. I	3-20
Notes on Some Outlying Coal-fields in the South-eastern Provinces of China	中国东南省份偏远地区的煤田	Kingsmill, Thomas William	VOL. III	3-546
Notes on Szechuen and the Yangtse Valley	四川及长江峡谷小记	Little, Archibald J.	VOL. XVIII	11-209
Notes on Temperatures in High Altitudes on the Tibetan Border	青藏高原边境高海拔气温观测记录	Edgar, J. Huston	VOL. XLV	23-353
Notes on the Agriculture, Botany and the Zoology of China	中国的农学、植物学和动物学(一)	Skvortzow, B. W.	VOL. L	25-315
Notes on the Agriculture, Botany and the Zoology of China	中国的农学、植物学和动物学(二)	Skvortzow, B. W.	VOL. LI	26-157
Notes on the Agriculture, Botany and the Zoology of China	中国的农学、植物学和动物学(三)	Skvortzow, B. W.	VOL. LII	26-341
Notes on the Agriculture, Botany and the Zoology of China	中国的农学、植物学和动物学(四)	Skvortzow, B. W.	VOL. LIII	27-223
Notes on the City of Yedo, the Capital of Japan	日本首都江户	Lindau, Rudolph	VOL. I	3-7
Notes on the Coal Fields and General Geology of the Neighbourhood of Nagasaki	长崎周边的煤田及地质概述	Kingsmill, Thomas William	VOL. V	4-302
Notes on the Early History of the Salt Monopoly in China	中国早期盐业垄断史	Hirth, F.	VOL. XXII	12-437
Notes on the Flora of the W. Ssŭch'uan Mountains	川西山区植物笔记	Ward, Francis Kingdon	VOL. XLVII	24-69
Notes on the Geology of the Great Plain	大平原地质简论	Lamprey, Dr.	VOL. II	3-221
Notes on the Geology of the Neighbourhood of Nagasaki	长崎及其周边地质概况	Guppy, H. B.	VOL. XVII	10-333
Notes on the Hydrology of the Yangtse, the Yellow River, and the Pei-ho	长江、黄河和白河的水文	Guppy, H. B.	VOL. XVI	10-7
Notes on the *Miao-fa-lien-hua-ching*, a Buddhist Sutra in Chinese	《妙法莲华经》述评	Werner, Edward Theodore Chalmers	VOL. IX	6-335

(续表)

题　　名	中译题名	责任者	卷期	页码
Notes on the Mineral Resources in Japan &c.	日本的矿藏及其他	Shock, W. H.	O. S. VOL. II No. I	2-500
Notes on the Mineral Resources of Eastern Shantung	山东东部的矿产资源	Becher, H. M.	VOL. XXII	12-406
Notes on the Nestorians in China	中国景教徒纪略	Parker, Edward Harper	VOL. XXIV	13-645
Notes on the North of China, it's Productions and Communications	华北记略：物产与交通	Williamson, A.	VOL. IV	4-39
Notes on the Opinions of the Chinese with Regard to Eclipses	中国人对月食的看法	Wylie, Alexander	VOL. III	3-523
Notes on the Productions, Chiefly Mineral of Shan-tung	山东物产（以矿产为主）	Williamson, A.	VOL. IV	4-70
Notes on the Provincial Examination of Chekeang of 1870, with a Version of One of the Essays	浙江1870年乡试（附范文一篇）	Moule, G. E.	VOL. VI	5-151
Notes on the Shantung Province, being a Journey from Chefoo to Tsiuhsien, the City of Mencius	山东纪略：从芝罘（烟台）到邹县之旅	Markham, John.	VOL. VI	5-23
Notes on the South Coast of Saghalien	库页岛南岸旅行记	Anderson, C.	VOL. XVII	10-345
Notes on the Symbolism of the Purple Forbidden City	紫禁城的象征主义之札记	Ayscough, Florence Wheelock	VOL. LII	26-313
Notes on the Ting-Chi, or Half-Yearly Sacrifice to Confucius	文庙丁祭评述	Moule, G. E.	VOL. XXXIII	19-133
Notes on the Tu T'ing Hui Held at Chinking on the 31st May, 1917.	1917年5月31日浙江的都天会	Ottewill, H. A.	VOL. XLIX	25-104
Notes sur les Alphabets Lü du Yünnan et les Denominations Ethniques Donnees aux T'ay	云南字母音律及民族名称资料	Rispaud, Jean	VOL. LXIV	33-173
Notices of Christianity in China: Extracted from Marco Polo	《马可波罗游记》中中国基督教史料评介	Moule, Arthur Christopher	VOL. XLVI	23-571
Notices of the Character and Writings of Meh Tsï	墨子述略	Edkins, Joseph	O. S. VOL. I No. II	2-187
Notices of the Mediaeval Geography and History of Central and Western Asia	中亚与西亚中古时代之史地考	Bretschneider, E.	VOL. X	7-95
Notions of Lok Ping Cheung, Late Governor General of Sze Chuen	前四川总督骆秉章	Preston, C. F.	VOL. V	4-345
Notions of the Ancient Chinese Respecting Music	古代中国人的音乐观念	Jenkins, B.	VOL. V	4-308

(续表)

题 名	中译题名	责任者	卷期	页码
O				
Obligations of China to Europe in the Matter of Physical Science Acknowledged by Eminent Chinese, The	中华先驱从欧人那里引进自然科学知识	Moule, G. E.	VOL. VII	5-387
Observatoire Météorologique et Magné-tique des Pères de la Compagnie de Jesus, à Zi-Ka-Wei.	徐家汇天文台1874年9月至1875年8月天气与地磁公报		VOL. X	7-363
Office of District Magistrate in China, The	中国之县官	Brenan, Byron	VOL. XXXII	18-564
Old Problems Concerning the Nestorian Monument in China Re-examined in the Light of Newly Discovered Facts	大秦景教碑相关老问题的新发现	Saeki, P. Y.	VOL. LXVII	34-123
Omei San: The Sacred Mountain of West China	华西圣山峨眉山	Shields, E. T.	VOL. XLIV	23-140
On a Large Meteorite Which Fell in the Sea near Video, Chusan Archipelago, on the 13th February, 1915	舟山列岛1915年2月13日坠落的大陨石	Tyler, William Ferdinand	VOL. XLVI	23-653
On a Method of Divination Practised at Foochow.	福州的"打童"民俗	Harding, H. L.	VOL. XLIX	25-100
On Chinese Names for Boats and Boat Gear with Remarks on the Chinese Use of the Mariner's Compass	船、舵之中文名及指南针的应用	Edkins, Joseph	VOL. XI	8-145
On Cyclones, or the Law of Storms	飓风之规律	Nicolson, F. W.	O. S. VOL. I No. I	2-27
On Some Wild Silkworms of China	中国野生蚕蛹	McCartee, D. B.	VOL. III	3-527
On the "Mutton Wine" of the Mongols and Analogous Preparations of the Chinese	蒙古的烤羊肉和酒	Macgowan, Daniel John	VOL. VII	5-477
On the Ancient Mouths of the Yang-tsï Kiang	古代长江入海口	Edkins, Joseph	O. S. VOL. II No. I	2-485
On the Banishment of Criminals in China	中国的流刑	Macgowan, Daniel John	O. S. VOL. I No. III	2-332
On the Building History of the Pao Shu T'a, Hangchow	杭州保俶塔的历史	Prip-Moller, Johannes	VOL. LXVII	34-86
On the Chinese Coins and Small Porcelain Bottles Found in Egypt	埃及发现的中国钱币和小瓷瓶	Rondot, Natalis	VOL. XXXII	18-594
On the Cosmical Phenomena in the Neighborhood of Shanghai, during the Past Thirteen Centuries	过去13个世纪上海周边地区观测到的特异自然现象	Macgowan, Daniel John	O. S. VOL. II No. I	2-453

(续表)

题 名	中译题名	责任者	卷期	页码
On the Introduction and Use of Gunpowder and Firearms among the Chinese	火药和火器在中国人中的引介和使用	Mayers, William Frederick.	VOL. VI	5-95
On the Limitations of Comparative Philology	比较语言学的局限	Möllendorff, P. G. von	VOL. XXXI	18-385
On the Musical Notation of the Chinese	中国的乐谱	Syle, Edward W.	O. S. VOL. I No. II	2-198
On the Sources of Chinese Taoism	中国道教源头考	Wilhelm, Richard	VOL. XLV	23-295
On the Stone Figures at Chinese Tombs and the Offering of Living Sacrifices	中国墓地中的石像和活祭品	Mayers, William Frederick	VOL. XII	8-217
On the Study of the Natural Science in Japan	自然科学学习在日本	Meerdervoort, Johannes Lijdius Catharinus Pompe van	O. S. VOL. I No. II	2-245
On the Style of Chinese Epistolary Composition	中国书信格式	Martin, William Alexander Parsos	VOL. XI	8-135
On Wen-ch'ang, the God of Literature, his History and Worship	文昌星的由来及文昌崇拜	Mayers, William Frederick	VOL. VI	5-53
One of the World's Literary Masterpieces: Introduction to a Great Chinese Epic or Religious Allegory by Ch'iu Ch'ang Ch'un	世界文学杰作《长春真人西游记》介绍	Richard, Timothy	VOL. XLIV	23-9
Operations and Manifestations of the Tao Exemplified in History or the Tao Confirmed by History, The	历史上"道"的作用及其表现形式	Morgan, Evan	VOL. LII	26-263
Oracle-bones from Honan, The	河南甲骨	Couling, Samuel	VOL. XLV	23-363
Oribatoidea Sinensi I	中华甲螨名录(一)	Jacot, Arthur Paul	VOL. LIII	27-152
Oribatoidea Sinensis II	中华甲螨名录(二)	Jacot, Arthur Paul	VOL. LIV	27-538
Oribatoidea Sinensis III	中华甲螨名录(三)	Jacot, Arthur Paul	VOL. LV	28-98
Origin and Growth of Deserts and the Encroachment of the Desert on North-China, The	沙漠的起源和发展及华北的沙漠化	Englaender, A. L.	VOL. LIX	30-204
Origin and History of the Irrigation Work of the Chengtu Plain, The	成都平原水利工程的起源和历史	Torrance, Thomas	VOL. LV	28-80
Origin of Loess, The	黄土的起源	Penniston, John B.	VOL. LXIV	33-136
Origin of the Chinese Priesthood, The	中国神职起源	Werner, Edward Theodore Chalmers	VOL. LIX	30-246
Overland Journey from St. Petersburg to Pekin, The	陆上之旅:从圣彼得堡到北京	Wylie, Alexander	VOL. I	3-53

(续表)

题　名	中译题名	责任者	卷期	页码
P				
Page from Ancient Chinese History: The Story of Kou Tsien—King of Yueh, A	中国古代史一页：越王勾践	Darroch, John	VOL. LIV	27-476
Painters Among Catholic Missionaries and Their Helpers in Peking	北京天主教传教士中的画家及其助手	Ferguson, John Calvin	VOL. LXV	33-307
Partial Bibliography of Chinese Birds, A	中国鸟类相关文献管窥	Riley, J. H. & Richmond, C. W.	VOL. LIII	27-230
Partial Bibliography of Chinese Birds, A	中国鸟类相关文献管窥（补遗）	Riley, J. H. & Richmond, C. W.	VOL. LIV	27-599
Passing of the R. A. S. Old Premises at Shanghai	亚洲文会旧会所的暂停使用	Mason, Isaac	VOL. LXII	32-225
Past Decade in Chinese Literature, The	近十年之中国文学	Lyon, David Willard	VOL. LXV	33-358
Patriarch Lü, Reputed Founder of the the Chin Tan Chiao, The	金丹教创建者吕洞宾	Couling, C. E.	VOL. LVIII	29-470
Periodical Change of Terrestrial Magnetism	地磁周期变化	Schulze, F. W.	VOL. XIII	9-81
Philippine Chinese Labour Question, The	菲律宾华人劳工问题	Mencarini, Juan	VOL. XXXIII	19-182
Philological Importance of Geographical Terms in the *Shi-Ki*	《史记》中地理名词的语言学意义	Edkins, Joseph	VOL. XXI	12-207
Philosopher Yang Hsiung, The	哲学家扬雄	Forke, A.	VOL. LXI	31-334
Philosophy of Tai Tung-yüan, The	戴震的哲学思想	Freeman, Mansfield	VOL. LXIV	33-80
Place of Music in the Platonic and Confucian Systems of Moral Education, The	柏拉图和孔子道德教育体系中音乐的地位	Phelps, D. L.	VOL. LIX	30-186
Plants from Peitaiho	北戴河的植物	Cowdry, N. H.	VOL. LIII	27-192
Poëte Chinios du XVIIIe Siècle, Yüan Tseu-ts'ai, sa Vie et ses Oeuvres, Un	诗人袁枚生平及其著作	Imbault-Huart, Camille	VOL. XIX	11-379
Poet-Monk of Modern China, A	当代中国的一个寺僧	Johnston, Reginald Fleming	VOL. LXIII	32-306
Political Idealists and Realists of China of the Fourth and Third Centuries B. C.	公元前三、四世纪时的中国政治理想主义者和现实主义者	Hughes, E. R.	VOL. LXIII	32-340
Political Intercourse between China and Lewchew	中国与琉球的政治关系	Williams, Samuel Wells	VOL. III	3-533
Political Parties of the Northern Sung Dynasty	北宋朋党	Ferguson, John Calvin	VOL. LVIII	29-332

(续表)

题　名	中译题名	责任者	卷期	页码
Porcelain Pagoda of Nanking, The	南京大报恩寺琉璃塔	Hobson, H. E.	VOL. XXIII	13-37
Porcelains of Successive Dynasties	中国历代瓷器	Ferguson, John Calvin	VOL. LXIII	32-293
Possible and Impossible Reforms	可能的改革与不可能的改革	Bourne, Frederick Samuel Augustus	VOL. XXXIII	19-9
Postscript on Tomb-destruction, A	关于皇陵被毁的备注说明	Werner, Edward Theodore Chalmers	VOL. LVII	29-223
Pottery Tomb Figures of Ancient China	中国古墓中的陶俑（会长演讲）	Sowerby, Arthur de Carle	VOL. LXIX	34-457
Prajna-Paramita Hridaya Sutra, The	《般若波罗密多心经》英译	Lee, Shao-chang	VOL. LXV	33-446
Prehistoric China	史前中国	Faber, Ernst	VOL. XXIV	13-497
Preliminary Notes on the Literary Background of "The Great River"	关于"大河"的文献的初步注解	Ayscough, Florence Wheelock	VOL. LIV	27-491
Preliminary Notes on the Natural History of Nanking	南京博物志初探	Ping, C.	VOL. LXII	32-79
Prevalance of Infanticide in China, The	中国溺婴的盛行		VOL. XX	11-471
Principles of Chinese Law and Equity, The	中国成文法与衡平法的原则	Parker, Edward Harper	VOL. XL	21-270
Putoshan: A Draught at the Wellsprings of Chinese Buddhist Art	普陀山：中国佛教艺术探源	Stanley, Arthur	VOL. XLVI	23-537

Q

Quelques Renseignements sur l'Histoire Naturelle de la Chine Septentrionale et Occidentale	华西和华北博物志	David, Armand.	VOL. VII	5-445

R

Rebuttal Notes on Chinese Religion and Dynastic Tombs	关于中国宗教和皇陵的辩驳	Werner, Edward Theodore Chalmers	VOL. LVI	28-550
Recent Books by a Chinese Scholar	罗振玉著作综述	Ferguson, John Calvin	VOL. L	25-398
Recent Discoveries in Ancient Chinese Sculpture	最近发现的中国古代雕塑	Segalen, Victor	VOL. XLVIII	24-407
Recent Research upon the Mammalia of Northern China	中国北部哺乳动物研究近况	Sowerby, Arthur de Carle	VOL. XLVII	24-83
Recollections of China Prior to 1840	在华往事（1840年前）	Williams, Samuel Wells	VOL. VIII	6-19

(续表)

题　名	中译题名	责任者	卷期	页码
Records of the Geological Committee of the Russian Far East	俄国远东地理学会报告	Ancell, B. L.	VOL. LIII	27－281
Relation of Chinese and Siamese, The	中国与暹罗关系	Dodd, W. Clifton	VOL. LI	26－21
Religion of The Ch'iang, The	羌族的宗教信仰	Torrance, Thomas	VOL. LIV	27－520
Religious Element in The Tso Chuan, The	《左传》中的宗教元素	Wright, Harrison King	VOL. XLVIII	24－445
Remains of Ancient Kambodia, The	高棉遗迹	Bastion, Dr.	VOL. II	3－347
Remarks on the Production of Salt in China	中国盐业述评	Carles, W. R. ; Zwehtkoff, P.	VOL. XXII	12－465
Reminiscences of a Chinese Viceroy's Secretary	总督秘书的回忆录：《张文襄公府纪闻》节译（一）	Ardsheal（pseud.）	VOL. XLV	23－409
Reminiscences of a Chinese Viceroy's Secretary	总督秘书的回忆录：《张文襄公府纪闻》节译（二）	Ardsheal（pseud.）	VOL. XLVI	23－613
Reply to Mr. H. J. Allen's Paper "Where was Ta-Ts'in?"	答啊查理"大秦在哪里？"	Hirth, F.	VOL. XXI	12－106
Reply to Mr. H. J. Allen's Paper Ta-Ts'in and Dependent States	《大秦及其属国》回应	Hirth, F.	VOL. XXI	12－217
Report of an Exploration of the New Course of the Yellow River	黄河新河道考察报告	Elias, Ney	VOL. V	4－537
Research Museum in Far Eastern Antiquities, A	瑞典远东文物博物馆	Murphy, Dagny Carter	VOL. LXIII	32－420
Researches into the Geology of Formosa	台湾地质研究	Kleinwachter, George	VOL. XVIII	11－73
River Problems in China	中国河流问题	Chatley, Herbert	VOL. XLIX	25－19
Roadside Religion in Manchuria	满洲的"路神"信仰	Macintyre, John	VOL. XXI	12－51
Rock Inscriptions at the North Side of Yentai Hill	雁荡山北麓的石刻	Rhein, J.	VOL. XIV	9－231

S

Saced Lamaist Dances, The	喇嘛教的圣舞	Fischer, Emil Sigmund	VOL. LXXII	35－400
Sacrifices in Ancient China	古代中国的祭仪	Morgan, Evan	VOL. LXX	35－86
Sailing Directions for the Yang-tsze Kiang, from Woosung to Hankow	长江航路指南：从吴淞到汉口	Ward, John	O. S. VOL. I No. II	2－265
Salt Administration of Ssǔch'uan, The	四川盐务管理	Rosthorn, Arthur von	VOL. XXVII	16－11

(续表)

题　名	中译题名	责任者	卷期	页码
Salt Revenue of China, The	中国之盐税	Parker, Edward Harper	VOL. XXII	12-451
Samshu-brewing in North China	华北白酒酿制	Guppy, H. B.	VOL. XVIII	11-207
Sang Huang-Yang, Economist of the Early Han	西汉经济学家桑弘羊	Ch'en, S. C.	VOL. LXVII	34-202
Scarcity of Copper Cash and the Rise in Prices	铜钱稀缺与物价上涨		VOL. XXXI	18-377
Science in Old China	中国古代科技	Chatley, Herbert	VOL. LIV	27-421
Sea-board of Russian Manchuria, The	俄占外东北（外满洲）的海岸线	Canny, J. M.	VOL. I	3-122
Sealing and Whaling in the Northern Pacific	北太平洋捕猎海豹与鲸	Brass, E.	VOL. XXXII	18-607
Seaports of India and Ceylon, The. Part I	《瀛涯胜览》所载印度与锡兰的海港（一）	Phillips, George	VOL. XX	11-655
Seaports of India and Ceylon, The. Part II	《瀛涯胜览》所载印度与锡兰的海港（二）	Phillips, George	VOL. XXI	12-38
Sei Yo Ki-Bun, or Annals of the Western Ocean	西洋纪闻	Brown, S. R.	VOL. II	3-275
Sei Yo Ki-Bun, or Annals of the Western Ocean	西洋纪闻（续）	Brown, S. R.	VOL. III	3-490
Sêrica of Ptolemy and its Inhabitants, The	托勒密笔下的"秦国"及其居民	Kingsmill, Thomas William	VOL. XIX	11-421
Shanghai Folk-lore	上海民俗（一）	Box, Ernest	VOL. XXXIV	19-489
Shanghai Folk-lore	上海民俗（二）	Box, Ernest	VOL. XXXVI	20-138
Shantung Foraminifera	山东有孔虫类	Jacot, Arthur Paul	VOL. LVI	28-486
Shapes of Porcelain Vessels	瓷器的形状	Ferguson, John Calvin	VOL. LIX	30-70
Short Notes on Chinese Instruments of Music	中国乐器简介	Dennys, N. B.	VOL. VIII	6-111
Short Notes on the Identification of the Yuè-ti and Kiang Tribes of Ancient Chinese History	中国古代"月底"和"羌"族考	Kingsmill, Thomas William	VOL. X	7-91
Short Sketch of the Chinese Game of chess, A	中国象棋	Hollingworth, H. G.	VOL. III	3-559
Shrines of History: Peak of the East-T'sai Shan	历史胜迹：东岳泰山	Ayscough, Florence Wheelock	VOL. XLVIII	24-291
Shuh Country, The	蜀地（一）	Hutson, James	VOL. LIII	27-71
Shuh Country, The	蜀地（二）	Huston, James	VOL. LIV	27-381

(续表)

题　名	中译题名	责任者	卷期	页码
Siamese Coinage	暹罗货币	Haas, Joseph.	VOL. XIV	9-235
Siege of Saianfu and the Murder of Achmach Bailo, The	阿合马事件(《马可波罗游记》两章相关内容)	Moule, Arthur Christopher	VOL. LVIII	29-297
Sinology in Italy	意大利的汉学	Nocentini, Ludovico	VOL. XX	11-601
Siün King, the Philosopher, and his Relations with Contemporary Schools of Thought	哲学家荀子及其与当代思想流派的关系	Edkins, Joseph	VOL. XXXIII	19-54
Six Horses of T'ang T'ai Tsung, The	昭陵六骏	Ferguson, John Calvin	VOL. LXVII	34-29
Sketch of a Journey from Canton to Hankow Through the Provinces of Kwangtung, Kwangsi, and Hunan, with Geological Notes	从广州出发穿越广东、广西、湖南到达汉口之旅(附地质笔记)	Bickmore, Albert S.	VOL. IV	4-7
Sketch of Tauist Mythology in its Modern Form, A	道教神话的现代形式概述	Edkins, Joseph	O. S. VOL. I No. III	2-345
Sketch of the Geology of a Portion of Quang-tung Province, A	广东省局部地质概述	Kingsmill, Thomas William	VOL. II	3-241
Sketch of the Life of Confucious, A	孔子的生平	Edkins, Joseph	O. S. VOL. II No. I	2-409
Sketches of the Miáu-tsze	苗族概述	Bridgman, Elijah Coleman	O. S. VOL. I No. III	2-301
Small Chinese Lark, The	中国的云雀	Swinhoe, Robert	O. S. VOL. I No. III	2-327
Snowstorm, A	《风雪》[汉诗英译]	Budd, Charles	VOL. LIV	27-357
Social Life of the Miao Tsï	苗族的社会生活	Betts, Geo. Edgar	VOL. XXXIII	19-97
Some Additions to my *Chinese Grammar*	《中文文法》补遗	Gabelentz, Georg Von der	VOL. XX	11-673
Some Chinese Animal Myths and Legends	中国动物主题神话	Sowerby, Arthur de Carle	VOL. LXX	35-47
Some Chinese Funeral Customs	若干中国丧葬礼仪	Walshe, W. Gilbert	VOL. XXXV	19-564
Some Chinese Sources for the Study of Northeastern Asia	东北亚研究的汉语文献	Gale, Esson Mcdowell	VOL. LXIV	33-142
Some Contributions to the Anthropology of the Buriats	布里亚特人人类学论稿	Kojeuroff, George P.	VOL. LVIII	29-446
Some Geological Notes on the Coal and Iron Ore Deposits in the Carboniferous Sediments of Central Shansi	山西中部石炭纪沉积物中的煤铁蕴藏	Norin, E.	VOL. LIII	27-129

(续表)

题 名	中译题名	责任者	卷期	页码
Some New Light on the Life and Times of Bishop Della Chiesa	意大利天主教士康和之生平	Heeren, John J.	VOL. LVI	28-503
Some Notes of a Trip to Corea, in July and August, 1883	1883年朝鲜旅行记	Morrison, G. James	VOL. XVIII	11-185
Some Notes on Asia's Ice Age	亚洲冰川纪释疑	Englaender, A. L.	VOL. LX	31-121
Some Notes on Land-birds, Including Also General Remarks on the Birds Observed at Sea on the Coast of China in 1916	陆禽,包括中国沿海地区1916年所见鸟类	Laver, H. E.	VOL. XLIX	25-31
Some Notes on the Blue Turkish Tongue	突厥语笔记	Gillett, Michael Cavenagh	VOL. LXXIII	35-581
Some Notes on the Geology of Takow, Formosa	台湾打狗地质记录	Guppy, H. B.	VOL. XVI	10-19
Some Notes on the History and Folk Lore of Old Shanghai	老上海历史与风俗笔记	Parker, Alvin Pierson	VOL. XLVII	24-117
Some Notes on the Remains of a Phallic Shrine in Japan	日本的一处生殖崇拜遗迹		VOL. LVII	29-229
Some Observations on China's International Relations	中国国际关系观察	MacNair, Harley Farnsworth.	VOL. LVI	28-405
Some Observations on the Agriculture of Inner Mongolia	内蒙古农业观察	Moyer, Raymond T.	VOL. LXVIII	34-351
Some Points on the History of Science in China	中国科技史要之管见:以数学为主	Vacca, Giovanni	VOL. LXI	31-232
Some Popular Religious Literature of the Chinese	中国广为流传的宗教文学作品	Williams, Mrs. E. T.	VOL. XXXIII	19-19
Some Remarkable Animals of China	中国珍稀动物	Sowerby, Arthur de Carle	VOL. LXXI	35-195
Some Remarks on Recent Elevations in China and Japan	关于近期中国和日本陆地上升的解释	Bickmore, Albert S.	VOL. V	4-336
Some Similarities in Chinese and Ancient Egyptian Culture	中国和古埃及文化的相似之处	Kliene, Charles	VOL. LIV	27-574
Some Types of Chinese Historical Thought	中国人的几种历史观	Chang, Hsin-hai	VOL. LX	31-21
Song of a Skirt, The	贫女[汉诗英译]	Fletcher, William John Bainbridge	VOL. LII	26-455
Sorgo, or Northern Chinese Sugar Cane	中国北方的甜高粱	Collins, Varnum D.	VOL. II	3-307
Southern Migration of the Sung Dynasty	宋朝的南渡	Ferguson, John Calvin	VOL. LV	28-34
Springs of Tsinanfu, The	济南的泉水	Barbour, George B.	VOL. LVI	28-478

(续表)

题名	中译题名	责任者	卷期	页码
Sramana-Shaman: Etymology of the Word "Shaman"	沙门—萨满:"萨满"一词的语源	Mironov, N. D.	VOL. LV	28-133
Standard Weights and Measures of the Ch'in Dynasty	秦朝标准度量衡	Chalfant, Frank Herring	VOL. XXXV	19-557
State Religion of China During the Manchu Dynasty, The	清朝的国教	Williams, Edward Thomas	VOL. XLIV	23-21
Stone Drums of the Chou Dynasty, The	周朝石鼓	Bushell, S. W.	VOL. VIII	6-151
Stone Implements on the Upper Yangtze and Min River	长江上游及岷江流域发现的石器	Edgar, J. Huston	VOL. XLVIII	24-321
Stories in Chinese Paintings	中国绘画中的故事（一）	Ferguson, John Calvin	VOL. LVI	28-526
Stories in Chinese Paintings, II	中国绘画中的故事（二）	Ferguson, John Calvin	VOL. LXI	31-266
Stories in Chinese Paintings, III	中国绘画中的故事（三）	Ferguson, John Calvin	VOL. LXIII	32-383
Story of the Emperor Shun, The	舜帝的传说	Kingsmill, Thomas William	VOL. XIII	9-169
Stray Notes on Corean History and Literature	朝鲜历史与文献散论	Scott, James	VOL. XXVIII	16-528
Studies in Conduct and Character	行为与性格研究	Morgan, Evan	VOL. LXIII	32-430
Study in the Life and Philosophy of Wang Yang Ming, A	王阳明的生平及其哲学思想	Henke, Frederick G.	VOL. XLIV	23-72
Sunspots and Sun-shadows Observed in China, B. C. 28-A. D. 1617	公元前28年至公元1617年在中国观测到的太阳黑子及太阳阴影	Hosie, Alex.	VOL. XII	8-307
Supplemental Memorandum on the Present State of the Magnetic Elements in China and Places Adjacent	中国及周边地区地磁学纪要补充	Shadwell, C. B.	O. S. VOL. II No. I	2-503
Supplementary Notes to the Intercourse between China and Lewchew	中国与琉球关系的补充说明		VOL. III	3-571
Sur les Institutions de Crédit en Chine	中国银行机构	Simon, G. Eug.	VOL. VI	5-75
Survey of the Work by Western Students of Chinese History, A	西方学者中国历史研究成果综述	Latourette, Kenneth Scott	VOL. XLVII	24-135
Symbolism of the Forbidden City, Peking, The	紫禁城的象征意义	Ayscough, Florence Wheelock	VOL. LXI	31-337

T

Table of the Emperors of the Yüan Dynasty, A	元代皇帝年表	Moule, Arthur Christopher	VOL. XLV	23-442

(续表)

题　名	中译题名	责任者	卷期	页码
Tableau Chronologique de la Dynastie Mandchoue-Chinoise Ta-Ts'ing	清朝帝王世系表	Hoang, Pierre; Tobar, Jérôme	VOL. XXXIII	19-210
Tablet of Yü, The	大禹碑	Medhurst, W. H.	VOL. V	4-356
T'ai Chi Shan Yuan—The Chinese Astrological Theory of Creation	太极上元——中国天文学的宇宙论	Chatley, Herbert	VOL. LXVII	34-41
T'ai Miao: A Description of the Supreme Hall of Sacrifices of the Forbidden City	紫禁城太庙	Fischer, Emil Sigmund	VOL. LXIV	33-102
T'ai Shan	泰山	Moule, Arthur Christopher	VOL. XLIII	22-299
Taoist Superman, The	道教真人	Morgan, Evan	VOL. LIV	27-603
Ta-Ts'in and Dependent States	大秦及其属国	Allen, Herbert J.	VOL. XXI	12-212
Teaching of Micius, The	墨子学说	Pott, Francis Lister Hawks	VOL. LVI	28-436
Technique and Spirit of Chinese Poetry, The	中国诗歌的技巧及其精神	Lin, Yu-tang	VOL. LXVI	33-577
Temperature of Hakodadi, from Observations Taken at the English Consulate, from October 1858 to September 1859	1858年10月至1859年9月函馆气温记录	Courtney, Charles	O. S. VOL. II No. I	2-504
Tent Theory of Chinese Architecture, The	中国建筑中的"帐幕理论"	Fries, S. Ritter Von	VOL. XXIV	13-659
Tenure of Land in China and the Condition of the Rural Population	中国佃制及农民状况报告	Jamieson, George	VOL. XXIII	13-65
Theistic Import of The Sung Philosiphy, The	宋代哲学中的有神论	Bruce, Joseph Percy	VOL. XLIX	25-129
Then-and Now	《今昔》[汉诗英译]	Hudson, Elfrida	VOL. LIV	27-370
Thermometrical Observations, Taken During a Passage from Nagasaki to Shanghai	从长崎到上海沿途温度记录	Fedorovitch, J.	O. S. VOL. I No. II	2-281
Thirty Thousand Miles in China.	中国三万英里行	Edmunds, Charle Keyser	VOL. L	25-263
Three Sites in Hunan Connected with the Classical Legendary History of China	湖南境内的三处上古史迹	Warren, Gilbert G.	VOL. XLIII	22-360
Through the Land of Deep Corrosions: from Batang to Menkong.	穿越荒漠:从巴塘河到湄公河	Edgar, J. Huston	VOL. XLV	23-326
Tibetan and His Environment: an Interpretation, The	藏民及其生存环境	Edgar, J. Huston	VOL. LVII	29-54
Times and Manners in the Age of the Emperor K'ang Hsi	康熙时代与当时的风尚	Morgan, Evan	VOL. LXIX	34-481

(续表)

题　名	中译题名	责任者	卷期	页码
Tone-accents of Two Chinese Dialects, The	中国两种方言的声调	Bradley, Cornelius Beach	VOL. XLVI	23－590
Trade Routes to Western China	华西商路	Hosie, Alex.	VOL. XIX	11－361
Translation of Inscription on Tablet at Hang Chow, Recording the Changing the T'ien Chu Tang (Roman Catholic Church) into the T'ien Hao Kung	杭州《天主堂改为天后官碑记》英译	Gardner, Christopher T.	VOL. IV	4－27
Translation of the Fragments of the Nestorian Writings in China, The	中国景教文献英译（《一神论》、《世尊布施论》）	Saeki, P. Y.	VOL. LXIV	33－117
Translation of the Inscription upon a Stone Tablet Commemmorating the Repairs upon the Ch'eng Hwang Miau or Temple of the Tutelary Deity of the City	英译郑板桥《重修城隍庙碑记》	McCartee, D. B.	VOL. VI	5－195
Translation of the Nestorian Writings in China, The	中国景教文献英译（《世尊布施论》续）	Saeki, P. Y.	VOL. LXV	33－407
Travels of Emperor Mu, The	《穆天子传》英译（一）	Cheng, Te-k'un	VOL. LXIV	33－154
Travels of Emperor Mu, The (Continued from Vol. LXIV, P. 142)	《穆天子传》英译（二）	Cheng, Te-k'un	VOL. LXV	33－424
Trip to Hua Kang, A	人日游花埭[汉诗英译]	Fletcher, William John Bainbridge	VOL. LII	26－454
Two New Species of Chinese Snakes	中国新发现的两个蛇类品种	Stanley, Arthur	VOL. XLVII	24－113
Two Zodiacs (Solar and Lunar), Their Origin and Connections: A Study in the Earlist Dawn of Civilisation, The	一项关于文明起源之研究——两个黄道带：太阳和月亮，它们的起源及联系	Kingsmill, Thomas William	VOL. XXXVIII	20－617
U					
Use of Cowries as Money During the Shang and Chou Periods, The	商周时代的贝壳货币	Gibson, Harry E.	VOL. LXXI	35－231
V					
Vertebrata of the Province of Chihli with Notes on Chinese Zoological Nomenclature, The	直隶的脊椎动物及中国动物命名法	Mollendorff, O. F. von.	VOL. XI	8－63
Visit to Simoda and Hakodadi in Japan	日本下田与函馆游记	Foote, A. H.	O. S. VOL. I	№.－Ⅱ39
Visit to the Agricultural Mongols, A	访蒙古农耕区	Edkins, Joseph	VOL. II	3－321

(续表)

题　名	中译题名	责任者	卷期	页码
Visit to the City of Confucius, A	孔子家乡曲阜之旅	Edkins, Joseph	VOL. VIII	6－97
Vows of Amida: A Comparative Study, The	《阿弥陀经》版本比较研究	Inglis, J. W.	VOL. XLVIII	24－231
Voyage de l'Ambassade Hollandaise de 1656 a Travers la Province de Canton, Le	1656年荷兰使团广东行记	Imbault-Huart, Camille	VOL. XXX	18－9

W

题　名	中译题名	责任者	卷期	页码
Wang An-shih	王安石	Ferguson, John Calvin	VOL. XXXV	19－603
Wang Mang, the Socialist Emperor of Nineteen Centuries Ago	王莽	Hu, Shih.	VOL. LIX	30－276
Wang-Chung and Plato on Death and Immortality	王充与柏拉图论死亡与永生	Forke, A.	VOL. XXXI	18－344
Was Chu Hsi a Materialist?	朱熹是唯物论者吗？	Warren, Gilbert G.	VOL. LV	28－48
Weather Report for 1873	徐家汇天文台1873年气候报告		VOL. VIII	6－13
Wei-ch'i	围棋	Volpicelli, Z.	VOL. XXVI	15－88
Western Appliances in the Chinese Printing Industry	中国印刷业中的西方设备	Hirth, F.	VOL. XX	11－609
Western Transcription of Chinese, The	汉语西式标音	Gardner, Charles S.	VOL. LXII	32－163
What Did the Ancient Chinese Know of the Greeks and Romans	古代中国对希腊和罗马的了解	Edkins, Joseph	VOL. XVIII	11－37
What is Filial Piety?	何为孝顺？		VOL. XX	11－561
Where was Ta-Ts'in?	大秦在哪里？	Allen, Herbert J.	VOL. XXI	12－97
Who are the Northern Chinese?	关于中国北方人的人类学研究	Shirokogoroff, Sergei Mikhailovich	VOL. LV	28－21
Why the Sinologue Should Study Manchu	汉学家为何应学满文	Hauer, Erich	VOL. LXI	31－386
Winds and Weather at Chefoo, during Seven Months of the Year 1859	1859年7个月中芝罘（烟台）的风与气候	Ward, John	O. S. VOL. II No. I	2－505
Witchcraft in the Chinese Penal Code	中国刑法中的巫术	Williams, Edward Thomas	VOL. XXXVIII	20－513
Word "One" in Chinese Poetry, The	中国诗歌中的"一"字	Lin, Tung-chi	VOL. LXVI	33－598
Worship of Earth in Ancient China, The	古代中国之土地崇拜	Bishop, Carl Whitney	VOL. LXIV	33－52

（续表）

题　　名	中译题名	责任者	卷期	页码
Worship of Lei Tsu, The, Patron Saint of Silk Workers	嫘祖崇拜	Williams, Edward Thomas	VOL. LXVI	33－547
Worshipping Imperial Ancestors in Peking	北京的皇家祭祖仪式	Williams, Edward Thomas	VOL. LXX	35－102
Wu Pan Tablet, The	武斑碑	Warren, Gilbert G.	VOL. XLVI	23－629

Y

题　　名	中译题名	责任者	卷期	页码
Yen Hsi Chai: A 17th Century Philosopher	颜习斋：17世纪的中国哲人	Freeman, Mansfield	VOL. LVII	29－96
Yü-li, or Precious Records, The	《玉历》英译	Clarke, Geo. W.	VOL. XXVIII	16－547

Z

Zoological Exploration in China.	中国动物学探险	Sowerby, Arthur de Carle	VOL. LXXII	35－389

书　评

题　　名	中译题名	责任者	卷期	页码

A

题　　名	中译题名	责任者	卷期	页码
A la Decouverte de la Musique Japonaise (Westarp, M. Alfred)	Westarp《日本音乐发现》	Ruffé, M. d'Auxion de	VOL. XLIV	23－221
Abridged Catalogue of Certain Scutelleroidea (Plataspidae, Scutelleridae, and Pentatomidae) of China, Chosen, Indo-China, and Twaiwan, An (Hoffmann, William E.)	何辅民《中国、朝鲜、印度支那及台湾盾蝽总科简目》	Chu, Y. T.	VOL. LXVII	34－240
Account of Tibet, The Travels of Ippolito Desideri of Pistoia, S. J., 1712—1727, An (de Filippi, Filippo)	费力比《德西迪利1712－1727年西藏纪行》	McIntosh, G.	VOL. LXIII	32－492
Across Mongolian Plains (Andrews, Roy Chapman)	安得思《穿越蒙古大草原》	M.	VOL. LII	26－486
Adversaria Sinica (Giles, Herbert A.)	翟理思《翟山笔记》	W., R. K.	VOL. XLIII	22－421
Adversaria Sinica (Giles, Herbert A.)	翟理思《翟山笔记》	Couling, Samuel	VOL. XLVI	23－678
Alphabetical Index to the Chinese Encyclopaedia Ch'in Ting Ku Chin T'u Shu Chi Ch'eng, An (Giles, Lionel)	翟林奈《钦定古今图书集成字顺引得》	Chalfant, Frank Herring	VOL. XLIII	22－424
America and the Far Eastern Question (Millard, Thomas F.)	密勒《美国与远东问题》	O'Shea, J.	VOL. XL	21－414

(续表)

题　　名	中译题名	责任者	卷期	页码
American Consular Jurisdiction in the Orient（Hinckley, Frank E.）	Hinckley《东方的美国领事裁判权》	Morse, Hosea Ballou	VOL. XXXVIII	20-691
American Woman's Club Annual 1919-1920, The	《花旗妇女总会1919-1920年刊》	M.	VOL. LII	26-468
Americans in Eastern Asia（Dennett, Tyler）	德涅特《美国人在东亚》	B.	VOL. LIV	27-645
America's Aims and Asia's Aspirations（Gallagher, Patrick）	Gallagher《美国的目的和亚洲的愿望》	M.	VOL. LII	26-464
Among the Tribes in South-West China（Clarke, Samuel R.）	陈牧师《中国西南部落地区传教纪事》	Wilson, J. Wallace	VOL. XLIII	22-428
Analects of Confucius, The（Waley, Arthur）	威利译《论语》	Chan, Wing-tsit	VOL. LXXI	35-310
Analytic Dictionary of Chinese and Sino-Japanese（Karlgren, Bernhard）	高本汉编《中日汉字分析字典》	Darroch, John	VOL. LV	28-278
Ancient Chinese Bronze Mirrors（Swallow, R. W.）	燕瑞博《古代中国铜镜》		VOL. LXVIII	34-405
Ancient Chinese Paper Money as Described in a Chinese Work on Numismatics	《华夏古钱币书中描述的中国古代纸币》	M.	VOL. L	25-484
Ancient History of China, The（Hirth, Friedrich）	夏德《中国古代史》	Ferguson, John Calvin	VOL. XXXIX	21-236
Ancient Na-Khi Kingdom of Southwest China, The（Rock, Joseph F.）	洛克《中国西南部古纳西王国》	Gillett, Michael Cavenagh	VOL. LXXIII	35-626
Ancient Philosopher's View of the Perfect Life, An（Morgan, Evan）	莫安仁《一位古代哲学家关于完美人生的观点——译自〈淮南子〉》	Shipway, G. W.	VOL. LVI	28-642
Anglo-Chinese Glossary for Customs and Commercial Use, An（Williams, C. A. S.）	威立师《海关语文津梁——海关及商用英汉词汇》	M.	VOL. L	25-490
Anglo-Chinese Glossary of Modern Terms for Customs and Commercial Use（Williams, C. A. S.）	威立师《海关商务华英新名词》	Gale, Esson Mcdowell	VOL. LXIV	33-192
Annals and Memoirs of the Court of Peking（from 16th to 20th Century）（Backhouse, E. & Bland, J. O. P.）	巴克斯与濮兰德合《清室外纪》	Anon.	VOL. XLV	23-444
Annotated Bibliography of Selected Chinese Reference Works, An（Teng, Ssu-yu）	邓嗣禹《中国参考书目解题》		VOL. LXVIII	34-406
Annual Customs and Festivals in Peiping（Bodde, Derk）	卜德译《燕京岁时记》	Brown, Margaret Helen	VOL. LXVIII	34-388

(续表)

题名	中译题名	责任者	卷期	页码
Annual Report on Reforms and Progress in Chosen（Korea）1912—13（Government-General of Chosen Keijo）	京城朝鲜总督府《朝鲜1912－1913年度改革与发展报告》	Ayscough, Florence Wheelock	VOL. XLVI	23－703
Anson Burlingame, and the First Chinese Mission to Foreign Powers（Williams, F. Wells）	卫斐列《蒲安臣与中国首次派遣外国的使团》	Ferguson, John Calvin	VOL. XLIV	23－233
Anthropology of Eastern China and Kwangtung Province（Shirokogoroff, S. M.）	史禄国《华东和广东省人类学》	Chatley, Herbert	VOL. LVII	29－240
Arabian Prophet-A Life of Mohammed from Chinese Sources, The（Mason, Isaac）	梅益盛《阿拉伯先知：一名中国回教徒的生活》	B., M. E.	VOL. LII	26－468
Arabic and Chinese Trade in Walrus and Narwhal Ivory（Laufer, Berthold）	劳费尔《阿拉伯与中国之间的贸易：以海象牙和鲸鱼齿为中心》	Couling, Samuel	VOL. XLV	23－468
Archaeological Investigations in the Aleutian Islands（Jochelson, Waldemar）	Jochelson《阿留申群岛考古调查》	Shirokogoroff, Sergei Mikhailovich	VOL. LVII	29－253
Art Funéraire a L'Epoque des Han, L'（Geuthner, Paul）	Geuthner《汉朝丧礼》	Ferguson, John Calvin	VOL. LXVIII	34－379
Arts and Art Crafts of Ancient China	《古代中国美术与工艺品》	Ayscough, Florence Wheelock	VOL. LIII	27－302
Arts Asiatica. 1.（Chavannes, E. & Petrucci, R.）	沙畹等编《亚洲艺术》卷一《1912年塞努齐博物馆中国绘画展图册》	Stanley, Arthur	VOL. XLV	23－466
Asbestos and Salamander（Laufer, Berthold）	劳费尔《石棉和蝾螈》	Stanley, Arthur	VOL. XLIX	25－181
Asian Odyssey（Alioshin, Dmitri）	Alioshin《亚洲奥德赛》		VOL. LXXI	35－313
Au Japon: Promenades aux Sanctuaires de l'Art（Migeon, Gaston）	Migeon《日本漫步艺术圣地》	Couling, C. E.	VOL. LIX	30－378
Autobiography of a Chinese Dog, The（Ayscough, Florence）	爱司克夫人《一条"中国狗"的自述》	Couling, C. E.	VOL. LVIII	29－541
Autobiography of a Chinese Historian, The（Ku, Chieh-kang）	顾颉刚撰《顾颉刚自传》	Millican, Frank R.	VOL. LXIII	32－489
Autumn Leaves（Werner, E. T. C.）	倭讷《秋叶》	Robinson, F. Alan	VOL. LIX	30－342
Awakening of Asia, The（Hyndman, H. M.）	Hyndman《亚洲的觉醒》		VOL. L	25－494
Awakening of China, The（Martin, W. A. P.）	丁韪良《中国之觉醒》	Bruce, Charence Dalrymple	VOL. XXXIX	21－232

(续表)

题　　名	中译题名	责任者	卷期	页码
B				
Basics of the Chinese Civilization (Gale, Esson M.)	盖乐《中国文明基础》	Cressy, M.	VOL. LXV	33-474
Bankwesen in China, Das (Dzen, Tien-yue)	陈田月《中国银行系统》	G.	VOL. LIX	30-325
Battle of Muddy Flat, The	《泥城之战》	Teesadale, J. H.	VOL. XLVI	23-699
Baukunst und religiöse Kultur der Chinesen, Die (Boerschmann, Ernst)	柏石曼《中国的建筑与宗教文化》	Johnston, Reginald Fleming	VOL. XLIV	23-199
Beans and Bean Products (Yen, Shih Chi)	Yen氏《豆及豆制品》	Shaw, Norman	VOL. XLIX	25-206
Beginnings of Porcelain in China, The (Laufer, Berthold)	劳费尔《中国陶瓷起源》	Stanley, Arthur	VOL. XLIX	25-181
Beschrijving der Javaansche, Balineesche en Sasaksche Handschriften (Brandes, J.)	Brandes《爪哇、巴厘岛和萨萨克族的手稿》	Berg, Jan van den	VOL. LIX	30-372
Bibliography on Far Eastern Numismatics and an Union Index of the Currency, Memorial Pieces, Charms and Amulets of the Far East, A (Coole, Arthur Bradden)	邱文明《远东钱币书目》	Sowerby, Arthur de Carle	VOL. LXXI	35-314
Big Game of Central and Western China, The (Wallace, H. F.)	华河力《华中和华西之大狩猎》		VOL. XLV	23-456
Biography of Shao Chin-han (Huang, Yün-mei)	黄云眉辑《邵二云先生年谱》		VOL. LXV	33-468
Botanische Reisen in den Hoch gebirgen Chinas und Ost-Tibets (Limpricht, W.)	Limpricht《中国内地和西藏东部的高山植物园之旅》		VOL. LV	28-289
Botany Dictionary	植物学大辞典	M.	VOL. XLIX	25-204
Boxer Rebellion, The (Clements, Paul H.:)	Clements《义和团运动》	M.	VOL. XLVII	24-168
Brave New China (Hosie, Lady)	谢福芸《义勇中国》	Read, Katherine L.	VOL. LXX	35-128
Brief Account of Diplomatic Events in Manchuria, A (Parlett, Harold)	帕雷脱《满洲外交史略》	L.	VOL. LXI	31-420
Brief History of Chinese Architecture, A (Mirams, D. G.)	Mirams《中国建筑简史》	Phillips, E. S. J.	VOL. LXXII	35-443
Brief Hisotry of Early Chinse Philosophy, A (Suzuki, Daisetz Teitaro)	铃木大拙《中国古代哲学简史》	Couling, C. E.	VOL. XLV	23-471
British in China and Far Eastern Trade, The (Smith, C. A. Middleton)	Smith《中国及远东贸易中的不列颠》	Wright, Harrison King	VOL. LIII	27-306

(续表)

题　名	中译题名	责任者	卷期	页码
British Jurisdiction in China（Kennett, W. B.）	开纳脱《英国在华司法管辖权》		VOL. LI	26－203
Bronze Vessels of Shan Chai（Jung Kêng）	容庚《善斋彝器图录》	Ferguson, John Calvin	VOL. LXVII	34－228
Bronzes of Chou and Shang, The（Jung Kêng,）	容庚《商周彝器通考》	Ferguson, John Calvin	VOL. LXXII	35－448
Buddha: His Life, His Doctrine, His Order（Oldenberg, Hermann）	奥尔登堡《佛的生平、学说与僧团》	Edkins, Joseph	VOL. XXI	12－241
Buddha and the Gospel of Buddhism（Coomara-Swamy, Ananda K.）	库马拉斯瓦米《佛陀与佛教的福音》	Johnston, Reginald Fleming	VOL. XLVIII	24－472
Buddhist Art in Its Relation to Buddhist Ideas with Special Reference to Buddhism in Japan（Anesaki, M.）	姉崎正治《日本佛教艺术及其与佛教思想的关系》	Johnston, Reginald Fleming	VOL. XLVIII	24－477
Buddhist China（Johnston, Reginald F.）	庄士敦《佛教徒的中国》	Richard, Timothy	VOL. XLV	23－454
Buddhist Sculptures at the Yun Kang Caves（Mullikin, Mary Augusta）	Mullikin《云冈石窟佛教造像》	Cressy, Earl Herbert	VOL. LXVII	34－222
Bulletin des Amis du Vieux Hué, Annam, Le	《故都顺化通迅》	Read, Bernard Emms	VOL. LXXII	35－451
Bulletin of the School of Oriental Studies	《伦敦大学东方研究院通讯》		VOL. L	25－493
Bulletin of the School of Oriental Studies London Institution	《伦敦大学东方研究院通讯》	M.	VOL. LXIII	32－488
Bulletin of the Shanghai Science Institute. Vol. I, No. 6. Upper Carboniferous Brachiopods from North China（Ozaki, Kin-emon）	尾崎金右卫门《华北晚石炭纪腕足动物研究》	Morgan, Evan	VOL. LXIII	32－506
Butinant: Scenes et Croquis de Mongolie, En（Oost, Josephe van）	彭嵩寿《蒙古自然景色》	M.	VOL. XLIX	25－200

C

Cadastrial Map of Peking	《清内为府藏京城全图》	Ferguson, John Calvin	VOL. LXXII	35－440
Carte de la Province du Kiang-sou（Dugout, Henry）	屠恩列《江苏省地图》		VOL. LIV	27－652
Catalogue of a Special Exhibition of Chinese Paintings at the Metropolitan Museum of Art in New York（Ferguson, John C.）	福开森编《纽约大都会艺术博物馆中国画特展展品目录》	Stanley, Arthur	VOL. XLVI	23－694
Catalogue of Chinese Paintings Ancient and Modern（Ayscough, Florence Wheelock）	爱司克夫人编《古今中国画目录》	Stanley, Arthur	VOL. XLVI	23－694

(续表)

题 名	中译题名	责任者	卷期	页码
Catalogue of Palace Bronzes, Supplement Pt. II	《西清续鉴乙编》	Ferguson, John Calvin	VOL. LXIII	32-497
Catalogue of the Maps and Charts Preserved by the Imperial Household, Peking	《清内务府造办处舆图房图目初编》	Ferguson, John Calvin	VOL. LXVIII	34-400
Catalogue of the Recorded Paintings of Successive Dynasties (Ferguson, John C.)	福开森编《历代著录画目》	Sun, Chien	VOL. LXV	33-463
Catholic Native Episcopacy in China	《中国本土的天主教主教》	Morgan, Evan	VOL. LIX	30-326
Central and Local Finance in China (Li, Chuan Shih)	李氏《中国中央与地方财政》	M.	VOL. LIV	27-659
Changing Chinese, The (Ross, E. A.)	罗辛甫《变化中的中国人》		VOL. XLIII	22-442
Chao Chün -Beauty in Exile (Mrs Wu, Lien-teh)	伍连德夫人黄淑琼《昭君出塞》	Morgan, Marion L.	VOL. LXVI	33-652
Character of Races as Influenced by Physical Environment, Natural Selection and Historical Development, The (Huntington, Ellsworth)	亨丁顿《受物理环境、自然选择和历史发展影响的种族特征》	Shirokogoroff, Sergei Mikhailovich	VOL. LVII	29-243
Character Study in Mandarin Colloquial, A (Goodric, Chauncey)	富善《官话特性研究》	Mason, Isaac	VOL. XLVIII	24-495
Chau Ju-Kua (Hirth, F. & Rockhill, W. W.)	夏德《赵汝适及其〈诸蕃志〉》	Ferguson, John Calvin	VOL. XLV	23-485
Chekiang Highways (Grow, Carl)	克劳《浙江公路》	Gale, Esson Mcdowell	VOL. LXVIII	34-375
Chemins de Fer Chinois, Les (Charignon, A. J. H. :)	沙海昂《中国铁路发展规划》	Ross, A.	VOL. XLVI	23-680
Chemins de Fer de Chine, Les (Laboulaye, Edouard de)	Laboulaye《中国铁路》	Shipway, G. W.	VOL. XLIII	22-425
Children of the Yellow Earth Andersson, J. Gunnar)	安特生《黄土地的子孙》	Plumer, James Marshall	VOL. LXVI	33-654
China and England (Soothill, W. E.)	苏慧廉《中国与英国》	G., A. J.	VOL. LIX	30-368
China and Foreign Powers (Whyte, Frederick)	怀德爵士《中国与列强》	Darroch, John	VOL. LVIII	29-533
China and Foreign Powers (Whyte, Frederick)	怀德爵士《中国与列强》	Darroch, John	VOL. LIX	30-367
China and Religion (Parker, E. H.)	庄延龄《惟天惟一:中国和宗教》	L., A. E. N.	VOL. XXXVII	20-392

(续表)

题　　名	中译题名	责任者	卷期	页码
China and the West (Soothill, W. E.)	苏慧廉《中国与西方》	Shipway, G. W.	VOL. LVII	29-237
China and the World War (Wheeler, W. R.)	Wheeler《中国与世界大战》	Wright, Harrison King	VOL. L	25-486
China Awake (Payne, Robert)	白乐达《中国觉醒》	Roberts, Frances M.	VOL. LXXIII	35-621
China in Revolution (An Analysis of Politics and Militarism under the Republic) (MacNair, Harley Farnsworth)	宓亨利《革命中的中国》	Millican, Frank R.	VOL. LXIII	32-484
China in Sign and Symbol (Crane, Louise)	鹤路易《中国招幌》	Ayscough, Florence Wheelock	VOL. LVIII	29-530
China Journal of Science and Arts, The (Sowerby, Arthur de C. & Ferguson, John C.)	苏阿德与福开森合编《中国科学和艺术杂志》		VOL. LIV	27-660
China Magnificent-Five Thousand Years of Chinese Art (Carter, Dagny)	贾德之夫人《瑰丽中华——五千年艺术》	Plumer, James Marshall	VOL. LXVI	33-654
China Mission Year Book 1912, The (Bondfield, G. H.:)	文显理《中国基督教年鉴》	M.	VOL. XLIII	22-447
China Moulded by Confucius (Cheng Tien-hsi)	郑天锡《孔子模型之中国——西方视野下的中国人》	Perry, Charles E.	VOL. LXXIII	35-622
China of the Chinese (Werner, E. T. C.)	倭讷《中国人之中国》	MacGillivray, Donald	VOL. LI	26-223
China Review, The (Couling, Samuel)	库寿龄编《中国评论》		VOL. LI	26-221
China under the Empress Dowager (Bland, J. O. P.)	濮兰德《慈禧外纪》	Leveson, W. E.	VOL. XLII	22-255
China under the Empress Dowager (Bland, J. O. P.)	濮兰德《慈禧外纪》	Read, Bernard Emms	VOL. LXX	35-133
China Year Book, The (Beel, H. T. Montague & Woodhead, H. G. W.)	伍德海《中国年鉴》	Stanley, Arthur	VOL. XLVIII	24-487
China Yesterday and To-day (Williams, Edward Thomas)	卫理《中国的昨天和今天》	Shipway, G. W.	VOL. LVIII	29-501
China, A Short Cultural History (Fitzgerald, C. P.)	费子智《中国文化简史》	Gale, Esson Mcdowell	VOL. LXVII	34-217
China, An Interpretation (Bashford, J. W.)	柏赐福《中国述论》		VOL. XLVIII	24-503
China, Her History, Diplomacy and Commerce from the Earliest Times to the Present Day (Parker, E. H.)	庄延龄《中国从古至今的历史、外交和商业》		VOL. XXXIII	19-313

(续表)

题　名	中译题名	责任者	卷期	页码
China, Japan and Korea (Bland, J. O. P.)	濮兰德《中国的日本与朝鲜》		VOL. LII	26-489
China, The Land and the People (Buxton, L. H. Dudley)	Buxton《中国土地与人民》	Chatley, Herbert	VOL. LXI	31-407
China, The Mysterious and Marvellous (Murdock, Victor)	Murdock《神秘而奇妙的中国》		VOL. LII	26-482
China, Then and Now (Escarra, Jean)	爱斯嘉拉《中国的过去和现在》	Millican, Frank R.	VOL. LXXII	35-446
China, Yesterday and To-day (Johnson, J. E.)	Johnson《中国的昨天和今天》	E., E. C.	VOL. LIX	30-357
China's Foreign Relations, 1917-1931 (Pollard, Robert T.)	浦纳德《中国1917至1931年对外关系》	Roberts, Donald	VOL. LXIV	33-197
China's Geographic Foundation (Cressey, George B.)	葛德石《中国之地理基础》	Arnold, Julean Herbert	VOL. LXV	33-450
China's International Relations and Other Essays (Farnsworth, Harley)	宓亨利《中国国际关系及其他论文》	Roberts, Frances M.	VOL. LIX	30-388
China's New Nationalism, and Other Essays (Farnsworth, Harley)	宓亨利《中国的新民族主义及其他论文》		VOL. LVII	29-241
China's Postal and other Communications Services (Chu Chia-hua)	朱嘉桦《中国邮政及其他通信服务》		VOL. LXVIII	34-405
China's Problems and Their Solution (Wang, Ching-wei)	汪精卫《中国之问题及其解决办法》	Wang, T. Ford	VOL. LXVI	33-656
China's Revolution: 1911-1912 (Dingle, Edwin John)	丁乐玫《中国的辛亥革命》	Stanley, Arthur	VOL. XLIII	22-438
Chine Contemporaine, Politique et Économique, La (Dubarbier, Georges)	巴尔比《当代中国政治和经济》	Grosbois, Ch.	VOL. LVIII	29-502
Chine et la Formation de l'Esprit Philosophique en France (1640-1740), La (Pinot, Virgile)	毕诺《中国对法国哲学思想形成的影响》	Grosbois, Ch.	VOL. LXIV	33-187
Chinese Abroad, The (McNair, Harley Farnsworth)	宓亨利《华侨志》	Shipway, G. W.	VOL. LVI	28-640
Chinese Altars to the Unknown God (de Korne, John C.)	狄靠恩《通向未知神灵的中国祭坛》	Couling, C. E.	VOL. LVIII	29-513
Chinese Ancestor Worship (Addison, James Thayer)	Addison《中国人的祖先崇拜》	Shipway, G. W.	VOL. LVI	28-644
Chinese and English Handbook of Business Expression, The (Gieter, L. de)	Gieter《汉英商业用语手册》	M.	VOL. XLIV	23-232
Chinese and Sumerian (Ball, C. J.)	包尔《汉人与闪族人》	Wilhelm, Richard	VOL. XLV	23-475
Chinese Art	《中国艺术》		VOL. LVI	28-650

(续表)

题　名	中译题名	责任者	卷期	页码
Chinese Art Motives（Tredwell, Winifred Reed）	Tredwell《中国艺术的主旨》		VOL. XLVII	24-183
Chinese Bridges（Fugl-Meyer, H.）	Fugl-Meyer《中国的桥梁》	Sowerby, Arthur de Carle	VOL. LXIX	34-561
Chinese Bronzes（Yetts, W. Perceval）	颜慈《中国青铜器》	Chatley, Herbert	VOL. LVI	28-650
Chinese Buddhist Monasteries（Prip-Møller, J.）	艾术华《中国佛教僧侣》	Millican, Frank R.	VOL. LXX	35-134
Chinese Clay Figures, Part 1（Laufer, Berthold）	劳费尔《中国泥塑》第一册	M.	VOL. XLVI	23-682
Chinese Drama, The（Johnston, Reginald F.）	庄士敦《中国戏剧》	Pott, Francis Lister Hawks	VOL. LIII	27-291
Chinese Eye. An Interpretation of Chinese Painting, The（Chiang Yee）	蒋彝《中国人的眼睛：中国绘画阐释》	Dunlap, Eva Wyman	VOL. LXVII	34-236
Chinese Farm Economy（Buck, John Lossing）	卜凯《中国农家经济》	Chatley, Herbert	VOL. LXII	32-245
Chinese First Reader, A（Sha, Chih-pei）	沙志培《汉文初阶》	Williams, Edward Thomas	VOL. LXVIII	34-391
Chinese Forest Trees and Timber Supply（Shaw, Norman）	余瑠璜《中国森林树木与木材供应》	Bourne, Frederick Samuel Augustus	VOL. XLVI	23-695
Chinese Free-Hand Flower Painting	《中国写意花卉画》	Dunlap, Eva Wyman	VOL. LXVIII	34-389
Chinese Game Birds（Jernigan, T. R.）	佑尼干《中国猎鸟》	Teesadale, J. H.	VOL. XLVI	23-698
Chinese Game Mammals（Jernigan, T. R.）	佑尼干《中国捕猎哺乳动物》	Teesadale, J. H.	VOL. XLVI	23-697
Chinese Ghouls and Goblins（Willoughby-Meade, Gerald）	Willoughby-Meade《中国的食尸鬼和地精》	Couling, C. E.	VOL. LIX	30-364
Chinese Grammar Self-taught（Darroch, John）	窦乐安《中文文法自学》	Wright, Harrison King	VOL. LIII	27-294
Chinese Grave Sculptures of the Han Period（Laufer, Berthold）	劳费尔《中国汉代墓葬雕塑》	Stanley, Arthur	VOL. XLIV	23-224
Chinese Heart Throbs（Hughes, Jennie V.）	胡遵理《中国的心跳》	Wright, Harrison King	VOL. LII	26-476
Chinese Hotch Potch（Kahler, William R.）	查立尔《中国的大杂烩》		VOL. XLII	22-254
Chinese Idea of a Garden, The（Ayscough, Florence）	爱司克夫人《中国园林理念》	Shipway, G. W.	VOL. LV	28-286
Chinese Idea of the Second Self, The（Werner, E. T. C.）	倭讷《中国人的心腹观念》	M.	VOL. LXIII	32-487
Chinese Idol, A（Lunt, Carroll）	龙塔《中国偶像崇拜》	M.	VOL. LII	26-473

(续表)

题　　名	中译题名	责任者	卷期	页码
Chinese Isles of the Blest，*The*（Yetts，W. Perceval）	颜慈《中国福岛》	M.	VOL. L	25－513
Chinese Jade，*Ancient and Modern*（Tanner）	单尔《中国古今玉器》	Chatley, Herbert	VOL. LVI	28－649
Chinese Jews（White, William Charles）	怀履光《中国之犹太人》	Abraham, R. D.	VOL. LXXIII	35－616
Chinese Junks（Donnelly, Ivon A.）	Donnelly《中式舢板》		VOL. LI	26－209
Chinese Language，*The*（Forrest, R. A. D.）	Forrest《汉语》	Gillett, Michael Cavenagh	VOL. LXXIII	35－624
Chinese Lyrics（Pai Ta-shun）	白大舜《中国抒情诗》	Kanno, Domei	VOL. XLVIII	24－483
Chinese Materia Medica，*Animal Drugs*（Read, Bernard E.）	伊博恩《中国医药名录：动物药品》	Maxwell, J. L.	VOL. LXIII	32－483
Chinese Materia Medica：*Fish Drugs*（Read, Bernard E.）	伊博恩《中医药名录：鱼药》	Sowerby, Arthur de Carle	VOL. LXX	35－124
Chinese Materia Medica：*Insect Drugs*（Read, Bernard E.）	伊博恩《中医药名录：昆虫药》	Sowerby, Arthur de Carle	VOL. LXXII	35－443
Chinese Materia Medica：*Turtle and Shell fish Drugs*（Read, Bernard E.）	伊博恩《中医药名录：龟药与贝类药》	Read, Bernard Emms	VOL. LXIX	34－559
Chinese Materia Medica：*Vegetable Kingdom*（Stuart, G. A.）	师图尔《中医药名录：草药》	Stanley, Arthur	VOL. XLIV	23－222
Chinese Mettle（Kemp, E. G.）	Kemp《中国秉性》	Wright, Harrison King	VOL. LIV	27－657
Chinese Migrations（Chen Ta）	陈达《华侨》	Shipway, G. W.	VOL. LVI	28－640
Chinese Mirror，*A*（Ayscough, Florence）	爱司克夫人《中国镜子》	E., E. C.	VOL. LVIII	29－539
Chinese Moral Sentiment Before Confucius（Rudd, H. F.）	Rudd《前孔子时代中国人的道德观》	Parker, Alvin Pierson	VOL. XLVII	24－180
Chinese Mythology（Ferguson, John C.）	福开森《中国神话》	K., J. C. D.	VOL. LX	31－165
Chinese Names of Plants（Matsumura, J.）	松村润《中国植物名称考》	M.	VOL. XLIX	25－205
Chinese on the Art of Painting，*The*（Sirén, Osvald）	喜仁龙《中国人论绘画艺术》	Dunlap, Eva Wyman	VOL. LXVII	34－223
Chinese Paintings（Ferguson, John C.）	福开森《中国国画》	Smith, H.	VOL. LIX	30－389
Chinese Peasant Cults（Day, Clarence Burton）	队克勋《中国农民的迷信》	Ferguson, John Calvin	VOL. LXXII	35－440
Chinese People，*The*（Moule, Venerable Archdeacon）	慕雅德《中华民族》		VOL. XLV	23－464

(续表)

题 名	中译题名	责任者	卷期	页码
Chinese Periodical Press 1800–1912, The (Britton, Roswell S.)	白瑞华《中国报刊1800–1912》	Ungern-Sternberg, L.	VOL. LXVI	33-638
Chinese Pictorial Art (Strehlneek, E. A.)	史德匿《中国绘画艺术》	Stanley, Arthur	VOL. XLVI	23-694
Chinese Political Thought (Thomas, Elbert Duncan)	Thomas《中国政治思考》	Pott, Francis Lister Hawks	VOL. LIX	30-338
Chinese Porcelains and Hard Stones (Gorer, Edgar)	Gorer《中国陶瓷与宝石》	Ayscough, Florence Wheelock	VOL. XLIII	22-441
Chinese Pottery and Porcelain (Hobson, R. L.)	何博逊《中国陶瓷》	Ayscough, Florence Wheelock	VOL. XLVI	23-691
Chinese Pottery in the Philippines (Cole, Fay-Cooper)	科尔《菲律宾之中国陶瓷》	Mooallen, A. A.	VOL. XLV	23-462
Chinese Pottery of the Han, Tang and Sung Dynasties	《汉、唐、宋朝瓷器》		VOL. L	25-495
Chinese Prose Literature of the T'ang Period, vol. I (Edwards, E. D.)	叶女士《唐代散文》卷一	Millican, Frank R.	VOL. LXIX	34-560
Chinese Prose Literature of the T'ang Period, vol. II (Edwards, E. D.)	叶女士《唐代散文》卷二	Millican, Frank R.	VOL. LXIX	34-568
Chinese Religion through Hindu Eyes (Sarkar, Benoy Kumar)	Sarkar《印度人眼中的中国宗教》	Chatley, Herbert	VOL. XLVIII	24-467
Chinese revolution, 1926—27, The (Chapman, H. Owen)	贾溥泉《1926–1927年中国革命》	Sowerby, Arthur de Carle	VOL. LX	31-163
Chinese Shadows (Bredon, Juliet)	裴丽珠《中国的皮影》	Stent, George Carter	VOL. LIII	27-304
Chinese Speaker; Readings in Modern Mandarin, The (Morgan, Evan)	莫安仁《汉语口语》		VOL. XLVII	24-186
Chinese Temple Frescces, a Study of Three Wall-paintings of the Thirteenth Century (White, William Charles)	怀履光《中国之庙宇壁画》	Sowerby, Arthur de Carle	VOL. LXXII	35-445
Chinese Treatise on Architecture, A (Yetts, W. Perceval)	颜慈《中国营造法式》	Morgan, Evan	VOL. LVIII	29-524
Chinese Women Yesterday and Today (Ayscough, Florence)	爱司克夫人《中国妇女的昨天与今天》	Reichelt, Karl Ludvig	VOL. LXIX	34-561
Chinese Writing in the Chou Dynasty in the Light of Recent Discoveries (Hopkins, L. C.)	金璋《周朝的中文书写新发现》	Couling, Samuel	VOL. XLIV	23-239
Chinese, Corean and Japanese Potteries (Hobson, R. L.)	何博逊《中国、朝鲜和日本的陶器》	Ayscough, Florence Wheelock	VOL. XLVI	23-691
Chinese: Their History and Culture, The (Latourette, Kenneth Scott)	赖德烈《中国人历史及其文化》	Gale, Esson Mcdowell	VOL. LXV	33-469

(续表)

题　名	中译题名	责任者	卷期	页码
Chinese-English Dictionary, A (Giles, Herbert A.)	翟理思编《华英字典》	Ferguson, John Calvin	VOL. XL	21-407
Chinesische Kunst	《中国艺术品》	Sowerby, Arthur de Carle	VOL. LX	31-164
Chinesische Kunstgeschichte (Münsterberg, O.)	敏斯德保《中国艺术史》	Hinckley, F. E.	VOL. XLII	22-259
Chinesische Kunstgeschichte (Münsterberg, O.)	敏斯德保《中国艺术史》	Hinckley, F. E.	VOL. XLIII	22-448
Chinesische Malkunsttheorie in der T'ang-und Sungzeit (Teng, Ku)	滕固《唐宋绘画史》	Contag, Victoria	VOL. LXVII	34-239
Chinesische Philosophie (Hackmann, Heinrich)	哈克曼《中国哲学》	B.	VOL. LIX	30-392
Christian Life and Message, in its Relation to Non-Christian Systems, The	《在非基督教体系下的基督徒之生命和使命》	Mason, Isaac	VOL. LX	31-159
Christian Missions and Oriental Civilization (Price, Maurice T.)	Price《基督教传教和东方文明》	Morgan, Evan	VOL. LVIII	29-512
Chuang Tzǔ, Mystic, Moralist and Social Reformer (Giles, Herbert A.)	翟理思《庄子——神秘主义者、道学家和社会改革者》	Morgan, Evan	VOL. LVII	29-231
Chung Yung or, the Centre, The Common, The (Lyall, Leonard A & King Chien-kun.)	赖发洛《中庸》	Morgan, Evan	VOL. LIX	30-322
Civil Code of the Republic of China, Books I, II, and III, The	《中华民国民法》	B.	VOL. LXII	32-241
Civilization of the Mayas, The (Thompson, John. Eric Sidney)	汤普逊《玛雅文明》	Sowerby, Arthur de Carle	VOL. LX	31-167
Class of Social Outcasts, A (Gee, N. Gist)	祁天赐《乞丐——被社会遗弃的阶层》	Teesadale, J. H.	VOL. XLVI	23-699
Coal and Mineral Resources of Shansi Province, China, The (Nyström, Erik T.)	新常富《晋矿》	Stanley, Arthur	VOL. XLIV	23-202
Code Pénal de la République de Chine (Escarra, Jean)	爱斯嘉拉《中华民国刑法》	B.	VOL. LXII	32-240
Coins in China's History (Coole, Arthur Bradden)	邱文明《中国古今泉币辞典》		VOL. LXVIII	34-404
Coins of the Ch'ing Dynasty	《故宫清钱谱》	Ferguson, John Calvin	VOL. LXIX	34-552
Collection and Disposal of the Customs Revenue, The (Wright, Stanley F.)	魏尔特《海关和常关税收的征收与处理》	Ferguson, John Calvin	VOL. LVIII	29-492

(续表)

题　　名	中译题名	责任者	卷期	页码
Colloquial Sentences with New Terms (Morgan, Evan)	莫安仁《口语句子与新词》	Wright, Harrison King	VOL. LIII	27-290
Combined Concordances to Ch'un-ch'iu, Kung-yang, Ku-liang and Tso-chuan	《春秋经传引得》	Ferguson, John Calvin	VOL. LXIX	34-550
Commercial Geography of China for Middle Schools, A (Coole, Arthur Bradden)	邱文明《中学用中国商业地理》	Chatley, Herbert	VOL. LXII	32-247
Commercial Handbook of China. vol. II (Arnold, Julean)	安立德编《中国商务指南》下卷	Fox, Harry H.	VOL. LII	26-456
Common Marine Food Fishes of Hongkong (Herklots, G. A. C.)	Herklots《香港常见海洋食用鱼》	Read, Bernard Emms	VOL. LXXI	35-312
Comparative Study of Life Ideals, A (Fung Yu-lan)	冯友兰《人生理想之比较研究》	Shipway, G. W.	VOL. LVI	28-652
Compte Rendus de Onze Années 1923-1933 de Sejour Et d'Exploration Dans Le Bassin Du Fleuve Jaune, Du Pai Ho Et des Autres Tributaires Du Golfe Du Pei Tcheu Ly (Licent, Emile)	黎桑《黄河流域1923-1833年勘察报告》		VOL. LXVIII	34-391
Confucianism and Modern China (Johnston, Reginald F.)	庄士敦《儒学与近代中国》	Morgan, Evan	VOL. LXVI	33-634
Confucius and Confucianism (Wilhelm, Richard)	卫礼贤《孔子和儒教》	Shipway, G. W.	VOL. LXIII	32-480
Confucius and New China (Wang Ching Tao)	王氏《孔子与新中国》	M.	VOL. XLIV	23-229
Constitution Building in China (Bevan, L. R. O.)	毕善功《中国的宪政建树》		VOL. XLII	22-255
Contemporary Politics in the Far East (Hornbeck, Stanley K.)	亨培克《远东现代政治》	Parker, Alvin Pierson	VOL. XLVIII	24-492
Couling-Chalfant Collection of Inscribed Oracle Bones, The (Britton, Roswell S.)	白瑞华编《库方二氏藏甲骨卜辞》	Gibson, Harry E.	VOL. LXVII	34-235
Country life in South China (Kulp, Daniel Harrison, II)	葛学博《华南乡村生活》	Shipway, G. W.	VOL. LVII	29-238
Course in the Analysis of Chinese Characters, A (Blakney, Raymond B.)	Blakney《汉字分析教程》	Morgan, Evan	VOL. LVIII	29-516
Course of Colloquial Chinese, A (Usoff. S. N.)	Usoff《汉语口语教程》		VOL. LXIX	34-567
Court Painters of the Grand Moguls, The (Binyon, Laurence)	彬雄《大蒙古宫廷画师》		VOL. LIII	27-308
Craft of the Japanese Sculptor, The (Warner, Langdon)	Warner《日本雕塑家之工艺》	Abraham, R. D.	VOL. LXXIII	35-618

(续表)

题　名	中译题名	责任者	卷期	页码
Critical Study of the First Anglo-Chinese War, A (Kuo, P. C.)	郭斌佳《第一次英中战争评论》	Roberts, Donald	VOL. LXVII	34－235
Cult of Dr. Sun, The (Sun Yat-sen)	孙中山《孙文学说》	Millican, Frank R.	VOL. LXIII	32－487
Cultural Contacts of the United States and China (1784－1844), The (Danton, George H.)	谭唐《中美文化接触(1784－1844)》	Morgan, Evan	VOL. LXIII	32－491
Cultural Relations on the Kansu-Tibetan Border (Ekvall, Robert B.)	埃克瓦尔《甘藏边的文化联系》	Read, Bernard Emms	VOL. LXXI	35－308
Currencies of China, The (Kann, Edward)	耿爱德《中国货币》	Abraham, R. D.	VOL. LVIII	29－542
Currency of the Far East, The (Schjoth, Fr.)	佘德《远东货币》	Gibson, Harry. E.	VOL. LXV	33－461
Current Chinese (Ratay, J. P.)	Ratay《当代汉语》	Ferguson, John Calvin	VOL. LIX	30－340

D

题　名	中译题名	责任者	卷期	页码
Dalai Lamas of Lhasa and Their Relations with the Manchu Emperors of China, 1644－1908, The (Rockhill, W. W.)	柔克义《拉萨达赖喇嘛及其与满清帝国的关系》		VOL. XLII	22－253
Democracy and Finance in China (Shaw, Kinn-wei)	寿景伟《中国的民主和财政》	Kliene, Charles	VOL. LIX	30－381
Democracy and the Eastern Question (Millard, Thomas F.)	密勒《民主政治与远东问题》		VOL. LII	26－482
Demonism Verified and Analyzed (White, Hugh W.)	白秀生《魔鬼崇拜验证和分析》	Wright, Harrison King	VOL. LIV	27－658
Derniers Barbares-Chine-Tibet-Mongolie, Les (D'Ollone)	多伦《中国禁地 1906 年至 1909 年之考察》	Bruce, Charence Dalrymple	VOL. XLIV	23－236
Descriptive Sociology; Chinese (Werner, E. T. C.)	倭讷《叙述社会学:中国人》	Couling, Samuel	VOL. XLVII	24－173
Dettes Publiques Chinoises, Des (Tcheou, Jeungens)	周鸿钧《中国的公共债务》	G., A. J.	VOL. LIX	30－361
Development of China, The (Latourette, Kenneth Scott)	赖德烈《中国之发展》	Lanning, George	VOL. XLIX	25－190
Development of Extraterritoriality in China, The (Keeton, G. W.)	Keeton《中国治外法权发展》	Mason, Isaac	VOL. LX	31－157
Dialecte Monguor parté par les Mongols du Kansou Occidental, Le (de Smedt, A.)	德斯迈《甘肃西部蒙古语蒙哥尔方言》	Gillett, Michael Cavenagh	VOL. LXXIII	35－612
Diamond Jubilee of the International Settlement of Shanghai, The (Kounin, I. I.)	Kounin《上海公共租界钻石庆典》	Sowerby, Arthur de Carle	VOL. LXXI	35－316

(续表)

题名	中译题名	责任者	卷期	页码
Diamond, a Study in Chinese and Hellenistic Folk-lore, *The*（Laufer, Berthold）	劳费尔《钻石:中国和古希腊民俗研究》		VOL. XLVII	24-183
Dictionary of Chinese Buddhist Terms, *A*（Soothill, William Edward）	苏慧廉《汉语佛教术语词典》	Reichelt, Karl Ludvig	VOL. LXXI	35-308
Dictionnaire des Formes Cursives des Caractères Chinois（Millot, Stanislas）	Millot《汉字草书字典》	Ferguson, John Calvin	VOL. XLI	21-611
Dictionnaire Monguor-Francais（de Smedt, A.; Mostaert, A.）	德斯迈与田清波合编《蒙语—法语词典》	G.	VOL. LXV	33-476
Dictionnaire Ordos（Mostaert, Antoine）	田清波《鄂尔多斯辞典》	Gillett, Michael Cavenagh	VOL. LXXIII	35-613
Diplomat in Japan, *A*（Satow, Ernest）	萨道义《一个外交官在日本》	Wilden, Henry Auguste	VOL. LIII	27-311
Discourses on Salt and Iron（Gale, Esson M.）	盖乐译《盐铁论》	Kliene, Charles	VOL. LXIII	32-507
Discoveries of the Kozlóv Expedition（Yetts, W. Perceval）	颜慈《哥司罗夫考古的发现》	Chatley, Herbert	VOL. LVIII	29-522
Diseases of China（Jefferys, W. Hamilton & Maxwell, James L.）	Jefferys 与马雅各《中国的疾病》	Houghton, Henry Spence	VOL. XLII	22-251
Documents inédits Relatifs à la Connaissance de la Chine en France de 1685 à 1740（Pinot, Virgile）	毕诺《法国与中国相关的未刊文献》	Grosbois, Ch.	VOL. LXIV	33-188
Dogs of China and Japan in Nature and Art（Collier, V. W. F.）	柯氏《自然与艺术中的中日狗犬》	M.	VOL. LIII	27-300
Douane Chinoise, *La*（Ting, Tsao-chao）	丁氏《中国海关》	Grosbois, Ch.	VOL. LXIII	32-494
Dr. F. Hirth and the Hiung Nu: Review of Hirth's Ueber Wolga-Hunnen und Hiung-nu	夏德与匈奴:评夏德《伏尔加河的匈人和匈奴人》	Kingsmill, Thomas William	VOL. XXXIV	19-524
Droit Chinois, *Le*（Escarra, Jean）	爱斯嘉拉《中国法制史》	Gale, Esson Mcdowell	VOL. LXVIII	34-383
Dschung Kuei, Bezwinger der Teufel（Du Bois-Reymond）	谛部《钟馗》	Cressy, M.	VOL. LIV	27-662
E				
Early Buddhist Scriptures（Thomas, Edward J.）	Thomas《早期佛教经典》	Gale, Esson Mcdowell	VOL. LXVI	33-655
Early Buddhist Theory of Man Perfected, *The*（Horner, I. B.）	Horner《早期佛教人论》	Millican, Frank R.	VOL. LXVIII	34-397

(续表)

题　　名	中译题名	责任者	卷期	页码
Early Chinese History. Are the Chinese Classics Forged?（Allen, Herbert J.）	啊查理《中国古代史——中国经书是伪造的吗?》	Kingsmill, Thomas William	VOL. XXXVIII	20－697
Early Chinese Painting（Gates, William E.）	Gates《早期中国绘画》	Stanley, Arthur	VOL. XLVIII	24－486
Early Chinese Writing（Chalfant, Frank H.）	方法敛《中国早期文字书写研究论文集》	Pearson, G. W.	VOL. XXXVIII	20－707
Early History of Chengtu, The（Torrance, Thos.）	陶然士《早期成都历史》	Mason, Isaac	VOL. XLVIII	24－495
Early Ming Wares of Chingtechen（Brankstow, A. D.）	Brankstow《明初景德镇瓷器》		VOL. LXIX	34－566
East India Co. Trading to China, The（Morse, Hosea Ballou）	马士《东印度公司对华贸易纪事》	Brett, H. J.	VOL. LVIII	29－498
East India Company Trading to China, The, v. 5（Morse, Hosea Ballou）	马士《东印度公司对华贸易纪事》卷五	Morgan, Evan	VOL. LXI	31－402
Eastern Odyssey, An（Le Fèvre, Georges）	卢飞凫《东方的奥德赛》	Platt, B. S.	VOL. LXVI	33－648
Economic Aspects of the History of the Civilization of Japan, The（Takegoshi, Yosaburao）	竹越与三郎《从经济角度看日本文明史》	Inui, K. S.	VOL. LXII	32－246
Economic History of China with Special Reference to Agriculture, The（Lee, Mabel Ting-hua）	李美步《中国经济史——以农业为主》	G., D. M.	VOL. LIII	27－295
Educational Directory of China 1914	《中国教育名录及1914年年鉴》		VOL. XLV	23－488
Educational Directory of China 1915, The	《中国教育名录及1915年年鉴》	Couling, Samuel	VOL. XLVI	23－704
Educational Directory of China 1916, The	《中国教育名录及1916年年鉴》	M.	VOL. XLVIII	24－494
Educational Directory and Year Book of China, 1918, The	《中国教育名录及1918年年鉴》	O., M.	VOL. XLIX	25－208
Educational Directory and Year Book of China, 1920	《中国教育名录及1920年年鉴》		VOL. LI	26－215
Educational Directory and Year Book of China, 1921, The	《中国教育名录及1921年年鉴》	M.	VOL. LII	26－470
Elements of Buddhist Iconography（Coomaraswamy, Ananda K.）	库马拉斯瓦米《佛教造像要素》	Millican, Frank R.	VOL. LXVII	34－226
Elements of Japanese Writing, The（Isemonger, Noel Everard）	Isemonger《日文写作基础》	Morgan, Evan	VOL. LXI	31－427

(续表)

题　　名	中译题名	责任者	卷期	页码
Encyclopaedia Sinica, *The*（Couling, Samuel）	库寿龄编《中国百科全书》	Fraser, E. H.	VOL. XLVIII	24－507
Encyclopaedia Sinica, *The*（Couling, Samuel）	库寿龄编《中国百科全书》	M.	VOL. XLIX	25－211
English-Chinese Dictionary of Peking Colloquial, *An*（Hillier, W.）	禧在明《袖珍英汉北京方言词典》	M.	VOL. L	25－474
English-Chinese Dictionary of the Standard Chinese Spoken Language（Hemeling, K.）	赫美玲《英汉标准口语词典及翻译手册》	Wright, Harrison King	VOL. LI	26－219
Epochs of Chinese and Japanese Art（Fenollosa, Ernest F.）	Fenollosa《中日艺术源流》	Ferguson, John Calvin	VOL. XLIV	23－208
Ethics of Opium, *The*（La Motte, Ellen N.）	La Motte《鸦片伦理》	Shipway, G. W.	VOL. LV	28－284
Ethnological and Linguistical Aspects of the Ural-Altaic Thesis（Shirokogoroff, S. M.）	史禄国《乌拉尔阿尔泰民族与语言学研究》	M.	VOL. LXIII	32－488
Etudes Sino-Mahométanes（Vissière, A.）	微席叶《中国伊斯兰教研究》	Merz, C.	VOL. XLIII	22－434
Etudes sur Âryadeva et son Catuhśataka（Vaidya, P. L.）	Vaidya《提婆菩萨及其〈四百论〉研究》	MacLeod, N.	VOL. LV	28－290
Etudes sur la Phonologie Chinoise（Karlgren, Bernhard）	高本汉《中国声韵学研究》		VOL. LI	26－222
Etudes sur l'Iconographie Bouddhique de l'Inde（Foucher, A.）	Foucher《印度佛教画像研究》	Stanley, Arthur	VOL. XLIV	23－220
Europe and China（Hudson, G. F.）	洪慈恩《欧洲与中国》	Morgan, Evan	VOL. LXIII	32－472
Evolution des Corporations Ouvrières et Commerciales dans la Chine Contemporaine, *L'*（Wou, Mon-feng）	吴氏《当代中国工商业团体的演变》	Grosbois, Ch.	VOL. LXIII	32－495
Examination of Chinese Bronzes, *An*（Ferguson, John C.）	福开森《中国青铜器考》	Couling, Samuel	VOL. XLVII	24－184
Examples of the Various Turki Dialects with Turki Text and English Translation（Hunter, G. W.）	胡进洁《各种突厥方言和文字与英语翻译实例》		VOL. LI	26－211
Exercise Book of the Geography of China, *An*（Sawdon, E. W.）	Sawdon《中国地理学练习册》	Mason, Isaac	VOL. LIV	27－651
Experiences with Man-Eating Tigers in China（Caldwell, H. R.）	Caldwell《在华与食人虎生活的经历》	Teesadale, J. H.	VOL. XLVI	23－696
Expounder of Dark Sayings, *An*: Review of Giles' Translation of *Chuang-tzŭ*	评翟理思译《庄子》	Playfair, G. M. H.	VOL. XXIV	13－580
Exterritorialité et Intérêts trangères en Chine（Soulie de Morant, Georges）	摩兰特《治外法权及外国对中国的兴趣》	Grosbois, Ch.	VOL. LVIII	29－504

(续表)

题　　名	中译题名	责任者	卷期	页码
Eyak Indians of the Copper River Delta, Alaska, The（Birket-Smith, K.）	Birket-Smith《阿拉斯加铜河三角洲的埃雅克－印第安人》		VOL. LXIX	34－567

F

题　　名	中译题名	责任者	卷期	页码
Facets of the Chinese Question（Gull, E. Manico）	葛罗《中国问题的各个方面》	Morgan, Evan	VOL. LXII	32－239
Famille d'Historiens et son Oeuvre, Une（Lo, Tcheng-ying）	罗氏《史学家之家庭及其作》	Grosbois, Ch.	VOL. LXIII	32－495
Family in Classical China, The（Wilkinson, H. P.）	威金生《古典中国的家庭》	Shipway, G. W.	VOL. LVII	29－242
Famous Chinese Plays（Arlington, L. C.）	阿灵敦编《中国名剧集》		VOL. LXVIII	34－405
"Fan Kwae" at Canton before Treaty Days, 1825－1844, Bits of Old China, The（Hunter, William C.）	亨特《广州番鬼录》、《旧中国杂记》		VOL. XLII	22－255
Fans Painted by Famous Artists	《名人书画扇面集》		VOL. XLIII	22－442
Far East, The（Little, Archibald）	立德《远东》	Ferguson, John Calvin	VOL. XXXVII	20－397
Far-East in World Politics, The（Hudson, G. F.）	赫达生《世界政治中的远东》	Millican, Frank R.	VOL. LXVIII	34－403
Far Eastern International Relations（Morse, Hosea Ballou & MacNair, Harley Farnsworth）	马士与宓亨利《远东国际关系》	Shipway, G. W.	VOL. LX	31－161
Festivals and Songs of Ancient China（Granet, Marcel）	葛兰言《中国古代的节日与歌谣》	Lyon, David Willard	VOL. LXIII	32－501
Fight for the Republic in China, The（Weale, B. L. Putnam;）	辛博森《为中国的共和而战》	Pott, Francis Lister Hawks	VOL. XLIX	25－216
Finance in China（Wagel, S. R.;）	Wagel《中国之财政》	Morris, H. C.	VOL. XLVI	23－702
Five Hundred Proverbs（Brace, A. J.）	布礼士《谚语五百句》		VOL. LIV	27－662
Flight of the Dragon, The（Binyon, Laurence）	彬雄《龙腾虎跃》	Ayscough, Florence Wheelock	VOL. XLIII	22－420
Folklore Odos, Dictionnaire Ordos（Mostaert, Antoine）	田清波《鄂尔多斯民俗》	Gillett, Michael Cavenagh	VOL. LXXIII	35－613
Folkways in China（Hodous, Lewis）	何乐益《中国的风俗》	Chatley, Herbert	VOL. LX	31－174
Food Habits of North American Diving Ducks（Cottam, Clarence）	Cottam《北美潜水鸭的进食习惯》	Sowerby, Arthur de Carle	VOL. LXX	35－123

(续表)

题　　名	中译题名	责任者	卷期	页码
Food of Game Ducks in the United States and Canada（Martin, A. C.）	马定《美加猎鸭之食》	Sowerby, Arthur de Carle	VOL. LXX	35-122
Foreign Financial Control in China（Overlach, T. W.）	Overlach《外国金融控制在中国》	Wright, Harrison King	VOL. L	25-497
Foreign Trade of China, The（See, Chong Su）	See 氏《中国对外贸易》	Wright, Harrison King	VOL. LI	26-221
Forests and Chihli Floods（Lin, D. Y.）	林氏《森林与直隶洪水》	Shaw, Norman	VOL. XLIX	25-209
Forgotten Tales of Ancient China（Dyson, Verne）	Dyson《被遗忘的古代中国故事》	Couling, C. E.	VOL. LIX	30-343
Formulaire Sanscrit-Tibétain du Xe. Siècle（Hackin, Joseph）	Hackin《梵藏汇编》	Chatley, Herbert	VOL. LIX	30-351
Forty-five Years in China（Richard, Timothy）	李提摩太《留华四十五年记》	B.	VOL. XLVIII	24-469
"Fou" dans le Wen-siuen, Le（Margoulies, G.）	Margoulies《〈文选〉中的"赋"》	Dubs, Homer Hasenpflug	VOL. LVIII	29-510
Foundations of Chinese Musical Art（Levis, John Hazedel）	来维思《中国音乐艺术之基础》	R., F. F.	VOL. LXVIII	34-399
Fur and Feather in North China（Sowerby, Arthur de C.）	苏阿德《华北之鸟兽》	Lanning, George	VOL. XLVII	24-171
Further Notes on the Birds of the Province of Fukien in South East China（Touche, J. D. D. de la）	德拉图什《福建省鸟类记录续》		VOL. XLIX	25-183

G

Gateway to China, The（Gamewell, Mary Ninde）	Gamewell《中国的大门：上海》		VOL. XLVIII	24-491
Gedankenwelt des Chinesischen Kulturkreises, Die（Forke, Alfred）	佛尔克《中国文化领域的知识界》	B.	VOL. LIX	30-392
Gems of Chinese Literature（Giles, Herbert A.）	翟理思编《古文选珍》	M.	VOL. LIV	27-649
Gems of Chinese Verse（Fletcher, W. J. B.）	佛来遮《英译唐诗选》	Couling, C. E.	VOL. XLIX	25-213
Gèographie de l'Empire de Chine（Richard, L.）	夏之时《中国坤舆详志》	Ridge, W. Sheldon	VOL. XXXVIII	20-685
Geography of China, The（Cressey, George B.）	葛德石《中国地理》	Mason, Isaac	VOL. LIX	30-350
Geology of Shanghai, The（Cressey, George B.）	葛德石《上海的地质》	Chatley, Herbert	VOL. LX	31-156

(续表)

题　名	中译题名	责任者	卷期	页码
George Eumorfopoulos Collection Catalogue of the Chinese and Corean Bronzes, Sculpture, Jades, Jewellery and Miscellaneous Objects, The, v. 1（Yetts, W. Perceval）	颜慈编《颜氏集古录》卷一	Morgan, Evan	VOL. LX	31－149
George Eumorfopoulos Collection Catalogue of the Chinese and Corean Bronzes, Sculpture, Jades, Jewellery and Miscellaneous Objects, The, v. 2（Yetts, W. Perceval）	颜慈编《颜氏集古录》卷二	Morgan, Evan	VOL. LXI	31－416
George Eumorfopoulos Collection. Catalogue of the Chinese and Corean Bronzes, Sculpture, Jades, Jewellery, and Miscellaneous Objects, The, v. 3,（Yetts, W. Perceval）	颜慈编《颜氏集古录》卷三	Morgan, Evan	VOL. LXIV	33－183
Geschichte der alten Chinesischen Philosophie（Forke, Alfred）	佛尔克《古中国哲学史》	B.	VOL. LIX	30－392
Geschichte des Chinesischen Reichs, v. 1（Franke, O.）	福兰阁《中华帝国史》（卷一）	Chatley, Herbert	VOL. LXII	32－244
Giles' Dictionary	翟理思编《华英字典》	Ferguson, John Calvin	VOL. XLV	23－483
Giraffe in History and Art, The（Laufer, Berthold）	劳费尔《历史和艺术中的长颈鹿》	Sowerby, Arthur de Carle	VOL. LX	31－169
Gleanings from Fifty Years in China（Little, Archibald）	立德《旅华五十年拾遗》		VOL. XLII	22－254
Glimpses of the Yangtse Gorges（Plant, Cornell）	Plant《长江三峡》		VOL. LII	26－472
Glossary of Bacteriological Terms（College, P. V. M.）	College编《细菌学名词草案》		VOL. LXI	31－424
Gods of Northern Buddhism, The（Getty, Alice）	Getty《北方佛教的神》	Johnston, Reginald Fleming	VOL. XLVI	23－672
Goh or Wei Ch'i（Cheshire, Horace F.）	Cheshire《围棋完整指导手册》		VOL. LIV	27－654
Gramatica Chino-Espanola（Gonzalez, P. A.）	Gonzalez《汉文－西班牙文文法》	Mencarini, Juan	VOL. L	25－505
Grammar of Chinese Lattice, A（Dye, Daniel Sheets）	戴但理《中国格子窗入门》	Read, Bernard Emms	VOL. LXIX	34－562
Grammata Serica, Script and Phonetics in Chinese and Sino-Japanese（Karlgren, Bernhard）	高本汉《汉字字形类纂》	Gibson, Harry E.	VOL. LXXI	35－315
Great Cultural Traditions: The Foundations of Civilization, The（Turner, Ralph）	Turner《伟大的文明传统》	Roberts, Donald	VOL. LXXIII	35－620

(续表)

题名	中译题名	责任者	卷期	页码
Great Earthquake of 1923 in Japan, The (Bureau of Social Affairs Home Office, Japan)	日本社会事务局编《1923年日本关东大地震》	Sowerby, Arthur de Carle	VOL. LX	31-173
Greek-Chinese-English Dictionary of the New Testament (Stuart, J. Leighton)	司徒雷登《希腊文—中文—英文新约辞典》		VOL. L	25-487
Grottes de Touen-Houang, Les	《敦煌壁画》		VOL. LIII	27-302
Grottes de Touen-Houang, Les (Pelliot, Paul)	伯希和《敦煌壁画》	Wright, Harrison King	VOL. LII	26-488
Guide to the Qutb, Delhi, A (Page, J. H.)	Page《德里古特伯旅行指南》	S., H. P.	VOL. LIX	30-371
H					
Hand-book of China (Von Landesen, A.)	Landesen编《中国手册》	Ferguson, John Calvin	VOL. XL	21-417
Handbook of Cultural Institutions in China (Chyne, W. Y.)	Chyne《中国文化机构手册》		VOL. LXVIII	34-405
Hand-book of New Terms and Newspaper Chinese (Mateer, A. H.)	狄文爱德编《中文报纸新词手册》	Mason, Isaac	VOL. XLIX	25-201
Hangchow, the "City of Heaven," with a Breif Historical Sketch of Soochow, "The Beautiful" (Cloud, Frederick D.)	云飞得《人间天堂杭州及美丽苏州》	Woodbridge, S. Isett	VOL. XXXVIII	20-687
Harvard Medical School of China Reports, 1911-1916	《哈佛医学堂1911-1916年报告》	Stanley, Arthur	VOL. XLIX	25-182
Heart of Asia: a History of Russian Turkestan and the Central Asian Khanates from the Earliest Times, The	《亚洲腹地:俄罗斯突厥斯坦及中亚汗国史》		VOL. XXXIII	19-64
Heiligtümer des Konfuzianismus (Tschepe, Albert)	彭亚伯《儒学圣地》	Kingsmill, Thomas William	VOL. XXXIX	21-227
Herald Wind, The (Candlin, Clara)	坎德林《信风——宋代诗词歌赋选译》	Ayscough, Florence Wheelock	VOL. LXV	33-477
Heritage of Hiroshige, The (Amsden, Dora)	Amsden《安滕广重画集》	Stanley, Arthur	VOL. XLIV	23-223
Hinduism and Buddhism (Eliot, Charles)	义律《印度教与佛教》	Wright, Harrison King	VOL. LIII	27-314
Hirth Anniversary Vol.	《夏德纪念文集》	Chatley, Herbert	VOL. LV	28-272
Histoire de la Concession Française de Changhai (Maybon, Ch. B. & Fredet, Jean)	梅朋、傅立德《上海法租界史》	B.	VOL. LXI	31-404

(续表)

题　名	中译题名	责任者	卷期	页码
Histoire du Commerce du Levant au Moyen-âge（Heyde, W.）	海爱德《中世纪东方商业史》	Hirth, F.	VOL. XXII	12-490
Histoire Général de la Chine Et de ses Relations avec les Pays Étrangers Depuis les Temps les Plus Anciens Jusqu'a la Chute de la Dyanstie Mandchou（Cordier, Henri）	高第《中外关系通史》	M.	VOL. LIII	27-287
Historic Shanghai（Montalto de Jesus, C. A.）	Montalto de Jesus《上海史》	Lanning, George	VOL. XL	21-413
Historical and Commercial Atlas of China（Herrmann, Albert）	Herrmann《中国历史和商用地图》	Arnold, Julean Herbert	VOL. LXVII	34-230
Historical Atlas of the Chinese Empire	《中华帝国历史地图集》	Ferguson, John Calvin	VOL. LXIX	34-554
Historical Development of Religion in China, The（Clennell, W. J.）	乐民乐《中国宗教历史沿革》	Hodges, Ada	VOL. XLVIII	24-482
History of Babylonia and Assyria, The（Winckler, Hugo）	Winckler《巴比伦和亚述之历史》		VOL. XXXIX	21-224
History of China's Pictorial Art, The（Giles, Herbert A.）	翟理思《中国绘画史》		VOL. L	25-498
History of Chinese Medicine（Wong, K. Chimin & Wu, Lien-teh）	王吉民、伍连德《中国医史》	Hagerty, M. J.	VOL. LXIV	33-200
History of Chinese Philosophy, A（Fung Yu-lan）	冯友兰《中国哲学史》	Millican, Frank R.	VOL. LXIX	34-559
History of Christian Missions in China, A（Latourette, Kenneth Scott）	赖德烈《基督教在华传教史》	Mason, Isaac	VOL. LX	31-158
History of Early Chinese Painting from the Han Dynasty to the end of the Yuan Dynasty, A（Sirén, Osvald）	喜仁龙《中国早期绘画史》（汉到元末）	Gale, Esson Mcdowell	VOL. LXVI	33-632
History of Later Chinese Painting, A（Sirén, Osvald）	喜仁龙《中国晚近绘画史》	Sowerby, Arthur de Carle	VOL. LXIX	34-565
History of Shanghai, The（Lanning, G. and Couling, S.）	蓝宁、库寿龄《上海志》	M.	VOL. LII	26-476
History of the Early Relations Between the United States and China, 1784-1844, The（Latourette, Kenneth Scott）	赖德烈《早期中美关系史1784-1844年》	Lanning, George	VOL. XLIX	25-192
History of the Finger-Print System（Laufer, Berthold）	劳费尔《手印制度沿革》	Stanley, Arthur	VOL. XLV	23-465
History of the Former Han Dynasty, The（Pan Ku）	德效骞译班固《汉书》	Millican, Frank R.	VOL. LXIX	34-558

(续表)

题 名	中译题名	责任者	卷期	页码
History of the Peking Summer Palaces under the Ch'ing Dynasty（Malone, Carroll Brown）	麻伦《清代皇家园林史》	Murphy, Henry Killam	VOL. LXVI	33－640
History, Customs and Religion of the Ch'iang, The（Torrance, Thos.）	陶然士《青衣羌——羌人的历史、习俗和宗教历史》	Mason, Isaac	VOL. LI	26－214
Hopkins Collection of Inscribed Oracle Bone, The（Chalfant, Frank H.）	方法敛《金璋藏甲骨卜辞》	Gibson, Harry E.	VOL. LXX	35－127
Hors d'Oeuvre（Michie, A.）	宓吉《插曲》	D., C. E.	VOL. XXXIX	21－238
Household Industries in Soochow（Love, Elizabeth A.）	Love《苏州家庭工业》	Shaw, Norman	VOL. XLIX	25－207
Household Insects（Kellogg, C. R.）	克立鸽《家庭昆虫》	Teesadale, J. H.	VOL. XLVI	23－699
How Chinese Families Live in Peiping（Gamble, Sidney D.）	甘博《北平的中国家庭生活》	Wang, T. Ford	VOL. LXV	33－465
How to Identify Old Chinese Porcelain（Hodgson, Willoughby）	Hodgson《如何识别中国古瓷器》		VOL. XXXIX	21－224
Hsi Shih（Beauty of Beauties）（Mrs. Wu Lien-Teh）	伍连德夫人黄淑琼《西施》	Morgan, Marion L.	VOL. LXIII	32－465
Hsün Tze—the Moulder of Ancient Confucianism（Dubs, Homer H.）	德效骞《荀子》	Mason, Isaac	VOL. LIX	30－353
Huafêng Lao Jên（Piggott, Francis）	毕葛德《华封老人宪法意见书》	Bourne, Frederick Samuel Augustus	VOL. XLV	23－473

I

I-Li or Book of Etiquette and Ceremonial, The（Steele, John）	Steele译《仪礼》	M.	VOL. XLIX	25－178
Imaginative Interpretation of the Far East in Modern French Literature, The（Schwartz, W. L.）	Schwartz《现代法国文学中的远东想象》	Grosbois, Ch.	VOL. LIX	30－358
Imperial Palaces of Peking, The（Sirén, Oswald）	喜仁龙《北京紫禁城》	Werner, Edward Theodore Chalmers	VOL. LVIII	29－486
Imperial Portraits（Book Review）	《中国历代帝后像》	B.	VOL. XLVII	24－185
In Search of Old Peking（Arlington, L. C.）	阿灵敦《寻找老北京》	Crow, Carl	VOL. LXVII	34－233
In the Footsteps of Marco Polo（Bruce, C. D.）	卜禄士《沿着马哥孛罗的足迹前行》	Bourne, Frederick Samuel Augustus	VOL. XXXIX	21－239
In the Footsteps of the Buddha（Grousset, René）	格鲁塞《沿着佛陀的足迹》	Millican, Frank R.	VOL. LXIII	32－505

(续表)

题　　名	中译题名	责任者	卷期	页码
Inconstancy of Madame Chuang and Other Stories, *The*（Howell, E. B.）	豪厄尔《不坚定的庄夫人及其他中国短篇小说》	Shipway, G. W.	VOL. LVI	28－655
Index to the China Review（Ferguson, John C.）	福开森编《中国评论引得》	Wright, Harrison King	VOL. L	25－488
Index to the Tso Chuan（Fraser, Everard and Lockhart, J. H. S.）	法磊斯与骆任廷合编《左传引得》	Hughes, E. R.	VOL. LXIII	32－467
India in Transition（Khan, Aga）	Khan《转变中的印度》	Chatley, Herbert	VOL. LII	26－484
India's Demand for Transportation（Weld, W. E.）	Weld《印度的运输需求》	Wright, Harrison King	VOL. LII	26－474
Indian Archaeology	《印度考古》	Chatley, Herbert	VOL. L	25－477
Industrial and Social Importance of Forestry in China, *The*（Sherffsee, Forsythe）	余佛西《中国森林的产业意义和社会意义》	Stanley, Arthur	VOL. XLVIII	24－485
Influences Iraniennes en Asie Centrale et en Extreme-Orient, *Les*（Pelliot, Paul）	伯希和《伊朗在中亚与远东的影响》	MacGillivray, Donald	VOL. XLIV	23－204
Inner Asian Frontiers of China（Lattimore, Owen）	拉铁摩尔《中国之亚洲内陆边疆》	Dent, Robert V.	VOL. LXXI	35－307
Inscriptions of Yin Dynasty Divination Bones（Harvard-Yenching Institute）	哈佛燕京学社编《殷契卜辞》	Ferguson, John Calvin	VOL. LXIV	33－196
Insect-Musicians and Cricket Champions of China（Laufer, Berthold）	劳费尔《中国的昆虫音乐家和蟋蟀冠军》	Sowerby, Arthur de Carle	VOL. LX	31－172
Instruction Féminine en Chine, *L'*（Lin Pao-tchin）	林氏《中国女性教育》	T., M. B.	VOL. LVIII	29－505
International Aspect of the Missionary Movement in China, *The*（Wu, Chao-Kwang）	吴氏《中国传教运动的国际问题》	Morgan, Evan	VOL. LXII	32－236
International Relations of the Chinese Empire, *The*（Morse, Hosea Ballou）	马士《中华帝国对外关系史》	Hinckley, F. E.	VOL. XLII	22－257
International Relations of the Chinese Empire, *The*（Morse, Hosea Ballou）	马士《中华帝国对外关系史》	F., K. H.	VOL. L	25－501
Introduction to Chinese Art（Silcock, Arnold）	Silcock《中国美术导论》	Dunlap, Eva Wyman	VOL. LXVII	34－238
Introduction to Literary Chinese（Brandt, J.）	Brandt《中国文学导论》	Morgan, Evan	VOL. LVIII	29－515
Introduction to the History of Chinese Picturial Art, *An*（Giles, Herbert A.）	翟理思《中国绘画艺术史导论》	Ferguson, John Calvin	VOL. XXXVII	20－396
Introductory Mandarin Lessons（McHugh, J. M.）	麦克猷《华语新捷径》	Morgan, Evan	VOL. LXIII	32－496

(续表)

题　名	中译题名	责任者	卷期	页码
Is Japan a Menace to Asia?（Das, Taraknath）	达斯《日本是亚洲的威胁吗？》	M.	VOL. XLVIII	24-508
Islam in China: *A Neglected Problem*（Broomhall, Marshall）	海思波《中国的伊斯兰教》		VOL. XLII	22-253
Isle of Palms, *The*（M., M. M.）	M.《棕榈岛》	M.	VOL. LI	26-210
J				
Jade: *A Study in Chinese Archaeology and Religion*（Laufer, Berthold）	劳费尔《玉：中国考古和宗教研究》	Ayscough, Florence Wheelock	VOL. XLIV	23-215
Japan（Murray, David）	墨雷《日本国》		VOL. LII	26-481
Japan, *a Short Cultural History*（Sansom, G. B.）	桑慎《日本文化简史》	Roberts, R.	VOL. LXXIII	35-619
Japan's Beziehungen Zu China（Tschepe, Albert）	彭亚伯《日本对华关系》	Thomas, James.	VOL. XXXIX	21-215
Japan's Financial Relations with the United States（Odate, Gyoju）	小伊达《日美金融关系》		VOL. LIII	27-294
Jehol, *City of Emperors*（Hedin, Sven）	斯文赫定《皇城热河》	Chatley, Herbert	VOL. LXIV	33-195
Jesuits at the Court of Peking（Allan, C. Wilfrid）	林辅华《北京宫廷的耶稣会士》	Millican, Frank R.	VOL. LXVIII	34-386
John Chinaman at Home（Hardy, E. J.）	哈代《国内的中国佬》	L., A. E. N.	VOL. XXXVII	20-392
Junks and Sampans of the Yangtze, *The*, vol. 2（Worcester, G. R. G.）	夏士德《长江上的帆船和舢板》卷二	Pringle, J. C.	VOL. LXXIII	35-614
Justizwesen in China, *Das*（Holzhauer, F.）	Holzhauer《中国的司法体系》		VOL. XLIV	23-214
K				
Kan Ying Pien, *The*（Webster, James）	魏雅各译《感应篇》	L., A. L.	VOL. L	25-483
Keng Chih T'u, *Illustration of Husbandry and Weaving*	《耕织图》		VOL. LIV	27-652
Kêng Tschi T'u（Franke, O.）	福兰阁译《耕织图》		VOL. XLV	23-467
Key to the Birds of the Lower Yangtze Valley, *A*（Gee, N. Gist）	祈天锡《长江下游流域的鸟类》	M.	VOL. XLIX	25-183
Kiangsi Native Trade and Its Taxation（Wright, Stanley）	魏尔特《江西地方商业与税收》	M.	VOL. LI	26-225
Kiao Ou Ki Lio（Tobar, Jerôme）	管宜穆《教务纪略》	Couling, C. E.	VOL. XLIX	25-183
Konfuzius und sein Kult（Biallas, Franz Xavier）	鲍润生《孔子及其崇拜》	Buchanan, J. U.	VOL. LXI	31-410

(续表)

题　　名	中译题名	责任者	卷期	页码
Korea's Fight for Freedom（McKenzie, F. A.）	麦庚锡《朝鲜为自由而战》	Wright, Harrison King	VOL. LIII	27－293
"Kou-wen" Chinois, Le（Margoulies, G）	Margoulies《古文》	Dubs, Homer Hasenpflug	VOL. LVIII	29－509
L				
Laboratory Manual: Division of Bacteriology（College, P. V. M.）	College 编《实验室手册:细菌学》		VOL. LXI	31－423
Labour Movement and Labour Legislation in China, The（Lin, Tung-hai）	林东海《中国劳工运动与劳工立法》	Wang, T. Ford	VOL. LXVI	33－659
Land Forms of Chekiang, China, The（Cressey, George B.）	葛德石《浙江土地形态》	Sowerby, Arthur de Carle	VOL. LXX	35－125
Land of the Blue Poppy, The（Kingdon-Ward, F.）	Kingdon-Ward《蓝罂粟之地:一个博物学家藏东旅行记》	Bruce, Charence Dalrymple	VOL. XLV	23－443
Land Tax in China, The（Huang, Han Liang）	黄韩亮《中国之土地税》	M.	VOL. L	25－504
Land Utilization in China（Buck, John Lossing）	卜凯《中国土地的利用》	Read, Bernard Emms	VOL. LXIX	34－556
Laotse（Yen Fu）	严复评点本《老子》	Kingsmill, Thomas William	VOL. XXXVII	20－395
Laute von Gau Ming. Ein Chinesisches Singspiel in Deutscher Sprache, Die（Handhausen, Vincenz）	Handhausen《高明之琵琶记》	Chatley, Herbert	VOL. LXIII	32－481
Lectures on Biology（Bayne, P. M.）	Bayne《生物学讲座》		VOL. L	25－498
Legende de l'Empereur Açoka, La（Przyluski, J.）	Przyluski《阿育王时期印度与中国的佛教》	M., N.	VOL. LVI	28－644
Lehrgang der Chinesischen Schriftsprache（Haenisch, Erich）	黑尼施《汉文文言文教程》	Chatley, Herbert	VOL. LXIII	32－482
Lessons of History, The（Leavenworth, C. S.）	Leavenworth《历史的教训》	Shipway, G. W.	VOL. LVI	28－643
Letters from China and Japan（Dewey, John and Dewey, Alice Chipman）	杜威《中国和日本来信》		VOL. LIII	27－308
Letters to a Missionary（Johnston, Reginald F.）	庄士敦《致传教士的几封信》	Pott, Francis Lister Hawks	VOL. L	25－507
Li Duke of Ch'ien（Jackson, J. A.）	蔡文才译《李洴公穷邸遇侠客》		VOL. LIII	27－293
Li Hung Chang（Bland, J. O. P.）	濮兰德《李鸿章》	M.	VOL. XLIX	25－197

（续表）

题　名	中译题名	责任者	卷期	页码
Library North China Union Language School Books on China	《华北协和语言学校图书馆汉学书目》	M.	VOL. LXIII	32-489
Lingnaam Agricultural Review, *The*	《岭南农业评论》		VOL. LIV	27-652
Links Between Ancient China and the West（Yetts, W. Perceval）	颜慈《古代中国和西方的联系》	Couling, C. E.	VOL. LVIII	29-523
Lion and Dragon in Northern China（Johnston, Reginald F.）	庄士敦《威海卫狮龙共存》		VOL. XLII	22-249
List of Chinese-Moslem Terms（Mason, Isaac）	梅益盛《汉语与穆斯林词汇对照表》		VOL. L	25-513
List of Plants Found in Fukien Province（Walker, J. E.）	和约瑟《福建省植物名录》	Teesadale, J. H.	VOL. XLVI	23-699
List of Plants Found in Kiangsu Province（Gee, N. Gist）	祁天赐《江苏省植物名录》	Teesadale, J. H.	VOL. XLVI	23-699
Literary Chinese by the Inductive Method（Creel, Herrlee Glessner）	顾立雅等编《文言文入门——〈孝经〉》		VOL. LXIX	34-567
Literary Chinese by the Inductive Method Vol. II（Creel, Herrlee Glessner）	顾立雅等编《文言文入门——〈论语〉》	Read, Bernard Emms	VOL. LXX	35-131
Literary Inquisition of Ch'ien Lung, *The*（Goodrich, Luther Carrington）	傅路德《乾隆时期文字狱》	Gale, Esson Mcdowell	VOL. LXVI	33-646
Little Garland from Cathay, *A*（Gaunt, T.）	恭思道《中国小花环——唐诗译注》	Wright, Harrison King	VOL. LIII	27-289
Local Post of China（Rosenberg, W.）	Rosenberg《中国地方邮政》	Read, Bernard Emms	VOL. LXXII	35-442
Lore of the Chinese Lute, *The*（Van Guilk, R. H.）	高罗佩《琴道》	Read, Bernard Emms	VOL. LXX	35-131
Lotus of the Wonderful Law, *The*（Soothill, W. E.）	苏慧廉译《妙法莲华经》	Shipway, G. W.	VOL. LXI	31-418
Lung Men. The Door of the Dragon（Freer, Charles）	Freer《龙门》	Ayscough, Florence Wheelock	VOL. XLIII	22-445
Lun-Heng, pt. 1（Forke, Alfred）	佛尔克译《论衡》上卷	Kingsmill, Thomas William	VOL. XXXIX	21-218
Lun-Heng, pt. 2（Forke, Alfred）	佛尔克译《论衡》下卷	Medhurst, C. Spurgeon	VOL. XLIII	22-429
M				
Mahayana Doctrines of Salvation（Schayer, Stanislas）	沙耶《大乘经典》	Darroch, John	VOL. LV	28-277
Makers of Cathay, *The*（Allan, C. Wilfrid）	林辅华《中国的缔造者》	Ferguson, John Calvin	VOL. XLI	21-612
Makers of Cathay（Allan, C. Wilfrid）	林辅华《中国的缔造者》	Millican, Frank R.	VOL. LXVIII	34-406

(续表)

题　名	中译题名	责任者	卷期	页码
Manchu Abdication and the Powers, 1908 - 1912, The (Reid, John Gilbert)	李约翰《清帝逊位与列强》	Roberts, Donald	VOL. LXVII	34 - 233
Manchuria Year Book, 1931, The (Toa-Keizai Chosakyoku)	南满洲铁道株式会社东亚经济调查局编《满洲年鉴》（1931年）	McIntosh, G.	VOL. LXIII	32 - 471
Mandarin and Missionary in Cathay (Borstsmith, E. F.)	Borstsmit《中国的官吏与传教士》	Mason, Isaac	VOL. XLVIII	24 - 495
Manual of Chinese Metaphor, A (Williams, C. A. S.)	威立师《中国隐喻手册》	Ayscough, Florence Wheelock	VOL. LII	26 - 457
Manuale Pratico di Corrispondenza Cinese, con Annotazioni, Regole, Tavole, Etc. (Guseo, Marco)	各塞额《义文释注函续汇编》		VOL. XLV	23 - 463
Manuel des Superstitions Chinoises (Dore, Henri)	禄是道《中国迷信手册》	Couling, C. E.	VOL. LVIII	29 - 518
Manuel du Code Chinois (Boulais, Guy)	Boulais《中国法律手册》	Buchanan, J. U.	VOL. LV	28 - 287
Marchands Europeens en Cochin Chine et au Tonkin (1600 - 1775), Les (Maybon, Ch. B.)	梅朋《交址支那和东京的欧洲商人》	Brenan, Byron	VOL. XLVIII	24 - 497
Matteo Ricci's Scientific Contribution to China (Bernard, Henri)	裴化行《利玛窦对中国科学的贡献》	Chatley, Herbert	VOL. LXVII	34 - 231
Maze Collection of Chinese Junk Models in the Science Museum, The	《科学博物院梅乐和爵士之中国帆船模型收藏》	Sowerby, Arthur de Carle	VOL. LXX	35 - 125
Medical Guide	《医药指南》	P., A. C.	VOL. LIX	30 - 332
Melanges d'Histoire et de Geographie Orientales (Cordier, Henri)	高第《东方历史地理杂记》		VOL. LIV	27 - 652
Melanges sur la Chronologie Chinoise	《中国纪年论集》		VOL. LI	26 - 211
Memoirs of Li Hung Chang (Mannix, William Francis)	Mannix《李鸿章回忆录》		VOL. XLV	23 - 487
Mencius (Lyall, Leonard A.)	赖发洛译《孟子》	Morgan, Evan	VOL. LXIII	32 - 468
Mentor Department of Art, The (Book Review)	《门特艺术部》	M.	VOL. L	25 - 488
Mi Fu on Ink Stones (Van Guilk, R. H.)	高罗佩《米芾"砚史"》	Sowerby, Arthur de Carle	VOL. LXIX	34 - 562
Millionaire's Courtship, A (Little, Archibald)	立德《百万富翁的求婚》	Ferguson, John Calvin	VOL. XXXVII	20 - 405
Mineral Wealth of China (Wong, William A.)	王氏《中国的矿产资源》	Chatley, Herbert	VOL. LIX	30 - 340

（续表）

题　　名	中译题名	责任者	卷期	页码
Mining Laws of the Republic of China	《中华民国采矿法》	Teesadale, J. H.	VOL. XLVI	23-699
Mirabilia Descripta. Les Merveilles de l'Asie (de Severac, Jourdain Catalene)	de Severac《亚洲的奇迹》	Scott, James	VOL. LVIII	29-507
Mischief-Working Metric System, The (Werner, E. T. C.)	倭纳《公制之祸害》	Mason, Isaac	VOL. LXII	32-246
Mission Archéologique dans la Chine Septentrionale (Chavannes, Edouard)	沙畹《华北考古图谱》	Warren, Gilbert G.	VOL. XLVI	23-687
Mission d'Ollone 1906-1909	多伦《中国禁地1906年至1909年之考察》	Merz, C.	VOL. XLIII	22-434
Mission to Heaven, A (Richard, Timothy)	李提摩太译《西游记》	Ferguson, John Calvin	VOL. XLV	23-486
Modern China. A Political Study (Cheng, Sih-Gung)	程锡庚《现代中国政治研究》	M.	VOL. LI	26-206
Modern Chinese History (McNair, Harley Farnsworth)	宓亨利《现代中国历史》	Shipway, G. W.	VOL. LV	28-288
Modern Japan-Social, Industrial, Political (Hershey, Amos. S. & S. W.)	Hershey《近代日本社会、工业和政治》	Mason, Isaac	VOL. LI	26-213
Modern Newspaper Chinese (Brandt, J. J.)	卜郎特《摩登新闻丛编》	Gale, Esson Mcdowell	VOL. LXVII	34-232
Moon Year, The (Bredon, Juliet & Mitrophanow, Igor)	裴丽珠与米托发诺《农历年》	Lester, E. S.	VOL. LIX	30-370
Moral Tenets and Customs in China (Wieger, L.)	戴遂良《中国之道德理念与习俗》		VOL. XLIV	23-231
More Gems of Chinese Verse (Fletcher, W. J. B.)	佛来遮《英译唐诗选续集》		VOL. LI	26-212
Most Noble and Famous Travels of Marco Polo Together with the Travels of Nicolo dé Conti, The (Penyer, N. M.)	Penyer译《马可波罗游记与孔蒂游记》	Moule, Arthur Christopher	VOL. LXI	31-399
Must We Fight Japan? (Pitkin, Walter B.)	Pitkin《我们必须与日本开战吗?》		VOL. LIII	27-308
My Chinese Marriage (F., M. T.)	F.《我的中国婚姻》	M.	VOL. LIV	27-644
My Nestorian Adventure (Holm, Fritz)	何乐模《我为景教碑在中国的历险》	Shipway, G. W.	VOL. LV	28-280
My Orient Pearl (Cotton, Charles)	Cotton《我的东方明珠》	M.	VOL. LII	26-481
Mythical and Practical in Szechuan (Hutson, James)	Hutson《四川的神话与现实》	K., L.	VOL. XLVII	24-179

(续表)

题　名	中译题名	责任者	卷期	页码
Mythologie des Buddhismus in Tibet und der Mongolei（Gruenwedel, A.）	Gruenwedel《西藏与蒙古的佛教神话》	Forke, A.	VOL. XXXIII	19－324

N

题　名	中译题名	责任者	卷期	页码
Nanking Journal, vol. 1, no. 1	《金陵学报》（第一卷，第一期）	Zia, Z. K.	VOL. LXIII	32－488
National Quarantine Service Reports, Series II, 1931（Wu, Lien-Teh & Wu, Chang-yao）	伍连德等编《国家检疫工作报告》（1931年第二期）	Maxwell, J. L.	VOL. LXIII	32－486
Nationalism and Education in Modern China（Peake, Cyrus H.）	毕格《近代中国之民族主义与教育》	Lyon, David Willard	VOL. LXV	33－454
Naturalist in Western China, A（Wilson, Ernest Henry）	威尔荪《一位博物学家在华西》	Stanley, Arthur	VOL. XLV	23－469
Nature in Chinese Art（Sowerby, Arthur de C.）	苏阿德《中国美术中的自然》	Read, Bernard Emms	VOL. LXXI	35－313
Nature Notes（Sowerby, Arthur de C.）	苏阿德《自然笔记》		VOL. LXXI	35－313
Nestorian Documents and Relics in China, The（Saeki, P. Y.）	佐伯氏《中国的景教文献与遗物》	Read, Bernard Emms	VOL. LXIX	34－565
Nestorian Monument in China, The（Saeki, P. Y.）	佐伯氏《中国的景教碑》	M.	VOL. XLVIII	24－463
Netherlands India, a Study of Plural Economy, The（Furnivall, J. S.）	Furnivall《荷属印度多元经济研究》	Read, Bernard Emms	VOL. LXX	35－131
New Atlas and Commercial Gazetteer of China, The（Dingle, Edwin John）	丁乐玫编《中国新地图和商业地名索引》	M.	VOL. L	25－469
New China Review for 1920, The（Couling, Samuel）	库寿龄编《新中国评论》（1920年）	Wright, Harrison King	VOL. LII	26－487
New China Review, The. Nos. 1 and 2.（Book Review）	《新中国评论》第一期和第二期	M.	VOL. L	25－491
New Fresh-Water Goby from Tientsin, A（Shaw, Tsen-hwang）	寿振黄《天津出现的新种淡水鱼》	Sowerby, Arthur de Carle	VOL. LX	31－170
New Mind and Other Essays, A（Morgan, Evan）	莫安仁《新思想及其他论文》	Shipway, G. W.	VOL. LXI	31－409
New New Terms（Morgan, Evan）	莫安仁《官话最新用词汇编》	Shipway, G. W.	VOL. LVII	29－241
New Terms and Expressions（Morgan, Evan）	莫安仁《官话新词语汇编》		VOL. XLV	23－477
New Terms for New Ideas（Morgan, Evan）	莫安仁《新思想新名词》		VOL. XLV	23－477
New Testament of Higher Buddhism, The（Richard, Timothy）	李提摩太《高等佛教新契约》		VOL. XLII	22－248

(续表)

题　名	中译题名	责任者	卷期	页码
Ninety Common Birds of the Lower Yangtze（Allison）	沈文蔚《长江下游常见鸟类90种》	Lanning, George	VOL. XLVI	23-699
Northeastern Asia, A Selected Bibliography（Kerner, Robert J.）	Kerner《东北亚选目》	Gale, Esson Mcdowell	VOL. LXXI	35-305
Noted Porcelains of Successive Dynasties	《历代名瓷图谱》	Morgan, Evan	VOL. LXIII	32-509
Notes from a Frontier（Ainscough, T. M.）	Ainscough《边境纪实——四川》	Porter, Karola	VOL. XLVII	24-174
Notes on Chinese Documentary Style（Hirth, F.）	夏德《中国公文格式》	Ferguson, John Calvin	VOL. XLI	21-619
Notes on Chinese Painting with Reproductions from My Collection（Abraham, R. D.）	亚伯拉罕《本人藏中国画之评论》	Ayscough, Florence Wheelock	VOL. XLVIII	24-500
Notes on Chinese Porcelain（Wilkinson, F. E.）	伟晋颂《中国陶瓷介绍》	Ferguson, John Calvin	VOL. XL	21-417
Notes on Turquois in the East（Laufer, Berthold）	劳费尔《东方绿松石》	Stanley, Arthur	VOL. XLV	23-467
O				
"O Mei" Moon and Other Poems（Lee, Alan W. Simms）	李爱伦《峨嵋月及诗》	Ayscough, Florence Wheelock	VOL. LIII	27-305
Old Chinese Porcelain and Works of Art in China（Bahr, A. W.）	鲍尔禄《中国古瓷美术谱》		VOL. XLII	22-252
Old Tartar Trails（Kent, A. S.）	Kent《鞑靼古道》		VOL. LI	26-207
On the Cephalic Index and Stature of the Japanese and their Local Difference（Matsumura, Akira）	松浦氏《日本人的头指数、身高以及当地的差异》	Shirokogoroff, Sergei Mikhailovich	VOL. LVII	29-249
On the Laws of Japanese Painting（Bowrie, Henry P.）	包理《论日本绘画风格》	Stanley, Arthur	VOL. XLIV	23-225
On the Trail of the Opium Poppy（Hosie, Alexander）	谢立三《鸦片问题探索:中国主要产烟省份旅行记》	Couling, Samuel	VOL. XLVI	23-700
On Three Antique Lutes（Van Guilk, R. H.）	高罗佩《三琴考古》	Read, Bernard Emms	VOL. LXX	35-128
Oracle Records from the Waste of Yin（Menzie, James Mellons）	明义士《殷墟卜辞》	Couling, Samuel	VOL. XLVIII	24-489
Origin of the Buddha Image, The（Ananda, K.）	Ananda《佛像起源》	Chatley, Herbert	VOL. LIX	30-376
Origin of Tibetan Writing	《藏文书写的起源》	T., J. Ch.	VOL. L	25-473

(续表)

题　名	中译题名	责任者	卷期	页码
Origine et Évolution de l'Écriture Hiéroglyphique et de l'Écriture Chinoise (Kenn, Won)	Kenn《中国象形文字的起源和演化》	Couling, C. E.	VOL. LIX	30-376
Our Eastern Question (Millard, Thomas F.)	密勒《我们的东方问题》		VOL. XLVIII	24-500
Outline of the Capital Reconstruction Work, The	《日本东京重建工程概要》	Chatley, Herbert	VOL. LXI	31-428
Outline of Universal History, An (Sokolsky, George Ephraim)	索克思《世界史大纲》	Roberts, Donald	VOL. LIX	30-358
Outline of Yin Bone Inscriptions, Yin Ch'i T'ung Shih (Hsü, Hsieh-chên)	徐协贞《殷契通释》	Ferguson, John Calvin	VOL. LXV	33-456
Outlines of Chinese Art (Ferguson, John C.)	福开森《中国美术大纲》	Stanley, Arthur	VOL. LI	26-204
Outlines of Chinese History (Li Ung Bing)	李文彬《英文中国史略》	M.	VOL. XLIX	25-194
Outlines of Chinese Symbolism (Williams, C. A. S.)	威立师《中国表号学解》	Brown, Margaret Helen	VOL. LXIII	32-490
P				
Pageant of Peking, The (Mennie, Donald)	Mennie《北京历史勾陈》	I., O.	VOL. LII	26-471
Painting in the Far East (Binyon, Lawrence)	彬雄《远东绘画》	Ferguson, John Calvin	VOL. XLIV	23-205
Paper Money in China (Kann, E.)	耿爱德《中国的纸币》	Sowerby, Arthur de Carle	VOL. LXX	35-125
Passing of the Dargon, The (Keyte, J. C.)	祈仰德《龙之消逝——陕西革命和救援军的故事》	M.	VOL. XLIV	23-230
Passing of the Manchus, The (Kent, P. H.)	甘博士《满族的消失》		VOL. XLIV	23-217
Pearl Chaplet, The (Fletcher, W. J. B.)	佛来遮《珍珠项链》	Mason, Isaac	VOL. XLVII	24-174
Peking (Bredon, Juliet)	裴丽珠《北京》	M.	VOL. LI	26-218
Peking the Beautiful (White, Herbert C.)	怀沛云《美丽的北京》	Ferguson, John Calvin	VOL. LIX	30-317
Peking to Paris: An Account of Prince Borghese's Journey Across Two Continents in a Motor Car (Barzini, Luigi)	巴兹尼《北京至巴黎汽车拉力赛80天》		VOL. XXXIX	21-224

(续表)

题 名	中译题名	责任者	卷期	页码
Peking, A Historical and Intimate Description of its Chief Places of Interest（Bredon, Juliet）	裴丽珠《北京》	M.	VOL. LIII	27－299
Peking, A Social Survey（Gamble, Sidney D.）	甘博《北京社会调查》	Kulp II, Daniel H.	VOL. LIII	27－309
Pencil Speakings from Peking（Grantham, Alexandra Etheldred）	葛量洪《北京笔谈》	Wright, Harrison King	VOL. LIV	27－642
Penetration of Money Economy in Japan and its Effects upon Social and Political Institutions, The（Takizawa, Matsuyo）	泷泽氏《货币经济对日本的渗透及其对社会和政治体制的影响》	Stedeford, E. T. A.	VOL. LVIII	29－536
Penetration of Yunnan, The（Stout, Arthur Purdy）	Stout《穿越云南》	Ridge, W. Sheldon	VOL. XLIII	22－432
Peoples of Asiatic Russia（Jochelson, Waldernar）	Jochelson《北亚的俄国人》	Sowerby, Arthur de Carle	VOL. LX	31－173
Philology and Ancient China（Karlgren, Bernhard）	高本汉《中国语言学研究》	B	VOL. LIX	30－373
Philosophie de la Nature dans l'Art d'Extrême Orient, La（Petrucci, Raphael）	Petrucci《远东艺术自然哲学》	Ayscough, Florence Wheelock	VOL. XLIII	22－419
Philosophie Morale et Politique de Mencius, La（Yuan Chaucer）	袁擢英《孟子的德政哲学》	Elia, Pascal M. d'	VOL. LIX	30－318
Philosophy of Human Nature, The（Chu Hsi）	朱熹《心性哲学》	Chatley, Herbert	VOL. LIV	27－647
Philosophy of Wang Yang Ming, The（Henke, F. G.）	Henke《王阳明的哲学思想》	M.	VOL. XLVIII	24－471
Photographic Intensification and Reduction（Dent, R. V.）	Dent《摄影密度和减薄》	Gillett, T. H.	VOL. LXXI	35－312
P'ing-tzǔ-lei-p'ien	《骈字类编》	Hirth, F.	VOL. XXII	12－493
Plantae Wilsonianae（Wilson, Ernest Henry）	威尔荪《威尔荪植物标本》	MacGillivray, Donald	VOL. XLIII	22－445
Poetry	《诗歌》	M.	VOL. L	25－506
Portrait of a Chinese Lady（Hosie, Lady）	谢福芸《中华女士》	Shipway, G. W.	VOL. LXI	31－407
Postage Stamps of Japan and Dependencies, The（Woodward, A. M. Tracey）	伍德华《日本邮票及附属品》	Sowerby, Arthur de Carle	VOL. LX	31－177

(续表)

题　　名	中译题名	责任者	卷期	页码
Practical Chinese（Aldrich，Harry S.）	Aldrich《华语须知》	Morgan, Evan	VOL. LXIII	32－476
Practical Sanskrit Dictionary, *A*（Macdonell, Arthur Anthony）	麦多纳《实用梵语字典》	MacLeod, N.	VOL. LV	28－292
Preliminary List of the Plants of Kiangsu Province, *A*（Gee, N. Gist）	祁天锡《江苏植物初录》	Stanley, Arthur	VOL. XLIX	25－182
Preliminary Report on Some Coals from Szechuan（Hubbard, Geo. H.）	许志高《四川煤矿初步报告》	Chatley, Herbert	VOL. LVIII	29－524
Premier Voyage de "L'Amphitrite" en Chine, *Le*（Pelliot, Paul）	伯希和《昂菲特里特号始航中国记》	Morgan, Marion L.	VOL. LXIII	32－498
Present Day Political Organization in China（Brunnert, H. S. & Hagelstrom, V. V.）	卜内特等《当前中国的政治组织》	Jowett, Hardy	VOL. XLIV	23－198
Present-Day China（Harding, Gardner L.）	哈尔定《今日中国》	B.	VOL. XLVIII	24－496
Present-Day Japan（Tsurumi, Yusuke）	鹤见氏《今日日本》	Mason, Isaac	VOL. LVIII	29－534
Problems of Chinese Education（Purcell, Victor）	伯塞尔《中国之教育问题》	Millican, Frank R.	VOL. LXVIII	34－395
Problems of Industrial Development in China（Vinake, Harold M.）	费纳克《中国工业发展问题》	Morgan, Evan	VOL. LVIII	29－525
Progress of Chinese Studies in the United States of America	《美国之中国研究的新进展》	Millican, Frank R.	VOL. LXIII	32－482
Prose Poetry of Su Tung-p'o, *The*（Le Gros Clark, Cyril Drummond）	李高洁译《苏赋》	Wang, T. Ford	VOL. LXVII	34－225
Protection of Trade-Marks, Patents, Copyrights and Trade-Names in China（Allman, Norwood F.）	阿乐满《贸易保护：中国的注册商标、图案、版权、商号》	Williams, Samuel Wells	VOL. LVI	28－651
Proverbs and Maxims in the Chinese Language（Grone, H. Dawson）	克勒纳《汉语中的谚语与格言》	M.	VOL. XLIV	23－229

Q

题　　名	中译题名	责任者	卷期	页码
Quarterly Bulletin of Chinese Bibliography（Yuan, T. L.）	袁同礼主编《中国图书季刊》	Read, Bernard E.	VOL. LXXI	35－318
Questions de Milinda Milindapanha, *Les*（Finot, Louis）	Finot《那先比丘经》	M., N.	VOL. LVI	28－653

R

题　　名	中译题名	责任者	卷期	页码
Railway Enterprise in China（Kent, P. H.）	甘博士《中国铁路发展沿革史》	Ferguson, John Calvin	VOL. XL	21－416
Recent Events and Present Policies in China（Bland, J. O. P.）	濮兰德《中国最近的事变和现在的政策》		VOL. XLIV	23－193

(续表)

题名	中译题名	责任者	卷期	页码
Recherches sur les Superstion en Chine（Dore, Henri）	禄是遒《中国迷信研究》	Chatley, Herbert	VOL. XLIX	25-188
Recherches sur les Superstitions Chine（Dore, Henri）	禄是遒《中国迷信研究》	Chatley, Herbert	VOL. LI	26-208
Recherches sur les Superstitions en Chine（Dore, Henri）	禄是遒《中国迷信研究》	M.	VOL. XLIV	23-227
Recherches sur les Superstitions en Chine（Dore, Henri）	禄是遒《中国迷信研究》	Wright, Harrison King	VOL. L	25-511
Recherches sur les Superstitions en Chine（Dore, Henri）	禄是遒《中国迷信研究》	Budd, Charles	VOL. LX	31-175
Reconstruction of Modern Educational Organizations in China（Yin, Chiling）	殷氏《中国现代教育机构重建》	W., E. W.	VOL. LV	28-286
Record of Buddhistic Kingdoms, A（Legge, Dr.）	理雅各译《佛国记》	Giles, Herbert A.	VOL. XXI	12-322
Recueil de Nouvelles Expressions Chinoises	《中文短语汇编》	M.	VOL. XLIV	23-227
Reindeer and its Domestication, The（Laufer, Berthold）	劳费尔《驯鹿及其驯化》	Stanley, Arthur	VOL. XLIX	25-181
Religion des Chinois, La（Granet, Marcel）	葛兰言《中国的宗教》	Jamieson, C. A.	VOL. LIV	27-654
Religion of the Chinese, The（Groot, J. J. M. de）	高延《中国的宗教》	Merz, C.	VOL. XLI	21-610
Religions of Ancient China（Giles, Herbert A.）	翟理思《古代中国宗教》	Ferguson, John Calvin	VOL. XXXVII	20-405
Remains of Lao-tzǔ, The（Giles, Herbert A）	翟理思重译《道德经》	Kingsmill, Thomas William	VOL. XXI	12-124
Remains of Yin Dynasty Inscriptions on Carapaces and Bones -Yin Ch'I I Ts'un（Shang Ch'êng-tsu）	商承祚辑《殷契佚存》	Ferguson, John Calvin	VOL. LXV	33-469
Reply Letters（Smith, S. P.）	Smith《复信》		VOL. LI	26-212
Report of the Division of Orientalia（Hummel, W.）	慕恒义《美国国会图书馆东方学部报告》	Read, Bernard E.	VOL. LXXI	35-317
Report of the Hon. Mr. Justice Feetham, C. M. G. to the Shanghai Municipal Council	《费唐递交给上海公共租界工部局的报告》	Pott, Francis Lister Hawks	VOL. LXII	32-229
Report on the Hydrographic of the Whangpoo	《黄浦江水文报告》	Tyler, William Ferdinand	VOL. XLVIII	24-498
Re-shaping of Far East, The（Weale, B. L. Putnam）	辛博森《远东之新调整》	L., A. E. N.	VOL. XXXVII	20-394

(续表)

题　　名	中译题名	责任者	卷期	页码
Review of the Scientific Work Done on Chinese Materia Medica, A (Read, Bernard Emms and Liu, Ju-chiang)	伊博恩与刘汝强《中国药物学研究述评》	Sowerby, Arthur de Carle	VOL. LX	31-171

S

题　　名	中译题名	责任者	卷期	页码
Sammlung (Von der Heydt, Eduard)	冯德海《收藏》	Dunlap, Eva Wyman	VOL. LXVIII	34-402
San Kuo or Romance of the Three Kingdoms (Brewitt-Taylor, C. H.)	邓罗译《三国演义》		VOL. LVII	29-235
San Kuo, or the Romance of the Three Kingdoms (Brewitt-Taylor, C. H.)	邓罗译《三国演义》	Morgan, Evan	VOL. LVIII	29-524
San Min Chu I & The Three Principles (Sun Yat-sen)	孙中山《三民主义》	Darroch, John	VOL. LIX	30-333
Sayings of the Mongols (Oost, Josephe van)	彭嵩寿《蒙古族谚语》		VOL. L	25-499
School Books (Commercial Press)	新式小学教科书	Darroch, John	VOL. XXXVII	20-398
Second Report of Progress in Manchuria (to 1930) (South Manchuria Railway)	南满洲铁道株式会社撰《南满洲铁道报告书》（二）	Shipway, G. W.	VOL. LXIII	32-481
Secret of the Golden Flower, The (Wilhelm, Richard)	卫礼贤译《太乙金华宗旨》	Shipway, G. W.	VOL. LXIII	32-477
Secrets told in the Bamboo Grove (Dutton, Helen Wiley)	Dutton《竹林中的秘密》	Read, Bernard Emms	VOL. LXXII	35-450
Sectarianism and Religious Persecution in China (Groot, J. J. M. de)	高延《宗教史的一页：中国的宗教教派和宗教迫害问题》	Ferguson, John Calvin	VOL. XXXVII	20-405
Sericulture (Gee, N. Gist)	祁天赐《蚕桑》	Teesadale, J. H.	VOL. XLVI	23-699
Shanghai Birds (Wilkinson, E. S.)	Wilkinson《上海鸟类》	Sowerby, Arthur de Carle	VOL. LXI	31-425
Shanghai, its Mixed Court and Council (Kotenev, A. M.)	郭泰纳夫《上海会审公堂与工部局》	Chatley, Herbert	VOL. LVI	28-649
Shanghai: its Municipality and the Chinese (Kotenev, A. M.)	郭泰纳夫《上海公共租界工部局与华人》	Sowerby, Arthur de Carle	VOL. LVIII	29-527
Shangtung, the Sacred Province of China (Forsyth, R. C.)	法思远《山东》	Warren, Gilbert G.	VOL. XLIII	22-446
Short History of Shanghai, A (Pott, F. L. Hawks)	卜舫济《上海简史》	Chatley, Herbert	VOL. LX	31-157
Short History of Shanghai, A (Clark, J. D.)	开乐凯《上海简史》	Mason, Isaac	VOL. LIV	27-651

(续表)

题　名	中译题名	责任者	卷期	页码
Short History of the Far East, *A* (Latourette, Kenneth Scott)	赖德烈《远东简史》	Perry, Charles E.	VOL. LXXIII	35-623
Silver Money (Leavens, Dickson H.)	Leavens《银两》	Sowerby, Arthur de Carle	VOL. LXX	35-124
Sinism (Creel, Herrlee Glessner)	顾立雅《中国世界观的演变》	Morgan, Evan	VOL. LXI	31-412
Sino-Iranica (Laufer, Berthold)	劳费尔《中国伊朗编：中国对古伊朗文明史的贡献》	O., M.	VOL. LI	26-215
Sino-Portuguese Trade from 1514 to 1644 (Chang, T'ien-tsê)	张天泽《1514-1644年间的中葡贸易》	Roberts, Donald	VOL. LXV	33-475
Sir Robert Hart (Bredon, Juliet)	裴丽珠《赫德爵士传奇》	Ferguson, John Calvin	VOL. XL	21-412
Sketch of Chinese Arts and Crafts, *A* (Strong, Hilda Arthurs)	Strong《中国艺术与手工艺概要》	Dunlap, Eva Wyman	VOL. LXIV	33-197
Sketch of Chinese History, *A* (Pott, F. L. Hawks)	卜舫济《中国史纲要》	Ferguson, John Calvin	VOL. XXXIX	21-237
Sketch of Chinese History, *A* (Pott, F. L. Hawks)	卜舫济《中国史纲要》	M.	VOL. XLVII	24-187
Small Collection of Japanese Lacquer, *A* (Orange, James)	柯伦治《日本漆器小收藏》	Ayscough, Florence Wheelock	VOL. XLIII	22-440
Social Organization of the Manchus (Shirokogoroff, S. M.)	史禄国《满族的社会组织》	Chatley, Herbert	VOL. LV	28-275
Some Aspects of Japanese Feudal Institutions (Asakawa, K.)	朝河贯一《日本封建制度的若干特色》	M.	VOL. L	25-504
Some Chinese Painters of the Present Dynasty (Hirth, Friedrich)	夏德《清代画家记略》	Ferguson, John Calvin	VOL. XXXVII	20-396
Some Industries of Soochow (Jones, E. V.)	龚士《苏州的若干产业》	Shaw, Norman	VOL. XLIX	25-207
Some West China Hunting Notes (Day, Dye-fu)	Day《华西狩猎笔记》	Teesadale, J. H.	VOL. XLVI	23-695
Sound and Symbol in Chinese (Bernhard Kalgren)	高本汉《汉语语音与汉语言字》		VOL. LIV	27-661
Souvenirs of a Journey Through Tartary, Tibet and China During the Years 1844, 1845 & 1846 (Huc, E.)	古伯察作《1844、1845、1846年鞑靼、西藏与中国内陆行记》	Roberts, Frances M.	VOL. LXIV	33-198
Spirit of Chinese Poetry, *The* (Purcell, V. W. W. S.)	伯塞尔《中国诗歌的神韵》	Sowerby, Arthur de Carle	VOL. LX	31-164
Sport and Science on the Sino-Mongolian Frontier (Sowerby, Arthur de C.)	苏阿德《中蒙边界渔猎爱好与科学》	Lanning, George	VOL. L	25-492

(续表)

题 名	中译题名	责任者	卷期	页码
Sportsman's Miscellany, A (Sowerby, Arthur de C.)	苏阿德《渔猎者杂记》	Lanning, George	VOL. XLIX	25-202
Statesman, Patriot, and General in Ancient China (Bodde, Derk)	卜德《古代华夏的政治家、爱国者和将领》	Ferguson, John Calvin	VOL. LXXI	35-302
Stewart Lockhart Collection of Chinese Copper Coins, The (NCBRAS)	亚洲文会编《洛任廷爵士的中国古铜钱币收藏》	S.	VOL. XLVII	24-184
Story of the "Pinna and the Syrian Lamb" and Other Three Stories, The (Laufer, Berthold)	劳费尔《栉孔扇贝与叙利亚羔羊的故事及其他故事三则》	Maybon, C. B.	VOL. L	25-479
Structural Principles of the Chinese Language, an Introduction to the Spoken Language (Northern Pekingese Dialect), The (Mullie, Jos)	Mullie《汉语结构性原则——汉语口语入门》	Gale, Esson Mcdowell	VOL. LXIV	33-189
Structural Principles of the Chinese Language, The (Mullie, J.)	Mullie《汉语结构性原则》		VOL. LXIX	34-563
Studien und Schilderungen aus China, no. 1 (Tschepe, Albert)	彭亚伯《中国研究》第一期《泰山》	Merz, C.	VOL. XL	21-409
Studies in History, Economics and Public Law (Columbia University Faculty of Political Science)	哥伦比亚大学政治学系编《历史、经济和公共法律之研究》	Medhurst, C. Spurgeon	VOL. XLV	23-450
Studies in Na-Khi Literature (Rock, Joseph F.)	罗克《纳西文学研究》	Read, Bernard Emms	VOL. LXIX	34-564
Studies in the Decorative Art of Japan (Piggott, Francis)	毕葛德《日本装饰艺术研究》	Stanley, Arthur	VOL. XLII	22-256
Study of Chinese Alchemy, A (Johnson, Obed Simon)	约翰逊《中国炼丹术考》	Chatley, Herbert; Couling, C. E.	VOL. LIX	30-346
Study of Chinese Paintings in the Collection of Ada Small Moore, A (Hackney, Louise Wallace)	哈克尼《摩尔收藏中的中国绘画研究》	Ferguson, John Calvin	VOL. LXXII	35-438
Study of Shintō, the Religion of the Japanese Nation, A (Katō, Genchi)	加藤源次《日本神道研究》	Shipway, G. W.	VOL. LXI	31-426
Study of the Grand Period of Growth in Bamboo, A (Porterfield, Willard Merritt, Jr.)	包达甫《竹子的生长大周期研究》	Sowerby, Arthur de Carle	VOL. LX	31-170
Sun Yat-sens Vermächtnis (Amann, Gustav)	Amann《孙中山的遗产》	Ungern-Sternberg, L.	VOL. LIX	30-360
Supplemental Notes on Walrus and Narwhal Ivory (Laufer, Berthold)	劳费尔《海象牙和独角鲸鱼齿贸易补充说明》	Stanley, Arthur	VOL. XLIX	25-181
Supplementary Notes to "The Study of Forged Books" of Yao Chi-hêng (Huang, Yün-mei)	黄云眉辑《古今伪书考补证》		VOL. LXV	33-468

(续表)

题名	中译题名	责任者	卷期	页码
Survey of Chinese Art（Ferguson, John C.）	福开森《中国艺术综览》	Gale, Esson Mcdowell	VOL. LXX	35-134
Sutra of the Lord of Healing, The (Liebenthal, Walter)	Liebenthal《治愈神之经》	Millican, Frank R.	VOL. LXVIII	34-385
Sva (Birdwood, George C. M.)	Birdwood《Sva》	Chatley, Herbert	VOL. LII	26-485
Swinging Lanterns（Enders, Elizabeth Crump）	Enders《摇摆的灯笼》	Shipway, G. W.	VOL. LV	28-282
Symbolism in Chinese Art（Yetts, W. Percrval）	颜慈《中国艺术中的象征主义》	MaGrath, C. D.	VOL. XLV	23-474
Symbols of Yi King or the Symbols of the Chinese Logic of Changes, The (Sung, Z. D.)	沈仲涛译《〈易经〉的符号》	Millican, Frank R.	VOL. LXVIII	34-393
Synopsis of Chinese History, and Friendly Books on Far Cathay (Ayscough, Florence)	爱司克夫人《中国历史纲要》	Mason, Isaac	VOL. XLVIII	24-494
Szechwan. Its Products, Industries and Resources (Hosie, Alexander)	谢立三《四川的物产、实业和资源》	M.	VOL. LIV	27-646

T

题名	中译题名	责任者	卷期	页码
T'ai Chan, Le (Chavannes, Edouard)	沙畹编《泰山志》		VOL. XLIII	22-436
Tai Shan (Baker, Dwight C.)	Baker《泰山》		VOL. LVI	28-643
Tanggu Meyen and other Manchu Reading Lessons (Fraser, Forbes A.)	Fraser《满文百话及其他满文阅读》	S.	VOL. LVIII	29-535
Tao: The Great Luminant, Huai Nan Hung Lieh (Morgan, Evan)	莫安仁《淮南鸿烈》	Chatley, Herbert	VOL. LXVI	33-631
Taoïsme, Le (Wieger, L.)	戴遂良《道教》	Merz, C.	VOL. XLV	23-445
Taoist Teachings from the Book of Lieh Tzu (Giles, Lionel)	翟林奈《列子中的道家学说》	Medhurst, C. Spurgeon	VOL. XLIII	22-430
Tariff Problem in China, The (Chu, Chin)	朱氏《中国海关关税问题》	Lanning, George	VOL. XLVIII	24-487
Temperature en Chine et a Quelques Stations Voisines, La	《中国及其邻国哨站气温》	Shaw, Norman	VOL. L	25-495
Temple Bells and Silver Sails (Enders, Elizabeth Crump)	Enders《庙钟与银帆》	Shipway, G. W.	VOL. LVIII	29-537
Temples of Anking and Their Cults, The (Shryock, John Knight)	施赖奥克《安庆的寺庙及其崇拜》	Morgan, Marion L.	VOL. LXIV	33-193
Temples of the Western Hills, The (Hubbard, Gilbert Ernest)	赫播德《西山的寺庙》	Shipway, G. W.	VOL. LV	28-283

(续表)

题名	中译题名	责任者	卷期	页码
Tentative Classification of the Races of China, A (Liu, Chungshee H.)	刘氏《试析中国种族分类》	Sowerby, Arthur de Carle	VOL. LXIX	34-563
Territoires et Populations des Confins du Yunnan (Siguret, J.)	奚居赫《云南边地问题研究》	Baude, R. L. P.	VOL. LXVIII	34-403
Text of Yi King, The (Sung, Z. D.)	沈仲涛译《易经》	Millican, Frank R.	VOL. LXVIII	34-394
Textes Oraux Ordos (Mostaert, Antoine)	田清波《鄂尔多斯口述文本》	Gillett, Michael Cavenagh	VOL. LXXIII	35-613
They Saw China's Far West (Roberts, Frances M.)	Roberts《他们看见了中国遥远的西部》	Read, Bernard Emms	VOL. LXX	35-133
Things Chinese (Ball, J. Dyer)	波乃耶《中国风物》		VOL. LVII	29-237
Three Hundred Precepts for Chinese Taoist Monks, The (Hackmann, Heinrich)	哈克曼《道士三百戒规》	Fuchs; Morgan, Marion L.	VOL. LXIII	32-512
Three Religions of China, The (Soothill, William Edward;)	苏慧廉《中国之三教》	Parker, Alvin Pierson	VOL. XLIV	23-219
Through Jade Gate and Central Asia (Cable, Mildred & French, Francesca)	盖群英、冯贵珠《玉门和中亚之行》	Burt, E. W.	VOL. LIX	30-377
Through the Chinese Revolution (Farjenel, Fernand)	Farjenel《辛亥革命亲历记》	B.	VOL. XLVII	24-181
Thunder Out of China (White, Theodore H.)	白修德《中国雷鸣》	Roberts, Frances M.	VOL. LXXIII	35-623
Tibetan Book of the Dead, The (Evans-Wentz, W. Y.)	Evans-Wentz《中阴闻教得度》	Chatley, Herbert	VOL. LIX	30-352
T'ien Hsia Monthly (Sun Yat-sen Institute for the Advancement of Culture and Education)	上海中山文化教育馆编辑《天下》		VOL. LXVI	33-661
Timber Rafts on the Lower Yangtze	《长江下游的木排》	M.	VOL. L	25-489
Title Index to the Catalogue of the Gest Oriental Library (Gillis, I. V.)	义理寿编《葛思德东方藏书库书目》	Ferguson, John Calvin	VOL. LXXII	35-438
Tomb Tile Pictures of Ancient China (Book Review, White, William Charles)	怀履光《中国古墓砖图考》	Gibson, Harry E.	VOL. LXX	35-126
Tombs of Old Lo-Yang (White, William Charles)	怀履光《洛阳故城古墓考》	Morgan, Evan	VOL. LXV	33-482
Totemic Traces Among the Indo-Chinese (Laufer, Berthold)	劳费尔《印度和中国图腾崇拜遗存》	T., J. Ch.	VOL. L	25-471
Tour in Mongolia, A (Bulstrode, Beatrix)	布斯卓《蒙古之旅》		VOL. LII	26-456

题　　名	中译题名	责任者	卷期	页码
Trade and Administration of China, *The*（Morse, Hosea Ballou）	马士《中朝制度考》修订版	M.	VOL. LII	26－460
Trade and Administration of the Chinese Empire, *The*（Morse, Hosea Ballou）	马士《中朝制度考》	Hinckley, F. E.	VOL. XXXIX	21－225
Tragedies of Eastern Life（Lim Boon Keng）	林文庆《东方人的悲剧》	Shipway, G. W.	VOL. LIX	30－345
Traité Manicheen Retrouvé en Chine, *Un*（Chavannes, E. et Pelliot, P.）	沙畹与伯希和合编《摩尼教流行中国考》	MacGillivray, Donald	VOL. XLIV	23－203
Trans-Himalaya: *Discoveries and Adventures in Tibet*（Hedin, Sven）	斯文赫定《横越喜马拉雅山——在西藏的发现和探险》	H., L. F.	VOL. XLI	21－612
Transmarine Emigration of Chinese and its Influence on the White and Yellow Races; a Study in Political Economy, *The*（Gottwaldt, H.）	Gottwaldt《海外中国移民及其对白种人和黄种人的影响》	Reymond, C. du Bois	VOL. XLV	23－461
Träume aus Chinas Frühlings-Herbst-Annalen, *I. Abschnitt*	《春秋经戏曲》第一部	Ferguson, John Calvin	VOL. XLI	21－618
Travels in China, *1894 to 1940*（Fischer, Emil S.）	斐士《1894－1940 年在华旅行记集》	Read, Bernard Emms	VOL. LXXI	35－307
Travels of a Chinese Poet, *Tu Fu*, *Guest of Rivers and Lakes*, vol. II（Ayscough, Florence）	爱司克夫人《一个中国诗人之旅:杜甫》	Fitch, R. F.	VOL. LXV	33－480
Travels of a Consular Officer in North-West China（Teichman, Eric）	台克满《领事官在中国西北的旅行》	M.	VOL. LIII	27－297
Travels of Marco Polo, *The*（Ricci, Aldo）	Ricci 译《马可波罗游记》	Morgan, Evan	VOL. LXIII	32－479
Triple Demism of Sun Yat Sen, *The*（Elia, Pascal M. d'）	德礼贤译《孙中山三民主义》	Shipway, G. W.	VOL. LXII	32－243
Triple Demisme de Suen Wen, *Le*（Elia, Pascal M. d'）	德礼贤译《孙中山三民主义》	Buchanan, J. U.	VOL. LXI	31－422
Truth and Tradition in Chinese Buddhism（Reichelt, Karl Ludvig）	艾香德《中国佛教中的真理和圣传》	K., J. C. D.	VOL. LIX	30－327
Tu Fu-the Autobiography of a Chinese Poet（Ayscough, Florence）	爱司克夫人《杜甫——一个中国诗人的传记》	Shipway, G. W.	VOL. LXI	31－411
Twilight Hour of Yang Kuei Fei, *The*（Grantham, Alexandra Etheldred）	葛量洪《杨贵妃的暮日》	Shipway, G. W.	VOL. LV	28－285
Twin Pagodas of Zayton, *The*（Ecke, Gustav）	艾克《刺桐双塔——中国晚近佛教雕塑研究》	Cressy, Earl Herbert	VOL. LXVII	34－220

(续表)

题　　名	中译题名	责任者	卷期	页码
Two Gentlemen of China (Hosie, Lady)	谢福芸《两位华人绅士》	Shipway, G. W.	VOL. LV	28-273
Two Hundred Common Birds of the Yangtse Valley (Baker, H. A.)	贝开文《长江流域常见鸟类百种》	Lanning, George	VOL. XLVI	23-699
Two Lamaistic Pantheons (Clark, Walter Eugene)	喀刺格《两座喇嘛教神殿》	Millican, Frank R.	VOL. LXIX	34-557
Two Years in the Forbiddent City (Princess Der Ling:)	德龄《清宫二年纪》	Morgan, Evan	VOL. XLIII	22-427
Typhoon of July 28th 1915 (Froc., L.)	Froc.《镇海1915年7月28日台风》		VOL. XLVII	24-176
Tzŭ-Chin Shan, an Alkali-Syenite Area in Western Shansi (Norin, E.)	Norin《紫金山：山西西部碱性正长岩区》	M.	VOL. LIII	27-299

U

Unknown Mongolia (Carruthers, Doughlas)	Carruthers《不为人知的蒙古》	Couling, Samuel	VOL. XLV	23-488
Untersuchungen über das Yüan-ch'ao Pi-shi (*Die Geheime Geschichte der Mongolen*) (Haenisch, Erich)	黑尼施《元朝秘史探究》	Chatley, Herbert	VOL. LXIII	32-475
Ursprung der Chinesen auf Grund ihrer alten Bilderschrift, Der (Forke, Alfred)	佛尔克《从古老的象形文字看中国人的起源》	B.	VOL. LVIII	29-519

V

Variètès Sinologiques. Nos. 27 et 30 (Tschepe, Albert)	彭亚伯《汉学丛书》第27和30号	M.	VOL. XLV	23-458
Variètès Sinologiques. Nos. 36, 39, 41, 42 (Dore, Henri)	禄是遒《汉学丛书》第36, 39, 41, 42期	M.	VOL. XLVI	23-676
Variètès Sinologiques. Nos. 44, 45, 46 (Dore, Henri)	禄是遒《汉学丛书》第44, 45, 46期		VOL. XLVIII	24-491
Vegetationsskizze der Taihu-Berge, Eine (Limpricht, W.)	Limpricht《太湖植被概要》	Ruffé, M. d'Auxion de	VOL. XLV	23-470
Village and Town Life in China (Leong, Y. K.)	梁氏《中国城乡生活》	Couling, Samuel	VOL. XLVII	24-178
Village in August (Hsiao Chun)	萧军《八月的乡村》	Roberts, Frances M.	VOL. LXXIII	35-621
Vocabularies to the Elementary Chinese Texts Used at Harvard University (Ware, James R)	魏鲁男《哈佛大学基础汉语教材词汇》		VOL. LXVIII	34-404
Voyages of American ships to China, 1784-1844 (Latourette, Kenneth Scott)	赖德烈《美国轮船1784-1844年中国之旅》	Couling, C. E.	VOL. LVIII	29-527

(续表)

题名	中译题名	责任者	卷期	页码
Vues du Honan	《陇海线中州风景》		VOL. LI	26-215
W				
Wang An Shih: a Chinese Statesman and Educationalist of the Sung Dynasty, vol. 1 (Williamson, H. R.)	魏礼模《王安石——宋朝政治家和教育家》卷一	Gale, Esson Mcdowell	VOL. LXVII	34-213
Wang An Shih, a Chinese Statesman and Educationalist of the Sung Dynasty, vol. 2-3 (Williamson, H. R.)	魏礼模《王安石——宋朝政治家和教育家》卷二和卷三	Gale, Esson Mcdowell	VOL. LXVIII	34-392
Ways That Are Dark (Walsh, W. G.)	华立熙《黑道》	Bitton, W. Nelson	VOL. XXXVIII	20-688
Wenli Styles and Chinese Ideals (Morgan, Evan)	莫安仁《文理文体与中文思想》	Ward, John	VOL. XLIII	22-449
Western Tibet and the British Borderland (Sherring, Charles A.)	Sherring 等《西藏西部与英印边界》	Kingsmill, Thomas William	VOL. XXXVIII	20-679
Western Travellers to China (Roberts, Frances Markley)	Roberts《西人中国游记》	Gale, Esson Mcdowell	VOL. LXIV	33-190
What's Right With China (Rasmussen, O. D.)	雷茂盛《中国之好——对外国人攻击的回应》	Roberts, Donald	VOL. LIX	30-337
"Where Chinese Drive": Student Life in Peking by a Student Interpreter	《中国向何处去:北京的学生生活》		VOL. XX	11-548
Who's Who in China	《中国人名录》		VOL. LII	26-464
Who's Who of the Chinese in New York (Van Norden, W. M.)	Van Norden《纽约华人名录》	M.	VOL. XLIX	25-202
Wild Life in China (Lanning, George)	蓝宁《闲话中国鸟兽》	Stanley, Arthur	VOL. XLIII	22-431
Winter Birds about Peking (Lanning, George)	蓝宁《北京冬季鸟类》	Teesadale, J. H.	VOL. XLVI	23-698
With the Russians in Mongolia (Perry-Ayscough, H. G. C. & Otter-Barry, R. B.;)	爱司格等《与俄罗斯人在蒙古》	G.	VOL. XLVI	23-679
Within the Walls of Nanking (Hobart, Alice Tisdale)	Hobart《南京城内》	Couling, C. E.	VOL. LIX	30-362
Wong's System for Analysing Chinese Characters	《王云五的四角号码检字系统》	Chatley, Herbert	VOL. LX	31-159
Wong's System of Chinese Lexicography (Wong, Y. W.)	王云五《王氏四角号码检字法》	Darroch, John	VOL. LVIII	29-517
Word of the Buddha, The (Nyanatiloka)	向智尊者《佛偈》	Budd, Charles	VOL. LX	31-176

(续表)

题 名	中译题名	责任者	卷期	页码
Work in Tibet (Sörensen, Theo.)	徐丽生《在西藏传教》		VOL. LII	26-472
Working Forces in Japanese Politics, The (Iwasaki, Uichi)	岩崎夘一《日本政治中的动力》	Wright, Harrison King	VOL. LII	26-474
Works of Hsün Tze, The (Dubs, Homer H.)	德效骞《荀子作品选译》	Mason, Isaac	VOL. LIX	30-355
World Conception of the Chinese, The (Forke, Alfred)	佛尔克《中国人的世界概念》	Shipway, G. W.	VOL. LVI	28-651
Writings on Chinese Architecture (Yetts, W. Perceval)	颜慈《中国建筑著作概要》	Lester, E. S.	VOL. LVIII	29-521

Y

题 名	中译题名	责任者	卷期	页码
Yang Kuei-fei (Mrs. Wu, Lien-teh)	伍连德夫人黄淑琼《杨贵妃》	Shipway, G. W.	VOL. LV	28-284
Yearbook of the Netherlands East Indies, 1916	《荷属东印度群岛1916年年鉴》	Shaw, Norman	VOL. XLIX	25-210
Yellow Rivers; Adventures in a Chinese Parish (Cressy, Earl Herbert)	葛德基《黄河——一个中国教友的历险》	Porter, Lucius Chapin	VOL. LXVII	34-219
Yenching Science Conference Papers (The Peking Society of Natural History Bulletin)	北京自然史学会通报社编《燕京科学会议论文》	Sowerby, Arthur de Carle	VOL. LXI	31-424
Yunnan, the Link between India and the Yangtsze	《云南——连接印度与长江的纽带》	Bruce, Charence Dalrymple	VOL. XL	21-406

释 疑

题 名	中译题名	责任者	卷期	页码
Ages of Candidates at Chinese Examinations; Tabular Statement	中国科举考试的考生年龄	Oxenham, E. L.	VOL. XXIII	13-298
Alleged Old Import of Porcelain in Europe, An	欧洲据称进口自中国之瓷器	Hirth, F.	VOL. XXIII	13-46
American School and Chinese History, The	美国学校与中国历史课程		VOL. LXIII	32-522
Analysis of Brick from the Great Wall of China	长城墙砖分析	Brazier, J. S.	VOL. XXII	12-240
Ancient China in America	古代汉人在美洲	Hirth, F.	VOL. XX	11-633
Ancient Use of Wheels for the Propulsion of Vessels by the Chinese	中国古代船只推进中轮子的使用	Volpicelli, Z.	VOL. XXVI	15-135
Andaman Cannibals in Chinese Literature, The	中国文献中的晏陀蛮人	Hirth, F.	VOL. XXII	12-487

(续表)

题　名	中译题名	责任者	卷期	页码
Areas of Races	民族区域	Edkins, Joseph	VOL. XXI	12-236
Attempt to Burn Books during the T'ang Dynasty, An	吴海焚书	Giles, Herbert Allen	VOL. XX	11-725
Beri-Beri	《成医会月报》中的"脚气"报告		VOL. XX	11-498
Bird Collection in the Shanghai Museum	亚洲文会博物院鸟类标本拾遗		VOL. XL	21-405
Birth of Tsêng Kuo-fan	曾国藩生辰指正	Imbault-Huart, Camille	VOL. XX	11-630
Book Trade in China	关于中国书业贸易的询问		VOL. XX	11-503
Burial Customs	葬俗		VOL. XLI	21-607
Burning-Lens Sent to China, A	询问一段关于马戛尔尼送给中国皇帝"取火镜"的文字	Taylor, F. E.	VOL. XX	11-732
Cement for Pasting Porcelain	瓷器的上色接合剂	Hirth, F.	VOL. XXII	12-488
Character 中 on Walls, The	关于上海等地街道房屋墙面上"中"字的询问		VOL. XX	11-503
China Monuments Society	中国碑刻研究会	Couling, Samuel	VOL. XLV	23-491
China Monuments Society	中国碑刻研究会		VOL. XLVI	23-705
China Society, The	伦敦中国学会	Ferguson, John Calvin	VOL. XXXVIII	20-678
China under the Empress Dowager	关于濮兰德著《慈禧外纪》的说明		VOL. XLIV	23-241
China's Monuments	中国石碑补遗	Ferguson, John Calvin	VOL. XLIV	23-241
Chinese Characters as Dress Ornaments	作为衣服装饰的中国文字	Playfair, G. M. H.	VOL. XX	11-540
Chinese for the Bar of a River, The	"Bar"的汉译再议	Playfair, G. M. H.	VOL. XXI	12-237
Chinese Glassware	关于中国玻璃制品的询问		VOL. XX	11-503
Chinese Inscription from Ceylon, A	锡兰出土的中国碑刻		VOL. XLV	23-489
Chinese Land Measure	中国土地量度	Kingsmill, Thomas William	VOL. XX	11-537
Chinese li, The	关于中国计量单位"里"的询问		VOL. XX	11-503
Chinese Proverb about Ship's Crews, A	中国航海谚语	Hirth, F.	VOL. XX	11-633

(续表)

题　　名	中译题名	责任者	卷期	页码
Chinese Rudeness	上海《画报》所载中国文人对西人的嘲讽	Giles, Herbert Allen	VOL. XX	11－533
Chinese Term for Bar	"Bar"的汉译——铁板沙	Edkins, Joseph	VOL. XXI	12－116
Christian Mounment at Hsi-an Fu, The	《论西安景教碑》勘误与补记	Moule, Arthur Christopher	VOL. XLIV	23－243
Colloquial Analysis of Chinese Surnames, The	中国姓氏的口语表达		VOL. XXI	12－232
Condition of the Rural Population in China, The	中国农业人口状况	Kingsmill, Thomas William	VOL. XXVI	15－134
Corean Mints	关于朝鲜货币的询问	Dennys, H. L.	VOL. XX	11－733
Corrigenda	勘误		VOL. XLVII	24－193
Criticism on a Work by the Late Chinese Minister to Russia	评王之春《使俄草》	Parker, Edward Harper	VOL. XXX	18－191
Death of Yang Kuei-fei, The	杨贵妃之死	Giles, Herbert Allen	VOL. XX	11－721
Derivation of the Word Hoppo	"河保"一词起源	Hirth, F.	VOL. XX	11－542
Dictionary Omissions	字典拾遗	Parker, Edward Harper	VOL. XXXVII	20－386
Difficult Passage, A	《东周列国志》中"鹄"歌的翻译	Giles, Herbert Allen	VOL. XX	11－726
Does Public Opinion Exist Among the Chinese?	中国人中存在公共舆论吗？	Kliene., R.	VOL. XX	11－733
Early Foreign Coins in China	中国之早期外国钱币	F., H. D.	VOL. XX	11－635
East Asiatic Society of Boston	波士顿东亚攻究会笔记杂谈		VOL. XL	21－405
Ephthalites, The	挹怛人	Edkins, Joseph	VOL. XXI	12－235
Errata, Etc.	勘误等		VOL. XLVI	23－706
Exhibition of Chinese Paintings and T'ang Sculptures, Collection Jessel	国画与唐朝雕塑展	Almblad, A. F.	VOL. XLV	23－489
Exhibition of Old Chinese Porcelain and Works of Art	中国古代瓷器和艺术品展		VOL. XL	21－403
Exhibitiong of Chinese Paintings, the	国画特展		VOL. XLIII	22－454
Extinct Title	废弃的称号——"文渊殿大学士"	Playfair, G. M. H.	VOL. XX	11－540
False Beard Worn by an Empress, A	女王武则天所戴的假胡须	T., C. B.	VOL. XX	11－732
Foreign Art in China	西方艺术在中国	Nye, Gideon	VOL. XX	11－624

(续表)

题 名	中译题名	责任者	卷期	页码
Formation of Hangchow Bay	杭州湾的形成	M.	VOL. XXIII	13－45
Fu-Lin, a Persian Word	波斯语词"拂菻"	Edkins, Joseph	VOL. XXI	12－117
German Word "Hühnerauge", The	德语词"鸡眼"	Hirth, F.	VOL. XX	11－633
Ginger in China	中国之姜	Playfair, G. M. H.	VOL. XX	11－537
Goethe and Chinese Fiction	歌德与中国小说	Morgan, Marion L.	VOL. LXIII	32－519
Guild Terrorism	官府对汕头行商林应坤的迫害	Playfair, G. M. H.	VOL. XX	11－627
Hereditary Jurisdiction in South-West of China	中国西南地区的土司制度	Playfair, G. M. H.	VOL. XX	11－628
Hereditary Monstrosities	关于遗传畸形的询问		VOL. XX	
History of Turko-Scythian Tribes	突厥部落的历史	Kingsmill, Thomas William	VOL. XXVI	15－129
Hu-man-ts'ao, a Chinese Poison	中国毒药胡蔓草	Giles, Herbert Allen	VOL. XX	11－498
Hung-lou-mêng, The	《红楼梦》	Giles, Herbert Allen	VOL. XX	11－497
Inspectorate of Customs in Peking	《申报》对北京海关税务司署外籍人士的蔑称	Giles, Herbert Allen	VOL. XX	11－541
Italian Sinologues	意大利的汉学家	Nocentini, Ludovico	VOL. XX	11－731
Journal, Re-issue of Early Volumes, The	早期《亚洲文会会刊》将重印		VOL. XLV	23－491
Kangaroos in Central Asia	关于《梦溪笔谈》"中亚袋鼠"（跳兔）的询问	F., H. D.	VOL. XXII	12－489
Kangaroos in Central Asia	关于"中亚袋鼠"（跳兔）的回答	Möllendorff, O. F. von.	VOL. XXII	12－613
Kennelly's Edition of Richard's *Comprehensive Geography*	甘沛澍增订翻译夏之时著《中国坤舆详志》	Kingsmill, Thomas William	VOL. XXXIX	21－201
Kuanyin Pusa and Attendants	观音造像		VOL. XLVII	24－193
Kung（公）as a Personal Pronoun by Han Kao-Tsu	汉高祖以"公"自称	Imbault-Huart, Camille	VOL. XX	11－630
Lecture on Mongolia, the	关于蒙古的演讲		VOL. XLIII	22－454
Letter to Society Secretary, A	致亚洲文会会长的信	Warner, Langdon	VOL. XLV	23－492
Library of the NCBRAS	亚洲文会北华支会图书馆	Ayscough, Florence Wheelock	VOL. XLVII	24－188
Library, The	亚洲文会北华支会图书馆		VOL. XXXIX	21－199

(续表)

题　名	中译题名	责任者	卷期	页码
Manchu Horse-breeding Grounds	满洲的养马场	Parker, Edward Harper	VOL. XXII	12-484
Marco Polo's Journey in Manzi	马可·波罗在"蛮子"的旅行	Ferguson, John Calvin	VOL. XXXVII	20-380
Military Superstition	军事迷信	T., C. B.	VOL. XX	11-732
Miryeks, or "Stone Men" of Corea, The	朝鲜的"石人"		VOL. XXII	12-608
Miscellaneous Notes	杂记	Parker, Edward Harper	VOL. XXXVII	20-387
Miscellaneous Notes	杂记	Parker, Edward Harper	VOL. XXXVIII	20-673
Miscellaneous Notes	杂记	Parker, Edward Harper	VOL. XXXIX	21-212
Mistranslation, A	"圆明园上路"误译	Playfair, G. M. H.	VOL. XX	11-540
Modern Sinology and the Tao Teh King	当代汉学与《道德经》	Kingsmill, Thomas William	VOL. XXXVII	20-382
Mongol Giant, A	蒙古巨人	Giles, Herbert Allen	VOL. XXI	12-118
More about Fu-lin	"茀林"("拂菻")考	Edkins, J. & Hirth, F.	VOL. XX	11-729
Mr. F. Kingdon Ward's Paper	关于本卷 Ward, F. K. 文章的说明		VOL. XLVII	24-190
NCBRAS New Publication	亚洲文会新近出版物		VOL. XLVI	23-705
Nestorian Relics in North Kiangsu	苏北的景教遗物	Patterson, B. C.	VOL. XLIII	22-452
New Star in Nebula Andromedae, The	仙女座星云中的新星	F., H. D.	VOL. XX	11-634
Note on the Ephthalites A. D. 450	再论"挹怛人"	Edkins, Joseph	VOL. XXII	12-611
Notes and Queries	释疑		VOL. XLVIII	24-509
Notes and Queries	释疑		VOL. XLIX	25-218
Notes and Queries	释疑		VOL. L	25-514
Notes and Queries	释疑		VOL. LI	26-226
Notes and Queries	释疑		VOL. LII	26-492
Notes and Queries	释疑		VOL. LIII	27-318
Notes and Queries	释疑		VOL. LIV	27-665
Notes on *Popular Gods*	关于《神仙杂记》的询问	Imbault-Huart, Camille	VOL. XX	11-637
Notes on Yule	关于裕尔著作的读书笔记	Parker, Edward Harper	VOL. XXXVII	20-385

(续表)

题　名	中译题名	责任者	卷期	页码
Nye on Filial Piety, Mr.	奈益论"孝敬"	Nye, Gideon	VOL. XX	11－732
Old Chinese Books	中国古书	Hirth, F.	VOL. XX	11－499
Opium Smokers in Prisons	大牢里的鸦片鬼		VOL. XX	11－498
Origin of the Word "Tangutan", The	"党项"一词的起源	Rockhill, W. W.	VOL. XX	11－724
Parker's Travels in Chekiang, Mr.	庄延龄《浙江行记》指正	Moule, A. E.	VOL. XX	11－501
Phallic Monuments in Shansi	山西的生殖崇拜石碑	Goodrich, Luther Carrington	VOL. LXIII	32－521
Physiology in the Shanghai Dialect	上海方言发音的生理学研究	Edkins, Joseph	VOL. XXI	12－114
Popular Designation of Chinese Radicals	汉语偏旁部首的俗称	Playfair, G. M. H.	VOL. XX	11－631
Prefectures, Districts and Chief Towns of Japan in Chinese and Romanised Japanese	日本府县市名称汉字与罗马字对照	Playfair, G. M. H.	VOL. XX	11－534
Professor Giles's "Adversaria Sinica," Nos. 4 and 5	翟理思著《翟山笔记》第四、五期	Kingsmill, Thomas William	VOL. XXXVIII	20－668
Proposal to Establish in China a School for Higher Chinese Studies	在中国建立中国学高等研究院的建议	MacGillivray, Donald	VOL. XLI	21－608
Proposed Admistrative Changes in Formosa	台湾行政区划变化	Playfair, G. M. H.	VOL. XXI	12－113
Quality of Silver	银的成色	Morse, Hosea Ballou	VOL. XXXVII	20－381
Rekem-Petra-Likan	古城佩特拉地名考	Galt, E. W.	VOL. XX	11－543
Rekem-Petra-Likan	古城佩特拉	Hirth, F.	VOL. XX	11－632
Reprint of Journal	《亚洲文会会刊》重印		VOL. XLVI	23－706
Reprints of Journal	《亚洲文会会刊》重印		VOL. XLVII	24－190
Review of the Far East, The	《远东时报》	Ferguson, John Calvin	VOL. XXXVIII	20－677
Sale of Office in China	中国之卖官鬻爵	Parker, Edward Harper	VOL. XXII	12－484
School-boy Days of Sun Yat Sen in Hawaii, The	孙中山在夏威夷的学习时光	Sharman, Lyon	VOL. LXIII	32－515
Siwangmu and K'wenlun	西王母与昆仑	Kingsmill, Thomas William	VOL. XXXVII	20－375
Sleeping Buddha, The	卧佛像		VOL. XLVII	24－193

(续表)

题　名	中译题名	责任者	卷期	页码
Snuff in China	中国之倭烟	Hirth, F.	VOL. XX	11-501
Snuff in China	中国之鼻烟	Hirth, F.	VOL. XX	11-541
South-Pointing Needle	关于指南针的询问		VOL. XX	11-503
South-Pointing Needle	指南针	T., C. B.	VOL. XX	11-543
Sunflower, The	关于向日葵在中国之种植及功用的询问		VOL. XX	11-544
Supplement to the List of Surnames in Williams' Dictionary	卫三畏《汉英韵府》姓名补录	Playfair, G. M. H.	VOL. XXI	12-114
Talé-Lamas, The	达赖喇嘛	Rockhill, W. W.	VOL. XX	11-723
Thousand Character Numerals Used by Artisans	手工艺人所使用的"千字文"	Giles, Herbert Allen	VOL. XX	11-725
Translation into Chinese	英诗汉译		VOL. XL	21-401
Translation of Two Familiar Letters	译袁枚书信两封	Giles, Herbert Allen	VOL. XX	11-726
Transliteration	音译问题	Merz, C.	VOL. XL	21-398
Tribe of Pu-lu-k'o-pa or Bhotan, The	川藏布鲁克巴部落	Imbault-Huart, Camille	VOL. XX	11-728
Two Yangs, The	二杨	Forke, A.	VOL. XXXVII	20-390
Water-tight Compartments in Chinese Vessels	中国船只的水密舱	Playfair, G. M. H.	VOL. XXI	12-114
Wei Yüan on the Mongols	魏源论蒙古人	Parker, Edward Harper	VOL. XXII	12-485
Were the K'i-tan Fire Worshippers?	契丹的"日火"崇拜	Imbault-Huart, Camille	VOL. XX	11-630
Who was Pu-to-li?	波多力是谁	Edkins, Joseph	VOL. XX	11-728
Yue-Ti or Massagetae, The	月氏/马萨格泰人	Edkins, Joseph	VOL. XXI	12-235
呢 Ni(Broadcloth)	呢	Playfair, G. M. H.	VOL. XXI	12-237
呢 Ni(Broadcloth)	再论"呢"	Hirth, F.	VOL. XXI	12-237

杂记和札记

题名	中译题名	责任者	卷期	页码
Barometric and Thermometric Observations Taken during the Month of September 1864, with a View to Determining the Height of the Lew Shan	庐山1864年9月气压气温观测和高度测量	Hollingworth and Piry	VOL. I	3-195
Century of American Commerce with China, A (Nye, Gideon)	奈益《百年中美商业往来》摘录		VOL. XX	11-736
Critical Notes on Some Translations from the Chinese by Mr. Parker	评庄延龄的谚语汉译	Giles, Herbert Allen	VOL. XXI	12-121
Extracts from a Report upon the Present Condition of the Sea Wall at the Head of Hang-chow bay	杭州湾海塘现状报告摘要	Edward, R. E.	VOL. I	3-188
Folk-lore Society, The	香港民俗学会	Lockhart, J. H. Stewart	VOL. XXI	12-128
Items	杂录		VOL. XX	11-509
Li Ki, The	书讯:理雅各译《礼记》		VOL. XX	11-548
List of Ferns Found in the Valley of the River Min, Foochow (Miscellaneous)	福州闽江河谷发现的几种蕨类植物		VOL. XVI	10-257
Literary Note	理雅各着手翻译新版《庄子》		VOL. XXIV	13-496
Literature	文献书目		VOL. XX	11-510
Miscellaneous	杂记		VOL. IV	4-272
New Historical Work, A	历史著作《圣训》刊行	Edkins, Joseph	VOL. XXII	12-614
North-China Herald: *A Trip to Corea*	北华捷报馆版《朝鲜纪行》介绍		VOL. XX	11-737
Notes on the Funeral Rites Performed at the Obsequies of Takee	Takee葬礼上的仪式	Butcher, H.	VOL. II	3-395
Notes on the Tao Teh King	《道德经》注释	Kingsmill, Thomas William	VOL. XXXI	18-514
Notices on New Books and Literary Notes	新书通告与文献札记		VOL. XX	11-735
Notices on New Books and Literary Notes	新书通告与文献札记		VOL. XXI	12-322
Peking Oriental Society, The	北京东方学会	Drew, E. B.	VOL. XX	11-547
Remarks Made upon exhibiting a Tolo pall to the Society	陀罗尼经被展示	Jamieson, R. A.	VOL. II	3-400
Remarks on Some Impressions from a Lapidary Inscription at Keu-yung-kwan, on the Great Wall near Peking	居庸关碑拓	Wylie, Alexander	VOL. I	3-185

(续表)

题　　名	中译题名	责任者	卷期	页码
Remarks on the Water We Use in Shanghai	上海的饮用水	Lamprey, Dr.	VOL. II	3-399
Report on the Appearance of the Rugged Islands	羊山(崎岖群岛)地貌报告	Wilds, Edward.	VOL. I	3-191
Respecting China Grass	中国草原	Jarvie, Robert	VOL. II	3-393
Sinological Notes	汉学札记		VOL. LXIV	33-205
Sinological Notes	汉学札记		VOL. LXV	33-485
Sinological Notes	汉学札记		VOL. LXVI	33-662
Sinological Notes	汉学札记		VOL. LXVII	34-242
Sinological Notes	汉学札记		VOL. LXVIII	34-407
Sinological Notes	汉学札记		VOL. LXIX	34-569
Sinological Notes	汉学札记		VOL. LXXI	35-320
Specimen of a New Font of Chinese Movable Type belonging to the Printing Office of the Ameican Presbyterian Mission	美华书馆新体华文活字印刷样本	Gamble, William.	VOL. I	3-197
Synopsis of *How to Awaken Faith in the Mahayana School*	马鸣菩萨《大乘起信论》纲要	Richard, Timothy	VOL. XXVII	16-273
Traces of the Judicium dei, or Ordeal in Chinese Law	中国刑罚	Stronach, W. T.	VOL. II	3-398

讣告和悼文

题　　名	中译题名	责任者	卷期	页码
Allen, Mr. Hebert James	啊查理讣告		VOL. XLIV	23-192
Baber, Edward Colborne	贝德禄讣告		VOL. XXIV	13-577
Biallas, Rev. Francis X.	鲍润生讣告	Ferguson, John Calvin	VOL. LXVII	34-256
Bretschneider, Dr. Emile Vasilievitch	贝勒讣告	Kingsmill, Thomas William	VOL. XXXIII	19-333
Chavannes, Edouard	沙畹讣告		VOL. L	25-519
Cordier, Henri	高第讣告		VOL. LVI	28-393
Couling, Samul	库寿龄讣告		VOL. LIII	27-284
Dent, Vyvyan Edmond John	邓德讣告		VOL. LX	31-9
Edins, Rev. Joseph, D. D.	艾约瑟悼文		VOL. XXXVI	20-165
Ferguson, Dr. John C.	悼念福开森	Ly, J. Usang	VOL. LXXIII	35-483
Forbes, Francis B.	福勃士讣告		VOL. XXXIX	21-213

(续表)

题名	中译题名	责任者	卷期	页码
Fraser, Sir Everard. D. H.	法磊斯讣告		VOL. LIII	27－283
Fryer, John	傅兰雅讣告		VOL. LX	31－10
Giles, Dr. Herbert Allen	翟理思讣告	Ferguson, John Calvin	VOL. LXVI	33－690
Gorden, E. A.	Gorden 夫人讣告		VOL. LVI	28－395
Gordon, General Charles George	戈登将军悼文	Giles, Herbert Allen	VOL. XX	11－505
Hance, Henry Fletcher	韩士悼文	Parker, Edward Harper	VOL. XXI	12－317
Hart, Sir Robert	赫德悼文	K., P. H.	VOL. XLII	22－247
Hirth, Friedrich	夏德讣告		VOL. LVIII	29－284
Hosie, Sir Alexander	谢立山讣告		VOL. LVI	28－393
John, Dr. Griffith	杨格非悼文		VOL. XLIII	22－460
Kingsmill, Thos. W.	金斯密悼文	Lanning, George	VOL. XLI	21－604
Laufer, Berthold	劳费尔讣告	Gale, Esson Mcdowell	VOL. LXVI	33－692
Little, Mrs. Archibald	立德夫人讣告		VOL. LVIII	29－283
Little, Robert W.	立德禄悼文	L., D.	VOL. XXXVII	20－410
Lo Chên-yü	罗振玉讣告	Ferguson, John Calvin	VOL. LXXI	35－319
March, Benjamin	马尔智讣告		VOL. LXVI	33－696
Mason, Isaac	梅益盛讣告		VOL. LXX	35－137
Maybon, Charles B.	梅朋讣告		VOL. LVII	29－14
Mayers, Sidney Francis	梅尔思讣告	Gale, Esson Mcdowell	VOL. LXV	33－506
McClatchie, Rev. Thomas	麦克开拉启牧师悼文	Kingsmill, Thomas William	VOL. XX	11－545
Medhurst, Sir Walter	麦都思悼文	Anderson, C.	VOL. XX	11－733
Möllendorff, Paul Georg von	穆麟德讣告	Kingsmill, Thomas William	VOL. XXXIII	19－329
Morgan, Rev. Evan	莫安仁讣告	Ferguson, John Calvin	VOL. LXXII	35－452
Morse, Hosea Ballou	马士讣告	Gale, Esson Mcdowell	VOL. LXV	33－504
Moule, Arthur Evans	纪念慕雅德		VOL. L	25－522
Moule, George Evans	慕稼谷悼文		VOL. XLIII	22－415

(续表)

题　　名	中译题名	责任者	卷期	页码
Muirhead, Rev. William, D. D.	慕维廉讣告	Kingsmill, Thomas William	VOL. XXXIII	19－331
Ohlmer, Mr. Ernst	阿理文讣告		VOL. LXI	31－209
Othmer, Professor Dr. Wilhelm	欧特曼讣告	Glathe, von A.	VOL. LXV	33－505
Parker, Edwaqrd Harper	庄延龄讣告		VOL. LVII	29－9
Parkes, Sir Harry	巴夏礼悼文	Hughes, P. J.	VOL. XX	11－506
Pott, Dr. Francis Lister Hawks	卜舫济讣告		VOL. LXXII	35－452
Prentice, John	潘约翰讣告		VOL. LVI	28－395
Richard, Timothy	李提摩太讣告	Morgan, Evan	VOL. L	25－525
Richtofen, Freiherr Ferdinand Von	李希霍芬悼文	Kingsmill, Thomas William	VOL. XXXVII	20－408
Rockhill, William Woodville	柔克义悼文	Hinckley, F. E.	VOL. XLVI	23－669
Simpson, Bertram Lennox	辛博森讣告	Chatley, Herbert	VOL. LXII	32－10
Soothill, William Edward	苏慧廉讣告	Gale, Esson Mcdowell	VOL. LXVI	33－695
Stanley, Arthur	史笪来讣告	Ferguson, John Calvin	VOL. LXII	32－9
Stent, George Carter	司登得悼文	Drew, E. B.	VOL. XX	11－504
Walk, Dr. Anton J.	Walk讣告		VOL. LXV	33－507
Warren, Gilbert G.	任修本讣告		VOL. LVIII	29－285
Wiiliams, Frederick Wells	卫斐列讣告		VOL. LIX	30－9
Williamson, Rev. Alexander, Ll. D.	韦廉臣讣告	Edkins, Joseph	VOL. XXIV	13－696
Wylie, Alexander	伟烈亚力悼文	Muirhead, W.	VOL. XXI	12－313

大　事　记

题　　名	中译题名	责任者	卷期	页码
Record of Occurrences in China	中国大事记		O. S. VOL. I No. I	2－148
Record of Occurrences in China	中国大事记		O. S. VOL. I No. II	2－282
Record of Occurrences	中国大事记		O. S. VOL. I No. III	2－384
Record of Occurrences	中国大事记		O. S. VOL. II No. I	2－513
Retrospect of Events in the North of China during the years 1861－1864	1861－1864年华北大事记	Jamieson, R. A.	VOL. I	3－161

(续表)

题　名	中译题名	责任者	卷期	页码
Retrospect of Events in China and Japan during the year1865	1865 年中国和日本大事记	Kingsmill, Thomas William	VOL. II	3-357
Retrospect of Events in the North of China during the year 1866	1866 年华北大事记	Butcher, H.	VOL. III	3-565
Retrospect of Events in China and Japan during the year 1867	1867 年中国和日本大事记	Kingsmill, Thomas William	VOL. IV	4-257
Retrospect of Events in China and Japan during the year 1868	1868 年中国和日本大事记		VOL. V	4-558
Retrospect of events in China and Japan during the years 1869 and 1870	1869 – 1870 年中国和日本大事记		VOL. VI	5-201
Retrospect of Events in China &c. during the years 1871 and 1872	1871 – 1872 年中国大事记		VOL. VII	5-481
Retrospect of Events in China for the year 1873	1873 年中国大事记		VOL. VIII	6-199
Retrospect of Events in China and Japan for the year 1874	1874 年中国和日本大事记	Thomas, James.	VOL. IX	6-429
Retrospect of Events in China for the year 1875	1875 年中国大事记	Little, Archibald J.	VOL. X	7-329

会　务

题　名	中译题名	卷期	页码
年　报			
Report of the Council for the Year 1864	1864 年年报	VOL. I	3-201
Report of the Council for the Year 1865	1865 年年报	VOL. II	3-411
Report of the Council for the Year 1866	1866 年年报	VOL. III	3-437
Report of the Council for the Year 1869	1869 年年报	VOL. VI	5-7
Report of the Council for the Year 1870	1870 年年报	VOL. VI	5-15
Report of the Council for the Year 1872	1872 年年报	VOL. VII	5-231
Report of the Council for the Year 1873	1873 年年报	VOL. VIII	6-7
Report of the Council for the Year 1874	1874 年年报	VOL. IX	6-213
Report of the Council for the Year 1875	1875 年年报	VOL. X	7-9
Report of the Council for the Year 1876	1876 年年报	VOL. XI	8-7
Report of the Council for the Year 1878	1878 年年报	VOL. XIII	9-7
Report of the Council for the Year 1879	1879 年年报	VOL. XIV	9-185
Report of the Council for the Year 1880	1880 年年报	VOL. XV	9-269

(续表)

题 名	中译题名	卷期	页码
Report of the Council for the Year 1881	1881 年年报	VOL. XVI	10 - 259
Report of the Council for the Year 1883	1883 年年报	VOL. XVIII	11 - 7
Report of the Council for the Year 1884	1884 年年报	VOL. XIX	11 - 249
Report of the Council for the Year 1885	1885 年年报	VOL. XX	11 - 740
Report of the Council for the Year 1886	1886 年年报	VOL. XXI	12 - 340
Report of the Council for the Year 1887	1887 年年报	VOL. XXII	12 - 674
Report of the Council for the Year 1888	1888 年年报	VOL. XXIII	13 - 304
Report of the Council for the Year 1889 - 1890	1889 - 1890 年年报	VOL. XXIV	13 - 675
Report of the Council for the Year 1890 - 1891	1890 - 1891 年年报	VOL. XXVI	15 - 182
Report of the Council for the Year 1892	1892 年年报	VOL. XXVI	15 - 224
Report of the Council for the Year 1892 - 1893	1892 - 1893 年年报	VOL. XXVII	16 - 201
Report of the Council for the Year 1893 - 1894	1893 - 1894 年年报	VOL. XXVII	16 - 226
Report of the Council for the Year 1896 - 1897	1896 - 1897 年年报	VOL. XXXI	18 - 467
Report of the Council for the Year 1897 - 1898	1897 - 1898 年年报	VOL. XXXI	18 - 501
Report of the Council for the Year 1898 - 1899	1898 - 1899 年年报	VOL. XXXI	18 - 505
Report of the Council for the Year 1899 - 1900	1899 - 1900 年年报	VOL. XXXIII	19 - 87
Report of the Council for the Year 1900 - 1901	1900 - 1901 年年报	VOL. XXXIII	19 - 359

年 会 纪 要

题 名	中译题名	卷期	页码
Proceedings of the Annual General Meeting, 1887	1887 年年会纪要	VOL. XXI	12 - 334
Proceedings of the Annual General Meeting, 1888	1888 年年会纪要	VOL. XXII	12 - 672
Proceedings of the Annual General Meeting, 1889	1889 年年会纪要	VOL. XXIII	13 - 302
Proceedings of the Annual General Meeting, 1889 - 1890	1889 - 1890 年年会纪要	VOL. XXIV	13 - 672
Proceedings of the Annual General Meeting, 1890 - 1891	1890 - 1891 年年会纪要	VOL. XXVI	15 - 149
Proceedings of the Annual General Meeting, 1894	1894 年年会纪要	VOL. XXVII	16 - 226
Proceedings of the Annual General Meeting, 1895	1895 年年会纪要	VOL. XXXI	18 - 425
Proceedings of the Annual General Meeting, 1903 - 1904	1903 - 1904 年年会纪要	VOL. XXXV	19 - 663
Proceedings of the Annual General Meeting, 1905	1905 年年会纪要	VOL. XXXVI	20 - 168
Proceedings of the Annual General Meeting, 1906	1906 年年会纪要	VOL. XXXVII	20 - 412
Proceedings of the Annual General Meeting, 1907	1907 年年会纪要	VOL. XXXVIII	20 - 717
Proceedings of the Annual General Meeting, 1909	1909 年年会纪要	VOL. XL	21 - 419
Proceedings of the Annual General Meeting, 1910	1910 年年会纪要	VOL. XLI	21 - 624

(续表)

题　名	中译题名	卷期	页码
Proceedings of the Annual General Meeting, 1911	1911年年会纪要	VOL. XLII	22-269
Proceedings of the Annual General Meeting, 1912	1912年年会纪要	VOL. XLIII	22-525
Proceedings of the Annual General Meeting, 1913	1913年年会纪要	VOL. XLIV	23-257
Proceedings of the Annual General Meeting, 1914	1914年年会纪要	VOL. XLV	23-285
Proceedings of the Annual General Meeting, 1915	1915年年会纪要	VOL. XLVI	23-525
Proceedings of the Annual General Meeting, 1916	1916年年会纪要	VOL. XLVII	24-9
Proceedings of the Annual General Meeting, 1917	1917年年会纪要	VOL. XLVIII	24-221
Proceedings of the Annual General Meeting, 1918	1918年年会纪要	VOL. XLIX	25-11
Proceedings of the Annual General Meeting, 1919	1919年年会纪要	VOL. L	25-253
Proceedings of the Annual General Meeting, 1920	1920年年会纪要	VOL. LI	26-9
Proceedings of the Annual General Meeting, 1921	1921年年会纪要	VOL. LII	26-255
Proceedings of the Annual General Meeting, 1922	1922年年会纪要	VOL. LIII	27-9
Proceedings of the Annual General Meeting, 1923	1923年年会纪要	VOL. LIV	27-347
Proceedings of the Annual General Meeting, 1924	1924年年会纪要	VOL. LV	28-11
Proceedings of the Annual General Meeting, 1925	1925年年会纪要	VOL. LVI	28-397
Proceedings of the Annual General Meeting, 1926	1926年年会纪要	VOL. LVII	29-17
Proceedings of the Annual General Meeting, 1927	1927年年会纪要	VOL. LVIII	29-287
Proceedings of the Annual General Meeting, 1928	1928年年会纪要	VOL. LIX	30-11
Proceedings of the Annual General Meeting, 1929	1929年年会纪要	VOL. LX	31-13
Proceedings of the Annual General Meeting, 1930	1930年年会纪要	VOL. LXI	31-211
Proceedings of the Annual General Meeting, 1931	1931年年会纪要	VOL. LXII	32-11
Proceedings of the Annual General Meeting, 1932	1932年年会纪要	VOL. LXIII	32-282
Proceedings of the Annual General Meeting, 1933	1933年年会纪要	VOL. LXIV	33-9
Proceedings of the Annual General Meeting, 1934	1934年年会纪要	VOL. LXV	33-257
Proceedings of the Annual General Meeting, 1935	1935年年会纪要	VOL. LXVI	33-527
Proceedings of the Annual General Meeting, 1936	1936年年会纪要	VOL. LXVII	34-11
Proceedings of the Annual General Meeting, 1937	1937年年会纪要	VOL. LXVIII	34-305
Proceedings of the Annual General Meeting, 1938	1938年年会纪要	VOL. LXIX	34-437
Proceedings of the Annual General Meeting, 1939	1939年年会纪要	VOL. LXX	35-9
Proceedings of the Annual General Meeting, 1940	1940年年会纪要	VOL. LXXI	35-175
Proceedings of the Annual General Meeting, 1946	1946年年会纪要	VOL. LXXII	35-361
Proceedings of the Annual General Meeting, 1948	1948年年会纪要	VOL. LXXIII	35-479

(续表)

题 名	中译题名	卷期	页码
会 议 纪 要			
Summary of Proceedings for the Year 1864	1864年会议纪要	VOL. I	3-198
Summary of Proceedings for the Year 1865	1865年会议纪要	VOL. II	3-404
Minutes of a Meeting, 12th March 1886	1886年3月12日会议纪要	VOL. XX	11-738
Minutes of a Meeting, 26th May 1886	1886年5月26日会议纪要	VOL. XXI	12-131
Minutes of a Meeting, 30th November 1886	1886年11月30日会议纪要	VOL. XXI	12-249
Minutes of a Meeting, 16th December 1886	1886年12月16日会议纪要	VOL. XXI	12-260
Minutes of a Meeting, 25th October 1887	1887年10月25日会议纪要	VOL. XXII	12-500
Minutes of a Meeting, 18th November 1887	1887年11月18日会议纪要	VOL. XXII	12-505
Minutes of a Meeting, 22nd February 1888	1888年2月22日会议纪要	VOL. XXII	12-669
Minutes of a General Meeting, 22nd October 1888	1888年10月22日会议纪要	VOL. XXIII	13-48
Minutes of a General Meeting, 19th November 1888	1888年11月19日会议纪要	VOL. XXIII	13-53
Minutes of a General Meeting, 22nd February 1889	1889年2月22日会议纪要	VOL. XXIII	13-183
Minutes of a General Meeting, 10th December 1888	1888年12月10日会议纪要	VOL. XXIII	13-300
Minutes of a General Meeting, 15th May 1889	1889年5月15日会议纪要	VOL. XXIII	13-301
Minutes of a General Meeting, 14th December 1889	1889年12月14日会议纪要	VOL. XXIV	13-590
Minutes of a General Meeting, 20th December 1889	1889年12月20日会议纪要	VOL. XXIV	13-596
Minutes of a General Meeting, 21st February 1890	1890年2月21日会议纪要	VOL. XXIV	13-665
Minutes of a General Meeting, 11th November 1890	1890年11月11日会议纪要	VOL. XXV	14-479
Minutes of a General Meeting, 6th April 1891	1891年4月6日会议纪要	VOL. XXV	14-488
Minutes of a General Meeting, 20th April 1891	1891年4月20日会议纪要	VOL. XXV	14-491
Minutes of a General Meeting, 11th May 1891	1891年5月11日会议纪要	VOL. XXVI	15-137
Minutes of a General Meeting, 9th November 1891	1891年11月9日会议纪要	VOL. XXVI	15-190
Minutes of a General Meeting, 24th November 1891	1891年11月24日会议纪要	VOL. XXVI	15-194
Minutes of a General Meeting, 29th January 1892	1892年1月29日会议纪要	VOL. XXVI	15-198
Minutes of a General Meeting, 15th February 1892	1892年2月15日会议纪要	VOL. XXVI	15-215
Minutes of a General Meeting, 30th March 1892	1892年3月30日会议纪要	VOL. XXVI	15-218
Minutes of a General Meeting, 1st June 1892	1892年6月1日会议纪要	VOL. XXVI	15-221
Minutes of a General Meeting, 28th December 1892	1892年12月28日会议纪要	VOL. XXVII	16-208
Minutes of a General Meeting, 27th February 1893	1893年2月27日会议纪要	VOL. XXVII	16-216
Minutes of a General Meeting, 26th April 1893	1893年4月26日会议纪要	VOL. XXVII	16-220
Minutes of a General Meeting, 29th November 1893	1893年11月29日会议纪要	VOL. XXVII	16-256

(续表)

题　　名	中译题名	卷期	页码
Minutes of a General Meeting, 24th January 1894	1894年1月24日会议纪要	VOL. XXVII	16－257
Minutes of a General Meeting, 5th February 1896	1896年2月5日会议纪要	VOL. XXXI	18－432
Minutes of a General Meeting, 8th March 1895	1895年3月8日会议纪要	VOL. XXXI	18－439
Minutes of a General Meeting, 21st October 1896	1896年10月21日会议纪要	VOL. XXXI	18－444
Minutes of a General Meeting, 26th November 1896	1896年11月26日会议纪要	VOL. XXXI	18－454
Minutes of a General Meeting, 3rd March 1897	1897年3月3日会议纪要	VOL. XXXI	18－460
Minutes of a General Meeting, 24th March 1897	1897年3月24日会议纪要	VOL. XXXI	18－464
Minutes of a General Meeting, 29th November 1897	1897年11月29日会议纪要	VOL. XXXI	18－474
Minutes of a General Meeting, 12th May 1898	1898年5月12日会议纪要	VOL. XXXI	18－475
Minutes of a General Meeting, 16th February 1898	1898年2月16日会议纪要	VOL. XXXI	18－490
Minutes of a Meeting, 26th October 1899	1899年10月26日会议纪要	VOL. XXXIII	19－75
Minutes of a Meeting, 9th November 1899	1899年11月9日会议纪要	VOL. XXXIII	19－78
Minutes of a Meeting, 14th December 1899	1899年12月14日会议纪要	VOL. XXXIII	19－80
Minutes of a Meeting, 18th January 1900	1900年1月18日会议纪要	VOL. XXXIII	19－83
Minutes of a Meeting, 4th April 1900	1900年4月5日会议纪要	VOL. XXXIII	19－84
Minutes of a Meeting, 28th June 1900	1900年6月28日会议纪要	VOL. XXXIII	19－86
Minutes of a Meeting, 5th October 1900	1900年10月5日会议纪要	VOL. XXXIII	19－337
Minutes of a Meeting, 18th October 1900	1900年10月18日会议纪要	VOL. XXXIII	19－338
Minutes of a Meeting, 24th October 1900	1900年10月24日会议纪要	VOL. XXXIII	19－340
Minutes of a Meeting, 21st November 1900	1900年11月21日会议纪要	VOL. XXXIII	19－341
Minutes of a Meeting, 29th November 1900	1900年11月29日会议纪要	VOL. XXXIII	19－347
Minutes of a Meeting, 17th January 1901	1901年1月17日会议纪要	VOL. XXXIII	19－350
Minutes of a Meeting, 28th March 1901	1901年3月28日会议纪要	VOL. XXXIII	19－353
Minutes of a Meeting, 17th April 1901	1901年4月17日会议纪要	VOL. XXXIII	19－356
Minutes of a Meeting, 22nd May 1901	1901年5月22日会议纪要	VOL. XXXIII	19－357
Minutes of a Meeting, 25th June 1901	1901年6月25日会议纪要	VOL. XXXIII	19－358
Summary of Proceedings for the Year 1902	1902年会议纪要	VOL. XXXV	19－641

会　员　名　录

题　　名	中译题名	卷期	页码
List of Members (Corrected to March 10th, 1865)	会员名录（更新至1865年3月10日）	VOL. I	3－208
List of Members, 1865	1865年会员名录	VOL. II	3－421
List of Members, 1866	1866年会员名录	VOL. III	3－446

(续表)

题　　名	中译题名	卷期	页码
List of Members, 1869	1869 年会员名录	VOL. VI	5－11
List of Members, 1870	1870 年会员名录	VOL. VI	5－19
List of Members, 1871－1872	1871－1872 年会员名录	VOL. VII	5－236
List of Members, 1873	1873 年会员名录	VOL. VIII	6－15
List of Members, 1874	1874 年会员名录	VOL. IX	6－233
List of Members, 1875	1875 年会员名录	VOL. X	7－18
List of Members, 1876	1876 年会员名录	VOL. XI	8－20
List of Members, 1877	1877 会员名录	VOL. XII	8－213
List of Members, 1878	1878 年会员名录	VOL. XIII	9－9
List of Members（May, 1880）	会员名录（更新至1880年5月）	VOL. XIV	9－187
List of Members（July, 1881）	会员名录（更新至1881年7月）	VOL. XV	9－272
List of Members（April, 1882）	会员名录（更新至1882年4月）	VOL. XVI	10－266
List of Members（Corrected up to 30th September 1884）	会员名录（更新至1884年9月30日）	VOL. XVIII	11－229
List of Members（Corrected up to 1st October 1885）	会员名录（更新至1885年10月1日）	VOL. XX	11－552
List of Members Having Joined from 1st October 1885	会员名录（1885年10月1日后加入的）	VOL. XX	11－761
List of Members, 1886	1886 年会员名录	VOL. XXI	12－371
List of Members（Corrected to 1st August 1888）	会员名录（更新至1888年8月1日）	VOL. XXII	12－705
List of Members（Corrected to 31st August 1889）	会员名录（更新至1889年8月31日）	VOL. XXIII	13－341
List of Members（Corrected to 20th October 1890）	会员名录（更新至1890年10月20日）	VOL. XXIV	13－699
List of Members（Corrected to December 20th, 1892）	会员名录（更新至1892年12月20日）	VOL. XXV	14－512
List of Members（Corrected to October 31st, 1893）	会员名录（更新至1893年10月31日）	VOL. XXVI	15－246
List of Members（Corrected to March 31st, 1897）	会员名录（更新至1897年3月31日）	VOL. XXVIII	16－295
List of Members（Corrected to December 31st, 1901）	会员名录（更新至1901年12月31日）	VOL. XXXIII	19－371
List of Members（Correceted to June 30th, 1906）	会员名录（更新至1906年6月30日）	VOL. XXXVII	20－426

(续表)

题　　名	中译题名	卷期	页码
List of Members (Coreceted to June 30th, 1907)	会员名录（更新至1907年6月30日）	VOL. XXXVIII	20-725
List of Members (Corrected to June 30th, 1908)	会员名录（更新至1908年6月30日）	VOL. XXXIX	21-243
List of Members (Corrected to June 30th, 1909)	会员名录（更新至1909年6月30日）	VOL. XL	21-429
List of Members (Corrected to August 1, 1910)	会员名录（更新至1910年8月1日）	VOL. XLI	21-631
List of Members (Revised to September 30, 1912)	会员名录（更新至1912年9月30日）	VOL. XLIII	22-553
List of Members (Revised to October 1, 1911)	会员名录（更新至1911年10月1日）	VOL. XLII	22-279
List of Members (Revised to June 5, 1913)	会员名录（更新至1913年6月5日）	VOL. XLIV	23-265
List of Members, 1914	1914年会员名录	VOL. XLV	23-503
List of Members, 1915	1915年会员名录	VOL. XLVI	23-719
List of Members, 1916	1916年会员名录	VOL. XLVII	24-201
List of Members, 1917	1917年会员名录	VOL. XLVIII	24-527
List of Members, 1918	1918年会员名录	VOL. XLIX	25-229
List of Members, 1919	1919年会员名录	VOL. L	25-527
List of Members, 1920	1920年会员名录	VOL. LI	26-232
List of Members, 1921	1921年会员名录	VOL. LII	26-499
List of Members, 1922	1922年会员名录	VOL. LIII	27-323
List of Members, 1923	1923年会员名录	VOL. LIV	27-671
List of Members, 1924	1924年会员名单	VOL. LV	28-305
List of Members, 1925	1925年会员名单	VOL. LVI	28-661
List of Members, 1926	1926年会员名单	VOL. LVII	29-258
List of Members, 1927	1927年会员名单	VOL. LVIII	29-548
List of Members, 1928	1928年会员名单	VOL. LIX	30-404
List of Members, 1929	1929年会员名单	VOL. LX	31-181
List of Members, 1930	1930年会员名录	VOL. LXI	31-433
List of Members, 1931	1931年会员名录	VOL. LXII	32-251
List of Members, 1932	1932年会员名录	VOL. LXIII	32-529
List of Members, 1933	1933年会员名录	VOL. LXIV	33-217
List of Members, 1935	1935年会员名录	VOL. LXVI	33-708

（续表）

题　　名	中译题名	卷期	页码
List of Members, 1936	1936 年会员名录	VOL. LXVIII	34－269
List of Members, 1938	1938 年会员名录	VOL. LXIX	34－577
List of Members, 1939	1939 年会员名录	VOL. LXX	35－145
List of Members, 1940	1940 年会员名录	VOL. LXXI	35－328

规　　章

题名	中译题名	卷期	页码
Rules of the NCBRAS, Passed at the Annual Meeting of the Society Held January 10th 1865	文会章程（1865 年 1 月 10 日年会上通过）	VOL. I	3－211
Rules of the NCBRAS	文会章程	VOL. IX	6－229
Revised Rules of the NCBRAS (Instituted 24th September 1857)	文会章程（1857 年 9 月 24 日修订）	VOL. XVIII	11－234
Rules for the Issue of Books from the Library	图书馆借书条例	VOL. XVIII	11－240
Rules of the Issue of Books from the Library	图书馆借书条例	VOL. XXX	18－207

演说和致辞

题名	中译题名	卷期	页码
Inaugural Address (Delivered Oct. 16th, 1857)	会长裨治文 1857 年 10 月 16 日就职演说	O. S. VOL. I No. I	2－11
Presidents Address(Delivered Feb. 19th, 1874)	会长福勃士 1874 年 2 月 19 日致辞	VOL. IX	6－237
Inaugural Address by the President (Delivered Feb. 20th, 1877)	会长金斯密 1877 年 2 月就职演说	VOL. XI	8－23
Address to the Members of the NCBRAS (Delivered Feb. 3rd, 1879)	会长金斯密 1879 年 2 月 3 日的演讲	VOL. XIII	9－25
President Address(December 2, 1937)	会长苏阿德 1937 年 12 月 2 日致辞	VOL. LXIX	34－455
President Address(February 2, 1939)	会长苏阿德 1939 年 2 月 2 日致辞	VOL. LXX	35－45
Presidential Address(February 15, 1940)	会长苏阿德 1940 年 2 月 15 日致辞	VOL. LXXI	35－193

图　书　目　录

题名	中译题名	卷期	页码
List of Books, Papers, Charts, &c. in the Society's Library	图书馆图书、论文、图表等目录	VOL. II	3－424
List of Societies, Public Institutions, etc. Exchanging Publications with the Society	社会团体机构名录及与亚洲文会交换图书目录	VOL. XVI	10－280
List of Works Added to the Library during the Year 1881	图书馆 1881 年新增图书目录	VOL. XVI	10－283

(续表)

题　名	中译题名	卷期	页码
List of Books and Papers on China, Published Since 1st January, 1884	中国专题书籍与论文目录（1884年1月后出版）	VOL. XX	11－681
Provisional Acknowledgement of Donations (Books and Periodicals) Received for the Society since 1st January, 1886	文会收到的书刊捐赠目录（自1886年1月1日起）	VOL. XX	11－753
List of Societies, Public Institutions, and Periodicals Exchanging Publications with the Society	社会团体机构名录及与文会交换图书、期刊目录	VOL. XXI	12－347
Catalogue of Chinese Books in the Library	图书馆中文图书目录	VOL. XXI	12－366
List of Works Added to the Library from 1st April 1887 to 31st March 1888	图书馆1887年4月1日至1888年3月31日新增图书目录	VOL. XXII	12－688
List of Societies, Public Institutions, and Periodicals Exchanging Publications with the Society	社会团体机构名录及与文会交换图书、期刊目录	VOL. XXIII	13－313
List of Works Added to the Library from 1st April 1888 to 30st April 1889	图书馆1888年4月1日至1889年4月30日新增图书目录	VOL. XXII	13－321
List of Works Added to the Society's Library from 1st April 1889 to 31st March 1890	图书馆1889年4月1日至1890年3月31日新增图书目录	VOL. XXIV	13－685
List of Works Added to the Society's Library during the Year 1891	图书馆1891年新增图书目录	VOL. XXVI	15－232
Catalogue of the Library (Including the Library of Alex. Wylie, Esq.) Systematically Classed	图书馆图书目录（包括伟烈亚力所藏）	VOL. XXVI	15－307
Addenda to the Catalogue of Library	图书馆图书目录补遗	VOL. XXVII	16－235
List of Additions to the Catalogue of the Library	图书馆图书目录补遗	VOL. XXX	18－209
List of Additions to the Catalogued Periodicals, etc.	图书馆期刊目录补遗	VOL. XXX	18－257
Recent Books on China	中国专题出版物书讯	VOL. XXXVII	20－406
Recent Books on China and the Far East	中国和远东专题出版物书讯	VOL. XXXVIII	20－715
Recent Books on China and the Far East	中国和远东专题出版物书讯	VOL. XXXIX	21－241
Recent Books on China and the Far East	中国和远东专题出版物书讯	VOL. XL	21－418
Recent Books on China	中国专题出版物书讯	VOL. XLI	21－623
Books Contributed to the Library	图书馆受赠图书目录	VOL. XLII	22－261
Recent Books and Re-publications on China	中国专题出版物及再版书书讯	VOL. XLII	22－262
Recent Accessions to the Library	图书馆新增图书目录	VOL. XLII	22－264
Books Presented to the Library	图书馆受赠图书目录	VOL. XLIII	22－455

(续表)

题 名	中译题名	卷期	页码
Recent Accessions to the Library	图书馆新增图书目录	VOL. XLIII	22-457
Books Presented to the Library	图书馆受赠图书目录	VOL. XLIV	23-249
Recent Accessions to the Library	图书馆新增图书目录	VOL. XLIV	23-252
Books Presented to the Library (May 31st, 1913 – May, 1914)	图书馆1913年5月31日至1914年5月受赠图书目录	VOL. XLV	23-495
Additions to the Library (May 1913 – May 1914)	图书馆1913年5月至1914年5月新增图书目录	VOL. XLV	23-498
Books Presented to the Library	图书馆受赠图书目录	VOL. XLVI	23-707
Additions to the Library (June 1914 – June 1915)	图书馆1914年6月至1915年6月新增图书目录	VOL. XLVI	23-710
Books Added to the Library of the NCBRAS by Exchange of Publications	图书馆交换所得图书目灵	VOL. XLVI	23-715
List of Books on China Recently Published	中国专题出版物书讯	VOL. XLVII	24-194
Additions to the Library	图书馆1916年新增图书目录	VOL. XLVII	24-196
Books Presented to the Library	图书馆受赠图书目录	VOL. XLVII	24-196
Additions to the Library (July 1915 – June 1916)	图书馆1915年7月至1916年5月新增图书目录	VOL. XLVII	24-198
Books Added to the Library by Exchange of Publications	图书馆交换所得图书目录	VOL. XLVII	24-200
Additions to the Library (July 1916 – June 1917)	图书馆1916年7月至1917年6月新增图书目录	VOL. XLVIII	24-522
Additions to the Library (July 1917 – June 1918)	图书馆1917年7月至1918年6月新增图书目录	VOL. XLIX	25-226
Additions to the Library (July 1918 – June 1919)	图书馆1918年7月至1919年6月新增图书目录	VOL. L	25-515
Additions to the Library (July 1919 – June 1920)	图书馆1919年7月至1920年6月新增图书目录	VOL. LI	26-229
Additions to the Library (July 1920 – June 1921)	图书馆1920年7月至1921年6月新增图书目录	VOL. LII	26-496
Additions to the Library (July 1921 – June 1922)	图书馆1921年7月至1922年6月新增图书目录	VOL. LIII	27-320

(续表)

题　　名	中译题名	卷期	页码
Additions to the Library (July 1922 – June 1923)	图书馆 1922 年 7 月至 1923 年 6 月新增图书目录	VOL. LIV	27-668
Additions to the Library (July 1923 – June 1924)	图书馆 1923 年 7 月至 1924 年 6 月新增图书目录	VOL. LV	28-302
Additions to the Library (July 1924 – June 1925)	图书馆 1924 年 7 月至 1925 年 6 月新增图书目录	VOL. LVI	28-657
Presentations to the Library (July 1924 – June 1925)	图书馆 1924 年 7 月至 1925 年 6 月受赠图书目录	VOL. LVI	28-658
Additions to the Library (July 1925 – June 1926)	图书馆 1925 年 7 月至 1926 年 6 月新增图书目录	VOL. LVII	29-255
Presentations to the Library (July 1925 – June 1926)	图书馆 1925 年 7 月至 1926 年 6 月受赠图书目录	VOL. LVII	29-256
Additions to the Library (July 1926 – June 1927)	图书馆 1926 年 7 月至 1927 年 6 月新增图书目录	VOL. LVIII	29-544
Presentations to the Library (July 1926 – June 1927)	图书馆 1926 年 7 月至 1927 年 6 月受赠图书目录	VOL. LVIII	29-546
Additions to the Library (July 1927 – June 1928)	图书馆 1927 年 7 月至 1928 年 6 月新增图书目录	VOL. LIX	30-399
Presentations to the Library (July 1927 – June 1928)	图书馆 1927 年 7 月至 1928 年 6 月受赠图书目录	VOL. LIX	30-401
Additions to the Library	图书馆 1929 年新增图书目录	VOL. LX	31-178
Presentations to the Library (July 1929 – June 1930)	图书馆 1929 年 7 月至 1930 年 6 月受赠书目	VOL. LXI	31-430
Presentations and Additions to the Library (July 1930 to June 1931)	图书馆 1930 年 7 月至 1931 年 6 月受赠及新增图书目录	VOL. LXII	32-248
Books Received, 1932	图书馆 1932 年新增图书目录	VOL. LXIII	32-513
Presentations and Additions to the Library (June 1931 – May 1932)	图书馆 1931 年 6 月至 1932 年 5 月受赠及新增图书目录	VOL. LXIII	32-524

(续表)

题　　名	中译题名	卷期	页码
Presentations and Additions to the Library (June 1932 – April 1933)	图书馆1932年6月至1933年4月受赠及新增图书目录	VOL. LXIV	33－213
Presentations and Additions to the Library, 1934	图书馆1934年受赠及新增图书目录	VOL. LXV	33－508
Presentations and Additions to the Library, 1935	图书馆1935年受赠及新增图书目录	VOL. LXVI	33－698
Presentations and Additions to the Library (June 1935 – May 1936)	图书馆1935年6月至1936年5月受赠及新增图书目录	VOL. LXVII	34－257
Presentations and Additions to the Library (June 1936 to May 1937)	图书馆1936年6月至1937年5月受赠及新增图书目录	VOL. LXVIII	34－424
Presentations and Additions to the Library (June 1937 to December 1938)	图书馆1937年6月至1938年12月受赠及新增图书目录	VOL. LXIX	34－571
Presentations and Additions to the Library (January to December, 1939)	图书馆1939年受赠及新增图书目录	VOL. LXX	35－138
Chinese Libraries	图书馆中文书目信息	VOL. LXXI	35－317
Presentations and Additions to the Library (January to December, 1940)	图书馆1940年受赠及新增图书目录	VOL. LXXI	35－323
Perodicals Received by the Library (January to December, 1940)	图书馆1940年受赠及所收期刊目录	VOL. LXXI	35－326
Presentations and Additions to the Library (January to December, 1941)	图书馆1941年受赠及新增图书目录	VOL. LXXII	35－454
Presentations and Additions to the Library (September 1945 to December 1946)	图书馆1945年9月至1946年12月新增图书目录	VOL. LXXII	35－457
A Descriptive and Bibliographical Catalogue of the European Books Printed Before 1800 in the Library of the R. A. S.	图书馆藏1800年前出版欧洲文献书目提要	VOL. LXXII	35－429
A Descriptive and Bibliographical Catalogue of the European Books Printed Before 1900 in the Library of the R. A. S.	图书馆藏1900年前出版欧洲文献书目提要	VOL. LXXIII	35－605
Presentations and Additions to the Library (January to December, 1948)	图书馆1948年受赠及新增图书目录	VOL. LXXIII	35－628
其他重要目录			
A Classified Index to the Articles Printed in the JNCBRAS, from the Foundation of the Society to the 31th of Dec., 1874	会刊自创立至1874年12月31日所刊文章分类索引	VOL. IX	6－447

(续表)

题　　名	中译题名	卷期	页码
List of Birds Represented in the Shanghai Museum	博物院陈列鸟类目录	VOL. XVIII	11－17
A Classified Index to the Articles Printed in the JNCBRAS, from the Foundation of the Society, 1858, to the end of 1893	会刊自1858年创立至1893年底所刊文章分类索引	VOL. XXVI	15－254
List of Societies, Public Institutions, etc. Exchanging Publications with the Society	与文会交换图书的社团及公共机构名录	VOL. XXX	18－248
List of Societies, Public Institutions, etc. Exchanging Publications with the Society	与文会交换图书的社团及公共机构名录	VOL. XXXVI	20－177
A Classified List of the Articles Printed in the JNCBRAS from 1892 to 1907	1892年至1907年会刊文章总目	VOL. XXXVIII	20－710
List of Articles Contributed to the JNCBRAS	会刊文章分类索引	VOL. XLIII	22－537
List of Eexchanges	与图书馆交换图书的机构名录	VOL. XLVI	23－717
Index to the JNCBRAS from Vol. I to Vol. LIV	会刊第1卷至第54卷索引	VOL. LV	28－323
List of Articles Which Have Appeared in the JNCBRAS, 1912－1931	会刊1912－1931年所刊文章目录	VOL. LXIII	32－453
通　　信			
Prof. Legge to the Editor of the Journal	理雅各教授致会刊编辑的信	VOL. XXI	12－245
The Marquis d'H. St. Denys to the Editor of the Journal	圣丹尼斯侯爵致会刊编辑的信	VOL. XXI	12－246
M. Rondot to the President of the Society	Rondot致文会会长的信	VOL. XXI	12－247
Rockhill to the Hon. Secretary, Mr. W. W.	柔克义致文会荣誉秘书长庄延龄信	VOL. XXII	12－497
Parker's Reply to Above, Mr. E. H.	庄延龄复柔克义之信	VOL. XXII	12－498
Dr. Edkins on Mr. Giles	艾约瑟与翟理思商榷	VOL. XXII	12－499
Letter from the Hon. Secretary to the Editor of the North-China Daily News	文会荣誉秘书马士致《字林西报》编辑的信	VOL. XXIII	13－58
Letter from the Belgian Consul－General to the Hon. Secretary	比利时总领事Max Goebel致文会秘书的信	VOL. XXIII	13－60
Letter from the Hon. Secretary to the Editor of the North-China Daily News	文会荣誉秘书马士致《字林西报》编辑的信	VOL. XXIII	13－60
Correspondence: The Preservation of the Nestorian Tablet and Other Ancient Monuments at Si-an-fu	关于西安景教碑与其他古迹保护的通信	VOL. XXIV	13－492
Correspondence	安大生致文会博物院长Vosy-Bourbon的信	VOL. XXX	18－196
Correspondence	计里布致文会秘书卫理的信	VOL. XXX	18－198

题 名	中译题名	卷期	页码
Correspondence	文会 1937 年会员通信	VOL. LXVIII	34-420

其 他			
Report of the Council on the Proposed Trade and Commerce Museum	拟建贸易与商业博物院的报告	VOL. XXIII	13-55
Second Report of the Council of NCBRAS on the Proposed Trade and Commerce Museum	拟建贸易与商业博物院的第二份报告	VOL. XXIII	13-183
Three Score Years and Ten: the Seventieth Anniversary of the NCBRAS	文会七十周年纪念	VOL. LIX	30-19
The New Building of the Royal Asiatic Society	文会新大楼	VOL. LXIII	32-277
The Reopening of the Shanghai Museum	博物院重新开放	VOL. LXV	33-247
The History of the Shanghai Museum	博物院史	VOL. LXV	33-249
Personal Notes	通告	VOL. LXVIII	34-423
Notice	通知	VOL. LXX	35-144
Library Report	图书馆报告	VOL. LXXII	35-453
Summaries of Lectures Delivered Before the Society 1933-1934	1933-1934 年演讲概要	VOL. LXV	33-496
Summaries of Lectures Delivered Before the Society 1934-1935	1934-1935 年演讲概要	LXVI	33-679

作 者 索 引

责 任 者	责任者中文名	页　码
Abraham, R. D.	亚伯拉罕	29-370, 29-542, 32-131, 35-616, 35-618
Alabaster, Ernest	阿拉巴德	20-273
Alexeieff, V.	阿莱克塞夫	21-261
Allen, Herbert J.	啊查理	11-644, 12-97, 12-201, 12-212
Almblad, A. F.	[阿木巴;阿兰布]	23-489
Ancell, B. L.	韩忾明	27-281
Anderson, A. L.	安大生	18-196
Anderson, Geo. C.	安德森	10-345, 11-733
Andrew, G. Findlay	安献令	33-604
Ankerson, W. A.	安克生	35-420
Annandale, N.		24-79
Anon.		23-444
Ardsheal (pseud.)		23-409, 23-613
Arnold, Julean Herbert	安立德	21-304, 33-450, 34-230
Ayscough, Florence Wheelock	爱司克夫人	22-419, 22-420, 22-440, 22-441, 22-445, 22-537, 23-215, 23-691, 23-703, 24-188, 24-291, 24-500, 26-121, 26-313, 26-457, 27-302, 27-305, 27-491, 28-159, 29-530, 31-337, 33-477
B.		24-181, 24-185, 24-469, 24-496, 27-645, 29-519, 30-373, 30-392, 31-404, 32-240, 32-241
B., M. E.		26-468
Balfour, Frederic Henry	巴尔福	9-621, 11-639
Barbour, George B.	巴博尔	28-478
Bastion, Dr.	巴斯琴	3-347
Baude, R. L. P.	保德成	34-403
Beath, Sterling S.		35-375
Becher, H. M.		12-406
Berg, Jan van den	范德溥	30-372
Betts, Geo. Edgar		19-97
Biallas, Franz Xavier	鲍润生	30-289

(续表)

责 任 者	责任者中文名	页　　码
Bickmore, Albert S.	贝克莫尔	4-7, 4-336
Bishop, Carl Whitney	毕士勃	33-52
Bitton, W. Nelson	毕腾	20-688
Bourne, Frederick Samuel Augustus	班德瑞	19-9, 21-239, 23-473, 23-695
Box, Ernest	包克私	19-489, 20-138
Bradley, Cornelius Beach		23-590
Brandt, M. Von	巴兰德	13-492
Brass, E.		18-607
Brazier, J. S.	白氏	12-240
Brenan, Byron	璧利南	18-564, 24-497
Bretschneider, E.	贝勒	7-95, 9-313, 10-24, 14-9, 17-13
Brett, H. J.	卜乐特	29-498
Brewitt-Taylor, C. H.	邓罗	11-646
Bridgman, Elijah Coleman	裨治文	2-11, 2-301
Britton, Roswell S.	白瑞华	34-248, 34-407
Brown, Margaret Helen	薄玉珍	32-490, 34-142, 34-388
Brown, S. R.	勃朗	3-275, 3-490
Bruce, Charence Dalrymple	卜禄士	21-232, 21-406, 23-236, 23-443
Bruce, Joseph Percy	卜道成	25-129
Bruce, Percy	步如旭	31-326
Buchanan, J. U.		28-287, 31-410, 31-422
Budd, Charles	卜德	27-357, 31-175, 31-176, 31-395, 31-396, 31-398
Burt, E. W.	白向义	30-377
Bushell, S. W.	卜士礼	6-151, 9-507, 18-154, 19-38
Butcher, H.	布彻	3-395, 3-565
Buxton, Dudley		31-219
Camajee, D. N.	卡姆杰	6-271
Canny, J. M.	甘霓仁	3-122
Carey, Fred. W.	甘福履	20-9
Carles, W. R.	贾礼士	12-465, 13-7, 18-406
Chalfant, Frank Herring	方法敛	19-557, 22-424

（续表）

责 任 者	责任者中文名	页　　码
Chan, Wing-tsit		35－310
Chang, Hsing-lang	张星烺	35－561
Chang, Hsin-hai	张歆海	31－21
Chao, T. Y.		32－453
Chatley, Herbert	查得利	24－246，24－467，25－19，25－188，25－477，26－67，26－208，26－484，26－485，27－421，27－647，28－65，28－272，28－275，28－649，28－650，29－240，29－522，29－524，30－340，30－346，30－351，30－352，30－376，31－99，31－156，31－157，31－159，31－174，31－302，31－407，31－428，32－10，32－105，32－244，32－245，32－247，32－475，32－481，32－482，33－107，33－195，，33－209，33－330，33－485，33－631，34－41，34－231，34－569
Ch'en, S. C.		34－202
Cheng, Te-k'un	郑德坤	33－154，33－424
Chu, Coching	竺可桢	32－52
Chu, Y. T.	朱元鼎	34－240
Clarke, Geo. W.	花国香	16－547
Collins, Varnum D.	葛林德	3－307
Contag, Victoria	孔达	34－239
Cordier, Henri	高第	6－361
Couling, C. E.		23－471，25－183，25－213，29－470，29－513，29－518，29－523，29－527，29－541，30－343，30－346，30－362，30－364，30－376，30－378
Couling, Samuel	库寿龄	23－239，23－363，23－468，23－488，23－491，23－597，23－678，23－700，23－704，24－173，24－178，24－184，24－326，24－353，24－489
Courtney, Charles		2－504
Cowdry, N. H.		27－192
Cressy, Earl Herbert	葛德基	34－220，34－222
Cressy, M.	葛履绥	27－662，33－474
Crow, Carl	克劳	34－233
D., C. E.		21－238
Darroch, John	窦乐安	20－398，27－476，28－277，28－278，29－517，29－533，30－333，30－367
David, Armand.	谭微道	5－445

(续表)

责 任 者	责任者中文名	页　　码
Dechevrens, M.	能恩斯	10-237
Dennys, H. L.		11-733
Dennys, N. B.	丹尼斯	6-111
Dent, Robert V.	罗伯特·邓德	35-307
Dickson, W.	迪克森	3-37
Dodd, W. Clifton	铎德	26-21
Dovey, J. Whitsed.	杜明德	28-455
Drake, F. S.	林仰山	33-588, 34-189, 35-246
Drew, E. B.	杜维德	11-504, 11-547
Du Bois-Reymond, C.	谛部	22-348, 23-401
Dubs, Homer Hasenpflug	德效骞	29-509, 29-510, 33-621, 34-98
Dunlap, Eva Wyman		33-197, 34-223, 34-236, 34-238, 34-389, 34-402, 35-269
E., E. C.		29-539, 30-357
Edgar, J. Huston	叶长清	23-326, 23-340, 23-353, 24-274, 24-321, 27-95, 29-54, 31-135
Edkins, Joseph	艾约瑟	2-117, 2-187, 2-345, 2-409, 2-485, 3-321, 4-249, 6-97, 8-145, 11-37, 11-641, 11-728, 11-729, 12-114, 12-116, 12-117, 12-207, 12-235, 12-236, 12-241, 12-333, 12-499, 12-611, 12-614, 13-609, 13-696, 19-54, 19-537
Edmunds, Charle Keyser	晏文士	25-263
Edward, R. E.		3-188
Eitel, E. J.	艾德	5-67
Elia, Pascal M. d'	德礼贤	30-318
Elias, Ney	爱莲斯	4-86, 4-537
Englaender, A. L.	恩格莱德	30-204, 31-121
F., H. D.		11-634, 11-635, 12-489
F., K. H.		25-501
Faber, Ernst	花之安	13-497, 20-549
Fauvel, A. A.	福威勒	9-39
Fedorovitch, J.		2-281, 2-381

责 任 者	责任者中文名	页　　码
Ferguson, John Calvin	福开森	19-603, 20-245, 20-380, 20-396, 20-397, 20-405, 20-677, 20-678, 21-236, 21-237, 21-407, 21-412, 21-416, 21-417, 21-611, 21-612, 21-618, 21-619, 23-205, 23-208, 23-233, 23-241, 23-307, 23-483, 23-485, 23-486, 24-21, 24-433, 25-398, 27-104, 27-411, 28-34, 28-526, 29-83, 29-332, 29-492, 30-70, 30-317, 30-340, 31-266, 32-9, 32-293, 32-383, 32-497, 33-72, 33-196, 33-247, 33-307, 33-456, 33-469, 33-612, 33-690, 34-29, 34-228, 34-242, 34-256, 34-379, 34-400, 34-411, 34-418, 34-550, 34-552, 34-554, 35-302, 35-319, 35-320, 35-369, 35-438, 35-440, 35-448, 35-452
Fischer, Emil Sigmund	斐士	27-439, 31-242, 33-102, 35-286, 35-400
Fitch, R. F.	费佩德	33-480
Fletcher, William John Bainbridge	佛来遮	26-454, 26-455
Foote, A. H.		2-139
Forke, A.	佛尔克	18-344, 19-324, 19-389, 20-390, 31-334
Forrest, Robert James.	富礼赐	4-193
Fox, Harry H.	傅夏礼	26-456
Francis, John de	德范克	35-493
Fraser, E. H.	法磊斯	15-9, 24-507
Fraser, F. A.	富美基	18-175
Freeman, Mansfield	费孟福	29-96, 30-130, 33-80
Fries, S. Ritter Von	费习孟	13-659
Fritsche, H.	费理饬	8-347
Fuchs		32-512
G.		23-679, 30-325, 33-476
G., A. J.		30-361, 30-368
G., D. M.		27-295
Gabelentz, Georg Von der		11-673
Gale, Esson Mcdowell	盖乐	33-142, 33-189, 33-190, 33-192, 33-205, 33-212, 33-369, 33-469, 33-488, 33-491, 33-494, 33-504, 33-506, 33-632, 33-646, 33-655, 33-666, 33-674, 33-692, 33-695, 34-213, 34-217, 34-232, 34-246, 34-375, 34-383, 34-392, 34-409, 34-417, 35-134, 35-305
Galt, E. W.	高厚儒	11-543

(续表)

责 任 者	责任者中文名	页 码
Gamble, William.	姜别利	3－197
Gapanovich, J. J.	噶邦福	32－198
Gardner, Christopher Thomas	嘉托玛	4－27，11－259，16－81
Gardner, Charles S.		32－163
Gaunt, T.	恭多马	27－127
Gee, Nathaniel Gist	祁天锡	23－151，25－446，29－136
Gibson, Harry E.	裘必胜	33－461，34－49，34－235，34－336，34－467，35－93，35－126，35－127，35－231，35－315
Giles, Herbert Allen	翟理思	10－311，11－447，11－497，11－498，11－505，11－533，11－541，11－643，11－721，11－725，11－726，12－118，12－121，12－263，12－322，12－328，12－329，27－272
Gillett, Michael Cavenagh	支乐德	35－581，35－612，35－613，35－624，35－626
Gillett, T. H.	吉勒德	35－312
Gillis, I. V.	义理寿	28－569
Glathe, von A.		33－505
Goebel, Max.		13－60
Goodrich, Luther Carrington	傅路德	32－521，34－367
Grabau, A. W.	葛利普	33－285
Gribble, Henry	记里布	18－198
Griffith, John	杨格非	2－428
Groot, J. J. M. de	高延	15－116
Grosbois, Ch.	高博爱	29－502，29－504，30－358，32－494，32－495，33－187，33－188
Guppy, H. B.	古庇	10－7，10－19，10－333，11－203，11－207,,
H., F.		12－332
H., L. F.		21－612
Haas, Joseph	夏士	9－235，15－254
Hagerty, M. J.		33－200
Hall, J. C.	贺若贤	21－447
Hallifax, T. E.		13－663
Harding, H. L.	哈尔定	25－100
Hauer, Erich		31－386
Haward, Edwin	何立德	32－146
Hayes, L. Newton.	海士	28－106，30－105

(续表)

责 任 者	责任者中文名	页　　码
Headland, Isaac Taylor	何德兰	20-340
Heeren, John J.	奚尔恩	27-552, 28-503
Heidenstam, H. von	海德生	27-39
Henderson, James	韩德森	3-20, 3-73
Henke, Frederick G.		23-72
Henry, Augustine	韩尔礼	12-617
Hers, Joseph	艾勒斯	27-139
Himly, K.	希姆利	5-127
Hinckley, F. E.		21-225, 22-257, 22-259, 22-448, 23-669
Hirth, F.	夏德	10-531, 11-499, 11-501, 11-541, 11-542, 11-609, 11-632, 11-633, 11-681, 11-729, 12-106, 12-217, 12-222, 12-237, 12-437, 12-487, 12-488, 12-490, 12-493, 12-513, 12-587, 13-46
Hoang, Pierre	黄汝梅	19-210
Hobson, H. E.	好博逊	8-55, 13-37
Hodges, Ada		24-482
Hodous, Lewis	何乐益	22-403, 23-610, 24-261, 25-94
Holcombe, C.	何天爵	7-75
Hollingworth, H. G.	荷魏尔	3-195, 3-559
Hosie, Lady	谢福芸	29-45
Hosie, Alex.	谢立山	8-267, 8-307, 11-361
Houghton, Henry Spence	胡恒德	22-251
House, I. E.		35-527
Howell, E. B.	好威乐	25-465
Hu, Shih	胡适	30-276, 31-40
Hudson, Elfrida		27-118, 27-369, 27-370, 29-382, 29-386, 30-312
Hughes, E. R.	修中诚	32-340, 32-467
Hughes, P. J.	许士	11-506, 13-492
Huston, James	哈司顿	25-111, 26-73, 27-71, 27-381
I., O.		26-471
Imbault-Huart, Camille	于雅乐	11-91, 11-379, 11-630, 11-637, 11-647, 11-728, 18-9
Inglis, J. W.	英雅各	24-231, 24-242

(续表)

责 任 者	责任者中文名	页 码
Inui, K. S.		32-246
Jacot, Arhtur Paul	贾珂	27-152, 27-538, 28-98, 28-486, 29-389, 30-258, 31-353, 32-116
Jamieson, C. A.	陈国将	27-359, 27-654
Jamieson, George	哲美森	13-65
Jamieson, R. A.	詹美生	3-161, 3-335, 3-400
Jarvie, Robert	贾维	3-393
Jenkins, B.	秦右	4-308
Johnston, Reginald Fleming	庄士敦	23-199, 23-672, 24-472, 24-477, 32-306
Jowett, Hardy	周永治	23-198
K., J. C. D.		30-327, 31-165
K., L.		24-179
K., P. H.		22-247
Kann, E.	耿爱德	31-104
Kanno, Domei	简野道明	24-483
Keer, J. G.	寇尔	3-513
Kellogg, Claude R.	克立鹄	25-420
Kemp, Emily Georgiana	葛安布	26-418
King, George E.	金文宽	25-461
Kingsmill, Thomas William	金斯密	3-241, 3-357, 3-546, 4-257, 4-302, 5-377, 6-41, 7-91, 8-23, 8-313, 9-25, 9-169, 9-201, 11-421, 11-537, 11-545, 12-124, 15-52, 15-129, 15-134, 18-365, 18-514, 18-529, 19-329, 19-331, 19-333, 19-524, 19-614, 20-211, 20-375, 20-382, 20-395, 20-408, 20-617, 20-668, 20-679, 20-697, 21-201, 21-218, 21-227, 21-472
Kleinwachter, George.	康发达	11-73
Kliene, Charles	葛麟瑞	25-162, 25-384, 26-401, 27-574, 30-381, 32-507
Kliene., R.	葛麟祥	11-733
Kojeuroff, George P.		29-446
Kulp II, Daniel H.	葛学溥	27-309, 32-402
L.		31-420
L., A. E. N.		20-392, 20-394
L., A. L.		25-483

(续表)

责 任 者	责任者中文名	页 码
L., D.		20-410
Lamprey, Dr.	兰普雷	3-221, 3-399
Lanning, George	蓝宁	21-413, 21-604, 23-699, 24-171, 24-329, 24-487, 25-190, 25-192, 25-202, 25-492, 26-103
Latourette, Kenneth Scott	赖德烈	24-135
Laver, H. E.		24-305, 25-31
Le Gros Clark, C. D.	李高洁	33-662
Leavenworth, Charles S.		20-111
Lee, Shao-chang	李绍昌	33-446
Legge, James	理雅各	12-245
Lester, E. S.	李淑德	29-521, 30-370
Leung, George Kin.	梁社乾	29-355
Leveson, W. E.		22-255
Lin, Tung-chi	林同济	33-598
Lin, Yu-tang	林语堂	33-577
Lindau, Rudolph	林道	3-7
Ling, Peter C.	凌爱国	25-71
Little, Archibald J.	立德	7-329, 11-209
Liu, J. C.	柳中兴	31-140
Lobinger, Charles Sumner	罗炳吉	23-428, 25-301
Lockhart, J. H. Stewart	骆任廷	12-128
Lu, Yen-Ying		32-174
Ly, J. Usang	李氏	35-483
Lyon, David Willard	来会理	32-501, 33-358, 33-454
M.		13-45, 22-447, 23-227, 23-229, 23-230, 23-232, 23-458, 23-676, 23-682, 24-168, 24-187, 24-463, 24-471, 24-494, 24-508, 25-178, 25-183, 25-194, 25-197, 25-200, 25-202, 25-204, 25-205, 25-211, 25-469, 25-474, 25-484, 25-488, 25-489, 25-490, 25-504, 25-506, 25-513, 26-206, 26-210, 26-218, 26-225, 26-460, 26-464, 26-468, 26-470, 26-473, 26-476, 26-481, 26-486, 27-287, 27-297, 27-299, 27-300, 27-644, 27-646, 27-649, 27-659, 32-487, 32-488, 32-489
M., N.		28-644, 28-653

(续表)

责 任 者	责任者中文名	页 码
MacGillivray, Donald	季理斐	21-608, 22-445, 23-203, 23-204, 26-223, 30-42
Macgowan, Daniel John	玛高温	2-113, 2-192, 2-332, 2-453, 5-145, 5-475, 5-477, 6-419, 11-649, 12-30, 12-141
Macintyre, John	马钦泰	12-51
Macklin, W. E.	马林	19-265
MacLeod, N.		28-290, 28-292
MacNair, Harley Farnsworth.	宓亨利	28-405
MaGrath, C. D.		23-474
Markham, John.	马安	5-23
Martin, William Alexander Parsos	丁韪良	3-476, 8-135, 20-191
Mason, Isaac	梅益盛	24-174, 24-494, 24-495, 25-201, 26-181, 26-213, 26-214, 27-651, 28-592, 29-534, 30-19, 30-350, 30-353, 30-355, 31-62, 31-157, 31-158, 31-159, 32-143, 32-225, 32-246
Maxwell, J. L.	马雅各	32-483, 32-486
Maybon, C. B.	梅伯	25-479
Mayers, William Frederick	梅辉立	4-165, 5-53, 5-95, 5-241, 8-217
McCartee, D. B.	麦嘉缔	3-527, 5-195
McCormick, Frederick		22-463
McIntosh, G.	金多士	32-471, 32-492
Medhurst, C. Spurgeon		22-429, 22-430, 23-450
Medhurst, W. H.	麦华陀	4-356
Meerdervoort, Johannes Lijdius Catharinus Pompe van		2-245, 2-493
Meerkerk, M. E. R. F.		30-182
Mencarini, Juan	绵嘉义	19-182, 20-128, 25-505
Merz, C.	梅泽	21-398, 21-409, 21-610, 22-434, 23-445
Millican, Frank R.	梅立德	32-482, 32-484, 32-487, 32-489, 32-505, 34-226, 34-385, 34-386, 34-393, 34-394, 34-395, 34-397, 34-403, 34-406, 34-557, 34-558, 34-559, 34-560, 34-568, 35-134, 35-446
Mironov, N. D.		28-133
Moffett, Lacy I. & Gee, N. Gist	慕维德、祁天锡	23-151
Mollendorff, O. F. von.	穆林德	8-63, 12-613

(续表)

责 任 者	责任者中文名	页 码
Möllendorff, P. G. von	穆麟德	9-145, 13-357, 16-141, 18-385
Moninger, M. M.	孟言嘉	26-302
Mooallen, A. A.		23-462
Moore, Alfred	穆信诚	25-438
Moore, Osborne		13-195
Morgan, Evan	莫安仁	22-427, 25-146, 25-525, 26-47, 26-263, 27-601, 27-603, 29-76, 29-231, 29-231, 29-76, 29-430, 29-512, 29-515, 29-516, 29-524, 29-525, 30-322, 30-326, 31-149, 31-287, 31-402, 31-412, 31-416, 31-427, 32-179, 32-236, 32-239, 32-430, 32-468, 32-472, 32-476, 32-479, 32-491, 32-496, 32-506, 32-509, 33-183, 33-482, 33-634, 34-481, 35-86
Morgan, Marion L.		32-465, 32-498, 32-512, 32-519, 33-193, 33-652
Moromastix		11-591
Morris, H. C.		23-702
Morrison, G. James	毛里逊	11-185
Morse, Hosea Ballou	马士	13-55, 13-58, 13-60, 13-183, 20-381, 20-443, 20-691, 26-399
Moule, A. E.	慕雅德	11-501
Moule, Arthur Christopher	慕阿德	21-11, 21-548, 22-299, 23-243, 23-442, 23-571, 29-297, 30-314, 31-399
Moule, G. E.	慕稼谷	5-151, 5-387, 6-247, 11-352, 13-15, 19-133
Moyer, Raymond T.	穆懿尔	32-359, 34-351
Muirhead, W.	慕维廉	12-313
Murphy, Dagny Carter	美斐	32-420
Murphy, Henry Killam	茂非	33-640
Nicolson, F. W.		2-27
Nocentini, Ludovico	诺琴蒂尼	11-601, 11-731, 12-474
Norin, E.		27-129
Nye, Gideon	奈益	11-624, 11-732
Nyström, Erik T.	新常富	34-173

(续表)

责任者	责任者中文名	页码
O., M.		25-208, 26-215
Old Cathay [pseud.]		25-434
O'Shea, J.	和若望	21-414
Ottewill, H. A.	奥泰蔚	25-104
Oxenham, E. L.	欧森南	13-298
P., A. C.		30-332
Palladius, Archimandrite.	鲍乃迪	7-21
Parker, Alvin Pierson	潘慎文	23-219, 24-117, 24-180, 24-492
Parker, Edward Harper	庄延龄	8-235, 11-285, 11-312, 11-333, 12-297, 12-317, 12-385, 12-451, 12-484, 12-485, 12-498, 13-645, 18-82, 18-114, 18-191, 18-305, 20-385, 20-386, 20-387, 20-673, 21-212, 21-270, 23-114, 24-147
Patterson, B. C.	卜德生	22-452
Pearson, G. W.	毕尔逊	20-707
Penniston, John B.		33-136
Perry, Charles E.		35-622, 35-623
Phelps, D. L.	费尔璞	30-186
Phillips, E. S. J.		35-443
Phillips, George	费笠子	11-655, 12-38, 13-29
Ping, C.	平文谦	32-79
Platt, B. S.		33-648
Playfair, G. M. H.	白挨底	11-515, 11-534, 11-537, 11-540, 11-627, 11-628, 11-631, 11-640, 12-75, 12-113, 12-114, 12-237, 13-580
Plumer, James Marshall	濮累玛	33-654, 33-665
Porter, Karola		24-174
Porter, Lucius Chapin	博晨光	34-219
Porterfield, W. M.	包达甫	32-61
Poston, Divid Gray		35-276
Pott, Francis Lister Hawks	卜舫济	25-216, 25-507, 27-291, 28-436, 30-338, 32-229
Preston, C. F.	丕思业	4-345
Pringle, J. C.		35-614
Prip-Møller, Johannes	艾术华	34-86

(续表)

责 任 者	责任者中文名	页 码
Pryer, W. B.	朴贲懿	4-80
Qin Shi Huang	嬴政	28-434
R., F. F.		34-399
Read, Bernard Emms	伊博恩	34-556, 34-559, 34-562, 34-564, 34-565, 35-71, 35-128, 35-131, 35-133, 35-218, 35-307, 35-308, 35-312, 35-313, 35-442, 35-450, 35-451
Read, Katherine L.		35-128
Reichelt, Karl Ludvig	艾香德	34-561, 35-308
Reymond, C. du Bois		23-461
Rhein, J.	来因	9-231, 11-646
Richard, Timothy	李提摩太	23-9, 16-273, 23-454
Ridge, W. Sheldon	李治	20-685, 22-432
Riley, J. H.		27-230, 27-599
Rispaud, Jean		33-173
Roberts, Donald	罗道纳	30-337, 30-358, 33-197, 33-475, 34-233, 34-235, 35-383, 35-620
Roberts, Frances M.		30-388, 33-198, 35-621, 35-623
Roberts, R.	饶伯师	35-619
Robertson, D. B.	罗伯逊	2-339
Robinson, F. Alan	罗宾生	30-342
Rockhill, W. W.	柔克义	11-723, 11-724, 12-497
Rondot, Natalis		12-247, 18-594
Ros, Giuseppe	罗斯	24-356
Ross, A.	罗辛甫	23-680
Rosthorn, Arthur von	罗士恒	16-11
Ruffé, M. d'Auxion de		23-221, 23-470, 35-412
S.		24-184, 29-535
S., H. P.		30-371
Saeki, P. Y.	佐伯好郎	32-323, 33-117, 33-407, 34-123
Scherzer, F.	师克勤	11-61
Schmidt, C.	史密德	6-49
Schulze, F. W.	舒尔兹	9-81
Schwarz, Kurt L.		35-429, 35-605

(续表)

责 任 者	责任者中文名	页 码
Scott, James	萨允格	16-528, 29-507
Segalen, Victor		24-407
Shadwell, C. B.		2-256, 2-503
Sharman, Lyon		32-515
Shaw, Norman	佘瑙满	25-206, 25-207, 25-209, 25-210, 25-495
Shields, E. T.		23-140
Shipway, G. W.		22-425, 28-273, 28-280, 28-282, 28-283, 28-284, 28-285, 28-286, 28-288, 28-640, 28-642, 28-643, 28-644, 28-651, 28-652, 28-655, 29-237, 29-238, 29-241, 29-242, 29-501, 29-537, 30-345, 31-161, 31-407, 31-409, 31-411, 31-418, 31-426, 32-243, 32-477, 32-480, 32-481
Shirokogoroff, Sergei Mikhailovich	史禄国	27-620, 28-21, 28-293, 29-149, 29-243, 29-249, 29-253
Shock, W. H.		2-500
Simon, G. Eug.	西蒙	4-215, 4-279, 4-365, 5-75
Sirén, Osvald	喜仁龙	33-561
Sjolander, David		27-165
Skvortzow, B. W.		25-315, 26-157, 26-341, 27-223
Smith, F. Porter.	师维善	5-161
Smith, H.	司美福	30-389
Soothill, W. E.	苏慧廉	31-318
Sowerby, Arthur de Carle	苏阿德	24-83, 27-17, 29-527, 31-163, 31-164, 31-167, 31-169, 31-170, 31-171, 31-172, 31-173, 31-177, 31-424, 31-425, 33-249, 34-329, 34-455, 34-457, 34-561, 34-562, 34-563, 34-565, 35-45, 35-47, 35-122, 35-123, 35-124, 35-125, 35-193, 35-195, 35-314, 35-316, 35-389, 35-443, 35-445
St. Denys, d'Hervey	圣丹尼斯	12-246
Stael-Holstein, Baron Alexander von	钢和泰	27-372
Stanley, Arthur	史笪来	22-256, 22-383, 22-431, 22-438, 23-93, 23-202, 23-220, 23-222, 23-223, 23-224, 23-225, 23-315, 23-376, 23-465, 23-466, 23-467, 23-469, 23-537, 23-694, 24-113, 24-319, 24-485, 24-486, 24-487, 25-181, 25-182, 26-35, 26-204
Stedeford, E. T. A.	施福德	29-536

(续表)

责任者	责任者中文名	页码
Stent, George Carter	司登得	5-333, 5-423, 8-165, 27-304
Stifler, Susan Reed		34-504
Stronach, W. T.		3-398
Sun, Chien		33-463
Swinhoe, Robert	郇和	2-167, 2-259, 2-327, 3-261, 5-265, 5-281
Syle, Edward W.	帅福守	2-198
T., C. B.		11-543, 11-732, 11-527
T., J. Ch.		25-471, 25-473
T., M. B.		29-505
Taintor, E. C.	廷得尔	6-299
Talbot, R. M.	铎博赉	31-147
Taylor, F. E.	戴乐安	11-732
Teesadale, J. H.	天赐德	23-695, 23-696, 23-697, 23-698, 23-699, 29-118
Teng, Kuei	藤圭	33-349
Thomas, James.	唐默思	6-429, 21-215
Thompson, J.	汤顺	5-437
Tobar, Jérôme	管宜穆	19-210
Toda, Ed.	多达	10-351
Tomkinson, L.	童克圣	35-256
Torrance, Thomas	陶然士	21-507, 27-520, 28-80, 28-80, 28-86, 29-139
Touche, J. D. D. de la	德拉图什	21-359
Tsai, Yuen-pei	蔡元培	32-157
Turner, F. B.	德辅廊	29-25
Tyler, William Ferdinand	戴理尔	23-653, 24-498
Ungern-Sternberg, L.		30-360, 33-638
Vacca, Giovanni		31-232
Vale, Joshua	斐焕章	19-118, 20-44
Viguier, S. A.	威基谒	6-85
Volpicelli, Z.	武尔披齐	13-260, 15-88, 15-135, 16-43
W., E. W.		28-286
W., R. K.		22-421

(续表)

责 任 者	责任者中文名	页 码
Walshe, W. Gilbert	华立熙	19-290, 19-564
Wang, Kuo-wei.	王国维	30-165
Wang, T. Ford		33-465, 33-656, 33-659, 34-225
Ward, Francis Kingdon		24-69
Ward, John	倭尔特	2-265, 2-505, 22-449
Warner, Langdon		23-492
Warren, Gilbert G.	任修本	22-360, 22-446, 23-629, 23-687, 24-42, 28-48
Watson, W. C. Haines	花荪	20-59
Wells, H. R.		31-307
Wen, Yu	闻宥	34-541
Werner, Edward Theodore Chalmers	倭讷	4-231, 5-405, 6-63, 6-335, 26-448, 27-624, 28-492, 28-550, 29-223, 29-486, 30-246
White, Laura M.	亮乐月	30-227
Wilden, Henry Auguste	韦礼德	27-311
Wilder, Geo. D.	万卓志	28-184, 29-210
Wilds, Edward.		3-191
Wilhelm, Richard	卫礼贤	23-295, 23-475
Wilkinson, Hiram Parhes	威金生	26-374
Williams, Charles Alfred Speed	威立师	25-291
Williams, E. T., Mrs.	卫理夫人	19-19
Williams, Edward Thomas	卫理	20-513, 23-21, 33-547, 34-61, 34-391, 35-102
Williams, Frederick Wells	卫斐列	22-15
Williams, Samuel Wells	卫三畏	2-214, 2-350, 3-533, 5-171, 6-19, 28-651
Williamson, A.	韦廉臣	3-451, 4-39, 4-70
Wilson, J. Wallace		22-428
Woo, Z. T.	吴	32-453
Woodbridge, S. Isett	吴板桥	20-687
Wright, Harrison King	励德厚	24-445, 25-486, 25-488, 25-497, 25-511, 26-219, 26-221, 26-474, 26-476, 26-487, 26-488, 27-289, 27-290, 27-293, 27-294, 27-306, 27-314, 27-642, 27-657, 27-658

(续表)

责 任 者	责任者中文名	页 码
Wu, Lien-Teh	伍连德	32-21, 33-29
Wylie, Alexander	伟烈亚力	2-54, 3-53, 3-185, 3-523, 4-93, 4-431
Yan-tsz Chiu		25-409
Yao, Shan yu	姚善友	35-532
Zia, Z. K.		32-488
Zwemer, Samuel Marinus	知味墨	25-56

附 录

皇家亚洲文会北华支会研究

王毅 著

目　录

绪论 / 201

第一章　创建与发展 / 207
第一节　创建背景 / 207
第二节　发展历程 / 216
　一　初创时期(1857－1861) / 216
　二　重建与发展时期(1864－1910) / 218
　三　兴盛时期(1911－1941) / 222
　四　结束时期(1946－1951) / 225

第二章　组织机构（一）/ 226
第一节　理事会 / 226
第二节　会员 / 229
　一　国籍与身份 / 230
　二　会员级别 / 232
　三　会员与文会 / 235
　四　会员的分布 / 236

第三章　组织机构（二）/ 240
第一节　图书馆 / 240
　一　馆藏书籍 / 240
　二　图书馆之利用及评价 / 247
第二节　博物院 / 249
　一　发展历程 / 249
　二　藏品与陈列 / 252
　三　活动 / 257

第四章　日常活动 / 262
第一节　例会和年会 / 262
第二节　演讲 / 263
第三节　会刊 / 264

一 会刊内容 / 265
　　二 会刊影响 / 269
　第四节 其他活动 / 274
　　一 国际交流活动 / 274
　　二 国内活动 / 276

第五章 对华调查研究之动态分析 / 280
　第一节 时间变化 / 280
　　一 在关注点上，对中国内政从有所关注发展到不再关注 / 280
　　二 由调查走向研究 / 282
　第二节 空间差异 / 289
　　一 不同国家会员对华之调查研究 / 290
　　二 时空差异分析 / 303

第六章 亚洲文会与中西文化交流 / 311
　第一节 亚洲文会与近代国际汉学 / 311
　　一 研究领域 / 311
　　二 研究机构 / 315
　　三 汉学研究工具书及相关资料的编纂 / 316
　　四 人才培养 / 319
　　五 研究方法 / 319
　第二节 亚洲文会与西学东渐 / 320
　　一 学术研究方面 / 320
　　二 社会方面 / 322

结语 / 326

附表
　亚洲文会历次演讲目录 / 334
　皇家亚洲文会北华支会会员表 / 356

参考文献 / 508

表　目

- 表 1-1　19 世纪 50 年代五口与香港外侨人数统计表 / 208
- 表 1-2　大不列颠及爱尔兰皇家亚细亚学会支会表 / 212
- 表 1-3　文会英文名不同之中文译称 / 215
- 表 2-1　文会历任会长 / 227
- 表 2-2　文会可考会员之综合信息表 / 230
- 表 2-3　文会名誉会员表 / 232
- 表 2-4　各类会员的历年年度构成统计表 / 235
- 表 2-5　文会各类会员投稿信息统计表 / 236
- 表 2-6　文会会员所及世界各地的时间表 / 237
- 表 3-1　文会图书馆各类图书历年馆藏量 / 241
- 表 3-2　博物院历任院长 / 250
- 表 3-3　博物院展柜所展之标本 / 256
- 表 3-4　博物院历年举办的艺术品展览 / 259
- 表 3-5　博物院举办的博物学讲座 / 260
- 表 4-1　会刊文章来源统计表 / 265
- 表 4-2　会刊内容分类统计表 / 267
- 表 4-3　20 世纪中外期刊转载、引用会刊情况表 / 271
- 表 4-4　20 世纪世界各地曾经收藏会刊的图书馆 / 273
- 表 4-5　文会交换机构国籍分布统计表 / 275
- 表 4-6　文会交流机构类别统计表 / 276
- 表 4-7　文会出版之书籍（一）/ 277
- 表 4-8　文会出版之书籍（二）/ 278
- 表 5-1　文会演讲、发表文章分类统计表 / 287
- 表 5-2　文会对中国的货币研究文章 / 288
- 表 5-3　英国籍会员文章类别及篇数表 / 290
- 表 5-4　英国籍会员语言研究篇目表 / 295
- 表 5-5　美国籍会员文章类别及篇数表 / 298
- 表 5-6　文会会员在华游历观察内容之时空表 / 303
- 表 5-7　文会会员在各省最早居住地点时间表 / 306
- 表 6-1　文会帮助或参与创建的汉学机构 / 315
- 表 6-2　会员翻译的文章篇目 / 317
- 表 6-3　20 世纪各国发行的汉学期刊 / 321

绪　论

一、学术回顾与问题的提出

本课题研究与中西文化交流史研究及西方汉学史研究均有学术上的关系，因此，在展开本课题研究之前，必须对这两种专门史的研究现状作一番学术上的回顾。

长期以来，国内外学者在中西文化交流史领域进行了广泛而深入的研究。就近代中西文化交流史而言，以往的研究多注重对相关的思想、学说、流派、人物的论述，[1]而对机构等实体的研究则很少；同时，以往更多的是对学术交流的研究，而缺乏对文化交流模式的注意。近代国门被打开以后，各殖民地宗主国在华建立了为数不少的各种文化机构，这些文化机构固然是列强侵略的产物，但客观上也不免成了中外文化交流的实体。因为外来文化机构本身就是西方文化的载体，代表着一种不同的文化，同时他们也在不同程度上向西方传播着中国的文化。这些文化机构，就类别而言，有教会、学校、新闻、出版和其他社会文化机构；就性质而言，有专门服务于殖民侵略的，也有从事中西文化交流的；就功能而言，有单一的，也有综合的。在文化交流方面，这些文化机构的效能并不比人物、思想、流派的影响小。像广学会，它在近代出版了许多中文西学书籍，对"西学东渐"就有所贡献。对于教会、学校、新闻、出版等比较专门的文化机构，学界已有所论述，[2]但是对于综合性的文化机构尚未见到专门的研究论著。因

---

[1] 主要论文有：顾长声的《传教士与近代中西文化交流：兼评〈剑桥中国晚清史〉关于基督教在华活动的论述》（《历史研究》1989 年第 3 期），徐明德的《明清来华耶稣会士对中西文化交流的贡献》（《杭州大学学报》，1986 年第 4 期），梁碧莹的《美国传教士与近代中西文化交流》（《中山大学学报》1989 年第 3 期），李志刚的《马礼逊与中西文化交流》（见李志刚：《百年烟云，沧海一粟——近代中国基督教文化掠影》，今日中国出版社 1997 年版，第 27 - 43 页），卓新平的《西方传教士与中国古代文化》（《世界宗教资料》1990 年第 2 期），陶飞亚的《基督教与近代中西文化交流》（《文史知识》1993 年第 4 期），罗志田的《传教士与近代中西文化竞争》（《历史研究》1996 年第 6 期），王立新的《英美传教士与近代中西文化会通》（《世界宗教研究》1997 年第 2 期），谭树林的《卫三畏与中美文化交流》（《齐鲁学刊》1998 年第 6 期）；专著则有：Paul A. Varg, Missionaries, Chinese and Diplomats, American Missionary Movement in China 1890 - 1952, Princeton University Press, 1958. James M. McCutcheon, The American and British Missionary Concept of Chinese Civilization in the 19th Century, Ph. D, Diss, University of Wisconsin, 1959. 顾长声的《传教士与近代中国》，上海人民出版社 1981 年版；罗秉祥、赵敦华的《基督教与近代中西文化》，北京大学出版社 2000 年版；顾卫民的《基督教与近代中国社会》，上海人民出版社 1996 年版。这些研究还是局限于几个著名历史人物的身上，而且也是以他们在华的活动为主要内容，文化交流之具体影响探讨得还比较薄弱。

[2] 教会方面的论著有：D. Willard Lyon, Sketch of the History of Protestant Missions in China, New York, 1895; Kennth Scott Latourette, A History of Christian Mission in China, New York, 1929; W. N. Lacy, A Hundred Years of China Methodism, New York 1948; Wallace C. Merwin, Adventure in Unity: The Church of Christ in China, Brand Raids, Mich: Eerdmans, 1974; Iron T. Hyatt, Jr, Protestant Mission in China 1877 - 1890, Papers on China, Vol. 17., 1963; Kimberly A. Risedorph, Reformers, Athletes and Students, The YMCA in China 1895 - 1935, Washington University, 1994;学校方面的主要论著有：John Z. Bowers, Western medicine in a Chinese palace: Peking Union Medical College, 1917 - 1951, Philadelphia: The Josiah Macy, Jr. Foundation, 1972. Brian Harrison, Waiting for China: the Anglo-Chinese College at Malacca, 1818 - 1943, and early nineteenth-century missions, Hong Kong: Hong Kong University Press, 1979. Mary Lamberton, St. John's University, Shanghai, 1879 - 1951, New York: United Board for Christian Coleges in China, 1955; Philip West, Yenching University and Sino-Western Relations 1916 - 1952, Cambridge, Mass.: Harvard Univiversity Press, 1976;章开沅主编的《文化传播与教会大学》，湖北教育出版社 1996 年版；王立诚的《美国文化渗透与近代中国教育——沪江大学的历史》，复旦大学出版社 2003 年版。其他文化机构的主要论著有：The mission press in China: being a jublee retrospect of the American Presbyterian mission press, with sketches of other mission presses in China, as well as accounts of the Bible and Tract societies at work in China, Shanghai: American Presbyterian Mission Press, 1895.

此,本课题选择一综合性的文化机构作为考察对象,以期通过对该机构作具体的微观分析,能够在中外文化交流史以及文化地理研究方面作出新的探索。

本课题选择的这个综合性的文化机构是皇家亚洲文会北华支会,即 The North-China Branch of the Royal Asiatic Society(以下简称文会),它是近代外侨在上海创建的一个公共文化机构,旨在"调查研究中国各项事情"。它组织完善、目标明确,在近代独此一家,并以其图书馆、博物院和大量的会员,形成了多元化的文化交流媒介。因此,对于该机构的研究不仅可以弥补以往文化交流史研究的不足,而且可以拓展文化交流史研究的领域,掘进文化交流史研究的深度,也有助于认识文化机构在文化交流中的作用、地位和意义。

专门论述文会的文章十分有限。日本的小竹文夫最早对文会图书馆当时的馆藏书籍做了初步的介绍,列出了比较有价值的馆藏东方学图书。[1] 1933年,胡道静对文会博物院做了较为详细的回顾,基本上勾勒出了文会博物院的发展历程。[2] 1988年,奥特尼斯(Harold M. Otness)对文会图书馆的历史、藏书量做了简单回顾,但未谈及馆藏书籍之构成、来此借阅的读者、图书馆的有关活动和图书馆在近代中西文化交流中的贡献。[3] 1996年,张海林初步论述了文会的活动和会刊的内容,但是由于所见材料的限制,还欠准确。[4] 此外,在有关新闻史及其他论著中也曾见到关于文会的介绍,但这些介绍在学术上意义不大。[5] 可以说,前此关于文会的研究成果均系介绍性的,而且由于写作时间和所见材料的限制,这些文章对文会的介绍还欠准确,对文会的组织结构、会刊、会员、活动、博物院的情况至今未有研究性的论述,文会在近代中西文化交流中的贡献更无人论及。

文会设在上海,处于近代中西文化交流的最前沿,在近代中西文化交流史上有着特殊的地位,但是以往有关上海史的研究论著几乎未对文会做过深入研究,遑论文会在近代中西文化交流中的地位和意义。1921年,兰宁、库寿龄撰写的《上海史》和1937年岑德彰编译的《上海租界略史》对该机构的描述寥寥不到百余字。[6] 20世纪30年代编纂的《上海通志馆期刊》也只是在"上海图书馆史"中对文会图书馆做一简单介绍;[7] 1999年,熊月之先生主编的《上海通史》对文会图书馆和博物院也专门予以描述,[8] 在准确性、全面性方面都较以往论著有所突破,但基本上仍处于介绍的层面上。因此,对该机构的研究,也有望填补上海史研究的一项空白。

文会在致力于调查研究中国各项事情的同时,也提出"为汉学提供令人满意的研究成果"。

---

[1] (日)小竹文夫:《上海の英国亚细亚学会北支会图书馆》,见东亚同文书院支那研究部:《支那研究》第十九号,昭和四年(1930年)五月发行,第313—342页。

[2] 胡道静:《上海博物院史略》,《上海研究资料续集》,第391—412页。见《民国丛书》第四编第81辑,上海书店1993年版。

[3] Harold M. Otness: The one bright spot in shanghai: A history of the Library of the North-China Branch of the Royal Asiatic Society. Journal of the Hong Kong Branch of the Asiatic Society(Hong Kong), Vol.28, 1988.

[4] 张海林:《上海亚洲文会述论》,《南京大学学报》,1996年第1期。

[5] 这些介绍详见:戈公振的《中国报学史》,《民国丛书》第二编49辑,上海书店1990年版,第87页;郭卫东主编的《近代外国在华文化机构综录》,上海人民出版社1993年版,第181页;方汉奇的《中国新闻事业编年史》(上),福建人民出版社2000年版;叶再生的《中国近现代出版通史》,华文出版社2002年版;(日)山口昇编的《欧米人の支那に于けろ文化事业》,佐原研究室出版,上海日本堂发行,大正十年(1921年);石田干之助的《欧米人に於けろ支那学の现况》,东亚同文会调查编辑部编《支那》,1929年7—9月号;满铁上海事务所编的《上海アヅア学会北支那支部の杂志编纂主任Gale の记事》,《满铁调查资料》,第十一所揭,昭和七年十二月;姊崎正治博士的《欧米人の东洋学の现况》,东亚同文会发行《支那》,昭和八年十二月号;石田干之助的《欧米人に於けろ支那研究》,东京创元社昭和十七年(1942年)刊行,第105—112页;

[6] George Lanning & Samuel Couling, The History of Shanghai, Shanghai: Kelly & Walsh, Ltd., 1921. pp433—434. 岑德彰编译:《上海租界略史》,劝业书局1937年版,第112页。

[7] 胡道静:《上海图书馆史》,《上海通志馆期刊》第2卷第4期,第1399—1401页。

[8] 熊月之主编:《上海通史·晚清文化》(第六卷),上海人民出版社1999年版,第194—195、205—206页。

该机构存在期间,不仅从事中西文化交流的活动,而且也为近代国际汉学作出了突出的贡献。因此对该机构的研究也有助于对近代国际汉学发展的全面理解。

就近代汉学发展史研究状况而言,1933年莫东寅的《汉学发达史》(上海书店)和1942年石田干之助的《欧人之汉学研究》(东京创元社昭和十七年刊行)基本上勾勒出了20世纪以前汉学发展的脉络。此后,大陆学界的汉学史研究一度沉寂,港台地区部分学者则继续了在该领域的研究。20世纪60年代,陶振誉等人论述了英、美、法、德、意、日、越、荷、瑞典等地的汉学发展简史。[1] 1975年香港又再版了李璜早年翻译沙畹的《法国汉学小史》(香港珠海学院出版委员会1975年)。[2] 80年代以来,大陆之汉学史研究再次热起来,涌现了不少的论文和专著。[3] 这些研究成果几乎复原了17世纪以来世界各国的汉学发展之简史,涉及到各个国家、各个时期的主要论著和部分汉学研究机构,但深入论述还是主要集中于明清时来华的耶稣会士对中国文化的研究及他们向西方传播中国文化的贡献,对近代西方汉学史研究还有待深化。

文会是近代的一个重要汉学机构,文会所发行的会刊也是著名的汉学期刊,其图书馆收藏的书籍多数是关于中国的西文图书,但是上述汉学史的研究对这个位居东方的汉学重镇却言之寥寥,因此,对文会的研究不仅可弥补一项汉学研究的空白,而且也有望能开辟汉学研究的一个新领域。

综上所述,对文会做深入分析和研究,不仅可弥补汉学史与上海史研究的一项空白,更为重要的是有助于推进和深入对中西文化交流史的研究。而且,文化的传播、扩散与交流本是文化地理的研究对象之一,本选题同时也属于历史文化地理的范畴。此外,该机构对中国历史和地理也作了大量调查和深入研究,因此对该机构的研究无疑也可对中国历史地理学的研究提供一些有用的资料。

由于本课题是对文化机构作具体、微观的研究,以往的一些研究文化机构的学术成果对本课题也起到了一定的帮助,具体如下:

斯蒙德斯(Stuart Simmonds)、狄格拜(Simon Digby)等人合著的《皇家亚洲文会:它的历史及宝贵财富》是一册追溯大英皇家亚洲学会 Royal Asiatic Society of Great Britain and Ire-

---

[1] 陶振誉等著:《世界各国汉学研究论文集》,台湾"国防研究院"1968年版。
[2] 《法国汉学小史》最早出现于李璜所译格拉勒(Grant, M. M.)之《古中国的跳舞与神秘故事》(中华书局1933年版)。
[3] 主要论著有:(法)阿尔等著、耿昇摘译的《十八世纪法国对中国科学与工艺的调查》(《中国史研究动态》1980年第4期),许敏的《明清之际耶稣会传教士与中国社会生活的西传:西方人眼里中国人的衣食住行》(《史学集刊》1992年第1期),吴孟雪的《明清欧人对中国文献的研究和翻译》(《文史知识》1993年第6、7、9期),吴孟雪的《明清欧人对中国历史的研究和介绍》(《文史知识》1994年第7、8、9期),郑天星的《传教士与中学西渐:以德国汉学家卫礼贤为中心》(《宗教学研究》1997年第2期),(法)戴密微的《法国汉学研究史》(见(法)戴仁主编、耿昇译的《法国当代中学》,中国社会科学出版社1998年版,第1—65页),阎纯德的《汉学和西方汉学》、《汉学和汉学研究漫议》(《汉学研究》第一集),(美)韩大伟的《西方古典汉学史回顾:传统与真实》(《清华汉学研究》第三辑),戴密微的《法国汉学研究史概述》(《汉学研究第一集》,吴孟雪的《中学西渐的第一页——16世纪欧洲汉学概况》(《汉学研究》第一集),钱林森的《法国汉学的历史与现状》(《汉学研究》第二集),熊文华的《荷兰的汉学研究》(《汉学研究》第二集)、《俄罗斯的汉学研究》、《瑞典的汉学研究》(《汉学研究》第三集),马树德的《汉学和中国文学在德国》(《汉学研究》第三集),张国刚的《从外交译员到汉学教授》(李学勤主编的《国际汉学漫步》(下),河北教育出版社1996年版,第838—865页),(德)傅吾康著、陈燕、袁媛译的《十九世纪的欧洲汉学》(《国际汉学》第七辑),(法)巴斯蒂著、胡志宏译的《十九、二十世纪欧洲中国史研究的几个主题》(《国际汉学》第八辑),胡志宏的《西方早期汉学发展脉络》(胡志宏的《西方中国古代史研究导论》(第一章,大象出版社2002年版)。专著则有:张静河的《瑞典汉学史》(安徽文艺出版社1995年),计翔翔的《十七世纪中期汉学著作研究》(上海古籍出版社2002年版),吴孟雪、曾丽雅的《明代欧洲汉学史》(东方出版社2000年版),张国刚的《德国的汉学研究》(中华书局1994年版),《明清传教士与欧洲汉学》(中国社会科学出版社2001年版),(法)安田朴的《中国文化西传欧洲史》(商务印书馆2000年版),何寅、许光华主编的《国外汉学史》(上海外语教育出版社2002年版),李庆的《日本汉学史》(上海外语教育出版社2002年版),刘正的《海外汉学研究》(武汉大学出版社2002年版),阎宗临的《阎守诚传教士与法国早期汉学》(大象出版社2003年版)。

land 发展历史的论文集,[1]该书对大英皇家亚洲学会发展历史之回顾、所藏珍贵文物之论述、重要人物之贡献等部分的内容为本研究提供了直接的借鉴作用。

英国的亨利·莱昂斯论述了英国皇家学会(The Royal Society)自 15 世纪到 20 世纪间从筹建、发展到成为科学学会的发展历程,并对不同时期皇家学会的会员之身份、数量及参与英国皇家学会之活动热情度进行了深入的分析,[2]该书为本研究分析文会的理事会和广大会员提供了思路。

美国的 R. K. 默顿通过对 17 世纪英国的科学发展的研究,探讨了社会、文化与科学之间相互影响的模式以及促使科学研究课题转移的社会原因。[3]书中对英国皇家学会的论述和《哲学会报》所刊文章的分析为本研究分析文会会员研究课题的转移也提供了借鉴。

台湾的陈以爱通过对北京大学国学门这个研究所发展历程的回顾,论述了中国近代学术体制从传统过渡到现代的转变过程,指出了学术研究的组织化、制度化和专业化在现代学术发展中的作用。[4]该书为本研究论述"文会与近代国际汉学"提供了一定的启迪。

此外,还有数篇关于文化机构的论文在不同程度上也启发了笔者的思路,它们是:张寄谦的《哈佛燕京学社》(《近代史研究》1990 年第 3 期)、董作宾的《历史语言研究所在学术上的贡献》(《大陆杂志》2 卷 1 期)、史复来的《〈燕京学报〉前四十期述评》(《燕京学报》第 1 期,1995 年)、王立新的《晚清在华传教士教育团述评》(《近代史研究》1995 年第 3 期)、张静的《广学会与晚清中外文化交流》(《历史教学》1997 年第 11 期)。

二、资 料 来 源

1. 与文会直接相关的报刊资料:《皇家亚洲文会北华支会会刊》(Journal of the North-China Branch of the Royal Asiatic Society)、《皇家亚洲文会中国支会纪要》(Transactions of the China Branch of the Royal Asiatic Society)、《中国丛报》(Chinese Repository)、《北华捷报》(North China Herald)、《字林西报》(North China Daily News)、《租界工部局年报》(Municipal Council, Report for the year 1870 – 1941)。

2. 近代西文汉学期刊:主要有《通报》(T'oung Pao)、《华裔学志》(Monumenta Serica)、《教务杂志》(The Chinese Recorder)、《中国评论》(China Review)、《哈佛亚洲研究》(Journal of Asiatic Studies)、《远东博物院集刊》(Bulletin of the Museum of Far Eastern Antiquities)、《远东季刊》(The Far Eastern Quarterly)、《华西边疆研究会会刊》(Journal of the West China Border Research)、《中国科学与美术杂志》(The China Journal of Science & Arts)、《美国东方学会会刊》(Journal of the American Oriental Society)、《大不列颠及爱尔兰皇家亚洲学会会刊》(Journal of the Royal Asiatic Society of Great Britain and Ireland)。这些期刊主要是英、

---

[1] Stuart Simmonds and Simon Digby, The Royal Asiatic Society: its history and treasures, Leiden: Published for the Royal Asiatic Society by E. T. Brill, 1979. "Royal Asiatic Society of Great Britain and Ireland",已有文献都习惯翻译为"大不列颠及爱尔兰皇家细亚学会"或"大英皇家亚细亚学会",简称"大英皇家亚洲学会"。本书中将"The North-China Branch of the Royal Asiatic Society"翻译为"皇家亚洲文会北华支会"而不是"皇家亚洲学会北华支会",这是有原因的,正文部分对此有解释。

[2] (英)亨利·莱昂斯著、陈先贵译:《英国皇家学会史》,云南省机械工程学会、云南省学会研究会 1985 年版。

[3] (美)R. K. 默顿著、范岱年、吴忠、蒋效东译:《十七世纪英国的科学技术与社会》(Robert K. Merton, Science, Technology and Society in Seventeen Century England, New York, Howard Fertig, 1970),四川人民出版社 1986 年版。

[4] 陈以爱:《中国现代学术研究机构的兴起——以北大研究所国学门为中心的探讨》,江西教育出版社 2002 年版。

美、法、德等欧美国家创办的研究中国及东亚的学术杂志,这些期刊多多少少都记载有关于文会的信息。

3. 民国年间国人创办的学术期刊:《"国立中央研究院"史语所集刊》、《国学季刊》、《史学消息》、《燕京学报》、《清华学报》、《国立北平图书馆馆刊》、《中法大学月刊》、《中华图书馆协会会报》等。

4. 档案:文会的原始档案尚未整理和公布,笔者只是参阅了1952－1956年上海市文化局接受亚洲文会的数件档案,这些档案提供了文会移交给中国政府的时间和当时文物标本之状况和数量。虽然未能参阅原始档案,但依据现有资料能够对文会进行较为完整的研究。

第一章 创建与发展

第一节 创建背景

探索异质文化是人类的本能。自古以来,中国在努力认识域外的同时,其他民族也在关注着中国,由此衍生出了绵延不绝、蔚为壮观的中外文化交流。以西方对中国的认识而言,古希腊、罗马时期西方的著作中已经有了相关的记载。真正来到中国,并对中国有较为丰富的感性认识的是13世纪的马可波罗,但"汉族两千多年的传统教化,他是知道得不多的",[1]后来出版的《马可波罗游记》也只能算是沿途的见闻,还谈不上研究。

15世纪新航路开辟后,东西方之间的交通已不像以前那样困难,伴随着殖民者东进的步伐,西方开始了对中国更为直接的探索与考察。首先东来的是意大利、西班牙和法国的传教士,由于明初的海禁政策,他们一直未能踏上中国土地,因此,整个15世纪"欧人关于中国之所认,非旅行之见闻,即事业之报告,距研究之域尚远"。[2]

16世纪西方开始其全球的扩张运动,基督教参与了这场运动。在中国,传教士们先于殖民者叩开了中华帝国的大门。1540年罗耀拉(Ignatius de Loyola)创建耶稣会(Jesu Societas),[3]1549年即派沙勿略(Francis Xavier)东来传教。然而沙勿略"壮志"未酬身先死,1552年病逝于中国南部沿海的上川岛。1578年,耶稣会又派利玛窦东来传教。利氏在华28年,深刻意识到中国是一个历史悠久的文明古国,要想使中国人信基督教,首先要了解中国文化、尊重中国文化。他在实践中开启了一套行之有效的传教方法,即说汉语、读典籍、着儒服、奉华俗的"适应"策略。传教的过程中,利玛窦(Matteo Ricci)、曾德昭(Álraro de Semedo)、卫匡国(Matin Martini)、柏应理(Philippe Couplet)等人深入观察了中国社会,在深度和广度上较之以前都有所突破,有人称他们为"近代史上的第一代汉学家",[4]他们的著作和书简集大大促进了西方对中国的认识与了解。16世纪,西方对中国的省份、周边国家都有了比较具体而准确的记载;语言文字方面也出现了中外对照的字典,学者们初步具备阅读汉语文献的能力,也开始了对中国的思想、制度、文化的探讨。

17世纪中叶至18世纪,西方对中国的认识较以前有很大深入。在开明运动、重农主义、开明专制的政治讨论、百科全书运动中,西方都曾用中国文化作为材料以表明观点。一些启蒙

---

[1] 柳存仁:《从利玛窦到李约瑟:汉学研究的过去与未来》,转引自林徐典的《汉学研究之回顾与前瞻》(文学语言卷),中华书局1995年版,第6页。
[2] 莫东寅:《汉学发达史》,上海书店1989年版,第60页。
[3] 本研究中的外文人名、专名之中文译称主要采自:黄光域编的《近代中国专名翻译词典》,四川人民出版社2001年版;中国社会科学院近代史研究所翻译室编的《近代来华外国人名辞典》,中国社会科学出版社1981年版。也有少数译称来源于其他资料中,鉴于比较分散,将不再一一注明。
[4] 李天纲:《中国礼仪之争:历史、文献和意义》,上海古籍出版社1998年版,第242页。

思想家如孟德斯鸠、伏尔泰和亚当·斯密也认真审视中国的古老文明。伏尔泰曾把中国的政治制度誉为"人类精神所能够设想出的最良好的政府"。在英国人眼中,中国已有了个性,他们"对中国的态度,既有亲善的,也有反对的,亲善者肯定中国的古代文明和科技,比较认同中国的自然宗教方式;反对者主张世界有神和进步,反对中国无神论和凝定的世界观"。[1]

由于18世纪发生了"礼仪之争",中外双方都禁止传教士来华传教,致使19世纪初"西方在华传教事业非常糟糕,1810年中国境内只有31位欧洲教士。北京的传教中心地位几乎已经荡然无存,1838年葡萄牙教士毕学源(Gaetano Pirès-Pereira)去世后,北京城内已无西洋传教士,利氏所开创的传教中心自此消失"。[2]

"礼仪之争"延缓了西方人直接了解认识中国的进程。18世纪末至19世纪初,除了1792年马戛尔尼使团访华外,西方与中国几乎中断了交往。直到19世纪30年代,中国沿海才出现寥寥几位西方商人和传教士。在近一个世纪中,西方对中国的研究实际上还是基于此前耶稣会士的报告和专著,没有新的调查资料和文献,这自然使得这个时期的研究带有很大的局限性和片面性。"他们了解的中国文化基本上限于儒家。他们了解的中国习俗基本上限于广东、福建沿海地区。他们了解的中国政治基本上限于康熙时代"。[3] 可以说,与利氏、卫氏等在华传教士对中国的研究相比,这一时期的研究无论是广度还是深度方面都难说有多大的突破。中西之间断绝往来,其后果是外国人对中国的认识处于空白状态,有关中国的报道有很多失实之处,如《广东记录报》(The Canton Register)所刊文章说,"中国的宝塔是用铜瓷包围而成的;旗杆用作电线机;桥有5 940尺长,104尺宽;山与山间有成千成万的桥,中国南部某古城即有12 000座"。[4] 鸦片战争前,"很多外国商人甚至不知道有厦门、上海、宁波、福州等地"。[5]

鸦片战争打破了中外隔绝的局面。1842年《南京条约》第二款规定:"自今以后,大皇帝恩准英国人民带同所属家眷寄居大清沿海之广州、福州、厦门、宁波、上海等五处港口,贸易通商无碍。"1844年美国、法国又分别逼迫清政府签订了中美《望厦条约》和中法《黄埔条约》。据此,英、美、法国等人可以携带家属居住于香港和五口通商城市。虽然游历内地还有种种限制,但是他们毕竟获得了亲自目睹中国的机会,为深入调查研究中国奠定了基础。

鉴于当时的交通不便,早年来华的外侨并不是很多,1842年共有259名,其中英国147名;美国49名;另外48名系港脚商和英属印度人。[6] 19世纪50年代,五口与香港外侨情况如下表:

表1-1　　　　　　　　　19世纪50年代五口与香港外侨人数统计表

年份	总数	上海	香港	广州	厦门	福州	宁波
1850	994	141	404	362	29	10	19
1855	1 038	243	377	334	31	28	25
1859	2 148	408	1 462	127	45	57	49

资料来源:马士:《中华帝国对外关系史》第一卷,生活·读书·新知三联书店1957年版,第389页。

---

[1] 陈受颐:《鲁滨孙的中国文化观》,《岭南学报》1卷3期,第30页。
[2] Kennth Scott Latourette, A History of Christian Mission in China, New York, 1929. pp180-181.
[3] 李天纲:《中国礼仪之争:历史、文献和意义》,上海古籍出版社1998年版,第254-257页。
[4] Chinese Repository, Vol. V(1836), P154.转引自王树槐的《卫三畏与〈中国丛刊〉》,见林治平编的《近代中国与基督教论文集》,台北,宇宙光出版社1981年版,第183页。
[5] S. W. Williams, Recollections of China prior to 1840. Journal of the North-China Branch of the Royal Asiatic Society, Vol. VIII, P16.(为引用方便,以后用"JNCBRAS"代 Journal of the North-China Branch of the Royal Asiatic Society)。
[6] 马士:《中华帝国对外关系史》第一卷,生活·读书·新知三联书店1957年版,第352页。

这些欧美国家的各色人等,包括他们的家属,远涉重洋,陆续来到中国各地。他们在通商口岸或工作,或访问,或旅行,或寓居,开始了另一种特别的异域生活。

中外直接沟通虽然实现了,但是由于中西传统文化不同,生活方式互异,当两种不同文化相遇时,便会因彼此缺乏了解、信任以及有效的沟通和相互适应而产生文化冲击(Culture Shock)现象。[1] 西方文化以宗教为主,中国文化以人文为主,二者之间虽有相同之理,但其融合一致起来却不是短时间能够做到的事。加以不平等条约的背景,中西之间存在较大的隔膜。自古形成的"华夷"观念和战争失败带来的民族屈辱感,使得作为"堂堂天朝"的子民难以接受惨败于"区区岛夷"的事实,而更加反对红毛番鬼出入于街市,因此,中外接触初期,摩擦与碰撞的现象不断出现。表现形式之一:鸦片战争前后,清官僚士大夫提出的各种制夷思想。"以夷制夷"、"以商制夷"、"以民制夷"、"以静制夷"等思想迭为先后,相继涌生,又彼此交错渗透。[2] 这种思想导致了政府官员的消极抵抗,通过回避、拖延的方法企图达到"以静制夷"的目的。例如两广总督叶名琛采取不战、不和、不守的"三不"政策,"拒不承认外国代表和不对他们作任何让步"。[3] 闽浙总督刘韵珂不愿英人入城,遂"阴加阻挠,密为牵制,使该夷不能即遂其谋"。[4] 表现形式之二:各地出现的"反入城"斗争。根据不平等条约,外人拥有在通商五口的居住权和一定区域内的自由活动权,然而福州、广州却出现了广大人民强烈的排外倾向——反对外人入城。在广州,民众揭帖"英夷居心险诈,桀骜鸱张,罪恶擢发难数";如果任其入城"终将导致夷人之进一步掠夺,最后造成战火复燃,互相残杀,不可遏止"。[5] 1846年7月8日,广州民众又向外人商馆投掷石块,引起暴乱。"外国商人只有冒着不断的挑战式的侮辱,才能越出商馆限定范围之外,只有冒着被殴打和可能受伤的危险,才能到甚至极短距离的乡村里去"。[6] 商人知道英人入城后,"人情惶恐,客心疑惑,在粤之商,早决归计,远方之客,闻风不来"。[7] 广州入城,前前后后拖延了15年。在福州,1850年仍拒绝外人入城,"传教士到城内租房居住,被华人围攻和赶出城"。[8] 英国驻福州领事李太郭(G. T. Lay)"被安置在城外一片泥地上用木杆架成的一个简陋房子里,用尽力量想要在城里找到一所适宜的住处都成徒劳"。[9] 实际上,整个反入城斗争是情绪支配理智,只是"盲目地反对英方提出的入城要求,而并没有客观地分析入城究竟会给民众带来何种利弊"。[10]

上海没有发生反入城斗争,外侨的生活环境也比广州和福州自由和宽松许多,他们可以到周围的乡村做短暂旅行。尽管如此,开埠初期英国人就一再发现"中国人深深憎恨外国商人、'冒险家'和其他侵略分子,把他们称作'鬼子',连小孩子看见他们都大喊'鬼子来了!'"。[11] 上海道台宫慕久采取隔离政策,"希望通过减少接触来避免中国人与西方人之间的冲突,试图

---

[1] Borton M. Scwartz, Robert H. Eward, Culture and Society, Taibei, 1972, pp23-24.
[2] 王开玺:《鸦片战争前后清政府制夷思路探论》,《近代史研究》,1995年第6期,第1页。
[3] 马士:《中华帝国对外关系史》第一卷,生活·读书·新知三联书店1957年版,第480页。
[4] 中国历史第一档案馆:《第一次鸦片战争后福州问题史料》,《历史档案》,1990年第2期,第47页。
[5] 广东文史研究馆译:《鸦片战争史料选译》,中华书局1983年版,第342—343页。
[6] 马士:《中华帝国对外关系史》第一卷,生活·读书·新知三联书店1957年版,第401页。
[7] 广东文史研究馆译:《鸦片战争史料选译》,中华书局1983年版,第478页。
[8] Miscellaneous, Chinese Repository, Vol. XIX, Aug., 1850, P460.
[9] 马士:《中华帝国对外关系史》第一卷,生活·读书·新知三联书店1957年版,第407页。
[10] 茅海建:《关于广州反入城斗争的几个问题》,《近代史研究》,1992年第6期,第55页。
[11] Robert Fortune: Three years' Wanderings in the Northern Provinces of China, pp107-108,转引自黄苇的《上海开埠初期对外贸易研究》,上海人民出版社1961年版,第129页。

阻止外国人与中国居民混合居住,尽可能多地限制外国人的活动";麟桂采取绥靖政策,划给法国租界地,"其思想基础仍然是以夷制夷传统观念"。[1]而普通上海人对西洋人到来的反应是新奇和费解,"在老百姓那里西洋人叫'鬼子',在士大夫那里,西洋人叫'夷'、'外夷'、'西夷',租界被称作'夷场'"。[2]"小孩子见了(洋人)就要哭,因为他们向来听人说这些都是极凶恶的洋鬼子"。[3]

面对中国人的抵制与冷漠,外侨除了依据不平等条约进行交涉外,就是希望尽快了解和认识中国,以方便他们在华生活和工作。

早期在华外侨主要是商人、传教士和外交官三类人,他们对中国的了解十分有限。据卫三畏回忆,"林则徐时代,只有五人懂汉语,这五人中能够胜任翻译的只有罗伯聃(Robert Thom)、马儒翰(John R. Morrison)和郭实腊(Gutzlaff)"。[4] 1858年,"美国公使列卫廉(W. Reed)致美国国务卿卡斯说,'在旅华美商中没有一个能够写成或朗读一句中文的'"。[5] 来华商人为了获取利益,传教士为了基督教中国化,外交官为了和中国政府打交道,他们都需要调查研究中国社会的方方面面。加以上述中外交涉的种种纠纷,来华外侨更加迫切地想要认识中国。1847年,大不列颠及爱尔兰皇家亚细亚学会(The Royal Asiatic Society of Great Britain and Ireland)创始人斯当东(George Staunton)寄信给香港总督德庇时(John Francis Davis),提出了关于中国的33个问题,[6]建议居住在香港和五个通商口岸城市的英国侨民关注这些问题。从这些问题看,当时西方对中国还知之甚少,他们急欲了解中国的风俗、贸易、思维习惯、历史观等多方面的知识。此外,"中国人的日常生活状况,他们的感情生活、内心世界、行为方式和那些难以言明却又对中国人生活有重要意义的无数点滴知识"[7]也一直是在华外人所渴望了解的内容。

在行动上,来华外侨创办了报刊和其他文化机构,希望借此途径尽快深入了解认识中国。在这方面传教士发挥着先锋作用,因为传教是西人来华的一个重要事业,传教士们始终没有放

---

[1] 梁元生著,陈同译:《上海道台研究——转变社会中之联系人物,1843-1890》,上海古籍出版社2003年版,第44、47页。
[2] 熊月之主编:《上海通史》(晚清文化卷),上海人民出版社1999年版,第33页。
[3] (美)霍塞著,越裔译:《出卖上海滩》,大地出版社1941年版,第7-9页。
[4] S. W. Williams, Recollections of China prior to 1840. JNCBRAS, Vol. VIII, P16.
[5] (美)泰勒·丹涅特著,姚广译:《美国人在东亚》,商务印书馆1959年版,第472页。
[6] 这33个问题是:1.所居住地的地理概况和地质情况。2.居住地的主要农业产品和工业制成品。3.上述物品是否适合英国市场? 4.这个国家急需欧洲哪些农工产品? 5.这个国家的人民吸鸦片吗? 哪个阶层吸鸦片? 占全国人口的比例是多少? 6.这种(吸鸦片)习惯对于他们的身体健康和道德原则有多大影响? 7.与中国其他地方相比,所居住地人民的道德、智力及性格特征是什么? 8.盗贼和土匪经常出没吗? 9.凶杀和海盗经常出没吗? 10.溺婴是否普遍? 11.中国老百姓对欧洲人是否热情? 是否喜爱欧洲的商品? 12.贸易是采用物物交换还是采用信用方式? 如果采取信用贸易方式,贸易额有多大? 以何种具体方式交割? 13.中外存在交往吗? 14.外国人的活动范围是否被限制在居留地内? 如果是,他们是否已经屈服于这种规定? 还是他们偶尔会突破限制深入内地活动,这种情况是否经常? 一般在何时行动? 15.当地的百姓是顺服于政府还是经常反抗政府? 16.当地百姓对鞑靼王朝(即清王朝)的统治认可程度有多大? 17.中外人民发生冲突时,政府对待中外人民是否有区别? 如果有,哪些法律是针对中国人的? 18.中国的官吏是否廉洁? 是否官吏腐败流行? 程度如何? 19.中国的法官是怎样审理案件的? 犯人有没有辩护人? 20.所在地内是否有巨额资产者? 土地占有是否平等? 21.所在地是否有公认的望族或大的家族? 22.是否有用于救济穷人的粮食? 如果没有,他们如何赈济穷人? 23.乞丐是否到处都有? 24.当地的教育情况怎样? 有多少人具备读写文字的能力? 25.人口是在增长还是在下降? 26.所在地的发展趋势是繁荣还是衰败? 27.当地的主要宗教信仰是什么? 28.他们有哪些娱乐活动和游戏方式? 29.是否见到过古代的碑刻或其他古迹? 30.贸易时,主要用哪种语言? 官话、广东话(粤语)、还是行话? 是否这三种语言在贸易中同时使用? 31.是否遇到基督教传教士、耶稣会士、天主教士,以及他们出版和发行的著作? 他们是否受到中国人的尊重? 多大程度? 32.他们是否遇到来自中国政府的阻挠? 当地的巫师是否嫉妒他们? 33.自从条约签订后,中外交往的进一步加深,中国人在生活习惯和使用的器具方面是否有显著的改变? 或者说他们是否采用了西方现在最新的科技成果? 各个阶层的人是否因此对外国人更加宽容和自由? 参见 Address, Transactions of the China Branch of the Royal Asiatic Society, Hongkong, 1847. pp7-8.
[7] Stent, G. C., Chinese Lyrics, JNCBRAS, Vol. VII, P93.

弃努力。"他们相信一旦旧有的藩篱被打破后,将有一个史无前例的机会——将基督教文明与信仰传播到中国人身上,基督教的仪式(生活方式)将会渗入中国人的日常生活和习俗中"。[1] 伟烈亚力(A. Wylie)创办《六合丛谈》起初就是以传教为目的的。[2]

在广东,当时比较著名的期刊有以下几种:《广东记录报》(The Canton Register)(1827)、《广东杂志》(Canton Miscellany)(1831)、《中国丛报》(The Chinese Repository)(1832)、《东西洋考每月统计传》(1833)。[3] 这些报刊大多旨在"透过报章杂志,中外人士可获得更清晰之了解,破除彼此间思想上之障碍"。[4] 一般来讲,英文杂志内容多为向西方介绍贸易情况,叙述中国风土人情,向本国报告有关消息;中文期刊则主要是服务于传教,同时也向中国传播西方的科学知识。《中国丛报》的创办人之一卫三畏回忆,创办该刊目的就是"为了获取关于中国的正确信息"。[5]《六合丛谈》创刊时就讲道:"溯自吾西人越七万余里航海东来,与中国敦和好之谊,已十有四年矣。吾国士民旅于沪者,几历寒暑,日与中国士民游,近沪之地,渐能相稔。然通商设教,仅在五口,而士人足迹未至者,不知凡几。兼以言语各异,政化不同,安能使之尽明吾意哉?是以必须藉书籍以通其理,假文字以达其辞,俾远方之民与西土人士,性情不至于隔阂,事理有可以观摩,而遐迩自能一致矣。"[6] 其意借此与中国各地之人民作思想上之沟通十分明显。

总之,鸦片战争后,外国在华的商人、传教士、领事及海关人员逐年增多,来华外人在从事经商、传教、侵略的同时也开始了对华探索与求知的历程,其主要方式便是建立各种文化机构、出版发行中外文刊物。皇家亚洲文会北华支会(为便于叙述,下文以"文会"代之)便是其中之一。

文会的创建,除了上述原因外,就文化机构本身而言,还要追溯到18世纪以来的东方学会。

18世纪以来,随着殖民扩张运动,西方对东方的研究也进入职业化阶段,其标志为拥有一批专门的研究人员和研究机构。西方各国先后在欧美和亚洲各地成立了各类"亚洲学会"(Asiatic Society),旨在对亚洲进行调查研究。1781年,荷兰人首先在爪哇成立巴达维雅学艺协会(Bataviaasch Genootschap van Kunsten en Wetenschappen)。1784年,英国人乔恩思(William Jones)在加尔各答成立孟加拉亚细亚学会(Asiatic Society of Bengal),该会先后发行《亚细亚研究》(Asiatic Researches)和《皇家亚细亚学会杂志》(Journal of the Royal Asiatic Society of Bengal)。英国人又在孟买创立孟买文学会(Bombay Literary Society),刊行《孟买文学会纪要》(Transactions of the Bombay Literary Society)。1822年,法国著名汉学家兰米利(Jean-Pierre Abel-Rémusat)和流寓法国的德意志东洋学家克拉勃洛德(Heinrich Julius von Klaproth)在巴黎发起亚细亚学会(Société Asiatique),该会研究"东方人之历史、哲学、科学、文学及语言之纪事、摘录及报告文汇编",发行《亚细亚学报》(Journal Asiatique)。[7]

---

[1] Kennth Scott Latourette, A History of Christian Mission in China, New York, 1929, P202.
[2] 周振鹤:《〈六合丛谈〉综论》,《中华文史论丛》第61辑,第129页。
[3] 谭卓垣:《广州的定期刊物调查》,《岭南学报》4卷3期,第3页。
[4] 王萍:《西方算学之输入》,《"中央研究院"近代史研究所专刊》第17辑,1966年版,第137页。
[5] S. W. Williams, Recollections of China prior to 1840, JNCBRAS, Vol. VIII, P17.
[6] 戈公振:《中国报学史》,《民国丛书》第二编49卷,上海书店1990年版,第75页。
[7] 石田干之助:《欧人之汉学研究》,《中法大学月刊》第4卷第5号,第98页。

1823年3月15日,曾任孟加拉亚细亚学会会长的著名梵文学者考尔勃克(Colerbrooke)、斯当东和约翰斯顿(Alexander Johnston)等人在伦敦共同组织大不列颠及爱尔兰皇家亚细亚学会,旨在"调查研究亚洲的历史(包括人类和自然)、古迹、艺术、科学及文学,其范围是人和自然,包括农业、(手)工业和商业"。[1] 成立大会上,考尔勃克说大不列颠及爱尔兰皇家亚细亚学会的研究范围也要包括亚洲各国的政治事务、哲学经典,也要注意他们的神话、地理方面的知识。该会会长多是一些颇有声望的人,他们都曾任过高官职务,或是与印度有关。大不列颠及爱尔兰皇家亚细亚学会成立后,先后有11个设在亚洲的东方学会加盟其中,成为其支会,详见表1-2。

表1-2　　　　　　　　　　大不列颠及爱尔兰皇家亚细亚学会支会表

名　称	地　点	起止年份	加入年份
孟加拉支会	加尔各答	1784－1950	1829
孟买支会	孟买	1804－1955	1829
马德拉斯支会	马德拉斯(印)	1812－1894	1830
比尔哈-奥丽萨支会	Bankipur(印)	1915－1943	1924
缅甸支会	仰光	1909－?	1924
斯里兰卡支会	锡兰	1845－?	1846
香港支会	香港	1845－1859	1847
日本支会	横滨	1872－?	1912
朝鲜支会	汉城	1900－1950	1901
海峡支会	新加坡	1845－?	1878
班加罗尔支会	班加罗尔(印)	1909－?	1924
北华支会	上海	1857－1952	1859
北京东方学会	北京	1885－1911	1888
麦吉尔大学东方学会	蒙特里尔(加)	1911－1916	1912

资料来源:Stuart Simmonds and Simon Digby, *The Royal Asiatic Society: its history and treasures*, Leiden: Published for the Royal Asiatic Society by E. T. Brill, 1979, pp13－19.

注:1. 除上海、北京、蒙特里尔三处已经彻底停止外,其余支会机构至今都还存在,起止年份表示这些机构隶属于伦敦总部的时间段。
2. 香港支会1859年停止,1960年重建。
3. 麦吉尔大学东方学会是唯一一个不在亚洲的支会。
4. 地名之中文译名采自中国地名委员会所编《外国地名译名手册》(中型本),商务印书馆1998年版。

在中国,首先成为大不列颠及爱尔兰皇家亚细亚学会支会的是1847年在香港成立的"中国亚洲学会"(The Asiatic Society of China)。1847年1月19日,香港总督德庇时、外国侨民史丹顿(Rev. V. Stanton)、梅塞(W. T. Mercer)、布雷顿(Colonel Breton)、坎贝尔(C. M. Campbell)、肯尼迪(Kennedy)、巴佛(Balfour)等人聚集在一起,大家一致表决"成立一个学会

---

[1] Frederick Eden Pargiter Compiled, *Centenary Volume of the Royal Asiatic Society of Great Britain and Ireland 1823－1923*, Published by the Royal Asiatic Society, London, 1923. Pviii.

以调查研究中国之艺术、科学、文学、天然产物"。[1]学会成立时命名为"中国亚洲学会",德庇时任会长。作为1823年成立的大不列颠及爱尔兰皇家亚细亚学会的最早成员之一,德庇时成为"中国亚洲学会"和"大不列颠及爱尔兰皇家亚细亚学会"之间的重要桥梁,在他的努力下,"中国亚洲学会"于同年加入"大不列颠及爱尔兰皇家亚细亚学会",成为其支会,中国亚洲学会遂改为"皇家亚洲学会中国支会"(The China Branch of the Royal Asiatic Society)。[2]

皇家亚洲学会中国支会成立时,大不列颠及爱尔兰皇家亚细亚学会会长奥克兰伯爵(Earl of Auckland)曾给香港支会一封信:"对我们来说,我们目前所拥有的关于中国政府、人民、艺术、物产等方面的知识和信息,几乎没有任何价值。"[3]基于此,中国支会曾对调查的项目作了详细的规定,语言9条、历史12条、文学8条、艺术10条、政府部门19条、中外关系12条,[4]较之斯当东给香港总督德庇时的33个问题更详细、更具体、更科学。中国支会出版《皇家亚洲学会中国支会纪要》(Transactions of the China Branch of the Royal Asiatic Society),共计6卷。1859年,由于香港总督包令(John Bowring)的离职和秘书哈兰德(W. A. Harland)的去世,皇家亚洲学会中国支会于同年停止活动。[5]

大不列颠及爱尔兰皇家亚细亚学会在中国的另一个支会即是设在上海的皇家亚洲文会北华支会。[6]

上海开埠后,首先抵沪的是英美商人和传教士。1844年在沪外侨主要有11个英国和美国商行的23个代表,另有2个英国籍的基督教传教士,1个英国籍的专任领事。1855年外侨总数增加到243人,其中有30个基督教传教士,其余多是商人。传教士主要是雒魏林(Willam Lockhart)、麦都思(W. H. Medhurst)、米怜(W. Milne)、伟烈亚力、文惠廉(W. J. Boone)等人。19世纪50年代,上海的各国领事多由商人充当,1857年葡萄牙、荷兰、普鲁士、丹麦等国还都是由英国人充当代表,瑞典和挪威则由一个美国人充当代表。[7]这些外侨与香港外侨一样也在业余从事对中国社会的调查与研究,但主要由传教士个人进行,《中国丛报》上面就有上海的传教士定期向本国政府撰写上海见闻和对中国社会方方面面的认识。

这一时期,寓沪外侨的生活比较枯燥。因为最初来华的外侨并未打算在中国长期定居,他们像候鸟一样奔波于中国与本国之间,在华目的不外乎赚钱、短期传教。随着租界的建立和特权的获得,上海也越来越像一座欧洲城市,来华外侨也逐年增多,长期定居已成趋势,上海事实上成为他们的第二家乡,他们强烈地意识到文化生活的重要性,也极力想把上海建成像西方一样的社会。因此,在上海开埠数年之后,文化娱乐机构与设施便逐渐产生。娱乐方面,先后建立了跑马总会(The Recreation Club of Shanghai)、上海赛船会(Shanghai Rowing Club),举办了划船比赛、板球比赛;文化方面,1849年工部局创建了读书会(Shanghai Book Club),1850

---

[1] Asiatic Society of China, Chinese Repository, Vol. XVI, Feb., 1847, P93.

[2] Isaac Mason, F. R. G. S., Three Score Years And Ten, JNCBRAS, Vol. LIX, 1928, P2.

[3] Address, Transactions of the China Branch of the Royal Asiatic Society, Hongkong, 1847, P8.

[4] Appendix—Suggestions for future Discussion, Transactions of the China Branch of the Royal Asiatic Society, Hongkong, 1847, pp73 – 77.

[5] Stuart Simmonds and Simon Digby, The Royal Asiatic Society: its history and treasures, Leiden: Published for the Royal Asiatic Society by E. T. Brill, 1979. P17; Proceedings, JNCBRAS, Vol. XXXV, 1903 – 1904, Pi.

[6] 上海的支会翻译成"皇家亚洲文会北华支会"而不是"皇家亚洲学会北中国支会",一是因为该会当时中文简称为亚洲文会,二是为了区别当时还存在皇家亚洲学会香港支会。

[7] 马士:《中华帝国对外关系史》第一卷,生活·读书·新知三联书店1957年版,第390页。

年《北华捷报》诞生,一定程度上推进了寓沪西人对上海的了解和适应,极大地方便了那些来沪不久,不懂中文、不会沪语的外国人。但是,除此之外,50年代其他文化设施却还很少,高第(Henri Cordier)回忆到"在那个时代,一些有声望的绅士们认为,无论茶、丝、曼彻斯特的货物在商业上多么重要,都无法满足精神上的需求。他们因此建立一个文学科学学会"。[1]

1857年9月24日,尼克逊从男爵(Capt. Sir Frederick W. Nicolson)、裨治文(E. C. Bridgman)、帅福守(E. W. Syle)、艾约瑟(J. Edkins)、纳尔逊(R. Nelson)、亚希逊(W. Aitchison)、戴威士(T. Davis)、雒魏林(W. Lockhart)、西柏多(Sibbald)、蒙克里夫(Moncreiff)、康普东(Compton)、荷巍尔(Howell)、凯丝威(Keswick)、卫三畏(S. W. Williams)、汉璧礼(Hanbury)、弗兰克(Franks)和立德(Reid)等18人聚集到互济会礼堂(Freemason's Lodge),讨论认识研究中国的重要性。经商议决定成立一个学会,以调查中华帝国及其周围的国家,学会命名为"上海文理学会"(Shanghai Literary and Scientific Society)。

如果我们看看该会成立时几位发起者的发言,便能说明该会成立的背景。

蒙克里夫:如果这个机构在上海得以创立,相信整个地区会受益。作为一个商人,关注上海文理学会可以看作使自己从日常生活与烦琐事务中恢复精神的方式。

艾约瑟:有更广阔的领域和范围等待上海文理学会去调查研究。我们生活于一个伟大国家的边缘,几个世纪以来这个国家引起了西方的极大兴趣。马可波罗和约翰·曼德维尔(John Mandeville)通过自己的描述把人们唤醒,他们的著作在中世纪被广泛传阅。现在,西方正向东方迈进,与任何时期相比更有必要研究这个伟大的帝国;上海文理学会不仅研究文学,也应致力于科学的研究,使那些不愿研究文学的人也有他们的研究领域,同时,也增加我们的自然、历史、地理学及其他方面的科学知识。来自远方的客人和本地的居民可以通过上海文理学会贡献他们的价值,进而也希望上海文理学会长久存在和更为实用。[2]

荷巍尔:目标之一即增加我们的中国知识:它的文学、它的艺术、它的商业。

次日,《北华捷报》对上海文理学会的成立发表短评:

我们欢呼这个学会的建立,没有比现在更合适来建立这样的学会了,相信它将成为迈向较高知识分子之路和便利公众的文化资源。

目前,我们处在这个古老而又特殊的帝国发生巨大变革的前夕。实际上,我们还不知道这个古老帝国为什么能够维持长久的专制,上帝又会通过哪种方式来打破这种体制。因此,目前为我们提供了一个机会,去了解中国人的性格与特征,他们长久远离真理、几乎没有受到较高文明的熏陶;去探知这个国家内的那些我们长久不知的资源。

现在来训练和指引我们的心智,以便时间来临时我们能够充分地利用它。毫无疑问,文会在初创办时会有困难。我们都习惯了繁忙生活的程序化,习惯了日常事务,习惯了平时的放松,很容易习惯一天辛劳之后认真地追求乍看上去像是心灵洗炼的状态。但是,朋友,长久的训练培养了心智,曾经不喜欢的,将成为我们的快乐。[3]

艾约瑟后来也回忆道:"我们学会是基于亚洲学会香港支会的创建者的理念建立的。那就

---

[1] (法)高第著,马军译:《对英国汉学家伟烈亚力的回忆》,《中国史研究动态》1998年第5期,第22页。
[2] Minutes of A Meeting Held in the Reading Room of the Shanghai Library, North-China Herald, Vol. III, No. 374, 26th, Sep., 1857. P34.
[3] North-China Heald, Vol. III, No. 374, 26th, Sep., 1857. P34.

是对这个国家研究的强烈愿望——欧洲对于亚洲这个大的帝国知之甚少。"[1]

综上所述,上海文理学会的创建原因可以归为以下几点:外人的求知与传教是本源,东方学的学术背景是其建立的外在条件,外侨自身的生活需要是创建的直接原因。

1859年,上海文理学会加盟大不列颠及爱尔兰皇家亚细亚学会,该会名称遂改为皇家亚洲文会北华支会。历史时期,上海文理学会的名称几经变化,但是"皇家亚洲文会北华支会"这一名称使用最久。[2] 20世纪初以来,中外学人对 The North-China Branch of the Royal Asiatic Society 有多种不同的译称(详见表1-3)。

表1-3　　　　　　　　　　文会英文名不同之中文译称

译　名	译　者	资　料　来　源	年份
亚细亚上海支会	陈潜	《东方杂志》	1908
英国亚洲文会华北支会	傅振伦	《东方杂志》	1914
英国皇家亚洲文学会	(不详)	《申报》	1923
英国亚细亚学会北支那支会	(日)小竹文夫	《支那研究》(19号)	1929
皇家亚洲学会华北分会	贝鲁士	《西文东方学报论文举要》	1933
英国亚洲文会北中国分会	(不详)	《上海通志馆期刊》	1933
皇家亚洲文会北中国支会	胡道静	《上海博物院史略》	1936
皇家亚洲学会华北分会	(不详)	《史学消息》	1936
亚洲文会华北支会	戚铭远	《中国博物学:上海博物院指南》	1936
亚洲文会北支分会	(日)原一郎	《上海的文化》	1941
皇家亚细亚文会北中国分会	方汉奇	《新闻研究资料》(第三辑)	1981
皇家亚洲文会华北支会	李志刚	《基督教与中国文化论集》	1989
亚洲文会北中国支会	(不详)	《上海文物博物馆志》	1997
皇家亚洲学会华北分会	蒋重跃	《十九世纪西方人眼中的中国》	1999
英国皇家亚洲文会北中国支会	薛理勇	《上海掌故辞典》	1999
亚洲文会北中国支会	(不详)	《上海文化通史》	2001

注:相同译称取时间早的。

---

[1] Proceedings, JNCBRAS, Vol. IIIV, P1.
[2] 该会成立后名称曾几经变化,不同时期的名称如下:

年　月	名　　称
1857.9—1859.9	上海文理学会(Shanghai Literary and Scientific Society)
1859.9—1882.3	皇家亚洲文会北华支会(The North-China Branch of the Royal Asiatic Society)
1882.3—1906.6	皇家亚洲文会中国支会(The China Branch of the Royal Asiatic Society)
1906.6—1952.6	皇家亚洲文会北华支会(The North-China Branch of the Royal Asiatic Society)

该会成立后，《北华捷报》经常以"The Royal Asiatic Society"为题目报道该会的有关情况，《申报》则以"亚洲文会"称之；该会大门口之匾额上的中文名字也是"亚洲文会"，[1] 演讲厅内悬挂的布料上也写着"亚洲文会"，[2] 所以该会在近代上海的通用名称应该是"亚洲文会"，为了叙述方便，本研究以"文会"指称。

第二节 发展历程

一、初创时期（1857-1861）

1857-1861年是文会的创建阶段。以裨治文为首的理事会领导文会召开40次会议，其中4次为年会。这一时期，文会的发展概况如下：

（一）初步制定了文会的规章制度，指明了文会的发展方向

1857年9月26日文会成立大会上制定了六条章程，这些章程初步规定了上海文理学会的研究对象和组织构成。

1. 协会的名称为"上海文理学会"，本会调查研究的领域主要是中华帝国及其周围的国家。

2. 所有出席这次会议的人只要表示其加入上海文理学会的愿望即可成为上海文理学会的会员，以后的会员必须在现有会员两人的提议基础上，并经上海文理学会投票同意方可加入。

3. 上海文理学会领导成员：会长一人，副会长一人，秘书一人，会计一人；任期一年，投票选举。

4. 每年的会费目前应固定为白银五两。每月的常会于星期二晚八点（或其他时间）举行。

5. 上海文理学会的日常事务授权理事会处理，文理学会理事会成员包括上述领导成员和三名理事。理事会所采取的一切措施解释权都属于文理会。

6. 现在主席应任命一个委员会（小组），由委员会推荐明年的官员。

1857年10月16日开幕式上，会长裨治文详细阐述了中国的历史和文会宗旨、目标、任务、发展方向。[3]

文学与科学是仅次于真教的最贵重、最崇高、最光亮的人类饰品。在文学与科学的领域中，一些重大的成就却是在没有上帝启示的真知下实现的。

在这个古老的帝国，由于缺乏神的感召，他们的文学与科学成就，尽管比近邻的民族及同类要高，但总体上看，仍然低于基督教国家。……这里有错误的宗教和伦理学说、错误的物理学和抽象论、错误的国内和国际政治理论，所有这一切都被误称的"科学"粘合在一起。这些谬论一定要被推翻、戳穿，也注定会在真知和正当理由前消失、让道。

上海文理学会将要在一些领域开展调查研究工作。对于科学和博学之士来说，在中国，有大量的课题可以做。他可以从事地理学的调查，随着帝国的开放，广阔的幅员将会

---

[1] Mason, I, Passing of the R. A. S. Old Premises at Shanghai, JNCBRAS, Vol.LXII, P201.
[2] The Annual Society of the Royao Asiatic Society, North China Branch, The China Journal, Vol. XXXIV, Jan., 1941, No. 1.
[3] Bridgman, E.C. Inaugural Address, Journal of the Shanghai Literary and Scientific Society, No. I, Jun., 1858. pp1-13.

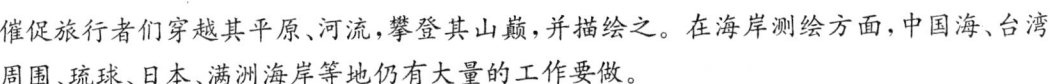

催促旅行者们穿越其平原、河流，攀登其山巅，并描绘之。在海岸测绘方面，中国海、台湾周围、琉球、日本、满洲海岸等地仍有大量的工作要做。

博物学家们将会非常高兴地记录岩石、丘陵和山谷，鸟类、兽类和鱼类，以及每一种树木、灌木、鲜花。博物学的三大门类，矿物、植物和动物，这里有成千上万的对象可以研究。……奥森伯格、雅裨理、福钧等人已经采集到了一些灿烂的标本，向西方世界告知全能的神在这个东方帝国境内做的工是多么丰富和绚丽！但是，西方所知的不到一半，甚至不及千分之一。

他也可以从事深入地表下之研究，挖掘永存的山脉，寻找古老的岩石，把这些证据与它们的创造者——上帝之力和智慧联系起来，给《圣经》的忠实以确凿的证据。

他也可以努力去解决更为微妙的流体问题，将会发展关于飓风中的规则，探讨巨轮航行的原理。

或许民族学的研究，应该优先于上述一些科目。……东亚部落与太平洋北部、东部岛屿上的族群来自哪里？

中国政治制度中的继承法则，他的立法、行政与司法制度，选官制度，竞争性的考试制度，税收制度，他在治理与统治间是如何平衡的？他对周围国家的政策是什么？尤其是在当前国内外处于重大变革的时代，任何课题都没有上述题目显得迫切。

作为一个文学与科学学会，我们将会责无旁贷地去探究：目前在这里出现的、似乎有加速趋势的民族间的较量，究竟仅仅是武力的角逐，还是智力的较量？被授权去和中国政府高官谈判的外国官员们在与这个帝国的主要有才智之人进行交涉时，在多大程度上做好了准备？……目前，由于对中国政治机制的无知，导致我们在与中国政府交往时变得十分无能。尽管我们拥有武力，但是与他们打交道时必须要审慎和有技巧，唯此，才能在最后获得尽可能大的成果。

必须研究他们的语言，无论多么艰难，都要展开，并掌握之，在这场战争中没有退伍令。……整理他们的法律和法规，许多延续朝代的统计数字，关于宗教、教育、音乐、医技方面的卷宗，以及其他类似的文献等，这些都是上海文理文会成员们需要较早和仔细关注的内容。

我们将从以下方法和途径来实施上述设想：首先，需要一些人来从事工作，尤其是那些喜欢文学和科学的学者，那些将致力于崇高知识追求的学者。其次，我们要建立图书存放处和放置自然与科学标本的储藏室。第三，随着学会科研的推进，为了展现我们自己在文学和科学方面贡献，我们要发行一份会刊。

开幕词反映出该会的宗旨在于：调查研究中国。调查研究的范围则包括博物学、地质学、物理学、地理学、民族学、人类学、历史学、哲学、文学的学科对象，以及中国的政治制度、法律、中外关系等。

具体的行动目标是：收集图书与标本、编辑出版会刊、吸纳会员。

发刊词也表明：该会不仅要加强对中国的认识与了解，而且也要把基督教文明传播到中国境内最远的地方；不仅要在中国开展调查研究活动，而且也要关注殖民者的利益。概言之，它包括文化交流、宗教传播、科学研究、服务侵略四个意向。

1857—1861年间裨治文主持的演讲和讨论涉及61个主题，基本上每月举行一次演讲，是文会历史上演讲、讨论最密集的时段之一。

（二）加盟大不列颠及爱尔兰皇家亚细亚学会

1857年9月26日，上海文理学会成立时荷巍尔就说："相信随着与大不列颠及爱尔兰皇家亚细亚学会的交往，我们将证明自己是它的一个重要分支。"章程第五条规定："如果可能的话，上海文理学会就加盟伦敦大不列颠及爱尔兰皇家亚细亚学会。"1858年7月20日，理事会宣布大不列颠及爱尔兰皇家亚细亚学会已同意接受上海文理学会作为其支会。1858年9月21日，上海文理学会第一次年会上，裨治文宣布该会正式成为大不列颠及爱尔兰皇家亚细亚学会的支会。由于此时香港的皇家亚洲学会中国支会尚未停止，文会遂更名为皇家亚洲文会北中国支会，"所以名为北华支会者，系立于香港的地位观之，上海居于北方故也"。[1]

上海文理学会加盟大不列颠及爱尔兰皇家亚细亚学会的意义是将文会纳入了世界学术网络之中，为文会以后的发展提供了很好的平台。因为大不列颠及爱尔兰皇家亚细亚学会是近代欧美所建的规模和影响最大的东方学会团体之一，借助于大不列颠及爱尔兰皇家亚细亚学会，文会大大提高了自己在国际东方学中的地位，多年来上海的中外人士因此而习称它为"亚洲文会"。近代有很多来华的西方著名学者都曾接受文会的邀请到文会演讲，文会实际上成为近代中西文化交流的桥头堡和近代外国学者来华交流的枢纽。

（三）提出了中西文化交流的具体内容

开幕词中，裨治文就提出要把中国的生物、地理标本传向西方，同时要把基督教传到中国的意愿，在近代文化交流史上，首次明确提出了中西交流的具体内容。虽然耶稣会士也为中西文化交流作出了巨大贡献，但是他们没有提出明确的交流内容，尤其是"中学西传"方面，耶稣会士多是撰写了一些零碎的见闻，文会则首次提出以科学方法来调查研究中国，并将其研究成果传向世界各地。

实践方面，对外，文会与奥地利科学考察团、奥地利帝国地质研究所（The Imperial Geological Institute of Austria）展开合作与交流；对内，1860年10月，文会理事会决定成立"汉语翻译出版委员会（A Chinese translation Committee），负责用汉语出版历史、科技书籍"。[2]

这一时期演讲或讨论的61个主题涵盖了中国的地理、历史、宗教、民俗、地质、气象、民族、动物、钱币、语言等学科的内容，可以说已打开了对中国调查研究的局面。

1861年，文会首任会长裨治文病重，11月2日病逝；同年艾约瑟北上，伟烈亚力回国。由于资金缺乏与核心组织成员的分离，1861年10月15日常会开后，文会就停止了活动。[3]

二、重建与发展时期（1864－1910）

1864年3月1日，在金斯密（T. W. Kingsmill）、伟烈亚力及英国驻上海领事巴夏礼（Harry Smith Parkes）等人的努力下，文会得以重建，并确立了文会的三个目标：①调查研究中国与其邻近国家各项事情；②出版会刊；③建立一个图书馆和博物院。[4] 此后，文会的三个目标一直未变，只是在1882年11月7日增加了"举行会议，在会议上宣读和讨论与上述目标相关的

---

[1] 胡道静：《上海博物院史略》，《上海研究资料续集》，上海书店1993年版，第393页。
[2] North-China Herald, Vol. XI, No. 533, 13th, Oct., 1860, P163.
[3] The Royal Asiatic Society, North-China Herald, Vol. XII, No. 586, 19th, Oct., 1861.
[4] The North-China Branch of the Royal Asiatic Society, North-China Herald, 12th, Mar., 1864.

论文。"[1]

1864年12月1日,会刊重新出版。前言中这样写道:"文会马上就要对那些掘壕据守的远东学术的要塞发动一场艰巨的、无疑也是无可抵挡的攻坚战,对于这支进攻部队的每个人而言,在未来的日子里都会处于一个自我满足的境地,因为他贡献了自己的努力去摧毁那些现在看来阻挡着西方文明传播的障碍,同时又熟识了东方学术的复杂的体系。"[2]这表明文会要对中国历史文化做深入的研究,而且这是一项长期的事业。

经过努力,文会获得了英国政府和后来的租界工部局(Municipal Council)、法董局(French Municipal Council)的财政支持。这一时期,文会没有自己的活动场所,主要在"上海图书馆"(Shanghai Library)[3]举行演讲会,讨论会员提交的文章。1868年英国驻上海领事阿礼国(Rutherford Alcock)上书英国政府,代表文会请求英国政府捐地一块,以建筑一座会所,包括图书馆、博物院和演讲厅。英国政府随后答应将下圆明园路(今虎丘路)和北京路交叉之东北一块地作为文会会所,但要求"这片土地不能改作捐赠之目的以外的用途,而且该会停止时或三年内不能建筑起房屋时,土地将归还英国政府"。[4]获得该地块后,文会遂向上海外侨募捐资金,汉璧礼(Thomas Hanbury)捐赠银500两,金斯密则免费提供会所设计图纸。1872年1月11日文会会所建成开放,分上下两层,一楼为演讲厅(长35英尺、宽28英尺),二楼为图书馆,存放伟烈亚力和文会的书籍,此外,还专门设有图书管理员和博物院管理员的房间。包括装修在内,整个建筑费用共计银3 000两。[5]

尽管如此,文会在上海的影响还很小。当时上海公众对文会的活动很少感兴趣,很少有人参加演讲,1879年只开两次演讲会议,参加的人也寥寥无几。[6]文会还被人"视为一群卖弄学问的人,互相吹捧而聚集在一起,相互标榜而博虚名"。[7]文会影响小的原因是:一、这一时期在华外侨对中国的认识还很肤浅,对文会的活动并不在意。"上海社会还很少有人对文学和科学感兴趣"。[8]文会的"许多演讲无疑都很有价值,然而只对中国充满浓厚兴趣的人才会感兴趣。非常明显的是,外侨对它们不感兴趣"。[9]相对单调、乏味的演讲导致"上海99%外侨都形成一种错误的认识:中国问题深奥而枯燥,他们也只能递交这类深奥又枯燥的文章"。[10]虽然演讲题目和会刊内容中也有不少游记类作品,但是早期"外侨大都担心自己的东西不加区别地公布于上海观众面前,所以对文会的呼吁也比较冷淡"。[11]二、资金困难。由于文会资金主要来自会员会费和工部局的支持,所以会员的多少反映了文会的社会影响。1881年文会仅仅有会员150名左右,其中居住在上海的只有38名,连文会自己都承认"文会的目标

---

[1] Report of the Council of the North-China Branch of the Royal Asiatic Society for 1882, JNCBRAS, Vol. XVII, Part 2, 1882. Pxiii.
[2] Preface, JNCBRAS, Vol. I. 此处引文系周振鹤师翻译,特此致谢。
[3] 这里的图书馆是指1849年3月上海西侨社会成立的"上海书会(Shanghai Book Club)",1851年改名为"上海图书馆(Shanghai Library)"。见胡道静的《外国教会和外国殖民者在上海设立的藏书楼和图书馆》,转引自李希泌、张淑华编的《中国古代藏书与近代图书馆史料(春秋至五四前后)》,中华书局1982年版,第514页。
[4] Isaac Mason, F. R. G. S., Three Score Years and Ten, JNCBRAS, Vol. LIX, 1928, P8.
[5] The North China Branch of The Asiatic Society, North-China Herald, 18th, Jan., 1872.
[6] Report of the Council of the North-China Branch of the Royal Asiatic Society for 1879, JNCBRAS, Vol. XIV, Pi.
[7] The Asiatic Society, North-China Herald, 26th, Feb., 1872. P174.
[8] The North-China Branch of the Royal Asiatic Society, North-China Herald, 30th, Oct., 1873, P361.
[9] Shanghai, The North-China herald and market report, North-China Herald, 15th, Apr., 1868, P172.
[10] The Royal Asiatic Society, North-China Herald, 10th, Dec., 1884, P651.
[11] The Royal Asiatic Society, North-China Herald, 18th, Jan., 1872, P37.

和文会给有文化修养的人所提供的好处还远远不被社会所承认"。[1] 而且文会早期没有会所,要租借场地开展活动,这笔资金成为文会的沉重负担。由于缺乏资金,会刊不能按时出版,1869－1873年每两年才出一期。图书馆也没有达到令人满意的程度,"人们感到文会没有达到他们所想象的目的,虽然文会图书馆收集图书的范围很大,但是没有很新的书和最新的科学类杂志,也没有小说之类的休闲性书籍"。[2] 三、文会的活动与当时外侨的生活习惯有冲突,这也是文会早期不受人注意的原因之一。文会演讲的时间是安排在周二晚上六点到八点,这一时间恰恰是外侨饭后散步的时间,所以参加或旁听演讲的人寥寥无几,每次也只有3－12人,并且多是会员,非会员很少参加。此外,一般人都因日常繁重工作而无暇关注文会,更不可能每周抽出1－2小时来为文会义务工作。

面对这种局势,会长福勃士(F. B. Forbes)提出:"要想发展、繁荣文会,我们不仅要增加收入,也必须扩大文会的影响,使更多的人参加文会的演讲,会刊有更多的读者。"[3] 在理事会其他成员的共同努力下,文会采取了以下措施,使文会转危为安,并取得了巨大成就。

(一)筹建博物院

博物院是文会的一个主要目标。文会从创立之始就收集动植物标本,1869年文会已任命比塞特(J. P. Bisset)负责标本的收集与管理。由于没有合适的馆舍和充裕的资金来聘请拥有专业水平的博物院负责人,所以未能正式成立博物院。1871年,文会会所建成后,筹建博物院遂提上日程,而且"博物院之设置,不独文会北支有此企图,即上海外侨社会当时亦坚强地有此盼望"。[4] 1874年2月13日,理事会举行会议,宓吉(A. Michie)提议"委托理事会组成一个博物院,并与上海运动事业基金会(Trustees of the Recreation Fund)协定借款银1 500两(借款系作开办费)",[5] 提议获得通过。同年3月14日,文会在会所召开会议,并通过以下决议:由宓吉、葛罗姆(Groom)、费子智(C. P. Fitzgerald)、朴赍懿(Pryer)4人组成一个委员会,委员会与文会理事会共同筹划建立博物院,并设法雇佣法国神父谭微道(Père David)的中国助手作为博物院管理人员。3月25日的文会年会上选出了博物院的各部负责人,他们是:植物学——麦华陀(W. H. Medhurst)和施敦力(Stronach);地质学与贝壳学——金斯密;爬虫学与动物学——克锡(Keswick);鳞翅类——普赖尔(Pryer);考古学与货币学——伟烈亚力;鱼类学——魁克特(Quekett);人种学——高第和福勃士;鸟类学——科提尔(Hawtrey)和费子智;实业与生产——廷得尔(E. C. Taintor)和谷特堡博士(Dr. Gottburg);显微镜检查——韩德森博士(Dr. Henderson)。[6] 馆址设在会所二楼的一间房中。1874年在华著名的法国博物学家谭微道路过上海,把他亲手培养的中国籍采集人员王树衡留下,帮助博物院收集标本。

博物院建成后,工部局很重视,从1877年开始每年都向博物院拨款资助其发展。从文会历年财务报表看,博物院早年的收入几乎全是来自工部局和法董局的财政拨款。1877年拨款银250两,1879年后增至每年500两,1906年后又增至每年1 000两。因博物院的地位和影

---

[1] Meeting of the North-China Branch of the Royal Asiatic Society, North-China Herald, Vol. XXVI, No. 725, 29th, Apr., 1881, P419.
[2] The Royal Asiatic Society, North-China Herald, 1st, Nov., 1871. P831.
[3] The North-China Branch of the Asiatic Society, North-China Herald, 19th, Feb., 1874. P159.
[4] 胡道静:《上海博物院史略》,《上海研究资料续集》,上海书店1993年版,第394页。
[5] The North-China Branch of The Asiatic Society, North-China Herald, Vol. XII, No. 355, 19th, Feb., 1874. P160.
[6] Report of the Council of the North-China Branch of the Royal Asiatic Society for 1874, JNCBRAS, No. VIII, 1874, Pxi-xii.

响,1886年工部局将文会所在地的下圆明园路改为博物院路。[1]

此间,文会理事会一度酝酿筹建中国艺术博物馆和上海商贸博物馆,虽然未能实现,但为博物院后来收藏艺术品和商贸之类的物品奠定了基础。

(二)筹建图书馆

图书馆是文会的三个主要目标之一。成立之初,文会就开始收集关于中国及远东方面的图书与资料,并将每年新进书目刊登于当年会刊上。1858年1月19日,裨治文捐赠了《中国丛报》、帅福守捐了一批个人藏书。同年这些书成为最早的藏书,合信(Benjamin Hobson)被推选为图书管理员。1866年理事会开会商议建立一个图书馆,并向公众开放。1869年4月,文会以1 767.5两银的低价收购了著名汉学家伟烈亚力的私人所藏718卷(册)西文书籍和1 023册中文书籍,[2]奠定了图书馆的基础。伟烈亚力的这些藏书是其在华20余年来收集的西人论中国的书籍以及汉文书籍的译本,而且是比较完善的,因此当1868年文会决定购买后,《北华捷报》就发表评论:"亚洲文会以伟烈亚力所提出的低价购买该图书馆,乃是一件值得庆幸的事。"[3]早年文会没有会所时,书籍先后存放在规矩堂(Masonic Hall)、宁波路前上海道台的房子、汇隆银行(Commercial Bank of India & the East)、上海图书馆等处。1873年,文会会所建成后才将图书移至二楼。

筹建中文阅览室。19世纪60－70年代,文会理事会"发现(上海)有一大批努力学习英国、法国、德国思想的身着华服之人。同时上海外侨又告诉我们,目前他们最关心的是点燃中国人对欧洲的认识"。[4]鉴于此,1874年3月24日文会召开会议,大家一致赞成建立一个华人阅览室,以便那些有身份、有名望的中国人可以来阅览。理事会任命麦华陀、福勃士、傅兰雅(John Fryer)等人成立专门委员会,负责筹建一个华人阅览室(a reading-room for the Chinese)。计划将每年欧洲出版的有价值的工程条款、基督教、数学、地理学及其他相关学科书籍翻译成中文,华人阅览室内主要存放这些书籍。文会希望"通过这种方式来改变这个国家的趣味风雅,并树立新的道德标准;通过这个途径来传播新的思想,并借此使双方能够更好地沟通"。[5]从《北华捷报》有关报道所反映出的信息看,该中文阅览室一度建立了起来,但不久便夭折,因为此后再也没有相关的信息,而文会的年度报告对此阅览室的情况也只字未提。这个中文阅览室很可能只是昙花一现。

文会图书馆和博物院的建立,大大提高了文会在上海的社会地位,经常有外侨光顾文会,或参观展品、或借阅图书,文会已成为上海的大众文化场所之一。

(三)努力扩大会员,吸收中国籍会员加入

最初会员每人每年交纳会费5墨洋,后来升到10墨洋。考虑到非居住会员比较分散的情况,1866年文会决定:"应鼓励会员申请终生会员的资格。终生会员每年要交纳会费10墨洋。非居住会员有权申请终生会员。"[6]1885年开始,会员每年会费降至5墨洋,当年就加入新会

---

[1] 熊月之主编:《上海通史》第十五卷(附录),上海人民出版社1999年版,第307页。
[2] The North-China Branch of the Royal Asiatic Society, North-China Herald, 30th, Oct., 1873, P362.
[3] The Asiatic Society, North-China Herald, 28th, Nov., 1868.
[4] Reading Room for Chinese, North-China Herald, Vol. XII, No.361, 2nd, Apr., 1874, P286.
[5] Summary News, North-China Herald, Vol. XII, No.360, 26th, Mar., 1874, P258.
[6] Report of the Council of the North-China Branch of the Royal Asiatic Society for the year 1866, JNCBRAS, Vol.III, 1868, P5.

员 61 名。[1] 而且会员也不再局限于英美侨民,1885 年新加入的会员来自 18 个国家,文会已呈现国际化趋势。

（四）改变会刊编辑方针,使其内容更加丰富多彩

从 1885 年开始,会刊上刊登了一些短小的论文,这些论文题目十分广泛,内容丰富、信息量大,给读者以更多的中国方面的知识,"会刊十分受到社会欢迎,它已不仅仅局限于学术圈内了"。[2]《北华捷报》也给会刊以很高的评价:"这是值得赞扬的出版物,它充分证明在中国的外国侨民对所有的科学研究有广泛的兴趣,同时也说明亚洲文会绝不是卖弄学问的机构。"[3] 会刊销售十分良好,1885 年开始在伦敦、莱比锡、巴黎设置代理处。此外,以前的旧刊也得以重印,会刊销售收入占文会收入的三分之一。

从 1893 至 1907 年夏士(Joseph Haas)编的会刊论文索引来看,这一时期文会调查研究的内容涉及到中国地理、地质、历史与考古、博物学、宗教、文学、风俗、货币、钱庄、游戏、娱乐等 12 门学科的知识。在人文和自然学科方面作了重要的调查研究,自然学科方面主要集中于杭州湾的海塘、中国海域的台风、中国的气候与地质等领域。

1880 年文会扭转了困境,进入稳健发展阶段,1886 年初步实现财务上的扭亏转盈。在此基础上,文会开展了一些对中国的全国性规模的调查活动,比如中国的度量衡调查、土地利用状况调查等。1886 年文会理事会又设立了一个 25 000 元墨洋的基金,资助远东,尤其是关于中国的课题研究。[4] 1910 年后,每月常会都能够正常召开,"参加演讲会议的人数也远远多于以前,主要是由于会员对文会有了新的兴趣,更为直接的原因是会所、图书馆、博物院大大改善的结果"。[5]

总之,这一时期文会健全了组织,成为一个拥有自己活动场所的文化实体。不仅扭转了社会对文会的偏见,而且逐步扩大了影响。从各个方面看,文会已摆脱了岌岌可危的状态,步入良性发展轨道,这为后期的兴盛奠定了基础。

三、兴盛时期(1911 - 1941)

经过半个多世纪的积累,19 世纪末 20 世纪初欧美各国的汉学研究开始进入一个新的发展时期。各国纷纷成立汉学研究组织、开设中国语言学校和课程、出版汉学研究杂志、定期召开国际东方学研究大会。具体而言,1890 年荷兰创设《通报》(T'oung Pao),1901 年法国在越南西贡创建法兰西远东语言学校,1887 年德国创设柏林东方语言学校,1912 年柏林大学开设汉学讲座,1900 年俄国成立皇家东方学会,1890 年加利福尼亚大学开设东方语言讲座,1901 年哥伦比亚大学设立中文讲座。到了 20 世纪上半期,汉学研究实现了从信息调查、语言学习转变到具体问题的学术研究层面上,"人们正在向其所熟悉的中国问题的各个分支进行深入研究,而不再是对中国文献做泛泛研究"。[6]

与此同时,上海也发展成为一个文化中心。30 年代上海已有 1 000 余所学校,其中高等院校 20 所,此外还有相当多的科研机构和文化机构,它们都与各个国家的办事处和有关团体保

---

[1] Proceedings, JNCBRAS, Vol. LXX, 1885, P295.
[2] 谭维理:《1830 - 1920 年美国人之汉学研究》,《清华学报》(台湾)新二卷第二期(1961 年),第 266 页。
[3] Review, North-China Herald, Vol. XII, No.364, 25th April, 1874, P358.
[4] The N. C. B of R. A. S., North-China Herald, Vol. XXXVI, No.974, 17th, Mar., 1886. P293.
[5] Royal Asiatic Society, North-China Herald, 5th, Aug., 1910.
[6] Proceedings, JNCBRAS, Vol. XLII(1911). pp256 - 257.

持着密切的联系。

立足于国际汉学的发展先锋和远东的中外文化交流中心地,文会也实现了由一个调查机构向国际学术机构的转变。1910年后,文会的演讲活动进入正常的发展轨道,平均每年演讲8次,已改变了此前演讲次数不稳定的现象。演讲者也更加国际化,不再像此前仅限于艾约瑟、玛高温(D. J. Macgowan)、金斯密、庄延龄(E. H. Parker)等几位关键人物,参与者除了英美在沪侨民外,还有来沪的中外国家的学者,比如法国的伯希和(Powl Pelliot)、俄国的史禄国(S. M. Shirokogoroff)、中国的竺可桢、江亢虎、丁文江等人。更为重要的是演讲者多是中外著名学者、大学教授和有关机构的专职研究员,"他们都是在各自研究领域内的卓越专家,演讲内容也多是各自研究领域内的最新的研究成果"。[1] 1933年9月29日,世界著名的古生物学专家兼国际地理学会会员格雷博博士(Dr. A. W. Grabau)演讲《人类的起源》,就是作者在北京考察后的最新研究成果。[2] 演讲也大都采用幻灯机、标本、图片等工具,生动而直观,改变了以前相对单调枯燥的宣读、讨论方式,传播效果非常明显;参加的人数每次在百人左右,而19世纪每次不过20-30人左右。通过面对面的接触和讨论,演讲促进了思想火花的迸发,成为中外学者进行直接学术交流的最佳途径,文会因此也成为国际汉学界在远东的学术交流中心。

1928年,文会拆除已历70余年而显破败不堪的会所。1933年2月23日,文会新楼正式落成,"工部局总董斐尔(A. D. Bell)主礼,宣告落成开幕,蔡元培、伍连德相继发表演说"。[3] 建筑费共计银40 000两,除了文会多年的积蓄外,工部局、法董局也拨了一大笔款。此外社会捐款也相当多,像英美烟草公司(British American Tobacco Ltd.)、沙逊洋行(Sasson, Sons & Co., Ltd.)都为文会新楼捐了款。其中中国著名的公共卫生学家、我国检疫防疫事业的先驱——伍连德博士,一人就向文会捐银20 000两,因此文会新楼的演讲厅(大会堂)就命名为"伍连德馆"。[4] 新楼六层,一楼为伍连德馆,二楼为图书馆,三楼为生物标本陈列室,四楼为文物、古董陈列室,五楼陈列美术品。后曾一度租给中国科学美术杂志社(The China Journal of Science & Arts)和沪江大学(Shanghai University)使用。新楼融合中西建筑术,下为石拱门,阳台栏杆,雕刻着中国传统的花纹。楼顶悬挂一块匾额,标有"R. A. S."三个英文字母;三楼窗户下则悬挂标有中文"亚洲文会"的匾额。[5]

30年代,文会最为强盛。会员人数每年都在700名左右,1933-1940年会员人数分别为:695、722、852、903、909、718、796、813名,而1910年才达326名。而且会员遍布全球六大洲30余个国家,理事会成员经常是来自五六个国家。[6] 文会的演讲会、图书馆、博物院都向公众开放。其图书馆被认为是上海市收藏关于远东及中国方面外文图书最多的图书馆,平均每月接待读者300余名,1939年图书馆接待读者45 000余人。更为难得的是,"七七事变"爆发后,文会图书馆还接待了许多中国学者和流亡上海的学生。

博物院最初以收藏自然历史标本为主,这一时期开始收藏中国文物古董、古画、刺绣、木工艺品等,逐渐成为远东地区中国生物标本和文物收藏最丰富的博物馆之一。而且"博物院的

---

[1] Proceedings, JNCBRAS, Vol. LXVI(1935). Pi.
[2] Proceedings, JNCBRAS, Vol. LXV(1934). Pxxvi.
[3] 《亚洲文会正式落成》,《申报》1933年2月25日。
[4] Proceedings, JNCBRAS, Vol. LXIII, 1932. PX.
[5] 见《会刊》23卷封二图片,JNCBRAS, Vol. XXIII.
[6] 1934-1940年理事会成员国有英、美、法、中、丹、加等。

方针是为上海社会所利用,使公众在闲暇的时间能够来参观博物院"。[1] 博物院每天都免费向公众开放,从上午八点到下午七点,节假日照常,平均每月逾1 000 人。1938 年后每月均在5 000人左右,1940年5月曾达8 254人,[2] 而 1910 年以前博物院每月参观人数仅 100 人左右。来参观的人三分之一为外侨,三分之二为华人,团体则有学校学生、童子军和上海的外侨妇女协会等。博物院还开展了与上海学校合作的活动,设立教育督导员,专门负责向来文会参观的学生和教师讲解藏品,由著名人类学工作者劳立尔(Y. Laurell)担任。两年内,他走访了上海的许多学校,向校长和教师讲解了文会(博物院)对于学校的作用,与学校建立了广泛的联系,促使上海的中外小学组织各级学生参观博物院。不仅上海社会对博物院钟爱不已,即使国内外的著名科学家对博物院也都是兴味十足,他们来到上海后,多会专程参观文会博物院。

文会通过自己的活动也赢得了上海社会的青睐。20 世纪 30 年代,"亚洲文会在上海(如果不能说全国的话)是唯一一个向公众提供文化需求的机构"。[3] 1930 年一名英国外交官赞扬"文会是上海的一盏明灯"。[4] 1940 年英国政府还从"庚子赔款"中向文会拨款 10 000 美元资助其活动及偿还大楼债务。

会刊每年一册,已改变了此前两年才出一册的情况。投稿人已不再是伟烈亚力、郇和(Robert Swinhoe)、金斯密、艾约瑟、玛高温、翟理思(H. A. Giles)等主要英美在华侨民,这一时期,美、英、中、德、日等国家的学者也纷纷向文会投稿,1933 - 1935 年会刊上刊登的论文来自7个国家:英国5篇、中国8篇、美国10篇、日本2篇、德国2篇、法国1篇、瑞典1篇,[5] 这些还不包括书评和汉学消息,会刊的作者日益呈现国际化的局面。文章的类型更加多样,最重要的是 1906 年以后每期会刊都刊登有 30 篇左右的新书评介,这些新书都是当年出版的关于远东尤其是关于中国的论著。书评的意义非常明显,以 30 年代每年 800 名会员计,加上 100 余个与文会交流的文化机构,通过会刊,这些关于远东的著作被迅速介绍到一个有千余人的庞大读者群。1933 年起的会刊又增设"汉学札记"(Sinological Notes)栏目,评述《通报》、《艺术》(ARTES)等汉学期刊上的论文,介绍国际汉学研究动态及国际东方学消息。会刊实际上向学术界传递了最新的研究动态,具备了学术期刊应有的功能。一些研究中国问题的权威也纷纷向文会投稿,会刊的内容越来越丰富、领域越来越广,论述更加深入。因此,会刊受到了国际学术界的重视,其影响力越来越大,"成为文会最有价值的出版物了,每一期都受到读者的青睐"。[6] 20 世纪 30 年代每年的发行量都在 1 000 册左右。许多科研机构都向文会索求会刊或者用自己的出版物与文会交换会刊,也有许多中国的大学和学术机构购买会刊。文会早期的会刊也不断重印,被世界各地 100 多个图书馆、博物馆等文化机构、团体所收藏。文会实际上已成为国际汉学研究的资源宝库。

由于中日战争和第二次世界大战的爆发,工部局对文会无暇顾及,加之 1941 年后许多欧美外侨纷纷离沪,文会资金较为短缺,这一时期上海能够资助文会的其他机构也不多,因此从1940 年 1 月 1 日起,文会就与尚贤堂(International Institute of China)合作,双方议定:"文会

---

[1] Proceedings, JNCBRAS, Vol. LXV, 1934. Pxviii.
[2] Proceedings, JNCBRAS, Vol. LXX, 1939. Pv.
[3] The China Journal of Science and Arts, Vol. XVII., Oct., 1932, No. 5, P32.
[4] Proceedings, JNCBRAS, Vol. LXIII, 1930, PViii.
[5] Proceedings, JNCBRAS, 1935, Pviii.
[6] Our Book Table, The Chinese recorder, Vol. XLIV, P773.

收藏尚贤堂的标本和书籍,为尚贤堂人员提供办公场所,双方共同管理文会的演讲活动,尚贤堂每月为这些活动支付经费,双方保持各自身份的独立性。"[1]

尽管如此,自1941年7月起,《字林西报》上已不再见到有关文会活动的消息了,而图书馆和博物院则于1941年6月1日暂时关闭。[2] 太平洋战争爆发后,日军占领上海英、美租界,文会图书馆之藏书遭到日军的掠夺,幸运的是抗战胜利后,所掠书籍被如数追回。

总之,20世纪文会已成为国际东方学尤其是汉学研究领域的著名学术机构之一。它为各种学术机构、教育团体的大量成员提供了学术交流的平台,在这里,来自世界各国的学者可以通过英语交流各自的观点。在这个国际性的城市中,文会的地位和意义更加突出,这正如《中国科学美术杂志》所说:"70年来,亚洲文会已成为中国境内外国侨民研究东方文化的主要中心。"[3]

四、结束时期(1946—1951)

1946年秋天,文会恢复活动,演讲活动基本上每月一次,向公众开放,演讲者和听众已不再局限于会员、学者,而有更多的其他人士参与,成为当时外侨社会的一个公共文化活动中心,截至1951年3月,共演讲54篇文章。由于解放战争的进行和在华外侨的迅速撤离,文会很少开展其他活动,博物院没有什么大的发展,只是接待一下来此参观的游客而已。会刊仅出版两册,1949年后没有再出版。"1949年前夕,该会将一部分图书、文物运出中国。"[4]1952年5月19日,文会关闭;同年8月,由上海市文化局接收。1954年6月3日,上海市文化局、上海市文物整理委员会又接收了亚洲文会博物院的文物、标本。[5] 1955年2月,上海图书馆接管文会图书馆。[6]

---

[1] Proceedings, JNCBRAS, Vol. LXX, 1939, Piii.
[2] From day to day, North-China Daily News, 1st, Jun., 1941.
[3] The China Journal of Science and Arts, Vol. XV., Nov., 1931, No.5.
[4] 马军:《博物院路与中西文化交流》,《读书》2002年第1期,第106页。
[5] 戚文娟:《上海文物整理仓库的历史功绩》,《上海文化史志通讯》,1994年第33期,第74页。
[6] 王世伟:《上海公共图书馆发展史略》,《图书馆杂志》,1998年第1期,第58页。

第二章　组织机构（一）

第一节　理　事　会

1857年文会成立时就规定，日常事务由理事会处理；理事会成员包括会长、副会长、秘书、会计和3名理事；理事会所采取的一切措施都向文会负责。1874年，文会新章程对理事会又作了详细规定：

第三条　领导成员

文会领导成员设：会长1名、副会长1名、理事4—6名、秘书1名、会计1名、图书馆馆长1名、博物院院长1名。他们必须在每年年会上选出。上述成员如果出现空缺，本年替补人员必须经剩余领导成员一致同意方可出任。如果会长去世，将由副会长接管会长职务，直到下年年会为止。

第四条　理事会

1. 理事会由当年领导成员组成，其职责具体如下：
2. 管理文会事务及文会财产；
3. 向文会推荐会员；
4. 确定常会上将宣读的论文；
5. 挑选论文、出版会刊，并监管会刊的印刷、分发与销售等工作；
6. 为图书馆和博物院购买书籍与标本；
7. 代表文会接受或拒绝他人捐献的物品；
8. 在文会年会上提交文会的年度总结报告；
9. 理事会每月召开一次会议，处理文会事务；或者在必要时召开。会议至少有5位成员出席；
10. 理事会有权在必要的时候实施上述规章制度，并提交文会常会批准；
11. 秘书有权先动用经费25元墨洋，然后再向理事会会议上呈报，如果超过25元，没有理事会的批准，会计不予支付。

概言之，理事会的主要事务即：定期召开演讲会议和文会年会、讨论演讲的文章、出版会刊、管理图书馆和博物院。早年年会一般在12月份或元月份举行，1889年后决定每年6月下旬召开年会。年会上，会长要宣读本年文会的工作总结，有时是文会秘书宣读的，主要内容有会员的变动情况、向去世的会员致哀、本年演讲之文章、会刊的发行情况。图书管理员要宣读本年图书馆的情况，主要是新进书目；博物院院长要宣读本年博物院新进标本和博物院的财务状况；会计则提交本年度收支明细账。之后，全体投票选出下一年的会长及理事会其他成员。年会报告刊登于每年年报上，向所有会员并向社会公布。文会日常事务并不轻松，尤其是会刊的编辑与发行,涉及很多细小的琐事。所以,理事会中的副会长、文会秘书、图书馆馆长、博物院院长、会刊编辑等人承担了文会的主要事务。这些人多为汉学修养较高的人,其中有金斯密、伟烈亚力、福勃士、艾约瑟、福开森(John C. Ferguson)等人。

历任会长主要由驻沪领事人员或学者担任,尤其是英、美驻沪领事(见表2-1)。任职最长的是霍必澜(Sir Pelham Warren)、巴尔敦(Sidney Barton)和法磊斯(E. D. H. Fraser),三人都是英国驻上海总领事,后两人还曾先后在福州、汉口、宜昌、九江等地任领事。其余会长中,系英国驻沪领事的还有巴夏礼、哲美森、许士、韩能、包克本,而美国籍会长也多是美驻沪领事。英、美领事担任会长、主导文会,一是因为文会是大英皇家亚洲学会的支会,创建和参与者主要是在沪的英美侨民,演讲和会刊所使用的语言主要是英语;其二,长期以来文会的经费主要来自于工部局和法董局的资助,以领事任会长自然容易获得租界当局财政的扶持。这些具领事身份的会长并不主管文会日常事务,演讲和投稿也不多,推选他们只是为了扩大文会的影响,这种情况在19世纪比较突出。除了领事外,会长一职也由那些在海关或其他部门的学者及汉学家担任,像海关的夏德(F. Hirth)、翟理思,工部局的史笪来(A. Stanley),还有北洋政府顾问福开森;至于苏阿德(A. De C. Sowerby)、伊博恩(Bernard E. Read)更是其各自领域内的杰出人士,卜舫济(F. L. Hawks Pott)和黎照寰则是20世纪上半期上海两大名校的校长。这种学者型会长的出现在后期十分明显。所有会长中,贡献突出的当属裨治文、金斯密和苏阿德这三人。

表2-1　　　　　　　　　　　　文会历任会长

年　　份	会　　长	国　籍	身　　份
1857—1859	裨治文	美	传教士
1859—1860	密迪乐	英	驻沪总领事
1860—1861	麦华陀	英	驻沪总领事
1864—1866	巴夏礼	英	驻华公使
1869—1870, 1875—1876	麦华陀	英	驻沪总领事
1866—1867 1868—1869	西华	美	美驻沪领事
1867—1868	温思达	英	英驻沪领事
1870—1872	古丁	不详	
1872—1875	福勃士	英	商人
1876—1877 1877—1879	金斯密	英	建筑师
1879—1880	布策	英	传教士
1880—1882	毛里逊	英	工程师
1882—1884	杜维德	美	海关人员
1884—1885	翟理思	英	海关人员
1885—1887	夏德	德	海关人员

续表

年 份	会 长	国 籍	身 份
1887—1889	哲美森	英	驻沪总领事
1895—1896	哲美森	英	驻沪总领事
1889—1891	许士	英	驻沪总领事
1891—1895	韩能(艾约瑟)	英	英驻沪领事
1896—1898	穆林德	德	领事人员
1898—1901	璧利南	英	驻沪总领事
1901—1903	班德瑞	英	大英按察使
1903—1911	霍必澜	英	驻沪总领事
1911—1912	福开森	美	中国政府顾问
1912—1920 1921—1922	法磊斯	英	驻沪总领事
1920—1921	史笪来	英	工部局医生
1922—1929	巴尔敦	英	英驻沪领事
1929—1931 1932—1933	卜舫济	美	圣约翰大学校长
1931—1932	查德利	英	工程师/洋员
1933—1934	莫安仁	英	传教士
1934—1936	包克本	英	领事参赞
1936—1941	苏阿德	英	博物学家
1941—1942	周尔执	英	领事人员
1946—1947	伊博恩	英	雷氏德研究院
1946—1947	奥格登		
1947—1948	尤桑	不详	
1948—1951	不详		
1951—1952	黎照寰	中	上海交大校长

资料来源:

1. 主要参照:会刊71卷中的插页。
2. 1874—1875,See,Summary News,The North-China Herald,19th,Feb.,1874,P151.
3. 1876—1877,See,The Royal Asiatic Sciety,The North-China Herald,25th,Jan.,1877,P84.
4. 1888—1889,See,The Royal Asiatic Sciety,The North-China Herald,1st,Jun.,1889,P249.
5. 1902—1903,See,The Royal Asiatic Sciety,The North-China Herald,9th,Jul.,1902,P75.

注:1. 1891—1895年间,主要由副会长艾约瑟负责文会日常事务,且艾约瑟曾担任短期会长。

2. 1865年1月10日巴夏礼当选1865—1866年文会会长,副会长是西华、韩德森。1865年6月7日,巴夏礼主持好文会第14次常会后赴日本,继任者尚难确定是上述哪位副会长。参见:Summary of Proceedings,JNCBRAS,Vol. II, pp182. Royal Asia Society,The North-China Herald,15th.,Jul.,1865,Vol. XVI,No. 781,P111.

3. 1870—1872年的古丁(C. W. Goodin)、1879—1880年的布策(C. H. Butcher)、1946—1947年的奥格登(A. G. N. Ogden),1947—1948年的尤桑(J. Ly. Usang)等人的中文名字都是音译。

裨治文，文会创始人之一。1801年生于美国马萨诸塞州，后受美部会（American Board of Commissioners for Foreign Missions）派遣来华传教。1830年2月19日到达广州，受到了当时中国境内的唯一传教士马礼逊（Robet Morrison）博士的热烈欢迎，遂从其学习汉语，并翻译《圣经》。然而，"裨治文不只是一个认真的传教士，对有益于中国人或外国人的任何事情也非常热心"，[1]他以非凡的能力，组织和参与了数个文化机构，如《中国丛报》、益智会（The School and Texbook Series Committee）、马礼逊教育协会（Morrison Education Society）、中华医药传教会（China Medical Missionary Society）。其中，《中国丛报》是由裨治文一手创办的英文期刊，裨治文在1832年的《创刊词》中说，该报的宗旨是："评介关于中国的外文书籍，观察这些书籍内容的变化过程；调查中国的气候、矿藏、河流、动植物、物产、商情；关于社会关系方面，要注意中国人的道德素质、教育制度、妇女地位、宗教情况等。"[2]文会的宗旨几乎与此相同。1857年，他又和伟烈亚力、雒魏林等人创办了上海文理学会。文会创办初期，几乎是他一人负责所有事务，去世前他曾在文会上演讲文章4篇。

金斯密，英国人，1862年到达中国，1864年加入文会，后来又当选为名誉会员，"多年来一直被外侨视为汉学方面的权威"。[3] 1861年11月裨治文病逝后，文会一度夭折。在金斯密的积极活动下，1864年3月1日，文会得以重建。[4] 他曾多次担任文会理事会理事，1887年至1889年担任会长。在他和文会其他成员的努力下，文会得以健康发展，逐渐摆脱了"曾被上海外侨视为卖弄学问的团体"的坏印象，并且获得了工部局和法董局的财政支持。从1865年到1907年，金斯密在会刊上共发表了27篇文章，[5]供稿数量居于前列。

苏阿德，博物学家。英国浸礼会（English Baptist Mission）教士苏道昧（Arthur Sowerby）之子，1885年生于太原。1905－1916年间，作为大英博物馆和美国自然历史博物馆（American Museum of Natural History）的代表，在山西、陕西、东北三省及蒙古等地采集自然标本。[6] 1916年当选文会会员，1923年当选文会博物院院长，1935年10月至1940年底担任文会会长。苏阿德担任会长后，他和其他理事一道采取各种方案，使文会获得极大发展。1937年文会会员达到909名，1937年6月到1938年12月，图书馆接待读者达5 702人次，博物院每月接待观众达2 000余人次。在苏阿德的主持下，博物院还开展一系列科学演讲活动，举办数次中国文物展，在上海引起极大轰动。为纪念他，1946年文会理事会决定将博物院所使用的房间命名为"苏阿德馆"。[7]

第二节 会 员

文会创建时就决定："所有出席这次会议的人只要表示其加入上海文理学会的愿望即可成为上海文理学会的会员，以后的会员必须由现有会员两人的提议，在文会常会上投票同意后，

---

[1] Obituary, The North-China Herald, Vol. VII, 9th, Nov., 1861.
[2] Introduction, The Chinese Repository, May, 1832. pp2-3.
[3] Obituary, The North-China Herald, 29th, Jul., 1910.
[4] The Royal Asiatic Society, The North-China Herald, 5th, Mar., 1864.
[5] In Memoriam: Thos. W. Kingsmill, JNCBRAS, Vol. XLI, 1910. pp116-117.
[6] 中国社会科学院近代史研究所翻译室：《近代来华外国人名词典》，中国社会科学出版社1981年版，第450页。
[7] Proceedings, JNCBRAS, Vol. LXXII, 1946. Pii.

方可加入。"[1]从创建到结束(1857—1952),文会曾经吸纳大量的会员。分析这些会员不仅有助于深入认识文会,而且也能透视出近代来华外侨的文化生活以及他们在近代中西文化交流中的贡献。

一、国籍与身份

据笔者统计,目前能够确定的会员共有3 115位。[2] 其中1 000余名会员之姓名、国籍、职业、学历可考,可以大致反映出整个文会会员的信息,详见表2-2。

表2-2　　　　　　　　　　　　文会可考会员之综合信息表

国　籍	人数	部　门	人数	身　份	人数	学　历	人数
英　国	498	公司/洋行	543	教士	344	博士	158
美　国	177	领事馆	294	教授	75	医生	61
德　国	74	学校	261	学者	42	医生/博士	108
中　国	61	教会	232	律师	19	硕士	1
法　国	51	海关	198	工程师	17		
俄　国	26	政府部门	173	记者	16		
日　本	25	银行	90	政府官员	10		
加拿大	23	报刊	71	法官	7		
意大利	19	研究机构	36	教师	6		
瑞　典	18	出版部门	29	船长	6		
丹　麦	12	医院	27	编辑	4		
奥、匈	10	俱乐部	20	建筑师	3		
瑞　士	9	图书馆	16	银行家	2		
挪　威	6	军事部门	10	会计师	2		
比利时	4	博物馆	9	药剂师	2		
澳大利亚	3	事务所	7	研究员	2		
芬　兰	3	慈善部门	3	大学校长	2		
古　巴	1	古玩行	2	化学师	1		
其他国家	17	其他部门	2	其他	2		
合　计	1 037	合计	2 023	合计	562	合计	328

资料来源:参见附表2。

注:1. 表中数字仅仅是可以确定的各类会员数量。
2. 会员身份未统计海关、领事、商人三种行业人的具体身份。
3. 身份参照了《近代中国专名翻译词典》。
4. 在所有通讯录中,标有PH.D的可以确定为博士,但是有些会员仅仅标有Dr.,目前尚难确定这些人是医生、博士,还是拥有博士学位的医生,所以只能把他们归入"医生/博士"。

---

[1] North-China Herld, Vol. III, No. 374, 26th, Sep., 1857. P34.
[2] 文会历年会刊后附有当年的会员通讯录。1864—1948年共计有67个年份的会员录,此前(1857—1861)会员统计来自《北华捷报》。1948年后加入的会员,由于无直接资料,故没有计算在内。所以,3 115位会员是在现有资料基础上统计出来的准确数字。

该表显示以下几点:

首先,文会是一个以英美在华侨民为主的国际性文化团体。鸦片战争后,外国在华商人、传教士、领事及海关工作人员逐年增多,他们在从事经商、传教和外交的同时,也创办了各种文化机构,但是很多文化机构仅限于在某个国家的成员中展开活动,不具备国际性质。如徐家汇观象台(Observation de Zi Ka Wei),其成员几乎是清一色的法国传教士;东亚同文书院(Tung Wen College)则全部是日本人的天下,哈佛燕京学社(Harvard-Yenching Institute)主要限于中美之间的文化交流。而文会则不同,会员国籍十分广泛,除了无人类居住的南极洲外,涉及六大洲34个国家,且主要来自于英、美、德、法、俄、日等国,这与近代各国在华的势力有密切关系,英、美、德、法、俄、日等国在近代中国是利益获得的大户,这些国家在华的侨民也是最多的。

文会中还有为数不少的中国籍会员,估计有百余名,目前所能确认的有61名。最初文会是不吸纳中国人的,1887年11月18日,理事会才决定向所有国家开放,但同时规定,"只吸收有名望的中国绅士加入文会,因为他们可以帮助文会在中国展开活动"。[1] 中国籍会员少的另一个原因是,"该会悬格甚高,限制极严,非有特别介绍保证,不准加入"。1923年,江亢虎加入时,有英、美大学教授10人联合推荐。[2] 1920年后中国籍会员才逐渐多起来,他们中很多是各界名流,如著名学者胡适、蔡元培、林语堂、伍连德;政府高官有晚清上海道台应宝时、北洋政府总理王宠惠、上海市市长吴铁城;工商名流有永安百货经理郭顺、中国银行的李伟;出版界则有王云五及中华书局和商务印书馆的编辑。

其次,以会员工作部门看,会员所在的部门比较广泛,但主要集中于洋行、领事馆、学校、教会、海关、银行、报刊等领域,基本都是一些知识层次和薪金收入较高的工作部门。文会对于会员的加入除了需要两名会员推荐之外,并无明确的资格限制,但实际上,要想成为文会会员,却需要两个基本的条件:①拥有一定的文化素养;②能够缴纳起会费(普通会员一般每年在5墨洋,终生会员要10墨洋)。不具备前者,难以参加演讲活动和参与文会开展的调查活动,而且也阅读不了会刊;不具备后者,则不会被吸纳,因为文会的日常开支一部分来自会员的会费,如果拖欠会费两年,则会被理事会宣布自动脱离文会。

文会不是单纯的学术机构,而是一个综合的文化机构,能够被各个领域和各个阶层的群体所接受,因此,它能够吸纳各色人群。对于大众来说,会刊充满知识性和趣味性,较之《华裔学志》和《通报》那样的学术刊物,更易为普通读者所接受。文会演讲选题多样,内容丰富,门槛也不是很高。所以具备上述两个条件的在华侨民也乐意加入文会来丰富他们的业余生活。

再次,以身份言,这里面不乏拥有较高素质的外交官、传教士、大学教授和一些著名的学者。如语言学家高本汉(B. Karlgren),人类学家史禄国,地质学家李希霍芬(Ferdinand Von Richthofen),探险家斯文赫定(Sven Anders Hedin),法学家古德诺(Frank J. Goodnow),汉学家儒莲(Stanislas Julien)、伯希和、卫礼贤(Richard Wilhelm)、佛尔克(A. Forke)、夏德;还有各个行业的专业人士,如工程师毛里逊(G. J. Morrison)、建筑师茂非(H. K. Murphy)、会计师鲍德(C. W. Poter);记者则有大名鼎鼎的莫理循(G. E. Morrison)、白瑞华;政府高官则有英国驻华领事阿礼国、法董局总董薄图(A. Bottu)、美国领事蒲安臣(A. Burlingame)、驻华武官步让

---

[1] Proceedings, JNCBRAS, Vol. XXII, P121.
[2] 《江亢虎当选亚洲文会会员》,《申报》,1923年11月2日。

(C. C. Brown)等人；大学校长则有圣约翰大学校长卜舫济、岭南大学校长晏文士(C. K. Edmunds)、上海交通大学校长黎照寰；出版界则有翻译巨擘傅兰雅、著名报人福开森、《字林西报》编辑詹美生(R. A. Jamieson)。正是这些人使得文会在近代汉学领域内拥有一席之地，也是在他们的努力下，会刊成了近代著名汉学刊物。

二、会员级别

文会会员最初设居住会员、非居住会员、通讯会员、终生会员四类。居住会员指长住上海的会员，非居住会员指居住在中国上海以外其他地方的会员，通讯会员则一般不在上海，终生会员指长期居住在外国的文会成员。后来，又简化为名誉会员、终生会员、通讯会员、普通会员四类。

名誉会员主要是指一些汉学家或是对文会作出巨大贡献的成员，他们多是在华著名的外交官、传教士、汉学家。如李希霍芬和普鲁捷维斯基(Col. N. Prejevalsky)，由于二人对中亚地理和中国地理作出巨大贡献，1880年文会授予他们名誉会员称号。许士"以其对文会作出了突出贡献"，[1] 1891年当选为名誉会员。一旦当选名誉会员则免交会费，并享有会员的所有权利。名誉会员人数非常有限，一共有65名，详见表2-3。

表2-3　　　　　　　　　　　　　文会名誉会员表

英　文　名	中文名	国籍	身份	在会年份
Rutherford Alcock	阿礼国	英国	领事	1859－1897
J. B. C. do Amaral	阿穆恩	葡萄牙	澳门总督	1865－1870
F. Ayscough	爱司克夫人	英国	不详	1920－1940
Sidney Barton	巴尔敦	英国	外交官	1906－1940
Adolph Bastian	巴斯琴	不详	博士	1865－1907
John Bowring	包令	英国	外交官	1866－1907
S. W. Bushell	卜士礼	英国	医师	1868－1908
Herbert Chatley	查得利	英国	工程师	1937－1946
Emmanuel Édouard chavannes	沙畹	法国	教授	1889－1917
Henri Cordier	高第	法国	教授	1886－1924
S. Couling	库寿龄	英国	牧师	1894－1921
John Francis Davis	德庇时	英国	外交官	1866－1873
M. De J. J. Groot	高延	荷兰	汉学家	1887－1922
E. J. Eitel	艾德	德国	教士	1887－1908
John C. Ferguson	福开森	美国	政府顾问	1896－1940
A. Forke	佛尔克	德国	外交官	1894－1946
John Fryer	傅兰雅	英国	编辑	1866－1927
Herbert Allen Giles	翟理思	英国	汉学家	1880－1934
Robert Hart	赫德	英国	海关	1864－1910
Sven Hedin	斯文赫定	瑞典	博士	1935－1940

[1] Proceedings, JNCBRAS, Vol. XXV, P481.

附录：皇家亚洲文会北华支会研究

续表

英 文 名	中文名	国籍	身份	在会年份
F. Hirth	夏德	美国	汉学家	1877－1926
Alexander Hosie	谢立山	英国	外交官	1877－1924
P. J. Hughes	许士	英国	外交官	1868－1901
Stanislas Julien	儒莲	法国	汉学家	1869－1870
T. W. Kingsmill	金斯密	英国	汉学家	1864－1907
Charles B. Lanman	兰曼	美国	教授	1908－1940
James Legge	理雅各	英国	汉学家	1864－1897
Mrs. Archibald Little	立德夫人	英国	不详	1906－1924
J. H. Stewart Lockhart	骆任廷	英国	外交官	1855－1936
Jose Martinho Marques	马吉士	葡萄牙	翻译	1866
W. A. P. Martin	丁韪良	美国	教士	1864－1916
Isaac Mason	梅益盛	英国	教士	1916－1938
T. T. Meadows	密迪乐	英国	外交官	1858－1868
Walter H. Medhurst	麦华陀	英国	教士	1864－1885
Evan Morgan	莫安仁	英国	教士	1901－1940
H. B. Morse	马士	美国	海关	1888－1930
G. E. Moule	慕稼谷	英国	教士	1864－1911
E. H. Parker	庄延龄	英国	外交官	1877－1924
Harry S. Parkes	巴夏礼	英国	外交官	1858－1884
Paul Pelliot	伯希和	法国	汉学家	1901－1946
Marques. A. F. Pereira		葡萄牙	不详	1866－1901
F. L. Hawks Pott	卜舫济	美国	大学校长	1913－1940
Herbert Putman		美国	国会图书馆	1908－1946
Major-General N. Pyjevalsky		俄国	军人	1880－1885
Timothy Richard	李提摩太	英国	教士	1894－1918
Baron Ferdinand von Richthofen	李希霍芬	德国	地理学家	1880－1897
D. B. Robertson	罗伯逊	英国	领事人员	1859－1880
W. W. Rockhill	柔克义	美国	外交官	1885－1912
De Arthur von Rosthorn		不详	不详	1888－1946
H. H. the Prince Sampatrao		印度	王子	1898－1940
Rt. Hon. Sir E. Satow	萨道义	英国	外交官	1906－1929
Rt. Rev. Schereschewsky	施约瑟	美国	牧师	1864－1906
Wilhelm Schott	许德	德国	东方学家	1887－1888
George F. Seward	西华	美国	外交官	1864－1888

续表

英 文 名	中文名	国籍	身份	在会年份
C. B. Shadwell		英国	船长	1858－1868
Arthur de C. Sowerby	苏阿德	英国	博物学家	1916－1946
A. Stanley	史笪来	英国	医师	1905－1930
Thomas F. Wade	威妥玛	英国	外交官	1864－1888
Pelham Warren	霍必澜	英国	外交官	1904－1926
S. Wells Williams	卫三畏	美国	外交官	1864－1881
E. T. Williams	卫理	美国	外交官	1889－1940
A. Wylie	伟烈亚力	英国	汉学家	1858－1885
W. Perceval Yetts	颜兹	英国	教授	1940－1946
H. Yule	裕尔	英国	汉学家	1874－1887
Père Angelo S. J. Zotolli	晁德莅	意大利	教士	1886－1897

资料来源：参见附表2。

可以看出，这些名誉会员除了少数几位未曾到过中国外，其余多为近代来华的外交官和传教士，他们工作之余从事中国历史文化的研究，归国之后又纷纷成为欧美各国汉学研究机构的创办者和中文教师，为近代欧美各国的汉学研究作出了突出的贡献，这在后文将有详述。

对于其他类型的会员，尚无发现理事会所作出的具体规定。1866年理事会作出决定："应鼓励会员申请终生会员的资格。终生会员每年要交纳会费10墨洋。非居住会员有权申请终生会员。"[1]这是因为普通会员年度会费为5墨洋，而终生会员则为10墨洋。文会设立终生会员纯粹是为了增加会费。通讯会员与其他会员之间的关系尚不清楚，从会员的通讯地址簿看，其级别要高于普通会员和终生会员，居住地多不在上海。但是1874年理事会制定的章程却规定名誉会员和通讯会员免交会费。

从历年会员发展情况看（见表2-4），名誉会员比较稳定，一直维持在14－16名左右；通讯会员呈逐渐减少之势，19世纪每年维持在20－30名，20世纪则逐年减少，1928－1933年只有加利福尼亚大学教授卫理（卫三畏之子）一人担任通讯会员，此后通讯簿上不再见到通讯会员名单。与此相反，终生会员和普通会员历年呈上升之势，终生会员1885年以前只有2人，1900年才突破20人，此后每年以5－10名的速度递增。普通会员从文会创建之日起，逐年增加，19世纪每年增加20名左右，20世纪则达到50名左右。终生会员和普通会员得以急剧增加，其原因是文会为了增加会费的收入以应付日常的开支，20世纪文会年度报告经常见到入不敷出的窘相，1932年文会新楼建成后更是负债累累，为此文会理事会经常呼吁社会各界人士的支持，"只要捐助钱款就可以成为文会会员"，30年代《中国科学美术杂志》、《字林西报》（North China daily news）、《大陆报》（China Press）、《大美晚报》（Evening Post and Mercury）、《上海泰晤时报》（Shanghai Times）等报刊上经常可以见到有关广告。

---

[1] Report of the Council of the North-China Branch of the Royal Asiatic Society for the year 1866, JNCBRAS, Vol. III, 1866. P5.

表 2-4　　各类会员的历年年度构成统计表　　（单位：人）

年份	名誉会员	通讯会员	终生会员	普通会员	总　计
1858	1	10	0	13	24
1868	14	33	1	113	161
1878	12	23	0	125	161
1888	9	25	4	222	260
1897	6	20	17	207	250
1908	18	18	27	234	297
1918	16	9	65	424	514
1928	13	1	97	506	617
1938	14	0	171	530	715
1941	16	0	190	597	803

资料来源：参见附表 2；数字系笔者一一统计而得。

文会还有一些团体会员，如徐家汇天文台、沪江大学图书馆、上海交通大学图书馆、雷氏德研究院、燕京大学图书馆、北京大学图书馆、北洋大学图书馆、之江大学图书馆、金陵大学图书馆、齐鲁大学图书馆、华西协和大学图书馆、福建协和大学图书馆、美国国会图书馆、哥伦比亚大学图书馆、斯坦福大学图书馆、康奈尔大学图书馆、新泽西的纽瓦克公共图书馆、加拿大蒙特利尔麦吉尔大学汉学研究中心、英国东印度公司图书馆、日本设在大连的满洲铁路株式会社、"中央研究院"社会科学研究所、上海自然科学研究所等。这些会员不同于个人会员，他们只是为了获取文会的会刊，不参与文会的任何活动。

三、会员与文会

各类会员参与文会活动的情况大不一样，居住在上海的会员参与演讲活动比较多，而不在上海的会员只能参与文会的调查活动和向文会投稿。虽然有时有二三十人参与调查活动，但这些人多是各地的传教士和领事，加之次数并不是很多，因此总体上参与的会员是屈指可数的，换言之，很多会员估计从未参与过文会的调查活动。

就投稿而言，从仅存的通讯簿中可以发现（见表 2-5），19 世纪名誉会员和终生会员几乎不向文会投稿。名誉会员只有两名投稿人——伟烈亚力、麦华陀，这二人都是伦敦会传教士。通讯会员投稿的比例很高，有一半以上的通讯会员向文会投稿，这些人有艾约瑟、贝勒（E. Bretschneider）、费理饬（H. Fritsche）、傅兰雅、翟理思、杨格非（Griffith John）、丁韪良、慕稼谷、麦嘉缔（D. B. McCartee）、慕维廉（W. Muirhead）、庄延龄和柏林的巴斯琴（Adolph Bastian）、林道（Rudolph Lindau），匈牙利的西切尼（Count Bela Széchényi）。上述在华的通讯会员中，除了庄延龄为英驻福州领事之外，其余的 10 人几乎都是在华的传教士，他们不仅是文会的主要撰稿人，而且也是当时外文报刊的主要撰稿人，《教务杂志》、《北华捷报》、《远东释疑》经常能见到他们的作品。

表 2-5　　　　　　　　　　　文会各类会员投稿信息统计表　　　　　　　　　　（单位：人）

年份	名誉会员		通讯会员		终生会员		普通会员	
	投稿人数	比例(%)	投稿人数	比例(%)	投稿人数	比例(%)	投稿人数	比例(%)
1885	2	20	12	46	0		24	12.9
1887			13	52	1	50	25	12.3
1888			13	52	1	25	26	11.7
1892			13	56.5	1	0.09	30	14.5
1893			12	54.5	1	0.08	25	12.8
1894			12	60	1	0.07	26	12.8
1897			12	60	2	0.11	26	12.5

资料来源：各类会员投稿人数来源于会刊 1885、1887、1888、1892、1893、1894、1897 各年份的会员通讯录。凡是曾经供稿的会员其名字前都标有"十"。数据系笔者一一统计而得。

注：比例指的是各类供稿人数与各类会员总数间的比值。如：1885 年名誉会员共计有 10 人，而名誉会员供稿人只有 2 人，比例即 20%。

普通会员只有不到 13% 的人向文会投稿，这些人不是领事、外交官，就是洋行、海关人员。他们中有啊查理（C. Alabaster，外交官）、安德森（J. Anderson，太古洋行商人）、卜士礼（领事人员）、贾礼士（W. R. Carles，领事人员）、杜维德（E. B. Drew，海关人员）、花之安（Ernst Faber，传教士）、嘉托玛（C. T. Gardner，领事人员）、哈巴安（Andrew P. Happer，海关人员）、韩尔礼（Augustine Henry，海关人员）、夏德（海关人员）、合信（医生）、马士（海关人员）、金斯密（建筑师）、葛显礼（H. Kopsch，海关人员）、立德（《北华捷报》工作）、穆林德（P. G. von Möllendorff，海关人员）、毛里逊（工程师）、诺思蒂尼（L. Nocentini，领事秘书）、白挨底（G. M. H. Playfair，领事）、柔克义（外交官）、太罗（George Taylor，海关人员）、武尔披齐（Comdr. Z. Volpicelli，领事人员）、卫理（外交官）。

通讯会员和普通会员之投稿总量目前尚难确定，但是依据这一时期的演讲目录看，前者的供稿数量要远远多于后者。上述通讯会员几乎每人至少有 3-5 篇文章，而普通会员除了金斯密、夏德和白挨底外，一般只有 1-3 篇。这也说明 19 世纪文会的主要参与者是在华的传教士，其他人尚不占主流；同时也反映出近代西方对中国社会的研究，传教士还是走在前列。

由于资料的缺乏，本研究对 20 世纪各类会员的投稿情况还无法作出准确的判断。但从演讲者和会刊文章作者的身份看，传教士已不再独领风骚，中外学者、汉学家及大学教授成为文会的主要撰稿人。

四、会员的分布

文会会员主要是在华的外侨，尤其是居住在上海的各国侨民。职业的关系使得很多会员会不定期地流动于世界各地，加之不时有新的外籍会员加入，在客观上文会会员已将他们对中国的调查研究成果传播到世界各地。换言之，文会会员向西方传播了中国的社会和文化信息，他们成为中西文化交流的桥梁。因此，考察不同时段会员的居住地分布情况，有助于我们认识文会对中西文化交流所做的贡献。

从文会的 24 482 个通讯地址中，可以确认居住地的有 20 019 个，这些地点分布于六大洲 49 个国家中。文会章程规定要向会员免费邮寄会刊，因此会刊是随会员而流动。会刊当在这

49个国家中出现过,姑且不论其影响力,至少可以说文会对中国的研究成果曾经辐射至48个国家(中国除外)。这48个国家中,欧洲19个,亚洲15个,南美洲5个,非洲4个,北美洲3个,澳洲2个(见表2-6)。除了欧美外,其他地点也都是欧美殖民者在世界各地的居留地,说明会刊的读者群体主要还是欧美人士。

表2-6　　　　　　　　　　　　　文会会员所及世界各地的时间表

年份	会员	城市	国家	部门
1860	Brown, Rev. S. R.	江华	朝鲜	
1864	Muller-Beeck, Geo	横滨	日本	德国领事馆
1878	Williams, Rev. S. Wells.	耶鲁	美国	
1878	Brown, H. O.	柏林	德国	
1878	Skatschkoff, his Ex. C. A.	圣彼得堡	俄国	
1878	Giquel, P., Esq.	巴黎	法国	
1878	Alcock, Rutherford.	伦敦	英国	
1878	Pereira, Marquis, A. E.	曼谷	泰国	
1878	Smith, The Hon. Cecil C.	新加坡	新加坡	
1880	Hepburn, J. C., M. D.	横滨	日本	
1881	Kreitner, Kieut. G.	维也纳	奥地利	
1881	Széchényi, Count Bela	Zinkendorf	匈牙利	
1881	Pereira, Marquis, A. E.	孟买	孟买	
1887	Nocentini, L	佛罗伦萨	意大利	
1887	Möllendorff, O. E. Von.	马尼拉	菲律宾	德国领事馆
1892	De Groot, Dr. J. J. M.	阿姆斯特丹	荷兰	
1892	Schjöth, Fr.	奥斯陆	挪威	海关
1892	Bethge, C.	贝林佐纳	瑞士	
1892	Gabriel, Hermann, JUR.	巴达维亚	印尼	德国领事馆
1894	Beaune, Th. Mercier	西贡	越南	学校
1897	Sampatrao Gaikward	巴洛达	印度	
1901	Lund, Hugo	赫尔辛基	芬兰	赫尔辛基大学
1901	Marques-Pereira, J. F.	里斯本	葡萄牙	大太阳报编辑部
1906	Eitel, E. J., PHD	阿得雷德	澳大利亚	
1906	Jamieson, J. W.	开普敦	南非	
1910	Tejldor, Manuel	哈瓦那	古巴	古巴领事馆
1910	Seco, R.	帕拉	巴西	西班牙领事馆
1910	Nord, Dr. H.	君士坦丁堡	土耳其	德国领事馆
1912	Carter, J. C.	麦克塔维什	加拿大	
1912	Gröne, H. Dawson	都柏林	爱尔兰	

续表

年份	会员	城市	国家	部门
1912	Bingham, H. T.	槟榔屿	马来半岛	
1913	Petrement, A.	阿亚库乔	玻利维亚	比利时领事馆
1915	Dorsey, W. Roderick	的黎波里	利比亚	美国领事办
1915	Hildebrandt, Adolf	奥利瓦	西班牙	
1918	Zwemer, Rev. Samuel M.	开罗	埃及	
1918	Bennett, E. S.	贝尔发斯特	北爱尔兰	
1919	Barton, Sidney.	亚的斯亚贝巴	埃塞俄比亚	英国领事馆
1919	Jorgenson, O.	哥本哈根	丹麦	大北电报公司
1919	Dorsey, W. Roderick	仰光	缅甸	美国领事办
1921	Du Monceau, comte L.	布鲁塞尔	比利时	
1921	Richert, G.	斯德哥尔摩	瑞典	
1923	Clementi, C.	科伦坡	锡兰	政府秘书处
1931	Little, Edward S.	凯里凯拉	新西兰	
1935	Groenman, F. E. H.	加拉加斯	委内瑞拉	荷兰领事馆
1938	Davis, Monnett B.	布宜诺斯艾利斯	阿根廷	美国领事馆
1939	Davis, John Ker	华沙	波兰	美国领事馆
1940	Groenman, F. E. H.	加拉加斯	委内瑞拉	荷兰领事馆

资料来源：参见附表2。

注：地名之中文译名采自：中国地名委员会编：《外国地名译名手册》（中型本），商务印书馆1998年版。

从会员在各国最早的居住地点看，19世纪文会会员主要在亚洲、欧洲和北美洲活动；20世纪文会会员足迹已达澳洲、非洲和南美洲，形成了全球网络格局。会员的不断流动客观上形成了一个文化的逐步扩散过程，而且这个过程几乎与西方在世界各地的殖民过程同步进行。

首先，扩散的地点是亚洲的朝鲜和日本。1860年，通讯会员、美国传教士勃朗（Samuel Robbins Brown）到朝鲜江华从事对朝鲜的调查活动，他是4年后的《江华条约》的主要参与者。此后，汉城、釜山的英、美、俄、日领事馆都有文会的成员。继1853年美国打开日本大门，1856年英、法、俄又先后和日本签订不平等条约，欧美各国人士纷纷进入横滨和东京。文会创建后，会员也就较早到达日本，最先到日本的会员是德国的Geo Muller-Beeck，1864年到横滨的德国领事馆工作。次年英国驻华公使兼文会会长巴夏礼到日本任英国驻日公使，后来还有不少英国、法国、德国等国的会员来到日本。1872年，这些来日会员和在日欧美侨民仿效文会模式在日本横滨（后移至东京）创建了文会的姊妹——皇家亚洲文会日本支会（The Asiatic Society of Japan），继续从事对中国和东亚的研究，日本支会会刊上发表有不少关于中国的文章。从这一点看，会员的流动客观上拓宽了中西文化交流的渠道，使欧美人士能够获得更多的关于中国的信息。

其次，文会会员也较早地向欧美带去了关于中国的第一手信息，并促进了欧美各国对中国的研究。最早回到欧美各国的5名会员是英国的阿礼国、美国的卫三畏、俄国的孔琪庭（C. A.

Skatschkoff)、法国的日意格(P. M. Giquel)和德国的布朗(H. O. Brown)，1878 年他们已经回到各自的国家，[1] 向当时的 5 个资本主义列强带去了自己对中国的认识。由于这 5 位会员在华期间的活动范围都比较大，较之普通在华侨民，他们对中国有更深的认识。阿礼国回国前曾经先后在广州、福州、上海的英国领事馆工作，并一度担任驻上海总领事，参与"青浦事件"的交涉。职业的关系使他认识到西方对中国的认识还远远不够，因此他于 1868 年上书英国政府为文会求得一方土地，建立会所。而以他本人经历为基础的《维多利亚时代在中国的英国人——以阿礼国的机遇为例证说明》[2] 一书也一度成为西方人认识中国的主要参考书。阿礼国在向西方传播中国文化和改善西方人对中国的认识方面功不可没。卫三畏，文会的创始人和名誉会员，也是《中国丛报》创始人之一。他来华先后 43 年，留居北京 17 年，与当政诸人董恂、文祥、徐继畬、郭嵩焘等友善，且与董恂为邻居。长期以来致力于对中国社会的调查研究，对于中国语言文字、风俗人情，靡不深研，其所著的《中国总论》(Middle Kingdom)一书，当时在华外交人士莫不奉为圭臬，其言行无不为当时中外士人所重视。[3] 1877 年回国后又担任美国耶鲁大学的汉学教授，直至 1884 年去世，为促进中美文化交流作出了巨大贡献。孔琪庭(1821-1883)，曾经任俄驻塔城、天津等地领事馆领事，也是俄国考古学会、地理学会会员，国际东方学会和民族学会会员。"居华期间，曾深入考察中国民情风俗、宗教仪式、农活家计、租赋典当、茶馆酒肆等，并与农民结交，亲自种植茶、瓜、豆、谷、花卉、草药、果树等共达 343 种"。[4] 1878 年代表文会参加在彼得堡召开的第三届国际东方学家大会，他一生著译丰富，是近代俄罗斯乃至西方的著名汉学家。

19 世纪末 20 世纪初，文会还有不少会员回到欧美参与各国的汉学研究机构的创建和教学工作，大大加速了西方对中国的认识与研究进程。到了 20 世纪，文会会员更是呈遍布全球之势，进一步拓展了中国文化西传的传播空间，他们的流动客观上将中国文化带向了世界。

---

[1] 1878 年以前文会会员的通信录未注明各个会员的居住地址，因此这几位会员也有可能在 1878 年前已经回到欧美各国。
[2] Alexander Michie, The Englishman in China During the Victorian Era, as illustrated in the Career of Sir Rutherford Alcock, Edingburg Blackwood, 1900.
[3] 胡光麃：《百余年来影响我国的六十名洋客》，《传记文学》第 35 卷第 3 期，第 80 页。
[4] 孙越生：《俄国的中国学家》，见中国社会科学文献情报中心所编《俄苏中国学手册》，中国社会科学出版社 1986 年版，第 85-86 页。

第三章　组织机构(二)

第一节　图　书　馆

图书馆是文会的一个重要实体。文会自创建之时就已经开始收集有关图书,1869年4月,收购伟烈亚力藏书后,图书馆正式建立,1952年关闭。图书馆一直致力于搜集东方学方面的图书,在近代汉学研究和文化传播方面作出了突出贡献。

一、馆藏书籍

文会图书馆图书主要靠会员与上海外侨的捐赠,多年来,"只要是关于中国及远东的中外文书籍、杂志、小册子、地图,以及未出版的手稿、私人的旅行日记、碑刻的拓片,甚至一份报纸、一张便笺都不拒绝"。[1] 其次是通过与其他文化机构交换刊物获得,也有作者本人和出版机构的赠送,1911年,金斯密就捐赠了自己收藏的100卷(册)书;[2] 1919年南通气象台向图书馆赠送了该台的气象观测资料,1928年日本政府捐赠了《1923年日本大地震》(The Great Earthquake of 1923 in Japan)。理事会也断断续续向图书馆拨款购买书籍,由于缺乏资金,购买的书籍很少。

新中国建立前文会曾运出一批珍贵书籍和文物,[3] 加之馆藏中文、满文图书和一些稿本一直都没有完整统计,所以文会图书馆的完整藏书情况目前已很难得其详。1933年,据国人调查,"藏书一万余册,以西文为主,中文约一百五十种,二千余册,余皆西文杂志,二百余种,全是西文,新闻纸数种,特藏中国古学、地质、史地、博物,均是孤本。"[4] 又据文会年度报告,截至1940年底,图书馆的西文书籍共计12 177卷(册),[5] 此外,期刊杂志、俄文、中文、满文以及地图等图书未计在内。不同时期馆藏书籍的构成见表3-1。

总体上看,文会图书馆藏书量并不是很大,甚至可以说很小,与工部局图书馆相比,简直少得可怜。后者1935年就有71 665册/卷书(小说57 858,非小说12 932,儿童图书823,中文23册/卷)。[6] 这主要是因为资金的问题,历年文会年报中,图书馆长总抱怨缺乏资金致使无力购买很多新出版的关于东方学的书籍。

藏书量虽然少,但文会图书馆比较专业,是上海所有图书馆中唯一不收藏小说的图书馆,也是"中国境内最好的东方学图书馆",[7] 文会图书馆内收藏有16、17世纪以来出版的关于中

---

[1] Introduction. President's Address, JNCBRAS, No. IX., 1874, Pxxxiii.
[2] Proceedings, JNCBRAS, Vol. XLII, P259.
[3] 马军:《博物院路与中西文化交流》,《读书》2002年第1期,第106页。
[4] 冯陈祖怡编:《上海各国图书馆概览》,中国国际图书公司1934年版,第105页。
[5] 1938年底馆藏书籍有11 796卷(册),1939、1940年新增书籍数分别为262、119(卷)册。
[6] Public Library, Shanghai Municipal Council, Report for the year 1935.
[7] 胡道静:《上海图书馆史》,上海通志馆期刊抽印本1935年版,第45页。

表 3-1　　　　　　　　　　文会图书馆各类图书历年馆藏量　　　　　　　　　　（单位：Title）

年份 类别	1872	1881	1894	1909	1934	1955
综合	105	84	243	324		702
哲学	6	23	46	54	11	110
宗教	20	20	39	120	161	479
社会科学	27	41	33	133	89	809
语言学	116	147	210	340	255	601
自然科学	57	78	38	278	178	1 084
艺术(useful arts)	8	15	39	65	38	
美术(fine arts)				52	58	334
文学	34	55	62	84	67	284
历史	449	523	637	675	559	2 856
中文书		48		67	131	
满文书				3		
地图			81	7		
合计	951	986	1 424	2 256	1 416	7 259

资料来源：（单位：Title）

1. 1872 年数据来源于：*A Catalogue of the Library of the China Branch of the Royal Asiatic Society including the Library of Alex Wylie*, Shanghai, Printed at the "Ching-Foong" General Printing office, 1872.

2. 1881 年数据来源于：*A Catalogue of the Library of the China Branch of the Royal Asiatic Society*, Shanghai, Printed at the "Shanghai Mercury" office, 1881.

3. 1894 年数据来源于：*A Catalogue of the Library of the China Branch of the Royal Asiatic Society*, Shanghai, Kelly and Walsh limited, 1894.

4. 1909 年数据来源于：Ayscough, Florence Wheelock, *Preface to the Fouth Edition in the Catalogue of the North-China Branch of the Royal Asiatic Society*, Shanghai, 1909, Ppvi-ix.

5. 1934 年数据来源于：*Proceedings*, JNBRAS, Vol. LXV(1934), Pxiv. 说明：本年统计未计各类期刊杂志和有关学会团体出版的会刊、纪要。而且有些书籍借出未归，也有丢失的，所以数量较少。

6. 1955 年数据来源于：上海图书馆编的《前亚洲文会图书馆图书目录》，1955 年打印稿。

注：数据系笔者根据上述馆藏目录一一统计而得。这里的单位（Title）不是册，从 1955 年馆藏书目看，同一作者关于同一内容的多册书编的是一个书号。而许多学会多年出版的会刊也只有一个书号。1881、1909、1934、1955 等年份的中文、满文以及地图等图书有可能是没有分开统计或者是没统计。

国和远东方面的外文图书，"此外还有许多文化机构的会刊、纪要、年刊等杂志，这些都是上海其他图书馆难以找到的，对于从事中国及远东研究的工作者和学者来说是最好的去处"。[1] 图书馆收藏的珍贵西文文献，现分类叙述之。

（一）综合类图书

主要是世界各地学术机构、文化团体发行的杂志、期刊。从 1955 年书目看，图书馆收藏了 297 种有关学会团体的会刊、纪要、年报，112 种期刊杂志，26 种报纸。这些连续出版物主要是英文，其次为法文、德文、俄文、日文、意文、葡文、西文等文字，发行地涉及英、法、俄、德、奥、匈、荷、丹、葡、西、意、澳、日、印、越、印尼、朝鲜等国。这里有比较完整的英国皇家亚洲学会及其各

[1] *The China Journal*, Vol. XXVIII, Feb., 1938, No. 2, P67.

个支会发行出版的会刊和纪要(1798 – 1948)、伦敦皇家地理学会会刊与纪要(1831 – 1941)、1599 – 1900 年西方殖民者在巴达维亚发行的 10 种纪要与会刊之类的法文系列出版物、1744 – 1938 年的美国费城哲学协会纪要与会刊、1849 – 1931 年俄国帝国科学院纪要及年刊。杂志期刊类则收藏很多 19 世纪以来西方汉学期刊,如:法国的《亚洲学报》、《法兰西远东语言学校校刊》;荷兰的《通报》(1890 – 1924)、《东方学报》;德国的《汉学杂志》、《东亚季刊》;英国的《皇家人类学会会刊》;日本的《东方学报》、《史学杂志》;美国的《哈佛亚洲研究》、《美国东方学会会刊》;在中国出版的有:《中国丛报》(1832 – 1851)、《中日杂纂》、《教务杂志》(1868 – 1941)、《中国评论》(1872 – 1901)、《华裔学志》、《中国科学美术杂志》,还有中国人创办的《中国政治经济学报》(1923 – 1941)、《中国经济月报》等。报纸类有近乎完整的《北华捷报》、《字林西报》、《大陆报》和英国出版的《伦敦–中国邮报》。

综合类图书中另一部分重要图书是关于上海的西文文献,这里有完整的上海海关年报与海关出版物、工部局年报(1868 – 1941)、《上海年鉴》(1857 – 1869)以及关于上海的专著,对于研究上海近代史十分有用。

此外还收藏有数百余册目录与索引,如《香港马礼逊图书馆馆藏目录》(1873 年版)、《大英博物馆馆藏目录》(1915 年版)、《剑桥大学馆藏中文、满文图书目录》、《葛思德东方藏书库书目》(1941 年版)、1914 年 5 月 2 – 21 日在纽约举办的"中国、日本、朝鲜陶瓷展"目录。还有被中外学者予以高度称赞的高第的《汉学书目》、[1] 库寿龄的《中国百科辞典》、[2] 德国汉学家穆林德编纂的《中国书目手册》。[3]

(二)专著

专著方面,图书馆收藏了近代西方出版的许多著名的汉学研究专著,涵盖了各个学科。现分类叙述之。

1. 哲学

佛尔克的三卷本《中国古代哲学》(也有人译为《中国哲学史》)(书号:180/F68.1)[4] 被德国学界评价为"长期以来它都是西文著述中有关中国哲学史的最便利、完备的参考书。可以称得上是一部后人难以企及的哲学史著作"。[5] 该书与嘎伯冷兹(G. von der Gabelentz)的《汉语语法》、葛鲁贝(Wilhelm Grube)的《中国文学史》和福兰格(Otto Franke)的《中国通史》(也有译为《中华帝国史》)一样是代表德国汉学研究水平的巨著。他本人也因此而长期享名于东方学界。

2. 宗教

艾约瑟的《中国之宗教》(209/Ed1),"这书先概述中国宗教情形,中国人怎么会相信耶稣。

---

[1] 中国学者很早就说它"提要钩元,学者欲要阅何种(西人所著中国)书籍,按此书以求之,则十可得其八九矣"。日本的石田干之助评价它是"研究东洋史的,没有一人不受这书的助益"。李约瑟也说此书"在查考一切较古的书籍时,它是必不可缺少的"。见:陈潜《西人译中国书籍及在中国发行之报章》,《东方杂志》,第 5 卷第 9 期,第 162 页;石田干之助《欧人之汉学研究》,《中法大学月刊》第 5 卷第 1 号,第 54 页;(英)李约瑟《中国科学技术史》第 1 卷第 1 分册,科学出版社 1975 年版,第 108 页。

[2] 该书 16 开本,共 633 页,上海别发洋行 1917 年版。词条按英文字母顺序排列,必要时附汉字。"该书在当时对于西人了解中国的历史文化确有裨益,在今天则是中西文化交流史研究者的必备书。库氏因此获得 1919 年度的儒莲奖(Prix Stanislas Julien)"。见马军《上海社科院西文汉学旧籍简介》(四),《史林》2003 年第 4 期。

[3] 该书分"中国语言和文字"、"中华帝国"和"中国边地"三大部分,介绍了 4 639 条文献,书后附人名索引。1876 年别发洋行发行,共 378 页。该书是最早的西方汉学书目,其学术地位仅次于高第的《汉学书目》。

[4] 括号内的书号来自《前亚洲文会图书馆图书目录》,书号是文会当时所编,而非后人所编。

[5] 张国刚:《德国的汉学研究》,中华书局 1994 年版,第 54 页。

一时盛传于欧西宗教学界"。[1]

高延（J. J. M. De Groot）的《中国的宗教》（299.51/G89.13），1912年纽约版。"这书可为孔教、道教研究的指针"。[2]

沙畹与伯希和合著的《中国摩尼教考》（273.2/C34），"为研究摩尼教之佳著"。[3]

艾德（E. J. Eitel）的《中国佛教研究者必读》（294.1/Eil.1），1870年香港版，"这是一册简便的梵汉字典，为研究吾们中国佛教史及西域佛教史时必备的东西"。[4]

义律（C. Eliot）的《印度教与佛教概要》（294.1/El3），1921年伦敦版，"这书里'中国西藏'一章可见内容的渊博，为治中国佛教史者所必读"。[5]

高延的《中国宗教体系》（299.51/G89.1），"尤为成名之作"。[6]

3. 社会科学

毕瓯（E. Biot）的《中国教育论》（370.951/B47），"近百年内（上世纪中叶以前）关于中国教育的唯一西文书籍"。[7]

4. 语言学

翟理思的《英华字典》（495.1/G37），"为外人常用之手册"，翟氏因此而获得1912年的欧洲汉学最高奖——儒莲奖。

德国著名语言学家、哲学家威廉密·冯·洪堡（G. de Humboldt）的《就总的语法形式的属性，特别是中国语言语法形式的属性而致阿贝尔—雷慕沙先生的信》（495.1/H88），该书"至今在许多方面仍被认为是有关汉语哲学和汉语学原理方面的最好的导论性著作"。[8]

嘎伯冷兹的《汉语语法》（495.1/G11），"是西方研究中文语法奠基性的作品。当时西方有人认为中文是没有语法可言的，这本著作第一次对古汉语语法作了初步的分析和归纳"，该书1953年曾再版。[9]

5. 纯科学

5.1 地质学

李希霍芬所著的《中国》（555.51/R53），此书系李氏在华4年（1868－1872）考察之结晶，李氏提出的黄土风成说和关于中国地层、地质构造的论述都有较高的学术价值。"东亚全般的地质学无论底层方面或构造方面，总算从他手里造成一个宏大坚实的基础"。[10]

美国地质学家维理士（B. Willis）及其助手在华进行地质考察的报告（1903－1904）——《在中国的研究》（555.51/W69）"在中国地层划分以及构造地质学方面具有一定影响"。

那琳（E. Norin）的《山西地层详考》（555.51/N77）"初步奠定了山西石炭、二迭系地层之确认"。[11]

---

[1] 石田干之助：《欧人之汉学研究》，第67页。
[2] 石田干之助：《欧人之汉学研究》，第66页。
[3] 莫东寅：《汉学发达史》，上海书店1989年版，第97页。
[4] 石田干之助：《欧人之汉学研究》，第68页。
[5] 石田干之助：《欧人之汉学研究》，第70页。
[6] 莫东寅：《汉学发达史》，第106页。
[7] （英）李约瑟著：《中国科学技术史》第1卷第1分册，科学出版社1975年版，第227页。
[8] （德）傅吾康（Wolfgang Franke）著，陈燕、袁媛译：《十九世纪的欧洲汉学》，《国际汉学》第7辑，大象出版社2002年版，第72页。
[9] 张国刚：《德国的汉学研究》，第24页。
[10] 章鸿钊：《中国地质学发展小史》，《民国丛书》第2编第88册，上海书店1989年版，第6页。
[11] 黄汲青：《中国地质科学的主要成就》，《中国科技史料》1983年第3期，第3页。

美国地质学家庞培烈(Raphael Pumpelly)的《中国蒙古及日本之地质研究》,该书是作者1862－1865年在华北、长江下游一带的考察成果,书中提出中国的主要地质构成线是东北——西南走向,命名为"震旦上升系",后来论及我国地质构造经常使用的震旦方向就是从这里开始的。[1]

5.2 植物学

杜亚泉等人编纂的《植物学大辞典》(580.3/C63),1918年商务印书馆出版,是书包括名称名词8 980条,记载植物1 700余种。每种植物下列有中名、拉丁学名、日名、形态描述、产地、用途以及中名别名的古书考证等项,并附有插图1 002帧。此《辞典》对于我国近代植物学的发展和普及近代植物学知识有重要的历史意义,曾多次再版。[2]

瑞士植物学家德堪多(A. E. De Candolle)父子主编的《植物界自然系统长编》(580/C11),为19世纪最著名的、综合性的世界植物区系著作,此书包括161科、58 000余种植物。书中首次引入"分类学"这个术语,其分类系统对20世纪的一些系统有很大影响。[3]

边沁与霍克(G. Bentham and J. D. Hooker)合著的《植物自然科属大全》(580.1/B35),是书"经22年之长期始成,所载之显花植物有100 320种、8 417属及210科,是巨著在今日(1922年)犹风行也"。[4] 该书对中国植物分类学更具指导意义。

俄国著名植物学家马希慕维支(C. J. Maximowicz)所著的8卷本《亚洲新种会要》(581.957/M1.11),该书"为探索东亚植物之名典"。[5]

英国植物分类学家福勃士和汉姆斯莱(F. B. Forbes and W. B. Homsloy)两人合著的《中国植物目录》(581.951/F74)是最早全面研究中国植物的专著之一,也是近代中国植物研究的重要参考文献。

贝勒的《欧洲人研究中国植物历史》(581.951/B76.11)和《中国古代植物学》(581.951/B76),前者"是研究外国人近两百年来在中国进行植物采集与研究活动的重要参考文献";[6] 后者当时就享誉欧洲学术界,曾多次在欧洲各国以多种文字再版。

此外,还有日本植物志、香港植物志及其他博物学著作及手稿。

5.3 动物学

谭微道的《中国鸟类志》(598.2/D27),记载中国鸟类807种,"为尔时法京名著"。[7]

威金生(E. S. Wilkinson)的《上海鸟类》(598.2/W62),是书"考订精博,叙次详审,足资程式,为并世名典"。[8]

6. 医学

有极为罕见的Andreas Cleyer之《中医标本》(Speimen Medicine Sinice)和狄康伦(D. Hanbury)的《中国药物志》(Notes on Chinese material medinca, 1862)(610/H11)。

7. 艺术

---

[1] 杜石然等编:《中国科学技术史稿》(下),科学出版社1983年版,第267页。
[2] 中国植物学会编:《中国植物学史》,科学出版社1994年版,第126、156页。
[3] 中国植物学会编:《中国植物学史》,第150页。
[4] 吴元涤:《植物学分类发达史》,《博物学杂志》1卷4期,第36页。
[5] 张孟闻:《中国科学史举隅》,《民国丛书》第1编第90册,上海书店1989年版,第62页。
[6] 中国植物学会编:《中国植物学史》,第154页。
[7] 张孟闻:《中国科学史举隅》,第61页。
[8] 张孟闻:《中国科学史举隅》,第60、76页。

卜士礼的《中国艺术手册》(709.51/B85,1904年),是书"无论就范围的博大看,或是就学术贡献看,都可以算是破天荒的工作,甚至到目前(1945年)为止,有些地方还没有人能超过"。[1]

安德逊(W. Anderson)的《大英博物馆中国和日本画目录》(759.9/An2,1886年),该书被誉为"可以算是第一本用英文写的研究中国画的著作"。[2]

劳费尔的《汉代陶器研究》(738.51/L36),"尤为世所称道","为研究中国考古学、美术学者必读的书"。[3]

福开森的《中国建筑史概论》(709.51/E32.11),国人很早就予以重视该书,并将其译成中文,"译者将这书译成中文,纯为给国人知道欧美人对于中国建筑之记述思想,已比较进步不少了"。[4]

8. 文学

伟烈亚力的《汉籍解题》(895.18/W97),被李约瑟评为是"研究中国文献的最好的入门书"。[5]

翟理思的《中国文学史》(895.1/G37)有1901年和1923年的两个版本。

格鲁贝的《中国文学史》(895.18/G75),"这是德国第一部由专家撰写的中国文学史著作"。[6]

《中国诗歌》(The Poetry of the Chinese.),被认为是关于中国诗歌最早的英文论著。[7]

9. 历史

9.1 考古学

劳费尔(Berthold Laufer)的《中国古玉考》(913.51/L36.12),"旁征博引,以考古方法寻绎古今玉之演进,以玉器为中心资料说明中国古代文明与礼教发展",[8]成为该领域内的经典之作。

沙畹的《两汉时代之石画像》与《北华访古录》(915.18/C34.1)"图像丰富,解说精细,由此开西欧研究中国古代艺术之风尚"。他的《西突厥史料》(915/C34)"为治西北史者不可缺少之书"。[9]

此外,理雅各的《大秦景教流行中国碑研究》(913.51/L52),是景教碑研究的必备之书。

9.2 通史

沙畹的5大册《司马迁史记》(951/C43):"为汉学界盖世名作,译文既正确详尽,且有丰富之底注;创见既多,考证及比较法亦复精细"。[10]

夏德的《中国古代史》(931/H52):该书是夏德在美国哥伦比亚大学之讲义,出版后被学界

---

[1] Perceval Yetts 著,汪家正译:《不列颠的中国研究》,《东方杂志》41卷22号,第37页。
[2] Perceval Yetts 著,汪家正译:《不列颠的中国研究》,第38页。
[3] 岑家梧:《中国艺术论集》,《民国丛书》第2编第66册,上海书店1989年版,第88页。石田干之助:《欧人之汉学研究》,《中法大学月刊》第5卷第1号,第75页。
[4] 福开森著,毛一心译:《中国建筑史概论》,《民国丛书》第5编第87辑,上海书店1989年版,第46页。
[5] (英)李约瑟《中国科学技术史》第1卷第1分册,科学出版社1975年版,第98页。
[6] 张国刚:《德国的汉学研究》,中华书局1994年版,第26页。
[7] Sophie. S. Lanneau: Chinese Poetry, The Chinese Recorder, Vol. LVI, P800.
[8] 莫东寅:《汉学发达史》,上海书店1989年版,第144页。
[9] 莫东寅:《汉学发达史》,第144页。
[10] 莫东寅:《汉学发达史》,第97页。

誉"为当时名著"、"可称是一部卓越的汉学著作"。"立论多少有些非难之点,然是著名的书"。[1]

福兰阁之最负声誉的 5 卷本《中华帝国史》(951.9/F84.1),李约瑟认为是关于中国历史的最好的西文书,"这部著作的百科全书式的特点,使它能够在一定程度上注意到某些有科学意义的事情"。[2]

赖德烈(Kenneth Scott Lataurett)的《中国历史及文化》(951/L11.2),"第一卷述先秦至现代史实,第二卷分述文化史各项,各章附有西文参考书目,颇便初学,为中国史入门之名著"。[3]

亨利·裕尔(Henry Yule)的《东域纪程录丛》(915/Y99)"为研究中西交通史之权威"。[4]

劳费尔的《中国伊兰篇》(931/L34)"为中西文化交通史上杰作,其书博大浩瀚,于中国植物金石称谓沿革,搜求中外记述,一名一物之微,详加疏证"。[5]

夏德的《中国与东罗马》(951/H52.1)"为研究中国与西亚交通史杰作"。是一本经典著作,为研究中西文化交流的"入门台阶"。[6]

德国克拉勃罗德(M. J. Klaproth)的《亚细亚杂考》(950/K66)"记清俄国境、满族起源、蒙古历史、运河原委、台湾琉球之地志,以及长白山攀登记,纸币起源考,所涉极广"。[7]

斯坦因(A. Stein)的《古和阗》(913.516/st3)详述作者 1900－1901 年间实地考察新疆塔里木盆地,并在和阗发掘尼雅、古里雅遗迹的过程,以及所获得古壁画、佛典、汉晋木简等。

马士的《远东国际关系史》(951/M84.1)更是近世国际关系史名著。

9.3 民族史

庄延龄的《鞑靼千年史》(951.8/P11.1)长期盛行于英语读者间。1937 年向达、黄静渊曾将之翻译成中文(商务版,1937 年)。

柏尔(Charles Alfred Bell)的《西藏人民生活》(915.15/B67),作者"深通藏语,久居拉萨,所记详密正确,转非汉籍中所可见者矣"。[8]

9.4 地图

1647 年南怀仁主编的《坤舆全图》。

1826 年德国克拉勃罗德主编的《亚细亚历史地图》(950/K66.1),"彩色地图二十七页,为东方历史地图之鼻祖"。[9]

内地会(China Inland Mission)编印的《中华帝国地图集》(912.51/C43.11)和著名植物学家贝勒绘制的《中国及邻近地区地图》(912.51/B72)都是较早的、比较准确的中国全国地图,"帝国境内的城市地点绘制得都比较准确,为后来的中国地图提供了基础"。[10]

---

[1] 石田干之助:《欧人之汉学研究》,第 62 页;(英)李约瑟著《中国科学技术史》第 1 卷第 1 分册,科学出版社 1975 年版,第 153 页;莫东寅:《汉学发达史》,第 143 页。此外,文会会刊 18 卷,艾约瑟也有评价。
[2] (英)李约瑟著《中国科学技术史》第 1 卷第 1 分册,第 152 页。
[3] 莫东寅:《汉学发达史》,第 146 页。
[4] 莫东寅:《汉学发达史》,第 126 页。
[5] 莫东寅:《汉学发达史》,第 144－145 页。
[6] (英)李约瑟著《中国科学技术史》第 1 卷第 2 分册,科学出版社 1975 年版,第 419 页。
[7] 莫东寅:《汉学发达史》,第 109 页。
[8] 莫东寅:《汉学发达史》,第 127 页。
[9] 莫东寅:《汉学发达史》,第 109 页。
[10] Lady Hosie, A Map of China in the Making, JNCBRAS, Vol. LVII, P23.

赫尔曼（A. Herrmann）的《中国历史与商业地图》（912.51/H42）"则清楚地表示出沙漠、黄土、冲击土、古森林等各种区域的特征。便于迅速查考，是必不可缺少的辅助工具，其中历史方面的材料较商业方面的为多，可惜已经绝版，不能买到"。李约瑟在《中国科学技术史》中就是借助此地图来叙述中国的地形概貌。[1]

除了书籍、杂志外，图书馆还收藏有一些原始的文件、档案和图片，主要有工部局纳税人会议记录，上海水厂年报，上海运动事业基金会年报，中国海关的关税价目表、灯塔浮标信号统计表，上海打猎协会（Hunt Club of Shanghai）档案等。图片则有北京故宫的图片。

文会图书馆还收藏了数量不少的中文文献，多为各地方志，从1887年图书馆出版的两页馆藏中文图书目录看，当时已有1 497卷。[2]后来又陆续收藏有《圣经》（中文版）、《李文忠公全书》、《崔东壁遗书》、《玉狮堂传奇十种曲》、《四库全书总目》、《字帖大王集》、《胡文忠公遗书》等。还有一些西译过来的科技类图书和国人未出版的手稿，如1861年裨治文翻译的《苗族概略》就是一位中国学者的手稿。但中文藏书"惟得资浏览者，殊无几人，于公众方面毫无裨益"。[3]

二、图书馆之利用及评价

图书馆在致力于藏书的同时，还通过以下渠道实现知识的传播功能：

（一）借阅与研究

文会图书馆自成立之日始，就决定办成一个公共图书馆，这是因为当时上海的外侨社会文化生活十分单调，除了工部局成立的上海图书馆外，几乎没有别的读书场所。而上海图书馆收费，且只对内部会员开放，所以上海外侨社会一直希望建立一个公共图书馆。文会图书馆建立初期，"由于没有完整的馆藏目录，一直难以向公众开放"，[4]读者主要限于文会会员。1872年高第编了《皇家亚洲文会北华支会图书馆馆藏目录》后，图书馆才向公众开放。1917年理事会决定"图书馆为大众服务，并尽可能地扩大非会员的权利"。[5]20世纪30年代图书馆每日上午9时至下午7时开放，任何人均可免费阅览，平均每日接待30－40人。

20世纪后，随着馆藏书籍的丰富，图书馆的地位也日益突出，来此阅读的人数也逐年增加，而且在上海的几个图书馆中，文会图书馆的读者人数一直居于前列。读者的身份也日益复杂，不仅有文会的会员，也有普通的外侨；不仅有外国人也有中国人；不仅有教授、学者出入，也有大中小学生来借阅。文会的阅览室是对社会开放的，会员可以自由翻阅图书，非会员则由图书管理员帮助调书。文会图书馆发挥出其应有的社会功效，真正成为文化传播的场所。1937年日军入侵上海后，上海"图书馆事业也随之呈现萧索的气象，市立图书馆和民众图书馆已成敌人占领区，租界内比较大的图书馆，像蚂蚁图书馆、量才图书馆、鸿英图书馆，都因战事而先后停办，仅存的只有去岁成立的国际图书馆和最近创设的丁香图书馆，而且藏书很少，令人失望"。[6]文会图书馆这时成为社会大众求知之地和上海乃至华东地区的学习研究中心，"阅览室可以看到来自金陵大学（University of Nanking）、东吴大学（Soochow University）、圣约翰

---

[1]（英）李约瑟著《中国科学技术史》第1卷第1分册，第109、117页。
[2] Proceedings, JNCBRAS, Vol. XXI, pp358－359.
[3]《文会致江苏教育会：倡设公共图书馆之商榷》，《申报》1922年4月14日。
[4] Perface, A Catalogue of the Library of the China Branch of the Royal Asiatic Society, Shanghai, Printed at the "Ching-Foong" General Printing office, 1872.
[5] Proceedings, JNCBRAS, Vol. XLVII, Pviii.
[6]《上海文化的现状》，《中华图书馆协会会报》13卷1期（1938年7－9月），第21页。

大学及其他学校的教授、学生和学者,无论男女老幼都专心阅读,书库中几乎已无存书"。[1]不仅如此,文会图书馆还保护了一批书籍文献,抗战期间之江大学(Hangchow Christian College)、沪江大学等学校的部分馆藏书籍因存放在文会图书馆内而避免了战火之灾。

图书馆还为学术研究——尤其是"热衷于亚洲的学者"——提供了多方面的帮助。高第曾经回忆道"文会给我最深的影响是使我产生了编纂《西人论中国书目》(Bibliotheca Sinica)的念头,在那里获得了不少知识,对我后来再版《西人论中国书目》和编纂其他书籍都起着作用。"[2]图书馆也通过各种途径,或租用或借调相关的资料文献来满足读者的需要。1873年图书馆就借到1871-1872年美国疏浚密西西比河的文件,为上海疏浚黄浦江提供参考咨询帮助。[3] 1895年图书馆从英国领事馆租借了13卷《蓝皮书》(Blue Books),使读者了解中国及其邻近地区详细可靠的商业贸易和自然历史信息。[4] 1919年图书馆"专门搜集了五四运动的有关资料,便于读者了解此事"。[5]文会图书馆还为上海市通志馆、雷氏德研究院(Henry Lester Institute)和燕京大学(Peking University)等文化机构提供帮助。[6]

研究方面,图书馆做得比较薄弱。但是对于学术研究,尤其是为近代汉学及东方学研究提供了帮助,这方面主要体现在图书馆出版的馆藏书目上。文会曾编过6次馆藏书目,[7] 1872年高第最早编辑了图书馆分类书目,采用的是克拉勃罗德(Klaproth)的分类法。高第所编之馆藏书目出版后,《北华捷报》和《中国评论》(China Review)都专门予以介绍,称赞"该书使得我们无需再咨询图书管理员,文会也将得到上海社会的进一步支持"。[8] 1881年予以补充,1894年夏士又做了修订再版。1907年"爱司克夫人对所有书籍进行重新编号、装订,并根据杜威分类法(Dewey System)将书重新放置"。[9]在当时很多中国人自己的图书馆还采用传统的四库分类法时,文会比较早的引进了这种科学的西文图书分类法。同年图书馆又制作现代书目卡片,这些卡片有作者索引卡片、同类书目卡片和书名卡片。"自从用了这种卡片制后,它的无限止展拓的可能性,包括它的广大和其他等等的长处是非常的明显"。[10]馆藏书目的出版和目录卡片的制作大大提高了文献检索的速度,从而也提高了馆藏书籍的利用率。

除了编辑馆藏书目,图书馆也不定期地编辑和修订有关索引工具书,对于出现于各类期刊杂志上关于中国及远东地区的论文都做了目录索引。图书馆先后编辑了《中国丛报》、《远东释疑》、《美国国家博物馆纪要》(1891-1925)、《美国国家博物馆年报》(1887-1932)、《斯密生博物馆年报》(1-80卷)、《美国东方学会会刊》(1849-1933)、《美国语言协会纪要》(1869-1917)、《美国历史学会年刊》(1889-1898)、《艾塞克斯研究院学刊》(1864-1894)、《哈佛大学动物学博物馆年刊》(1884-1908)、《菲律宾科学杂志》(1916-1930)、《皇家亚洲学会纪要》(1827-1835)、《皇家亚洲学会会刊》(1834-1933)、《皇家人类学会会刊》(1872-1933)、《中

---

[1] Proceedings, JNCBRAS, Vol. LXIX, 1938, Pxiii.
[2] Proceedings, JNCBRAS, Vol. XXXV, 1903-1904, Px.
[3] The Asiatic Society, North-China Herlad, Oct. 30, 1873, P365.
[4] Proceedings, JNCBRAS, Vol. XXXI, P119.
[5] Proceedings, JNCBRAS, Vol. L, 1919, Pix.
[6] The R. S. A. Library, China Journal, Vol. XXI, Jul. 1934, No. 1, P12.
[7] 这六次官藏书目的出版时间分别是1872年、1881年、1894年、1909年、1921年、1934年。
[8] Short notices of new books, The China Review: or Nortes and Queries of the Far East, Vol. I-no. 4, 1873, P270.
[9] The Royal Asiatic Society Library, North-China Herald, Vol. LXXXVIII, No. 2135, 11th, Jul. 1908, P95.
[10] 胡道静:《上海图书馆史》,《上海通志馆期刊》,第2卷4期,1935年,第1457页。

国科学美术杂志》等期刊上面的关于中国及远东方面的论文索引。这些书目和索引,大大便利了相关专题文献的查阅,促进了汉学研究的进程。

(二)合作与交流

文会图书馆在加强馆内工作的同时,也不断与其他图书馆合作,加强彼此交流。文会图书馆曾先后与三个图书馆合作,实现资源共享。1880年与上海图书馆(即后来的工部局图书馆)达成协议,两个机构的会员可以互相阅读对方的图书。[1] 1884年至1893年,上海图书馆又长期租借文会会所二楼作为藏书场所。两馆合作之后,效果非常明显,不仅文会会员得以免费借阅上海图书馆图书,扩大了他们的阅读范围,而且整个上海社会(外侨)的读者群体也大为增加,据上海图书馆馆长毛里逊说"两馆合作后,上海图书馆成为上海地区最好的图书馆,也是上海地区唯一的一个公共图书馆"。[2] 这样的合作,还有1935年加入的中国科学美术协会图书馆和1940年加盟的尚贤堂图书馆。其次,图书馆积极展开与世界各地文化团体之间的交流,通过互赠出版物实现资源共享。1936年世界各地的出版社曾向文会捐赠200册书。此外,举办书展、画展等活动来传播有关文化知识。1938年12月29日的新年晚会上就举办了"老上海"作品展,包罗了上海古代、现代、旅游、艺术、青铜、翡翠、社会风俗等方面的著作。

综上所述,文会图书馆在图书采集上,不仅收藏古代典籍与近世新学书籍,而且也订购各类杂志和报刊;在服务对象上,不仅向学者开放,更注重面向大众;不仅面向外侨,也向华人开放。从功能上看,不仅为上海儿童及在校学生提供了校外学习的资源和场所,也为社会公众提供了保护与传播知识的方便和机会;它不仅承担了上海外侨社会的文化、教育的功能,而且也引进了崭新的文化传播体制——社会公共文化机构。因此,它不仅是中外文化交流的基地,而且也是社会教育的课堂。

第二节 博 物 院

博物院又称"上海博物院"(Shanghai Museum),也是文会的一个重要实体。由于没有合适的馆舍和缺乏充裕的资金,1874年3月25日博物院才建立。

一、发展历程

博物院创建时,按照近代西方自然科学学科设立了数个收藏部门:植物学、地质学与贝壳学、爬虫学与动物学、考古学与钱币学、鱼类学、鸟类学、人种学、事业与生产等七大部门,而且各个部门也都是由比较专业的人管理(见第一章)。实际上,有些部门由于藏品有限,也是形同虚设。20世纪,博物院内场设有负责人的部门主要是鸟类学、鱼类学、植物学、钱币、考古、贝壳6大部门,说明博物院藏品也是主要集中于这6个方面。

早期博物院实行名誉监院制(Honorary Curator),1932年才改为名誉院长(Honorary Director)制。监院就是院长,负责博物院的日常事务。年会上递交博物院年度报告,内容包括博物院的年度财务情况,标本的收集、制作、贮存、陈列与展览活动,馆际之间的交流等。监院在每年年会上选出,任期一年,亦可连任。历任监院多为著名学者,见下表:

---

[1] Proceedings, JNCBRAS, Vol. XV, Pxii.
[2] Municipal Council, Shanghai: Report for the year ended 31st Dec. 1885, Kelly & Walsh, Limited, 1886, P135.

表 3-2　　　　　　　　　　　　　博物院历任院长

任职年份	院长	职业/身份
1874－1875	朴赉懿	
1876	丁韪良	传教士
1877－1879	福威勒	动物学者,短吻鳄的发现者
1880、1882、1892－1893	健生	不详
1881	金斯密	汉学家
1883	史密斯	不详
1884－1885	史丹阳	博物学家
1886－1888	好博逊	瑞典外交官,业余从事动植物研究
1889－1891	柏固	不详
1894－1895、1897	沃斯·布儒邦	良济药房医师
1896	克罗瑟	不详
1898－1900、1902	莱曼	格致书院教授
1901、1903	巴切特	美国领事馆医生,博士
1904、1906	李治	中国公论西报编辑
1905、1907－1920	史笪来	医生、爬虫类专家
1921－1927	谈维士	工部局卫生处处长
1923－1941	苏阿德	博物学家
1947－1948	裘必胜	钱币收藏家

资料来源：
1. 文会历年年会报告,见历年会刊。
2. 胡道静:《上海博物院史略》,见《上海研究资料续集》,第 391－412 页,上海书店 1993 年版。
3. *The history of the Shanghai Museum*. The China Journal, Vol. XIX, No. 5., pp219－227.
4. Sowerby, Arthur de Carle, *Presidential Address*: *Some Remarkable Animal of China*, JNBRAS, Vol. LXXI, pp1－22.
5. 黄光域编:《中国近代专名翻译词典》,四川人民出版社 2001 年版。
注：从 1923 年 5 月份开始,苏阿德就已经和谈维士一起执掌博物院,1928 年后主要由苏阿德一人负责。
表中:健生(D. C. Jansen)、史密斯(H. L. Smith)、史丹阳(F. W. Styan)、沃斯·布儒邦(H vosy-bourbon)、克罗瑟(F. A. de st. Croix)、莱曼(E. R. Lyman)、巴切特(S. P. Barchet, M. D.)等人的中文名字是笔者音译。

　　文会最初的目的是将博物院建成中国博物学的信息储藏中心,[1]收藏中国动植物和地质标本就成为博物院的一个主要目标。初期搜集的多是上海附近的各种鸟类——主要由在华外侨运动员提供的各种野鸭。1876 年上海野鸽协会(Shanghai Clay Pigeon Club)向博物院捐银 750 两,用于布置中国鸟类及其他动物标本陈列的背景设置。1877 年丁韪良在徐家汇博物院韩德禄(Pierre Heude)神甫的帮助下,将博物院内收藏的珍稀动物标本进行分类。1881 年健生(D. C. Jansen)任监院时,英国 Hornet 号船上医生古庇(H. B. Guppy)捐赠了一批完整的地质标本。同年,博物院将一部分原为图书馆的面积改为标本陈列室。

　　1884 年,著名的博物学家史丹阳担任监院,他在任期间搜集了大批的鸟类标本并为许多中国鸟类和动物作了命名,使得博物院鸟类标本系列收藏初具规模,大大提高了博物院的影响

[1] Report of the N. C. B. of the R. A. S. for the year 1875, JNCBRAS, Vol. X, Pvii.

力。1886 年,好博逊任监院后,进一步加大了鸟类标本的收藏,为博物院日后成为远东地区著名的自然历史博物院奠定了基础。因此苏阿德称"这一时期是博物院历史上辉煌的一页"。[1] 1891 年博物院从一在华军人扬考斯基(Yankowsky)手中购买一批蝴蝶标本,这批标本几乎包括了远东地区蝴蝶的大部分物种。随着标本的增多,1897 年博物院雇佣一位姓周的中国人作为专职管理员,负责标本的放置、贮存。博物院已由此前的标本储藏所发展为初具规模的陈列室。

1906 – 1920 年公共租界的卫生行政长官史笪来任博物院的监院。这是博物院的又一个辉煌发展时期。史笪来任职监院 15 年,为博物院作出了重大贡献。他通过多种渠道增加博物院的藏品,在任期间收藏品大大增加,尤其是中国爬行动物。1906 年,史笪来又将博物院内标本重新分类,所有标本都制作了标签,上面用英文注明标本之名称、来源、种属。1907 年,他又邀请著名的中国鸟类学权威德拉图什(J. D. D. de la Touche)将馆藏的鸟类标本重新布置,并作了妥善分类。德氏还帮助博物院搜集了一大批鸟类标本,并编辑了《博物院馆藏鸟类标本名录》,该书一直为文会所用。到 1920 年"博物院有鸟类标本 3 000 余种,代表 500 个种类,估计价值在 10 000 元;哺乳动物之收藏价值已达到 1 500 元;爬行和两栖动物有 1 500 余种中国标本,代表 100 个物种,价值在 2 000 元;矿石和化石价值达 2 000 元,总计达 20 000 元"。[2] 这一时期内博物院的标本制作也取得了进展,博物院制作了栩栩如生的各种动物标本,除了展览和存储外,多余的予以出售,仅 1904 – 1920 年间出售转让的鸟类标本复制品价值达 1 000 元。1914 年博物院第一次实现了盈利。[3]

史笪来之后,博物院的监院几乎一直由著名博物学家苏阿德担任。1927 年废弃名誉监院称号,改为名誉院长制,苏阿德任名誉院长,在他任职期内博物院获得大发展,进入鼎盛时期。首先,改组博物院机构,扩大博物院规模。苏阿德到任后,在加大对动植物和自然标本搜集的同时,也加强了对历史文物的收藏。1934 年他将博物院分为四个部门:植物部——包达甫(W. M. Porterfield)、鸟类部——威金生(E. S. Wilkinson)、考古部——柏达(Harold Porter)、钱币部——裘毕胜(H. E. Gibson)、鱼类部——朱元鼎(Yuanting Chu)。各部负责人均为拥有教授称号的专业人士。包达甫为圣约翰大学植物学教授,长期研究中国的竹子等草本植物,是这一方面的权威;柏达则热衷于收藏和研究中国的文物艺术品,对古董研究情有独钟;威金生则是上海地区鸟类的权威。裘必胜专门收藏和研究中国货币,是远东地区的著名货币收藏鉴定专家;朱元鼎是鱼类学家。20 世纪 30 年代博物院从以收藏动植物标本为核心开始向收藏文物古玩为中心转移。1936 年由苏阿德牵头在博物院内成立了中国钱币学会,并将博物院作为该团体的活动场所。其次,雇佣专职剥制师,制作标本。文会很早就曾聘剥制师为博物院制作标本,多余的标本出售,但是这些剥制师经常是候鸟型的,每年只在博物院工作数月,这就使得文会搜集的原始标本往往不能及时处理而腐烂掉。鉴于此,苏阿德决定永久雇佣唐仁宫为博物院剥制师,专门负责处理收集来的原始标本。他还指导唐制作了一套几乎涵盖了所有种类之中国鱼类标本,成为院中珍贵的陈列品。第三,他邀请俄国著名人类学家史禄国参与整理院中的所藏标本。他们共同设计了一套方案,对标本进行了重新分类、编号,并制作卡片索引。在此

---

[1] Sowerby, Arthur de Carle, Presidential Address: Some Remarkable Animal of China, JNCBRAS, Vol. LXXI, P16.
[2] Proceedings, JNCBRAS, Vol. LI, Pxv.
[3] Proceedings, JNCBRAS, Vol. XLV, Pxi.

基础上重新摆放柜子和标本,按类集中收藏、陈列,从而改变了以前陈列房间杂乱无章和拥挤的局面,腾出来摆放大型哺乳动物骨骼的空间,使得陈列效果更为明显,展览也颇具吸引力。此外,苏阿德还开展了一系列的活动,真正发挥了博物院的储藏、展览、研究、教育四大功能。苏阿德以其渊博的专业知识和杰出的管理才能为博物院的发展作出了巨大贡献,使得博物院不仅受到中外学者所瞩目,而且也成为大众的文化殿堂。

二、藏品与陈列

经过多年积累,博物院收藏了中国各地的动植物标本,早期的陶器、古代的青铜器、河南的甲骨、少数民族的服装,也有碑刻、砖石、珠宝、古玩、头盔、钱币等零碎文物,不但种类繁多,而且数量也是同时代中国境内的其他博物馆所无法企及的。1951年6月上海市文管会接收时,博物院内"生物标本(包括小部分矿物标本)共20 328件,历史文物及艺术品共6 663件",具体如下:[1]

(一)人类学标本

中国地质考察所赠的一具完整的北京人头盖骨、近代西藏人头盖骨、上海发现的近代华人头盖骨;

居住于松花江流域的通古斯族所用的鲑鱼皮上衣和皮靴、满族服装、藏兵战袍、四川白族少女之裙、四川苗族早期所用的两种乐器、四川土著所用之弩、竹子雕刻的木偶、中国女婴的小鞋;

中国往昔之兵器:铠甲、剑、矛、弓、矢、盾、盔甲、明代之甲胄;

澳大利亚及新几内亚土著居民所用之木器、骨器、鲨鱼齿、海螺号和曾经使用的旧式武器;

史前之兵器:商、周、秦时代及以前的石器和铜制兵器;

旧时官吏之首饰:清朝官吏之服装、朝珠;

宗教器物:喇嘛教供神之杯——饰以金属之头盖或脑壳、和尚之念珠、崇拜之石、佛教祈祷藏文、红木佛杖、饰有黄金、珊瑚宝石的蒙古喇嘛教之圣剑;

中药材:虎骨、鹿角、蝎子、蜈蚣、蛇、蜥蜴、昆虫、介壳化石、龙骨以及甘草等植物药材;

中国旧式外科用具:针灸之针、粗皮针、刮刀、钳子、称药之天平、皮下注射器、吹药粉入鼻孔之喷射器、角质边之水晶眼镜。

北京之玩具、堪舆家之罗盘仪、中国之烟具;

西北各省所用之骨制、木制烟管;

(二)考古与钱币

中国历代钱币:商代之珍珠贝、骨币,战国之帛币、刀币、剑形货币,西汉的五铢钱,辽金时期圆形方空小钱,明清时期流通于中国的西班牙银币、墨西哥鹰洋、印度银币,明代使用的银票,清朝各省铸造的铜钱,太平天国发行的货币,清代的钱庄汇票,民国时期广东普遍使用的香港银元、豪洋,中共根据地发行的布币,中共在四川发行的银元。

外国货币则有:早期俄国的铜币、一战前后俄国各个银行发行的61种不同面值之卢布、一战后德国发行的10万亿面额的马克纸币。

---

[1] 这些标本名称参见:①文会历年年度报告;②苏阿德著,戚铭远译的《中国博物学:上海博物院指南》,亚洲文会华北支会1937年;③《自然博物馆情况报告(1956年3月3日)》,见《上海市文化局·社文:文化部关于召开全国博物馆工作会议的通知及我局汇报上海各博物馆的工作报告》,上海市档案馆,档案号:B172-1-220。各类标本分类标准参照《中国博物学:上海博物院指南》。

古代铜器:戟、剑、匕首、带钩、马具、铃、秤、铜箭头;古代铜镜、铜碗(周朝)、铜壶(周朝)。

陶制墓像:人俑、家畜陶制墓像(猪、狗、鹅、鸭;南京明代墓出土的狗和狮子)、汉、魏、唐等朝代的墓像(包括马、牛、羊、猪、狗、鹅、鸭、鸡)、陶制器具——明代之官轿、旅行箱、桌等。

古代陶器:汉代龙首陶壶、济南出土之陶罐、甘肃出土的仰韶文化陶器。

先秦至清代各个时期各种式样之陶瓷:汉代之彩陶、来自波罗州的宋代陶瓷、明代之彩陶。

石刻像:来自云岗之佛教石刻像;古代中国商船模型。

其他古董:象牙、玻璃杯、刻有麒麟之汉砖、上海城墙的砖、河南之甲骨、[1]安阳商代之石器、新西兰石斧、太平天国印、南京贡院的瓦、安德森博士捐赠的石器。

(三)博物学标本

哺乳动物:

灵长类——云南的白眉猿、各地(热河、四川、福建、海南等地)所产的猕猴、西藏的短尾猴、两广及海南的长尾猴、四川的金丝猴、两广之灰狐猿;

翼手类——台湾、香港、上海、四川、福建等地的蝙蝠,其中福建一处就有11种;

食虫类——上海地区的猬、福建的大麝鼠、云南的树鼠;

食肉类——上海的金色鼬鼠,华北的鼬鼠、四川的大小熊猫、东北虎、福建的幼虎、东南亚的虎、福建的豹、华南的云豹、东北的狸猫、华东的野猫、福建山林所产的托契猫、上海近郊的斑点麝猫、四川、云南、海南等地的棕榈麝猫、西藏的山猫、海南的食蟹猫鼬、长江中游的水獭、华南的野狗、中国境内的沙獾、雪獾、福建的山獭、来自巴基斯坦的西藏灰熊、中国境内的狗熊(黑熊);

犬科——华北地区的狼,东北及华东地区的狐狸,西部的沙漠狐、日耳曼羊、犬、北京的卷毛犬、西藏的狮犬,产于西伯利亚的巨齿海豹;

鲸类:在上海捕获的卢多尔夫鲸、长江下游的河豚、黄浦江中的海猪、来自日本海的下颚鲸;

有蹄动物——绥远的野绵羊,中国马鹿、蒙古的麋鹿、东北的梅花鹿、喉肿黄羊、喜马拉雅山中的野山羊、印度支那的野牛、马来亚的貘、蒙古的四角绵羊、四川野牛、白犍野驴、浙江之羚羊、四川的扭角羚羊、青羊、长江流域的獐子、华东地区的吠鹿、来自四川、湖北、广东、福建的簇鹿、毛冠鹿、有冠鹿、东北的麋鹿、北京的四不像、山东的野猪、海马;

啮齿动物——黄河流域的冠毛箭猪、福建的竹鼠、白腮鼠及鼹鼠,各类石鼠和巢鼠的标本、松鼠标本,河北、江苏、陕西、甘肃的野兔,西藏东部的鼠兔;

贫齿类——上海法租界内捕获的穿山甲。

鸟类:

馆藏十分丰富,有数十类的标本:野禽类(天鹅类、鹅类、鸭类及凫类)、猎禽类(孔雀类、雉类、鹧鸪类、鹤鹑类、及山鸡类)、猛禽类(兀鹰类、鹫类、鹰类、雕类、大鸱鸺类)、鸮类、鹤类、苍鹭类、鹳类、鹭鸶类、塘鹅类、鸥类。

栖鸟标本有:乌鸦、喜鹊、樫鸟、山雀、鸥掠鸟、黄鸟、燕雀、伯劳、啭鸟、鹟、画眉、夜劳、小莺燕、鹡鸰、天鹅、百灵、颊白、梅花雀。

三宝鸟类——啄木鸟、鱼狗、戴胜鸟、舠斗鸽、食蜂鸟、杜鹃、鹦鹉;

---

[1] 文会博物馆是世界上最早收藏甲骨的博物馆。见:Gibson, H.E., Reviews of Recent Books, JNCBRAS, Vol. LXVII, P193.

枭类——大鸱鸺、长耳枭、短耳枭、日本小枭；

鹫鹰——华北山区的金鹫、蒙古的版鹫、山西的大雕；

兀鹰——灰兀鹰、小兀鹰（隼）、髭兀鹰、黑颈阿比；

猎鸟——缅甸之孔雀、彩颈雉、红背雉、红腿鹧鸪、有须鹧鸪，日本的鹌鹑及其他各种鹧鸪鹌鹑标本，东北黑山鸡、金色野鸡、东方大鸨；

鹤类——丹顶鹤、白鹤、灰鹤；

天鹅——大天鹅、黑色洋口天鹅、白鹤鹅及其他野鹅；

塘鹅——蒙古塘鹅，福建的白塘鹅、海鸬鹚、彩鸬鹚；

野鸭——丝绒海番鸭、普通冠鸭、红冠鸭、潜水鸭、秋沙鸭、鸳鸯凫、并通凫；

水鸟——鹭鸶、矶鹬、朱鸡、秧鸡、鹬鹡、海燕、海鸥、燕鸥、鹮鹈、黑鹳、彩鹳、日本的朱鹮鹭、苍鹭、鸭色紫鹭、小池鹭、夜鹭、潜水鸟、北戴河的军舰鸟；

国外鸟类——澳大利亚的食火鸡、鹦鹉、白鹦鹉、极乐鸟；

鸟卵、鸟巢——来自爪哇的燕窝、来自东北的山雀巢。

爬虫类：

龟类——黄浦江中的蠵龟、日本的绿蠵龟、东方棱龟、玳瑁龟、河鳖、泥鳖、大头龟；

鳄鱼——产于长江中游的短吻鳄、扬子鳄、湾鳄、印度与南美洲的鳄鱼；

蜥蜴——华北六种蜥蜴标本、马来半岛之巨蜥、壁虎、蟾蜍、六种中国石龙子、武夷山的无肢蛇蜴；

蛇类——眼镜蛇、蝮蛇、致渴蛇、褐蛇、赤练蛇、竹蛇、上海地区的无毒蛇、蟒蛇、细小的掘穴盲蛇、两头蛇、海蛇；

两栖类——墨西哥之蝾螈，中国的大鱼蛙、大鲵鱼（娃娃鱼），北戴河的马鲅，香港产的娃娃鱼，密西西比河所产的娃娃鱼，中国西藏、云南、浙江等地所产的鲵鱼，各地出产的蝾螈，东北出产的大腹蛙，蒙古、浙江等地的蟾蜍。

鱼类：

热河的鲟鱼，四川及西北山水中的泥鳅鱼，乌苏里江的白鱼、岩鱼，满洲的鳟鱼；

鲤鱼标本有鲉鱼、白鱼、白扬鱼、鲷鱼、鳍鱼（池鳍、刺鳍）、鲙鱼、长江与黄河中的剑鼻鳣鱼、鲈鱼、鲑鱼、鲱鱼、比目鱼、鲭鱼、鳗鱼（黑龙江的八目鳗鱼）、琵琶鱼、黄嗜河豚、中国鲨鱼。

原始脊椎动物：

无脊椎动物——蜈蚣、马陆、蛞蝓；

甲壳类——斑节虾、蟹龙虾、泥蚕、水蚤、福建的毛蟹、螺蛳、蛛蟹、日本的大蛛蟹；

蜘蛛类——各种蜘蛛及华北蝎。

昆虫类：

上海的白蚁、蜉蝣、虻虱、蝇、蚊、有益的飞蝇、黄蜂、穿木虫。

鳞翅类——蝴蝶（有完整的温州地区蝴蝶标本）、白蝶、粉蝶、蚁、蜀、飞蛾；

甲壳类——萤火虫、蜣螂、蛴螬、蜗牛、花金龟、虻虫、水螳螂、蜡虫、乌舌、鹦鹉贝、白垩贝、牙贝、螺旋贝、镏贝、牡蛎、花贝、砗磲、剃刀贝、灯形蛤、簾蛤、文蛤、曰没贝、大天蚕；

棘皮动物——鸡爪鱼、海胆、海参、崔星鱼、石连。

植物：

馆藏植物标本不是很多,所藏标本多来自上海及附近地区,此外也有福建所产各种树之木条、四川峨眉山上的火绒草、中国各种树干之截面。也有一些植物的种子和树叶,如橡胶种子、橡胶树叶。

地质学与矿物标本:

主要是世界各处不同之矿物、宝石、半宝石。如:青藏高原的砾岩,山西泰谷县的黄土,浙江的锑矿石,1906年维苏威火山爆发的火山灰,[1]加利福尼亚的岩石和矿石。

古生物学:

三叶虫化石、蝙蝠化石及海产化石、羊齿化石、各种哺乳动物之化石、龙骨及植物化石、安阳出土的贝壳化石、香港的海贝化石;

此外还有:中国地图模型、马来半岛橡皮业有关标本。

博物院藏品不仅数量与种类在近代中国境内的博物馆中是屈指可数的,而且许多藏品收藏得十分完整,这为科学研究提供了便利的条件。爬行和两栖动物标本有中国大多数省份内之种类。鸟类标本则是中国境内收藏最丰富的博物馆,1924年博物院中的动物标本显示几乎已经涵盖了中国境内的主要动物。[2]这些系列完整的藏品为许多相关研究提供了第一手的参考资料。1938年1月20日,威金生做了题为《说鸟》的演讲,讲述鸟类的进化史,就是运用博物院所收藏的鸟类标本来做的例证。[3]后来他又以博物院内的鸟类标本为基础撰写了《上海鸟类年鉴》。而博物院中大量的钱币则促成了钱币学会的建立,1936年钱币学会在博物院成立,并且在演讲论文时经常以收藏的钱币做实物演示。博物院还用馆藏品为学生传授博物学知识,下文详述。

博物院不仅藏品丰富,而且也非常注重藏品的陈列,其藏品的陈列方式在近代中国境内的博物馆中是走在前列的,为我国近代博物馆陈列方法提供了模式。

首先,文会博物院最先推出复原陈列法——按照动植物所处时代的原型设置天棚、墙壁,布置有关的家具,把相关的藏品置于科学的背景和恰当的自然环境中。在近代中国境内,文会博物院最早采用这种陈列法,效果非常明显,并成为博物院吸引观众的一大亮点。如熊猫展柜内装一只罕见的大熊猫和一只小熊猫,代表了两类濒临绝灭的食肉动物,它们被置于尽可能相似于它们的栖息地环境中,周围是中国西部川藏高原山地的石楠灌木丛和竹林。[4]北京人头盖骨标本后面附有一透视画,"男女两北京人在一洞口袭击一利齿之猛虎",[5]鸟类标本则多在其背后置一风景画。

其次,设置玻璃柜,置放藏品。中国的传统收藏法主要是将藏品放置于格子橱中,虽然错落有致,但同类藏品不能置于一起,不利于观众的观赏和学者的比较。1924年,文会博物院已采用分门别类、井然有序的陈列方式,将展柜置于展厅两侧,展台上有层次地布置展品,在相互的衬托之下,如同一个个"圣地",整体效果光彩夺目。博物院制作100余个漂亮的玻璃展柜,放置各类由剥制师制作好的各种同类标本。所有收藏品都做有标签,上面写有名称、来源、分

---

[1] Proceedings, JNCBRAS, Vol. LXVI., Pvi.
[2] Proceedings, JNCBRAS, Vol. LV, Pxiv.
[3] The China Journal, Vol. XXVIII, Feb., 1938, No.2, P99.
[4] See pictures in The China Journal, Vol. XIX, (1933), No.6.
[5] 苏阿德著、戚铭远译:《中国博物学:上海博物院指南》,第5页;Proceedings, JNCBRAS, Vol. LXVI, Pvi.

类等内容。这些展柜的藏品具体见表3-3。

表3-3　　　　　　　　　　　　博物院展柜所展之标本

柜　号	标　本　名　称	柜　号	标　本　名　称
1	东北黑山鸡	51	澳大利亚土著居民所用的兵器
2	海鸥	51	日耳曼羊、犬
3、6-13	各类栖鸟标本	52	北京人头盖骨、西藏人头盖骨
5	棘皮动物（鸡爪鱼、海胆、海参）	52	西藏狮犬、北平卷毛犬
14-17	水鸟	53	中国猿猴：白眉猿、狝猴等
18-19	野鸭	54	蠵龟
21	燕鸥、野鸭	55	河鳖、泥鳖
22	猎鸟	56-57	短吻鳄、湾鳄
23-24	鹤类	58	巨蜥
25-26	鹫类；猎鸟	59	中国蜥蜴及两栖类动物
27	兀鹰、天鹅	60-61	各类蛇
28	猎鸟、鹳、朱鹭	63-64	中国鱼类
29	东方大鸨、野鹅	65	昆虫类（白蚁、蜉蝣）、虻虱类
30	竹	66	甲壳类
31	野鹅	67-69	鱼翅类
32-33	猛禽类	70	软体动物、木材与橡皮业植物
34	托契猫	71	各类种子及干果
35	云豹	73	中药材
35	华东吠鹿	74	罗盘、中国旧式医用外科用具
36	大熊猫、小熊猫	75	斑节蟹类
37	狸猫、西藏灰熊	76	四川土著民族之服装和乐器
38	中国东部之野猫	76	日本大铁蟹
39	四川野牛	77	旧时官吏之服装与首饰
40	鲸、海豚	78	海产双壳类及中国淡水牡蛎
41	印度江猪	81-82	珊瑚
42	巨齿斑点海豹	84	黄土
43	蝙蝠、水獭；犬科	85	海产生物标本
44	中国貂鼠、鼹鼠及地鼠	86	古生物学标本
45	贫齿类：中国鲮鲤（穿山甲）	87	各种哺乳动物之化石
46	四川白犍野驴	88-90	矿物标本
47	中国青羊、华东之羚羊	91	宝石及半宝石
48	中国的野兔	92	中外钱币
49	竹鼠、鼹鼠	93	明代之甲冑
50	食蟹猫鼬	94	东亚人之各类服装

续表

柜 号	标 本 名 称	柜 号	标 本 名 称
95	中国古代之兵器	112	中国烟管
96－97	中国古镜	113	非洲黑人之长矛
98	秦以前中国所用之铜兵器	113	东北虎
98	古代铜器	114	豹
99	商、周、秦中国所用之铜兵器	115	猸
99－100	商代遗物：石器、骨器、玉器	115	簇鹿、冠毛吠鹿
100	甲骨	116	麇鹿
101	石刻像	117－118	古生物标本
102	北平玩具	120	天鹅
103	汉砖	121	中国地图模型
104－105	中国古代陶器	122	中国二足及多足类动物
106－107	陶制墓像	124－125	蟹类
108－109	中国陶瓷	126	鸟卵
110	佛教、喇嘛教之礼器	130	马来西亚獏
111	官吏之朝珠	132	麋鹿（四不像）

资料来源：苏阿德著，戚铭远译：《中国博物学：上海博物院指南》，亚洲文会北华支会，1937年。

第三，除了原始藏品外，博物院还陈列有仿真的标本。这些仿真的标本主要是一些难以获得的藏品，就依据原型尽可能复原。博物院内"有木制之模型曰猪生之象，体似猪，首如象，且有长鼻"。[1] 还"藏有英国女王皇冠上的宝石仿制品，虽系仿制，但是非常精美，它的原材料是来自南非的红宝石"。[2] 这些仿真标本生动而逼真，向观众传播了有关知识和信息。

可以说，文会博物院在收藏和陈列方面都向中国带来了近代西方的博物馆学知识，不仅收藏的范围大为增加，也大大不同于中国社会对于文物古董的"藏"重于"观"的传统观念。

三、活动

博物院还举办一系列活动，充分发挥了它应有的教育、研究功能，从而使博物院真正成为大众的文化殿堂。这些活动有：

（一）面向学者——为学者提供标本，编辑出版相关论著

1878年，文会就提出"上海博物院不仅要为公众服务，而且要在科学研究领域占一席之地"。[3] 1924年，博物院就提出"努力加强和国内外有关机构的联系，以使博物院能够为生物学家提供帮助，也使博物院为大众所利用"。[4] 博物院每年都通过文会会刊向社会公开年度新收藏品之细目，也不定期地出版部分藏品名录。这些藏品名录提供了大量的学术信息，为有关学者进行科学研究提供了帮助。1906年，德拉图什编辑《上海博物院鸟类标本名录》(The

---

[1]《上海指南》卷三《公共事业》，商务印书馆1930年版。
[2] 2003年4月11日上午复旦大学校史办公室许有成老师口述，地点：复旦大学文科图书馆港台阅览室。
[3] Report of the N.-C. B. of the R. A. S. for the year 1878, JNCBRAS, Vol. XIII, Pxvii.
[4] Proceedings, JNCBRAS, Vol. LV, Pxiv.

Collection of Birds in the Shanghai Museum),该文不仅在文会会刊上发表,而且也出版了单行本。该名录列出了院内所藏鸟类标本的具体详目:20 目,7 个亚目;51 科、38 亚科;254 类,共计 1 717 个,代表 431 个鸟类,实际上提供了当时中国境内已为人知的鸟类状况。博物院的这类标本目录出版之后马上引起了国内外学者的重视,"不仅上海社会对博物院钟爱不已,而且国内外的著名科学家也都对博物院兴趣十足"。[1] 1932 年冬季澳大利亚墨尔本大学解剖学系教授、北京协和医科大学(Peking Union Medical College)兼职教授琼斯(Dr. Frederic Wood Jones)专程赴文会博物院,依靠博物院收藏的动物标本来研究他的"中国博物学"课题。同年美国纽约自然历史博物馆副馆长、著名蒙古探险家安德鲁斯(Roy Chapman Andrews)也来信咨询博物院馆藏爬行动物标本情况。类似这样的咨询来信,博物院会不停地收到。[2] 文会收藏库寿龄(S. Couling)在山东等地搜集的甲骨一直是中外学者所希望见到的重要历史文物,鉴于此,1935 年方法敛(F. H. Chalfant)和白瑞华二人合力将这些甲骨上的文字一一临摹,出版《库氏方氏二氏藏甲骨卜辞》。该书出版后,裘必胜就予以很高评价:"对于那些热衷于中国文字和古代文明的学者来说,该书给予他们的是无比珍贵的商代甲骨文献。"[3] 董作宾在论述甲骨文研究现状时,就专门提到该目录。但是博物院在这方面做得并不够,像这样的名录编得太少。

除了编辑出版藏品名录外,博物院还出版了《上海博物院史略》、《博物院手册》、《中国博物学:上海博物院指南》(中英文版均有)等数种介绍博物院的小册子和著作,这些书同样介绍了藏品的内容,而且比单纯的藏品目录,更加详细和深入。尤其是《中国博物学:上海博物院指南》一书,不仅介绍了博物院,而且向中国传播了博物学知识。作者在前言中就指出"使学者便于研究各种自然科学(特别是人类学、古生物学、化石学、地质学、植物学、动物学)起见,上海博物院特将陈列柜子及所有标本按照自然次序,加以整理"。该书内容分为三编:第一编,"人类学",16 页,理论;第二编,"艺术与考古",17 页,也是理论;第三编,"博物学",145 页,先讲定义和博物学概要,然后叙述各种动植物之分布,最后才是博物院中之标本介绍。

(二)面向社会——免费向公众开放、举办各种展览会

向社会开放及举办展览会是博物院的基本工作,博物院也只有通过这些渠道才能实现其传播知识的功能。文会博物院是近代中国境内最早向社会开放的博物馆之一。中国近代不乏文物收藏者,但是多系收藏,而不展览,更不用于研究,"沪上好古虽多,如康有为、唐绍仪辈,家藏丰富,然不能供外人之浏览,即好友亦不获一见"。[4] 徐家汇天主教博物馆必须有证明才能观看,不像文会博物院成立后就向公众开放。19 世纪 90 年代博物院已是天天向公众开放,更为重要的是文会博物院最早向华人开放,而且"愈来愈受到中国人的欢迎,他们经常来参观。文会决定周一、周二下午向华人开放,并设专门督导员予以安排讲解"。[5] 20 世纪 30 年代博物院方针是为上海居民利用,参观的人"主要是学校儿童、高校学者及大学生,无疑显示了博物院的价值和其为社会所提供的价值"。[6] 博物院受到了社会的瞩目,来参观的人数呈逐年增

---

[1] Proceedings, JNCBRAS, Vol. LXIV, Pxiv.
[2] Proceedings, JNCBRAS, Vol. LXIII, Pxiv.
[3] Gibson, H. E., Reviews of Recent Books, JNCBRAS, Vol. LXVII, P193.
[4] 《主设美术博物院之继起》,《申报》1922 年 7 月 10 日。
[5] Proceedings, JNCBRAS, Vol. XLVII, Pxii.
[6] Proceedings, JNCBRAS, Vol. LXVIII, Px-xi.

加之势。1930年:5 942人次;1937年:3 077人次;1938年:24 000人次;1939年:45 000人次;1940年:65 049人次,"而同时期上海其他文化机构的参观人数尚未有如此观众"。[1] 为了能让观众了解馆藏品,博物院还设了专职解说员,免费向观众讲解。

举办各种展览会也是博物院向社会传播知识的一个重要途径。博物院很早就举办展览会,有免费的,也有收费的。从文会会议记录看,主要举办的是中国艺术品展览,尤其是中国画展。详见表3-4。

表3-4　　　　　　　　　　　博物院历年举办的艺术品展览

年份	名　　称	年份	名　　称
1907	中国陶瓷展	1917	地毯展、中国昆虫展
1908	中国陶瓷与艺术品展	1917—1918	两次绘画艺术展
1911	上海昆虫展	1922	北京版画、水彩画展
1911—1912	中国画展(六次)	1935	参加伦敦展览会
1913	中国画展	1936	15天中国画展
1914	画与石雕展	1937	邮票展览
1916	煤炭的形成过程	1937	中国画展

资料来源:1907—1938年文会历年会刊。

这些展览活动一般都会注明展品的有关信息,以达到整洁、清晰、分类有序的效果。1917年举办中国昆虫展览,在展板上就注明了各类昆虫的特点。举办的中国艺术品展览会大大加深了外国人对中国的认识,并激起了他们对中国动物的兴趣和艺术的爱好。[2] 1912年文会资助的中国画展,包含了唐、宋、元、明、清各个朝代不同绘画艺术风格和类型的164幅画,参观的人数达550人次,画展后来又在大德国新闻纸馆(Ostasiatische Lloyd)举办了讨论会。"外侨对中国的风景画予以肯定,尤其是山水画所赋予那明朗的线条、适度的着色、灵巧的搭配,更是令外侨由衷地佩服,改变了以前对西人中国风景画的反感"。[3] 1935年3月,文会还挑选部分馆藏艺术品参加伦敦展览会,在欧洲引起了轰动。"外国人对中国了解与认识最大的进步可能来自于对中国伟大的古代艺术的了解,在这个过程中文会起了重要作用"。[4] 通过这些展览活动,文会不仅推动了西方人对中国艺术的研究(后期文会的演讲题目多与中国文物和艺术品有关),而且借助于中国艺术品也加深了西方人对中国文化的认识。

(三)面向儿童——组织学生参观博物院、举办座谈会

博物院非常注重对儿童的教育。1878年博物院就邀请天主教神甫带领教会学校的儿童参观博物院的藏品。1920年博物院在整理标本时,考虑到"收藏的习惯要从小培养,它可以训练人的有序、清洁和分类能力。小孩是天生的科学家,对于周围自然环境有着热烈的求知欲,

---

[1] Proceedings, JNCBRAS, Vol. LXXI, Pii.
[2] 1908年的"中国陶瓷与艺术品展"当时影响就很大,后来又专门编辑成书在伦敦和纽约发行。见:Old Chinese Porcelain and Works in China:being description and illustrations of articles selected from an exhibition held in Shanghai, Nov., 1908, by A. W. Bahr, London, New York:Cassell and Company Ltd., 1911.
[3] The Exhibition of Chinese Paintings, JNBRAS, Vol. XLIII, P120.
[4] Proceedings, JNCBRAS, Vol. LI, 1920, Pviii.

因此以后的标签上要用一些推理的语言,借此来启发他们的想象力"。[1] 为了加强对学生的教育功能,1933年福开森任会长时又提出"博物院要成为上海和附近地区学校的一个活动中心,使每个小学生都有机会来参观博物院。小孩不仅需要进行物理操作训练,也需要动物学知识,而博物院是提供这方面学习的最佳场所。博物院要和上海的学校紧密合作,这样才能向公众显示出其价值所在"。[2] 1936年博物院专门设立教育督导员,其职责主要是向来文会参观的学生和教师讲解藏品,由著名人类学工作者劳立尔担任,劳立尔曾在瑞典斯德哥尔摩自然历史博物院工作10年,后又到非洲和澳洲作过长期的探险考察,拥有丰富的民族学和考古学知识。两年内他与上海很多中小学校(主要是外侨学校)建立了广泛的联系,"传播博物院在教育上的益处之可慰效果",[3] 促使上海的中、小学学生参观博物院,效果非常明显。"博物院很受欢迎,特别是中外(学校)儿童,他们会成群结队地来参观博物院中所陈列的他们家乡的动物标本",[4] 经常有学校全体师生一同来参观博物院。

为进一步扩大博物院影响,获得社会对博物院的支持。1935－1936年博物院还向上海各个学校学生开设了一系列博物学讲座,旨在向他们宣传生物标本和文物古董方面的知识,主要由苏阿德主讲,详见表3-5。

表3-5　　　　　　　　　　　　博物院举办的博物学讲座

日　期	题　目	日　期	题　目
1935.3.6	博物学概论	1936.3.4	智人、猿人、猴子
1935.3.13	博物院中的哺乳动物	1936.3.11	中国的巨型哺乳动物
1935.3.20	中国钱币	1936.3.18	中国的小型哺乳动物
1935.3.27	中国的鸟	1936.4.1	中国爬行动物和两栖类动物
1935.4.3	化石及其价值	1936.4.15	中国的甲壳类动物和昆虫
1935.4.10	蛇与蜥蜴	1936.4.22	中国软体动物
1935.4.17	蝴蝶与飞蛾	1936.4.29	中国的化石
1935.4.24	中国的鱼	1936.5.6	中国的考古学
1936.2.26	北京人	1936.5.13	中国的艺术

资料来源:Proceedings, JNCBRAS, Vol. LXVI, Pxii.
　　　　　Proceedings, JNCBRAS, Vol. LXVII, Pxiii.

苏阿德在讲解时用博物院中的藏品做演示例证,使得这种谈话方式的交流更为生动、深刻。讲述《北京人——中国人的祖先》时,苏阿德以博物院收藏的人类标本为演示,先谈史前人、北京人,通过整个动物的分类,从灵长类到最低的动物,最后谈到中国考古学和艺术的脉络。这些讲座反应很好,参加的学生也十分踊跃。"虽然是面向学校儿童,许多成年人也来旁听,包括许多上海市内大专院校的中国学生"。[5]

---

[1] Proceedings, JNCBRAS, Vol. LI, 1920, Pxv.
[2] Ferguson, Dr. John C., The Reopening of the Shanghai Museum (R. A. S.), JNCBRAS, Vol. XV, Pii.
[3] 《亚洲文会经济极感困乏》,《申报》1937年6月26日。
[4] Proceedings, JNCBRAS, Vol. LXX, 1939, Pv.
[5] Museum talks well attended, China Journal, Vol. XXIV, Apr., 1936, No.4, P238.

博物院以其丰富的藏品、科学的陈列和全方位的活动在近代中西文化交流中作出了一定的贡献,这主要表现在以下两个方面:

1. 藏品的交流

博物院与世界其他地区的相关机构一直保持着密切的联系,仅 19 世纪与上海博物院有过交流的相关机构就有 22 个,著名的有美国斯密生博物馆、纽约首都艺术博物馆(Metropolitan Museum of Art)、美国自然历史博物馆(American Museum of Natural History)、波士顿精美艺术博物馆(Boston Museum of Fine Art)、芝加哥户外自然历史博物馆(Field Museum of Natural History)、哈佛的弗格艺术博物馆(Fogg Art Museum)、法国的基美博物馆(Musée Guimet)。交流的方式之一就是互赠藏品。1874 年博物院就向大英博物馆寄赠了上海附近的候鸟皮;1881 年美国的华盛顿自然历史博物馆向上海博物院赠送了香港水域的 66 种鱼类标本;1935 年大英博物馆向文会赠送一小部分 17 世纪收集的矿物/矿石标本。

博物院也经常将搜集来的中国各类标本送到英美博物馆作鉴定,通过这种方式很多生物标本、矿石标本的名称和类别得以确定。1881 年博物院就将在上海地区购买的 30－50 种鱼类标本送到大英博物馆作鉴定,1923 年苏阿德也将博物院收藏的原始鱼类标本送到美国著名的斯密生博物馆命名。在近代中国生物标本的鉴定方面,博物院远远走在国人前面。

2. 中外学者与博物院

随着收藏的增多,博物院地位也日益上升,在远东地区颇为著名。1922 年,博物学家所和亚摆爱氏就说"亚洲文会之事业,驰誉世界"。[1] 20 世纪 30 年代国内学术界对文会博物院评价也很高,说它"收藏颇富"。[2] 一些西方学者来到中国后,多会参观文会博物院。1927 年瑞典王子曾专门赴上海参观文会博物院,对博物院内收藏的一些考古文物和租借的河南殷墟出土的甲骨表现出了浓厚的兴趣。欧美科学界不断向博物院来信索求有关标本。1936 年博物院就应英国科学界请求向英国一位著名的鸟类学家赠送了一套东方鸣禽蛋,向一位古生物学家送了一个鸵鸟蛋化石,[3] 以帮助他们完成相关的研究项目。

中国人自己创办的博物院是否直接受到文会博物院的影响?博物院的藏品是否促成了有关科学研究的诞生?由于资料的限制,这里无法予以论述。但是从博物院的参观人数来看,博物院向中国不仅传播了自然历史文化知识,而且传播了公共文化观念。因为"博物馆本身即是一个'公共的'空间,而同时它又参与塑造着一个更为广大的公共空间。"[4] 作为一个公共文化空间,文会博物院通过上述活动,在实现博物院应有的功能同时,也成功地塑造了一个世界性的文化空间,从而将中国自然和历史文化知识传播到了世界各地。

---

[1]《上海应该设美术科学博物院谈》,《申报》1922 年 7 月 7 日。
[2]《亚细亚协会图书馆将停办》,《中华图书馆协会会报》6 卷 2 期,第 30 页。
[3] Proceedings, JNCBRAS, Vol. LXVII, Pv.
[4] 杨志刚:《博物馆与中国近代以来公共意识的拓展》,《复旦学报》1999 年第 3 期,第 56 页。

第四章 日常活动

第一节 例会和年会

文会每年要召开四类会议:每月常会、每年年会,理事会专门会议以及年末举行的茶话会,现分类叙述之。

1857年上海文理学会创建之时就决定:"每月的常会于星期二晚八点举行,或者由理事会决定在其他时间召开。"[1]后来又提前到下午五点半或六点。一般在每月的第三周举行,基本上可以做到每月正常召开,但也有些年份每季才召开一次。常会的议程一般为:①审阅并通过上次例会的笔录;②宣告理事会成员与重要会员离任、去世及职务变更等情况;③公布新当选的会员名单及其身份;④演讲(宣读)并讨论理事会通过的文章。有时也处理来往信件及其他相关事宜,会议时间长短不定,一般为两个小时。

19世纪常会参加者有20-30人,多是居住在上海的文会会员或在上海的外国侨民。由于见不到会议的原始记录,所以无法确定整个历史时期常会出席者的身份,也难以衡量理事会成员及社会人士对文会兴趣程度之高低。从1910年前的《北华捷报》和会刊中的部分会议报告、记录看,这一时期理事会成员及文会会员出席会议的比例较高,其他人士较少。理事会成员中的伟烈亚力、理雅各、翟理思、金斯密、玛高温、郁和、艾约瑟等人都经常出席常会,他们也是这一时期的主要演讲者和讨论者。从文会年会记录和《字林西报》相关报道看,[2]1911年后常会参加者人数有明显上升,有时达到百人左右;参加者的身份也越来越多元化,社会公众明显增多。

年会即文会的年度总结会议,早期一般在9月份举行,1874年章程规定年会在每年1月举行,1884年又决定在6月份举行。年会要处理以下事务:①会长(有时是秘书)向大会宣读文会本年度发展概要,内容包括会员变更情况、演讲文章之篇目;②各部门述职报告:图书馆长宣读本年新进书籍及读者借阅情况;博物院监院则要宣读本年标本之搜集与制作进展;会计要宣读年度财务收支明细账;会刊编辑要宣读年度会刊的编辑与销售情况;③选举的下届领导成员名单;④有文章的话,还要演讲讨论。

文会对年会有严格的要求,至少要有11名会员参加才能达到法定人数。年会记录(报告)则刊登在会刊和《北华捷报》上,以使会员了解文会的发展情况。

理事会专门会议指的是理事会成员不定期地召开会议,就文会的有关事务进行协商处理,一般每年召开数次。

此外,文会在年终召开茶话会,多邀请上海外侨社会的名流参加,诸如工部局总董和英美

---

[1] Minutes of A Meeting Held in the Reading Room of the Shanghai Library, North-China Herald, Vol. III, No. 374, 26th, Sep., 1857. P34.
[2] 1911年后《北华捷报》已不再像此前那样"热切"关注文会的事情,很少再刊登文会演讲或者年会的消息。《字林西报》的"每周时事"(From time to time)栏目刊登有文会每周的演讲消息。1911年后文会会刊刊登有完整系统的年会记录。

驻沪领事,会议内容以娱乐、联系感情为务。

第二节 演 讲

演讲是文会的主要活动,文会也非常重视,1882年文会将其作为第二个目标。因为它是文会日常的主要活动,也是社会能看得到的表现方式,所以文会对演讲文章审阅得比较严格。文会规定:所有来稿必须由理事会决定是否具备演讲资格或能否在会刊上发表。

演讲一般由作者本人宣读自己的论文,如果作者本人不在上海或文章是从外地邮寄来的,会议主席就任命他人代为宣读。文章读完后要进行讨论,所有出席会议的人都可以向作者提问或提出自己的见解,作者要针对所有的问题一一做解答。最后表决该文章是否通过以及能否在会刊上发表,或者达成修改的意见。

除了在常会和年会举行固定演讲外,"文会理事会也不时会举办一些文学和科学的演讲活动,一般会在常会之外的晚上举行"。[1] 这类演讲属于临时性和特邀性的,多是莅临上海的一些重要人物或者是文会特别邀请的学者。1873年,卫三畏到上海审阅印刷他的《音节辞典》(Syllabic Dictionary)之际,文会邀请他演讲了《在华往事(1840年前)》;[2] 1932年12月15日,法国著名汉学家伯希和来华路过上海,文会邀请他演讲了《中国境内的土耳其斯坦民族》,讲述其1907年在敦煌进行的考古发掘。[3] 这样的演讲20世纪后比较多。

演讲者并不限于文会会员,只要文章被理事会认可,非会员作者也可以到文会演讲自己的文章。目前所知有388人曾在文会演讲过762篇文章,其中非文会人士140人、演讲157篇(参见附表一)。

19世纪文会的影响还不够大,参加演讲的人也比较少。演讲者都是在华的文会会员,主要来自英、美、法、德、俄、奥六国,身份主要是传教士、外交官及海关工作人员。由于这个时期在华外人的中文修养普遍低下,所以这一时期的演讲主要集中于数名文会会员,他们是金斯密(30次)、艾约瑟(29次)、玛高温(27次)、庄延龄(10次)、卫三畏(6次)、爱司克夫人(10次)、伟烈亚力(5次)、慕稼谷(7次),此外裨治文、郇和、梅辉立(W. F. Mayers)、李提摩太等人也都有四五篇文章演讲(参见附表一)。非文会人士有48篇文章演讲,这些文章多是个人的游记,文会会员的文章则多是对中国社会的各个领域所作出的开拓性研究,比如《中国的乐谱》、《汉语方言比较研究》、《中国的戏剧调查》、《翰林院中的四夷馆》。这些文章虽然很多也只是相关资料的堆积,但它们向在华外人传播了中国30多个方面的初步知识,应该说,这一时期的演讲大大帮助了在华外人对中国社会的认识。

较之19世纪,20世纪文会的演讲群体日益壮大、演讲内容更加广泛和深入。越来越多的欧美人士参加文会的演讲,演讲者的国籍也扩大到16个,他们有来自欧洲的丹麦、荷兰、挪威、意大利、瑞士,北美的美国、加拿大,听众也常达百余名左右。这一时期演讲者的身份更多的是相关专业的学者、工程师和大学教授,传教士、外交官已不再是主流。尤其值得注意的是,文会还不断邀请中国学者参加演讲,目前能够确认参加演讲的中国学者有蔡元培、张铨、竺可桢、梁

---

[1] Report of the Council of the North-China Branch of the Royal Asiatic Society for 1874, JNCBRAS, No. VIII, Pxx.
[2] Proceedings, JNCBRAS, Vol. XXXV, 1903–1904, Pxix.
[3] Societies and Institutes, The China Journal of Science & Arts, Vol. XVIII, Feb., 1933, No. 2.

社乾、林同济、林语堂、丁文江、蒋廷黻、黄继祥、胡适、吴经熊、伍连德、江亢虎、姚善友、朱元鼎,其中胡适、伍连德、姚善友、朱元鼎都是两度被邀请到文会演讲。20 世纪 30 年代,每年来文会演讲的会外人士都有六七名,这些人也多是学者和教授,如日本东京大学的铃木(D. T. Suzuki)、南京金陵大学的贝德士(M. S. Bates)、史迈士(Lewis Smythe),上海圣约翰大学的傅统先(Foo Thongsien)。这些中外学者的演讲内容大都是建立在对有关问题深入分析的基础之上,他们告诉世人的是一个更加真实的中国。这些演讲不仅带动了更多的欧美人加入到研究中国的队伍中,而且也使得文会在 20 世纪能够保持一定的学术含量,并在世界汉学领域拥有一席之地。

从 1857 年 9 月到 1951 年 3 月,文会共演讲文章 700 余篇,目前所能确定的有 725 篇。[1] 文会规定每月演讲一次,但是还要看稿源和经费如何。从已有的资料看,最多时每年曾演讲 19 篇文章,最少时仅演讲 3 篇文章。演讲主题涉及 38 个学科与门类,人文社会科学居多,其中地理游记、历史、宗教居于前列,这三类文章占演讲篇目总数的比例分别为:15.7%、9.8%、6.7%,其余各类学科的内容比例从 1.5%—3.5% 不等。自然科学类文章主要集中于地质、天文、气象、动植物方面,关注的是中国矿藏、气候、动植物物种的发掘和采集。这充分说明近代来华外侨更多还是关注对中国社会的认识和了解。

文会的一些演讲受到了国内外学者的注意,欧美汉学家只要经过上海,多半会参加文会的演讲活动。1897 年 11 月 29 日,德国柏林大学教授格鲁贝路过上海,就参加了卜士礼的《西夏的货币及其独特文字》一文之演讲,并对该文提出了修改的建议。[2] 一些演讲的文章也受到学者的赞扬和引用。1900 年 10 月 24 日,绵嘉义(J. Mencarini)演讲的《菲律宾华人劳工问题》,演讲前主持人艾约瑟宣读了张之洞的来信,张赞扬该文有很高的价值。[3] 1870 年罗伯逊(J. Barr Robertson)演讲《1860 年的北京谈判会议》,该文中关于第二次鸦片战争的论述受到学者注意,丹特涅的《美国人在东亚》(Tyler Dennett: Americans in Eastern Asia, P510)一文就引用了罗伯逊对战后中外关系的论断。[4] 1872 年 6 月 12 日,玛高温演讲了《中国人用鲻鱼治瘰病、用碘酒治淋巴病的方法》。该文发表后,受到中国医学界的重视,近代中国医史权威伍连德认为,"从此,中国人才更多听到关于淋巴病症的特性和治疗方法"。[5] 1924 年 11 月 27 日,苏阿德演讲的《中国境内的蝾螈及其类属》被当时中外学界誉为"首次将中国部分两栖类植物划归为一纲"。[6]

限于资料的关系,文会演讲活动对上海外侨、欧美学者之于中国的研究所产生的具体影响和作用,目前还难以更加清晰地展现出来。但是对于作者本人和听众来说,演讲、讨论活动无疑加速了在华外侨对于中国的认识和了解,其文化传播的效用不言自明。

第三节 会 刊

发行会刊是文会的三个目标之一。1857 年上海文理学会成立时,裨治文就提出要办一份

---

[1] 数字来源于历年会报、《北华捷报》、《字林西报》,1908—1910 年目前尚未发现文会演讲的完整记录。
[2] Proceedings, JNCBRSA., Vol. XXXI, P166.
[3] Proceedings, JNCBRSA., Vol. XXXIII, P311.
[4] A.L. Warnshuis: Christian Missions and Treaties with Chinese, The Chinese Recorder, Vol. LIV, P705.
[5] K. ChiMin Wong and Wu Lien-the, History of Chinese Medicine, Southern Materials Central, INC., P. O. Box13 - 342, Taipei, 1985, P121.
[6] Societies and Institutes, The China Journal of Science & Arts, Vol. III, Jun., 1925, No.2, P50.

期刊,发表学会成员的研究成果,次年会刊诞生。截至1948年,《皇家亚洲文会北华支会会刊》持续出版75卷,发行91年,是近代中国境内发行时间最长的西文期刊。[1]

一、会刊内容

统计历史时期该刊全部内容,有633篇文章(Article)、791篇书评、17篇调查报告、34篇汉学文摘、163个问题释疑、65个著名汉学家和重要会员的讣告、75年的文会年度报告和会议记录、14年的中国和日本大事记、34年的图书馆新进书目、26篇杂纂类文章,此外还有十余封读者或会员的来信,两份图书馆藏书目录。可以说,会刊记载了文会的整个历史。

会刊所发表的文章中有335篇演讲过,占所刊文章总数的52%(参见表4-1)。19世纪会刊文章主要来自于演讲,尤其是1890年前,90%的文章选自演讲。20世纪后由于会员的增多,文会影响的扩大,参加演讲和投稿的人也随之增加,会刊更多的文章来自投稿,1905—1948年来自投稿的文章达65%。而且会外投稿人士也急剧增加,1904年前只有12人、文章12篇;1905年后则有51人、投稿58篇。

表4-1　　　　　　　　　　会刊文章来源统计表　　　　　　　　　　(单位:篇)

时　间	演讲文章	投稿文章	总　计
1857—1904	194	91	285
1905—1948	123	225	348
合　计	317	316	633

资料来源:《北华捷报》(1857—1910)、《字林西报》(1946—1951)、附表1。
注:选取1904年作为界点是因为此前会刊出版并不定期,而1905年后则每年一卷。

20世纪中国学者也曾向会刊上投稿。仅发表的就有:王国维:《中国过去19个世纪的量具》(冯友兰译);胡适:《王莽》、《汉代儒家思想统治地位的确立》;伍连德:《西医传入中国的早期阶段》、《早期中国之旅行家及其后继者》;竺可桢:《中国历史时期的气候变化》;蔡元培:《中华民族与中庸之道》;Lu Yen-Ying:《儒家思想、民主政体和民族主义》;郑德坤(翻译):《穆天子传》(英译);李绍昌(翻译):《般若波罗蜜多心经》(英译);林语堂:《中国诗歌的技巧及其精神》;林同济:《中国诗歌中的"一"字》;姚善友:《董仲舒的天人观》;张星烺:《景教主教伊斯来华原因及时间考》。

文会吸纳中国籍会员,并发表他们的作品,无疑促进了西方对中国的研究,加深了西方对中国的认识,文会之中西文化交流媒介之效能也凸现了出来。

文会对会刊历来要求很严,"编辑多为饱学之士"。[2]文章要经过数次讨论和修改方能在会刊上发表。会刊文章主要来自演讲会上一致通过的文章,也有他人的投稿,但是后者必须经过理事会讨论一致投票通过才予刊登。会刊所载文章,学术价值和史料都很高。作者多会大量引用中国的文献及西方的相关研究成果,并采用近代科学方法进行分析研究。象夏德的《古代陶瓷:中世纪中国工商业研究》论述了中国各个时期的陶瓷特点、制作技术、使用情况和部分官窑、民窑的历史、地位、产品、贸易等内容,引证资料包括正史、方志、私人笔记、西人著作。费理饬的《东亚气候》分析了1858—1875年东亚的气温、洋流、季风、云量、风雪等气候因素,每一

---

[1] 根据1959年出版的《全国西文期刊联合目录》,该刊是近代中国境内出版时间最长的西文期刊。
[2] Proceeding, Journal of the North-China Branch of the Royal Asiatic Society, Vol. LXIII, 1932, ppix.

种因素都做了日变化和年变化的分析,文中保存有 1858 – 1875 数个地方的观测资料,制作了数十页的洋流、气温变动图,此文对于研究"丁戊奇荒"时期的气候情况非常有用。论文中还有许多颇有价值的综述类文章,如赖德烈的《西方学者中国历史研究成果综述》、史禄国的《通古斯语文献研究综述》、苏阿德的《中国北部哺乳动物研究近况》,该类文章为相关学者的进一步研究奠定了基础,受到学界的重视,曾被多次引用和转载。

会刊中的 35 篇游记类文章更是难得珍贵的历史资料,它们多是按日期写的,内容非常丰富,记载了不少关于近代中国乡村社会的信息。1858 – 1875 年,每册会刊还设有专栏"远东大事回顾",主要刊登当年的中国及日本大事记和在华外侨的生活内容,多由理事会成员联合执笔,"对于热衷于远东事务的学者来说,其价值可谓不菲,对于普通读者也是非常有趣的"。[1]

除了文章外,会刊还有一大内容——书评。会刊十分关注学界的最新动态,尤其是对学术界最新出版的有关论著,尽可能的进行评介。1906 年起每期会刊上都对本年度 20 – 30 册的西方汉学新书做评介。这些书评信息量很大,有时能够占到整个会刊的 1/3 版面,平均每篇书评有两页左右的篇幅。而且一般都是由比较著名的汉学家执笔,点评精彩而到位,他们会指出该书的优缺点及其学术价值。17 卷中,夏德评介了德国著名汉学家嘎伯冷兹的《汉语语法》一书,由于原书是用德文出版的,没有拉丁文和英文版,夏德用英文对该书作了评介,将该书中的三大汉语语法作了详细叙述。夏文被认为"大大帮助了德国之外人士对于汉语语法的学习,推动了国际汉学的发展"。[2] 21 卷(1887 年)艾约瑟的《评〈佛的生平、学说与僧团〉》(原书作者系柏林大学教授),认为"作者指出了基督教和佛教的相似之处,对于佛学研究言,此书是一重要贡献"。[3] 这些书评不仅在当时为学者提供了最前沿的学术信息,而且现在看来它们基本勾勒出了近代欧美汉学发展的概况。

因为文章的内容往往同时涉及到好几个领域,所以对会刊上的文章进行分类有相当的难度,以下略参照文会 1912 和 1932 年的"总目分类索引",将诸文作一个大致的划分,为的是说明会刊上的文章主要分布在那几个领域。对于 75 卷会刊,按 5 年为期分类排列的全部结果如下表(表 4-2),这里可以大致发现会刊的编辑方向及前后变化。

可以看出,历史学和学术动态类的文章数目高居前列,但在演讲篇目中历史学文章并不是最多的,这说明会刊偏重于刊登中国历史方面的文章。学术动态主要是刊登世界汉学界的一些活动和消息,借此,在华外人得以迅速获知各种学术资源,作为学术讨论和进一步研究的参考。1885 年就刊登了世界各国的汉语文学和语言的研究状况,"它们是由世界各国的首席汉学家所撰写,简单叙述本国的汉学研究进展情况。《意大利汉学》一文谈到了意大利传教士的功绩,在此我们知道意大利在汉学领域所做的贡献"。[4]

值得注意的是,所有演讲中占比例较大的游记类文章在会刊中的篇幅却较小,说明会刊还是偏重于研究型的,而不是大众型的。不过学术类文章和游记类随笔在整个时期内,二者的比例几乎是稳定的,这也说明会刊在聚焦于学者的同时,也没有放弃普通读者,这也正是会刊能够长久发行下去的原因之一。

---

[1] The North-China Stunday News, 19st, Jan., 1930, pp11.
[2] Notices of Recent Publications, The Chinese Recorder, Vol. XIII, P477.
[3] Literary Notes, JNCBRAS, Vol. LXXI, 1886, P233.
[4] Italian contributions to Sinology, North-China Herald, 13 th, Jan., 1886.

表 4-2 会刊内容分类统计表

年份	1857-1861	1864-1870	1871-1875	1876-1880	1881-1885	1886-1890	1891-1895	1896-1900	1901-1905	1906-1910	1911-1915	1916-1920	1921-1925	1926-1930	1931-1935	1936-1941	1946-1951
卷号	1-2 (O.S)	1-6 (N.S)	7-10	11-15	16-20	21-25	26-30	31-33	34-36	37-41	42-46	47-51	52-56	57-61	62-66	67-71	72-73
哲学	2	0	0	1	0	4	0	4	1	0	1	2	2	3	3	3	1
历史学	9	17	15	8	22	27	9	5	5	12	14	19	13	17	12	13	5
游记	2	15	5	0	7	0	1	1	2	1	4	1	5	3	3	2	0
文学	0	1	2	2	18	10	0	2	0	5	2	4	13	13	11	6	2
医学	0	3	2	0	2	1	0	0	0	0	0	0	0	0	1	1	1
艺术类	1	1	1	0	1	0	0	1	0	2	5	5	1	2	2	3	0
宗教	2	5	4	0	2	5	2	0	3	0	4	8	13	9	10	2	4
社会学	2	1	3	1	14	6	2	4	3	4	3	9	9	4	5	0	0
政治经济	0	5	0	0	11	8	4	3	1	1	1	0	1	1	2	0	0
地学	7	13	2	3	5	2	1	1	0	1	2	5	5	5	4	2	2
生物学	3	8	1	3	3	5	1	2	1	3	2	10	10	7	2	5	0
物理科学	0	4	0	1	1	3	1	1	0	1	3	1	1	0	5	2	0
科学综合	0	0	2	0	1	0	1	1	1	0	0	2	3	0	1	0	0
学术动态	1	0	0	0	13	1	1	0	0	15	15	14	11	10	26	16	5
文会会务	0	0	2	1	6	4	0	3	0	4	12	8	10	9	18	5	4
其他	0	0	0	0	0	0	0	0	0	1	0	3	0	0	2	0	0

注：1. 由于会刊上的文章类型多样，其分量也难有一个统一的标准，所以统计时对篇幅的大小不作考虑。
2. 由于书评难以归类，所以表中未列书评之数目。

如果以1901年为节点,学术动态、艺术类、生物学、宗教类的文章明显比前一个时期增多,学术动态增多说明文会更加关注世界汉学界的动态和消息。20世纪文会与世界各地交流的学术刊物就达100余家,通过会刊,文会已进入国际汉学乃至东方学的阵营中,并积极向会员及汉学研究者传递了最新的学术信息。

艺术类文章增多的原因是:20世纪后外国人对中国的认识和研究上了一个台阶,经过近半个世纪的努力,研究中国的最大障碍——汉语对于许多外国人来讲已不是那么陌生,各种字典和工具书已经相继出现;有关中国的概况,经过先驱们的开拓,很多人能够直接在相对较高的平台上从事中国的研究。与此同时,中亚考古和敦煌文献的发掘,使得古老的中华文明再次焕发出诱人的魅力,并引发了国际汉学界对中国古代文化——尤其表现在古代文物和艺术品上——的研究热潮,艺术类内容的文章比较多见也正是当时学术发展的结果。

生物学类文章的增多主要是个人的原因。1921年著名博物学家苏阿德主管博物院,1928-1941年出任文会会长,在他的影响下文会博物院获得较大发展,或许是出于个人的专业,在他任会长期间无论是演讲题目还是所刊发的文章,动植物方面的文章尤其多。

宗教一直是外人研究的热门课题。尤其是来华传教士,本着传教的使命,较之于其他行业的人群,他们更加执著于研究中国境内的宗教。19世纪会刊宗教类文章刊登的少有两个原因,一是有《教务杂志》这个刊物,有关传教及宗教研究的文章主要发表在这个刊物上,20世纪初"大多数传教士看上去仍然喜欢阅读《教务杂志》,对于拥有许多传教士撰写中国考古、文学、宗教、地理等方面信息的资源宝库——文会会刊——却不多浏览"。[1]二是近代来华外人对于中国的各类宗教有一个逐渐认识的过程,最初他们都把儒学当作中国的主要宗教,纷纷致力于孔子及儒家学说的研究。近代外人在编写各类期刊杂志上所刊文章的索引时,都把儒学列入中国宗教一栏。[2] 20世纪后,佛教、伊斯兰教及中国人的其他宗教信仰才真正进入外人的视野中。这一时期,传教士也不再是研究中坚,更多来自其他职业的人加入到对中国宗教的研究中。比如人类学家史禄国的《通古斯的萨满教通论》、梵文学家钢和泰(Alexander von Stael-Holstein)的《玄奘及其现代研究》、考古学家毕士勃(Carl Whitney Bishop)的《古代中国之土地的崇拜》、汉学家翟理思的《〈历代神仙通鉴〉中的基督》、政府顾问庄士敦的《当代中国的一个寺僧》。会刊刊登这些类文章反映了外人对中国的认识大大深入,同时也说明会刊的方向主要还是在于研究中国的历史文化而不是宗教传播。

19世纪社会学、政治经济学类和地学类文章较多,原因是这一时期外人对中国的各个方面都不熟悉,他们的主要从事是传教、经商和搞外交,职业本身决定他们必须先对中国的地质矿藏、交通贸易、物产、气候、民族风俗有所了解和认识,所以来华外人首先要调查研究这些内容。

此外,这两个时期会刊文章的风格前后也有差异。19世纪许多文章是资料整理,数十万、甚至上百万字数的文章很多。每卷会刊文章篇数并不多,但是容量却有400-500页。20世纪则大不一样,虽然每卷会刊有六七篇文章,但是整卷内容总在200页左右,所刊文章短小精悍,多是就一些小题目写的分析论证的学术性论文。

---

[1] Couling, S., The Ideal Missionary, The Chinese Recorder, Vol. XLXII, Oct., 1916, No. 10. pp671.
[2] See, Cordier, Henri, A Classified Index to the Articles printed in the Journal of the North-China Branch of the Royal Asiatic Society from 1858 to 1874, JNCBRAS, VOL. IX, pp200-218.

二、会刊影响

会刊以其较高的学术含量,从创刊起就受到了国内外的注意。不仅有众多的知名学者关注和投稿,而且有很多刊物刊登会刊的有关消息、评论会刊的学术价值、转引会刊上的文章。

(一)会刊有一些文章受到当时国内外学界的好评。

1936年《史学消息》辟专栏介绍世界汉学有关杂志,对文会会刊作了详细介绍,高度评价会刊,称赞"在许多方面都有佳作和珍贵资料。百余年间,对中国有价值之探讨数见不鲜。"[1]会刊出版之后,国内外学术界总会对上面的一些具有较高学术价值的文章予以肯定。

动植物方面:穆林德(O. F. von Möllendorff)的《直隶的脊椎动物及中国动物命名法》,被当时中国科学界誉为"虽非巨著,要为名作"。[2]贝勒的《先辈欧人对中国植物的研究》一文,"遥遥领先于同时代同类的研究,并且被公认为后来研究的奠基石",[3]该文还获得了汉学最高奖"儒莲奖"。祁天锡(N. Gist Gee)的《苏州及其周边地区动植物初探》,列举了各类植物名录,在此基础上,作者修订出版了《江苏植物名录》,1921年由我国著名植物学家钱崇澍译成中文,由中国科学社出版。"凡研习植物分类学者,莫不手执一卷"。[4]里利(J. H. Riley)和里士满(C. W. Richmond)合编的《中国鸟类相关文献管窥》"为从事中国鸟类学研究的学者扫除了多年的障碍"。[5]苏阿德的《中国博物学》、海德生(H. Von Heidenstam, C.E)的《长江三角洲的成长》被誉为"具有永久的价值"。[6]就连50年后的今天还有人肯定该文的价值。[7]

历史文化方面:佛尔克的《王充与柏拉图论死亡与永生》刊出不久就被中国学者予以赞赏。[8]司登得之《中国的(民间)传说》与汤顺(J. Thomson)《柬埔寨古迹》刚出来就被《北华捷报》誉为"都是新颖之作"。[9]卫三畏的《卫三畏日记》,"对于所有热衷远东事务的学者来说,其价值可谓不菲"。[10]福开森的《中国历史要览》系"作者多年的研究心得,无疑为进一步研究中国历史奠定了基础,尤其是面对浩繁的中国文献,该文为深入研究打开了便捷之道"。[11]

宗教方面:钢和泰的《玄奘及其现代研究》一文,提出了"西藏和土耳其佛教都源于中国而非印度"的观点,"为下一步佛教研究打开了局面"。[12]季理斐(D. Macgillivray)的《河南犹太人》在当时是"关于此主题最好的论述"。[13]金陵大学哲学系教授亨克(F. G. Henke)的《王阳明的生平及其哲学思想》,1916年又印成《王阳明的哲学》,"这是美国学者研究中国哲学的杰作"。[14]

对于会刊文章的评价,除了部分来自中国学者外,主要来自《北华捷报》、《教务杂志》及《中国科学美术杂志》。这可能难以真实反映会刊所载文章的水准,但是由于这三家报刊都是近代

---

[1] 《西洋汉学论文提要》,《史学消息》,第一卷第一期,第10页。
[2] 张孟闻:《中国科学史举隅》,《民国丛书》第一编第90册,上海书店1989年,第63页。
[3] Ferguson, J. C., Bretschneider, The China Journal of Science & Arts, Vol. XIII, Oct., 1930, No. 4, P248.
[4] 王志稼:《祁天锡博士事略》,《科学》24卷1期(1940年1月),第70页。
[5] Biological notes and Reviews, The China Journal of Science & Arts, Vol. I, Nov. No. 6, pp604.
[6] Recent Literature, The New China Review, Vol. IV, Oct. 1922, No. 5. P422 - 424. P422.
[7] 胡道静:《历史上以上海为研究对象的学术团体》,《档案与历史》,1998年第2期;
[8] 陈潜:《西人译中国书籍及在中国发行之报章》,《东方杂志》,第五卷第九期,第162页。
[9] Review, North-China Herald, 20th, Feb., 1872. P163.
[10] 《北华捷报》1911年12月2日,No. 2312, pp578 – 579.
[11] Societies and Institutes, The China Journal of Science & Arts, Vol. IV, April, 1926, No. 4, P204.
[12] Our Book Table, The Chinese Recorder, Vol. LIV, P497.
[13] Our Book Table, The Chinese Recorder, Vol. LIX, P794.
[14] 宋晞:《美国的汉学研究》,见陶振誉等著:《世界各国汉学研究论文集》(第一辑),台湾"国防研究院"1968年印行,第148页。

上海乃至远东最著名的外文报刊,因此他们的评论也反映出了这些文章在远东(汉学)学术界的地位。从上述评价看,会刊中的历史文化、动植物学及宗教方面的文章水平较高,而会刊主要撰稿人的文章却没有受到学者(读者)的欣赏。

关于会刊不利方面的声音也不时出现。第50卷就遭到《中国评论》的批评,"我们怀疑此卷会使很多读者失望,不仅印刷错误百出,而且内容平淡",指出该卷的《台湾》一文实在是毫无新意。[1] 52卷中的《海南的苗族》"对于科学家来说,仅仅六周的参观是很难获得翔实、可信的科学资料"。[2]而66卷中的《螺祖崇拜》一文中则"把杜佑之《通典》的编纂年代和乾隆年间《皇朝通典》的编纂年代弄混了";林仰山的《中国西北通道》一文,"作者没有参考沙畹、伯希和等人的研究成果,尤其是伯希和的《〈史记〉考释》。"[3]

尽管如此,正如很多评介所说,"它仍充满了许多有价值的信息",会刊还是受到了学界和社会的好评。

(二) 会刊受到国内外学术刊物的重视。

笔者检索了20世纪国内外十余种重要的学术期刊,中文期刊涵盖了20世纪中国境内社会科学研究水平最高学术期刊,外文刊物则挑选了19世纪以来各国研究中国的主要汉学刊物(详见表4-3)。[4]发现这一时期国内外学术界的许多期刊杂志都辟专栏,或介绍、或评价会刊所载之文章,并将会刊列为各自刊物的主要参考文献之一或交流刊物。以下数篇文章,在这些期刊中曾被他人直接引用:

艾约瑟之《中国的建筑》,"叙述中国建筑之文献、技术、装饰等,受到中国学界注意"。[5]

1924年姚从吾的《欧洲学者对于匈奴的研究》一文在论述当时西方人的研究现状时就专门提到了金斯密的《夏特与匈奴》(34卷)和查得利的《中华文明源于埃及吗?》(60卷)。[6]

董作宾在《方法敛博士对于甲骨文字之贡献》提到了方法敛的《秦朝标准度量衡》(35卷)[7]

陆懋德的《中国人发明火药火炮考》引用梅辉立的《火药和火器在中国人中的引介和使用》(6卷)。[8]

1948年芮逸夫《僚(獠)为仡佬(犵狫)试证》一文在论述犵狫族时首先就引用会刊1859年老刊第3卷14页裨治文关于倮倮的翻译,并指出裨氏错误"但因白列居门氏(按:即裨治文:E. C. Bridgeman)英译《黔庙图说》(Sketches of the Miautsze)译倮罗(即倮倮)为Lolo,……本应为犵狫(Toleman or Coloman)"。[9]

《直隶的脊椎动物及中国动物命名法》和陶然士(Thomas Torrance)的《四川的丧葬习俗》、

---

[1] The New China Journal, Vol. I, Oct., 1919, No. 5, P542-544.
[2] The New China Review, Vol. III, Oct., 1921, No. 5, P403.
[3] Harvard Journal of Asiatic Studies, Vol. 1, July, 1936, No. 2, pp276-278.
[4] 注:未刊登会刊任何消息的中文期刊有:《地学杂志》、《国闻周报》、《岭南大学学报》、《图书评论》、《社会科学》(清华)、《史地学报》、《史学年报》、《史学集刊》、《北平图书馆月刊》、《国立中山大学语言历史研究所集刊》、《国立武汉大学文哲季刊》、《国立武汉大学社会科学季刊》、《大夏学报》。
[5] 福开森著,毛一心译:《中国建筑史概论》,《民国丛书》第五编第87辑,上海书店1989年,第37页。
[6] 姚从吾:《欧洲学者对于匈奴的研究》,《国学季刊》二卷三期,第494页。
[7] 《图书季刊》二卷三期,第229页。
[8] 《清华学报》五卷一期,第1489页。
[9] 芮逸夫《僚(獠)为仡佬(犵狫)试证》,《国立中央研究院历史语言研究所集刊》第二十册,上册,商务印书馆民国三十七年版,第344页。

表 4-3　20 世纪中外期刊转载、引用会刊情况表

期刊名称	录目录	评介会刊	论文转引	文献参考
国立中央研究院史语所集刊			√	
国学季刊			√	
史学消息	√	√		
燕京学报			√	
清华学报			√	√
辅仁学志			√	
国立北平图书馆馆刊			√	
中法大学月刊		√		√
图书季刊			√	
中华图书馆协会会报			√	
中国社会及政治学报(中国)			√	
辅仁学志(北京)	√	√	√	√
亚洲艺术评论(德国)			√	
远东季刊(美)	√	√	√	√
中国评论和新中国评论	√	√	√	√
斯德哥尔摩远东博物院集刊			√	
中国华西边疆研究会会刊(成都)			√	√
中国科学与美术评论(上海)	√	√	√	√
教务杂志(上海)	√	√	√	√
哈佛亚洲研究(美)	√	√	√	√
美国东方学会会刊(美)	√	√	√	√
通报(荷、法)	√		√	√
亚洲学报(法国)			√	√
华裔学志	√	√		
东方学报(日)			√	

注：1. 西文刊物一般都在最后列出参考文献(或交流文献)的英文缩写字母，在上述西文期刊提到文会的会刊时，都用统一的缩写语"JNCBRAS"。中文期刊由于在体例上没有西文期刊规范，无从谈起它们是否将文会会刊以统一的形式列为参考文献，因此只能看其论文中是否引用了会刊作为他们对会刊重视的标志。

2. 各项指标含义如下：
录目录：指该刊物仅仅列出会刊每期文章之篇目，不介绍每篇文章之内容；
评介会刊：指该刊物对会刊所刊文章之学术价值予以评介；
论文转引：指该刊物所刊之文章中曾经引用会刊上之文章；
文献参考：指该刊物将会刊列为必要参考文献和交流刊物。

《羌族的宗教信仰》一文被许多人引用。[1]

(苏俄)聂斯克著的《西夏语研究小史》一文中评价了卜士礼的《西夏的货币及其独特文字》

---

[1]《直隶的脊椎动物及中国动物命名法》见 Hubbard, A. W. A Frigate bird at Peitaiho 和朱元鼎的《中国鱼类论著》，见 The China Journal of Science & Arts, Vol. II, Nov., 1924, No. 6, P561; Vol. IV, Jan. 1931, No. 1. P84;《四川的丧葬习俗》见 Graham, D. C., The Ancient Caves of Szechuan Province, The China Journal of Science & Arts, Vol. LXI-61, pp 437.《羌族的宗教信仰》见 Graham, D. C. Litholatry in West Chine; Torrance, T., Work Among the Ch'iang Tribesmen; The China Journal of Science & Arts, LX, P42; LXI-61, pp104.

对40个西夏文字的贡献和不足。[1]

柯老斯(Prof. Dr. F. A. Krauze)著,姚从吾译《蒙古史发凡》,该文附录《西文蒙古史重要史源与参考书举要》中列了会刊45卷124页中慕阿德的《元代皇帝年表》一文。[2]

日本佐伯好郎《北京城午门楼门に於て发现せりろれたるシリヤ文古钞本に就いて》一文中引用会刊1885年20卷会刊中《大秦之谜:评夏德〈中国和罗马人的东方〉》一文。[3]

可以看出,这些文章已经被当时国内外相关专业的一流学者所认可。文章被引用说明会刊在当时已进入国内外学者的视野中,而且拥有比较稳定的读者群体。当然会刊的引用率并不是很高,甚至有许多期刊数十年只被引用一次,但是正如葛兆光先生所言,一份杂志"被允许用缩略号意味着它已经司空见惯,常常被引用则表明它在学界人心目中的分量"。[4]

除了期刊杂志外,一些相关索引和专著还大量引用会刊所载之文章。1933年贝德士从19种西文东方学报中一一精选出那些"材料丰富、解释精当、观念准确,且能引起研究中国文化各方面之兴趣,中国学者可参考之中国问题之论文",共计281篇。其中来自会刊之文有55篇,数量仅次于《通报》,位居第二。[5] 1935年国立北平研究院出版的《中国地质文献目录》中就收录了会刊上金斯密、艾约瑟等人撰写的中国地质学论文。[6] 1956年中科院编辑的地貌学文献目录内收录了会刊上的9篇地质学文章。[7] 李约瑟的巨著《中国科学技术史》前5册就引用会刊文章达39篇文章之多。

(三)会刊成为学术交流和学术竞争的平台。

借助会刊,国内外学者得以及时交流和沟通。会刊为学者提供了学术交流的空间,使分散在世界各地的学者能通过文会会刊就有些问题进行讨论乃至辩论,大大推动了相关领域向前发展的速度与研究深度。1900年夏德在慕尼黑发表《伏尔加河的匈人和匈奴人》(Ueber Wolga—Hunnen und Hiung-nu),该文依据《魏书·西域传·粟特国》内所载的匈奴西迁的记载,认为欧洲的匈人就是《史记》、《汉书》中的匈奴人。次年10月金斯密在会刊上发表《夏德与匈奴:评夏德〈伏尔加河的匈人和匈奴人〉》一文,对夏德的考证提出质疑。夏德后撰文《金斯密先生与匈奴》(Mr. Kingsmill and the Hiung-nu)刊登在《美国东方学会会刊》上,对金斯密之文做了答复。[8]

会刊不仅成为学者论战的地方,而且也为学者提供了信息交流的平台,成为学术信息的资源库之一。1932年美国斯密生博物馆的考古学家毕勃士来信与苏阿德探讨中国古代中原的野牛问题,苏阿德认为中原地区出现野牛的可能性很小,所以难以解释中国古代文献中关于野牛的记载。后来一名读者——美国在华海关人员阿灵顿来信说文会会刊59卷已有一篇文章早已解决了这个问题。[9]

(四)会刊的一些文章由于具有较高的学术价值,后来曾经被国内外单独出版。

10卷(1876年)会刊中的贝勒的《中亚与西亚中古时代之史地考》一文,后在伦敦再版

---

[1] (苏俄)聂斯克著,张玛丽译:《西夏语研究小史》,《国立北平图书馆馆刊》四卷三期3页。
[2] 柯老斯(Prof. Dr. F. A. Krauze)著,姚从吾译:《蒙古史发凡》,《辅仁学志》一卷二期,第67页。
[3] 东方文化学院、东京研究所编辑《东方学报》第四册(昭和八年十一月)。
[4] 葛兆光:《域外中国学十论》序,复旦大学出版社2002年,第9页。
[5] 贝德士编:《西文东方学报论文举要》,金陵大学中国文化研究所印行,民国二十二年。
[6] 杨遵仪编:《中国地质文献目录》,国立北平研究院总办事处出版课印行,民国二十四年。
[7] 中国科学院地理研究所编:《中国地貌学文献目录 1855-1958》,科学出版社1960年。
[8] See: T. W. Kingsminn, Dr. F. Hirth and the Hiung Nu, JNCBRAS., Vol. XXIV(1901-1902), pp136-141.
[9] The China Journal of Science & Arts. Vol. XVIII, Jan., 1933, No. 1, pp17.

(Notes of the Mediaeval Geograpgy and History of Central and Western Asia, London, Trübner, 1877)。

15 卷中贝勒的《先辈欧人对中国植物的研究》一文,1881 年上海美华书馆出版。

16 卷(1881 年)中的贝勒的《中国植物志》一文,1882 年在伦敦再版。

25 卷(1890)和 26 卷(1891)的《中国植物志》,上海别发洋行于 1892、1895 年分别再版。

54 卷中的《伊大仁主教和他失踪坟墓的故事》后被单行出版,并被《教务杂志》(1923 年 7 月号)摘录。

39 卷(1908 年)中慕阿德的《中国乐器及其他发声器之目录》(1908 年)次年在上海单独重印。

63 卷中福开森的《中国历代瓷器》(1932 年),同年由别发洋行再版。

以上说明,文会会刊以一定的学术含量,受到国际学术界的注目,成为中外学者进行学术交流的一道重要桥梁。

(五) 会刊受到国内外学术研究机构的重视。

由于会刊之学术价值和资料价值受到学术界的认可,所以许多大学及科研究机构的图书馆都收藏会刊。据不完全统计,20 世纪国内外就有 30 余家图书馆都收藏有会刊(见表 4-4)。其中大连满铁图书馆还专门编辑了 1941 年前所有会刊内容之索引,供该机构人员之利用。[1]

表 4-4　　20 世纪世界各地曾经收藏会刊的图书馆

图书馆	地点	图书馆	地点
东方图书馆	上海	福建协和大学	福州
东亚同文书院	上海	岭南大学	广州
复旦大学图书馆	上海	之江大学图书馆	杭州
工部局图书馆	上海	齐鲁大学图书馆	济南
广学会	上海	中央研究院社会科学研究所	昆明
沪美学堂	上海	南京大学中国文化研究所	南京
花旗妇女总会	上海	金陵大学图书馆	南京
雷氏德医学研究院	上海	南满铁路图书馆	大连
明复图书馆	上海	麦吉尔大学图书馆	蒙特利尔
上海交通大学图书馆	上海	仰光大学图书馆	仰光
上海自然科学研究所图书馆	上海	纽瓦克公共图书馆	新泽西
徐家汇藏书楼	上海	斯坦福大学图书馆	加利福尼亚
中华书局	上海	艾塞克斯学院图书馆管理员	麻萨诸塞
北洋大学图书馆	天津	东印度公司图书馆	伦敦
厦门大学	厦门	哥伦比亚大学	纽约
燕京大学图书馆	北京	印度图书馆	伦敦
清华大学	北京	美国国会图书馆东方学部	华盛顿
华西协和大学	成都	康乃尔大学图书馆	纽约

资料来源:
1. 参见附表 2;
2. 1881、1907、1915 年文会交流机构名录;
3. 全国图书联合目录编辑组:《全国西文期刊联合目录》,北京图书馆 1959 年,第 1452 页。

[1] 参见满铁调查部《英国王立亚细亚学会北支支部志索引》,昭和十五年十二月。

（六）会刊是近代外人认识中国的重要媒介。

19世纪60年代,有位上海外侨曾说:"自从《中国丛报》停刊以来,尽管还有广阔的领域可以研究,然而一直未出现相似的期刊,一度有《中国见闻》(Chinese Magazine)、《远东疑释》、《中国丛报》等杂志。他们满足了我们对中国文化的好奇心……除了《皇家亚洲文会北华支会会刊》外,最近二十年没有像《中国丛报》那样的期刊出现。"[1]

20世纪20年代,欧美人士曾评出40种对于"理解和认识中国最有帮助的英文书籍",这里面只有文会会刊和《中国教会年刊》(China Mission Year Book)两种连续出版物,其余全是专著,如理雅各的《中国经书》、卫三畏的《中国总论》、库寿龄的《中国百科辞典》、卜舫济的《中国历史概要》、马士的《中华帝国对外关系史》等。[2]

因此,可以说会刊是近代来华外人学习研究中国文化、传播知识的重要媒介。会刊上面所发表的文章实际上反映了近代以来在华外人对中国文化研究认识的总体水平,对于后来外人认识研究中国,会刊起了奠基的作用。

第四节 其他活动

除了上述主要活动之外,文会还不定期地举办一些其他活动,这些活动也是旨在促进对中国的调查与研究,客观上促进了近代中西文化的交流。

一、国际交流活动

（一）参加国际有关学术会议,了解国际学术界最新的研究动态以便对学会会员研究起指导作用。

1874年12月理事会推选阿礼国和谭微道参加巴黎国际地理学大会(Cengress of Geographical Societies)。[3] 1881年9月文会理事会派克雷特纳(L. G. Kreitner)参加了在威尼斯召开的第三届国际地理学会(International Geographical Congress),并在会上提交了一份关于中亚和东亚的论文。同年,夏德代表文会参加了柏林举行的东方学大会(Oriental Congress)。通过参加这些会议,文会不断把中国介绍到西方,在改变西方人对中国的认识方面起到了积极作用。更为重要的是通过参加国际学术会议,使文会能够及时了解世界汉学动态,为会员的研究提供帮助。1892年9月1日,国际东方学大会在伦敦召开,艾约瑟代表文会出席了这次会议。1893年艾约瑟回来后马上在文会年会上做了长篇演讲——《国际东方学会议讨论之热点》(Popular Lecture on the Oriental Congress),向文会会员传达了当时东方学研究的五大热点:①印欧语系之研究,尤其是汉语语言岛问题;②佛教进入中国的过程及其对中国和东方社会的影响;③蒙藏语言研究的必要性;④古代埃及文明及其对中国的影响;⑤中国的三大宗教;⑥中国的哲学研究。[4] 该文全文刊登于会刊27卷的会议记录中,这在所有会议记录中是十分罕见的,目的是使会员能够迅速地了解到国际学术动态,拓宽了他们的研究范围。1893—1898年间穆麟德的《比较语言学的局限》、李提摩太的《〈大乘起信论〉纲要》、艾约瑟的

---

[1] Literature in China, The North-China China and Market Report, North-China Herald, 12th, Dec., 1868.
[2] L. Newton Hayes: The Most Helpful Books on China, The Chinese Recorder, Vol. LVI(1925), pp302.
[3] Summary News, North-China Herald, Vol. III, NO.397, 17th, Dec., 1874.
[4] Proceedings, JNCBRAS, Vol. XXVII, pp231-246.

《华南土著:他们的历史、宗教及语言》(演讲稿)显然是本次会议的结果。

(二)接待来华学者和有关国际机构,与国外有关机构合作进行调查研究。

近代,凡是来到远东的西方学者和文化团体多会在上海短暂驻足。"文会会接待一些来自南北的杰出人士,一般会邀请他们到文会演讲"。[1] 1932年法国著名汉学家伯希和路过上海之际,文会便邀请他演讲了1907年的敦煌考古发掘过程;文会还接待过地理学家李希霍芬、语言学家高本汉、探险家斯文赫定等人。

与国外机构合作方面,缘于经费的关系不是很多。1858年8月10日文会召开专门会议迎接奥地利科学考察船"Novara"号上的官员及奥地利帝国科学院的成员,双方达成协议交流各自的自然历史标本。[2] 后来文会还帮助该机构考察中国华南地区之人体体质项目。19世纪70年代,文会也曾帮助德国柏林天文研究机构观测记录了涵关、烟台、北京、牛庄等地区的气温、风向、湿度等气象信息。[3] 20世纪尚未见到类似的信息,更多的表现在与有关机构交换出版物。

(三)与世界各地文化机构交流彼此的出版物。

最初文会与世界各国文化机构交换出版物目的是为了获得相关的资料,尤其是关于中国的研究文献,以便于充实文会的图书馆和方便会员的研究。1885年图书馆管理员曾向世界各地有关出版社、文化机构寄信索取对方的出版物。20世纪后文会在国外的声誉逐渐上升,有关机构都主动与文会交换期刊及其出版物。

根据文会记录,1881年有66个,1886年有109个,1896年有128个,1915年有155个文化机构和文会交换各自的出版物。据笔者计算,截至1915年,共有32个国家的204个机构曾与文会交换出版物(见表4-5)。这些机构主要集中在欧美国家和欧美列强在亚非的殖民地国家,应该说文会的出版物(主要是会刊)已经流入欧美人群主要聚集区域中了。

表4-5　　　　　　　　文会交换机构国籍分布统计表　　　　　　　(单位:个)

国　家	数量	国　家	数量	国　家	数量
德　国	32	中　国	27	美　国	29
英　国	18	印　度	9	加拿大	3
法　国	14	日　本	7	墨西哥	3
奥地利	12	越　南	4	澳大利亚	3
俄　国	11	马来西亚	2	阿根廷	2
荷　兰	4	朝　鲜	1	埃　及	2
瑞　典	4	菲律宾	1	巴　西	1
葡萄牙	3	泰　国	1	乌拉圭	1
意大利	3	锡　兰	1	智　利	1
比利时	1	新加坡	1		
丹　麦	1	印　尼	1		
瑞　士	1				

资料来源:会刊1881、1886、1896、1905、1915年。

注:奥匈帝国计入奥地利内。

[1] Proceedings, JNCBRAS, Vol. XXXV, 1903-1904, Pxix.
[2] The Asiatic Society, North-China Herald, Vol. VIII, No. 420, 14th, Aug., 1858.
[3] The Asiatic Society, North-China Herald, 16th, July, 1870;会刊7-12卷中的气温测量资料。

从交换的机构看（见表4-6），欧美各国的各类学会（包括支会）是主要交换单位，这是因为这些机构与文会属于同一性质的文化机构。这些学会主要是各国的地理学会、人类学会、动植物学会和东方学会，但是这里面与文会交换刊物最多的单位不是东方学会，而是地理学会。[1] 各类地理学会共有34个，若再加上科研机构中的地理研究所，地理学类机构共计达41个，地理类机构如此众多是一个非常奇怪的现象。不过美国的《国家地理杂志》却不是文会的交换对象，目前尚难解释其真正的原因，笔者认为会刊是以其历史文化和动植物学之类的文章受到了学术界的重视，地理和游记类文章在会刊中的篇幅虽然仅次于历史，但这类文章资料价值有余，学术价值不高，在当时几乎没有受到国内外学界的重视。

科研机构主要是欧美各国皇家科学院（国家科学院）、大学及各种专业研究所，博物馆中主要有华盛顿斯密生博物馆、芝加哥自然历史博物馆、巴黎基美博物馆、莱比锡民族博物馆（Museum für Völkerkunde）、维也纳自然历史博物馆（K. K. Naturhistorisches Hofmuseum），它们的科研能力在当时也都是世界知名的；期刊则几乎涵盖了19世纪以来所有东方学会的会刊。

表4-6　　　　　　　　　　　　　　文会交流机构类别统计表　　　　　　　　　　　　（单位：个）

类　别	数　量	类　别	数　量
学　会	100	政　府	4
科研机构	33	海　关	3
报　纸	16	教　堂	2
博物馆	16	天文台	2
期　刊	16	孤儿院	1
不　详	11		

资料来源：会刊1881、1886、1896、1905、1915年。

通过这些机构，文会实际上打造了一个世界性的学术网络，借助于交换而来的会刊和其他出版物，广大会员、在华外人及中外学人得以迅速获得各种最新学术信息和各类学术资源。通过交换出版物，汉学也进入到了东方学主流队伍中，从而大大推动了欧美各国对中国之研究。

总之，这些活动使得文会拥有了更宽的学术网路，更快的获取国外学术资讯的速度，从而也有了更多的文化交流内容。

二、国内活动

在国内，文会策划了一些调查活动，举办了中国文物及艺术品展览。前者放在第五章中论述，后者由于主要由博物院承办，前文已有论述，这里无需重复。

除了上述活动外，文会还有一项活动——出版书籍。历史时期文会出版的书籍很少。主要由以下几类：

（一）文献类

1868年翻印了早年裨治文、卫三畏等人主办的《中国丛报》，目的是为了便于上海外侨认

---

[1] 即便将东方学会和东方学会所创办的刊物叠加计算，也没有地理学会、地理研究院的数量多。

识中国国情,此后文会没有再出版印刷此类书籍;

1882年的《中国与远东之书目》(Catalogue of Books Relating to China and the East),该书出版于1884年以前(包括1884年),作者和定价不详。

可以看出,该类书籍是了解与研究中国之工具书。

(二)与文会自身有关的书籍(见表4-7)

这些书籍主要是让社会知道文会是一个什么样的机构。馆藏书目是根据杜威图书分类法编排的。《博物院指南》则告诉世人博物院藏有哪些标本和文物,并对博物院内每个展柜都一一作了介绍。《章程》主要是向世人公布1906年修改后的新章程。1864—1900年(此后未见)文会年度报告曾单行出版,内容比《北华捷报》上刊登的报告多了一份会员通讯录。

表4-7　　　　　　　　　　　文会出版之书籍(一)

编著者	书　名	年份	价格	备　注
高　第	皇家亚洲文会北华支会图书馆藏目录	1872	8vo	
	皇家亚洲文会北华支会图书馆藏目录	1881		文汇报馆印制
夏　士	皇家亚洲文会北华支会图书馆藏目录	1893	3$	别发洋行印制
爱司克夫人	皇家亚洲文会北华支会图书馆藏目录	1910	1$	
	皇家亚洲文会北华支会图书馆藏目录	1921		
	皇家亚洲文会北华支会章程	1911		上海泰晤时报印制
苏阿德	中国博物学:上海博物院指南(英文)	1936	3—4	精装本
苏阿德	中国博物学:上海博物院指南(中文)	1937		
苏阿德	中国博物学:上海博物院指南(中文)	1939	0.30	平装
	文会年度报告			仅部分年份

该类书籍的出版,一是文会之义务,因为文会是工部局财政资助下的社会文化机构,它是非营利性单位,[1]免费向社会开放,有责任定期向社会公开其事宜,以便于社会利用;二是文会为了扩大自己的影响,使更多的人能够支持文会,目的是为了获取更多的社会捐款和会费收入,以减轻债务负担。《馆藏书目》(1872年版)和《博物院指南》(中文版)就是在这种背景下出版的。为了宣传博物院,1939年文会还专门发行一套"博物院标本明信片"(Picture Post Cards of Museum Specimens 18 kinds)。[2]

(三)学术书籍

这些书主要是资助部分会员出版他们的学术研究成果,由于财力有限,资助得并不多。详见下表(见表4-8):

[1] 上海档案馆编:《工部局董事会会议录》(第5册),上海古籍出版社2001年版,第665页。
[2] Proceedings, JNCBRAS, Vol. LXX, Pxvii.

表 4-8　文会出版之书籍（二）

作　者	书　名	年份	定　价
西　蒙	中日之地质学与古生物学略论	1869	8vo
伟晋颂	中国陶瓷概要	1908	0.35 us/£/$
骆任廷	中国钱币综录	1915	8net(1924)
爱司克夫人	中国及远东研究文献综述	1921	0.35
史禄国	华北人类学研究	1923	1.5
史禄国	满族的社会组织	1924	2.5
史禄国	民族内部之组织单位	1924	0.7
史禄国	华东及广东人类学考察	1925	3
倭　讷	中国的武器	1932	2（精装）
伊博恩	上海的食用鱼	1938	1.5
罗德民、卫思克	五台山的土地利用	1939	

资料来源：1886年、1915-1948年各卷会刊封底广告；1939年年度报告。

这些作者都是文会会员，他们的著作都未曾演讲过，而且只有西蒙（G. E. Simon）之著作在第5卷会刊（1868年）上发表过。

他们中西蒙、伟晋颂、骆任廷和倭讷都是在华的外交官。西蒙（法国人）曾在会刊上发表一篇关于中国农业物产的文章；骆任廷只有一篇介绍香港民俗学会（Hongkong Folk-Lore Society）成立一事的短文，这主要还是因为他是该会会长，民俗学会需要和文会交流以促进彼此的研究。其他两人虽然是文会会员，但是既未来文会演讲过，也未在会刊上发表过文章。

史禄国，俄国人。1917年来华，从事民族学、人类学、文字学等方面的研究，先后担任清华、厦门、中山、辅仁各大学人类学、社会学教授，多年来致力于中国东北和华北的人类学研究，为研究通古斯民族之权威。[1] 他在会刊上发表3篇文章。

伊博恩，英国人，博士，系上海雷氏德研究院医学教师，1939-1947年曾相继担任文会副会长、会长职务。在会刊上发表2篇关于中医的文章。

爱司克夫人，多年担任文会图书管理员，主编过1921年的馆藏书目。在会刊上发表5篇文章，都是关于中国历史文化的探讨，如《紫禁城的象征主义》《关于"大河"文献的初步注解》，这些文章不仅视角新颖，而且也具有一定的深度。

罗德民（W. C. Lowder）是金陵大学教师，卫思克（Dean R. Wickes）是美国公理会（American Board Mission）教士，二人都是普通会员。

目前看来，上述著作在各自学术领域内能够拥有一席之地的只有史禄国和爱司克夫人的论著，这是两人多年学术生涯和职业生涯积累的结果。史禄国曾在西伯利亚、东北、华北、华东进行多年的人类学和民族学调查，出版了一系列专著。《华北人类学研究》《满族的社会组织》是其主要成果，也是该领域的代表作，为以后的研究奠定了一个坚实的基础；《满族的社会组织》一书作者考察了满族的起源和历史，论述了满族语言、风俗、信仰以及满族与通古斯之间的关系。"是他首次将ethnos（同种同文之民族）解释为：'说同种语言，且拥有与其他群体不

---

[1]《史禄国博士逝世》，《科学》24卷3期，第238页。

同的共同习俗起源和社会体系起源的群体'。"[1]《华北人类学研究》"是作者在多年实地考察的基础上,运用了社会学、人类学和民族学的理论研究华北人类,其基本方法是抽样调查,成为该领域内的水平最高的论著。"[2]

其他6册著作之学术水准,现在还很难断言。

骆任廷的《中国钱币综录》"收录了古代至民国时期的1 800个钱币图像,已经远远超过了大英博物馆库普尔La Couperie编的《钱币目录》,该书的出版无论是对于业余收藏者还是研究者都具有极大的价值。"[3]这是文会自己给的评价,但是"中国钱币"一直是近代来华外人的研究热点,类似这样的论著仅会刊上就有3篇,《中国评论》、《中国科学美术杂志》中关于中国货币的文章则更多,有些文章也是长篇累牍,绝不亚于一本专著。目前尚不知骆著究竟发行多少册,从会刊1915年的封底广告看,1914年的版本已经脱销;而1937年的广告则说会员半价购买,其他人八折优惠。说明该书曾经再版过,但后来销售十分不佳。

伟晋颂(F. E. Wilkinson)和倭讷(E. T. C. Werner)之论著尚未见到相关的书评,不过论及陶瓷,福开森的《中国历代陶瓷》和夏德的《古代陶瓷:中世纪中国工商业研究》都是不错的文章;后来学者论及武器时,也多会提到梅辉立的《火药和火器在中国人中的引介和使用》,很少见到引用伟晋颂和倭讷二人之作,说明这二人之著作并未受到当时学界的重视。

剩余3本专著都是比较冷僻的选题,应该说有一定的学术价值,否则文会也不会予以出版,而且罗德民与卫克思合著的《五台山的土地利用》(History of Soil Use in the Wu Tai Shan Area, By W. C. Lowder milk and Dean R. Wicks.)还是在American Council of learned Societies的资助下出版的。

总之,从这些书籍可以看出,文会主要帮助会员出版他们的未曾发表的学术著作,尽可能地把中国文化介绍到西方。同时也说明,参加演讲和发表文章的人只是文会成员的一部分,还有很多会员也参与了对中国的调查研究。

此外,1935年文会还出版了T. F. Chu编的《新版上海电话号码簿》(0.35),由于和文会关系不大,无需多费笔墨。

---

[1] 原文是:a group of people speaking the same language, recognizing their common origin possessing a complex of customs and social system which is differentiated from those of other groups. 见:Scientific notes and Reviews, The China Journal of Science & Arts, No. 5, 1924, pp486 – 487.

[2] Scientific notes and Reviews, The China Journal of Science & Arts, No. 3, 1944, pp290 – 291.

[3] Notes and Queries, JNCBRAS, Vol. XLVI, P153.

第五章 对华调查研究之动态分析

1857年文会制定的目标是"The field of whose **investigations** shall be the Empire of China and the surrounding nations",1864年文会复会时正式确立文会的目标为"The **investigation** of subjects connected with China and the neighbouring countires",胡道静将之译为"调查中国与其邻近国家的各项事情",实际上"**investigation**"包含了"调查"和"研究"之义,而且从文会的主要成果——演讲主题和会刊文章来看,除了调查报告外,更多的还是研究型的学术论文,所以文会的目标的准确含义应该是"调查研究中国与其邻近国家各项事情",这样才全面。95年里文会调查研究了中国自然和社会的方方面面,内容涉及30多个学科。本章通过对这些调查研究成果(以演讲篇目和会刊篇目为例)的时空分析来展现文会在近代中西文化交流中的贡献。

第一节 时间变化

近百年中,文会的关注点、文会的功能和调查研究的内容都发生不同的变化,这些变化具体如下:

一、在关注点上,对中国内政从有所关注发展到不再关注

1857年文会创建时,裨治文就在开幕词中指出:"在中国,就像在印度一样,一场大的暴乱正在来临。"希望会员关注和了解中国局势的发展,以便外国能够顺利地和中国政府处理中外事务。因此文会在初期对中国内政比较关注,具体表现为:

(一)编辑中国大事回顾,帮助在华外人了解中国的局势

1858-1875年间理事会每年都专门编辑当年中国境内大事记,并刊登于会刊上。这些大事记主要有三方面的内容:

1. 中外交往中每年发生的重要大事。对于这些事情往往叙述得十分详尽,比如1858-1859年英、法、俄、美四国公使在天津与清政府间的修约谈判,《天津条约》和《北京条约》之签订与部分条款之内容,"反洋教"斗争与"马嘉理事件",洋务运动时期的中外关系,这些内容每年都有大量笔墨予以详述。从叙述的笔调看,其重点在于中外交往中的种种"困难"和所取得的"成就"。当清政府拒绝帝国主义的修约要求或不能满足列强要求时,作者会说"专制与傲慢的中国政府是中西交往的主要障碍",[1]不断抱怨中国政府仍然拒绝西方的思想,中国的步伐太慢了,与他们的期望相差太远了,"中国的许多事业仍然不允许外国人涉入,基隆煤矿,外国公司是没有权利去开采的"。为此他们提出"开启中国人和能够让外国企业与资本进入中国

---

[1] Editoral Committee, Record of Occurrences in China, JNCBRAS, O.S. Vol.I., No.3, P254.

最有效的方法是通过外交压力来革除中国官员的阻挠,这样才能实现中外间的自由交往"。[1]当《天津条约》签订后,他们则欢呼是"英国在东亚外交的新纪元","因为,这些涉及政治、宗教、商业等内容的条款具有重要的价值,未来西方基督教国家与中国之间将呈现自由贸易的环境"。[2]作者还不断呼吁各国在中国修建从矿藏资源地到各口岸间的铁路线,开发内河航运、开采各地矿藏、创设电报通讯网络。

2. 关注中国的内政和动乱。内政方面也是立足于中外关系的角度,来看待中国发生的大事。辛酉政变后他们认为是中外交往的一个新时代的来临;1866年清王朝的一些官员和蒲安臣一起出使欧美各国,作者对此评价很高:"标志着中国政府顽固排外意识已开始发生改变,我们不能低估它的意义。"[3]对于太平军在常州、镇江、苏州地区的杀戮予以谴责,也指出八旗兵和绿营兵已经腐朽不堪,难以"剿灭太平天国叛乱"。称赞中外联合绞杀太平天国之行动,"其效果十分明显,通过太平天国叛乱,我们获得了中国政府的认可,从此中国政府不敢轻视我们的帮助"。[4]大事记中也有关于捻军与西南西北的少数民族起义的记载,指出太平天国和这些叛乱对清政府的打击很大,使中国元气大伤,但这些叛乱也促使中国政府走上"自强新政"的道路。他们对"中兴名臣"曾国藩、李鸿章评价较高,认为他们不仅帮助清政府渡过难关,而且在建设军工企业方面贡献很大。"曾国藩为帝国作出了巨大贡献,他受到了皇室的高度评价和中外人士的尊敬"。[5]灾害方面注意了中国各地的水旱之灾,如1871-1872年的永定河泛滥造成的直隶水灾和1874年的山西大旱。

3. 关注各国在华的考察活动。鸦片战争后,外人纷纷来华考察、探险中国之地质与动植物等有关信息,文会十分关注这些活动,或在上海接待他们,或参与他们的考察活动。1874年李希霍芬在华考察结束,文会专门予以评论,"在华的商人将会记住他的功绩,因为他的探险活动所揭示的中华帝国那些未开发的资源信息将给商人们手中的企业一个巨大的希望"。[6]而"马嘉理事件"发生后,他们则认为大大影响了对西藏云南地区的地理考察。1865年英国支持的阿古柏入侵新疆的失败,文会认为它造成了英国对新疆和中亚的地理考察落后于俄国。

除了大事回顾外,这一时期文会还专门举办了三场关于中国时政的演讲:卫三畏的《美国公使团赴京记》、艾约瑟的《苏州暴乱记》、耿惠廉(W. G. E. Cunningham)的《从上海到南京——穿越暴乱区》,这都是作者亲身经历。其中艾约瑟之文是他本人专门到苏州考察的结果,当时外侨非常关心战乱对商业的影响程度,他正是本着这个目的而去的。

总之,这一时期文会对于中国的内政是比较关注的,尤其是对中外关系有重大影响的事情。文会热衷于讨论这些问题的原因与当时的中外局势有巨大关系,两次鸦片战争使西方列强在华获得了一系列特权,但是由于中国社会固有的特性,并没有出现资本主义商品在中国倾销的现象,这不是英法等工业相对发达的西方列强所期望的,因此他们一直渴望中国能够尽可能地开放,从而真正实现其商业利益。文会这一时期又恰处于初创阶段,会员不是领馆内的外交人员就是来华商人。雒魏林、麦都思等人不仅是传教士,同时也兼任各个领使馆内的翻译、

---

[1] Little, Archibald John, Respect of Events in China for the year 1875, JNCBRAS, P316.
[2] Editoral Committee, Record of Occurrences in China, JNCBRAS, O. S. Vol. I, No. 3., P248.
[3] Bucher, C. H., Retrospect of Events in the North of China during 1866, JNCBRAS, Vol. III, P118.
[4] Jamieson, R. A., Retrospect of Events in the North of China during 1861 to 1864, JNCBRAS, Vol. I, P157.
[5] Canny, J. M., Respect of Events in China, etc., 1871 and 1872, JNCBRAS, Vol. VII, P249.
[6] Little, Archibald John., Respect of Events in China for the year 1875, JNCBRAS, Vol. X, P323.

领事等职务。可以说,这一时期文会成员代表了当时在华的英美侨民的主要阶层,自然会提出上述商业侵略色彩较浓的言论。

1876年后文会会刊没有了"中国大事回顾"这个栏目,虽然也偶有关于中国社会的大事的讨论和研究,但是这些文章属于专门研究的很少,多数则散见于个人的旅行日记中。中国此后发生的数个重要事情都未予以关注,1883—1884年中法战争爆发,但这两年文会演讲题目和会刊的文章既没有云南地区的调查报告,也没有中国政治与外交方面的研讨文章,相反这两年关于佛教和中西交通方面的研究论文有数篇。对中国近代社会和中外关系产生重要影响的甲午战争爆发后,文会同样没有对此表现出一丝的关怀。1893—1895年主要讨论的是当时国际东方学关注的宗教、民俗、语言等问题,如李提摩太的《〈大乘起信论〉纲要》、穆麟德的《比较语言学的局限》、艾约瑟的《华南土著:他们的语言、宗教和风俗》(演讲稿)。戊戌维新后,只有英国领事班德瑞(F. S. A. Bourne)在一次演讲中随便提到,希望在华外人关注中国发生的大事,此年的演讲却没有与中国政治事件有紧密关系的文章。对于随之发生的许多在华外侨和传教士死于战乱的"庚子事变"和次年的《辛丑条约》,文会同样没有这方面的内容,即便是间接性的。这两年他们讨论和研究了成都平原的灌溉设施、孟子及其他中国古代哲学家、苗族的风俗等问题。此后半个世纪文会演讲和发表的文章更趋向学术化,勉强能够与中国内政拉上关系的也只有1936年耿爱德(Edward Kann)的《中国通货之发展与最近的货币改革》、1940年的《中国历史上的战争与和平观》、1949年4月7日演讲的《中国战胜封建主义:帝国的终结》,但这三篇文章是以学术论文的形式出现,根本不同于以前大事回顾中的研讨风格,作者在言谈之间更没流露出时政对中外关系的影响。因此,可以说1876年后文会已不再关注中国的时政问题。

文会自创立至结束,历经95年,此间中国经历了第二次鸦片战争、太平天国运动、洋务运动、中法战争、中日战争、戊戌变法、义和团运动、辛亥革命、五四运动、抗日战争、解放战争、新中国成立等一系列重大事件。文会在整个近代历史时期曾经一度关注过第二次鸦片战争、太平天国和洋务运动,但这只是文会工作中很少的一部分,文会的重心还是在对中国历史、地理、风俗、文化的调查研究上,1876年后对华调查研究的学术色彩日益浓厚。文会经历一个从对中国时政有所关注到不再关注的演变过程。

二、由调查走向研究

文会对中国的调查研究共计有944个题目。[1] 这些题目既有调查报告、地理游记,也有规范的学术论文。通过对这些文章内容的分析发现文会经历了一个由调查走向学术研究的演变过程。19世纪,尤其是1895年以前,文会是以调查为主,研究为辅。

文会对中国的调查活动有三种形式:一是由文会理事会发起,以文会名义组织的调查活动,这类调查经费由文会承担,参与的会员最多。调查结果以报告的形式刊登于会刊上,有的调查报告也发行单行本。一种是文会委托他人代替文会调查,调查者多由所在地之外侨担任。另外一种是会员个人的调查活动,该类调查多系作者个人搜集的一些地方资料或是游记性质的观察记录。

1895年前的调查活动主要是前两类。这些调查具有明确的考察目标、详细的考察过程、

---

[1] 注:会刊676篇文章(包括17篇调查报告、26篇杂纂类文章),演讲共计703个题目(已确知)。其中335篇文章是演讲后又发表在会刊上的,所以共计有944个题目。

规范的考察报告,因而有很高的科学价值。文会理事会发起的调查活动主要有:

黄河新河道考察。1867年文会组织了黄河新河道考察委员会,由爱莲斯(Elias)和荷魏尔(H. G. Hollingworth)两人担任。1867年9月24日到11月20日,两人徒步到江苏、河南、山东三省,考察了1855年铜瓦厢决口后黄河河道的变迁情况,绘制了清晰的黄河新河道图(张秋镇—入海口)。对于黄河新河道的水文特征、航运能力、河道沿岸的商业贸易、山东境内的物产情况均做了详细的记录,本次考察耗银565.81两银。[1] 由于贡献杰出,爱莲斯因此获得了英国皇家地理学会(Royal Geographical Society)金奖。[2]

1884-1885年的"中国各地溺婴陋俗"调查。本次调查由文会理事会向广东、江西、湖北、福建、安徽、直隶、北京、上海、山西、辽宁等地外国侨民发函,要求他们调查所在地的溺婴陋俗。目标是"为何出现溺婴陋俗? 与其他地方相比,程度如何?"共有17人回信。调查结果为:①溺婴现象的根源:贫困、生育观念、夫权思想、灵魂转世说;②溺婴的时间:一般在出生后不久;③性别:主要是女婴,男婴很少;④溺婴的方式;⑤溺婴的阶层:主要集中于中下层社会;⑥溺婴的地域差异:农村远远多于城市。后者少的原因是女性在城市容易销售,而且城市有慈善机构可以收养弃婴。⑦中国法律对于溺婴的处罚:有条文,但不执行,也不受重视。结论:溺婴在中国十分普遍,其动机和程度为世界其他地方所罕见。

1885年的"何为孝"的调查。1885年6月由当时的《北华捷报》编辑巴尔福(F. H. Balfour)提议,向各地外侨发出45件信函,调查各地对于孝的看法。针对以下问题作了调查:①孝观念产生的历史与发展;②孝观念的涵义;③中国人是如何灌输孝观念的;④中国人是如何履行"孝"的;⑤"孝"对中国社会产生了哪些正、负影响;⑥如何将基督教和孝观念融合,或是用前者改造后者,其中主要就"孝对中国社会产生的正、负影响"作了详细的调查。在这次调查中,参与者几乎都基于西方的近代平等思想,对中国的孝观念予以猛烈批评。他们承认孝是一种美德,对中国民族的凝聚力和家庭的稳定与和睦方面起了重要作用,但是更多的人还是认为孝对中国社会的负面作用要远远大于正面影响。其负面影响有:①它不符合法律的平等性;②在现实社会中,孝流于说教和伪善,这样不仅发挥不了应有的优点,反而阻碍了中国政府和社会迈向文明的步伐;③"父母在,不远游"限制了中国社会的人口流动,也丧失了中国人到外国学习先进文明的机会;④"不孝有三,无后为大"导致了女婴的遗弃;⑤"敬老"、"崇贞"剥夺了丧偶妇女再婚的权力;⑥"父母之命"压制了青年人追求幸福婚姻的愿望;⑦守孝时间太久,对于官员个人和国家来说都是浪费;⑧对孝要求太高,阻碍了有才能的人获取治理国家的机会。

1887年的"中国合伙企业成员的责任和义务"调查。上海、汉口、广州、天津、牛庄等地的英国(H. B. M.)领事和其他会员参与了本次活动。他们调查了以下内容:①在一个三人组成的股份制商号中,根据中国法律和惯例,三人如何来承担共同的债务? 各自的比例应该是多少? ②在一个家族商号中,家族财产和商号财产如何区别? 是否用家族财产来偿还商号债务?[3]

1886年的"用汉语传播西方知识的正反效果"调查。该项调查是由翟理思提议、夏德发起,参加者有丁韪良、狄考文(C. W. Mateer)、慕维廉、傅兰雅、玛高温、花之安、白挨底、费习孟

---

[1] Report of the Council of the North-China Branch of the Royal Asiatic Society for 1868, JNCBRAS, No. V, Pxi.
[2] The North-China Branch of the Royal Asiatic Society, North-China Herald, 30th, Oct., 1873. P361.
[3] Chinese Partnership: Libertrary of the Individual Members, JNCBRAS, Vol. XXII, P39.

(S. Ritter Von Fries)、邓罗（C. H. Brewitt-Taylor）、啊查理、詹美生等人，几乎全是在华的著名传教士。他们针对汉语在传播西方文明，尤其是在传播自然科学中的效果展开了调查和讨论。一方认为汉语难以精确表达西方文明的原意，比如化学翻译中出现的元素符号，汉语就很难有合适的对应词汇，因此反对用汉语传播西方文明；另一方持肯定态度，认为汉语可以吸取其他语言的词汇，完全能够传播西方文明。最终达成"面对中国知识阶层对西方文明持惊奇的眼光时，必须让中国人学习掌握外国语言，培养一个有学问的阶层，这样才能真正地向中国传播西方文明"。[1]

1888年的"中国佃制及农民状况"调查。参与者为文会各地会员和各地传教士，他们中有李提摩太、欧森南（E. L. oxenham）、费笠子（George phillips）、哲美森（George Jamieson）等人。本次调查文会制定了调查问卷，设计了以下问题：[2]①中国各地农庄的面积；②这些农庄内地主和劳动者之间的比例是多少？采用何种雇佣方式？③如果是租借方式，每亩租金是多少？是用银两还是其他方式付租金？或者是用哪种农作物付租金？地主占有土地的数量是多少？是否存在拥有1 000亩、10 000亩土地的地主？④每亩谷物的产量有多少斤？当地的谷物价格是多少？⑤每亩土地的平均赋税是多少？政府是如何收取赋税的？是直接收取还是间接缴纳？

从调查报告看，内容涉及16个省份的土地所有权的历史及变更，租佃的具体方式，地方官、地主、自耕农之间的关系，不同形态土地的产量，不同作物的产量、各地的粮食价格和各地的农业人口等。调查得十分详细，李提摩太对山东莱州、河北武清的调查项目达32项，细微到佃农的日工资和不同等级的土地产量，无论其调查方法还是调查成果，现在看来仍具参考价值。

1889年的"中国的货币与度量衡"调查。1889年文会向各地传教士及文会会员发出通知，要求他们调查各自所在省份的度量衡，经过近一年的调研，1890年由马士汇总出初稿，内容涵盖17省39府的银两名称、重量及所含的标准实银量；14省30府的重量单位及差异；11省19府的土地单位——亩的差异。[3]

1890－1894年的"中国之内陆交通"调查。本次调查旨在考察清楚内地各省的陆路交通路线，"因为当时世界其他国家的铁路路线证明大都是沿着已有几千年历史的人类、骡子所行走的路线"。1892年收到各个省份报告有云南5篇，江苏4篇，甘肃3篇，山西3篇，直隶2篇，安徽2篇，台湾、广东、河南、陕西、海南、广西、蒙古各1篇。[4]调查项目涉及各地商路（古今道路之演变）、矿藏及其开发、货物的运输成本、主要运输货物、重要的桥梁（包括桥梁的跨度、石块的重量）、栈道以及各地电报部门制作的旅游地图。调查报告中所绘制的地图使用了李希霍芬、马士等人的最新的度量单位，而不再是中国的"里"。[5]本次调查报告究竟是否被19世纪末在华争夺铁路修建权的列强所利用，目前尚不清楚，但是从本次调查的操作和参与者的只言片语所透出的信息看，文会实际上已经意识到列强在华修建铁路的时代已经来到。

---

［1］Giles, H. A., The Advisability or the Reverse of endeavouring to convey Western Knowledge to the Chinese through the medium of their own Language, JNCBRAS, Vol. XXI, P1.
［2］Jamieson, George, Tenure of Land in China and the Condition of the Rural Population, JNCBRAS, Vol. XXIII, pp59－118.
［3］Morse, Hosea Ballou, Abstract of Information on Currency and Measures in China, JNCBRAS, Vol. XXIV, pp1－96.
［4］Proceedings, JNCBRAS, Vol. XXV, P470.
［5］Emil S. Fischer, Modern Travel From Tai Yuan Fu via Mount Wu Tai to the Mongolian Frontier, JNCBRAS, Vol. LIV, P81.

这一时期文会委托他人的调查活动主要集中于对中国地质、气象、水文等方面信息的考察。

1857—1858年,由英国的各个船长负责观察、记录所在地的地磁倾角,他们调查了上海、宁波、香港、新加坡、广州等地不同时期的地磁倾角变化情况。

1859年的上海和日本长崎气温变化。由船长约翰·伍德(John Ward)负责调查,内容包括1859年上海和长崎两地每天的气压、温度,早上、上午、晚上三个时间点的风向、干湿情况。

1887年9月至1889年4月,理事会委托 H. M. M. "Rambler"海军中校莫尔(R. N. Moore)对杭州钱塘江海潮作了详细的考察。主要内容有:①海潮的次数、海潮到达的具体地点、海潮的高度、到达时的具体时间、速度及状态;②钱塘江海潮现象的原因。

1859年罗伯逊调查了湖北、湖南、江西、安徽、福建、广东、云南、浙江等省份的具体产茶地,对于安徽、浙江的绿茶做了较详细的叙述。

这一时期个人的单独考察,与文会组织的调查活动相比,个人考察更加随意、自由,没有规范的调查报告,调查内容也比较随机,主要是关于中国各地的地理地质概况、天文气象、动植物和民俗风情。

1866年丁韪良的《1866年2、3月间北京至上海的陆上之旅》。作者路经北京、保定、开封、徐州、上海,建议"修一条大沽至开封的铁路,这样华北地区的煤铁资源便可以得到开发利用,河北的铁用来做铁轨,山西的煤做燃料。有了铁路,军队可以迅速调遣,举子可以赴京考试,商人转运商品不必再走运河、雇推车"。"从政治和商业方面看,考察黄河是当务之急。如果开放黄河航运,中外都可受益。对于外商而言,可以打开一片长江难以所及的广阔市场;对于中国而言,盗匪之抢劫行为可以被消除。希望我们的外长在1866年修约时记住这些"。[1]

1866年韦廉臣(A. Williamson)的《北京出发经大运河、兖州府等至芝罘之旅》。作者详细观察了临清等地的商业情况,重点还是考虑黄河新河道的航运能力,"这条新河道为我们打开了通向富庶而繁荣的华北大地之路。通过黄河与其他几条小河流,我们可以进入鲁西南、河南、苏北、山西"。"以前烟台的外国商品要经过陆路托运至黄河,现在可以经新黄河河道水运,从而避免了转运之繁琐"。

1872年英国驻汕头领事郇和的《海南探险记》。作者考察沿途河流和城市,内容涉及街道、城墙、寺院、语言、服饰等,但更重要的还在于各个港口的水深,新安江、南渡江等河流的航运能力,海南东北山地的矿藏资源。作者提出"回去之后,要告诉欧洲人,并希望他们获得开采当地铜矿的权利"。"道台希望根据条约开放海口港口,这样当地的商业贸易可以得到刺激,尤其希望外国蒸汽火轮驶来,这正是我们要调查的重要商业信息"。[2]

1875年美国公理会教士、外交官何天爵(Chester Holcombe)的《陕西和山西旅行记》。作者经北京、正定、获鹿、固关、平定、太原、霍州、蒲州、西安,描写了沿途之地貌、聚落、桥梁、城墙、矿藏、人口、市场等内容。作者也提出了山西煤炭资源的价值,认为"山西中部将成为中国的匹兹堡和伯明翰"。[3] 不过,这不是全文的重心所在,也不是作者观察的焦点,确切地说,是作者的旅行见闻记录。

---

[1] Martin, W. A. P., Account of an Overland Journey from Peking to Shanghai, JNCBRAS, Vol. III, P27、36.

[2] Swinhoe, R., Narrative of an Exploring Visit to Hainan, JNCBRAS, Vol. VII, P83、46.

[3] Holcombe, Chester, Notes made on a Tour through Shang-his and Shen-his, JNCBRAS, Vol. X, P19.

1883—1884年英国驻福建领事庄延龄的福建、浙江旅行记,对沿途观察得十分详细,所到城镇都要考察其历史、街道、民风、人口、建筑、交通、土地、物产、方言、风俗等基本情况,但是作者尤其注重各地商业状况、物价差异、河道运输能力、外国商品的影响范围、矿藏开发等商业信息。该文不同于何天爵的山西、陕西旅行考察记,庄氏流露出对福建、浙江沿途各种潜在商业信息的关注。

除了地理、矿藏调查外,会员还对各地的自然资源作了调查。1859年郇和就调查了台湾地区发现的新鸟类物种。

这一时期文会成员对中国其他方面也进行了初步的研究。但是由于作者大多来华不久,语言的限制使他们对中国历史、语言、文献的研究处于初步的水平,很多文章都是泛泛概述和注释,没有引用相关的资料予以深入佐证。如裨治文的《苗族概述》、玛高温的《中国的文献学》,前者只是翻译了一本中国人的手稿,列出了当时中国的28支不同苗族的大致情况;后者只是提出对中国方志的收集与研究。也有一些对具体问题做初步探讨的文章,如艾约瑟的《孔子的生平》、金斯密的《关于周朝建立者周文王的传说》,但是这些文章也都十分肤浅,限于介绍的水平,都是简单的叙述一下主人公的生活年代、官职与地位等情况。当然也有一些水平较高的论文出现,这些文章一般资料比较丰富、论证相对严密,如伟烈亚力以实地考察和史料结合的方法指出"古代的云梦泽和洞庭湖无联系","荆江河道的历史变迁",[1]但是这类文章数量极为有限。

相对而言,这一时期对自然科学方面研究的水平要高于对历史文化的研究。如,费理饬的《东亚气候》(1877)分析了1858—1875年东亚的气温、洋流、季风、云量、风雪等气候因素,每一种因素都做了日变化和年变化的分析,文中保存有1858—1875数个地方的观测资料,制作了数十页的洋流、气温变动图,此文对于研究"丁戊奇荒"时期的气候情况非常有用。福威勒(A. A. Fauvel)的《中国的短吻鳄》(1878)一文,先查找中国文献中的"鳄",然后叙述中外有关研究成果,再从动物学的角度研究它,解剖并分析它的各个部分,全文不仅资料丰富,而且绘图准确,至今看来仍不失其科学性。自然科学方面水平较高的论文还有西蒙的《中国和日本古生物学和地质学研究刍议》;能恩斯(M. S. J. Dechevrens)(徐家汇天文台台长)的《上海的气候》、安德森(Anderson, G. C)的《福州闽江河谷发现的几种蕨类植物》、古庇的《南口关岩层小析》、F. W. Schulze 的《地磁周期变化》。但是自然方面更多的也是考察与收集地质、气象、矿藏、动植物等方面的信息。

总之,1857—1895年文会对于中国还处于调查认识阶段,对华的认识图像还相当粗略,会员的研究也比较肤浅和初步。这是因为,一,鸦片战争打开了中断百余年的中西交往,这次开放的广度和深度是以前所未有的,战后来华外侨已不像以前那样仅限于传教士,还有商人和外交官,他们不仅要传教,还要从商谋利、扩张殖民侵略。所以,对中国各方面有一个大致的、初步的了解是来华各色外人先做的事情。二,这一时期来华外人尚不具备娴熟运用汉语的水平,大多数人还难以读懂中国的文献典籍,语言的限制使他们只能从事资料的收集和自然的考察等方面的工作,还没达到深入研究分析中国社会的阶段。三,对华自然的调查和研究相对深入,是因为近代欧美自然科学体系的建立使他们拥有相对完备的科学手段和方法来对中国的自然做科学的调查和分析,相对人文而言,困难要小得多。所以这一阶段对中国的自然界的考察和研究要远远多于对人文社会的调查和研究,而且水平也高于后者。

---

[1] Wylie, A., Itnerary of a Journey through the Provinces of Hoo-pih, Szechuen, and Shen-se, JNCBRAS, Vol. V, P190.

20世纪后,文会进入了研究的时代。从调查到研究也不是一蹴而就的,从会刊内容和演讲主体看,1895年以后已经呈现出由调查走向研究、由自然走向人文的趋向。1900年,班德瑞就对文会粗浅介绍中国提出了批评:"我们不能仅仅满足于翻译、评论、删节,这样的后果是传承下来的知识难以扩大,并存在对于许多知识的误解和不合适的使用。……我们不能仅仅再编目录和索引,而要贡献出坚实的硕果。……我们是一个亚洲学会,我们在上海,我们理所当然地研究中国和中国人。我们决不允许我们成为仅仅记录中国、读写汉语的人,这是我们首先要改革的。"[1]在文会理事会的努力和学术本身的推动下,20世纪文会发表演讲的文章已不再是简单的调查资料和文献整理,而有了研究型的文章了。这一时期文会演讲篇目之内容很能反映这一趋向(详见表5-1)。

此表反映文会研究的两个趋势:一是自然类的调查研究1895年后逐渐退缩,中国历史、语言、考古、艺术方面的研究逐步占据主流;二是调查类的文章已不再是会员的主要贡献,研究型的论文占据主流,这从地理与游记可以反映出来,虽然1895年后的此类文章比1895年前还多,但是年平均数量却要大大少于以前,而且文章的篇幅也很短。

表5-1　　　　　　　　　　文会演讲、发表文章分类统计表　　　　　　　　　　(单位:篇)

类　别	1857－1895年	1896－1951年
地理、游记	53	54
地　质	24	14
气　象	9	5
天　文	6	6
历　史	36	37
考　古	3	8
艺　术	2	46
陶　瓷	1	10
民　俗	11	24
民　族	11	24
文　学	7	9
中医史	1	8
文　字	2	6

注:分类标准参照会刊1912年、1924年之分类标准,篇数系笔者自己统计。

这一时期,文会对于中国历史的研究已不再是大而化之的简单讨论,已转入具体问题的论述。同样是论及孔子,前后明显能够看出学术的进步。1860年艾约瑟只是简单地介绍一下孔子的小传。1886年,啊查理则对孔子本人的真实历史地位提出了质疑,作者认为孔子的地位、声望及其著作多由其门人造作而成。[2] 1925年杜德明(J. W. Dovey)论及孔子时,已从其生

---

[1] Bourne, Frederick Sarmuel Augustus, Possible and Impossible Reforms, JNCBRAS, Vol. XXXIII, pp1－2.
[2] Allen, Harbert. J., Is Confucius a Myth? JNCBRAS, Vol. XXI, pp193－198.

平年代来考察这个历史人物了,分析得比较深入和客观。[1]文会对中国货币的研究,更能反映出这种变化趋势,参见表5-2:

表5-2　　　　　　　　　　　文会对中国的货币研究文章

篇　名	作　者	年　份
大清货币	伟烈亚力	1858
中国小型钱庄概要	西　蒙	1868
大清钱币	卜士礼	1880
安南及其钱币	多　达	1883
中国货币考	马　士	1907
中国货币综录(专著)	骆任廷	1915
民国的铸币	罗　斯	1917
中国的黄金	耿爱德	1929
商周时代的货币贝壳	裘必胜	1940

资料来源:1858、1868、1880、1885、1907、1915、1917、1929、1940年会刊。

伟烈亚力的《大清货币》只是列举了1644—1857年间中央及各个省份发行的各类货币,对于每个货币列举其名称、金属含量、制造时间、主要标记以及部分货币的发行量。文中所选货币"多数《大清会典事例》已收录,部分罕见特殊之货币资料则来源于《选青小笺》、《钱币考》、《钱谱提纲》"。[2]可以看出该文旨在向外国人介绍大清货币,还谈不上研究。西蒙的《中国小型钱庄概要》也只是列举了各类制钱与主币之间的换算数量,目的在于方便在华外人的商业贸易。卜士礼的《大清钱币》是延续和补充伟烈亚力之《大清货币》,主要是1857—1880年间清朝各地新发行的货币,而且也是转抄于中文文献,"所有货币资料来源于《古今钱略》和《大泉图录》"。[3]1883年多达的《安南及其钱币》主要是介绍1877年版《古今钱略》中描述的当时中国人收藏的早期外国货币,实际上主要是历史时期各个边疆少数民族发行的货币。

1907年马士的《中国货币考》已经显示出研究的水平,该文在翟理思、艾约瑟和骆任廷等人的研究成果基础上比较系统地论述中国货币的沿革史,先后述及物物交换、无字货币、刀布货币、雕饰货币(有字和图,如秦半两钱、楚蚁鼻钱、唐宋元明清各朝发行的主要铜钱),纸币则论述了唐之飞钱、北宋之交子和便钱、南宋之关子与会子、金之宝钞、元明之宝钞、清之汇票;银两货币则有元朝的银锭、明清的马蹄银及各种银两货币。每一种货币都论述了发行的背景、流通的时间、存世情况与收藏价值。作者还对各个时期主币与辅币、银两与铜钱间的换算比例进行了详细的论述,尤其是清朝时期各地银两货币所含标准实银的差异和换算标准,如库平银与行化银、漕平与市平间的具体换算方法,上海的九八规银与标准实银间的换算公式都作了详细的列举。该文共计60页,已大大突破了此前只简单地列举各种货币图案的水平,可以说是一

---

[1] Dovey, J. W., The Life and Times of Confucious, JNCBRAS, Vol. LVI, pp51-69.
[2] Wylie, A., Coins of the Ta-Ts'ing or Present Dynasty of China, Journal of the Shanghai Literary and Scientific Society, No. I, Jun., 1858, P44.
[3] Bushell, S. W., Coins of the Present Dynasty of China, JNCBRAS, Vol. XV, P195.

部中国货币简史。

1917年罗斯(G. Ros)的《民国的铸币》已经是一篇像样的学术论文了。该文一开始就是学术史的回顾,"在中国有许多关于旧钱币的论著,但是至今仍没有一篇是论述关于当今货币的文章;欧洲人还无暇关注中华民国的货币,关于这方面的欧洲语言作品太少了,也难说有什么学术贡献"。[1] 然后又谈了《日本钱币与集邮杂志》(The Numismatic and Philatelic, Journal of Japan, 1912 – 1914)、美国钱币学会(American Numismatic Society)主办的《货币学家》(The Numismatist)上的两篇涉及民国铜钱的论文。全文论述了民国初年新旧货币体制的转变过程及其对民国货币的影响。主要内容则有财政部币泉司的建立,"袁大头"银元的发行、各省制作的银元、铜钱及这些货币的内容与发行背景。

《商周时代的贝壳货币》作者已经能够运用《卜辞通纂》、《缀遗斋彝器考释》、《说文句读》、《古籀汇编》等中文相关专著,通过文字的变化论证了贝壳从商以前的装饰品到商时代的货币和周朝货币市场的形成这一演变过程。提出"商以前,中国人存在迷信和崇拜,用已雕饰的贝壳挂在腹部作为装饰品和辟邪物,并逐渐成为爱与美之神的象征,商朝时期这种风俗逐渐失去"。[2]

1920年后文会更呈现出个案研究的色彩,很多文章都是从小处入手,做深入分析和论证。这在下文各国对华之研究将有详细论述。

由资料整理到具体问题论证的转变,这主要还是学术本身的发展的结果。经过半个多世纪的发展,外人的足迹已经涉入中国的各个地方和各个领域,虽然还谈不上深入认识中国,但是前文(第一章)所述外人进入中国时所要求了解的数十个问题(即香港支会要调查的各个项目)已经得以解决。在文化领域,中外词典已经编纂出版,中国经书已经被翻译到西方世界,关于中国哲学、语言、历史三方面的通史著作也已在欧美面世。在此基础上学者们对于中国的研究自然无需再做文献方面的泛泛译介,自然会转入较为具体的问题讨论。这个时期"汉学在各个领域正走向专业化"。[3] 就文会本身而言,虽然规定其目标是致力于对中国社会的调查研究,但是缺乏明确详细的规则和目标,只要是关于中国的研究达到一定的水平,就能够演讲和发表,这样的后果是会员研究什么课题纯属个人意愿。进入20世纪后,在华外人亦不同于19世纪,许多人要为生活而奔波,能够专门做学问的时间已经很少了,转入具体问题之研究也是时代所决定的。

第二节 空间差异

由于各国文化背景的不同和各国外侨在华流动区域的差异,文会中来自各个国家的会员对华的调查研究,无论是内容还是地点,都存在着明显的差异。这里选取英、美、法、德、俄作为主要考察对象,不仅仅是因为文会中这几个国家的会员最多、供稿最多,更重要的是因为这几个国家在近代世界舞台上最为活跃,与中国接触也最为密切。这几个国家对中国的认识能够代表近代西方对中国的认识,也能够反映出近代中西文化交流的主要脉络和线索。

---

[1] Ros. Giuseppe, Dr., Coins of the Republic of China, JNCBRAS., Vol. XLVIII, P118.

[2] Gibson, Harry E., Cowries as Money During the Shang and Chou Periods, JNCBRAS, Vol. LXXI, P35.

[3] Proceedings, JNCBRAS, Vol. XLIII, P189.

一、不同国家会员对华之调查研究

（一）英国

无论在自然还是人文方面,英国人之对华调查研究所涉及的领域都是最广的,已知英国籍会员的文章有379篇,他们的成果涉及36个学科。

地理和游记方面:英国人的足迹几乎遍布中国的各个省份,这是近代其他国籍的在华外人所没有的。从时间上看,很多地方英国人也是走在其他国家的前列。19世纪英国人的足迹主要是两个地带,一是长江流域:他们主要沿着长江顺水而上,从上海一直到四川。一是华北、华东地区,包括东北、直隶、山东、江苏、浙江、湖南、广东、海南省份,这一地区他们的旅行路线有三条:1.京杭大运河,杭州以南走金华、衢州,翻越仙霞岭,然后沿闽江经建宁、延平进入福州;2.南北官道:沿太行山经保定、大名、开封、洛阳、襄樊、荆州、宜昌、汉口、岳阳,沿湘江经长沙、湘潭、衡阳、郴州、越南岭、过韶关到广州;3.俄罗斯——蒙古草原——晋北、北京。

表5-3　　　　　　　　　　英国籍会员文章类别及篇数表

类别	篇数	类别	篇数	类别	篇数
历史	68	人类学	7	地质	18
游记	44	社会学	6	自然科学	14
宗教	41	文献	6	动物	14
民俗	23	音乐	6	天文	11
文学	13	法律	5	建筑	6
经济	13	钱币	5	医学	6
语言	12	碑刻	3	气象	5
艺术	11	雕塑	1	植物	5
哲学	10	机构	1	博物	1
民族	10	教育	1	水文	1
考古	9	东方学	1	生物	1
政治	7	其他	1	农业	1

资料来源:文会会刊和附表1。
注:分类和统计是由笔者自己完成的。

这一时期他们所注意的主要是各地的基本信息,比如:人口、交通、语言、地理位置、服饰、地貌等,但是作者在这些游记中也流露出了对各地商业信息的浓厚兴趣。1869年英国外交官马安(J. Markham)的《山东纪略:从烟台到邹县之旅》考察的内容除了沿途各个城市的概况外,主要还是各地的商业状况和矿藏资源。作者对潍县和博山煤矿煤层之厚度、开采技术、工人数量、产量、价格、运费、税收都作了详细的记录。对于各个城市的商业店铺、主要商品、商业习惯、官商关系、文明程度、对外态度、交通要道也都一一描述。[1] 英国驻福建领事庄延龄在《浙江行记》、《福州行记》中同样详细叙述了沿途的商业行情。作者述及青田与温州之间的贸易往来时,提出"中国政府应早日开放温州,对外建成一个自由港,这样就可以充分发挥瓯江的

---

[1] Markhan, J., Notes on the Shanntung Province, being a Journey from Chefoo to Tsinhsien, JNCBRAS, Vol. VI, pp1–30.

运输能力"。[1] 他还了解到"中国各地都有定期的集市,北京为'会',广东为'墟',四川为'场'"。[2]

除了商业信息,英国籍会员也会注意一些社会现象,如贾礼士经过对大运河航运能力详细调查后,指出"就整个大运河而言,漕运的功能是失败的。……1850 年黄河决口和 1878 年黄河再次改道入侵运河,结果是内陆航运已彻底废弃"。结论是"由西方来帮助中国修建铁路,才能使这个悲惨贫困的国家迈向幸福的生活"。[3]

20 世纪后英国人在华的旅行主要集中于西南数省和新疆地区。对于新疆主要是放眼于中亚考古,以斯坦因考古为主。西南地区,英国人所到之地较多,大多是由长江到成都,然后北经岷江河谷进入松潘草原,南沿乌江进入黔、滇。西南地区,他们主要观察和记录各地各民族的民俗。如花荪(W. C. H. Waston)的《松潘行记》就描述了四川的挑夫、成都的街道、警察的制服、灌县的概况、都江堰、李冰祠堂,汶川县苗民的村落、风俗,松潘草原的景色、藏人的管理机构——厅,苗民的舞蹈、娱乐。甘福履(F. W. Carey)的《从思茅至仰光纪行》则对云南境内的掸族作了详细的描述,包括他们的语言、生活习惯、外貌与体型特征、服饰、信仰(多数是佛教徒)。爱司克夫人的《四川及长江峡谷小记》主要叙述四川境内长江沿岸的历史故事,比如杜甫、关羽等历史人物和祠堂建筑。

历史方面,内容主要集中于历史地理、考古和历史人物三方面。

1. 历史地理

19 世纪英国人对中国古代的漳州、南京、绍兴、和林、西安等城市展开了初步研究。费笠子通过《元史》、《三山续志》、《福建通志》等文献再现了元朝时期福建地区的政区沿革,考证出漳州在元朝时曾一度做过福建地区的分省治所,从而纠正了裕尔编的《马可波罗》和《不列颠百科全书》(Encyclopaedia Britannican)中关于漳州记载的谬误。华立熙(Willam Gilbert Walshe)的《古代绍兴》则详述了自尧到清咸丰年间的绍兴城的沿革简史及其周围的舆地、形胜、传说、艺文等。此外,他们也初步论述了元代蒙古旧都和林及附近聚落遗址和明代之南京。但这几篇城市沿革研究文章水平很一般,既没有新的资料,也没有运用新的方法,即便是近代欧洲学者所擅长的历史语言学方法,换言之,这些文章实际上仅仅是翻译、转述中国的文献而已。

令人疑惑的是近代汉学史上的研究热点——中西交通史,英国人并没有太多的贡献。他们只是论及了两汉时期的"大秦"和历史时期的丝绸之路。19 世纪金斯密、艾约瑟和白挨底、啊查理等人只是在夏德的《中国与东罗马》一书基础上,对"大秦"和中亚至阿拉伯交通路线做了一些质疑和补充,实际上并没有开拓出新的研究领域。[4] 1928 年英国人又依据《史记》、《汉书》、《后汉书》中的《张骞传》、《大宛传》、《西域传》重现了两汉对西域的经营。但是英国人是以欧洲中心主义的观点来看待中外之间的交流,艾约瑟在《古代中国对希腊和罗马的了解》一文中就说"欧洲的思想和希腊的艺术正是通过这些道路(波斯——印度——中国)传入到中国"。[5]

---

[1] Parker, E. H., A Journal in Chekiang, JNCBRAS, Vol. XIX, P29.
[2] Parker, E. H., A Journal from Foochow to Wenchow through central Fukien, JNCBRAS, Vol. XIX, P86.
[3] Carles, W. R., The Grand Canal of China, JNCBRAS, Vol. XXXI, P107、115.
[4] Kingsmill, T. W., Review: Dr. F. Hirth and the Hiung Nu, JNCBRAS, Vol. XXXIV, P154.
[5] Edkins, J., What did the Ancient Chinese Know of the Greeks and Romans? JNCBRAS, Vol. XVIII, P15.

林仰山(F. S. Drake)的《中国西北通道》则说"西汉对西域的控制和西去道路的开辟,其结果,外国的物品是通过中亚国家进入中国,对中国人的生活产生了重要的影响,那个时代的艺术便是明证"。[1]

2. 考古与文物方面

19世纪英籍会员参与了俄国人对叶尼塞河实地考察和考古的工程,收集了许多碑刻。[2] 20世纪英国人主要致力于出土文物的文字、陶俑的研究。他们研究了周代石鼓和陶俑上的文字、河南出土的甲骨文、西夏文字和一些碑刻上的铭文。卜士礼结合唐代陕西凤翔府出土的周代石鼓和中国文献,追溯了历代中国学者对石鼓年代的考证和每条石鼓上的文字及释义。卜士礼依据西夏的数枚铜钱上的文字,确认了60个西夏文字之含义。[3] 库寿龄则对文会博物院内收藏的甲骨作了详细的描述,作者在中外论著的基础上探讨了部分甲骨文字的含义和商代的占卜。林仰山根据《史记》、《战国策》、《武英殿彝器图录》等文献解读了1939年8月在山东济南大辛庄出土的一件周代陶瓷上的文字。

3. 历史人物

金斯密的《关于周朝建立者周文王的传说》叙述了周文王创立周朝的历史,并与印度、埃及和德国的早期历史相对比,指出"从东方的中国到西方的威尔斯,从北欧的条顿人到尼罗河的埃及人,都流行着一个重要历史人物(国王),而且几乎都在大洪水时代之后的年代"。[4] 该文颇具宗教色彩,估计是为在华传教提供相关依据。艾约瑟的《郭子仪》只是依据《旧唐书》翻译、叙述了郭子仪小传和他平定"安史之乱"的过程,并无任何创新。天锡德(J. H. Teesadale)的《忠王李秀成》详细介绍了英国海关译员李华达的《忠王自传》,实际上就是李秀成的狱中自述。莫安仁的《周公》是借助《孟子》、《淮南子》、《绎史》、《史记》、《书经》及梁启超等人的著作与文献,详述了周公的生平及别人对他的评价。莫安仁还摘抄了《东华录》中关于康熙的生平事迹。

总体而言,英国人对中国历史之考察研究还处在叙述的层面上,实证性的研究要少于法国人、德国人,总体上的把握又不及美国人,显得零乱而肤浅。

民族方面:英国人的研究重点在于藏族及其他西南少数民族,在时间上,前后没有太大变化。庄延龄的《满洲与西藏的关系》叙述了藏族的历史、唐以来汉藏之交往、清朝对藏族的统治与管理、各种机构的设置、藏族的宗教、地理环境和人口,可以说是一册西藏简史。金斯密的《古代西藏及其前沿地带》则利用中国文献和已有的研究成果,结合人类学和民俗学的方法,考证了汉至元时期今西藏地区和川藏结合部的主流统治民族、中亚西亚地理的变化与古代藏族部落迁移的关系,纠正了沙畹的错误。叶长清通过实地考察指出地理环境对人的成长影响很大,它可以解释人们的思维、行为和性格。"高原气候使得这里的人们成为自然的奴隶,藏民逐渐形成一种野蛮的性格,这种环境使藏民既是牧民、农民也是商人"。[5]

对于西南的主要少数民族——苗族和羌族,英人大多是将中国史书中关于这些民族的记载罗列出来,只有部分在叙述中使用了"审音原则"加以考证,如金斯密的《四川的傈傈族》(演

---

[1] Drake, F. S., China's North-West Paeeage: A Chapter in Its Opening, JNCBRAS, Vol. LXVI, P49.

[2] Proceedings, JNCBRAS, Vol. XXVII, pp198 - 205.

[3] Bushell, S. W., The His Hsia Dynasty of Tangut, JNCBRAS, pp142 - 160.

[4] Kingsmill, T. W., The Legend of Wen Wang, Founder of the Dynasty of Chows in China, JNCBRAS, Vol. VIII, P29.

[5] Edgar, J. H., The Tibetan and His Environment: An Interpretation, JNCBRAS, Vol. LVII, P29.

讲稿)、普鲁恩夫人(Mrs. Pruen)的《族群的聚集:贵州黑苗的舞蹈》(演讲稿)。此外,英人也运用了田野调查的方法来研究苗、羌族。叶长清实地调查了四川威州和茂州地区的氐、羌、戎、吐蕃、夷、蛮等少数民族的当时生活状况,对羌族的宗教信仰,新年祭祀的时间、地点、祭祀物品、祭祀的具体方式都做了详细的记载。[1] 陶然士的《川西羌族》、王树德(W. H. Hudspeth)的《云南贵州的花苗》、《印度支那地区的华裔》更是从田野调查来考察这些民族的。

民俗学方面:英国会员比较注意中国人的民间信仰、称呼和葬礼。空间上集中于上海和西南地区。民间信仰,他们注意中国人所崇拜的各种神,其中以苏阿德的《中国动物主题神话》最具代表,该文将中国动物神话的历史渊源、种类、各种动物神话所衍生的图画、雕塑及寓意都作了深入的论述。苏阿德将中国的动物神话分为四类:宗教色彩的英雄和小丑;具有特殊疗效的中医动物;以农村日常生活所见到的各种鸟、鱼、爬行动物为基础而衍生出来各类神话;部分特殊的动物神话(比如《聊斋志异》中的人与动物的互相转变),并指出"中国的动物神话与道教、佛教紧密地联系在一起,也与史前时期各个民族的图腾、狩猎生活有密切的关系"。[2] 包克私(Ernest Box)则专门论述了上海及周边地区民间信仰,包括土地神、季节神和生死、婚嫁、鬼魂说等。[3] 丧葬习俗也是他们注意的一个方面。陶然士的《四川的丧葬习俗》采用田野考察的方法对四川成都地区的丧葬习俗作了深入的论述。作者描述了近代四川葬礼的习俗和方式、墓葬构成、不同阶层的坟墓建筑、殉葬品、明代以前的墓穴。并探究了两汉三国以来的丧葬习俗,从孝文化方面论证了中国人重视葬礼现象。[4]

宗教方面:1920年以前研究的几乎全部是佛教,此后才扩展至基督教、道教、伊斯兰教、景教和其他宗教信仰。佛教方面是比较具体的小课题,比如艾约瑟论述的佛经《壹输卢迦论》、倭讷对《妙法莲华经》的初步研究,慕稼谷则翻译了一张佛教版画及版画上的佛教说贴。但是由于语言的原因,19世纪"在华外人,除了少数几人外,很少注意中国人的宗教和相关的宗教文献",能够阅读和评述佛经内容的人更少了,他们几个也是仅有的关注中国佛教的外人了。倭讷的《〈妙法莲华经〉述评》之所以能够深入论述,还是因为艾约瑟、儒莲、毕欧(Edouard Constant Biot)等人对此佛经已经做了翻译和注释,尽管如此,如同作者所说,"由于佛教专有名词和术语仍是困扰学界的一大障碍","现有的注释成果也仅仅只有一些涉足了《妙法莲华经》的主要内容,还有更多的空间留待我们去研究"。[5]

20世纪随着佛教研究的成果日益增多,佛经的研究也逐步深入。英雅各(J. W. Inglis)对5种不同版本的《阿弥陀经》做了比较研究,包括《佛说无量清净平等觉经》、支谦译本《阿弥陀经》以及菩提流支、康僧铠、法贤等人的译本和及一个英文翻译的版本,通过比较这些版本的经文风格、翻译的差别,作者确认"《佛说无量清净平等觉经》和支谦的《阿弥陀经》是比较早的版本,佛之信仰也最早来源于这两个版本"。[6] 英国人还研究了大乘佛教和藏传佛教等佛教分支的经义,李提摩太不仅介绍了大乘佛教,而且将马鸣菩萨的《大乘起信论》予以翻译和详细介绍,从而将大乘佛教之渊源、经义清晰地呈现出来。内地会传教士徐丽生(Theodore

---

[1] Edgar, J. H., Notes on Ch'ing Sacrifice and Litholotry, JNCBRAS, Vol. LIII, P68.
[2] Sowerby, Arthur de C., Presidential Address: Some Chinese Animal Myths anf Legends, JNCBRAS, Vol. LXX, pp1-20.
[3] Box, Ernest., Shanghai Folk-Lore, JNCBRAS, Vol. XXXIV, pp101-135.
[4] Torrance, T., Burial Customs in Sz-chuen, JNCBRAS, Vol. XLI, pp57-75.
[5] Watters, T., Notes on the Miao-Fa-Lien-Hua-Ching, A Buddhist Sutra in Chinese, JNCBRAS, Vol. IX, P114.
[6] Inglis, J. W., The Vows of Amida, JNCBRAS, Vol. XLVIII, P10.

Sörensen)则向外人介绍了藏传佛教。

1920年后英国人对中国宗教的研究所涉及的课题远多于以前,他们研究了道教、伊斯兰教、摩尼教、基督教以及羌人和汉人的宗教信仰。这些研究中,伊斯兰教相对深入。梅益盛依据中国史书、阿拉伯商人旅行游记、碑刻等文献和清真寺的建筑风格全面考察了伊斯兰教进入中国的时间和途径,对公认的刘介廉的《穆斯林的生活》一文中关于穆斯林已经于公元546年来到中国提出质疑,作者在详细分析的基础上指出:"依据可信史料证明,穆斯林第一次为官方所知道是公元651年,这一年哈里发遣唐使来到中国。在此之前已经有阿拉伯商人经海路到达广州,并将伊斯兰带到广州及中国沿海的城市,但是这些早期来华的商人并不是宣道者。阿拉伯征服中亚后,穆斯林才真正接近中国西部边境。"梅益盛进而提出"离开具体的历史背景必然会产生断裂和不确定性,希望大家不要轻易接受传统的说法。"[1]此外,他还论述了中国伊斯兰教文献、伊斯兰教年表、中国伊斯兰教徒的生活等内容。

道教、民间信仰以及羌人的宗教,英人也有论述,但很肤浅。令人困惑的是他们对基督教相关内容并没有太多的研究,仅有牧作霖(G. W. Sheppard)的《马礼逊来华之前的〈圣经〉汉译本》和倭讷、翟理思对徐光启在《历代神仙通鉴》中所撰写的救世主予以探讨,目的还是在于传教。

人类学方面:郇和对台湾和海南的土著居民作了详细的实地调查,他考察得非常仔细,内容很广泛。郇和注意到台湾土著的语言中"R"的音节很多,作者专门列举了16个字的发音。作者认真记录海南土著的房屋建筑、周边环境、发型、服饰、体型、当地的神话传说、黎族的宗教信仰、风俗和习惯、方言和词汇以及中国文献关于海南人群的描述。在19世纪,这样系统、深入的调查是比较罕见的。

文学方面:主要表现在诗歌上。司登得(G. C. Stent)的《中国的抒情诗》收集了中国街头见到的歌谣如《王大娘》、《十二月歌谣》、《烟花柳巷》、《玉美针》、《小刀子》,并将这些歌谣翻译成英文,并配以五线谱,提出"这是了解和认识中国人内心世界的重要渠道"。[2]爱司克夫人的《中文诗及其内涵》探讨了中国古体诗文所蕴含的象征意义和写作背景,由于每首诗歌的具体含义都不同,所以作者也只能以几首诗歌为例来讨论,未能从总体上予以评述。除了诗歌,翟理思和李提摩太还分别简述了《红楼梦》和《西游记》的故事概要;威妥玛则论述了韩愈生平及其著作。总的来说,文学方面各国研究的都不是很深入,英国研究的相对多一些而已,也谈不上有什么突破。

艺术方面:英国人对中国的音乐比较感兴趣。先后论述了中国的乐谱、乐器、中国古代的音乐,其中帅福守的《中国的乐谱》和丹尼斯(N. B. Dennys)的《中国乐器简介》都是这方面的开拓之作,尤其是丹尼斯详细介绍了中华民族的79种乐器,内容包括形制、材料、功能、演奏方法、用途,每种乐器还附有图。而慕阿德的《中国乐器及其他发声器之目录》仅导言部分引征的就有《律吕精义》、《文庙乐书》、《御制律吕正义》、《琵琶谱》、《文庙祀典考》、《文庙丁祀谱》、《阙里纂要》、《七修类稿》、《增补事类赋统编》、《对相杂字》、《尔雅图》、《康熙字典》等文献,还用五线谱写出中国的传统乐曲。袁同礼在《西洋人对中国音乐的研究》一文中就对上述两篇文章予以赞扬。[3]

---

[1] Mason, I., The Mohammedans of China: When, and How They First Came, JNCBRAS, Vol. LX, P77, 78.

[2] Stent, G. C., Chinese Lyrics, JNCBRAS, Vol. VII, P135.

[3] 袁同礼:《中国音乐书举要》,《图书馆季刊》第4卷第3期。

除了音乐,哲美森、金斯密、艾约瑟等人还论述了中国的书法;史笪来图文并茂地论述了刺绣和金属艺术品;爱司克夫人初步探讨了中国书法、绘画、诗歌三者间的关系,提出"中国的古代艺术家通常是集书法、绘画、诗歌于一体,而他们的文化根基则是中国阴阳文化"。[1]

语言方面:选题研究比较随意,但是看得出英国人比较注重语言背后的历史文化现象。见表5-4。

表5-4　　　　　　　　　　　　英国籍会员语言研究篇目表

作者	题目	年份
金斯密	周朝的语言和文化	1878
金斯密	希腊文中"中国"与"中国人"之词源	1878
艾约瑟	《史记》中地理名词的语言学意义	1886
威立师	汉语修辞中的动物学	1919
阿礼国	日语之结构	1860
庄延龄	汉语方言比较研究	1878
艾约瑟	亚洲语言的演变	1892
艾约瑟	亚洲的语言(国际东方学大会综述)	1893
金斯密	用现代英语诗歌的形式翻译的中国古代民谣	1900
蓝宁	汉语和英语的近似特征	1917
莫安仁	语言与新思想	1929
支乐德	突厥语笔记	1948

资料来源:文会会刊和演讲篇目(见附表1)。

经济方面:英国对中国经济信息的关注程度要超过任何其他国家,尤其是关于中国的货币与财政。1876年,金斯密就揭示了中国的铜元贬值问题。1896年戴乐安(F. E. Taylor)又依据葛雷欣法则论述了中国当时铜元贬值所造成的货币危机与物价上升现象。马士和班德瑞则论述了20世纪初中国的货币紊乱状况。在财政税收方面,庄延龄论述了19世纪90年代中国各省财政税收情况以及各省向中央的解款数量。英国人也较早地研究了中国各地的物产和商路。艾约瑟、金斯密对山东和东南数省的物产和矿藏都作了调查。韦廉臣论述了华北的物产、贸易和交通,谢立山叙述了四川、云南的人口、物产和两省间具体的商业贸易道路。麦士尼(G. W. Mesny)深入调查研究了云南各府的农产品、矿藏资源、对外交通、官道和水路及云南与四川、两湖、两广之间的道路和贸易,云南可开发的潜力,急需建设的项目等。可以看出,经济方面英国调查研究得比较深入和细致,其广度也是其他国家难以比拟的。但是,英国人的目的不在学术而在商业发展上,具有较强烈的商业侵略色彩。

地质学方面:主要是19世纪对中国沿海及华北的地质与地磁的考察。这一时期对地质的考察和研究有两类人,一是商船船长,1858－1859年H. B. M. Highplyer号船长沙德韦尔(Capt. Shadwell, C. F. A.)就记录了新加坡、香港、广州、上海、宁波、吴淞等地不同时间的地

[1] Summaries of Lectures, JNCBRAS, Vol. LXV, pp204－205.

磁偏角。还有一类人是来华的领事馆翻译，如艾约瑟、金斯密等人对于中国地质的探索。古庇（H. B. Guppy）观察了淡水附近山区的地质，认为当地山区中的石灰石是最近形成的，而不是1873年英国《皇家地理学报》中所提出的"长时间形成的"，作者认为山中所见到的贝壳化石是山体抬升的结果，而且也不会太久远。山体抬升的另一个后果是淡水港的逐渐形成。[1] 古庇还就李希霍芬认为最能代表中国地质构造的南口岩层做了探讨。1910年叶长清对黄河在山东入海口的泥沙堆积现象，金沙江、怒江等河流对横断山区的切割侵蚀现象作了较为详细的论述，并附有清晰的彩色地质构造图。1925年燕京大学地理系教授巴尔博（G. B. Barbour）从济南的地理位置、岩层构造等方面分析了济南泉水的水温和水源，该文是一篇严谨的学术论文，在整个地质学中也是少见的。总的来说，英国人对中国地质的调查研究仅限于台湾、沿海、西南、华北几个点的研究，没有对一个地区的地质做全面地考察研究。

气象学方面：早期英国人和其他国家的人一样比较关注中国及周边地区的气候。1857年10月16日，文会演讲的第一篇文章就是尼克逊（F. W. Nicolson）船长提交的《飓风之规律》，作者根据自己的航海经历和航海日志分析了印度洋、南海、东海和上海附近海面上的飓风特征，飓风来临时所携带的气旋方向。韩德森（James Henderson）的《影响气候的物理因素》论述了上海、天津等地一年四季气候变化情况，作者对上海租界居留地的气候分析得尤为详细，提出"如果采取适当的措施，那么上海将是地中海以东最适合居住的地方"，其目的主要还在于服务于上海的外国侨民。[2] 20世纪后气象被关注得很少，只有叶长清在西藏旅行时对西藏的气候作了观测记录。

天文学方面：主要有以下几个人的成果：伟烈亚力对中国史书上所记载的日月食之研究、谢立山对历史时期太阳黑子的研究、金斯密对中国历法的起源与发展的研究、查得利对中国古代星相学的研究，这几人的研究成果几乎代表了该领域的最高研究水平。1866年9月发生了一次月食，有人向对中国科技史颇有研究的伟烈亚力询问："中国人对于日月食有没有一个科学的看法？他们记录多少？"伟烈亚力答复："中国历史上很早就有一个专门负责记录日月食的机构，日月食的定期记录大约始于公元前8世纪，且一直持续至今。"他还阐述了中国的历法演变及占星术，并对耶稣会士向中国传入陈旧的托勒密体系所造成中国天文在近代的落后表示遗憾。[3] 谢立山通过对《图书集成》中记载的历史时期的旱灾和太阳黑子出现年份的排比，对中国古代占星家普遍认为的"黑气（太阳黑子）是旱灾的前兆"提出质疑，作者提出"太阳黑子出现的周期为11年，与中国历史上的旱灾并没有必然的联系"。[4] 金斯密详细论述了中国古代历法的形成发展历史，并初步探讨历法与文明产生的关系。查得利论述了二十八星宿理论产生的历史及其与每周7天的关系，提出"这（星期的历史）是早期中国文化和西方文化为数不多的共同点之一"。[5]

动物学方面：它是英国人的一个研究热点，英国人对中国动物学的调查和研究集中于鸟类、哺乳动物两个领域。1911年之前中国的动物学还是一片荒原，"尤其是哺乳动物、鸟类、爬

---

[1] Guppy, H. B., Some Notes on the Geology of Takow, Formosa, JNCBRAS, Vol. XVI, P16.
[2] Henderson, James, Notes on some Physical Causes which Modify Climate, JNCBRAS, Vol. I, P27.
[3] Wylie, Rev. A., Notes on the Opinions of the Chinese With Regard, JNCBRAS, Vol. III, pp71-74.
[4] Hosie, Alexander, Sunspots and Sun-shades observed in China, B.C. 28, A.D. 1617, JNCRAS, Vol. XII, P92.
[5] Chatley, H., The History of the Days of the Week, JNCBRAS, Vol. LXII, P83.

行类、两栖类等脊椎型动物刚刚开始标本的收集和整理阶段",[1]主要由一些在华外人业余从事对中国动物标本的收集,贡献较大的是英国的郇和。郇和曾在厦门、宁波、台湾、杭州等地英国驻华领事馆工作,对中国的鸟类很感兴趣,一生收集不少鸟类标本。所到之处见到鸟类物种,郇和都认真考察和研究。他不仅翻译了《台湾府志》中的鸟类,而且实地调查搜集了尚未被记载的"新"鸟类物种。自己难以辨认的物种,就将标本送到大英博物馆予以鉴定。他曾专门撰写《中国的云雀》一文,对云雀作了解剖式的描写,详细又精确地描写了云雀的羽毛、四季活动、习性、巢穴,读起来简直不亚于法布尔的《蝉》。

20世纪后期,西方各国在加强对中国动物标本调查和搜集的同时,也开始了个案研究,整个上半期各国的对华研究都有很大贡献,其中法国以徐家汇博物馆韩德禄神父为代表,美国以斯密生博物馆在华的研究员为代表,英国则是著名博物学家苏阿德。苏阿德曾经参与多项动物考察,所到之地几乎遍及全国,不仅为文会博物院搜集了数量众多的动物标本,而且在文会会刊、《中国科学美术杂志》上发表多篇研究论文,可以说他代表了近代英国人对中国动物的研究水平和研究特点。从其演讲和发表的论文看,哺乳动物是他的主要研究对象,该项研究可以说是走在世界前列。1916年他的《中国北部哺乳动物研究近况》一文,列举了中国从东北到甘肃、直隶、山西、陕西、山东等地7种22亚种100余类哺乳动物的特征、习性、主要活动区域,该文成为多年来研究中国哺乳动物的奠基之作,经常被转载和引用。

植物学方面:英国人比较薄弱,韩尔礼(Augustine Henry)对宜昌地区的植物名称做了统计,以补充贝勒对该地区的记载,嘉托玛对湖北宜昌地区的植物、动物和化石做了统计。

建筑学方面:主要是从文化上探讨中国建筑所蕴含的文化信息。艾约瑟的《中国的建筑》一文勾勒出了中国建筑的发展简史。该文认为儒家和佛教思想对中国的建筑产生重大影响,同时这些传统价值观也阻止了铁路在中国的建设。[2]库寿龄的《中国的塔》论述了各地不同的塔,提出"中国的塔绝不仅仅是一种建筑,或是钟楼,而是佛教徒的圣骨存放地"。"佛教是中国塔的起源","风水也是中国各地建塔的原因之一"。[3]爱司克夫人则探讨了紫禁城布局所体现出的文化内涵。

医学方面:只有1864年传教医生韩德森的《中医和中药》和雷斯德研究院的伊博恩教授对中医的几篇研究文章。韩德森论述了中国历史时期的医学著作、部分中草药之效用、把脉、针灸等医疗技术,一方面肯定了"中医是古代世界的几个最早付之于实践的医学之一,有可能是当时最先进的医学",另一方面认为"近代以来,中国医生完全不了解西方的医学知识;中国人也乐于接受西方的医学和其他科学知识,但必须是用欧洲的语言来教授他们"。[4]伊博恩对中医研究得比较全面,包括中医的发展历史、中药中的动物和龙骨、中医对化学的贡献等。1929年南京国民政府出台限制使用中医令后,医学界"中医不科学"的论调甚嚣尘上,尤其在大城市和上流社会。在上海,西医已是占据了医疗界的主流,中医十分受歧视,在此情况下,作者在《中医的发展历程》一文中说"客观地讲,中国的医药进化历程是世界其他地区难以比拟

---

[1] Sowerby, Arthur de C., Zoological Exploration in China, JNCBRAS, Vol.LXXII, P20.
[2] Edkins, J., Chinese Architecture, JNCBRAS, Vol.XXIV, pp253 – 287.
[3] Couling, S., Chinese Pagodas, JNCRAS, Vol.XLVII, pp56 – 57.
[4] Henderson, J., The Medicine and Medical Practice of the Chinese, JNCBRAS, Vol.I, pp61, 104 – 105.

的。虽然现在许多中药不被人使用,但这些中药仍有很大的价值"。[1]他在《中药中的龙》一文中指出"龙骨的医疗效用是非常有限的,许多古代的医疗学家用龙骨治病是基于神话和迷信,使用龙骨的后果之一是病人误认为龙具有至高无上的力量,可以驱除他们身上的病魔,其心理效果不可忽视"。[2]在华外侨中像他这样对于中医有如此客观评价的人是不多的。

此外,英国还对中国的军事科技和造船技术也做了研究,像梅辉立的《火药和火器在中国人中的引介和使用》和艾约瑟的《船、舵之中文名及指南针的应用》都是著名的论文,经常被转载和引用。

(二)美国

美国籍会员的文章共计175篇,仅次于英国。这些文章有27个学科(见表5-5),各个学科有多有寡,研究的水平也深浅不一。地理游记最多,其次为历史、宗教、民族。相比较而言,社会学、人类学研究的水平要高一些,经济、文物、艺术方面的研究深度也高于同时期的其他国家。

表 5-5　　　　　　　　　　　　美国籍会员文章类别及篇数表

类别	篇数	类别	篇数	类别	篇数	类别	篇数
游记	30	人类学	6	法律	3	动物	14
历史	28	陶瓷	5	文献	3	地质	4
宗教	12	经济	4	音乐	3	建筑	4
民俗	10	农业	4	钱币	2	气象	2
政治	8	艺术	4	民族	2	植物	1
文学	8	青铜器	4	碑刻	2	天文	1
哲学	6	社会学	4	东方学	1		

资料来源:文会会刊和演讲篇目(见附表1)。注:分类和统计是由笔者自己完成的。

地理和游记方面:从空间上看,美国人主要集中于东部地区(京广铁路以东)和西藏地区。从时间上看,19世纪主要是山东运河沿岸,20世纪后才扩展到蒙古和西藏地区。从内容上看,19世纪以前在华东地区主要是大运河沿岸见闻,他们的观察焦点主要是各地的商业贸易情况。丁韪良考察黄河山东入海后,提出"从政治和商业的角度看,开放黄河已成为当务之急,因为轮船航行于黄河,中外都能受益。对于外国商人,它将提供一个巨大的市场;对于中国人来说,它将消除泛滥千年的洪水灾害"。[3]

20世纪以后,美国人主要游历于中国边疆的省份,注意力主要放在民俗和人类学方面。1908年安立德(J. H. Arnotd)的《攀登玉山山脉》(The Assent of Mt. Morrison),记录了山中的土著居民服饰、饮食起居、丧葬习俗、娱乐方式、打猎生活等。类似的还有葛德石(G. B. Cressey)的《鞑靼、鄂尔多斯、阿拉善旅行记》(演讲稿)、史德文(A. L. Shelton)的《西藏每日见闻》(演讲稿)。

历史学方面:美国人研究热点在于政治史上重要的历史人物和中外关系。历史人物方面,

---

[1] Summaries of Lectures, JNCBRAS, Vol. LXV, P201.
[2] Read, Bernard, E., The Dragon in Chinese Medicine, JNCBRAS, Vol. LXX, P29.
[3] Martin, W. A. P., Account of an Overland Journey from Peking to Shanghai, JNCBRAS, Vol. III, P36.

美国人研究了大禹、刘邦、项羽、王安石、骆秉章及明清来华传教士。较之早期英国人对中国历史人物的介绍,在研究对象上已经从皇帝、孔孟等名流转移到个别时期重要的官员身上;美国人也不再是简单介绍人物生平,而能够客观地分析和评价历史人物。对于这些非皇帝、圣人的历史人物,他们也给予很高的评价。福开森在《王安石》一文中详细叙述了王安石生平,尤其重视王安石仕途中的重要环节,并将其生平和当时时代背景联系起来予以考察,指出他是时代的产物。"王安石富有思想和博大的爱心,他不仅是一位务实者(积极推行改革),而且对于以往的优秀传统依旧予以保留,并做进一步的改进。他为北宋的繁荣和国力增强打下了基础"。[1] 丕思业(C. F. Preston)在骆秉章去世不久就撰文,"他以自己的政治和廉洁赢得了世人的尊重,他正是这个时代帝国所需的人才典范,他的行为将在社会和军营中大放光彩"。[2]

中外关系史方面,美国人尤其关注中国与邻近国家的关系。傅路德(L. C. Goodrich)撰写了《朝鲜对中国历史编纂的抵触》;利维沃思(Leavenworth)教授的《琉球群岛的历史》和卫三畏的《中国与琉球的政治关系》都以琉球为中心探讨了中日关系;铎德(W. C. Dodd)则写作了《中国与暹罗的关系》。对中外关系史研究最深入的是宓亨利(H. F. MacNair),他的《中国国际关系观察》一文从地理角度探讨了历史时期中国与周边及西方各国之间的关系。文章认为中国所处的独特地理环境使它与世界各国处于隔绝的状态,并且这种地理环境造就了中国人"天朝大国"的优越心态,这种心理又影响了18世纪以来中国与西方各国之间的交往,使得中国的统治阶级不能变化自己的政体,进而阻止了近代民主政治在中国的发展,在某种程度上讲,也正是这种优越感和政治体制造成了鸦片战争后的各个不平等条约。[3]

美国人比较注重对中国历史总体的把握,认为这是研究具体问题的基础。这方面的作品主要有盖乐(Esson M. Gale)的《三千年来的中国历史及历史学家》、福开森的《中国历史要览》、罗道纳(Donald Roberts)的《中国的历史诠释学》。福开森曾提出"对于中国历史没有一个总体认识,要进行具体问题的研究是不可能的","中国历史进程中各种局面是由内外因素共同促成的,而不仅仅是外部政治原因。因此,把中国作为一个统一的民族国家来看待是非常重要的"。[4] 赖德烈也抱怨"在西方的中国历史学中,关于中国历史整个朝代综论性论著是最贫瘠的,即便有,也是主要集中于个别历史时期的论述。对于中国大历史的论述还是处于总结中国古代历史学家的层面上"。[5] 盖乐和福开森都还对中国历史要籍做了大致介绍和分类,为学者研究中国历史提供了建议和指南。美国人在追求大历史的同时,也注意到欧洲学者泛泛讨论中国大历史所存在的缺陷,赖德烈及其他美国学者提出,不能过多地泛泛研究中国大历史,要加强对具体问题、具体时间段的研究。

宗教方面:美国人提出"中国人的宗教信仰必须从时空两方面去看待。因为在中国,无论是历史时期的各个朝代,还是各个地区、各个阶层都不存在统一的宗教信仰"。[6] 不过,美国人对中国宗教信仰考察研究的广度和深度都十分有限。他们仅仅对佛教、儒学、伊斯兰教和中国人对天、地的崇拜做了初步的描述和探讨。虽然研究佛教的相对多一些,但是这些文章还是

---

[1] Ferguson, J. C., Wang An-shih, JNCBRAS, Vol. XXXV, pp74-75.
[2] Preston, C. F., Notes of Lock Ping Cheung. Late Governor General of Szechuen, JNCBRAS, Vol. V, P71.
[3] MacNair, Harley. Farnsworth, Some Observations on China's International Relations, JNCBRAS, Vol. LVI, P2、7、15.
[4] Ferguson, J. C., General Survey of Stanfard Chinese Histories, JNCBRAS, Vol. LVII, P67.
[5] Latourette, K. S., A Survey of the work by Western Students of Chinese History, JNCBRAS, Vol. XLVII, P105.
[6] Bishop, Carl Whiting, The Worship of Earth in Ancient China, JNCBRAS, Vol. LXIV, P24.

处于介绍和泛泛而谈的水平，如葛德基（E. H. Cresst）的《佛教的朝圣者》、费佩德（R. Fitch）的《佛教寺院的一天》、慕天恩（R. Mortensen）的《中国的佛教》等都是就一些零碎的现象进行描述。相对而言，对中国的祖先崇拜和其他信仰还有一些深度的论述。毕士勃论述了新石器时代至东汉中国各个地方、各个时期民间与官方对天和地的信仰。卫理在详细叙述清朝皇帝祭孔、祭天与祭地繁琐礼节的基础上，探讨了这些信仰的文化根源——"儒家对个人道德（仁、义、礼、智、信）的强调，促使在中国形成了三纲社会伦理体系，而追求三纲必然要求人们对祖先、天、地，乃至鬼神的崇拜和信仰"。[1]

民族方面：美国学者比较注意苗族的生活习俗。他们研究了浙江、海南、四川的苗族。19世纪，他们主要依据中国文献来论述中国的苗族情况。裨治文的《苗族概述》就是以一部中国人的手稿为基础，叙述了中国境内的82支苗民生活及习俗，反映了18、19世纪初中国苗族的大致情况；玛高温的《浙江苗族》则通过《金华府志》、《浙江通志》、《处州府志》中有关苗族的资料回溯了浙江山区中苗族的渊源。20世纪后，美国有些学者运用田野调查的方法来对苗族进行研究，蒙宁娜（M. M. Moninger）亲自进入海南山区，深入苗族的生活中，她叙述了苗族的祖籍、迁移、方言、服饰、分支、居住环境、建筑式样、房屋布局、生活习惯、待客方式、打猎捕鱼（与汉人不一样，他们居于山谷中，生活主要靠狩猎，不从事农耕）。[2] 葛维汉（David C. Graham）以同样方式调查了川西苗族的习俗、宗教和艺术。

经济方面：美国人也比较注重对中国经济状况的了解，主要是中国的彩票、商业团体和银行机构，尤其是近代的货币金融市场，这主要由在海关工作的马士完成的，其他人的相关研究并不多见。

自然方面：除了1858年裨治文和玛高温对中亚地质和东北地震的初步研究外，就是20世纪20、30年代以来对中国动植物的调查研究，尤其是对中国鸟类的调查。主要有万卓志（G. D. Wilder）与胡本德（H. W. Hubbard）合著的《直隶鸟类目录》、祁天锡的《苏州及其周边地区的动植物初探》、贾珂（Arthur Paul Jacot）的《山东有孔虫类》和里利（J. H. Riley）与里士满（Dr. C. W. Richmond）合著的《中国鸟类相关文献管窥》。美国人对自然的研究领域远不及英国人的十分之一，但是这几篇却都是名作，作者也都是著名专家。祁天锡是来华的美国著名生物医学家，曾任东吴大学生物学系教授、燕京大学驻美副校长，也是中国科学社、静生物研究所董事和美国卫生学会、美国寄生学会等多个中外科学团体的成员，他的《苏州及其周边地区动植物初探》在中国植物学界影响很大。[3] 里利和里士满则是著名的美国斯密生博物馆的研究员，专门来华考察中国的鸟类标本，上述文章正是他们的考察报告的一部分。

（三）法国

文会中来自法国人士的文章，主要集中于历史学和博物学两方面。

历史学方面：法国学者比较注重历史地理考证。如高第的《安南东京近事记》（这里的东京指的是法属印度支那殖民地越南北部的省会东京），该文探讨了东京的地理位置与自然概貌，涉及内容有：①西汉至清代该地区的行政沿革，各个时期的历史关系及政区划分；②该地区之语言、民俗、奴隶制度；③该地区的河流：布拉马普特拉河、伊洛瓦底江、沙尔瓦江、湄公河，以及

---

[1] Williams, Edward Thomas, The State Religion of China during the Manchu Dynasty, JNCBRAS, Vol. XLIV, P43.
[2] Moninger, Miss M. M, The Hainanese Miao, JNCBRAS, Vol. LII, P45.
[3] 王志稼：《祁天锡博士事略》，《科学》24卷1期（1940年1月），第69-70页。

这些河流的航运能力、沿岸的矿藏资源;④历史时期当地政权的更迭情况及各政权与中国的政治关系和商贸往来。[1]该文参照了中文历史文献、16世纪以来的耶稣会士记录和19世纪以来的西方人的考察报告,对法属殖民地的历史地理作了详细的考证,充分反映出作者的学识。托马森(Déchiffrées par Vilh Thomsen)在儒莲对突厥史研究的基础上,借助突厥语、蒙古语和羊皮书的记载解释了鄂尔浑河碑之铭文,从而重现了历史时期匈奴和突厥在北部边疆的发展历史。[2]伯希和的《中国境内的土耳其斯坦民族》和列维(Sylvain Lévi)的《喜马拉雅山之行,其历史、宗教、山脉》也是经典之作,对于所见地点,都要用突厥语、梵语和汉语文献相互参引来证古今地名,明其沿革。而美国人对中国历史地理还谈不上研究,因为他们只是将有关的文献按时间顺序连起来,很少引用其他相关资料相互印证。如福开森的《古都洛阳》,只是依据《书经》、《诗经》、《洛阳伽蓝记》、《资治通鉴》、《太平御览》、《唐两京城坊考》、《河南通志》、《洛阳县志》(民国)等文献中关于洛阳城的记载,叙述了从西周到唐朝洛阳城的大致变迁,并没有深究城址变迁的原因。利维沃思的《琉球群岛的历史》也只是依据中国的文献,而没有利用日本和早期西方殖民者关于琉球岛的记载资料。

在自然方面,法国主要讨论的是中国自然历史方面的内容。如著名博物学家谭微道的《华西和华北博物志》、西蒙的《中国和日本古生物学和地质学研究刍议》、福威勒的《中国的短吻鳄》。《华西和华北博物志》系作者在华北实地考察的结果,该文论述了直隶、山东、蒙古、山西、陕西、河南等地的地质与动植物,"尤其是本地区的鸟类,是谭氏最早将其予以分类的",[3]成为研究该地区鸟类物种的奠基之作。福威勒最早发现了长江下游珍稀动物短吻鳄,遂撰文《中国的短吻鳄》,他不仅查阅了中国文献关于"鳄"的解释,而且从动物学的角度来研究、解剖并分析它,绘出了科学的图样,从而使短吻鳄这一鳄类得到了世界学术界的承认。西蒙的《中国农业物产图》则统计了华北、上海江南牧场饲养的牛、骆驼、马、山羊、绵羊等各类动物的畜产量;小麦、玉米、水稻、棉花、黑麦、高粱等农作物在河南、湖北、山西、陕西、山东、四川、湖南、江西、福建、江苏、浙江、广西、云南、广东等省份的种植面积、产量,并绘出上述各类动植物的分布图。能恩斯的《上海的气候》利用徐家汇天文台的观测资料分析了上海的温度、湿度、气压、太阳辐射等因素的变化规律和趋势。

(四)德国

近代德国人对中国的调查研究主要集中于历史、语言、哲学、地质四方面。

历史方面:主要有夏德对中国古代史的研究。夏德对于中国历史的论述,主要是将中国典籍中的同类史料予以筛选,所选课题视角相对新颖,但较少进行考证与纠谬。其《古代陶瓷:中世纪中国工商业研究》一文论述了唐、宋陶瓷之特点,青瓷之质地、颜色,古代主要陶瓷之分类:柴、汝、官、哥、定、龙泉、均州、章生、乌泥、宣、成;各类瓷器的色泽、厚度、材料、产地、流通等内容。其《中国早期盐业垄断史》一文则按时间顺序论述了从《禹贡》到唐末刘晏推行盐务改革之间,中国盐税征收制度、盐官形成的历史。

语言方面:主要有赫爱礼(Erich Hauer)的《汉学家为何应学满文?》,该文论述了满语的发展历史、满语特点与相关的语法著作、学习满语的必要性,指出"满语是理解中国文献的一个重

---

[1] Cordier, H., Narrative of Recent Events in Tong-king, JNCBRAS, Vol. IV, pp114-172.

[2] Thomsen, Déchiffrées par Vilh, Parker, E. H. translated, Inscriptions de l'Orkhon, JNCBRAS, Vol. XXXI, pp1-38.

[3] 经利彬:《谭微道在中国生物学上之贡献》,《真理杂志》1卷4期(1944),第455页。

要途径。如果我们仅仅懂得汉语,那是难以真正理解中国的文献。如果我们借助于满文经书,那么我们就会更加容易和准确理解汉文经书的真正含义。满语知识有助于我们理解汉语文献中的满语专有名称。要想真正了解1644—1912年的中国历史必须得懂满语,正如研究蒙元历史要懂得蒙古语一样。通过满语文本能够真正理解许多专有名词的含义,因为满语比汉语要好学一些"。[1]此外,夏德的《外国名称中字母"R"的中文对应词》、穆麟德的《比较语言学的局限》也都对东方学研究中的语言问题作了有益的探讨。

哲学方面:只有佛尔克的三篇文章。《王充与柏拉图论死亡与永生》简述了王充的生平和《论衡》的内容,并将柏拉图对于灵魂和生死的论证与王充的观点相比较。指出"与其说王充是一个武断的哲学家,不如说他是一个优秀的辩论手。他反驳了儒家和道家思想中毋庸置疑的错误和当时流行的迷信思潮。他是中国的伏尔泰,他启迪了中国的思维"。[2]《中国之辩士》一文分别列举了名家尹文子、公孙龙、邓析、惠子、黄公、毛公等人的观点;对于《荀子·不苟篇》、《列子·仲尼》、《名实论》、《坚白论》、《通变论》、《白马论》、《指物论》、《庄子·天下》篇、《庄子·转辞》篇、邓析的《无厚》篇都做了简单述评,第一次比较全面地向西方介绍了中国先秦时期的诡辩家及其思想。《哲学家扬雄》则提出"扬雄已经超越了孟子和荀子等玄思派,他是宋代以前儒家中最伟大的形而上学者"。[3]

自然方面:目前所能知道的只有康发迭(G. H. J. Kleinwächter)的《台湾地质研究》、穆林德的《直隶的脊椎动物及中国动物命名法》、费理饬的《东亚气候》三篇文章,但是这三篇文章都是经典佳作。《直隶的脊椎动物及中国动物命名法》叙述了直隶地区48种哺乳动物、14种爬行动物、316种鸟、27种鱼的特征、体型、习性、种属,以及中文文献对这些动物的记载和谭微道等西方人士的相关研究成果,一度被学界誉为该领域内的名作。《东亚气候》分析了1858—1875年东亚的气温、洋流、季风、云量、风雪等气候因素,每一种因素都从日变化和年变化两方面研究,文中不仅保存有1858—1875年数个地方的观测资料,而且制作了数十页不同时期的东亚洋流、气温分布图,此文对于研究"丁戊奇荒"时期的气候情况非常有用。

(五)俄国

俄国人的研究主要集中于植物学和人类学方面,以贝勒和史禄国二人为代表,史禄国对中国人类学的研究,前文已有详述,这里不再重复。

贝勒(1833—1901),1886年加入文会,在会21年。1866—1883年担任俄国驻北京使馆的医生,此间他研究中国植物和中西交通史,尤其热衷于对中国植物的研究,他收藏很多中国植物学的书籍,撰写了不少关于中国植物学的论著,这些论著在瑞典、德国、丹麦、法国、英国、俄国分别再版。贝勒曾在文会演讲三次:1875年11月29日的《中亚与西亚中古时代之史地考》;1880年11月19日的《先辈欧人对中国植物的研究》;1881年9月26日的《中国植物志》。这三篇文章是他一生的代表作,都发表于文会会刊上。其中《先辈欧人对中国植物的研究》一文,"遥遥领先于同时代同类的研究,并且被公认为后来研究的奠基石"。[4]该文还获得了法国"儒莲奖",并被上海美华书馆和伦敦以单行本再版。他的《中亚与西亚中古时代之史地考》

---

[1] Hauer, Erich. Dr., Why the Sinologue should Study Manchu? JNCBRAS, Vol. LXI, pp162–163.
[2] Forke, A., Wang-Chung and Plato on Death and Immortality, JNCBRAS, Vol. XXXI, P43.
[3] Forke, A., The Philosophy Yang Hsing, JNCBRAS, Vol. LXI, P110.
[4] Ferguson, J. C., Bretschneider, The China Journal of Science & Arts, Vol. XIII. Oct., 1930, No. 4, P248.

和《中国植物志》更是闻名于世。

此外,俄国人对蒙古也做过考古调查,1889年俄国地理学会西伯利亚支会对鄂尔浑河河谷探险,考察了元朝时期的蒙古旧都和林及附近的聚落。

(六)其他国家

奥地利学者在历史和货币方面有数篇研究性的文章,如夏士的《中国古代历史编纂学》、耿爱德的《中国的黄金:历史、应用及财政功能》。

瑞典则有斯文赫定、安特生(J. G. Anderson)、高本汉、喜仁龙(O. Siren)等人,他们几乎集中了当时瑞典的主要汉学家,这里有斯文赫定的《1934—1935年新疆考古记》、高本汉的《从发音学看中国文字》、安特生的《匈奴的青铜器》、喜仁龙的《中国人如何看待绘画艺术》。他们都是著名学人,上述文章也都是相关领域内的杰作。

西班牙人只注意菲律宾群岛,他们研究了菲律宾的华人。

二、时空差异分析

(一)调查上的时空差异

将地理和游记类文章作为来华外人对中国的考察记录,最能反映他们对中国的考察情况,把这些文章按时间编排起来(详见表5-6),能比较清楚地看出近代在华外人在不同时期和不同地域所注目的内容之差异。

表5-6　　　　　　　　　　文会会员在华游历观察内容之时空表

时间	题目	主要内容	主要地点
1858	雪窦山游记	物产(农业情况)	宁波
1858	台湾行纪	物产、习俗、方言	台湾
1859	长江航路指南:从吴淞到汉口	航运	长江下游
1861	长江旅行记:从汉口到荆州	物产、航运	长江流域
1861	陆上行纪:从广州经湖南至汉口	物产、交通	粤、湘、汉口
1864	天津第一印象	不详	津
1864	俄占之满洲海岸	地理位置、物产、土著	东北
1864	杭州湾海塘	海塘	浙
1864	陆上之旅:从圣彼得堡到北京	交通、贸易、食宿	蒙、京
1865	安徽绿茶区浏览记	茶叶	徽
1865	旅行记:南京—苏州—上海	太平天国战事	苏
1866	从北京到上海	商业、贸易、交通	京、直、鲁、苏
1866	运河见闻:从北京到烟台	商业、贸易、交通	京、直隶、鲁、
1867	从广州到汉口	矿藏、地质	粤、赣、湘、鄂
1867	黄河古河床	商业、航运	直、鲁、豫
1867	山东的物产	物产	鲁
1868	华西、西藏等地的道路与交通	交通	川、滇、藏
1868	从天津到镇江	不详	华东
1868	黄河	不详	黄河

续表

年份	题目	主要内容	主要地点
1869	黄河新河道考察记	商业、航运	鲁
1869	从烟台到邹县	地理、物产、矿藏	鲁
1869	湖北、四川、陕西三省旅行记	物产、交通、地理环境	长江中游
1872	海南探险	物产、交通、民风	琼
1873	孔子家乡曲阜之旅	历史文化、交通、商业	鲁
1873	最近杭州游览记	历史文化	杭州
1874	鄱阳湖、白鹿书院游览记	历史文化	鄱阳湖
1875	陕西、山西旅行记	物产、交通、地理环境	晋、陕
1877	辽河	不详	辽宁
1878	三角测量上海及周边的突起点	地理	沪
1880	长江中游游览记	不详	长江中游
1881	萨哈林岛(库页岛)旅行记	地理、土著	东北
1881	长江上游的急流	河流	长江上游
1881	萨哈林岛、阿尼瓦湾及俄国属鞑靼海岸旅行记	不详	东北
1882	苏州及其周围农村	地理、城廓	苏州
1883	四川及长江峡谷小记	历史、交通	长江上游
1884	从福州到温州	物产、交通、城廓	浙江、福建
1884	华西商路	商业、交通	川、滇、陕等
1884	浙江旅行记	物产、交通、城廓	浙
1891	云南:其财富与商路	商业、交通	滇
1892	神秘的叶尼塞河	古迹	蒙
1895	西藏旅行记	不详	藏
1896	中国之大运河	商业、航运	直隶、鲁、苏
1899	四川	不详	川
1905	从思茅至仰光纪行	交通、贸易、物产	滇
1905	松潘行记	习俗、物产、土著	川
1908	攀登玉山山脉	风景、习俗、土著	台
1911	从杭州到温州	不详	浙
1911	中国、印度旅行印象	不详	川、藏、滇
1913	峨眉山	风景、历史文化	川
1913	西藏每日见闻	习俗、气候、风景	藏
1914	大伤痕:圣诞节黄河入海口之行	物产、习俗	鲁
1914	蒙古游记	风景	蒙
1915	普陀山:中国佛教艺术探源	风景、宗教文化	浙
1917	历史胜迹:东岳泰山	风景、宗教文化	鲁
1919	中国三万英里行	交通、商业、地图	中国

续表

年份	题　　目	主要内容	主要地点
1919	甘肃概说	生产、生活、地理	甘
1919	台湾	习俗、土著	台
1920	云南探险记	不详	滇
1921	贵州的大道与小径	交通、习俗、物产	黔
1921	浪白窀:远东的不解之谜	风景、历史文化	鲁、闽
1922	西安印象	城廓、民风、历史文化	陕(西安)
1922	山西中部含煤沉积物中的煤铁蕴藏	矿藏	晋
1922	蜀地	历史、文化	川
1922	从太原府经五台山至蒙古边境纪行	历史文化、交通、物产	晋、蒙
1923	拉萨旅行记	宗教文化	藏
1923	蜀地再论	历史、文化	川
1925	甘、藏和蒙古地区的地质、地理调查	地质学、地理考察	甘、藏、蒙、疆
1926	从北京到蒙古	不详	京、蒙
1927	喜马拉雅山之行:其历史、宗教、山脉	历史文化、宗教	藏
1928	驮驼、鄂尔多斯、阿拉善旅行记	不详	蒙
1929	西藏日记摘要	不详	藏
1930	西藏及其自然环境	风景、地理概貌	藏
1931	攀登喀拉昆仑山	不详	藏
1934	1933年云南、贵州旅行记	习俗	滇、黔
1934	西藏边缘考察记	土著、宗教	藏
1935	黄土高原上的居民和物产	物产	晋
1935	俄国、新疆、甘肃、西藏、印度旅行记	风景、宗教文化	疆、甘、藏
1937	西康旅行记	风景、民俗、宗教	川
1937	内蒙古农业观察	农业情况	蒙
1940	热河(避暑山庄)	建筑、宗教、历史	冀
1949	从北京经包头和宁夏到青海	不详	蒙、宁、甘

资料来源:篇目来自附表1和文会会刊;
注:1. 笔者是参照文会1912、1932年对文章的分类标准将这些文章划归为游记的。
　　2. 主要内容是笔者依据文章内容大致划分的,且以多寡为顺序依次排列文章所涉及的有关信息;部分文章见不到原文,只能以"不详"处理。
　　3. 地点以作者描述地点为主。

　　划分出一条前后截然的时间界限既不可能也不科学,因为近代来华外人对中国的调查必然有一个相互交错和彼此消长的推移过程,从上表看,这个过程大体上在1895－1900年间。
　　如果将会员在各地考察记录的内容分为三个方面:一、商业信息,主要指各地的物产、交通、矿藏资源信息;二、地理风景,主要指作者对各地地理、地质和风景的描述;三、历史文化,指作者对各地民俗、方言、历史、宗教的描述。在此基础上,对表5-6各地所记载之信息之次数按这三类标准予以分类统计,则可以透视出19世纪和20世纪外人对中国各地所关注内容上的变化:19世纪,文会成员的个人调查主要集中于山东、浙江、直隶、江苏等省份和长江流域,这一时期关注的主要是各地商业信息。1900年后，从空间上看已由东部转移到西部内陆省份，如四川、云南、西藏、甘肃、新疆、陕西等地。所关注的主要内容也不再是各地的商业信息，而是历史文化，尤其是在云南、四川和西藏地区。

就国籍而言，英国人活动的范围最大，19世纪已经达到山西、陕西、四川及长江流域，这些地方他们所瞩目的还是商业贸易的潜力；20世纪后到达西藏和四川，但是对这些地区之民族的考察水平很一般，仅仅是介绍性的。其余国家的会员只是在有限的范围内游历。美国人主要集中于东部地区（京广铁路以东）和西藏地区。从时间上看，19世纪主要是山东运河沿岸，观察焦点主要是各地商业贸易情况；20世纪后才扩展到蒙古、西藏地区，这时期倾向于考察民族学和人类学方面的信息。

文会会员在华游历考察的时空差异与近代中国开放的进程相适应。中英《天津条约》第九款规定："英国民人准听持照前往内地各处游历通商"，自此，外人才开始在华旅行。当时南方正处于太平天国管辖范围内，所以早期旅行之地主要是北方。19世纪70年代，外人才真正进入江南各地旅行。清政府由于政治原因，广大内陆地区仍然禁止外人游历。光绪二年（1876年）河南官府就下令禁止各处旅店收留来豫的英国传教士，也不容英教士停留。川、滇及西藏地区，开放得更晚，光绪十二年（1886年）驻藏大臣仍拒绝英人入藏游历。光绪三十三年（1907年），英人帕沃洛克曾持甘肃西宁护照混进西藏，被当地官员发现劝回。[1] 到了民国后，外人进入内地才比较自由。

以文会会员的居住地为例，19世纪主要是在沿海和长江沿岸省份中设有海关和领事馆的城市，20世纪才进入到内陆省份的主要城市，而且还是以传教为目的，参见下表。

表 5-7　　　　　　　　　　　文会会员在各省最早居住地点时间表

年份	省份	城市	部门	年份	省份	城市	部门
1864	安徽	芜湖	海关	1878	直隶	天津	
1864	直隶	北京	西班牙领事馆	1892	广西	龙州	法国领事馆
1864	福建	厦门	海关	1897	云南	蒙自	海关
1864	江苏	镇江	海关	1901	黑龙江	哈尔滨	华俄道胜银行
1864	江西	九江	海关	1906	湖南	长沙	伦敦会
1864	台湾	台南		1908	吉林	吉林	海关
1864	浙江	宁波	英国领事馆	1913	河南	开封	
1878	广东	广州		1915	山西	忻口	美部会
1878	湖北	汉口		1916	贵州	铜仁	
1878	辽宁	牛庄		1919	甘肃	兰州	
1878	山东	烟台		1925	新疆	喀什	
1878	四川	重庆		1936	陕西	西安	内地会

注：1. 本表指的是文会会员最早居住于各个省份的地点，而不是游历之地点。
　　2. 1878年前文会通讯簿未列居住地，所以1878年只能作为参考的时间点。

---

〔1〕《晚清欧人在华游历历史资料》，《历史档案》2002年第2期，第64页。

(二) 研究上的时空差异

1. 英国

英国研究的范围甚广,这是其他国家都无法比拟的。英国人尤其侧重长江流域和西南地区的自然和人文研究。前者是英国在华的势力范围,自然关注得多一些;后者则缘于与其殖民地——印度的关系。英国一直垂涎西藏和云南,希望能够从印度直接进入中国,从而将其殖民地和在华势力范围连接起来,扩大其殖民侵略的范围。因此,从马嘉理到叶长清,无论是旅游、考察还是作专题研究,英国对该地区的关注一直未断,而且很多研究都是开拓性的。

在研究水平上,英国人由于太注重商业贸易,导致研究深度很不够,很多论文都比较肤浅,与其说是历史考证,不如说是史料搜集。经济学研究文章最能反映这一点。同样的课题——盐,英国领事庄延龄的《中国之盐税》一文堆积了清朝山东、四川、两淮、广州、直隶等地盐的年产量、盐税数目、运销地;德国学者夏德则论述了《中国早期盐业垄断史》,作者按时间顺序论述了从《禹贡》到唐末刘晏推行盐务改革之间中国盐税征收制度、盐官形成的历史演变,重点在于反映各历史时期中国盐业管理制度的演变。俄国兹切科夫(Archimandrite P. Zwehtkoff)的《中国盐业述评》追溯了历史时期盐的生产和清朝的盐税收,但重点在于盐的生产情况。作者分别叙述了海盐、池盐、井盐三种具体生产方式在中国的分布、各自的技术指标和生产具体步骤。从中可以看出,英国人的商业色彩浓于其他国家,而德国人的学术色彩高于他国。

英国研究性论文水平不高与英国汉学本身无根基有密切关系。英国人对于中国文化和语言的研究,最初起因于商业的发展,19世纪英国东印度公司到东方后,英国商人发现语言成为贸易的主要障碍,而中国方面又禁止中国人向外人教授汉语。于是1825年创设伦敦东方语言学校(London Oriental Institution),聘请马礼逊教授汉语,该校只存在3年,1828年马礼逊重返广州后就倒闭了。后来大英皇家亚洲学会创始人斯当东又经过努力,于1837和1845年分别在大学学院(University College)和国王学院(King College)创设汉语讲座,然而前者由于缺乏教师于1843年就停止了,后者由在华传教数年的萨默斯(James Sammers)牧师任教,不仅学生较少,而且所教授的是广东话和上海话。1859年,英国外交部发现该校学生听不懂官话后,决定直接派学生到中国学习中文,该校遂不了了之。到了19世纪末,英国才有真正优秀的汉语教师,他们都是在华多年的传教士、外交官,如理雅各、翟理思等人,于是剑桥、牛津、伦敦等大学相继设立了汉语讲座,然而学生并不多。翟理思在剑桥凡33年,一共只有3个汉语学生,[1] 牛津、伦敦大学的汉语系学生也为数不多。由于英国只是注意培养商业翻译人才,而不将汉学作为高深学问来对待,加以汉语教师师资较差,所以英国虽然早在1825年就已经开始了对中国文化及语言的研究,但是直到第二次世界大战结束,其汉学的研究水平远不及法、德和美国,也没有培养出像沙畹、伯希和、马伯乐、佛尔克那样的一流汉学家。

2. 美国

整体而言,美国人的研究水平19世纪不如20世纪。这是因为19世纪主要是几个来华传教士在华考察和研究;20世纪后参与者的素质较高,很多是拥有博士学位的专业学者或是大学教授,他们的水平自然要高一些。美国人的研究主要集中于20世纪之后,这是因为1898年门户开放政策提出之后,美国才开始真正关注中国,此前由于国内事务和忙于入侵菲律宾而无

---

[1] 陈尧圣:《英国的汉学研究》,见陶振誉等著:《世界各国汉学研究论文集》(第一辑),第189页。

暇顾及中国。1895年以前在文会活动的主要是玛高温、卫三畏、裨治文三人,而且演讲和发表的文章也主要是这三人,尤其是玛高温几乎占了90%。

研究内容方面,美国人比较注重对中国国际关系的研究;空间上关注的是台湾、琉球和中国沿海地区。不过美国人比较重视各个学科的文献整理,为学者下一步研究提供了帮助。历史学方面有赖德烈的《西方学者中国历史研究综述》,法律方面有罗炳吉(Charles Sumner Lobingier)的《中国法律研究文献介绍》、盖乐的《东北亚研究的汉语文献》,动物学方面有里利与里士满合著的《中国鸟类文献》,文学方面有来会理(D. W. Lyon)的《近十年之中国文学》,以及福开森的《罗振玉著作综述》、卫理夫人(Mrs. E. Williams)的《中国广为流传的宗教文学作品》。

3. 法国

空间上主要集中于云南、印度支那半岛(东南亚)和上海地区;前一个地区是其势力范围,法国人一直希望将两广和云南纳入其印度支那版图之内,地缘政治关系自然使其对该地区的研究会十分深入。加以法兰西远东语言学校设在西贡(后移至河内),该校是远东地区的一个汉学重镇。"在这个中国和印度文化接触的交通中心里面,这个学院自然将它大部分精力都用在中国方面,并且它已养成好些将来最有希望的支那学者"。[1]地利之便使得该校学生几乎都参与云南、广西边陲地区的自然与人文调查研究,该校校刊——《法兰西远东语言学校校刊》除印度支那内容外,很多篇幅也都是刊登该校学生关于云南等地的研究文章,伯希和、马伯乐的早期汉学论文都是发表在该刊物上。后一个地点是因为徐家汇学术中心的缘故,近代很多来华法国学者、耶稣会士都集中在徐家汇天主堂,他们除了传教之外,还从事对中国的研究,设有书局,出版《汉学杂纂》,该刊物与《通报》相媲美,是近代著名的汉学出版物。

在时间上,法国人对中国的调查研究前后数量上并没有明显的变化,只是1895年前对中国的地质、河流、气候、自然历史关注的多一点,此后对中国历史、政治、法律、文学、民族关注的多一些,但是前期也有对中国历史和文学的研究,后期也有关于中国地质与建筑方面的文章。

相比而言,法国人的研究成果更为严谨和规范,人文方面比较注重运用不同语言来相互参证考察古今地名的变化,自然科学方面比较注重实地调查和分析。伯希和与托马森等人运用"审音和勘同"[2]的方法考证了西北地区古今地名变迁和民族迁移。

法国研究的水平较高主要是因为法国国内汉学基础要远远高于同时代的其他国家。1814年法国皇家科学院(法兰西科学院)就设置了西方第一个汉学讲座(汉族和鞑靼——满族语言与文学讲座),这是一个纯学术的研究机构,首任教授雷慕沙开课时就"将汉语知识建立在牢固的语言学基础上"作为该讲座的首要目标。[3]从雷慕沙到沙畹,执掌该讲座的教授也都是同时代赫赫有名的汉学家,这样使得该校出来的学生汉语基础扎实,并兼通满语和其他语言。鸦片战争后,出于专门培养通商、传教目的,1843年巴黎东方语言学校也设立了中文讲座。由于有安东尼·巴赞、儒莲等人执教,"不仅数代法国汉学家,而且来自欧美所有领域内的汉学家,

---

[1] 沙畹著、李璜译:《法国汉学小史》,见李璜译述的《古中国的跳舞与神秘故事》,上海中华书局1933年版,第132页。

[2] 这是一种语言学的比较研究方法。从19世纪后期起,西方学者,包括一些汉学家与东方学家不断用这种方法来解决历史研究中的疑难问题,获得愈来愈多的显著成果。其中,法国的伯希和称得上是这方面的巨匠,他用这种方法破解了东方史、宗教史和中外关系史的许多疑团,推进了这些学术领域的深入研究。见黄时鉴《东西文化交流史论稿》序言,上海古籍出版社1998年版,第9页。

[3] 戴密微:《法国汉学研究史》,见(法)戴仁主编、耿昇译的《法国当代中国学》,中国社会科学出版社1998年版,第27页。

他们都来此初步学习中国的语言和文化基础知识,即使那些专职从事研究汉学的人也如此"。[1]一个主要培养商业和传教的语言训练学校也成为一个汉学机构,这种情况是欧美其他国家所没有的。而英国的汉学讲座直到1876年才进入大学殿堂,并且多年来学生也很少。

4. 德国

从时间上看,19世纪德国人对中国的调查研究门类较多,有地质、法律、宗教、历史、语言等,主要有夏德的中国历史与文献研究,穆林德、赫爱礼的中国语言研究,佛尔克的中国哲学研究。20世纪以来调查研究的篇目不及此前的三分之一,主要集中于哲学和文学。哲学方面的研究德国人是走在世界前列的,这与德国浓厚的哲学学术传统有极大关系。

总体上看,德国人在文会演讲和发表的文章所涉及的内容要远远少于英美两国,19世纪德国学者在文会发表演讲30篇文章,夏德一人就有20篇。这主要归于德国国内的政治情况。1871年德国才实现统一,1890年德国才真正加入到侵略中国的列强之中。"整个19世纪上半叶,德国人学习中文,不是靠自学就是就读于巴黎。德国人自己的中文教学和研究机构要晚半个世纪到一百年"。[2] 19世纪末德国汉学才算刚刚确立,但仍"缺乏完备之中文书籍及应有之中文基本学识,德国境内最为有名的汉学家卡拉普罗特(即克拉伯罗德)及贵茨拉夫(Gütalaff)之著作均为利用他国之参考书而以法文写成"。[3] 1887年柏林大学成立东方语言研究所(Seminar fuer Orientalische Sprachen),主要还是培养实用语言人才,真正的汉学研究机构要到卫礼贤回到德国之后才建立起来。德国汉学虽然起步较晚,但是德国的东方学却颇为悠久。早在1846年,普鲁士就成立了"德国东方学会"(Deutsche Morgenlaendische Gesellschaft),德国人东方学的治学道路是"开始学习神学,继而东方学、汉学","研究梵文、阿拉伯文者亦兼习中文,是相当平常的事"。[4]这样使得德国学者掌握了多种语言的功底,因此夏德等人能够运用历史语言学来研究中国的历史、民族和宗教。20世纪,德国与法国籍人士在文会演讲的都不多,原因是德、法在华也都有自己的学术研究中心,前者有中德学会(Das Deutschland-Institut),后者有徐家汇天主堂。本来就没有几个人真正从事对中国的研究,加之语言的原因,德、法籍人士更少去文会演讲。

总之,德国学者对中国涉猎的范围虽然不广,但研究水平要高于英、美,这就是德国汉学能够拥有一席之地的原因,并造就出夏德、佛尔克、卫礼贤等杰出的汉学家。

5. 俄国

文会中俄国籍人士的研究主要集中于西北和东北地域。这与近代俄国在华势力范围和侵略图谋有极大关系,殖民侵略需要对这两地区地理、历史的了解与研究。中国西北部边疆及西域、中亚考古主要是由俄国人开拓的,贝勒的《中亚与西亚中古时代之史地考》可谓是奠基之作。随着俄国对中国土地的侵占,大批俄国学者、商人、军官、旅行家进入这两地区,进而带动了对这些地区的调查研究。1899年10月在罗马召开的第十二届国际东方学大会就采纳了俄国东方学家拉德洛夫院士的建议,决定成立中亚和远东历史学、考古学、语言学和民族学研究

---

[1] 《法国当代中国学》,第32页。
[2] 张国刚:《德国的汉学研究》,第20页。
[3] 胡隽吟:《中德学会与中德文化》,《中德学志》,第5卷第1、2期合订本(1943),第115页。
[4] 张国刚:《德国的汉学研究》,第21—22页。

国际协会,而以彼得堡俄国委员会为协会的中心委员会。[1] 该会的成立大大加速了国际学界对中国西北地区的考察和研究,当然也导致了中国大量文物和历史文献的流失。

6. 其他国家

西班牙主要研究菲律宾,显然与菲律宾是西班牙的殖民地关系极大。意大利只有武尔披齐的数篇文章,由于"意大利的汉学家大多是天主教司铎,非如英法德美,大都为世俗人;而且意大利在远东没有殖民地,所以努力也赶不上各国",[2] 因而意大利的汉学水平远不及英、法、德、美。瑞典对中国的研究主要集中于语言和历史考古,这纯粹是由高本汉和安特生两人所带动的。

日本人供稿的不多,原因是日本在华有自己的调查研究机构,如东亚同文书院、上海自然科学研究所和"东亚攻究会"。其中,"东亚攻究会"成立于1919年,其目标和文会不无二致,"这个会和图书馆处处是在针对着亚洲文会北中国支会及其图书馆"。[3] 日人有自己的机构,所以他们在文会演讲和发表的文章极少。

综上所述,从各国对华调查研究时空差异的原因分析中可以看出:各国对华研究的区域,在空间上表现出与各国在华划定的"势力范围"和传教有密切的关系。各国汉学基础的强弱直接关系到各国学者治学成就之高低。具体研究内容的取材方面,虽然也受到各国文化背景、学术传统及国内政治的影响,但是个人喜好所起的作用更为突出。

---

[1] 孙越生:《俄国的中国学主要机构》,见中国社会科学文献情报中心编《俄苏中国学手册》,中国社会科学出版社1986年版,第119页。
[2] 吴宗文:《意大利的汉学研究》,见陶振誉等著《世界各国汉学研究论文集》,台湾"国防研究院"1968年版,第273页。
[3] 胡道静:《上海图书馆史》,《上海通志馆期刊》第2卷第4号,第1403页。

第六章　亚洲文会与中西文化交流

第一节　亚洲文会与近代国际汉学

文会创建时就提出"希望为西方的汉学提供令人满意的成果"。[1]汉学是与"东学西传"和"西学东渐"同时发生、同时进行的中外文化交流的一个组成部分。汉学本是东方学的分支,东方学是历史上形成的研究东方的历史、经济、语言、艺术,以及物质和精神文化的古文物的各种学科的总体。[2]16—18世纪西欧殖民者在向东方扩张的同时,开始对所谓的东方(亚洲和非洲)国家作专门的研究,相继产生了埃及学(Egyptology)、巴比伦学(Babynology)、叙利亚学(Syrialogy)、印度学(Indialogy)、日本学(Japanology)、汉学(Sinology),东方学即是对这些学科的总称,18世纪欧美成立的各种东方学会就是专门从事上述研究的文化机构。目前"Sinology"一词,学界尚有不同的具体解释,分别有汉学、中国学、华学等不同的翻译和注释,[3]日本将之称为支那学,但一般都将19世纪以来外国人对中国历史、文化、民族、语言、文字、宗教、艺术等方面的研究称之为汉学。

从已有的中外汉学史论著看,无论是莫东寅的《汉学发达史》、方豪的《中西交通史》、袁同礼的《西方论述中国文献目录:续高第〈中国书目〉》(China in Western Literature: a continuation of Cordier'a Bibliotheca Sinica, Yuan Tung-li, Cordier, Henri. Far Eastern Publications, Yale University, 1958.),还是日本石田干之助的《欧米人に於けろ支那研究》、美国谭维理的《1830—1920年美国之汉学研究》、法国高第的《西方汉学研究:1895—1898》(Les Etudes Chinoises: 1895—1898),论及近代汉学的发展都会提到文会及其会刊,尤其是会刊,几乎被一致认为是近代国际汉学的重要园地之一。但是这些著作也仅仅是简单介绍文会与会刊,没有论及文会与近代国际汉学,尤其是与西方汉学的关系。因此,本节专门探讨文会与近代国际汉学间的关系。

这里从近代西方汉学的研究领域的开辟、研究机构的建立、汉学人才的培养、汉学研究方法的探索、汉学工具书与相关研究资料的编纂等方面来论述亚洲文会的成就与不足,进而展现文会在近代国际汉学发展史中的位置。

一、研究领域

文会是否为近代国际汉学提供了新的风气,这要从近代国际汉学发展的脉络谈起。遗憾的是至今尚未有一册全面系统的近代国际汉学发展通史,已有的各国汉学史几乎都是列举历

---

[1] Preface, Journal of the Shanghai Literature and Scientific Society, No.1 (1858).
[2] 苏联大百科全书选译,丁则良译:《东方学》,人民出版社1954年版,第1页。
[3] 详见:阎纯德的《汉学和西方的汉学研究》,《汉学研究》第3辑,中国和平出版社1998年版;张国刚的《德国的汉学研究》,中华书局1994年版;李学勤的《法国汉学·序》第1辑,清华大学出版社1996年版。

史时期的主要人物及其著作,对于前后的学术变化尚未谈及,各国间的汉学互动更无分析。而且,19－20世纪的国际汉学史更少有深入论述和分析,已有的论著也多是简单介绍近代欧美各国国内的汉学发展史,却对欧美人士在东方各国侨民定居地内所做的汉学研究鲜有触及。近代,欧美各国在亚洲各地建立了不少研究机构,如法国设在越南的法兰西远东语言学校、德国设在日本的东亚研究机构和英国亚洲文会在东亚各地的支会。中国境内,除了文会外,还有中德学会、哈佛燕京学社、俄国的传教士团、中法大学汉学研究所(Centre Franco-chinois d'Etudes Sinologiques)。从已有的研究成果看,这些欧美设在东方居住地境内的汉学研究与各国境内的汉学发展密切相关,因为很多著名的汉学大师都曾经在这些侨居地的汉学机构中工作和学习过。伯希和是法兰西远东语言学校最早的成员之一,他的学术生涯头几年就是在那里度过的(1900－1904);[1]鲍乃迪(O. Palladius)则于1849－1858年任俄国东正教驻北京第十三、十四届传教士团领班;[2]傅吾康(Wolfgang Franke)一度担任中德学会的学术秘书和学术研究员;[3]戴德华(Goerge Edward Taylor)、饶大卫(David Nelson Rowe)等人曾在哈佛燕京学社北平办事处(北京部)工作和学习过,费正清则受哈佛燕京学社的资助来华进行研究。[4]至于在文会中工作过的著名汉学家前文已有叙述。这些著名的汉学家在侨居地的学习和工作经历,对于他们各自国家的汉学发展的促进作用,应该是汉学史研究不可回避的课题,也是近代中西文化交流史值得注意的内容。

全面分析欧美设在东方各个侨居地的汉学机构与所属国的汉学发展关系,目前还存在困难。文会则为我们提供了一个窗口,结合文会对华调查研究的成果和各国近代的汉学发展史,一定程度上可以透视出近代欧美各国在东方的侨居地的汉学研究与各国境内汉学发展的互动状况。

文会创建时就希望为汉学作出贡献,那么近百年来文会为汉学具体提供哪些内容呢? 就新风气而言,笔者认为一些汉学研究领域是由文会开辟或带动起来的。文会对中国的调查和研究,就其范围而言,是近代其他任何机构所不能比拟的,在此过程中,文会开辟了汉学的一些研究领域。

就哲学而言,佛尔克在华期间(1897年)就在文会会刊上发表了《王充与柏拉图论死亡与永生》一文,该文叙述了王充的生平和《论衡》的内容,而且比较了王充和柏拉图两人对生死、永恒的论述。在此基础上,佛尔克于1906年翻译出版了《〈论衡〉——王充哲学散文选》英文本,张国刚在《德国的汉学研究》一书中说这是《论衡》"第一次被译成欧洲文字,在中国哲学概念术语的翻译和界定上具有示范性意义"。[5]那么,上述文章应该也是最早介绍和分析《论衡》的西文作品了,换言之,佛尔克开辟了对王充和《论衡》的研究。佛尔克在华期间还研究了战国时期的诡辩派、扬雄、杨朱等人的哲学思想,并发表在文会会刊上,这些专题研究也是近代汉学(哲学领域中)较早的。经过对中国多位哲学家思想的不懈钻研,佛氏于1927年出版了《中国古代哲学史》、于1934年完成三卷本的恢宏巨著《中国哲学史》,由此他也成为汉学史上的一颗

---

[1] 戴密微:《法国汉学研究史》,见戴仁主编、耿昇译的《法国当代中国学》,中国社会科学出版社1998年版,第50页。
[2] 孙越生:《俄国的中国学家》,见中国社会科学文献情报中心编的《俄苏中国学手册》,中国社会科学出版社1986年版,第39页。
[3] 丁建弘、李霞:《中德学会与中德文化交流》,见黄时鉴主编的《东西交流论谭》,上海文艺出版社1998年版,第282页。
[4] 张寄谦:《哈佛燕京学社》,《近代史研究》,1990年第3期,第155－161页。
[5] 张国刚:《德国的汉学研究》,中华书局1994年版,第54页。

璀璨明星。

俄国著名汉学家贝勒开辟了近代西方人对中国植物的研究。贝勒在华期间对中国植物作了认真研究,先后在文会演讲和发表了数篇文章。其中《先辈欧人对中国植物的研究》论述了从晚明来华耶稣会士到林奈植物分类法诞生期间欧洲人对中国植物的研究。全文分为6个部分:第一部分介绍16-18世纪来华耶稣会士利玛窦、曾德昭、J. Nieuhof、Dr. Dapper等人对中国植物的记载,主要是曾德昭的 Relation Della Grande Monarchia Della Cina(1643)、杜赫德(J. B. du Halde)的《中华帝国全志》(Description de L'empire de la Chine)以及卜弥格(Michael Boym)的《中华植物》(Flora Sinensis)等书中记载的近600种植物名称及简介,包括这些植物的产地、性状、颜色、中葡名称、用途(食用、医用),很多特点作者都引用原文;第二部分再现了1702-1703年英国《哲学会报》(Philosophical Transactions)上坎立安(James Cunningham)讨论中国植物的两封信,并且收录了坎立安收集的其他耶稣会士在华期间记录和收集的600种中国植物;第三部分记录了瑞典博物学家林奈和其学生奥斯伯克(Peter Osbeck)等人于1751-1766年间在华南收集的400余种中国植物标本;第四部分介绍索南劳特(P. Sonnerat)关于中国植物的论著;第五部分介绍了 Loureur 的 Flora Cochin-chinensis 一书内容及书中所列的680种植物;第六部分介绍格鲁索尔(Grosier)的 Description Generale de la Chine (1785)。该文"遥遥领先于同时代同类的研究,并且被公认为后来研究的奠基石",[1]因此获得了汉学最高奖——"儒莲奖"(Prix Stanislas Julein),1881年上海美华书馆又单行出版,后来在伦敦和巴黎多次再版。贝勒的另一巨著是《中国植物志》,该文洋洋洒洒1 200余页,会刊16卷大半,25、29卷两册都是该文内容。该文第一部分介绍了近百种中国医学与植物学文献、农学典籍,早期中国与印度、西亚的植物交换,日本的医学和植物简史,朝鲜、满洲、蒙古、西藏的植物知识;第二部分记录了汉语植物文献中的科学论断;第三部分介绍了1 148种与植物有关的中国典籍,包括他们的出版年代及作者;第四部分介绍了欧人对中国植物学文献之翻译和研究述评;第五部分介绍了《尔雅》、《诗经》、《书经》、《礼记》、《周礼》及其他经书中所记载的植物及《神农本草经》和《别录》中记载的药用植物。第六部分介绍了中国植物之类别。该文是中国植物研究的开创之作,也是研究中国植物学不可或缺的参考资料。

文会会员还带动和促进了一些汉学领域的研究进展。最明显的就是文会会员对开封犹太遗址的考察,使犹太人成为近代汉学研究的一个重要议题。对于开封的犹太人,1605年利玛窦在北京会见赴京赶考的举子艾田后,外国入华传教士便开始了调查研究。利玛窦、龙华民(Niccolo Longobardi)都曾派人到开封调查当地犹太人的情况,艾儒略(Jules Aleni)和毕方济(Francois Sambiasi)还亲自到开封实地调查,"礼仪之争"使得外人对开封犹太人的调查中断。鸦片战争后,伦敦基督教会为了将基督教传播到中国大地,尤其希望"那些中国犹太人成为基督徒,1849年在华传教士斯密斯(Bishop Smith)、麦都思遂派遣两个中国基督徒到开封考察,他们收集到一些希伯来文手稿和汉文碑刻拓片抄件"。他们的旅行游记,后来由艾约瑟译成英文,即《英国伦敦基督教和犹太教促进会对开封犹太人的调查报告》,[2] 1851年在上海出版。

---

[1] Ferguson, J.C., Bretschneider, The China Journal of Science & Arts, Vol. XIII, Oct., 1930, No.4, P248.

[2] Martin, W. A. P., Account of an overland Journey from Peking to Shanghai, Journal of the North-China Branch of the Royal Asiatic Society, Vol. II(1866), P30. 按:笔者未见到该书英文名称,这里的译名引自耿昇的《西方汉学界对开封犹太人调查研究的历史与现状》,《西北第二民族学院学报》,2000年第4期。

这些材料公开后引起了争论,19世纪50-80年代《北华捷报》和《教务杂志》上有不少文章讨论开封犹太人和西安景教碑的问题以及二者之间的关系,仅伟烈亚力前前后后就撰写了11篇文章。[1] 伟烈亚力认为中国史书所记载的"祆教"就是犹太教。[2] 有人认为是摩尼教,或者是波斯火神教(Persian fire-worshippers)。[3] 由于没有定论,开封犹太人的现象愈益增加其神秘性,文会会员遂着手对开封犹太人调查研究。

1866年丁韪良由北京到上海,路过开封时,专门考察了犹太教堂的遗迹,并与当地的犹太人交谈。根据丁韪良回忆,他是近代第一个亲历实地考察的外国人。此后文会会员施约瑟(S. I. J. Schereschewsky)、精琦(J. W. Jenks)、万卓志分别于1870、1904年到开封考察犹太人,1905年丁韪良又将内地会传教士毕斐然(Bevis)收集的开封犹太碑拓片翻译成英文《开封府的犹太教纪念碑》(The Jewish Monument at Kaifengfu)发表在会刊37卷(1906年)上。丁韪良等人都发现开封犹太人不仅十分贫困,而且犹太人社群处于不断解体之中,已成为贫穷无助的群体,更为严重的是他们很多也放弃了自己的宗教,为了生存还卖掉了当地所藏的希伯来文献和其他经文。[4]

文会会员的调查结果引起了西方学者和世界犹太人的注意,他们在实施援助开封犹太人的同时,也纷纷致力于开封犹太人的调查研究。1905年法国外交官贝特络就在《法兰西远东语言学院校刊》上发表了他实地考察开封犹太人的调查报告《一个赴中国的外交使团之科学考察结果》。[5] 但是对开封犹太人研究最深入的还是徐家汇耶稣会士管宜穆(Jerorme Tobar),他经过多年潜心搜集、调查研究,1900年出版《开封犹太人碑刻之研究》——作为《汉学杂纂》(Variétés Sinologiques)第17卷专辑出版。该书分为九章:第一章:开封犹太教堂内遗留之碑刻;第二章:开封犹太教堂的匾额;第三章:教堂之对联;第四章:犹太教堂内所收藏的经文与流传情况;第五章:明弘治碑(《重建清真寺记》,1498年)译注;第六章:明正德碑(《尊崇道经寺记》,1512年)译注;第七章:清康熙碑(《重建清真寺记》,1663年)译注;第八章:中外学者对这些碑刻的研究文章目录及摘要;第九章:关于犹太人的一些拓片。[6] 由于开封犹太教堂已经破败不堪,该书收录的文献在当时就已很难见到,因此该书资料价值非常高,成为研究开封犹太碑的必备书。

文会还有一些研究,虽然不是开创之作,但其开拓之功亦为当时汉学界所称赞。1881年德国汉学家嘎伯冷兹出版德文《汉语语法》(Gramnatik der Chinesischen Schriftsprache),该书是近代西方第一次对古汉语语法做的初步分析和归纳,成为西方研究中文语法的奠基性作品。[7] 由于该书是用德文出版的,没有拉丁文和英文版,夏德用英文对该书作了评介,将该书中的三大汉语语法予以详细叙述,被认为"大大帮助了德国之外人士对于汉语语法的学习,推动了国际汉学的发展"。[8]

---

[1]《伟烈亚力著述目录》,见汪晓勤:《中西科学交流的功臣——伟烈亚力》,科学出版社2000年版,第150-151页。
[2] Wylie, A., The Jewish Roll from Kai-Fung-Foo, Notes and Queries on China and Japan, Vol. II, Oct., 1868, P159-160.
[3] Martin, W. A. P., The Jewish Monument at Kaifungfu, JNCBRAS, Vol. XXXVII(1906), P2.
[4] Martin, W. A. P., The Jewish Monument at Kaifungfu, JNCBRAS, Vol. XXXVII(1906), P19-20.
[5] 耿昇:《西方汉学界对开封犹太人调查研究的历史与现状》,《西北第二民族学院学报》,2000年第4期。
[6] LEP. JERôME TOBAR. S. J., Inscriptions Juives de K'Ai-Fong-Fou, Chang-Hai Imprimerie de La Mission Catholoque Orphelinat de T'ou-SÈ-Wè, 1900.
[7] 张国刚:《德国的汉学研究》,中华书局1994年版,第24页。
[8] Notices of Recent Publications, The Chinese Recorder, Vol. XIII, P477.

1922年文会与美国斯密生博物馆合作进行的《中国鸟类相关文献管窥》出版后,《中国科学美术杂志》就评价该成果"为从事中国鸟类学研究的学者扫除了多年的障碍"。[1]而钢和泰在《玄奘及其现代研究》一文中提出的"西藏和土耳其佛教都源于中国而非印度"的观点被《教务杂志》评为"为下一步佛教研究打开了局面"。[2] 1928年季理斐的《河南的犹太人》在当时被誉为是"关于此主题最好的论述"。[3]

可以说,文会为学者们提供了学术交流的机会,促使他们迸发出学术研究的火花,进而推进汉学研究领域的不断扩大和深度的不断增加,文会所造就的近代汉学学术空间大大推进了近代汉学的发展。

二、研究机构

文会是远东地区较早建立的汉学研究机构,远远早于俄国设在海参崴的东方语言学校(1898)、法国在河内创建的法兰西远东语言学校(1901)以及中国科学美术协会(1923)、哈佛燕京学社(1934)、中法大学汉学研究所(1938)等,说它历史悠久一点都不过分。文会不仅创建得早,而且还参与和帮助不少汉学研究机构的创建。如果我们回顾一下西方各国在远东地区创建的汉学研究机构,可以看出,这些机构多是在文会的引导和帮助下建立起来的,见下表。

表6-1　　　　　　　　　　　　文会帮助或参与创建的汉学机构

年份	名　称	说　明
1874	教务杂志	本系传教士办的宗教刊物,后一度停刊。1874年伟烈亚力将其复刊,扩展范围,刊登许多中国历史与地理方面的论文,并成为著名的汉学期刊之一。
1885	北京东方学会	旨在研究东方(特别是中国)的各项事情。创建人全是文会会员,会长:丁韪良;秘书:柔克义;会员:艾约瑟、阿恩德、卜士礼。
1886	香港民俗学会	会长是文会名誉会员骆任廷
1908	中国碑刻学会	文会会员慕稼谷、夏德、傅兰雅、甘伯乐、精琦、佛尔克、翟理思等人参与创建。
1914	北京美国学校	旨在建立一个远东调查中心,由此获得更准确的东方知识,另一个目的就是研究中国历史、文化、艺术、文学、伦理、民俗等问题。该机构成立时受到了文会的帮助。见该会会长致文会的信。
1922	华西边疆研究会	六名创始人中5名是文会会员,他们是:会长莫尔思(W. R. Morse)、副会长赫文德(G. G. Helde)、秘书冬雅德(E. Dome)、理事 J. Hutson、名誉会员叶长清(J. H. Edgar)。只有会员 E. C. Wilford 不是文会成员。
1935	中国钱币学会	该会是在文会帮助下成立的,会所就设在文会博物院,演讲时就用博物院收藏的钱币,并采用博物院编的《中国钱币目录》,代替他们自己编的目录。

资料来源:1. 宋晞:《美国的汉学研究》,见陶振誉等著:《世界各国汉学研究论文集》(第一辑),台湾"国防研究院"印行,1968年版。第143页。
2. *The Peking Oriental Society*, JNCBRAS, Vol. XX., P101.
3. *Notes and Queries*, JNCBRAS, Vol. XL., P115.
4. *Proceedings*, JNCBRAS, Vol. LXVI., Piv.
5. Lockhart, Jams. Haldance. Stewart., *The Folk-Lore Society*(*of Hongkong*), JNCBRAS, Vol. XXI., P120.
6. Journal of the West China Border Research, Vol. I., Pii.

---

[1] Biological notes and Reviews, The China Journal of Science & Arts, Vol. I, Nov., No. 6, P604.
[2] Our Book Table, The Chinese Recorder, Vol. LIV, P497.
[3] Our Book Table, The Chinese Recorder, Vol. LIX, P794.

还有一些汉学机构，文会虽然没有参与创建工作，但是这些汉学机构中也有文会的成员。如法兰西远东学校中的伯希和在该校创建的同年(1901)就加入了文会，哈佛燕京学社的戴德华很早就是文会会员。

文会也推动了近代西方各国国内汉学机构的创建与发展。文会的很多会员回国后参与或帮助了欧美各国汉学研究机构的创建。高第回国后创办了当时西欧唯一的汉学杂志《通报》，终身会员伯希和担任巴黎法兰西学院亚细亚考古学讲座教授。1924年卫礼贤任法兰克福大学首任汉学讲座教授，并创办《汉学杂志》。1902年文会会长夏德到了美国后任哥伦比亚大学华学教授，1897年翟理思担任剑桥大学汉学讲座教授。1876年卫三畏任耶鲁大学中文教授，是美国创设最早的中文讲座首任教授。1896年傅兰雅任加州大学首任东方语文讲座教授，1915年他退休后，由文会会员江亢虎和卫理担任。劳费尔后到芝加哥自然历史博物馆(The Field Museum of Natural History)工作，继续从事对中国的研究，"成为美国汉学界的泰斗，学术界的第一流人才"。[1] 1928年宓亨利在芝加哥大学教授亚洲历史、宗教及国际关系课程。

文会会员也帮助西方的汉学机构搜集中文图书。"劳费尔多次到中国考察，受芝加哥各学术机构之托，搜集重要图书，经多年之搜集，于1907—1910年间带回了中、日、满、蒙和藏文等书籍；为纽贝里图书馆(Newberry Library)搜集21 403册的古典文学和历史的书籍；为约翰·克里拉图书馆(John Crerar Library)搜集12 819册的社会和科学的图书；为芝加哥自然历史博物馆搜集了数千册的考古和人类学的书籍"。[2] 部分会员还把自己的藏书捐献给欧美各图书馆以资助当地的汉学研究。容闳去世前就将自己的藏书捐献给了耶鲁大学，是该图书馆最早的中文图书，构成该图书馆中文藏书的基础。1916年江亢虎则把自己的约13 000册藏书捐献给加利福尼亚大学。

文会会员还担任一些汉学研究项目主要负责人。1931年赖德烈就担任美国"远东研究促进委员会"(Committee on the Promotion of Far Eastern Studies)发行的《美国的中国研究年报》(Progress of Chinese Studies in the United States)首任主编。1960年，傅路德、恒慕义担任美国亚洲学会主持的"明代名人辞典编纂计划"(The Ming Biographical Dictionary)顾问。[3] 恒慕义(A. W. Hummel)还曾担任美国国会图书馆东方部主任，主持编写过《清代名人传略》。

从个人的零散研究发展到有组织、有系统的科研行动，汉学形成了全球化的学术交流网络。在这个过程中，文会的确起了不小的作用。

三、汉学研究工具书及相关资料的编纂

中文是汉学的基础，无论是田野调查还是书斋研究。文会创始人裨治文在开幕词中也提到要重视对汉语的学习，它是了解与研究中国的基础。编纂各类中外词典和相关工具书是汉学研究的初步工作，在近代尤为迫切。翟理思之所以能够蜚声汉学界，主要还在于其编纂的《英华词典》。然而文会既没有组织会员编纂中外词典，也没有像哈佛燕京学社那样编纂名人辞典和相关中文文献索引之类的学术工程，因此这方面文会没有任何贡献。

其他汉学研究资料方面，文会方面所做的贡献主要体现在图书交换、编印汉学重要典籍及

---

[1] 谭维理：《1830—1920年美国人之汉学研究》，《清华学报》第2卷第2期，第277—278页。
[2] 宋晞：《美国的汉学研究》，第151—152页。
[3] 宋晞：《美国的汉学研究》，第149页。

出版汉学研究论著目录索引、翻译出版相关文献几方面,但是由于资金不足,文会在这些方面所作的贡献十分有限。图书交换方面:文会曾与世界100余个文化机构交换各自的出版物,借此,文会向世界汉学界提供了一些最新的汉学研究成果。文会所编辑的"图书馆馆藏目录"、"文会会刊论文索引"和《中国评论》论文索引"无疑为学术界提供了学术资讯。

珍贵典籍方面:1868年文会再版了《中国丛报》这套鸦片战争前后最能反映外人对中国认识的重要文献;此后,还曾资助徐家汇天文台出版上海气象观测资料和骆任廷的《中国货币综录》。

遗著方面:整理出版了《卫三畏日记(1858-1860)》这份关于第二次鸦片战争中美国公使入京谈判的重要史料,还有在美国国会图书馆发现的中国学者王国维的未刊稿《中国过去19个世纪的量具》。

翻译方面:文会会员翻译了一些中文文献,不仅为汉学界提供了资源,也使中学得以西传。这些译文详见表6-2。此外,文会会员也翻译了一些中国境内的碑刻文献,如大禹碑、汉口天主教堂内的碑、黄土高原上的庆典碑、雁荡山北部的石刻、西安的大秦景教流行中国碑、开封的犹太碑。

表6-2　　　　　　　　　　　　　　　会员翻译的文章篇目

年份	译者	中文名	篇名	备注
1858	不详		中国土著居民	译自中文手稿
1858	J. Edkins	艾约瑟	《壹输卢迦论》译稿与注释	
1860	E. C. Bridgman	裨治文	苗族概述	一位中国人的手稿
1861	G. E. Cunningham	耿惠廉	《从上海到南京——穿越暴乱地区》	一位中国人的手稿
1865	Revd. Mr. Brown	勃朗	日本手稿译文	
1865	Robert Swinhoe	郇和	台湾鸟兽	译自《台湾府志》第18卷
1865	Rev. S. R. Brown	勃朗	西洋纪闻	
1867	G. T. Gardner	嘉托玛	杭州《天主堂改为天后宫碑记》英译	
1868	Dr. Jenkins	秦右	古代中国人的音乐观	译自一位中国人的手稿
1871	D. B. McCartee	麦嘉缔	英译《重修城隍庙碑记》	原作者:郑板桥
1883	Monsieur F. Scherzer	师克勤	法译《朝鲜志》	译自《朝鲜志》
1884	G. E. Moule	慕稼谷	一张佛教画	
1885	C. B. T.		《镜花缘》节译	《镜花缘》第四回英译
1887	E. H. Parker	庄延龄	中国1842年前之军事组织	译自魏源《圣武记》
1888	G. E. Moule	慕稼谷	元阳子真空直指	
1888	H. E. Hobson	好博逊	南京大报恩寺琉璃塔	译自南京报恩寺主持雕刻的画卷
1892	M. F. A. Fraser	富美基	鄂尔浑河上游与古代蒙古帝国旧都遗迹考察记	译自俄国考察团考察报告

续表

年份	译者	中文名	篇名	备注
1893	Rev. Geo. W. Clarke	花国香	《玉历》英译	
1910	J. C. Hall	贺若贤	18世纪日本的儒家改革者	原文作者是日本思想家太宰春台(1680－1747)
1914	Adsheal	阿谢尔	一个总督大臣的回忆录	译自《张闻襄公府纪闻》
1916	Rev. A. P. Parker	潘慎文	义和团运动期间清朝政府的官方文件	
1917	Samuel. Couling	库寿龄	《雁塔圣教序》译文	原著：李世民
1919	Charles Kliene	葛麟瑞	《桃花源记》译文及短评	
1921	W. J. B. Fletcher	佛来遮	汉诗英译：《人日游花埭》、《贫女》	
1922	Mrs. Elfrida Hudson		《孔雀东南飞》英译	
1923	Charles Budd	卜德小姐	汉诗英译：《风雪》	明代诗人沈周作品
1923	C. A. Jamieson	陈国将	诸葛亮与《草船借箭》	京剧英译
1923	Elfrid Hudson	赫德森	云诗英译：《云汉》、《今昔》、《宿天》	来源分别为：《诗经》、公元3世纪一位无名氏、陶翰作品
1924	Rev. T. Torrance	陶然士	蜀地的历史	译自《蜀志》
1927	Elfrida Hudson	赫德森	陌上桑	
1927	Elfrida Hudson	赫德森	杜甫题王宰《戏题画山水图歌》	诗歌
1928	Arthur William Hummel	恒慕义	中国过去19个世纪的量具	译自王国维的作品
1928	Elfrida Hudson	赫德森	《风筝误》节译	
1930	Charles Budd	卜德小姐	汉诗选译：《秋风辞》、《风雪》、《南溪》	原作者分别为刘彻、沈周、元遗山
1932	P. Y. Saeki	佐伯好郎	《喜听谜诈所经》英译	
1932	P. Y. Saeki	佐伯好郎	中国景教文献英译（《一神论》《世尊布施论》）	
1933	Cheng Te-K'un	郑德坤	《穆天子传》英译	
1934	Esson M. Gale	盖乐	《盐铁论》第20－28卷	布德伯格、林振翰参与翻译
1934	Lee Shao-Chang	李绍昌	《般若波罗蜜多心经》英译	
1936	S. C. Chen		西汉经济学家桑弘羊	译自：青年协会书局出版的《中国杰出人物传》
1938	Morgan, Evan	莫安仁	康熙时代与当时的风尚	译自《东华录》

资料来源：文会《会刊》和附表1。
注：《盐铁论》1－19卷由盖乐翻译，1931年由 E. J. Brill, Ltd., Leyden 出版，一部分发表在《中国社会及政治科学报》(1934－4)上。该文出版后，该书才全部被翻译出来。见 Discoursis on Salt and Iron, JNCBRAS, Vol. LXV, P73.

上述翻译都是出于文会会员自己的兴趣和个人行为，这些作品也被有些学者所引用，因此不能忽视他们在"东学西传"方面所作出的贡献。但是由于文会没有组织统一的文献翻译工程,文献翻译工作也不是文会工作的重点,会刊上所刊出的翻译作品只能是点缀而已,影响是很有限的。这些文献的刊布是否促进了相关研究的进程,现在尚无直接见证材料,但是一定时期内汉学领域内的研究热点并没有导致文会对相关中文文献的翻译和刊布。因此,在资料翻译方面文会贡献不是很大。

四、人才培养

文会是一个松散的团体,其经费主要来源于会员会费和工部局拨款,不像欧美各国境内的皇家学院、研究所、大学等机构拥有较为强大的政府财力的支持,文会连一个培训语言的功能都不具备,又何谈专门培养学术人才。就汉学发展而言,19世纪以来欧美产生两支汉学家队伍,一支是完全在欧美各个国家内培养成长起来的汉学家,如法国的沙畹、雷慕沙,德国的嘎伯冷兹,他们多半是通过自学中文,然后在本国大学等研究机构中成长起来的汉学家,可以称之为半自学半经院式汉学家。另一支是19世纪中叶中国门户被武力打开后,涌入而来的各国传教士、外交官及部分商人,他们在工作之余从事对中国的研究,并逐渐成长为汉学家,如美国的卫三畏、裨治文,英国的伟烈亚力、庄延龄,德国穆林德、卫礼贤,俄国的贝勒、孔琪庭,意大利的晁德莅、武尔披齐。他们可以称为侨居地汉学家。

文会为那些后来成为汉学家的早期在华外交官、传教士、部分商人提供了学习交流的外部环境,促成他们进入了汉学的研究领域。很多近代汉学家都有一段在中国尤其是上海工作的经历。工作之余他们光顾文会的图书馆、博物院,参加文会的演讲会,一些人的研究成果就是依据文会图书馆的藏书和博物院的标本做出来的。浏览会刊便会发现一些汉学家的作品最初就是发表在会刊上的,尤其是那些来华旅行者,文会给了他们发表作品的机会,这在近代外国在华文化机构中是不多见的。可以说,文会客观上促使越来越多的来华从事考察、探险的军官、学者、旅行家等人加入到介绍、研究中国历史文化的队伍中,并引导他们走向汉学研究的道路。当然,成为汉学家更多的还是归功于他们自己的勤奋和努力,他们对于汉学研究几乎也可以说是个人行为。不过,文会为他们提供的学习交流的平台对他们走向汉学研究所起的作用也不可忽视。

五、研究方法

这方面至今尚无可资借鉴的学术史论著,已有的相关研究论及汉学发展史,也只是收录论著目录而已,却没有触及百余年来学术的传承和内在关系。这是由近代汉学和现今汉学史研究的水平决定的。近代百年汉学研究虽然不乏精品,但更多的成果还是搜集、翻译和整理资料,汉学的真正发展还是二战之后的事,而对世界汉学史的研究,现在还是在收集以往的汉学研究资料,整理阶段尚未达到。

17世纪以来西方学术的发展为研究东方学提供了方法,与中国学者相比,19世纪西方学者对于中国的研究已经采用了17世纪以来形成的语言学、民族学、考古学、社会学等新兴学科的方法来研究中国历史和社会,为中国传统的学术研究注入了新的血液,这已经为20世纪20、30年代中国学者所承认。

就文会而言,会员们在运用上述方法来调查研究中国的同时,也将汉学研究带向规范化和制度化。文会的调查报告是建立在完备的资料和可靠的数据基础上的,个案论述则注重实证的方法,研究型的文章一般都是立论有据、引文规范。文会会员以自己辛勤汗水和不懈努力将汉学研究纳入到了国际学术平台上,成为东方学中的一支显学。但是必须看到能够称得上研究型的论文不多,只有少数关于民族和民俗学的论文能够将田野考察和历史文献相结合来论述,其余多数论文还是"只事阐幽,不知博览;只事辑佚,而无根本"。[1]因此在方法上面,文会对汉学的贡献不能过高评价。

综上所述,文会在近代国际汉学的发展中具有特殊的地位,它为近代在华外侨的汉学研究提供了一个良好的环境,客观上培育了一些汉学家,并通过广大会员的努力,汉学被纳入到了欧美学术阵营中,成为东方学中的一门显学。文会也因此成为世界汉学在远东的学术交流中心。

第二节 亚洲文会与西学东渐

文化交流是双向的。文会的宗旨虽然是调查研究中国,而不是向中国传播西方的文明和科技,但文会建立在上海,设有图书馆、博物院并发行会刊,成员足迹又遍布中国和欧美各国。因而文会在调查研究中国、向西方世界提供中国社会知识的同时,也向中国传播了一些西学,这主要表现在以下两方面。

一、学术研究方面

文会向中国学界传播了部分领域内的西方研究成果。文会的一些研究成果受到中国学者的称赞,有的也成为中国学者相关研究领域的主要参考文献。

穆林德的《直隶的脊椎动物及中国动物命名法》叙述了直隶地区48种哺乳动物、14种爬行动物、316种鸟、27种鱼的特征、体型、习性、种属以及动物的中文记载和西方人士的相关研究成果。该文50年后还被中国科学界誉为"虽非巨著,要为名作"。[2]

苏阿德的《中国博物学》、海德生的《长江三角洲的成长》当时就被誉为"具有永久的价值",就连50年后的今天还有人肯定该文的价值。[3]祁天锡的《苏州及其周边地区动植物初探》列举了各类植物名录,在此基础上,作者修订出版了《江苏植物名录》,1921年由我国著名植物学家钱崇澍译成中文,由中国科学社出版,"凡研习植物分类学者,莫不手执一卷"。[4]

1936年《史学消息》辟专栏介绍世界汉学有关杂志,高度评价会刊,称赞"在许多方面都有佳作和珍贵资料。百余年间,对中国有价值之探讨数见不鲜。"对文会会刊作了详细介绍,对1936、1937年会刊上的论文一一作了提要。[5]

会刊上的一些文章为中国学者的相关研究提供了帮助,这可以从中国学者编纂的有关学科的论文索引反映出来。袁同礼编的《中国音乐书举要》收录了会刊中的两篇音乐文章;杨遵仪编的《中国地质文献目录》收录了会刊上发表的地质学论文。1960年中国科学院地理研究所编的《中国地貌学文献目录 1855－1958》收录了9篇。至于引用的文章就更多了,前文已有论述。

从现有的资料看,文会在自然方面,尤其是地质学的研究成果受到中国学界的重视,对于

---

[1] 伯希和曾提出汉学研究者有四弊:一、只凭对音,不考实事;二、只凭类书,不察史料;三、只事阐幽,不知博览;四、只事辑佚,而无根本。见《世界各国汉学研究论文集》,第200页。
[2] 张孟闻:《中国科学史举隅》,《民国丛书》第一编第90册,上海书店1989年版,第63页。
[3] Recent Literature, The New China Review, Vol. IV, Oct. 1922, No.5. pp422－424. 胡道静:《历史上以上海为研究对象的学术团体》,《档案与历史》,1998年第2期。
[4] 王志稼:《祁天锡博士事略》,《科学》24卷1期(1940年1月),第70页。
[5] 《西洋汉学论文提要》,《史学消息》,第1卷第1期,第10页。

中国相关学术领域的发展应该说是起了一定推动作用。但是在人文方面,文会的研究成果被中国学者引用的次数屈指可数。前文(第四章)所列举的中国学术期刊对文会会刊上文章的引用情况是:几乎都是只有一次,三次以上者极为罕见。

20世纪中外之间的学术交流已经形成,中国学者对西方学者的研究是比较注意的。1914年蔡元培就十分惊叹欧美人士所开拓的汉学研究新领域,为此感慨"庖人不知庖,尸祝越俎而代之"。[1] 就连早期对西方汉学评价不高("其用功甚苦,而成功殊微")的胡适也认为,"然其人多不为吾国古代成见陋说所拘束,故其所著书往往有启发吾人思想之处,不可以一笔抹煞也"。[2] 二三十年代,陈寅恪、王国维、赵元任等人与西方汉学家都保持着密切的联系,冯承钧、张星烺还翻译了不少西方汉学家的论著。然而这一时期,中国学者对于这个设在中国的远东汉学重镇却记录得不多。曾经被文会邀请去演讲并发表过文章的蔡元培、胡适二人在日记中对自己参加演讲一事均有记载,而对该机构,除了"亚洲文会"四字之外,没有任何过多的说明。曾经设有"学界消息"栏目——专门记载国内外学界消息的《国学季刊》和《清华学报》,从创刊到停止从没有提到任何有关文会的消息;相反对于伯希和的去世,有数家报纸和期刊都登了讣告和悼念文章。因此可以说文会对中国学术的影响是极为有限的。

文会未能进入多数中国人文学者视野的主要原因在于:对于中国学者来说,文会人文研究成果之学术含量相对较低,在整个汉学领域,文会的水平尚未进入顶尖行列。翻阅一下20世纪的中外汉学杂志,便能看出文会在整个汉学领域中的地位。笔者参阅1933年贝德士编的《西文东方学报论文举要》中列举的19种欧美汉学杂志,并加上1934年《远东季刊》所附的汉学杂志目录表,列出以下22种当时汉学界比较著名的西文杂志,见表6-3。

表6-3　　　　　　　　　　　20世纪各国发行的汉学期刊

名　称	代　号	发行地	文　字	创刊年份
东方语言学会会刊	MSOS	德国	德	1898
亚洲艺术	ArA	德国	德、英、法	1905
大亚细亚	AM	德国	德、英	1924
亚洲艺术杂志*	OZ	德国	德	1912
汉学杂志*	Sinica	德国	德	1924
东洋文库研究纪要	MTB	东京	英	1926
亚洲学报	JA	法国	法	1922
亚洲艺术评论	RDAA	法国	法	1912
法兰西远东学院校刊*	BEFEO	河内	法	1900
东方学报	AO	荷兰	法、英	1922
通报*	TP	荷兰	法、英	1890
东方艺术	EA	美国	英	1928

---

[1] 蔡元培:《学风·发刊词》,见高平叔主编的《蔡元培文集——卷八·语言文字》,锦绣出版事业公司1995年版,第329页。
[2] 曹伯言整理:《胡适日记全编》(二),安徽教育出版社2001年版,第315页。

续表

名　　称	代　号	发行地	文　字	创刊年份
远东季刊*	FEQ	美国	英	1934
哈佛亚洲研究*	HJAS	美国	英	1936
远东博物院汇刊*	BMFEA	瑞典	英	1929
东方学院学报	BSOS	英国	英	1917
皇家亚洲学会会刊	RAS	英国	英	1827
华裔学志*	MS	北京	英、法	1933
中国科学与美术杂志*	CJSA	上海	英	1923
中国评论*	C-Re	上海	英	1872
教务杂志*	CR	上海	英	1861
文会会刊*	JNCBRAS	上海	英、法	1858
新中国评论*	NC-Re	上海	英	1919

注：1. 选自贝德士编：《西文东方学报论文举要》，金陵大学中国文化研究所印行，民国二十二年。
2. 这里未列举俄国的《学士院汇报》(IAN)、《亚细亚论纂》(AN)两份期刊，因为笔者翻阅上述期刊时发现俄文杂志被学界引用比较少。
3. 标 * 的杂志，笔者翻阅了1950年以前出版的全部期刊，未标的只是见到每份刊物的部分卷册。

这些汉学杂志大体上可以分为两大类：法国、荷兰、德国创办的刊物所刊登的论文大多是针对个别问题所做的深入研究，很少就大问题做泛泛之论，可以归之为考证派；英美所创办的刊物所刊登的文章翻译多于论述、理论多于考证，可以归之为翻译派。现在看来这两派的贡献各有千秋，难分高低，但是在20世纪二三十年代就不同了，因为当时中国学术界，尤其是国学方面，"整理国故"是学者们所追求的方向。所以《通报》、《法兰西远东语言学校校刊》、《汉学》（中法大学汉学研究所创办）、《华裔学志》等考证色彩较浓的刊物能为中国学者所重视。而文会就不同了，无论其演讲还是会刊，都有很大篇幅的游记和一些泛泛而论的文章，这自然不会被中国学者所重视。严格意义上讲，文会并不是一个严谨的学术机构，20世纪20年代后文会为了吸纳社会资金，对于会员的要求已大为放松，文会理事会经常呼吁社会人员加入文会，借此来增加文会的收入。

二、社会方面

文会向中国人传播了近代西方的公共文化观念。文会拥有图书馆、会员、博物院，而且发行会刊、举办演讲、接待来往学者，在近代上海社会文化生活中有着特殊的地位。文会的会员近一半在上海，19世纪末每年平均在150人左右，20世纪每年平均在300人左右，他们参加演讲、免费获得会刊。文会的演讲活动是向社会敞开的，20世纪《北华捷报》和《字林西报》刊登文会演讲的消息，都有一句"Open to the Public"，具体每次参加的人数现在已很难得知，根据文会理事会记录，19世纪在20－30人左右，20世纪上升到百余人左右，1935年在天安堂举办的《台湾》演讲就有100余人。

近代上海，外侨办有三家较大的图书馆：徐家汇藏书楼、租界工部局图书馆和文会图书馆。但是徐家汇藏书楼"只准本教堂之人入观或借阅，其非本堂之人，无论何人均不准观"；工部局图书馆需要会员方可借阅，西人"无论何时均可入会，至于华人入会极难，非体面之人介绍不可"。[1]文会图书馆虽然没有工部局图书馆和徐家汇藏书楼藏书丰富,[2]但是文会图书馆藏书专业,且对外开放,"在会者可借出,不在会者可入览"。[3]对于那些热衷于远东事务——尤其是中国——的中外学者来说,文会图书馆的功效自然要大于前者;对于那些在华的外人来说,如果要了解和认识中国,文会图书馆之便利更是不言自明了。开放的文会给国人的启示是:文化资源应该向社会开放。这大大冲击了中国人之"藏"重于"看"的传统观念,为晚清沪上公共图书馆的建立起了示范作用。此外,图书馆还向中国人传入了近代图书馆学及相关思想,前文已有论述。

文会博物院最早向中国人传播了近代博物学知识。1871年,文会建立博物院后便致力于收集中国及远东地区的自然标本和历史文物,逐渐成为远东地区著名的博物馆。该馆免费向世人开放,影响极大。在近代,上海博物院的名声要远远大于文会,《北平博物馆馆刊》就不时刊登有上海博物院消息,《东方杂志》、《申报》也时常单独报道博物院的有关消息。民国年间论述上海近代文化机构的中外文专著也经常是把"上海博物院"作单独词条予以介绍。[4]

文会为中国近代博物馆的发展提供了模式。历来中国人对于文物古董的收集都系私人行为,只藏不展,大大降低了藏品的价值。鸦片战争后,来华外人向中国引进了"博物馆"这种文化设施。最早建立的是1868年天主教耶稣会创建的徐家汇博物院,但是1883年才建立馆舍。而且该馆附属于宗教事业,藏品虽然丰富,却不公开开放,游人参观还有种种限制,"起初须有熟识之人引导介绍方可入门参观,以后规定每日午后准人参观,但须负责管理的法国传教士准许后方可入内"。[5]1874年文会会所建成后,就在二楼设立了标本陈列室,并向社会开放,每日上午九点到下午五点,周六下午两点到四点,任人入览,不取游资。实际上,文会博物院是上海最早建成并向社会开放的博物院。与徐家汇博物院相比,文会博物院开放程度更大,其藏品又多靠社会捐助,更加体现了公共文化机构的社会性之本质。

文会博物院建成后就向中国传播了西方的近代博物学知识。文会博物院建成后不久,《申报》就予以报道:

> 泰西各大城池夙有成例,凡在该地方人,必公建一院,将飞禽走兽以及各动物并列于内,以便博物者随时赏玩。如在府城,则将阖郡之物实之;如在都城,则将天下之物实之,名曰博物院。现在旅居上海之西商亦仿效泰西规模,在本埠设立一院,将中国与东洋各物齐集聚院中,事虽创始,而所罗列者亦不少。计属毛虫者,有震泽湖旁之野猪小鼠等;羽族者,有鹰鹊麻雀等;又有水族中名物,不能殚述。余如螳螂、蚱蜢、蝴蝶之类亦各分其种,各表其名。每一物件系从何处得来,何人相赠,必署明悬贴于上。中外人有往观者,俱不取值也。珍藏羽毛各类,西国向有妙法,虽皮已干枯而毛可不落。现在此法华人已得之。且有从外国购到玻璃眼镜,故无论是何异兽珍禽,已经装点,便栩栩大有生气。[6]

该报道表明文会博物院向中国人传播了以下西学:

---

[1]《上海指南》卷四《公益团体》,商务印书馆,宣统元年。
[2] 文会图书馆是不收藏小说之类的文学图书。工部局图书馆则藏有大量的英文小说,因而后者的借阅次数要远远多于前者。
[3]《上海指南》卷三《公益事业》,1914年。
[4] 参见:W. Y. Chyen(庄文亚)Compiled and Edited, Handbook of Cultural Institutions in China, Chinese National Committee on Intellectual Co-operation, Shanghai, 1936. 和冯陈祖怡的《上海各图书馆概览》,中国国际图书公司1934年。
[5]《上海通史·晚清文化》第6卷,上海人民出版社1999年版,第204页。
[6]《创设博物院》,《申报》1875年11月4日。

1. 博物院这一新生事物的概念,换言之,中国人知道了什么是博物院。
2. 博物院之功能,即收藏、展览,供人欣赏。
3. 动植物分类学,中国的动植物分类学首先是由法国传教士谭微道建立的,"以科学方法研究鸟类,在吾国当推谭氏"。[1] 19世纪50、60年代谭微道在华北等地采集中国鸟类标本,后撰写《中国鸟类图谱》(David et Oustalet, *Les Oiseaux de Chine*, Pairs, 1877),该书是最早对中国鸟类做科学分类的研究论著,可惜它未在中国出版,中国学界真正了解动植物分类,是到了20世纪的事了。谭氏也是文会会员,且是首任博物院监院(馆长),他虽未将其著作传向中国,但是博物院内标本的最早制作、分类和早期整理都是由他完成的,这些标本的分类恰是体现他个人在动植物分类学方面的思想。
4. 标本制作方法,文会博物院的标本制作是由谭微道传授给中国人王树衡的,而王树衡又专任文会剥制师,标本制作技术已通过文会博物院传到了中国人手中。
5. 藏品之摆放,即分类摆放,并置标签;展品要尽可能地生动活泼。
6. 博物馆之性质,博物馆是公共事业,向社会开放,人人均可免费参观。可以说,博物院将人人有受教育权利的民主观念传播给了中国人。

博物院的建成不仅将这一新生事物即博物学知识传播到中国,而且其"鸟类标本颇有可观,时时举行展览会、讲演会,为国人所注意"。[2] 实物是博物馆传播知识信息的载体,它在传递信息中具有极大的说服力、可信性、简捷性。20世纪30年代每年都有数万观众来参观博物院,这说明已经有不少的中国人接触到了博物学知识。也正是在文会博物院的示范作用下,中国人自己也创办了博物院。1905年张謇在南通创建了南通博物苑,分天然、历史、美术三部,并设有陈列馆。1912年教育部设立历史博物馆。1912年中央观象台、农商部地质调查所陈列室成立。中国人自己的自然与历史博物馆正是在文会博物院和其他在华西人创办之博物馆的影响下产生的。

需要指出的是,19世纪时,公共文化机构的示范作用并没有促成中外文化之间的交流。主要原因是文会是由外人创办,藏书又系英文,演讲也是英语,又不翻译、发行西学书籍。这一时期中国人能够熟练听懂和读写英文的人可以说是寥寥无几,文会只是在外侨中有些影响,它只是促进了中国文化的西传。就引进西学方面,除了中国人了解到的一些初步的博物学和动植物学知识外,文会对于"西学东渐"贡献甚微。20世纪后,随着文会的日益壮大和更加开放,客观上文会向中国人传播的西学在深度和广度上也超过了19世纪。这一时期,文会的研究成果已为中国学者所注意,中国学者在研究相关问题时也都会吸取文会成员的研究成果,并进一步推进。会刊上的"汉学新书评"专栏和图书馆实际上向中国学者传播了西方学者对于中国研究的最新成果和信息;博物院则通过出版《中国博物学:上海博物院指南》进一步加深了国人的博物学知识;通过展览、讲解又向国人传播了西方近代自然科学知识,尤其是地质学和动植物分类学。文会的演讲、接待来往学者,尤其是邀请中国学者演讲,使得中国学者认识到文会这种文化机构存在的价值——它能为同行提供理论探讨和技艺切磋,促进开展学术交流和学术发展,造就社会学术氛围,提高大众科学素养。正是在文会的示范作用下和学者的认识基础

---

[1] 经利彬:《谭微道在中国生物学上之贡献》,《真理之光》第1卷第4期(1944),第459页。
[2] 傅振伦:《中国博物馆史略》,《东方杂志》11卷15号,第36页。

上，20世纪中国学者纷纷自筹经费、聚集同仁创建了各类学术团体和文化机构，如1910年成立的中国医学研究会，1914年成立的中国科学社。这些学会的运作方式很多与文会并无二致，也都建立图书馆、博物馆、举办演讲活动、发行刊物、出版研究论著。因此也可以说文会向中国提供了学术研究机构的模式。

总之，由于文会主要是研究中国而不是向中国传播西学，文会没有采取直接的西学东渐行动，所以文会向中国传播西学只是其客观效果。

结 语

　　皇家亚洲文会北华支会是近代外侨在上海创建的一个文化机构,无疑,它是殖民侵略的产物,但它却不是为殖民侵略服务的文化机构,这是文会的一个显著特征。文会建立的最初动机是帮助在华外侨了解中国的社会,方便他们在中国的生活。正如创建者所说,"把它看作使自己从日常生活和烦琐事务中恢复精神的方式","它将成为迈向较高知识分子之路和便利社会的公共资源"。1858年,文会加入大英皇家亚洲学会,并成为其支会,但是前者与后者必须区别看待,因为后者为殖民侵略服务的倾向要大于前者。大英皇家亚洲学会的建立有着浓厚的东方学背景。18世纪以来,随着殖民扩张运动,西方对东方的研究也进入职业化阶段,标志是拥有一批专门的研究人员和研究机构。西方各国先后在欧美和亚洲各地成立了各类"亚洲学会",旨在对亚洲进行调查研究。1781年,荷兰人首先在爪哇巴达维雅设立巴达维雅学艺协会。1784年,英国人乔恩思在加尔各答成立孟加拉亚细亚学会。此后,英国人又在孟买创立孟买文学会(Bombay Literary Society)。1823年3月15日,考尔勃克、斯当东和约翰斯顿等人在伦敦创建了大不列颠及爱尔兰皇家亚细亚学会(简称"大英皇家亚洲学会")。成立大会上,考尔勃克说大不列颠及爱尔兰皇家亚细亚学会的研究范围要包括亚洲各国的政治事务、哲学经典,也要注意他们的神话、地理方面的知识。[1] "政治事务"是大英皇家亚洲文会首要关心的问题,而上海文理学会创建时的目的主要在于丰富寓沪外侨的精神生活,创建动机上已经反映出二者的差异。此外,历史上二者间的联系并不密切。文会的发展历程显示,除了加入大英皇家亚洲学会成为其支会外,二者之间没有其他的联系。而加入的目的也只是为了借助后者以便获取更多的社会资源,"文会会员若在伦敦可以参加总会的会议,有权使用总会的图书馆"。[2] 从文会的会议记录看,除了交流各自的会刊外,并没有其他方式的交流记录。从各自会刊的内容看,也发现不了太多的关联,《大英皇家亚洲学会会刊》几乎不转引文会会刊的文章,也从不在书评栏目中介绍、评价文会会刊上所刊登的文章。[3]《大英皇家亚洲学会会刊》上不乏关于中国的文章,但是内容和风格与文会会刊都完全两样。前者学术性见长,后者可读性较强。文会虽然加入大英皇家亚洲学会,但自己的风格并没有改变,可以说,文会是完全独立于大英皇家亚洲学会之外的。当然,大英皇家亚洲学会为殖民侵略服务的程度究竟有多大,还有待于学界来研究,不过其背后英国政府的背景是比较明显的,因为它和英国皇家学会一样,虽然也是学者自己创立的,但是"政府可以自由地就各种科学问题请求学会提供咨询意见

---

[1] Frederick Eden Pargiter Compiled, *Centenary Volume of the Royal Asiatic Society of the Great Britain and Ireland 1823-1923*, Published by the Royal Asiatic Society, London, 1923, Pviii.

[2] Royal Asiatic Society, *North China Herald*, Vol. XVI, No. 848, 27th, Oct., 1866, P171.

[3] 相反,《通报》则对文会会刊每期的目录都会做简单介绍。

和帮助"。[1]而文会却无这方面的功能,尽管从成立到结束,文会与工部局关系密切,数任会长也是英美等国驻上海领事,但是文会从向英国政府申请土地建立会所起,实际上已经被定位是社会公共文化机构。[2]作为一个社会公共文化机构,文会不同于欧美各国在亚洲各地建立的东方学会,也不同于日本的满铁调查机构,可以说文会没有强烈的殖民侵略色彩。因此文会在文化交流方面,尤其是向西方传播中国的方方面面知识相对要客观许多。不可否认,文会会刊中也有不少能够为殖民侵略服务的文章,但是这并不是文会的主观目的,只是客观上的效果。

文会也不等同于那些近代外国在华建立的宗教文化机构。近代外国传教士在中国建立了为数不少的宗教文化机构,这些机构也从事对中国的调查研究,在向西方传播中国的真实信息方面也做出了巨大的贡献。如《教务杂志》对中国的历史文化也都有不错的研究文章,它在改变西方人对中国的认识方面起了重要作用。但是,不言而喻,宗教机构的主要任务在于宗教传播,它有着明显的关注领域和研究目标。文会则不同,它旨在"调查研究中国各项事情",从文会会刊所刊登的内容看,文会的调查研究涉及到地理、历史、民俗、动物、植物、哲学、语言、宗教、法律、音乐、考古、医药、化学、物理、工程、地磁、地质、绘画、交通、商业贸易、社会经济、科学总论、图书馆学、人类学、政治学、文献学、星象学、碑刻、货币、陶瓷等30余个学科,宗教只是其一部分内容。值得注意的是,文会会员也有很多传教士,但是他们在文会的活动几乎没有宗教色彩。因此,可以说,文会关注的对象和调查研究的内容要比宗教文化机构宽泛。

文会的第二个特征是:它在发展过程中逐渐形成了综合型的文化交流模式。

鸦片战争后,来华外人先后创办了各种文化机构,这些文化机构在近代中外文化交流的整个过程中发挥了它们各自的功能。但是许多机构只具有单一的职能,以上海为例,1843年传教士们就创设了墨海书馆,1849年西侨创建了上海图书馆,但前者早期主要从事于《圣经》的印刷,目的在于传教;后者只是一个读书会,不仅圈子十分狭小,而且不对公众开放,所以二者文化交流的功能非常有限。文会则不同,与上述机构相比,虽然建立相对较晚,但是其组织之完善、目标之明确,近代独此一家。以其图书馆、博物院和大量的会员,形成了多元化的文化交流媒介。

文会图书馆收藏了各类外文杂志报刊和中国古代典籍。它向社会开放,非文会会员也可以免费进入图书馆阅览室阅读文献。它不仅为学者的学术研究提供了专业的资源和信息,而且也成为上海儿童及在校学生校外学习的场所,客观上成为中外文化交流的基地和社会教育的课堂,为社会公众提供了保护与传播知识的方便和机会。

博物院则收藏了数万件中国的文物艺术品和动植物标本,成为远东地区著名的自然历史博物馆之一。博物院举办专题讲座、文物艺术品展览,与世界各地交流各自的藏品。不仅向中国传播了自然历史文化知识和公共文化观念,而且把有关中国的自然历史信息和文化遗存信息传向世人,增加了外人对中国的感性认识。可以说,博物院成功地塑造了一个世界性的文化

---

[1] 安德拉德著,中国科学院图书馆情报室供稿:《英国皇家学会简史》,中国科学院计划局1979年版,第1页。
[2] 阿礼国代文会向英国政府申请土地时是以"建立一个包括图书馆、博物馆、演讲厅之用的土地"为名,"它能够帮助英国人民了解中国"。见1928年会刊:Alexander Michie, The Englishman in China During the Victorian Era, as illustrated in the Career of Sir Rutherford Alcock, Edingburg Blackwood, 1900. 工部局也一直把文会作为租界社会公共文化机构看待,在性能上将文会与工部局图书馆等同,见上海档案馆编:《工部局董事会会议录》(第5册),上海古籍出版社2001年版,第665页。

空间,从而将中国自然和历史文化知识传播到了世界各地。

众多的会员使得文会形成了全球化的中外文化交流网络。近代在华设立的各类文化机构,像文会这样拥有3 000余名会员的是不多的,这些会员来自34个国家,其足迹则遍及六大洲49个国家。由于文会和会员是通过会刊联系的,所以文会会员已经将文会对中国的认识和研究成果带到了48个国家(中国除外),大大提高了欧美各国对中国的认识。

组织机构的多元化和会员的广泛性形成了交流媒介的多元化。图书馆、博物院、会员三大模块使文会在近代文化交流中独具特色,在文化交流的效果方面,文会要比学校、书局等功能较为单一的文化机构大得多。

在活动上,文会不仅在中国开展调查研究活动,而且举行演讲活动,参加世界有关学术会议和举办文物展览活动。文会定期举办演讲会,演讲者多是文会会员,演讲内容多是对中国的研究或是近代外人在华之旅行游记。演讲是向公众开放的,听众由最初的会员发展到各色人群。演讲这一文化交流的渠道,使交流双方在较短的时间内传播了最新的研究成果,与单纯的文字符号传播相比,它更加生动、深刻、简捷,效果十分明显。文会曾派人出席国际地理学会、东方学大会等国际学术会议。通过参加这些会议,文会不断地把中国介绍到西方,在改变西方人对中国的认识方面起到了积极作用。在中国,文会经常举办中国文物及艺术品的展览活动,大大推进了在华外人对中国艺术的研究,而且借助于中国艺术品使西方人加深了对中国文化的认识。此外,文会还出版会刊和书籍。会刊是汉学研究的资源宝库之一,受到中外学者的关注。学术圈外也拥有广泛的读者群体,这是因为它不仅有研究型的学术论文,也有大量充满趣味性的散文和游记;不仅有人文社会的调查研究,也有自然科学的探险考察。因此其不仅可以成为科学研究的重要参考文献,也可以成为普通百姓的床头休闲用书。并且就传播符号而言,会刊以英文为主,读者群体自然会比《通报》(法文为主)、《东亚杂志》(德文为主)这样的汉学杂志多,文会会刊曾经在巴黎、伦敦、莱比锡、法兰克福四地设立销售点。通过文字文本,文会已经将关于中国的知识和信息传播到了西方,成为西方认识中国的重要参考文献之一,在改变一般西方人对中国的认识方面起了重要作用。

这种集演讲、展览、出版、发行于一身的文化机构,采用多元化的文化交流方式在近代文化交流过程中是不多见的。同样是文化交流,很多机构却形式单一,要么仅仅做编译出版工作,如广学会与《万国公报》;要么仅仅是传授知识,如教会学校。许多文化机构的传播对象也非常狭小,如教会组织和一些专业的学术团体,这些机构一般是不对公众开放的,工部局图书馆举办的演讲会和徐家汇天主教博物馆举办文物、标本展,在很多情况下华人是难以接近的。所以,在文化交流途径方面,文会是唯一的多元化渠道的机构,自然其影响和效果也是其他机构难以达到的。

文化传播的最大效果在于,"传播者和受播者的某些属性应该是相似的,而在另外某些方面是相异的"。[1] 文会与其他文化机构相比,在文化交流方面并无本质上的差异,但是在交流媒介的多样化、交流途径的多元化以及交流内容的丰富性方面,它是独有的,因而所取得的效果自然是其他机构不能比拟的。它不仅为较高层次的学术研究提供了资源和信息,也满足了社会文化生活的需要;它不仅加速了西方对中国的认识和了解,也为国内外对我国的自然科学

---

[1] 朱增补:《文化传播学》,中国广播电视出版社1993年版,第18页。

调查研究起了先锋作用。文会虽然只存在95年,但它延续和拓展了文化交流的时空,它所形成的文化交流的综合模式至今仍值得借鉴。从某种意义上看,文化交流不能只停留于学术交流研究的层面上。

文会主要调查研究中国,而不是致力于西学东渐。因此,它在近代中西文化交流方面的贡献也主要体现在它在近代汉学史上的地位。文会在近代汉学史,尤其在近代西方汉学史上的地位是本课题需要总结的第三个问题。因为汉学是与"东学西传"和"西学东渐"同时发生、同时进行的文化交流的一个组成部分,而文会在汉学方面也作出了一定的贡献,前文已有论述,这里主要再深入探讨一下文会在近代西方汉学史上的地位。

汉学,英文名称Sinology,目前学界尚有不同的解释。[1]已有的概念对于汉学研究对象之界定侧重于强调外国人对中国历史、地理、语言、文化的研究,亦即主要还是人文社会科学方面,而且尤其强调的是对中国古代方面的研究。至于外国人对中国的自然科学研究和外国人对当时中国现象的研究,学术界有不同认识。[2]实际上,这样的汉学概念界定过于狭隘,因为16世纪以来,西方人对中国的研究有很多是针对中国当时的现象,如费正清等人对近代中国的研究;还有的是在科学方面,如李希霍芬对中国地质的考察。这些研究成果,无论是当时还是现在,其学术价值并不低于那些对中国古代史地语文的研究,同样释放出璀璨的光芒。因此,汉学研究对象的界定从时空两方面都应该予以延伸和拓展,研究方法也不能仅仅拘泥于考证之法。

论述文会在近代西方汉学史上的地位,首先要涉及到整个汉学史的发展脉络,尤其是19世纪以来的西方汉学发展史。目前学术界对汉学史的发展阶段尚有不同的看法,但是也大都认为19、20世纪是汉学的繁荣、发达、建立时期。[3]实际上,西方汉学19世纪与20世纪有明显的不同。[4]笔者认为,对这两个阶段作如下划分比较合适。

第一阶段:汉学初创时期,19世纪初至1890年《通报》创办。

一个学科或者说一门学问的建立要有三个条件:1.建立专门的研究机构、培养专门的研究人才,如各国汉学机构的建立、大学汉语系的创建;2.学科体系的建立:研究对象相对明确、研究方法相对成熟、研究队伍比较稳定;3.相关资料、工具书、专著的编纂和出版。就汉学而言,19世纪还没有达到上述三要件。虽然法国、英国、德国也建立了汉学研究机构,几个大学也设立了汉语系,但是远没有达到培养汉学人才的功能。这一时期各国还是兼学满语,通过满语来

---

[1] 详见:阎纯德《汉学和西方的汉学研究》,《汉学研究》第3集,中国和平出版社1998年版;张国刚《德国的汉学研究》,中华书局1994年版;李学勤《法国汉学·序》第1辑,清华大学出版社1996年版;计翔翔《十七世纪中期汉学著作研究》(前言部分),上海古籍出版社2002年版。计翔翔对学术界关于汉学之不同概念和汉学史之不同分期做了梳理。张国刚对"汉学"和"中国学"二者做了论述。

[2] 李学勤认为sinology专指有关中国历史文化、语言文学等方面的研究。有些学者则把外人对作者当时所处的中国社会现象的研究称之为"中国学",而不能称之为"汉学"。周晓红甚至认为中国学只是在二战之后才出现。

[3] 莫东寅将18世纪前的都写"西方人关于中国的知识",19-20世纪则写"鸦片战争后汉学之发达"。阎春德的划分是:汉学萌芽时期(公元前后至15世纪)、汉学初创时期(16至18世纪)、汉学繁荣扩展时期(18世纪末至20世纪中叶)、汉学的当代意识和发展趋势(20世纪中叶以后)。计翔翔对近代西方汉学史的发展阶段是这样划分的:前汉学阶段(公元前后—16世纪80年代)、早期汉学时期或古典汉学时期(16世纪末至18世纪)、现代汉学时期或发达汉学时期(19世纪以后)。张国刚则说:西方汉学发轫时期是16至18世纪,19世纪汉学在欧洲形成为一个学科。吴孟雪认为欧洲汉学缘起于明中后期,即16世纪中叶至17世纪中叶这百年间。张西平把西方汉学划分为"游记汉学"(《马可波罗游记》到耶稣会入华)、"传教士汉学"(1601年利玛窦进京到19世纪初)、"专业汉学"(以1814年法兰西学院正式任命雷慕沙为"汉族、鞑靼、满语言文学教授"为标志)三个阶段。以上见张西平的《应重视对西方早期汉学的研究》,《中华读书报》2000年11月9日。

[4] 周振鹤先生将1815年法兰西学院汉学讲座正式开始以后的汉学界分为两个阶段:第一阶段的汉学是学习介绍型的汉学,第二阶段则是研究型的汉学。两个阶段的分点以《通报》创办的1890年为标志。详见《马伯乐对中国历史地理学的贡献》。

解读中国经书,1814年法兰西学院设置的汉学讲座全称是"汉族和鞑靼——满族语言与文学讲座"。而且汉语的学习主要是为培养通商、外交人才,并不完全当成学问来研习,即便如此,学习汉语的人也不多。1888年剑桥大学就设立了汉语系,但翟理思在汉学教授任上33年,也不过才收了3个汉语学生。[1] 1887年柏林创立东方语言学校,内设华、日语两部,只为造就外交及通商人才,至于汉学的高深之研究则付之阙如。1893年嘎伯冷兹死后,汉学科也没有了。[2] 因此这一时期各国的汉学机构在汉学上的贡献并不大,很多人的汉语主要是在中国学习掌握的,他们在专攻本业之余,又兼治汉学。

这一阶段,各国的汉学成果主要还是"学习介绍型的汉学,也就是西方的汉学家通过学习中国的语言与文献,了解了中国的历史与文化,并将中国的有关文献以翻译的形式介绍给西方读者。这些翻译往往要加上一些必要的注释,如沙畹对《史记》的译注。这种介绍还包括对中国现状的介绍,这一方面是英美的汉学家做得较多。这一时期的汉学还有一个特点,那就是汉语与欧洲语言对照的双语词典与汉语语法书籍以及其他工具书的编纂出版,这也是为了学习汉语文献与了解中国的需要。"[3] 汉学的研究方法还处于摸索阶段,各个汉学家也都是各自为战,研究内容五花八门,学界缺乏共同探讨的主题。由于多是翻译介绍中土文献于西方,精深的研究寥寥无几。

第二阶段:1890年,《通报》创办之后,汉学进入一个新的发展阶段,尤其到了20世纪20年代,汉学几乎在欧美各国正式建立。这一阶段称之为汉学建立时期。这一时期,汉学在很多方面都明显超越19世纪。

就汉学机构而言,这一时期欧美各国大学的汉语系远多于前期,而且执教者也多是汉学领域内的著名汉学家,他们几乎都有在中国工作的经历,汉语水平远高于19世纪的执教者。如1896年到美国成为加州大学首任东方语文讲座教授的傅兰雅,1902年到哥伦比亚大学任华学教授的夏德,1909年执教于汉堡殖民地学院中国语言文化系的福兰阁,1918年任教于柏林大学东方语言学校汉语教师佛尔克,1924年法兰克福大学汉学首任讲座教授卫礼贤,此外还有曼彻斯特大学汉语讲座教授庄延龄、耶鲁大学的赖得烈、哈佛大学的嘉托玛、奥斯陆大学的喜仁龙、维也纳大学的倭色讷。

除了在大学设立汉语系之外,各类专业水准较高的汉学研究机构也纷纷出现,如哈佛燕京学社、法兰克福汉学研究中心。这一时期也涌现出了一批高水平的汉学杂志,除了1890年高第创办的《通报》外,还有德国的《柏林东方语言学校校刊》(1903)、《东亚杂志》(1912)、《全亚季刊》(1924)、《汉学》,荷兰的《东方学报》,美国的《哈佛亚洲研究》、《远东季刊》,英国的《东方学院报》(1917),瑞典的《远东博物馆学报》,法国的《亚洲学报》(1922)等等。这些汉学专业刊物的主编也都是当时著名的汉学家,如《通报》的伯希和、高第,《哈佛亚洲研究》的嘉托玛,《汉学》的卫礼贤,他们的加盟大大推动了汉学的研究水平。

在研究方法上,"新的一批汉学家在语言能力方面已经大大超越于前人,不但用中国传统的考证手段在历史编纂学方面取得突出的成就,而且还用语言知识为武器,做出中国学者不能解决的问题来。在法国这方面可以伯希和与马伯乐为代表,他们的研究论文与中国乾嘉时期

---

[1] 陈尧圣:《英国的汉学研究》,见陶振誉等著《世界各国汉学研究论文集》(第一辑),台湾"国防研究院"印行,1968年,第186—189页。
[2] 莫东寅:《汉学发达史》,第112页。
[3] 周振鹤:《马伯乐对中国历史地理学的贡献》(该文系周振鹤老师2004年2月7日在北京大学的演讲稿)。

的考证文章可以说没有实质性的分别。"审音、勘同、考证等方法的掌握也为学界所掌握。[1]在研究对象上,19世纪末学界对汉学研究的对象已初步达成共识,语言、哲学、三大宗教、蒙藏及中西交通成为西方汉学界的主要研究对象。[2] 20世纪初敦煌文献发现后,中亚史地也成为学界研究的热点。可以说整个汉学界有了大家共同研究的问题,这大大不同于以前各个汉学家单兵作战的局面,自然在有关问题的研究深度上也超过以前。

此外,经过19世纪资料的整理工作,欧美学者已经认识到"撰写一部全面的、完整的中国历史的时机到了……现在我们应该将我们的精力平均分布于中国历史的各个方面"。[3]因此19世纪末20世纪初,中国通史和专史与其他方面专门著作也纷纷面世,如贝勒的《中国植物志》(1892)、赖得烈的《中国基督教史》(1892)、格鲁贝的《中国文学史》(1902)、福兰阁的《中华帝国通史》(1930)、夏德的《中国古代史》(1908)、马士的《中华帝国对外关系史》(1910)、翟理思的《中国文学史》(1901)、李希霍芬的《中国》(1912)、高本汉的《中国音韵学研究》(1916)、戴遂良(Léon Wieger)的《中国宗教之信仰及哲学思潮史》(1917)、劳费尔的《中国伊朗篇》(1918)、福开森的《中国艺术总览》(1920)、葛兰言(Paul Marcel Granet)的《中国人之宗教》(1922)、密亨利的《现代中国史》(1923)、佛尔克的《中国哲学史》(1927)、卫礼贤的《中国文学史》(1928)、马伯乐(Henri Maspero)的《中国古代史》(1928)、卡德(Thomas Francis Carter)的《中国印刷术源流史》(1934)等等。这些通史和专史的出现,无论是研究领域还是研究深度,都反映出汉学进入一个新的阶段。可以说,20世纪二三十年代,汉学作为一门学科所要求的条件已经达到,汉学已经确立。

文会是一个重要的汉学研究机构,它在汉学上的具体贡献,前文已有论述。文会的发展与近代西方汉学的发展是同步的,19世纪,文会也是处在资料搜集和整理的阶段,很多文章是翻译介绍中国的文献,少有深入研究具体问题。20世纪后,文会会刊上刊登的文章除了游记外,其余多是就中国历史、语言、考古、艺术等方面某个具体问题作的分析和论述。但是在19、20世纪这两个阶段,文会在近代西方汉学史上的地位和贡献却有着明显的不同。

19世纪,文会在西方汉学发展史上的地位,主要表现为以下两方面:第一,文会为汉学初创时期培养不少汉学家。前文已述,19世纪欧洲各国的汉学机构并不具备培养高水平汉语的功能,19世纪的汉学家多数在华工作过,在华工作,客观上促使他们掌握了汉语,并达到了治汉学的语言要求。文会为在华工作的外人提供了一个治汉学的环境和成为汉学家的途径,为他们提供了语言学习的平台、学术交流的机会和发表研究成果的园地。很多后来成为各个汉学机构的负责人和汉学家都曾经在上海呆过,并且是文会的会员,如英国的伟烈亚力、庄延龄、威妥玛、翟理思、理雅各、傅兰雅;法国的高第、沙畹、伯希和;俄国的贝勒、史禄国、孔琪庭、阿莱克斯夫;德国的卫礼贤、夏德、福兰阁、佛尔克、梅泽;美国的卫三畏、丁韪良、赖德烈、密亨利、德效骞、恒慕义、马士;瑞典的安特生、高本汉、喜仁龙、斯文赫定;意大利的武尔披齐,他们早年的学术生涯与亚洲文会有着密切的关系。亚洲文会是当时上海唯一一个机构健全、学术氛围较

---

[1] 周振鹤,《马伯乐对中国历史地理的研究》。
[2] 1892年国际东方学会议上已提出当时东方学研究的五大热点:1.印欧语系之研究,尤其是汉语语言孤岛的问题;2.佛教进入中国的过程及其对中国和东方社会的影响;3.蒙藏语言研究的必要性;4.古代埃及文明及其对中国的影响;5.中国的三大宗教;6.中国的哲学研究。实际上,主要还是汉学。见:Proceedings, JNCBRAS, Vol. XXVII, pp231-246.
[3] Latourette, K. S., A Survey of the work by Western Students of Chinese History, JNCBRAS, Vol. XLVII, P113、114.

强的文化机构,文会为他们提供了科研环境和图书资料,他们很多人经常光顾文会图书馆。他们早年的研究成果也是在文会演讲的,演讲过程中他们得到听众的指正与批评,获得了修改的建议。这些成果又通过文会会刊而声名远扬,进而确立这批人在汉学界的地位。如贝勒对中国植物学的研究就是首先在会刊上发表的(百余万字,共计1 398页,几乎占满了4大卷会刊),后来才被欧美各国单行出版。可以说,文会促成了很多在华外人走向汉学研究之路,客观上,培养了一批汉学家,而且这批汉学家在20世纪又成为各国汉学机构的主要负责人。因此,文会为近代西方汉学的建立作出了重要的贡献。

第二,19世纪亚洲文会居于汉学研究的前沿。这一时期,侨居地的汉学水平要高于欧美各国内的汉学水平。从这一时期的汉学成果看,多是在侨居地完成的,尤其是在中国完成的,至少也是作者在华期间完成的初步工作。如马礼逊的《英华词典》、理雅各翻译的中国经书(由王韬协助在香港英华书院完成)。这一时期文会处于调查阶段,和整个近代西方汉学发展是同步的,但是水平是居于前列的。由于文会设在中国,在资料编纂和调查方面明显要比欧美国内的汉学研究有优势,有关成果也相对客观真实,学术价值相对较高。事实上,这一时期一些重要的汉学成果也都是先出现在文会会刊上,除上述贝勒对中国植物学的研究外,梅辉立关于中国火药及火器的研究也是如此。文会会员还作了不少的资料整理工作,如伟烈亚力的《中国典籍中关于日月食的记录》,玛高温的《中国的文献学》,裨治文翻译的《苗族概述》,夏德的《古代陶瓷:中世纪中国工商业研究》,穆麟德的《论满洲文献》,慕阿德的《中国乐器及其他发声器之目录》,勃郎翻译的《西洋纪闻》,庄延龄翻译的《圣武记》(军事部分),还有中国皇帝年表、孔子与周公等历史人物之小传。这些文章在介绍中国和文献整理方面的贡献均处于当时的汉学前列。文会关于当时中国社会的调查,更是西方各国在国内不能完成的工作。所以,在学习介绍中国的语言文献、了解中国的历史与文化方面,文会是居于前列的,也可以说,在汉学初创时期,文会在近代西方汉学发展史上是领头羊。

20世纪文会在整个西方汉学中的地位不同于19世纪,已经落伍于欧美各国国内的汉学研究水平。这与20世纪西方汉学发展状况有极大关系。如同周振鹤先生所言,这一时期汉学已经是研究型汉学。欧美各国国内的汉学水平超过了侨居地的汉学研究水平,尤其是以法国的伯希和、马伯乐为代表的法国汉学。而且这一时期各个领域内的研究专著也多是在各国国内完成的。当然侨居中国境内的欧美各国人士的汉学研究也在发展,20世纪文会也从调查走向了研究,文会会刊上的文章也是一些论述型的文章。但是文会的发展速度落后于欧美各国的汉学发展速度,并渐渐退出了整个西方汉学研究的前列。其原因有三:第一,文会是英美人士的天下,整个20世纪在文会演讲的主要是英美人士,而20世纪以来国际汉学的最高水平在法国,英美汉学水平要远远低于法国。20世纪法国在华人士也从事汉学研究,并取得非凡的成就,但是法国汉学家很少参与文会的活动,因为法国人在远东有自己的汉学研究机构,上海有徐家汇的《汉学杂纂》(Variétés Sinologiques),北京有中法大学汉学研究中心,河北有献县教堂,越南还专门设有法兰西远东语言学校,伯希和、马伯乐都曾在远东语言学校做过汉学研究。这一时期远东的欧美人士主编的汉学刊物和法国人主办的刊物及欧美各国国内的汉学杂志在内容和风格上有明显的区别。文会会刊、《教务杂志》、《中国评论》都是研究型论文和游记、调查报告并重;而《通报》、《汉学》(Sinica 德国卫礼贤主编,法兰克福大学出版)、《东亚杂志》(Ostasiatische Zeitschrift)、《法兰西远东语言学校校刊》、《汉学》(中法大学出版)主要是研究型文章,没有游记类文章,从汉学的学术价值看,自然后者要高于前者。二次世界大战结束后,美国人的汉学水平逐渐上升,沪江大学和圣约翰大学的美籍教授、讲师经常参加文会的演讲,但这时候文会已是夕阳西下,濒临结束。第二,经费短缺。缺乏资金使得文会在20世纪没能成为一个高水平的汉学学术研究机构。文会本身就不是一个单纯的学术研究组织,创建时期就把外人在华的游记列为主要收集的对象之一,游记和研究型文章都可以在文会演讲,《会刊》也发表有大量的游记。20世纪后文会愈加变成一个社会公共文化机构,其图书馆、博物院的社会效能已经远远超过该机构在汉学研究上的影响。20世纪20年代后,会刊编纂方针改变后,游记的文章占了较大篇幅,书评也是多评介那些捐赠的书籍,文会为了生存而日益走向世俗性、社会性,遂逐渐退出了汉学研究的前列。文会的学术研究水平大大降低,已不能与同时期的欧美各国汉学研究机构相比拟。第三,20世纪,汉学水平高的刊物是《通报》、《东亚杂志》,著名汉学家一般多在这几个刊物上发表他们的大作,而不再到文会会刊上发表。本来当时整个汉学界水平高的学术文章也就没有几篇,多数都被《通报》录用,文会会刊已不再是西方汉学界重视的头等学术刊物,而变成一个西方知识界了解中国认识中国的英文期刊。失去学界的注意,更加速了文会地位的下降。新中国的建立正好适时地结束了它近一个世纪的中国研究历程。换句话说,即使中国没有发生政权的更迭,皇家亚洲文会北华支会也会自行终结,如果它不改弦更张的话。

附　表

亚洲文会历次演讲目录

演讲时间	英文名	中文名	题　目
1857.10.16	Bridgman, Rev. E. C.	裨治文	开幕词
1857.10.16	Nicolson Bart, F. W.	尼克逊	飓风之规律
1857.11.17	Macgowan, D. J.	玛高温	远东人类学
1857.11.17	Wylie, A.	伟烈亚力	大清货币
1857.11.17	Edkins, J.	艾约瑟	《壹输卢迦论》译稿与注释
1857.12.15	Foot, A. H.		日本下田与函馆游记
1857.12.15			1857年9月之月食
1857.12.15			汉籍中记载的北太平洋中的国家
1858.1.19	Bridgman, E. C.	裨治文	宁波雪窦山游记
1858.1.19	Nelson	内尔森	地质一瞥
1858.1.19	Edkins, J.	艾约瑟	墨子述略
1858.2.16	Syle, E. W.	帅福守	中国的乐谱
1858.3.16	Macgowan, D. J.	玛高温	中国文献学
1858.3.16	Wylie, A.	伟烈亚力	中国的石棉
1858.4.20	Bridgman, E. C.	裨治文	中亚之地质
1858.4.20	Macgowan, D. J.	玛高温	中国东北（满洲）的地震
1858.4.20	Syle, R.	帅　礼	中国的音乐
1858.5.18	不详		中国的土著居民（译自中文手稿）
1858.6.1	Editorial Committee	编辑委员会	中国大事回顾（1858年）
1858.7.20	M. N. Rondot	罗纳特	关于海宁绿色颜料的来信
1858.7.20	Swinhoe, Robert	郇　和	台湾旅行记
1858.8.10	Scherzer, F.	师克勤	人类学家的考察
1858.9.12	Shock, W. H.		日本的矿藏及其他
1858.9.21	Macgowan, D. J.	玛高温	中国之流刑
1858.10.26	Williams, S. W.	卫三畏	关于日本的演讲
1858.12.1	Editorial Committee	编辑委员会	中国大事回顾（1859年12月）
1858.12.23	Meerdevoort, Pompe van		自然科学学习在日本
1858.12.23	Macgowan, D. J.	玛高温	过去13个世纪上海周边地区观测到的特异自然现象
1859.1.15	Shadwell, R. N. C. B.		中国及周边地区地磁纪要

附录:皇家亚洲文会北华支会研究

续表

演讲时间	英文名	中文名	题　目
1859.1.15	Ward	伍德	从汉口到上海
1859.2.15	Swinhoe, Robert	郇和	台湾岛上新发现的鸟类
1859.3.15			奥地利科学考察团之来信
1859.3.15	Montigny, M. C. de H. I. M.		从长崎到上海
1859.3.15	Hobson	好博逊	中国的谚语
1859.4.19	Macgowan, D. J., M. D.	玛高温	大禹与中国的水
1859.4.20	Editorial Committee	编辑委员会	中国大事回顾(1859年4月)
1859.5.17	Edkins, J.	艾约瑟	道教神话的现代形式概述
1859.6.28	Robertson, D. B.	罗伯逊	中国的产茶区
1859.7.17	Robertson, D. B.	罗伯逊	中国的棉花
1859.7.19	Swinhoe, Robert	郇和	中国的云雀
1859.9.27	Hon'ble T. Harris		日本江户的气象观测记录
1859.9.27	不详		中国古代文献中记载的犹太人
1859.10.18	Edkins, J.	艾约瑟	孔子的生平
1859.10.18	不详		一封来自日本的信(描述日本的情况)
1859.10.25	Williams, S. W.	卫三畏	美国使团北京纪行
1859.11.15	Griffith John	杨格非	中国人的伦理观:关于人性和罪的信条
1859.12.27	Courtney, Charles. F. A.		1857-1859年函馆气温观测纪录
1859.12.27	Meerdevoort, Pompe van		日本的凌迟
1860.1.24	Shadwell		中国及周边地区地磁学纪要补充
1860.1.24		多人讨论	论采用统一系统——罗马字母和变音符号,来表示汉语及其方言中的所有词汇之必要性和可行性
1860.3.18	Edkins, J.	艾约瑟	古代长江口
1860.8.13	Editorial Committee	编辑委员会	中国大事回顾(1860年8月)
1860.8.28	Edkins, J.	艾约瑟	苏州暴乱记
1860.9.25	Alcock, Rutherford	阿礼国	日语之结构
1860.10.16	Lindau, Rudolph		日本首都江户
1860.11.20	Syle. E. W.	帅福守	苏州日记
1860.12.18	Bridgman, E. C.	裨治文	苗族概略
1861.1.15	不详		试论中国农业
1861.2.26	Cunnyingham, W. G. E.	耿惠廉 译	从上海到南京——穿越暴乱地区
1861.3.26	Actaeon, H. M. Ship		朝鲜沿海考察记
1861.4.23	不详		舟山群岛农业调查

续表

演讲时间	英文名	中文名	题 目
1861.5.21	Major Sarel		长江旅行记:从汉口到荆州
1861.5.21	Henderson, James	韩德森	影响气候的物理因素
1861.8.20	Dickson, W.	迪克森	陆上行纪:从广州经湖南至汉口
1864.5.6	Wylie, A.	伟烈亚力	长城附近的四张碑拓
1864.6.8	Lamprey		中国建筑学
1864.7.6	Henserson, V. P	韩德森	中国人的性格
1864.8.5	Major Edward	美 查	当前杭州湾海塘
1864.8.5	Wilds		浙江沿海的小岛
1864.9.5	Canny, J. M.	甘霓仁	俄占外东北(外满洲)的海岸(一)
1864.10.12	Bowra, E. C.	包 腊	天津第一印象
1864.11.29	Canny, J. M. Esq	甘霓仁	俄占外东北(外满洲)的海岸(二)
1864.12.13	Kingsmill, T. W.	金斯密	广东省局部之地质概述
1865.2.10	Collins, V. D.		华北的高粱及其用途
1865.2.10	Lamprey		平原地质简论
1865.3.10	Bastian	巴斯琴	高棉遗迹
1865.3.10	Jarvie, R. Esq.		论以中国禾本植物(谷、芦苇、竹)为棉花替代品的可行性
1865.4.3	Little, A. Esq	立 德	景德镇与中国皖南绿茶产茶区旅行记
1865.4.3	Parkes, Harry Smith	巴夏礼	读杜赫德《中华帝国全志》
1865.4.3	Sampson, T. Esq.	三 顺	向西印度群岛贩卖苦力
1865.6.7	Noëtzli.	那礼士	柬埔寨之旅行
1865.7.6	Brown, Revd.	勃 朗	一则来自日本手稿之译文(一)
1865.8.8	Stronach		神判法
1865.8.8	Edkins, J.	艾约瑟	访蒙古农耕区
1865.9.8	Grant.		内外蒙古
1865.9.8	Kingsmill, T. W.	金斯密	读文章摘要《旅行记:南京-苏州-上海》
1865.10.9	Swinhoe, Robert	郇 和	台湾动物志
1865.11.13	Brown, Revd. Mr.	勃 朗	一则来自日本手稿之译文(二)
1865.11.13	Jamieson	哲美森	中文书法——草书
1866.3.13	Williamson, A.	韦廉臣	北京出发经大运河、兖州府等至芝罘之旅(一)
1866.3.29	Martin, W. A. P	丁韪良	从北京到上海
1866.4.13	McCartee, D. B.	麦嘉缔	中国野生蚕蛹
1866.4.16	Williamson, A.	韦廉臣	北京出发经大运河、兖州府等至芝罘之旅(二)
1866.5.14	Brown, Rev. S. R.	勃 朗	西洋纪闻译文(一)

续表

演讲时间	英文名	中文名	题目
1866.6.13	Moule, G. E.	慕稼谷	杭州一天主教堂内所发现的石碑
1866.10.13	Williams, S. W.	卫三畏	中国与琉球的政治关系
1866.10.13	Hollingworth		中国象棋
1866.10.13	Wylie, A.	伟烈亚力	中国人对月食的看法
1866.11.13	Keer.	基尔	广东贡院
1866.11.13	Kingsmill, T. W.	金斯密	中国东南省份偏远地区的煤田
1866	Alabaster, C.		江西与长江数省间的盐业贸易
1867.2.17	Bickmore, Aibert S.	贝克莫尔	陆上之旅:从广州到汉口
1867.3.13	Buthcer, C. H.		1866年华北大事记回忆
1867.4.18	Williamson, A.	韦廉臣	华北的物产与交通
1867	Macgowan, D. J., M. D.	玛高温	日本海军舰船统计
1867	Forrest, R. T.	富礼赐	太平天国的宗教
1867	Pryer, W. B.	朴赉懿	上海的昆虫
1867	Thin		太平天国的宗教释疑
1867	Elias, Ney	爱莲斯	黄河古河床
1867.11.5	Bickmore, Aibert S.	贝克莫尔	关于近期中国和日本陆地上升的解释
1867	Kingsmill, T. W.	金斯密	铜元贬值论
1867	Mayers, W. F.	梅辉立	中国历史年表
1867	Simon, G. Eugene.	西蒙	中国农业物产图
1867	Edkins, J.	艾约瑟	北京西部的烟煤
1868.2.15	Watters. T.	瓦特斯	中国人关于鸽子的看法
1868	Parker, E. H.	庄延龄	从天津到镇江
1868	Weber		黄河
1868	Medhurst, W. H.	麦华陀	黄土高原上的古代庆典碑刻
1868	Hall, E. Hepple		埃塞俄比亚人
1868	Kingsmill, T. W.	金斯密	长崎附近的煤矿及地质
1868	Simon, G. Eug.	西蒙	中国古代的合伙团体
1868.12.21	Cooper, T. T.		华西游记
1868	Macgowan, D. J., M. D.	玛高温	论在吴淞观测到的太阳黑子现象
1868.6.9	Jenkins	秦右	古代中国人的音乐观念
1868	Macgowan, D. J., M. D.	玛高温	长江河道上的雾
1868	Gardner, Chas.	嘉托玛	大禹碑
1868	Sibbald, W.		1867年12月18日的台湾北部地震

续表

演讲时间	英文名	中文名	题目
1868	Macgowan, D. J., M. D.	玛高温	浙江的苗族
1868	Sibbald, W.		台湾北部的煤矿
1868.11.13	Preston, C. F.	丕思业	四川总督——骆秉章
1868.12.21	Cooper, T. T.		华西游记
1868.12.27	Cooper, T. T.	库珀	华西、西藏等地的道路与交通
1869.5.5	Simon, G. Eug.	西蒙	中国和日本古生物学和地质学研究刍议
1869.5.5	Wylie, A.	伟烈亚力	湖北、四川、陕西三省游览
1869.5.18	Mayers, W. F.	梅辉立	火药和火器在中国人中的引介和使用
1869	McDonald, N. A.		暹罗的最后一位皇帝
1869	Elias, Ney	爱莲斯	黄河新河道考察记
1869	Markham, John	马安	山东纪略：从芝罘（烟台）到邹县之旅
1869	Simon, G. Eug.	西蒙	中国的银行机构
1869	Eitel, E. J.	艾德	黄河的源头
1869	Mayers, W. F.	梅辉立	文昌星的由来及文昌崇拜
1870.6.10		多人讨论	中西交往中出现的矛盾
1870	Macgowan, D. J., M. D.	玛高温	中国的彩票
1870.3.16	Himly, K.	希姆利	中国的棋类游戏
1870	Robertson, J. Barr	罗伯逊	1860年的北京谈判会议
1870.5.30	Macgowan, D. J., M. D.	玛高温	中国人发现美洲说
1870.6.10		多人讨论	中西交往中出现的矛盾
1870.6.13	Hass, Joseph	夏士	中国古代历史编纂学
1870	Kingsmill, T. W.	金斯密	第三纪晚期的华北
1870	Macgowan, D. J., M. D.	玛高温	中国的"牛战"
1870.12.5	Macgowan, D. J., M. D.	玛高温	中国男人的地位
1870.12.16	Moule, Rev. G. E.	慕稼谷	论1870年浙江乡试
1871.1.25	Smith, F. Porter.	师维善	中国化工制造
1871.2.27	Williams, S. W.	卫三畏	1801年使琉球记
1871.4.1	McCartee, D. B.	麦嘉缔	潍县《重修城隍庙碑记》
1871.6.5	Stent, George Chater.	司登得	中国抒情诗
1871.10.3	Mayers, Wm, Frederick	梅辉立	海南简史
1872.1.11	Thomson, J. M. R. G. S.	汤顺	柬埔寨古迹
1872.2.9	Solbé, E.		汉语的发音规则
1872.2.9	Kingsmill, T. W.	金斯密	周朝的起源

续表

演讲时间	英文名	中文名	题　目
1872.3.25	Swinhoe, R.	郇　和	海南土著居民
1872.3.25	Macgowan, D. J., M. D.	玛高温	蒙古的烤羊肉和酒
1872.4.17	Watters, T.	倭　讷	韩愈生平及著作
1872.5.13	Swinhoe, R.	郇　和	海南探险调查记
1872.5.13	Macgowan, D. J., M. D.	玛高温	中国的艺术展览
1872.6.12	Moule, G. E.	慕稼谷	中华先驱从欧人那里引进自然科学知识
1872.6.12	Stent, G. C.	司登得	中国的(民间)传说
1872.6.12	Macgowan, D. J., M. D.	玛高温	中国人用鲋鱼治瘘病、用碘酒治淋巴疾病的方法
1872	David, Père Armand	谭微道	华西、华北之博物志
1873.1.13	Williams, S. W.	卫三畏	1840年前中国回忆录
1873.3.26	Schmidt, Carl	史密德	上海史摘要
1873.3.26	Kingsmill, T. W.	金斯密	关于周朝建立者周文王的传说
1873.4.18	Watters, T.	倭　讷	中国神狐故事
1873.6.2	Edkins, J.	艾约瑟	孔子家乡曲阜之旅
1873.6.2	Francis Garnier	威基谒	法国1866年远征印度支那概要
1873.10.21	Dennys, N. B.	丹尼斯	中国乐器简介
1873.11.18	Bushell, S. W. M. D.	卜士礼	周朝石鼓上的文字
1873.12.8	Moule, G. E.	慕稼谷	最近杭州游览记兼论《马可波罗游记》中的相关记录
1874	Forbes, F. B.	福勃士	1857年以来文会的工作回顾
1874	Shearer, G.		鄱阳湖、白鹿书院游览记
1874.5.20	Camajee, H. D.		古代胡腊玛教先知的传说和琐罗亚斯德的故事
1874.6.18	Taintor, E. C.	廷得尔	台湾北部土著
1874.11.14	Cordier, H.	高　第	最近东京大事记
1874.11.23	Watters, T.	倭　讷	《妙法莲华经》述评
1874.12.16	Macgowan, D. J., M. D.	玛高温	中国的剧毒物质——砒霜
1875.1.20	Palladius, Archimandrite	鲍乃迪	马可波罗游历的华北:用中国材料诠释
1875.6.7	Hocombe, C.	何天爵	陕西、山西旅行记
1875.6.7	Kingsmill, T. W.	金斯密	中国古代"月底"和"羌"族考
1875.11.29	Bretschneider, E. M. D.	贝　勒	中世纪的中亚西亚之史地考证
1876	Kingsmill, T. W.	金斯密	舜
1876	Kingsmill, T. W.	金斯密	四川的倮倮族
1876.4.3	Hobson, H. E.	好博逊	热兰遮城及荷兰对台湾的殖民

续表

演讲时间	英文名	中文名	题目
1876.11.12	Kingsmill, T. W.	金斯密	中亚西亚地理的变化与古代藏族部落迁移的关系
1876.11.12	Martin, Rev. W. A. P.	丁韪良	中国书信格式
1876.12.8	Edkins, J.	艾约瑟	船舵之中文名及指南针之应用
1877.1.20	Möllendorff, O. F. von.	穆林德	直隶的脊椎动物
1877.2.20	Kingsmill, T. W.	金斯密	地质学和历史学的交汇领域
1877.3.26	Stent, G. C.	司登得	中国的宦官
1877	Ross, J.	罗士	辽河
1877	Macgowan, D. J., M. D.	玛高温	明朝时期鸦片的所谓应用
1877	Edkins, J.	艾约瑟	8－12、17世纪的各种指南针
1877	Ross, J.	罗士	满族的迷信
1877.10.16	Little	立德	中国人的自然崇拜(天、地)
1878	Kingsmill, T. W.	金斯密	公元前2世纪中国与中亚国家的政治经济往来
1878.2.12	Fritsche	费理饬	东亚气候
1878.2.12	Macgowan, D. J., M. D.	玛高温	疍民:浙江一个值得关注的族群
1878	Hosie, Alex. M. A.	谢立山	公元620－1643年间中国的干旱
1878.3.12	Mayers, W. F.	梅辉立	中国墓地中的石像和活祭品
1878.4.9	Kingsmill, T. W.	金斯密	周朝的语言和文化
1878.5.7	Möllendorff, P. G. von	穆麟德	中国的家法
1878.5.14	Parker, E. H.	庄延龄	汉语方言比较研究
1878.5.14	Hosie, Alex. M. A.	谢立山	公元前28年至公元1617年在中国观测到的太阳黑子及太阳阴影
1878	Kreitner, Lieut. G.		三角测量所确定的上海附近12个突起点
1878	Schulze, F. W.		地磁的周期变化
1878	Hosie, Alex. M. A.	谢立山	再论太阳黑子与中国历史上的饥荒
1878	Rhein, J.	来因	雁荡山北侧石刻
1878	Kingsmill, T. W.	金斯密	希腊文中"中国"和"中国人"之词源
1878.12.13	Fauvel, A.	福威勒	中国的短吻鳄
1879	Kingsmill, T. W.	金斯密	东亚人种学
1879	Hass, Joseph	夏士	暹罗货币
1880.1.27	Hass, Joseph	夏士	暹罗货币补遗
1880.3.8	Macgowan, D. J., M. D.	玛高温	长江中游游览记
1880.6.7	Bushell, S. W. M. D.	卜士礼	大清钱币
1880.9.21	Balfour, Frederic H.	巴尔福	中国的自然主义哲学

续表

演讲时间	英文名	中文名	题　　目
1880.9.21	Guppy, H. B. M. B.	古　庇	台湾打狗地质纪录
1880.9.21	Guppy, H. B. M. B.	古　庇	美国佩斯卡德罗之地质
1880.9.21	Guppy, H. B. M. B.	古　庇	长江、黄河和白河的水文
1880.9.21	Yuen		无与伦比的爱国者
1880.11.19	Macgowan, D. J.	玛高温	中国的著作权
1880.11.19	Bretschneider, E. M. D.	贝　勒	先辈欧人对中国植物的研究
1881.3.16	Schulze, F. W.		台湾海峡沙滩上的淡水
1881.3.16	Anderson, Geo. C.	安德森	萨哈林岛(库页岛)旅行记
1881.4.26	Parker, E. H.	庄延龄	长江上游的急流
1881.6.9	Butler, John		现今中国的佛教
1881.9.26	Bretschneider, E. M. D.	贝　勒	中国植物志
1881.9.26	Anderson, G. C.	安德森	萨哈林岛、阿尼瓦湾及俄国属鞑靼旅行记
1881.10.28	Dechevrens, Rev. Father Mare S. J.	熊恩斯	上海的气候
1881.10.28	Giles, Herbert A.	翟理思	汉语修辞
1881.12.15	Toda, E.		安南及其小钱币
1882.1.27	Kreitner, Lieut	克里特那	威尼斯第三届世界地理大会概要
1882.3.31	Guppy, H. B. M. B.	古　庇	长崎及其周边地质概况
1882.3.31	Schulze, F. W.		台湾海峡沙滩上的淡水
1882.8.29	Hirth.	夏　德	1753年的河泊书(粤海关报告)
1882.11.7	Imbault-Huart, C.	于雅乐	苏州及其周围农村
1883.1.9	Edkins, Rev. J.	艾约瑟	古代中国对希腊和罗马的了解
1883.2.27	Scherzer Monsieur F.	师克勤	朝鲜——译自《朝鲜志》
1883.4.17	Kleinwächter, G. H. J.	康发达	台湾地质研究
1883.11.8	Happer, A. P.		佛学与儒学之关系及世界上佛教徒的数量
1883.11.22	Morrison, G. James	毛里逊	1883年朝鲜旅行记
1883.12.3	Little, A. J.	立　德	四川及长江峡谷小记
1884.1.22	Moule, G. E.	慕稼谷	一张蕴含人生哲理的佛教帖
1884.3.14	Macgowan, D. J. M. D.	玛高温	关于中国人是火炮及其他火武器发明者的论断
1884.3.25	Hosie, Alex.	谢立山	华西商路
1884.3.28	Parker, E. H.	庄延龄	浙江旅行记(一)
1884.4.4	Hirth, F.	夏　德	古代中国与大秦之间的商路
1884.4.16	Parker, E. H.	庄延龄	浙江旅行记(二)
1884.10.20	C. Imbault-Huart	于雅乐	袁子才:18世纪中国的诗人

续表

演讲时间	英文名	中文名	题　目
1884.10.27	Parker, E. H.	庄延龄	从温州到福州
1884.11.10	Parker, E. H.	庄延龄	从福州到温州
1884.11.24	Kopsch, H.	葛显礼	中国人笔下的麦加圣石:兼论古代阿拉伯人之贸易
1884.12.2	Kingsmill, T. W.	金斯密	托勒密笔下的"秦国"及其居民
1884.12.15	Schulze, F. W.		朝鲜汉江航行记
1884.12.15	Macgowan, D. J. M. D.	玛高温	中国境内电话之应用
1885.4.16	Giles, H. A.	翟理思	《红楼梦》一书
1885.5.14		多人讨论	中国溺婴之盛行
1885.10.15		多人讨论	何为孝顺?
1885		多人讨论	中国戏剧调查
1886.3.12	Phillips, Geo.	费笠士	《瀛涯胜览》所记载的印度和锡兰附近的海港城市
1886.5.26		多人讨论	用汉语传播西方知识的正反效果
1886.11.30	Allen, Herbert J.	啊查理	孔子是虚构的吗?
1886.12.16	Macgowan, D. J. M. D.	玛高温	中国的行会制度
1887.5.6	Carles, W. R.	贾礼士	朝鲜
1887.10.25	Becher, H. M.		山东东部的矿藏资源
1887.11.18	Parker, E. H.	庄延龄	1842年前的中国军事组织
1887.11.18		多人讨论	中国合伙企业成员的责任和义务
1888.2.22	Hirth, F.	夏　德	翰林院中的四夷馆
1888.4.4	Hirth, F.	夏　德	古代陶瓷:中世纪中国之工商业
1888.10.22	Carles, W. R.	贾礼士	朝鲜大清皇帝功德碑
1888.10.22	Moule, G. E.	慕稼谷　译	元阳子真空直指
1888.11.19	Phillips, Geo. F. R. C. S.	费笠士	元时福建省会漳州
1888.11.19	Hobson, H. E.	好博逊	南京大报恩寺琉璃塔
1888.12.10	Moore, Usborne R. N.		钱塘江涌潮
1889.2.22	Jamieson, Geo.	哲美森	中国的佃制及农民状况调查报告
1888－1889	Volpicelli, Z.	武尔披齐	中国象棋
1889.12.14	Macgowan, D. J. M. D.	玛高温	东亚女性掌权的政府
1889.12.20	Faber, Ernst	花之安	中国文字反映出的史前中国信息
1890.2.21	Edkins, J.	艾约瑟	中国的建筑
1890.5.19	Parker, E. H.	庄延龄	中国景教徒记略
1890.5.19	Fries, S. Ritter von	费习蒙	中国建筑中的"帐幕理论"

续表

演讲时间	英文名	中文名	题 目
1890.11.11	Edkins, J.	艾约瑟	3500年前的中国
1891.4.6	Fraser, M. F. A.	富美基	鱼皮鞑靼
1891.4.20	Mesny, General W.	麦士尼	云南:其财富与商路
1891.5.15	Macgowan, D. J. M. D.	玛高温	中国的驴、猫和羊可能来自外国
1891.6.22	Williams		洪武和明代的首都
1891.11.9	Kingsmill, T. W.	金斯密	古代月亮星群及时辰对照表
1891.11.9	Thwing, M. D., Phd.		东方学的范畴
1891.12.24	Hitchcook		古代日本的坟丘和墓碑
1892.1.29	Fraser, M. F. A.	富美基	鄂尔浑河上游及古代蒙古帝国旧都遗迹考察记
1892.2.15	Volpicelli, Z.	武尔披齐	围棋
1892.3.30	Groot, J. J. M. de	高 延	中国佛教僧侣的尚武精神
1892.6.8	Edkins, J.	艾约瑟	亚洲语言之演变
1892.12.28		多人讨论	中国内陆交通
1892.12.28	Kingsmill, T. W.	金斯密	内地会通讯摘录:神秘的叶尼塞河
1893.2.27	Volpicelli, Z.	武尔披齐	早期在华的葡萄牙人之商业及其殖民地
1893.4.26	Volpicelli, Z.	武尔披齐	唐代阿拉伯在中国的贸易
1893.5.16	Edkins, J.	艾约瑟	国际东方学大会综述
1893.11.29	Scott, J.	萨允格	朝鲜历史与文献散论
1894.1.24	Edkins, J.	艾约瑟	史前考古
1894.1.24	Richard, Timothy	李提摩太	大乘佛教是如何兴起的?
1894—1895	Edkins, J.	艾约瑟	生命之轮回
1894—1895	Gardner	嘉托玛	朝鲜货币
1894—1895	Möllendorff, P. G. von	穆林德	中国的方言
1894—1895	Bishop	毕晓普	西藏旅行记
1896.2.5	Landis	兰迪斯	东学党人与他们的信仰
1896.3.8	Edkins, J.	艾约瑟	西南土著:历史、宗教与语言
1896.3.8	Pruen	普鲁恩	族群的聚集:贵州黑苗的舞蹈
1896.6.10	Rondot, N.		埃及出土的中国小瓷瓶和钱币
1896.6.10	Bullock, T. L.		评柔克义的《蒙古、西藏旅行记》
1896.10.21	Edkins, J.	艾约瑟	中国铜钱与银两的关系
1886.11.26	Kingsmill, T. W.	金斯密	从古代碑刻看中国书法的起源
1897.1.13	Bowra, C. A. V.	包 罗	唐代武则天
1897.2.16	Martin, W. A. P.	丁韪良	中国的陶器

续表

演讲时间	英文名	中文名	题　目
1897.3.3	Cox, R. H.	柯罗巴	X光射线
1897.3.24	Edkins, J.	艾约瑟	古代书法
1897.4.21	Volpicelli, Z.	武尔披齐	中国银两与物价的变动问题
1897.11.29	Bushell	卜士礼	西夏的货币与独特文字
1898.1.19	Möllendorff, P. G. von	穆麟德	比较语言学的缺点
1898.2.16	Fraser, M. F. A.	富美基	一张满文谕旨
1898.2.16	Kingsmill, T. W.	金斯密	《诗经》中的神话
1898.3.9	James, F. H.	秀耀春	中国圣人的道德规范
1898.4.6	Brass, E.	布拉斯	北太平洋的猎豹和捕鲸业
1898.5.12	Edkins, J.	艾约瑟	中国古代的宗教、政治和思想
1898.10.12	Box, Rev. E.	包克私	各地民俗
1898.11.16	Richard, Tomothy	李提摩太	中国的音乐
1898.12.14	James, F. H.	秀耀春	中国的文学/文献
1899.1.11	Brenan, Byron C. M. G.	璧利南	中国的县官
1899.4.5	Kingsmill, T. W.	金斯密	《道德经》与早期佛教的关系
1899.5.3	Lewis, R. E.	刘易斯	日本的教育
1899.6.28	Edkins, J.	艾约瑟	最近一位中国僧人的游历印度记
1899.10.26	Hickman, J.	希克曼	四川
1899.11.9	Bourne, F. S. A.	班德瑞	改革的可能性与否
1899.12.14	Edkins, J.	艾约瑟	荀卿：一位思想家
1899.12.14	Kingsmill, T. W.	金斯密	亚洲的心脏
1900.1.18	Williams, E. T.	卫理夫人	中国广为流传的宗教文学作品
1900.4.5	Kingsmill, T. W.	金斯密	中国的日历
1900.5.25	Little, Archibald	立　德	四川人的性格
1900.10.5	Vale, Joshua	斐焕章	成都平原的灌溉体系
1900.10.18	Kingsmill, T. W.	金斯密	用现代英语诗歌的形式翻译的中国古代民谣
1900.10.24	Mencarini, J.	绵嘉义	菲律宾华人劳工问题
1900.11.21	Macklin, W. E. M. D.		孟子及其他中国改革者
1900.11.29	Betts, Edgar		苗族的社会风俗
1901.1.17	Moule, G. E.	慕稼谷	丁祭考
1901.3.28	LEMIÈRE, J. EM.		日本戏剧及其历史
1901.4.17	Walshe, W. Gilbert	华立熙	古代绍兴
1901.5.22	Forke, A. Jur	佛尔克	中国之辩士
1901.10.17	Mencarini, J.	绵嘉义	菲律宾群岛
1901.11.21	Edkins, J.	艾约瑟	最近北京的变化
1901.12.12	Richard, Tomothy	李提摩太	中国的社会风俗
1902.4.17	Woodbridge, Rev. S. Isett	吴板桥	八股文及其对中国人思想和性格的影响

续表

演讲时间	英文名	中文名	题　　目
1902.5.8	Parker, A. P.	潘慎文	苏州的寺院和佛塔
1902－1903	Ferguson, J. C.	福开森	王安石
1902.10.16	Edkins, J.	艾约瑟	文会45年回顾
1902－1903	Jesus, Montalto de	杰　斯	澳门的历史
1902－1903	Edkins, J.	艾约瑟	中国的葬礼——以总督刘揆一为例
1902－1903	Edkins, J.	艾约瑟	佛教偈语
1903.12.11	Montalto de Jesus on Siy Kuang Ki	杰　斯	中国西部的米西奈斯；赵匡胤
1904.1.11	Edkins, J.	艾约瑟	郭子仪——唐朝的杰出军事将领
1904.1.12	Kingsmill, T. W.	金斯密	蛮子与黄金半岛（胖㭕地区）
1901.1.17	Chalfant, F. H.	方法敛	秦朝标准度量衡
1903－1904	Walshe, W. Gilbert	华立熙	若干中国丧葬礼仪
1904.11.17	Kingsmill, T. W.	金斯密	中国植物学释疑
1904.12.15	Vale, Joshua	斐焕章	再论成都平原的灌溉体系
1905.2.16	Mencarini, J.	绵嘉义	爪哇
1905.3.2	Davidson, J. W.	达飞声	台湾猎人之头目
1905.4.20	Leavenworth, Chas. G.	利维沃思	琉球群岛的历史
1905.6.1	Box, Ernest	包克私	上海民俗
1905.6.15	Smith, Arthur	明恩溥	中国的现状
1905.11.25	Martin, W. A. P.	丁韪良	开封府的犹太教纪念碑
1905.12.14	Jesus, C. M. de	杰　斯	上海的崛起
1906.1.18	Kingsmill, T. W.	金斯密	古代西藏及其前沿地带
1906.2.22	Ferguson, J. C.	福开森	上海华资银行体系
1906.4.5	Alabaster, Ernest	阿拉巴特	修订前的中国法律及其实施
1906.5.17	Headland, Isaac Taylor	何德兰	中国儿童游戏
1906－1907	Morse, H. A.	马　士	中国货币考
1906－1907	Williams, E. T.	卫　理	中国法律术语
1906－1907	Mencarini, J.	绵嘉义	不详
1908－1909	Parker, E. H.	庄延龄	中国成文法与衡平法的原则
1908－1909	Arnold, Julean H.	安立德	攀登玉山山脉
1908－1909	Kingsmill, T. W.	金斯密	中国的音乐
1908－1909	Torrance, Thomas	陶然士	四川的丧葬习俗
1908.10.10	Jesus, C. Montalto de	杰　斯	上海的开放
1908－1909	Hedin, Sven	斯文赫定	不详（在兰心大剧院演讲）

续表

演讲时间	英文名	中文名	题目
1909－1910	不详		中国的爬行动物
1910.11.23	Gipperich, H.	吉勃利	《道德经》的作者
1910.12.15	Williams, S. W.	卫三畏	卫三畏日记
1911.2	Moule, A. C.	慕阿德	泰山
1911.5	Schiener, K.	希 那	从杭州到温州
1911.6	Wendell, Barrett	温德尔	中国、印度旅行印象
1911－1912	Reymond, Du Bois	谛 部	射箭在中国
1911－1912	Stanley, A.	史笪来	中国的金属艺术品
1912.3.7	Bondfield, G. H.	文显理	蒙古与蒙古人
1911－1912	Warren, G. G.	任修本	湖南境内的三处上古史迹
1912.10.17	Henke, Frederick G.	亨 克	王阳明的生平及其哲学思想
1913.1.9	Shields, E. T.	希尔德斯	峨眉山
1913.3.6	Richard, Tomothy	李提摩太	丘处机之史诗
1913.3.28	Liu Sung-fu		清代画展
1913.4.4	Stanley, A.	史笪来	中国刺绣及其他艺术纺织品
1913.10.3	Shelton, A. L.	史德文	西藏每日见闻
1913.10.8	Ferguson, J. C.	福开森	古代中国画
1913.11.13	Stanley, A.	史笪来	中国的动物
1913.12.4	Edgar, Rev. J. H.	叶长清	穿越深深的侵蚀地带：从东川巴塘到湄公河
1914.2.20	Couling, S.	库寿龄	河南甲骨
1914.4.8	Gull, E. Manico	葛 罗	蒙古游记
1914.5.7	Rockhill, W. W.	柔克义	元、明时期的海上贸易
1914.6.25	Stanley, A.	史笪来	中国木雕
1914.11.5	Richard, Tomothy	李提摩太	佛教艺术的几个问题
1914.11.27	Dorsey, G. A.	多尔森	从文化人类学看文化的价值
1915.1.19	Maybon, C. B.	梅 伯	吴哥旅行记
1915.3.15	Tyler, W. F.	陶守谦	1915年2月12日舟山岛降下的一块大陨石
1915.5.13	Couling, Samuel M. A.	库寿龄	中国的塔
1915.10.28	Sarkar, Benoy Kumar	萨卡尔	中国宗教初探
1915.11.26	Louderback, C. D.	劳德巴克	东亚与美国西部地质上的关联
1916.1.13	Ferguson, J. C.	福开森	中国古代青铜器
1916.2.17	Parker, Rve. A. P.	潘慎文	老上海与历史与风俗笔记
1916.3.30	Sowerby, A. de C.	苏阿德	最近华北哺乳动物研究

续表

演讲时间	英文名	中文名	题目
1916.10.26	Carter, J. C.	卡 德	太平军在江苏
1916.11.23	Bowser, H. C.	鲍 泽	朝鲜的佛教寺院
1916.12.14	Chatley, Herbert	查得利	中国的巫术实践
1917.1.18	Edgar, J. Huston F. R. G. S.	叶长清	四川蛮子地区及其习俗
1917.2.22	Ayscough F.	爱司克夫人	东岳泰山
1917.4.26	Lanning, George	蓝 宁	汉语和英语的近似特征
1917.5.4	Segalen, Victor		最近发现的中国古代雕塑
1917–1918	Wilton, E. C.		中国西部省区的边界
1917.12.6	Chatley, H.	查得利	中国的河流问题
1917–1918	Sayee, A. H.	塞 伊	耶路撒冷
1918.1.17	Kliene, Charles	葛麟瑞	中国之谜局
1917–1918	Fox, H. H.	傅夏礼	一位领事记事簿中的数页内容
1918.4.18	Morgan, Evan	莫安仁	祭礼仪式的个案研究
1917–1918	Lobingier, Judge C. S.	罗丙吉	早期的马来人及其周边文化
1917–1918	Edmunds, C. K.	晏文士	中国人的身体特征
1918.5.30	Zwemer, S. M.	兹维莫	穆斯林祷告中的泛灵论元素
1918.10.31	Daniel, G. M.	丹尼尔	"阿勒山"之地
1918.12.5	Hall, W. L.	霍 尔	与中国接触
1919.1.17	Kliene, Charles	葛麟瑞	《桃花源记》
1919.2.13	Catchpool, E. St. John	卡奇普尔	高加索地区和附近的居民
1919.2.26	Chatley, H.	查得利	中国的化石能源
1919.3.20	Edgar, J. Huston	叶长清	查塔姆群岛(新西兰)
1919.4.29	Mason, Isaac	梅益盛	一个回教徒的中式生活
1919.5.8	Gist, N. Geo.	祁天锡	一个地方生物的调查报告
1919.10.23	Stanley, A.	史笪来	论希腊、中国的艺术思想
1919.11.20	Morgan, Evan	莫安仁	中国文学中的宿命论
1919.12.12	Lanning, George	蓝 宁	上海租界的地名和别名
1920.1.15	Andrews, R. C.	安德斯	云南探险记
1920.3.4	Sörensen, Theo.	徐丽生	藏传佛教
1920.3.26	Ayscough, F.	爱司克夫人	中国诗及其内涵
1920.4.1	Ferguson, J. C.	福开森	中国的山水画家
1920.10.21	Fitch, R. F.	费佩德	西藏的边界
1920.11.25	Powell, Robert	鲍威尔	中国的黑苗

续表

演讲时间	英文名	中文名	题　　目
1920.12.23	Kliene, Charles	葛麟瑞	媒婆
1921.1.27	Wilkinson, H. P.	威金生	中国古代的人名与避讳称呼
1921.2.24	Morgan, Rev. Evan	莫安仁	历史上"道"的作用及其表现形式
1921.3.24	Ayscough, Mrs, F.	爱司克夫人	紫禁城的象征主义
1921.4.21	Chatley, H.	查得利	中国古代科技
1921.11.23	Ayscough, Mrs. F.	爱司克夫人	中国古诗新译
1922.1.5	Sowerby, A. de C.	苏阿德	中国博物学
1922.1.19	Siré, Osvald PH. D.	喜仁龙	西安印象
1922.3.30	Heidenstam, H. von	海德生	长江三角洲的形成
1922.4.18	Fisher, E. S.	斐　士	从太原经五台山至蒙古边境纪行
1922.4.27	Cressy, Rev. E. H.	葛德基	中国佛教的朝圣者
1922.10.19	Darroch, John	窦乐安	中国古代史一页:越王勾践
1922.11.2	Karlgren, Bernald	高本汉	从发音学看中国文字
1922.11.16	Kliene, Charles	葛麟瑞	中国埃及太古文化之比较观
1923.1.18	Torrance, Thomas	陶然士	羌人的宗教信仰
1923.2.14	Ferguson, J. C.	福开森	文化:中国艺术的基石
1923.3.8	Sowerby, A. de C.	苏阿德	福建生物考察记
1923.3.22	Ayscough, Mrs. F.	爱司克夫人	"大河"文献的初步注解
1923.4.19	Morgan, Rev. Evan	莫安仁	道教真人
1923.5.21	Pereira, Brig-Gen. G. E.		拉萨旅行记
1923.10.25	Chatley, H.	查得利	中国不散的阴魂
1924.1.10	Shirokogoroff, M.	史禄国	关于中国北方人的人类学研究
1924.2.12	Thompson, H. Gordon	谭　信	在西藏发现的巴西边子树(Pereira治疟疾用)
1924.3.6	Illingworth, J. F.		应用昆虫学
1924.3.19	Ferguson, J. C.	福开森	宋代的杭州移民
1924.4.17	L. Newton Hayes		中国之神佛
1924.11.27	Sowerby, A. de C.	苏阿德	中国境内的蝾螈(火蜥蜴)及其类属
1924.12.18	Mironoff	迈伦诺夫	中国境内"土耳其斯坦人"的考古发掘
1924	Ayscough, Florence	爱克司夫人	城隍老爷崇拜
1925.2.19	Pott, Hawks	卜舫济	墨子学说
1925.3.12	Dovey, A. Whitsed	杜明德	孔子生平及其时代
1925.4.9	Cressey, Geo. B.	葛德石	甘肃、西藏和蒙古地区的地质、地理调查

续表

演讲时间	英文名	中文名	题目
1925.4.30	Wilbur, H. A.		国外的中国艺术珍宝
1926.1	Yamada, K.	山田谦吉	儒学与现代文明
1926.1	Jules, Rev. Bro.	朱尔斯	从北京到蒙古
1926.2	Teesdale, J. H.	天赐德	忠王李秀成的自传
1926.2	Chapin, Helen B.	柴平	中国艺术中的佛教因素
1926.3	Shirokogoroff, M.	史禄国	北通古斯族在远东的迁移
1926.3	Ferguson, J. C.	福开森	中国历史要览
1926.6	Edgar, Rev. J. Hutson	叶长清	藏民及其生存环境
1926.11.24	Reischauer, A. K.	赖肖尔	当今日本的佛教势力
1926.12.16	Ayscough, Mrs. F.	爱司克夫人	中国的祠堂
1927.1.13	Abraham, R. D.		中国的艺术主旨
1927.2.10	Leung, George Kin	梁社乾	梅兰芳其人其艺
1927.4.28	Couling, C. E.	库美龄	吕洞宾：金丹教的创始人
1927－1928	Mason, Isaac	梅益盛	文会七十周年纪念
1927－1928	Hayes, L. Newton	海士	中国的长城
1927－1928	Wong, K. C.	黄继祥	玉的习俗与中国早期文化
1927－1928	Macgillivray, Rev. D.	季理斐	河南的犹太人
1927－1928	Fitch, Rev. Robert	费佩德	佛教寺院的一天
1927－1928	Cresst, Rev. E. H.	葛德基	在日本富士山度假
1927－1928	Freeman, Mansfield B. A.	费孟福	清朝对宋代理学的批判
1927－1928	Chatley, H.	查得利	见证中西文化的古物
1927－1928	Englaender, A. L.	恩格莱德	沙漠的起源和发展及华北的沙漠化
1927－1928	Biallas, F. X. S. V. D.	鲍润生	屈原生平及其诗歌
1928.4.19	HuShih	胡适	王莽
1927－1928	Kato, H.	加藤日吉	实施科技和工业的日本
1927－1928	Lévi, Sylvain	列维	喜马拉雅山之行：其历史、宗教、山脉
1928－1929	Chatley, H.	查得利	中华文明源于埃及吗？
1928－1929	Englaender, A. L.		亚洲冰川纪释疑
1928－1929	Cressey, George B.	葛德石	鞑靼、鄂尔多斯、阿拉善旅行记
1928－1929	Chang Hsin Hai, PH. D.	张歆海	中国人的历史观
1928－1929	Kann, Edward	耿爱德	"金"（货币）在中国：其历史、现实与财政影响
1928－1929	Mason, Isaac	梅益盛	中国的回教徒：他们首次入华在何时，以什么方式？

续表

演讲时间	英文名	中文名	题　目
1928－1929	Edgar, J. H.	叶长清	西藏日记摘要
1928－1929	Sheppard, Rev. G. W.	牧作霖	马礼逊之前的《圣经》汉译本
1928－1929	Fearn, Anne Walter	斐尧臣	"吴哥"（柬埔寨）
1928－1929	Hu Shih	胡　适	儒学在西汉被确立为国教
1929.9.26	Fisher, Email S.	斐　士	被亵渎的东陵
1929－1930	Hu Shih	胡　适	中国禅宗之发展
1929－1930	Wong, K. M. M. D.	王吉民	中医历史概要
1929－1930	Tschepourkovsky, Prof. E.		论亚洲的某些科技问题
1929－1930	Englaender, A. M. D.		北方的干旱与香港的水荒
1929－1930	Wu, John C. H. LL. B.	吴经熊	谈中国法制史
1929－1930	Chatley, H.	查得利	汉字可以简化吗？
1929－1930	Seligman, C. G. M. D.	塞利格曼	远东考古印象
1929－1930	Sowerby, A. de C.	苏阿德	中国动植物之分布
1929－1930	Morgan, Rev. Evan	莫安仁	语言和新思维
1929－1930	Gibbons, Herbert Admas PH. D.		土耳其帝国的创建
1929－1930	Peterson, R. A. M. A.		西藏及其环境
1929－1930	Dutcher, G. M.	达　彻	亚洲历史地理论述
1929－1930	Chu, T. F.		一种新的中国古代文字分类法
1929－1930	Margouliés, Georges		韩愈在中国文学史上的地位
1930－1931	Chatley, H.	查得利	一周七日的起源
1930－1931	Visser, C. PHD.	维　琴	攀登喀喇昆仑山
1930.11.20	Tsai Yuan-Pei	蔡元培	中华民族与中庸之道
1930－1931	Wu Lien-tie	伍连德	早期西医在中国
1930－1931	Sowerby, A. de C.	苏阿德	爪哇和巴厘岛
1930－1931	Reddan, Miss S. M. B. A.		台湾的山脉
1930－1931	Abraham, R. D.	亚伯拉罕	中国的陶瓷器鉴赏
1930－1931	Porterfield, W. M. PH. D.	包达甫	中国的竹子
1930－1931	Chi Ping, PH. D.		南京的博物志
1930－1931	Coching Chu	竺可桢	中国历史时期气候变迁论
1930－1931	Morgan, Rev. Evan	莫安仁	宇宙元气
1930－1931	Haward, E	何立德	印度边界
1931.10.29	Johnston, Reginald F.	庄士敦	二十世纪的一位中国寺僧
1931－1932	Hughes, Rev. E. R.	修忠诚	三、四世纪中国的政治理想主义者和现实主义者

续表

演讲时间	英文名	中文名	题　　目
1931—1932	Dolan, Brooke		西藏边缘的大型狩猎活动
1932—1933	Pelliot, Paul	伯希和	中国境内的土耳其斯坦民族
1933.2.23	Wu Lien-tie	伍连德	早期中国之旅行家及其后继者
1932—1933	Abraham, R. D.		观赏中国画
1932—1933	Chatley, H.	查得利	再论每周天数的历史
1932—1933	Penniston, John B.		黄土的起源
1932—1933	Ferguson, J. C.	福开森	中国历代瓷器
1932—1933	Sowerby, A. de C.	苏阿德	中国的动植物资源
1932—1933	Gale, Esson M.	盖乐	中国人源自何处？——过去和现在的理论
1932—1933	Allan, Rev. C. W.	林辅华	早期的犹太人
1933.9.29	Grabau, A. W.		人类的起源
1933.10.19	Chatley, H. C.	查得利	六十甲子——中国古代历法
1933.11.12	Borrows, D. Bourke		亚洲森林学的重要性
1933.12.14	Sowerby, A. de C.	苏阿德	中国动植物之分布
1934.1.1	Read, Bernald E.	伊博恩	中医的发展历程
1934.1.15	Norwood, F. W.		世界及其困境
1934.1.25	Fisher, Emil S.	斐士	1933年云南、贵州旅行记
1934.2.8	Lyon, Willard D.	来会理	近十年中国文学之发展
1934.3.14	Carter, Dagny		游牧民族的艺术
1934.3.22	Dent, R. Vivian	罗伯特·邓德	吴哥遗址
1934.5.3	Kuei, Teng	藤圭	竹与竹画
1934.5.10	Suzuki, D. T.	铃木	大乘佛教
1934.5.17	Ayscough, Mrs. F.	爱司克夫人	中国书法、绘画、诗歌之间的相互关系
1934.11.15	Gale, Esson M.	盖乐	三千年以来的中国历史及历史学家
1934.11.23	Young, Jack T.	杨杰克	西藏边缘考察记
1934.12.6	Torrance, Thomas	陶然士	川西羌族
1934.12.13	Lin Yu-tang	林语堂	中国诗歌之内涵与技巧
1934.12.20	Chatley, H.	查得利	罗马日历
1935.1.16	Ting, V. K.	丁文江	陕西省水旱之记录与中国西北部干旱化之假说
1935.1.24	Andrew, G. Findlay	安献令	黄土高原上的居民和物产
1935.1.28	Bade, William F.	巴德	巴勒斯坦墓穴考古
1935.2.14	Sirén, Osvald	喜仁龙	中国人如何看待绘画艺术
1935.2.28	Hedin, Sven	斯文赫定	1933—1935年新疆中国考察记

续表

演讲时间	英文名	中文名	题　目
1935.3.7	MacNair, H. F.	宓亨利	1799年卡罗来娜的"广州到美国新大陆"沿海航行记
1935.3.21	Read, Bernard E.	伊博恩	古代中医中所蕴藏的化学
1935.4.18	Ayscough, Mrs. F.	爱司克夫人	从杜甫诗歌看唐代宫廷生活
1935.5.8	Reichelt, Rev. Karl L.	艾香德	佛学一观
1935.5.23	Filchner, Wilhelm	费通起	俄国、新疆、甘肃、西藏、印度旅行记
1935.10.17	NystrÖm, E. T.	新常富	中国黄金和其他金属矿藏及石油勘探和开采的可能
1935.10.31	Fearn, Anne Walter	斐尧臣	南非旅行记
1935.11.14	Barker, A. F.	巴克	印加版图
1935.11.27	Dolan Ⅱ., Brooke	多兰	鲜为人知的东藏
1935.12.5	Applrtion, John B.	阿普里顿	中华文明的地理背景
1935.12.12	Britton, Roswell S	白瑞华	中国报纸
1936.1.9	Kiang Kang Hu	江亢虎	中西间的文化关系
1936.1.30	Schafer, Herr Ernest		东藏的博物
1936.2.13	Kann, Edward	耿爱德	中国通货之发展与最近的货币改革
1936.2.27	Fithch, Robert F.	费佩德	佛寺的吸引力
1936.3.19	Chatley, H.	查得利	太极上元——中国天文学的宇宙论
1936.4.2	Gibson, H. E.	裘必胜	殷商甲骨
1936.4.23	Menzies, James M.	明义士	商周的艺术
1936.4.30	Menzies, James M.	明义士	商代的宗教与文化
1936.10.15	Sowerby, A. de C.	苏阿德	中国艺术中的动物
1936.11.5	Graham, D. C.	葛维汉	四川苗族的习俗、宗教及艺术
1936.11.25	Chang, P. C.	张铨	关于中国文化嬗变的争论
1936.12.3	Hughes, A. J.	郁赐	爪哇：无与伦比的自然吸引力
1936.12.10	Anderson, J. G.	安特生	匈奴的青铜器
1936.12.17	Laurell, Y	劳立尔	拉普兰人：斯堪底那维亚的一个亚洲前哨
1936.12.23	Griffin, C.	格里芬	在台湾土著中的日子
1937.1.14	Cressy, Rev. E. H.	葛德基	日本版画的魅力
1937.1.28	Gibson, H. E.	裘必胜	商代的音乐和乐器
1937.2.18	Bernard, M. Henri S. J.	裴化行	晚明基督教人文主义与新中国运动的领导者
1937.3.11	Zen, W. T.		湖州的石器发掘
1937.3.25	Levis, J. H.	来维思	中国音乐艺术之基础
1937.4.8	Kao Yu-Shih		吾国吾民
1937.4.22	Hudspeth, Rev. W. H.	王树德	云南、贵州的花苗

续表

演讲时间	英文名	中文名	题 目
1937.4.26	Pinching, H. C.		橡胶园参观记
1937.5.6	Stuebel, N.		海南土著
1937.5.20	Chungshee, H. Liu		试析中国民族之划分
1937.12.2	Sowerby, A. de C.	苏阿德	中国古墓中的陶俑(会长演讲)
1937.12.16	Dorf., V. C.	多尔夫	西康旅行记
1938.1.20	Wilkinson, E. S.	威尔金森	说鸟
1938.2.10	Abraham, R. D.	亚伯拉罕	三件古代艺术品
1938.3.10	Whatman. A. B.	惠尔曼	1935－1936年牛津大学北极科考活动中之东北探险考察记
1938.5.26	Gibson, H. E.	裘必胜	商代甲骨文以降汉字的演变
1938.10.27	Sowerby, A. De C.	苏阿德	上海公园之生态
1938.11.10	Cressy, E. H.	葛德基	中国的陶俑
1938.11.24	Gisbon, H. E.	裘必胜	商代驯养的动物及殉葬的动物
1938.12.15	Read, Bernald E.	伊博恩	中药中的动物
1939.1.5	Chu, Yuanting T.	朱元鼎	上海的淡水鱼
1939.2.2	Sowerby, A. De C.	苏阿德	中国动物主题神话
1939.2.16	Hubert, Richard	休伯特	荷属东印度游览记
1939.3.9	Roberts., Donald	罗道纳	正在华西的几位旅行者
1939.3.23	Dent, R. Vivian	罗伯特·邓德	摄影的科学
1939.4.6	Miorini, A. von		穿越北极地带
1939.4.27	Skyreme, F. H. E.	斯克姆	圣约翰时代的耶城勇士与马耳他
1939.5.18	Read, Bernard E.	伊博恩	中医中的"龙"
1939.6.8	MacNair, Henry Farnsworth	宓亨利	维多利亚中期执政官之变更
1939.10.12	Reifler, E.	赖费尔	汉语新学习法
1939.10.26	Read, Bernard E.	伊博恩	中国:丝的产地
1939.11.26	Laurell, Y.	劳立尔	所谓的中国黑陶
1939.11.30	Fisher, Emil, S.	斐 士	西藏的建筑奇观
1940.2.15	Sowerby, A. De C.	苏阿德	中国的珍稀动物
1940.3.14	Tomkinson, L.		中国人的战争与和平观
1940.3.28	Dunlap, E. W.		丹青人生
1940.4.11	Gibson, H. E.	裘必胜	商周的贝壳货币
1940.4.25	Huber, Richard S.	休 伯	金矿的故事
1940.5.16	Poston, David Gray	波斯顿	古代苏州散记
1940.5.30	Haughwout, Frank G.	霍沃特	台风规律
1940.9.12	Graham, D. C.	葛维汉	中国西部考古

续表

演讲时间	英文名	中文名	题 目
1940.10.24	Read, Bernard E.	伊博恩	昆虫在中药中的使用
1940.10.31	Penmington, W. B.	佩明顿	从印度支那到祖鲁兰（非洲）
1940.11.14	Sowery, A. De C.	苏阿德	中国的食虫动植物
1940.11.28	McCarthy, G. J.	麦卡锡	印度游记
1940.12.12	George, A. H.	周尔执	亚洲文会之过去与现在及其贡献
1940.12.19	Dent, R. V.	邓 德	显微镜下的事物
1941.1.30	Day, C. B.		中国的民间宗教
1941.2.13	Kann, Edward	耿爱德	明代的象牙雕刻
1941.3.20	Hudspeth, Rev. W. H.	王树德	印度支那地区的华裔
1941.4.15	Beath, S. S.		景德镇——中国的瓷都
1941.4.24	Sanger, F. J.	桑 格	天然飞行
1941.5.1	Ferguson, J. C.	福开森	宋代陶瓷
1941.5.15	Ruffé, D'Auxion de		中国古代刑法
1941.5.29	Roberts, Donald	罗道纳	中国历史诠释
1941.12	Sowerby, A. de C.	苏阿德	日本的哺乳动物
1946.5.23	不详		不详
1946.10.17	Read, Bernard E.	伊博恩	中国的饥荒根源
1941.11.28	Ankerson, W. A.	安克生	中国的皮影戏
1946.10.31	Pickens, Rev. Claude L.	毕敬士	中国与伊斯兰教的传播
1946.11.14	Gherzi, Father E.		台风
1946.11.28	Dent, R. V.	邓 德	彩色摄影术的基本原理
1946.12.28	Wise, E.	怀 斯	美国的自然公园
1947.1.16	Mortensen, Ralph	慕天恩	中国的佛教
1947.2.27	Boye, Teng Kwei	博 伊	中国的手指绘画
1947.3.27	Hudspeth, Rev. W. H.	王树德	华南地区的民间宗教
1947.4.17	Tsing	蒋廷黻	中国的生命线
1947.4.24	Russell, Rev. F. S.	路 思	西安简史
1947.5.15	Hudspeth, Rev. W. H.	王树德	基督徒与国际政治
1947.5.22	Worcester, Me. G. R. G.	夏士德	中国帆船集锦
1947.6.5	Yao, S. Y.	姚善友	复兴中的道教
1947.6.19	Millican, Rev. F. R.	梅立德	佛教与基督教的比较研究
1947.10.2	Beath, S. S.		上海早期历史
1947.10.16	Perry, Prof. Charles E.	佩 里	中国游览记
1947.10.30	Djang, Y. S.		重建中的社会力量
1947.11.13	Foo Thong-sien	傅统先	当代中国哲学发展趋势

续表

演讲时间	英文名	中文名	题　目
1947.11.22	FitzGerald, C. P.	菲茨杰拉德	唐朝的统治基础
1947.12.11	Dent, R. V.	邓　德	试论中国与西方的素描
1948.1.17	Ling, Helen D.	林海伦	中国早期的陶瓷
1948.2.19	Worcester, Me. G. R. G.	夏士德	中国帆船补注
1948.3.4	Chao Chen		中国哲学的某些方面
1948.4.1	Gillett, M. C.	支乐德	突厥语概要
1948.6.10	Graham, Darid C.	葛维汉	倮倮族的宗教
1948.6.24	Flowers, W. S.		中国的盲人
1948.10.21	Yao, S. Y.	姚善友	董仲舒的宇宙观
1948.11.14	Lin Tung. chi	林同济	一个中国人眼中的世界
1948.11.18	Abraham, R. D.		中国绘画导论
1948.12.2	Chen, C. Z.		中国建筑学
1948.12.16	Loo Yu. Tao, PhD		中国人的智慧
1948.12.30	Grosbois, Charles	高博爱	法国文学所受中国的影响
1949.1.13	Breuvery, Reverend Father de	贝　勒	台湾经济的特点和面临的问题
1949.1.27	Gadsby, J.		黎明之瓷:青瓷及其他瓷器
1949.2.10	Lawry, R. E.	劳　里	从北京经包头和宁夏到青海
1949.3.24	House, I. E.	休　斯	寻找野生动物
1949.4.7	Roberts, Donald	罗道纳	上海《天下月刊》社
1949.4.19	Bates, M. S.	贝德士	中国战胜封建主义:帝国的终结
1949.5.19	Zwetsloot, A. M.		一项地理调查:世界的20个大海
1949.12.8	Smythe, Lewis	史迈士	中国家族继承制之原因
1950.1.5	Griffin, Clarence	格里芬	造访台湾原住民
1950.1.19	Raguin, Father Y. E. S. J.		西方大学汉语研究的方法和趋势
1950.3.2	Zwetsloot, A. M.		地球上的河流系统
1950.4.6	Wu, Y. T.		新中国的前景
1950.5.27	不详		中西建筑学比较研究
1950.6.15	Chu, Diana		中国解放与志愿机构之儿童福利计划
1950.6.29	不详		暹罗和华南民族尤其是广州人的血缘关系
1950.7.27	Chu Yuan-ting T.	朱元鼎	中国石首鱼:生态学与经济价值
1950.9.14	Delza, Sophia	德尔泽	中国传统戏剧欣赏
1950.10.26	Meier, H.	美　亦	印度支那境内的"中国安南"居民(一)
1950.11.9	Meier, H.	美　亦	印度支那境内的"中国安南"居民(二)
1950.11.21	Abraham, R. D.		中国的青铜器
1951.1.1	Abraham, R. D.		中国玉(翡翠)之艺术价值

续表

演讲时间	英文名	中文名	题　目
1951.1.15	Wong, K. Chimin		中药中的艺术
1951.2.5	Leppich, Editha	莱伯奇	汉人、藏人及东方的地毯

1. 资料来源:《皇家亚洲文会北华支会会刊》(42－73卷)、《北华捷报》(1857－1910)、《字林西报》(1945－1951)。
2. 因资料限制,1871、1907－1908、1909－1910、1951.2－1952.6等时间段内之演讲目录只能付诸阙如。
3. 表中作者之中文名字主要采自黄光域的《近代中国专名翻译词典》。

皇家亚洲文会北华支会会员表

说明:

1. 该表主要依据《北华捷报》(1857－1861)所刊登的会员信息、《皇家亚洲文会北华支会会刊》(1－73卷)中的67个年份的文会会员通讯录,这些资料共计有24 482条会员之信息,经过统计,目前可以确认的会员有3 158名。笔者对每个会员尽可能地予以考证,详细列表于后。会员表格内容主要是:会员之英文名字、中文名字(译称)、国籍、身份、工作部门、居住地点、在会时间段、会员级别。

2. 会员的名字和工作部门之中文译称主要参照黄光域编的《近代中国专名翻译词典》(四川人民出版社2001年版)。

3. 会员国籍参照《近代中国专名翻译词典》和会刊中会员名录所包含的信息。

4. 会员身份参照《近代中国专名翻译词典》和通讯录中会员工作部门所反映出的信息。

5. 居住地点:

① 中文译称主要参照中国地名委员会编的《外国地名译名手册》(中型本)(商务印书馆1998年版);部分名称参照梁实秋主编的《远东英汉大辞典》(商务印书馆1994年版)及其他资料;一些英文地名和中文名称尚难确认,只能暂不翻译。

② 会员居住地点在历史时期曾经不断变更,本表所采用的标准是以居住年限的长短依次排列。由于表格所限,只列四个居住地点。

6. 在会时间:

① 在会时间系笔者就每个会员按在会的年份一一统计出来,如1901－1940年,笔者就要统计40个年份,所以以现有资料来说,在会时间应该十分准确。

② 由于部分会员中途曾经退出又再次加入,所以这些会员存在有两个或两个以上的在会时间段。

③ 由于文会有时候是两年统计一次会员名录,这样有些会员退出的具体年份只能暂缺;1946年后没见到会员名录,所以只能截止到该年份。1946年未与文会保持联系的,则以1940年为截止年份。

7. 会员类别中的英文字母含义如下:RM:居住会员;NRM:非居住会员;OM:普通会员;CM:通讯会员;LM:终生会员;HM:名誉会员。部分会员曾经先后当选通讯会员、普通会员、名誉会员,则按顺序依次排列,由于表格所限,会员类别的变更年份不再一一列出。

英 文 名	中文名	国 籍	身份/职业	部 门	居 住 地 点	在会时间	会员类别
Aalst, Jules A., van	阿理嗣	比利时	海关人员	海关	湖口,厦门,北京,上海	1886-1912	OM
Ababater, C.					上海	1861	RM
Abbott, R. J.	阿保德	英国	海关人员	海关	上海	1888-1892	LM
Abbott, W. E., M SC.				卜内碱公司,工部局化学处	上海	1926-1946	OM
Abbott, W. G.				工部局化学处	上海	1926-1929	OM
Abend, Hallett	安培德	美国	记者	《纽约时报》办事处	上海	1933-1946	OM
Abraham, D. E. J.					上海	1935-1940	OM
Abraham, Miss A.					上海	1933-1940	OM
Abraham, R. D.					上海	1914-1946	LM
Acheson, Guy			海关人员	海关	汕头,北京,苏州,伦敦	1908-1921	OM
Acheson, James, Esq.	阿岐森	英国	海关人员,领事人员		广州,上海,琼口	1880-1907	RM
Adam,Miss Edith M.				育才书社,公谊会	上海	1920-1946	OM
Adams, A. J.	阿淡斯	英国	海关人员		上海	1864-?	RM
Adams, Dr. H. C.				密西根大学	密西根	1914-1916	OM
Adams, Rev. A. S.	姚宣德	美国	牧师	美国浸礼会	汕头,宁波,上海,纽约	1889-?	OM
Adamson, Mrs. A. Q.	鄢盾生	英国	牧师	基督教育青年会	上海	1919-1921	OM
Addington The Rt. hon. Lord		英国	商人	汇丰银行	香港	1924-1929	OM
Addis, Charles Stuart	阿迪斯	英国	外交官		上海	1885-1888	OM
Adkins, T.	雅妥玛	英国	商人	泰和洋行	上海	1864-1877	RM
Adler, Max		德国	教授,教士	齐鲁大学	上海	1885-1887	OM
Adolph, W. H., PH. D.	窦维廉	美国		工部局卫生处	济南,费城	1917-1924	OM
Adrianoff, N. W.		美国	牧师	美以美会	上海	1935-1936	OM
Aeschliman, Rev. Ed. J	艾礼门				北京,天津	1936-1940	OM

续表

英 文 名	中文名	国 籍	身份/职业	部 门	居 住 地 点	在会时间	会员类别
Agar, Luis d'	阿噶	西班牙	领事人员		上海	1881－1885	OM
Ai, Dr. Henry, K. F.					上海	1946－?	OM
Aikin, R. P.				新丰洋行	上海	1939－?	OM
Ainger, Mojor E.				英军驻沪司令部	上海	1935－1936	OM
Ainscough, T. M.		英国		锦隆洋行	上海、北京	1909－1917	OM
Aitchison, W.			海关人员			1857	RM
Akehurst, A.	鄂克思	英国	外交官		上海	1906－1913	OM
Alabaster, C.	阿查立	英国				1866－1877	OM
Albertsen, K.				电报处	北京	1920－1929	OM
Alcock, Rutherford	阿礼国	英国	外交官	领事馆	上海、日本	1864－1897	HM
Alcott, Carroll D.		美国			费城	1941－?	OM
Alemann, Otto von				顺利洋行	上海	1910－1913	OM
Alexander, John A. C. C.	雷森德	英国	外交官	英国领事馆	上海、南京、青岛	1932－1940	OM
Alexéieff, Prof. Vassili	阿莱克斯夫	俄国	教授	圣彼得斯堡大学	北京、圣彼得堡	1907－1913	OM
Alford, R. G., Esq.	柯尔福	英国	教士	安立甘会	香港	1878－1885	OM
Allan, Dr. D. J.	林大卫	英国	教士	英国领事馆	上海、天津	1935－1940	OM
Allan, Rev. C. W.	林辅华	英国	牧师	卫理公会	上海	1935－1940	OM
Allen, E. L.			领事人员	工部局税务处	上海	1921－1927	OM
Allen, E. L. B., Esq.			外交官	领事馆	福州	1877－1885	OM
Allen, H. J.	阿赫伯	英国	外交官	领事馆	芜湖、上海	1872－1910	OM
Allen, K. E.				怡和洋行	汉口	1922－1924	OM
Allen, W. J.	欧伦		商人	太古洋行	上海	1939－1940	OM

附录：皇家亚洲文会北华支会研究

续表

英 文 名	中文名	国籍	身份/职业	部门	居住地点	在会时间	会员类别
Allman, Norwood F.	阿乐满	美国	外交官		上海	1932－1940	OM
Alway, Mrs. C.				太古洋行	青岛	1917－1924	OM
Amaral, J. R. C. do	阿穆恩	葡萄牙	领事人员	领事馆	澳门	1865－1875	HM
Ambrose, F. W.				工部局卫生处	上海	1925－1934	OM
Amelunxen, E. A., Esq.						1882－1883	OM
American Women' Club, Literary	图书馆	美国	图书馆	花旗妇女总会	上海	1922－1927	OM
Anand, A. S.					天津	1879－1901	OM
Ancell, Rev. B. L.	韩忤明	美国	牧师	大美圣公会	扬州、上海	1911－1930	OM
Andersen, N. P.	安得生	丹麦	海关人员	海关	上海	1883－1897	OM
Anderson, Dr. J. G.	安特生	瑞典	学者		北京	1919－1934	OM
Anderson, E.				老公茂洋行	上海	1864－?	RM
Anderson, F.			商人	太古洋行、怡和洋行	上海	1905－1911	OM
Anderson, G. C.	安德森	英国	海关人员	海关、大清银行	厦门	1880－1908	OM
Anderson, J.	安德森			燕京大学女校	北京	1864－1897	OM
Anderson, Miss E.			海关人员	海关	上海	1925－1929	OM
Anderson, P. B.		奥地利	领事人员	德国领事馆	北京、上海、南京	1915－1918	OM
Andes, Konrald J.	安得士	德国			上海	1903－1916	OM
Anding, W.		英国	教士	太古洋行	上海	1887－1893	OM
Andrew, G. Findley	安献令	美国		海关	旧金山	1935－1940	OM
Andrew, Miss L.		英国	海关人员		上海	1925－1929	OM
Andrew, W. M.	安乐					1891－1893	OM

续表

英 文 名	中文名	国籍	身份/职业	部门	居住地点	在会时间	会员类别
Anspach, P. P.	安保罗	美国	教士	美路德会	青岛	1927–1929	OM
Anstic, E. H.					上海	1936–?	OM
Appleman, L.				万泰保险公司	上海	1933–1934	OM
Archer, Allan	阿尔敦	英国		英国领事馆	北京,济南,青岛,重庆	1915–1932	OM
Arendt, C.	阿恩德	德国	外交官			1874–?	NRM
Argelander, F.	姚国伦	美国	教士	美以美会	九江	1930–1936	OM
Arlington, L. C.	阿灵敦	美国	邮局人员	中国邮局	汉口,杭州,北京	1917–1940	OM
Arnold, H. H.	亚诺尔	美国	工程师		上海	1932–1934	OM
Arnold, Julean H.	安立德	美国	外交官	美国领事馆	汉口,北京,厦门,烟台	1904–1940	OM
Arnold, Julian A.		美国	领事人员	美国领事馆	台湾,汕头	1904–1908	OM
Arnold, Miss D. M.				培成女校	上海	1927–1929	OM
Arnold, Robert			海关人员	海关	上海	1858–?	RM
Arnoux, Comte G d'	德达那	法国			上海	1882–1887	OM
Artindale, R. H.						1877–?	OM
Ashe, S. P. C.				永隆保险公司	上海	1937–1940	OM
Augustine, Library	图书馆	中国	图书馆	齐鲁大学图书馆	济南	1922–1946	OM
Ayrton, W. S., Esq.	爱尔敦	英国	外交官	英国领事馆	汉口,牛庄	1877–1885	OM
Ayscough, Mrs. F.	爱司克夫人	英国			上海	1906–1940	OM/HM
Baber, E. C.	贝德禄	英国	外交官	英国领事馆	上海,重庆,北京	1877–1888	OM
Bacci, E.				利威洋行	香港	1934–1936	OM

续表

英 文 名	中文名	国 籍	身份/职业	部 门	居 住 地 点	在会时间	会员类别
Backhouse, Edmund	巴克斯	英国	外交官		北京	1911–1913	OM
Badeley, J. E.					上海	1938–1940	OM
Baeser, Jos., Esq.						1882–1883	OM
Bahnson, J. J.	彭森	丹麦	商人	大北电报公司	上海	1909–1935	OM
Bahr, A. W.				壳件洋行	纽约、伦敦	1909–1940	OM
Bahr, P. J.		美国	外交官	壳件转运及拖轮有限公司	上海	1909–1928	OM
Bailey, David, H.	贝礼					1878–1880	OM
Bailey, J. A.					上海	1920–1929	OM
Bailey, R. M.					上海	1925–1932	OM
Bailler, Thos. G. B. SC.					上海	1920–1924	OM
Baillie, T. G.	蓓蕾		教师	工部局格致公学	上海	1931–1933	OM
Baily, R. M.				汇丰银行	上海	1925–1936	OM
Baker, A. E.				美以美会	泰安、天津、济南	1924–1929	OM
Baker, D. C.	贝克尔	美国	教士	中央银行	上海	1923–1936	OM
Baker, J. E.	贝克	美国		时评西行	上海	1935–1936	OM
Baldwin, Mrs. J. W.				北华捷报	上海	1920–1927	OM
Balfour, F. H.	巴尔福	英国	商人/编辑	法院	上海	1868–1885	RM
Ball, J. Dyer	波乃耶	英国	汉学家	字林西报	香港	1882–1918	LM
Ball, H. T. Montague		英国		格致书院	上海	1907–1911	OM
Ballie, T. G., B. SC.				爱礼司洋行	上海	1931–1935	OM
Balthaser, Waldemar					上海	1939–1940	OM

续表

英文名	中文名	国籍	身份/职业	部门	居住地点	在会时间	会员类别
Bamford, Rev. A.J.			牧师		上海	1881–1888	OM
Bandinel, J.J.F., Esq.	班迪诺	英国	商人		牛庄	1878–1881	NRM
Bao, Miss Dju Yu				工部局实业处	上海	1939–1940	OM
Barbour, E. d.						1869–1874	NRM
Barchet, Dr. S.P.				美国领事馆	上海	1899–1909	OM
Barchet, Miss H					宁波	1931–1946	OM
Bard, Eugene				永兴洋行	上海	1894–1897	OM
Barff, Richard				工部局	上海	1920–?	OM
Barker, Prof. A. F.			教授	上海交通大学,墨尔本大学	上海,墨尔本	1935–1940	OM
Barnett, Eugene E.	鲍乃德			国际基督教青年会	上海	1926–1939	OM
Barr, John. S.	白约翰	英国	教士	伦敦会	上海	1946–?	OM
Barrie, Howard				中华普仁医院	上海,牯岭	1920–1936	OM
Barrow, E. P. Graham				天主教学校	上海	1915–1919	OM
Bart, R. N.					上海	1857–?	RM
Bartlet, R. M.				燕京大学	北京	1927–1929	OM
Bartlett, W. W.				美国学堂	上海	1921–1925	OM
Bartley, H. S.					上海	1935–1936	OM
Barton, Miss E.				美国领事馆	上海	1936–?	OM
Barton, Mrs. Henry				美孚公司	上海	1940–?	OM
Barton, Rev. E. T.		英国	牧师	英国卫理公会	唐山	1934–1939	OM

续表

英 文 名	中文名	国 籍	身份/职业	部 门	居 住 地 点	在会时间	会员类别
Barton, Sir Sidney	巴尔敦	英国	外交官	英国领事馆	北京，上海	1906–1940	OM/HM
Barton, Rev. E. Tomlin			牧师	英国卫理公会	唐山	1934–1940	OM
Basset, Major A.				颐中烟草股份有限公司	上海	1934–1940	OM
Bastian, Prof. Dr. A.		德国	教授	柏林民族博物馆	柏林	1865–1907	CM/HM
Bataille, L.					比利时	1941–1946	OM
Batcher, H. S.						1864–?	RM
Bateman, E. F.				正广和洋行	上海	1933–1946	LM
Bateman, Rev. T. W.			牧师		重庆	1916–1919	OM
Bates, J. A. F. Sanders				中华大学图书公司	上海	1919–1940	OM
Batheke, Dr. M.				德国领事馆	重庆	1910–1916	OM
Battison, J.						1865–1874	RM
Baude, R. L. P.	保德成	法国	海关人员	海关	上海	1937–1946	OM
Bauer, L.	巴尔	奥地利	外交官	奥匈帝国领事馆	北京	1911–1917	OM
Baumber, J.				通用电器公司	上海	1926	OM
Baux, G.				旗昌缫丝厂	上海	1885–1893	OM
Bayne, Paker M.		加拿大	大学教师	华西协和大学	成都	1910–1946	OM
Bazin, J. Hervé			大学教师	震旦大学	上海	1917–1919	OM
Beal, Mrs. L.			教士	循道会	浏阳	1922–1927	OM
Beale, N. G.	毕尔	英国	商人	通用电器有限公司	上海	1932–1940	OM
Beaman, W. F.	斐继益	美国	教士	教士公所	上海	1921–1940	OM

续表

英 文 名	中文名	国籍	身份/职业	部 门	居 住 地 点	在会时间	会员类别
Beath, S. S.				沪江大学	上海	1939－1946	OM
Beaune, Th. Mercier			教授	法兰西远东语言学校	西贡	1894－1901	OM
Beauvais, J.	伯威	法国	外交官	法国领事馆	海口、广州	1900－1946	OM
Beauvais, M. A.					云南府	1900－1901	LM
Beauvais, M. J.	伯伟	法国	外交官	法国领事馆	龙州	1892－1897	OM
Bebenin, V. S.				工部局警署	上海	1935－1936	OM
Becher, H. M.			矿业工程师	怡和洋行、别发洋行	上海	1885－1892	OM
Beck, G.						1866－？	RM
Beck, H.			商人		上海	1885－1893	OM
Beck-Friis, H. E. Baron John	培克飞利思	瑞典	外交官	瑞典领事馆	上海	1937－1940	OM
Beckon, Rev. Oscar			牧师	北美瑞挪会	并州	1937－1940	OM
Beebe, R. C.	比必	美国	医生		上海、南京	1889－1940	OM
Behrens, L.				大北电报公司	上海	1935－1946	OM
Belcher, H. B.				工部局	上海	1917－1924	OM
Bell, A. D.	斐尔	英国	总董		上海	1933－1936	OM
Bell, F. H. Esq.						1865－？	OM
Bell, F. Hayley	贝渤	英国	海关人员	海关	上海、烟台	1908－1916	OM
Bell, H. T. Montague	毕尔	英国	报人	字林西报	上海	1907－1905	OM
Beltchenko, A. T.	贝勒成科	俄国	外交官	俄国领事馆	汉口	1918－1940	OM
Belvenetz, Peter, Lieut					彼德斯堡	1906－1907	OM

续表

英 文 名	中文名	国 籍	身份/职业	部 门	居 住 地 点	在会时间	会员类别
Bendixen, N. P.				大北电报公司	上海、北京、烟台、长崎	1913—1930	OM
Benham, Miss G. M.					上海	1925—1929	OM
Benjamin, Mis. M.					上海	1919—1920	OM
Bennett, C. R.	贝纳德	美国	银行家	花旗银行	北京	1933—1938	OM
Bennett, Capt. N. R.		英国		领江公司	上海	1928—1934	OM
Bennett, E. L.					上海	1939—1940	OM
Bennett, E. S.	贝纳特	北爱尔兰			贝尔发斯特	1918—1920	OM
Bennett, Mrs. E. L.					上海	1939—1940	OM
Bentley, Rev. W. P.			牧师		上海	1894—1897	OM
Bentley, Rev. W. T.			牧师		上海	1888—1901	OM
Berbom, T.				大北电报公司	上海	1908—1911	OM
Berg, Jan van den	范德溥	荷兰	外交官	荷兰大使馆	南京	1941—？	OM
Berge, Finn					上海	1940—？	OM
Bergen, Rev. Dr. P. D.	柏尔根	美国	牧师/博士	北长老会	潍县(山东)	1903—1915	OM
Bergling, Rev. R. M.				信义神学院	聂口	1936	OM
Bergman, Miss M					上海	1940—？	OM
Berlin, Arthur	柏林	美国	海关人员	海关	天津、上海	1936—1939	OM
Bernrd, Rev. Henri	裴化行	法国	牧师	徐家汇光启社	上海	1937—1940	OM
Bersani, O.					上海	1924—1929	OM
Bess, D. C.		美国	记者	上海泰晤时报	上海	1924—1929	OM
Bessell, F. L.	弼素乐	英国	海关人员	海关	天津、上海、香港、广州	1905—1946	LM
Betheke, M.				德国领事馆	重庆、上海	1910—1915	OM

续表

英 文 名	中文名	国籍	身份/职业	部 门	居住地点	在会时间	会员类别
Bethge, C.		瑞士			天津	1887－1897	OM
Betz, H.	贝斯	德国	外交官	德国领事馆	济南	1900－1915	OM
Bevan, Rev. H. W. L.	裴文	英国	牧师	伦敦会	上海	1906－1913	OM
Beveridge, H.						1865－1877	RM/NRM
Beytagh, L. M.				老公茂洋行	上海	1910－1934	OM
Biallas, Dr. F. X.	鲍润生	德国	牧师	辅仁大学	上海,北京	1927－1935	OM
Bidwell, H. S., Esq.						1865－?	OM
Biehl, Lieut. F. W.		美国			俄亥俄州	1929－1931	OM
Bielke, J. de		荷兰				1878－?	RM
Bierens de Haan, D.				好时洋行	汉口	1920－1924	OM
Bigel, Emile				佛兰西火轮船公司	上海	1925－1940	OM
Billingham, A.					上海	1937－1940	OM
Billinghurst, Dr. W. B.				沙逊洋行	上海	1908－1922	OM
Billinghurst, J. F.					上海	1891－1892	OM
Billinghurst, W. B.				西童书院	上海	1908－1911	OM
Billings, G. M.				义品放款银行	天津	1908－1913	OM
Binet, Marcel						1920－1929	OM
Bingham, Dr. Woodbridge	宾板桥	美国		加利福尼亚大学、美国雅礼会	加利福尼亚	1936－1940	OM
Bingham, H. T.					上海	1910－1912	OM
Bingley, C. K.		美国			加利福尼亚	1934－1940	OM
Birdwood, Christopher				卜内门公司、老公茂洋行	上海	1921－1928	OM
Birt, Wm.			商人		上海	1882－1885	OM

续表

英 文 名	中文名	国籍	身份/职业	部门	居住地点	在会时间	会员类别
Bishop, Carl Whitney	毕士勃	美国	考古学家	费城博物馆	费城	1919–1920	OM
Bishop, J.D.						1878–?	RM
Bisset, J.P.						1868–1877	RM
Bitton, Rev. W.N.	毕先生	英国	牧师	伦敦会	上海	1902–1913	OM
Biume, W.W.					上海	1921–1923	OM
Bixby, H.M.				中国飞运有限公司	上海	1935–1936	OM
Bjornson, E.	贝恩深	挪威	海关人员	海关	上海	1894–1897	OM
Bjorsvik, Rev. Lars			牧师	中华信义会湘中总会	安化	1939–1940	OM
Black, C.H.				美孚公司	上海	1914–1920	OM
Black, S.		丹麦		大北电报公司	北京、上海、天津	1910–1946	OM
Blackburn, A.D.	包克本	英国	外交官	英国领事馆	上海、北京	1917–1940	RM
Blair, J.H.						1870–1875	NRM
Blair, R.			军官			1877–?	NRM
Blakiston, Capt.	白拉克斯顿	英国				1865–1873	OM
Bland, Hubert					上海	1911	OM
Blickle, K.	布立克		商人	天福洋行	上海	1911–1919	OM
Blix, Peter				上海自来水公司	上海	1936–1939	OM
Block, M.S.	贝乐		商人	贝乐洋行	上海	1935	OM
Blume, W.W.	刘伯穆	美国	律师	密西根大学法律系	山西、上海	1921–1929	OM
Bock, Carl	柏固	瑞典	外交官	瑞典和挪威领事馆	上海	1888–1897	OM
Boerschmann, Ernst					北京	1908–1909	OM

续表

英 文 名	中文名	国 籍	身份/职业	部 门	居 住 地 点	在会时间	会员类别
Boey, P. L. Mingcheng				香港大学	香港	1929–1936	OM
Boezi, Dr. Guido	包安济	意大利	海关人员	海关	哈尔滨	1920–1936	OM
Bogomoloff, His Ex D. V.	鲍格莫洛夫	苏联	外交官	苏联领事馆	上海,南京	1936–1940	LM
Bois-Reymond, C. Du			教授		上海	1907–1919	OM
Bojesen, C. C.				工部局实业处	上海	1939–1940	OM
Bojko, V. F.						1941–?	OM
Boland, Capt. B.			船长	领江公司	上海	1925–1936	OM
Boleslawski, Chevalier C. de	卜理挖楷	奥匈帝国	外交官			1878–1881	RM
Bollerup-Sorensen, A.				大北电报公司	香港	1913–1916	OM
Bolton, R. L.				元芳洋行		1913	OM
Bondfield, Rev. Dr. G. H.	文显理	英国	牧师	大英圣书公会	上海	1900–1925	OM
Bondini, A. de		美国		美国通用电器公司	芝加哥	1937–1940	OM
Bonin, Dr. G. Von				北京协和医科大学	北京	1926–1936	OM
Boning, G. D.		荷兰		礼和洋行	上海	1894–1895	OM
Boode, E. P.					上海	1920–1936	OM
Bookless, A.	蒲兑礼士	英国		中国盐务稽核所	重庆	1933–1940	LM
Boone, Right Rev. Bishop			牧师		上海	1860	RM
Boosack, S. B.					上海	1933–1935	OM
Booth, A. S.				海关	厦门	1884–1887	OM
Boothby, B.		英国		英国领事馆	汉口,北京	1933–1940	OM

附录：皇家亚洲文会北华支会研究

续表

英 文 名	中文名	国籍	身份/职业	部 门	居住地点	在会时间	会员类别
Border, Commdr Lee Scott					上海	1926	OM
Borkowsky, P.			商人	顺发洋行	上海	1886—1888	OM
Bornestein, Dr. Jakob					上海	1939—1940	OM
Borrett, Mrs.					上海	1921—1924	OM
Borst-Smith, Rev. E. F.			牧师		上海	1928—1933	OM
Bos, W.		荷兰		隆茂洋行	上海	1922—1936	OM
Bosack, S. B.	白瑞克			普益地产公司	上海	1933—1940	OM
Bosustow, Miss J. C.				工部局	上海	1905—1940	OM
Bosworth, S. M.	卞珊兰(女)	美国	教士	美以美会	上海	1919—1934	OM
Botham, Rev. Mark E.	濮马可	英国	牧师	内地会	兰州,上海	1921—1924	OM
Bottu, A.	薄图	法国	总董	法董局	上海	1889—1897	OM
Bouinais, A. P.	濮义耐	法国	海关人员	海关	九江	1900—1909	OM
Bourgeois, Rev. A. M.			牧师		上海	1947—?	OM
Bourne, F. S. A.	班德瑞	英国	外交官	英国领事馆	上海,芜湖,厦门	1885—1917	OM
Bournonville, C. de		美国	商人	茂隆洋行,利和洋行	上海	1920—1924	OM
Bowden, V. G.				商务证信印刷所	上海	1928—1940	OM
Bowen, F. A.					上海	1935—1940	OM
Bowen, Mrs. A. J.	包文	美国		金陵大学,美以美会	南京,上海	1929—1936	OM
Bowker, H. F.		美国			纽约	1935—1940	OM/LM
Bowker, J. L.				亚细亚火油公司	上海	1938—1940	OM

续表

英 文 名	中文名	国籍	身份/职业	部 门	居 住 地 点	在会时间	会员类别
Bowker, J. T. E.						1864	RM
Bowra, C. A. V.	包罗	英国	海关人员	海关	北京、牛庄、沈阳、九江	1897－1932	OM
Bowra, E. C.	包腊	英国	海关人员	海关		1864－1874	RM
Bowring, Sir John	包令	英国	外交官			1866－1870	HM
Bowser, Miss H. C.					上海	1914－1922	OM
Box, Rev. Ernest	包克私	英国	教士	伦敦会、麦伦书院	上海	1897－1940	OM/LM
Boyé, Dr.	博耶	德国	外交官		柏林	1902－1909	OM
Boynton, C. L.	包引登	美国	教士	沪美学堂、基督教青年会、协进会	上海	1925－1929	OM
Brace, Capt. A. J.	布礼士	加拿大	教士	基督教青年会	上海	1921－1946	OM
Bradford, O. B.	巴剌佛	美国	外交官/牧师			1868－1877	RM
Bradlee, Rev. Caleb D.		美国	牧师		波斯顿	1890－1897	OM/LM
Bradley, H. W.	柏德立	美国	海关人员	海关	汉口、青岛、上海、宁波	1912－1920	OM
Brahn, C.				海关	上海	1939－1940	OM
Brand, J. K.				祥茂洋行	上海	1939－1940	OM
Brand, W.				义源洋行	上海	1887－1894	OM
Brandt, Carl T.	巴兰德	德国	海关人员	中国海关	汕头、重庆	1896－1922	OM
Brandt, Mrs.					上海	1913－1917	OM
Brandt, Mrs. Dorothea				古沃公馆	上海	1913	OM
Brandt, W. R.					上海	1913－1916	OM
Brass, E					上海	1894－1901	OM
Braun, Mrs. R.					上海	1939－1940	OM

续表

英　文　名	中文名	国　籍	身份/职业	部　　门	居　住　地　点	在会时间	会员类别
Brazier, Henry W.	白莱寿	英国	海关人员	海关	上海	1905—1920	OM
Brazier, James R.	白莱喜	英国	海关人员	福公司	天津、北京	1906—1913	OM
Brede, A., Jr.	裴德安			金陵大学	南京	1927—1929	OM
Bredon, M. Boyd	裴式模	英国	海关人员	海关	上海、烟台	1883—1897	OM
Bredon, Robt. E.	裴式楷	英国	海关人员	海关	北京、汉口	1885—1917	OM
Bremer, Miss M. A.	卜德明（女）	美国	教士	笃志女校	扬州、上海	1929—1940	OM
Bremner, Mrs. A. S.		英国	外交官	渣打银行	上海	1909—1920	OM
Brenan, Byron	璧利南	英国	外交官	英国领事馆	北京	1873—1912	OM
Brenan, J. F.	璧约翰	英国		平和洋行	上海、北京	1921—1936	OM
Brenneman, Mrs. J. J.				法国领事馆	上海	1922—1936	OM
Breteuil, Viscomte de					北京	1898—1901	OM/CM
Bretschneider, E.	贝勒	俄国	医生		北京	1880—1907	RM
Brett, G. A.						1864	OM
Brett, H. J.	卜乐特	英国	外交官	英国领事馆	上海	1906—1908	OM
Brett, Mrs. J. H.				花旗银行	上海	1920—1924	OM
Breuell, J. Esq.						1865	OM/LM
Brewitt-Taylor, C. H.	邓罗	英国	海关人员	海关	北京、福州、沈阳	1885—1938	OM
Bridge, F. S.				英商亚细亚火油公司	上海	1936—1940	OM
Bridgman, E. C.	裨治文	美国	教士		上海	1857—1862	RM
Brietow, H. H.				英国总领事馆	上海	1897—1907	OM
Bright, William	布莱德	英国	海关人员	海关统计局	上海	1885—1912	OM/LM

续表

英 文 名	中文名	国籍	身份/职业	部 门	居 住 地 点	在会时间	会员类别
Brind, B.				泰和洋行	上海	1935－1936	OM
Brisker, M. G.				渣大银行、利华公司	上海、汉口	1921－1936	OM
Bristow, H. B.	宝士德	英国	外交官	英国领事馆	烟台、上海、杭州、牛庄、九江	1887－1929	OM
Bristow, H. H.	宝述德	英国	外交官	英国领事馆	杭州、汉口、牛庄、上海	1909－1933	OM
Bristow, John A.				美孚公司	上海、九江	1933－1939	OM
Britland, A. J. D.	毕雅德	英国	教士	圣公会	北京	1924－1940	OM
Britte, Miss Edith M.	白玉德			基督教青年会	上海、北京	1932－1940	OM
Britton, Roswell S.	白瑞华	美国	记者		纽约	1931－1940	NRM
Brenan, Byron						1874－1875	OM
Broad, Wallace					上海	1903－1909	OM
Brockman, F. S.	巴乐满			基督教青年会	上海	1902－1909	OM
Brockman, W. W.	巴克蒙			基督教青年会	苏州	1927－1933	OM
Brooke, C.				雀巢奶品公司	上海	1918－1920	OM
Brooke, J. T. W.				新瑞和洋行、建兴建筑事物所	上海	1915－1940	OM
Brosche, H.	薄显理		海关人员	海关	汉口	1881－1888	OM
Browett, Harold				博易律师事务所	上海	1891－1936	OM
Brown, C. C.	步让	美国	驻华武官	美国领事馆		1936	OM
Brown, Geo.				英国领事馆	上海	1887－1888	OM
Brown, Geo. W., PH.D		美国		印第安纳波里教会大学	印第安纳波里	1926－1929	OM
Brown, H. O.		德国			柏林	1874－1878	NRM
Brown, I. S.	卜浪	美国	海关人员	海关、美国领事馆	上海	1927－1946	OM

续表

英 文 名	中文名	国 籍	身份/职业	部　　门	居 住 地 点	在会时间	会员类别
Brown, J. McLeavy	柏卓安	英国	海关人员	海关	上海、厦门、广州、九龙	1865－1926	OM/LM
Brown, J. L. Rev.		英国	牧师	大礼拜堂	上海	1935－1940	OM
Brown, L. S.		美国		英国领事馆	上海	1927－1934	OM
Brown, M. Rev.			牧师	上海抗大学校	上海	1933－1940	OM
Brown, M. W. Rev.	班可马		教士	卫理公会	天津	1916－1917	OM
Brown, Miss M. H.	薄玉珍(女)	加拿大		加拿大长老会	上海	1931－1940	OM
Brown, N. S.	卜隆			太古洋行	上海	1930－1936	OM
Brown, O.						1866－1870	NRM
Brown, R. C.					斯塔福德部	1865－1866	RM
Brown, Rev. J. L.			牧师		芜湖	1935－1939	OM
Brown, Robert E.	包让	美国	医生	博爱医院		1937－1940	OM
Brown, S. R. Rev.	勃朗	美国	牧师		江华	1860－1880	CM
Brown, Thomas		英国	出版商	别发洋行	上海	1885－1940	OM
Brown, W. P.	柏琵良	英国	海关人员	海关	上海	1890－1894	OM
Bruce, Col. C. D.	卜禄士	英国	军人	公部局	上海、威海卫	1900－1919	OM
Bruce, Edward B.		美国			纽约	1918－1946	LM
Bruce, Hon'ble F. W. A.						1859	RM
Bruce, Rev. J. P.	卜道成	英国	牧师	齐鲁大学	青州、济南	1916－1934	OM
Bruder, Mrs. F. F.					上海	1935－1936	OM
Bruehl, H. H.				信义会	汉口	1939－1940	OM
Brune, H. Prideaux				英国领事馆	上海、北京	1914－1929	OM
Bryan, H.					上海	1916－1918	OM

续表

英 文 名	中文名	国 籍	身份/职业	部 门	居 住 地 点	在会时间	会员类别
Bryant, P. L.				远东时报	上海	1917－1929	OM
Bryner, J., Esq.						1878－1883	RM/OM
Bryson, Dr. A. C.	贝来生	英国	医师		上海,北京	1932－1940	OM
Buchanan, E. M.				颐中烟草股份有限公司	北京,上海,青岛	1933－1946	LM
Buchanan, J.				长利洋行	上海	1887－1901	OM
Buchanan, J. U.					上海	1901	OM
Bucher, W.		英国			伦敦	1930－1934	OM
Buckens, F.	柏耿士	比利时			郑州	1915－1946	LM
Bugge, Rev. Sten	穆格新	挪威	牧师	陇海铁路	益阳,滠口,汉口	1924－1940	OM
Bullock, T. L.	布勒克	英国	外交官	湖北滠口信义神学院	北京	1885－?	OM
Buma, C. W. A.		荷兰		英国领事馆	巴黎	1921－1946	LM
Burdick, Miss S. M.	裴迪克(女)	英国	教士	美国浸礼会	上海	1909－1936	OM
Buri, Paul von	白礼	德国	外交官	德国领事馆	上海	1909－1916	OM
Burkhardt, Miss E.		英国			上海	1940－?	OM
Burkhardt, Mrs. L.				祥茂生洋行	上海	1911－1912	OM
Burkill, A. W.					上海	1912－1936	OM
Burling, Arthur H.	柏龄	美国	海关人员	海关	上海	1936－1940	OM
Burlingame, Hon. A.	蒲安臣	美国	外交官			1865－1869	NRM
Burnett, W. J.		新加坡		英国无线电公司	新加坡	1923－1936	OM
Burnice, C. M. G.				扬子公司,中国联合保险公司	上海	1923－1933	OM
Burns, Mrs.				茂生洋行	上海	1916－1926	OM

续表

英 文 名	中文名	国 籍	身份/职业	部 门	居 住 地 点	在会时间	会员类别
Burrows, T. D.				海关	九龙	1886－1888	OM
Burt, Rev. E. W.	白向义	英国	牧师	浸礼会	青州	1928－1933	OM
Bushell, Dr. S. W.	卜士礼	英国		英国领事馆	北京	1868－1909	OM/HM
Bushell, W. M. D.						1868－1873	NRM
Busse, F. W. K.	卜斯	德国	外交官	德国领事馆	成都	1904－1908	OM
Butcher, Rev. C. H.		英国	牧师			1866－1884	RM
Butland, C. A.				亚细亚火油公司	镇江、济南、宜昌	1920－1940	OM
Butler, Count A., von	毕第兰	德国	商人	泰来洋行	上海	1886－1901	OM
Butler, G. Hamilton				美国领事馆	上海、天津、广州	1908－1911	OM
Butler, M. C. P.					上海	1860	RM
Butrick, R. P.				美国领事馆	上海	1936	OM
Butt, D. M				祥泰洋行	上海	1935－1936	OM
Buttles, Prof. E. K.			教授		天津	1881－1885	OM
Byerly, Miss A. E.	巴道源		教士	美国圣公会	武昌	1928－1934	RM
Byramjee, D.				福利有限公司	上海	1859	OM
Byrne, E.					上海	1886－1887	OM
Byrne, P. L.				茂生洋行	上海	1913－1917	CM
Cachon, L'Abbe Mermet de						1866－1875	OM
Calder, A. Bland	高尔德	英国	外交官		上海	1934－1936	OM
Calder, J.		英国		北华捷报	上海	1890－1897	LM
Caldwell, Master J. C.				沪美学堂	上海	1930－1934	OM

续表

英 文 名	中文名	国 籍	身份/职业	部 门	居 住 地 点	在会时间	会员类别
Caldwell, Rev. H. R.	柯志仁	美国	牧师	美以美会	延平,福州	1920-1940	OM
Callado, His Ex., E.	喀拉多	巴西	外交官			1882-1883	OM
Camajee, H. D.						1874	RM
Cambiagi, Miss Y. G.					上海	1918-1920	OM
Camera, L.				怡和洋行、延昌洋行	上海	1891-1901	OM
Cameron, L.						1868-1873	RM
Campbell, C. W.	甘伯乐	英国	外交官	英国领事馆	北京,广州	1890-1913	OM
Campell, A. S.	甘伯操	英国		岭南大学	广州	1922-1924	OM
Camplin, A. B., M. SC., PH. D.						1939-1940	OM
Canady, F. H.				华北协和华语学校	北京	1920-1929	OM
Candlin, Rev. G. T.	甘淋	英国	牧师	圣道公会	唐山	1911-1913	OM
Cannan, A. M.				长利洋行、泰和洋行	上海	1908-1912 1933-1936	OM
Canny, J. M.	甘霓仁	英国	领事人员	法国驻镇江领事馆	镇江	1866-1877	NRM
Canny, T.						1864	RM
Cansey, B. D. Jr.						1939-1940	OM
Caraier, F.						1874-?	RM
Carbone, A. S.					上海	1931-1934	OM
Cardeillac, P.				华俄道胜银行	上海,牛庄	1920-1924	OM
Carey, H. Foote				华老大船务行	上海	1928-1940	OM

续表

英 文 名	中文名	国籍	身份/职业	部门	居住地点	在会时间	会员类别
Carl, Francis A.	柯乐尔	美国	海关人员	海关	汉口、广州、北京、牛庄	1906-1932	OM
Carles, W. R., C. M. G.	贾礼士	英国	领事人员	英国领事馆	上海、烟台、镇江、汉口	1887-1901	OM
Carlesen, N. P. V.				大北电报公司	天津、上海	1928-1936	OM
Carpenter, G. B.				新旗昌洋行	云南府	1906	LM
Carpenter, P. S. P.				北美洲保险公司	上海	1920-1940	OM
Carr, John					上海	1935-1936	OM
Carr, Paul R.		美国			纽约长岛	1940-?	OM
Carrall, James W.	贾雅格	英国	海关专员	海关	上海、烟台	1928-1940	OM
Carriere, J. D.	贾礼露	荷兰	商人	渣华油船公司	云南府	1885-1901	OM
Carruthers, A. G. H.	查德禄	英国	海关人员	海关	上海	1932-1940	OM
Carter, J. C.				大英医院药房有限公司	上海	1908-1915	OM
Carter, Lieut. A. F.				礼查饭店	纽约长岛	1912-1927	OM
Carvalho, Dr. A. de				海关	上海	1914-1917	OM
Casati, A.	克萨梯	意大利	海关人员		思茅	1935-1936	OM
Cass, Frank					厦门	1919-1929	OM
Cassat, Rev. Paul C.			牧师	齐鲁大学	济南、青岛	1895-1897	OM
Cassels, W. C.	盖威廉	英国	外交官	英国领事馆	上海、汉口、北京、汕头	1916-1920	OM
Castila, Capt.			船长			1921-1940	OM
Caughey, Lohn Lyons, D. D.						1865	OM
						1940-1946	OM

续表

英文名	中文名	国籍	身份/职业	部门	居住地点	在会时间	会员类别
Causey, B. D., Jr.				圣约翰大学	上海	1939-1940	OM
Chadsey, Mrs. Roy				科发药房	上海	1930-1934	OM
Chalfant, Rev. F. H.	方法敛	美国	教士		潍县(山东)	1904-1908	OM
Challoner, Mrs. G. T.						1921-1924	OM
Chalmers, James L.	湛玛斯	英国		海关	广州	1885-1893	OM
Chamber, Mrs. R. E.				西童女书院	上海	1935-1940	OM
Chambers, Rev. R. E., D. D.	湛罗弼	美国	教士	教士工所	上海	1928-1931	OM
Champan Ⅲ, F. J.				盐务稽核所	上海	1934-1936	OM
Chang King Fong M. A.				开滦煤矿办事处	上海	1939-1940	OM
Chang Shuh Ling				名尚实业公司	上海	1936-1940	OM
Chang Ying-hua				大华火油公司	天津	1933-1940	OM
Chang, F.				美亚保险总公司,俄商银行		1920-1936	OM
Chang, Hsin-hai, PH. H. D.				外交部	上海,南京	1928-1940	OM
Chang, Joseph Tsung-ping	张宗炳	中国	博士	东吴大学	上海,苏州	1940-?	OM
Chang, K. P.				明华银行	上海	1934-1936	OM
Chang, Kwang Tou		中国		复旦大学	上海	1933-1935	OM
Chang, S. C.					上海	1934-1936	OM
Chang, Sherman H. M., PH. D.	张郑敏	中国	留美博士	上海商业储蓄银行	上海	1933-1936	OM
Chapin, Miss H. B.				美国领事馆	青岛	1924-1929	OM
Chardin, Père T. De				地质调查所	北京	1935-1936	OM
Charles, A, A.				江南高中	南京	1909-1910	OM

续表

英　文　名	中文名	国　籍	身份/职业	部　　门	居　住　地　点	在会时间	会员类别
Charnely, J. R.					镇江	1914 – 1916	OM
Chase, Dr. Lewis, PH. D.				北京大学	北京	1923 – 1929	OM
Chatley, Herbert	查得利	英国	工程师	南京—湖南铁路、黄浦运输公司	上海、南京	1916 – 1946	OM/HM
Chatley, Miss M. H.				公理会	天津	1924	OM
Chavannes, Prof. Edouard	沙畹	法国	教授	法兰西学院	巴黎	1889 – 1917	LM/HM
Cheang, K. C. M. A. (CANTAB)					上海	1936 – 1946	OM
Cheang, K. Z.					上海	1836 – 1940	OM
Cheeloo University		中国	机构	齐鲁大学	济南	1922 – 1935	OM
Chen, Arthur Y. S.	陈叔源	中国	留美博士		上海	1916 1926 – 1929	OM
Chen, C.				中国旅行社	上海	1936 – 1946	OM
Chen, H. C.				工部局教育处	上海	1936 – 1940	OM
Chen, H. K.				之江大学	杭州	1939	OM
Chen, K. H.					上海	1946	OM
Chen, K. P.				上海商业储蓄银行	上海	1933 – 1946	LM
Chen, Kenneth K. S.	陈观胜	中国	留美博士	夏威夷大学	夏威夷	1937 – 1939	OM
Chen, Kuo-Chuan				中英美联谊会	上海、南京	1913 – 1928	OM
Chen, L. T.				金诚银行	上海	1932 – 1936	OM
Chen, Shao Yin				中国保险协会	上海	1946	OM
Chen, Ssu Tu					上海	1939	OM
Chen, W. Hanming	陈汉明	中国	记者	字林西报、孖剌西报	上海、香港	1923 – 1946	OM/LM

续表

英文名	中文名	国籍	身份/职业	部门	居住地点	在会时间	会员类别
Chen, W. Y., PH. D	陈文渊	中国		花旗银行、基督教青年会	上海	1937-1940	OM
Chen, Ya-ting				德和洋行	上海	1946	OM
Cheng Tsee Yoong					上海	1933-1940	OM
Cheng, Harry H.				基督教青年会	上海	1937-1940	OM
Cheshire, F. D.	哲士	美国	外交官	美国领事馆	广州、上海	1906-1915	OM
Cheshire, Wm.						1864-1866	RM
Chiao Tung University, Librarian	图书馆	中国	图书馆	上海交通大学图书馆	上海	1935-1946	LM
Chien Soo-Chun, Miss					上海	1935-1936	OM
Chieri, Cav. Uff. Dott Vi.				意大利厂商代理处	上海	1923-1939	OM
Chieri, V.	齐尔利			邮政局	上海	1908-1929	OM
Ching, William					上海	1937-1940	OM
Chiu Pei-hao				社会局	上海	1929-1931	OM
Chou Yao				江苏银行	上海	1935-1936	OM
Chou, Mrs. U. T. Bang				警卫报	上海	1933-1936	OM
Chow, Koo-chen	周谷城	中国		大北电报公司	上海、北京	1937-1940	OM
Christiansen, J. P.				瑞典挪威联盟领事	上海	1913-1930	OM
Christiernsson, Dr. B.	葛德生		外交官	领事馆	上海	1878-1880	RM
Christopher, Prof. J. W.			教授		南安普敦	1946	OM
Chrystall, W.				社会局		1875-?	RM
Chu Pei-hao					上海	1929-1934	OM
Chu, Tso-chih				上海中医学院	上海	1935-1936	OM

续表

英 文 名	中文名	国 籍	身份/职业	部 门	居 住 地 点	在会时间	会员类别
Chu, Dr. Yuanting	朱元鼎	中国		圣约翰大学	上海	1932－1940	OM
Chu, Philip	朱家祥	中国	律师		上海	1939－1940	OM
Chun, Dr. J. W. H.	陈永汉	中国	医生	国家检疫所	上海	1935－1936	OM
Chung Hwa Book Co., Library	图书馆		图书馆	中华书局	上海	1939－1940	OM
Claiborne, Miss Elizabeth				文汇报	上海,苏州	1908－1934	OM
Clair, A. B. St.	喀剌尔	英国			上海	1859	RM
Clark, J. D.	开乐凯	英国	报人	文汇报	上海	1864	RM
Clark, John W.					上海	1895－1922	OM
Clark, T. B.				美国领事馆		1921－1924	OM
Clarke, B. A.						1922	RM
Clarke, E. G.				永德洋行	上海	1866	OM
Clarke, Miss M. H.	柯雅德(女)	美国	教士	中西女塾	上海	1932－1940	OM
Clayson, W. H.	葛雷森	英国	海关人员	海关	广州	1928－1934	OM
Cleland, H. R.				克左时洋行	上海	1885－1888	OM
Clementi, C.	金文泰	英国	官员	殖民地秘书处	香港,新加坡	1935－1940	OM
Clennell, W. J.	乐民乐	英国	外交官	英国领事馆	九江,杭州,福州,镇江	1905－1911 1921－1928	OM/LM
Cleveland, Mrs. F. A.	葛佛伦	美国	盐税局	盐务稽核所	上海	1933－1934	OM
Clifford, Prof. O. C.			教授	南洋公学	上海	1909	OM

续表

英文名	中文名	国籍	身份/职业	部门	居住地点	在会时间	会员类别
Clifton, Baroness		英国	外交官	英国领事馆	上海	1921–1934	OM
Cloud, Fred D.	云飞得	美国	外交官	美国领事馆	上海、沈阳	1908–1913	OM
Clubb, O. Edmund, A. B.	柯乐博	美国	外交官	美国领事馆	汉口、北京、长春	1931–1936 1941–1946	OM
Canny, J. M.						1869–1870	NRM
Coales, O. R.		英国	外交官	英国领事馆	上海、腾越、长沙、牛庄	1906–1925	OM
Cochran, W.	王九德	美国	医师	美北长老会		1865	OM
Cockell, Capt.					上海	1919–1920	OM
Cocker, T. E.	哥嘉	英国	海关人员	海关	广州、上海、九龙、厦门	1885–1897	OM
Coelho de Carvalho, J.			领事人员	葡萄牙领事馆	上海	1886–?	OM
Coghill, J.G.S., M.D.						1868–1869	RM
Cohen, A.						1866	RM
Coifford, J.		法国	外交官	法国领事馆	上海	1934–1940	OM
Coignet, F., Esq.						1878–1882	OM
Cole, A. B.				卫理公会	天津	1906–1926	OM
Cole, Rev. W. B.	邬温柔		牧师		仙游（福建）	1917–1946	OM/LM
Coleman, N. L.					上海	1934–1936	OM
Collin de Plancy, V.	葛林德	法国	外交官	法国领事馆	上海	1877–1888	OM
Collins, D. J. Dr.		美国			上海	1939–1940	OM
Collins, Miss K.					上海	1936–1940	OM
Collins, Mrs. D. J.					上海	1939–1940	OM
Collyer, Rev. Chas. T.			牧师	大英圣公会	上海	1891–1901	OM

续表

英　文　名	中文名	国籍	身份/职业	部　　门	居　住　地　点	在会时间	会员类别
Columbia University	图书馆	美国	图书馆	哥伦比亚大学	纽约	1921–1924	OM
Commijs, A.J.	葛枚士	荷兰	海关人员	海关	上海	1917–1931	OM
Compton						1857	RM
Conger, E. H.	康格	美国	外交官	美国领事馆	北京	1902–1907	OM
Connell, C. C.				上海总会	上海	1914–1916	OM
Conrad, H.				矮克发洋行	上海	1935–1936	OM
Contag, Dr. Victoria				德国领事馆	上海	1935	OM
Cook, Capt A.			船长	太古洋行	上海、香港	1929–1940	OM
Cook, Cyril B.				卜内门洋碱股份有限公司	上海	1933–1940	OM
Cook, H. M.				友邦人寿保险公司	上海	1915–1917	OM
Cook, Rev, Thos.			牧师		万县	1921–1924	OM
Coole, A. B.	邱文明	美国	教士	天津汇文中学、卫理公会	天津	1926–1940	OM
Cooper, G.F.C.				华童公学	上海	1905–1907	OM
Cooper, Miss G. L.	顾环林(女)	美国		圣约翰大学、圣公会	上海	1928–1940	OM
Cooper, T. T.						1866–1870	NRM
Cooper, W. M.	固威林	美国	外交官	英国领事馆	宁波	1877–1888	OM
Cooverjee, P., Esq.						1881–1883	RM
Copper, W. A Duncan, M.D.				美孚煤油公司	上海	1896–1897	OM
Corbett, R.J.				工部局	上海	1933–1935	OM
Corbett-Smith, A.					上海	1909–1911	OM
Corder, G. A.	唔达	英国	海关人员	海关	广州	1885–1888	OM
Cordes, Aug. C.		德国	商人	公司	天津	1877–1893	OM

续表

英 文 名	中文名	国 籍	身份/职业	部 门	居 住 地 点	在会时间	会员类别
Cordier, Prof. Henri	高第	法国	教授	法兰西学院	巴黎	1873-1924	RM/CM/HM
Cornaby, Rev. W. A.	高葆真		牧师	广学会,循道会	上海	1903-1913	OM
Cornell University Libersity	图书馆		图书馆	康乃尔大学图书馆	纽约	1922-1928	OM
Corner, A. W.						1864-1877	NRM
Corner, G. R.						1865-1868	RM
Corrie, R. C.				太古洋行	上海	1930-1934	OM
Cory, A. E. Rev.	柯锐	美国	牧师		芜湖	1908-1913	OM
Cory, J. M.						1878-?	OM
Costenoble, H.				爱礼司洋行	上海	1928-1934	OM
Couch, Mrs. Esther G.						1940-?	OM
Coughtrie, J. B.				中华火烛保险公司	香港	1879-1897	OM
Couling, Miss	库美龄（女）	英国	文会成员	亚洲文会藏书楼	上海	1922-1926	OM
Couling, Mrs. C. E.		英国			上海	1916-1940	OM
Couling, Rev. S. M. A.	库寿龄	英国	牧师	麦伦书院	上海、青州	1894-1921	OM/HM
Count D'Escuyrac De L'Auture						1866	CM
Courier, Mme					上海	1915-1919	OM
Coushnir, I. S.					上海	1931-1935	OM
Cousing, L. G.				颐中烟草股份有限公司	上海	1935-1940	OM
Cousland, Dr. P. B.	高易		律师	长老会	上海	1908-1930	LM
Cowie, G. J. W.						1864-1866	RM
Cox, Dr. S. M.	柯罗巴	英国	海关人员	海关	上海	1908-1917	OM

续表

英 文 名	中文名	国 籍	身份/职业	部 门	居 住 地 点	在会时间	会员类别
Cox, Mrs. Charles				其来洋行	宜章	1924–1929	OM
Cox, Rev. Josiah	柯格	英国	牧师	循道会		1864–1888	CM
Craig, A.	柯礼克	英国	大学教师	马尼拉大学	马尼拉	1914–1924	OM
Craig, Rev. C. Stuart. B. A.			牧师	伦敦会	汉口	1939–1940	OM
Crampton, C. L.		美国		西亚库斯大学地理系	上海	1930–1933	OM
Crawford, J.						1869–1877	NRM
Creagh, E. Fitzgerald	格类	英国	海关人员	海关	汉口,广州	1886–1897	OM
Creighton, G. W.	柯瑞敦	英国	外交官	英国领事馆	上海,重庆	1939–1940	OM
Cressey, Prof. G. B.	葛德石	美国	教授	沪江大学,美国西那库斯大学	上海	1925–1940	OM/LM
Cressy, Rev. Earl H.	葛德基	美国	牧师	大美浸礼会	上海	1928–1940	OM
Crisler, C. C.	蒯思乐	美国	牧师		上海	1935	OM
Crockett, O. R.						1864	RM
Crofts, Geo.				永福洋行	天津	1921–1929	OM
Croix, C. de St.						1868–1874	NRM
Crokam, W. G.				怡泰洋行	上海	1932–1934	OM
Cross, A. A.						1864	RM
Crossman, Major, R. R.						1868–1869	RM
Crow, C.	克劳	美国	记者	大陆报	上海	1913–1940	OM
Crum, Stanley				美国总统轮船公司	上海	1940–?	OM
Cucherousset, Henri					上海	1912–1913	OM

续表

英 文 名	中文名	国 籍	身份/职业	部　门	居 住 地 点	在会时间	会员类别
Culbertson, Rev. M. S.	克陛存	美国	牧师	长老会		1859	RM
Cull, J.					上海	1864–1866	RM
Culpin, Dr. Millais				公裕太阳火险公司	上海	1908–1913	OM
Cumberbatch, L. H.				锦明洋行	上海	1939–1940	OM
Cumine, H. M.	顾敏	英国	海关		上海	1929–1940	OM
Cunningham, A.	康达	美国	报人	南清早报公司	香港,上海	1895–1910	RM
Cunningham, E.	克能翰	美国	商人	美国领事馆,瑞典挪威领事馆	上海	1866–1877	RM
Cunningham, E. S.	柯银汉	美国	外交官	美国领事馆	上海	1922–1938	OM
Cunningham, Rev. R.	顾福华		牧师	内地会	打箭炉	1913–1920	OM
Cupelli, M.	辜贝利	意大利	海关		上海,兰州,龙州	1918–1929	OM
Currelly, C. T.		加拿大		安大略皇家考古博物馆	多伦多	1923–1940	OM
Cushnie, G. S. B.				保家行	上海	1916–1919	OM
D'Alton, Mrs. F.				中国邮政局	满洲,天津	1930–1936	OM
D'Alton, V. L.				中国邮政局	上海	1924–1936	OM
D'Anty, Pierre Bons	安迪	法国	外交官	法国领事馆	重庆	1889–1919	LM
D'Elia, Rev. Father P. M., S. J.	德礼贤	意大利	耶稣会士	徐家汇光启社	上海	1928–1936	OM
Dale, Dr. C. L., M. D.						1941–?	OM
Dale, Rev. Alan T.	戴立义	英国	牧师	卫理公会	唐山	1934–1940	OM
Danforth, A. W.	丹士	美国	工程师	华胜棉纺公司	上海	1887–1907	OM
Daniel, W. H.						1875–1877	RM
Danner, Mrs.				客利饭店	上海	1920–1924	OM

续表

英 文 名	中文名	国籍	身份/职业	部 门	居 住 地 点	在会时间	会员类别
Danton, G. H.	谭唐	美国	教授	清华大学	北京	1918–1934	OM
Darch, O. W.		英国		青年协会书局,亚细亚火油公司		1922–1940	LM
Darroch, Rev. John	窦乐安	英国	牧师	中国圣教书会	汉口	1906–1913 1928–1933	OM
Das Chagas, J. F.	沙福斯图		外交官	葡萄牙领事馆	北京	1910–1913	OM
Davenport, A.	达文波	英国			上海	1858–1881	RM
Davey, W. J.	狄维生	英国	海关人员	文汇报	上海	1920–1940	OM
Davidson, J.	达飞声	美国	外交官	海关	上海	1938–1940	OM
Davidson, J. W.	达维森	英国	外交官	英国领事馆	明尼苏达州	1904–1908	OM
Davidson,J. W. O., O. B. E.	德焕文	英国	海关人员	英国领事馆	爱丁堡	1933	OM
Davidson, R.		英国			上海	1914–1933	LM
Davies, Eric	戴咸士			渣打银行	上海	1939–1940	OM
Davies, T.	谈维泗	英国	医师		上海	1857	RM
Davis, Dr. C. Noel	戴伟士	美国	外交官	海关	吉林,沈阳	1910–1936	OM
Davis, Grone H.				美国领事馆	上海	1908–1910	OM
Davis, J. K.		美国	外交官	同仁医院		1864–1866	RM
Davis, John Ker	戴维斯			美国领事馆	上海	1927–1940	OM
Davis,Miss Emily				宁林西报	上海	1921–1924 1935	OM
Davis, Monnett B.					上海	1935–1938	OM
Davis, R. W.					上海	1924–1940	OM
Davis, Sir John, K. C. B., Bart.	德庇时	英国	外交官			1866–1873	HM

续表

英 文 名	中文名	国籍	身份/职业	部 门	居 住 地 点	在会时间	会员类别
Dawber, R., B. A.					上海	1861	RM
Dawson, Brian				维昌洋行	上海	1925—1929	OM
Dawson, J. J.						1864	RM
Day, L. G.				上海电力公司	上海	1941—1946	OM
Day, Rev. C. B.	队克勋	美国	牧师	美北长老会	上海	1939—1940	OM
De Korne, Rev. John C.	狄靠恩		牧师	归正基督会	Jukao 甘肃,上海	1927—1940	OM
Deas, Stuart		英国		太古洋行	汉口,芜湖	1919—1940	LM
Deas, W. S. P.				太古洋行	上海	1919—1920	LM
Deighton-Braysher, C.	戴敦	英国	海关人员	海关	上海,牛庄,九江	1870—1893	OM
Delaplace, Mgr. L. G.		法国	教士		北京	1881—1884	CM
Delhaye, L. G.	田类思			比利时领事馆	上海	1935—1936	OM
Delius, Dr.				德国领事馆	上海	1902—1907	OM
Denby, Charles	田夏礼	美国	外交官	美国领事馆	上海	1908	OM
Denham, Mrs. J. E.	迪纳姆	英国	建筑师	纶华缫丝公司	上海,北京	1919—1924	OM
Denigri, E.					上海	1895—1897	OM
Dennys, H. D.			律师	港督秘书处	香港	1869—1870	NRM
Dennys, H. L.			编辑			1877—1913	OM
Dennys, N. B., PH. D.	丹尼斯	英国				1866—1875	NRM
Dent, H. W.	典题	英国	外交官	怡和洋行	上海	1864	RM
Dent, R. V.	罗伯特·邓德	英国	商人	怡和洋行	上海	1933—1939	OM
Dent, V.	维维安·邓德	英国	商人	中国海关	上海	1912—1928	OM
Deschamps, G.						1868—1877	NRM

续表

英 文 名	中文名	国 籍	身份/职业	部 门	居 住 地 点	在会时间	会员类别
Dew, G. C.				通和工程局	上海	1905-1907	OM
Dichson, A. L.				颐中烟草股份有限公司	上海	1935-1936	OM
Dick, L. S.				高林洋行	上海	1920-1924	OM
Dick, Thos.	狄妥玛	英国	海关人员	海关		1864-1877	NRM
Diehr, C. O. M.	铁迈士		盐务	盐务稽核所	上海	1929-1933	OM
Diemer, Miss C.				路透社新闻办	上海	1934-1936	OM
Dillon, C.	狄隆	法国	外交官	法国领事馆		1865-1873	RM
Dillon, Gustave		法国	地图专家	远东地理学会		1911-1913	OM
Dingle, Edwin J.	丁格尔				上海	1917-1936	OM
Dingle, Lilian M.					上海	1917-1924	OM
Dixwell, G. B.	狄思威		工部局	工部局董事会	上海	1864-1877	RM/NRM
Djou, G. G.				建兴建筑事物所	汉口,上海	1941-1946	OM
Dmitrevsky, P. A.	德密特	俄国	外交官	俄国领事馆	汉口	1882-1897	OM
Dobbs, F. E. L.	窦溥思		盐务	盐务稽核所	上海,汉口	1936-1940	OM
Dobrovolsky, S.					上海	1935-1936	OM
Docodha, N. B.					上海	1935-?	OM
Dodd, J.	多政	英国	商人	海关	厦门	1872-1893	NRM/OM
Dodson, Miss S. L.				圣玛利亚书院	上海	1909-1924	OM
Dome, A. Earl	冬雅德	英国	记者	基督教青年会	上海	1920-1929	OM
Donald, William H.	端纳			远东时报,上海泰晤时报	北京,沈阳,上海,汉口	1911-1940	OM
Dones, Dr.					上海	1861	RM

续表

英 文 名	中文名	国 籍	身份/职业	部 门	居 住 地 点	在会时间	会员类别
Donnelly, Ivon A.				隆茂洋行、大沽驳船公司		1923－1936	OM
Donovan, J. P.	多诺分	英国	海关人员	中国邮局	济南、上海、汉口	1891－1917	OM
Doodha, N. B.	杜德	英国	海关人员	海关	上海	1935－1940	OM
Dore						1864	RM
Dorrance, A. A.				美孚公司	上海	1934－1936	OM
Dorsey, W. Roderick				美国领事馆	上海、利比亚、意大利	1911－1924	OM
Douglas, J. C. E.				英国当局最高法院	上海	1905－1915	OM
Douglas, Miss L.					上海	1921－1924	OM
Douthirt, Mrs J. B.					纽约	1934－1940	OM
Doven, J. T.					上海	1860	RM
Dovey, J. W.	杜明德	英国		协和书局、亚细亚火油公司	上海	1918－1929	OM
Dowdall, Chas			律师		上海	1881－1897	OM
Dowie, Robert G.				育才学校、嘉道理中文学校	上海	1906－1919	OM
Doyle, J. E.				商文印刷有限公司	上海	1921－1924	OM
Drago, G. D.					纽约	1918－1924	OM
Drake, Noah F., PHD.				北洋大学	天津	1911－1919	LM
Drake, Rev. F. S., B. A., B. D.	林仰山	英国	教士	齐鲁大学	济南、青州	1930－1940	OM
Drew, E. B.	杜维德	美国	海关人员	海关	上海、北京、广州	1882－1933	LM
Drummond, W. V.	担文	英国	律师		上海	1864－1877	NRM
Drury, Rev. C. M.			牧师			1924－1926	OM
Du Monceau, comte L.				华比洋行、道胜银行、俄国银行	上海、横滨、布鲁塞尔	1909－1930	OM

续表

英 文 名	中文名	国 籍	身份/职业	部 门	居 住 地 点	在会时间	会员类别
Dubail, G.	吕班	法国	外交官	法国领事馆	北京	1894－1901	OM
Dubs, Homer H. Ph. D.	德利美	美国	汉学家			1946－?	OM
Ducken, A. C.						1870－1875	NRM
Dülberg, F. W. E.	涂理博	德国	海关人员	海关	九龙	1880－1893	OM
Dulcken, A. C.						1865－1868	NRM
Dumaresq, P. K.	杜玛理		外交官	瑞典挪威荷兰领事馆	宁波	1870－1874	RM
Dumon, F.		法国		法董局	上海	1910－1926	OM
Duncan, A.	邓铎	英国	海关人员	海关	上海、汉口、宁波	1896－1909	OM
Duncan, A. Mcl	邓铿	英国	海关人员	海关	上海	1922－1940	OM
Duncan, Chesney				香港电报局	香港	1889－1897	OM
Dunlap, Mrs. A. M.					上海	1933－1940	OM
Dunn, Dr. T. B., M. D.				公司	上海	1935－1940	OM
Dunn, J. G.	郭约翰	英国	商人			1864	RM
Dunn, J. W.						1869－1874	NRM
Dunphy, Capt. C. L. Austin				路透电报公司	上海	1925－1929	OM
Dunscombe						1865	OM
Duyvendak, Prof. Dr. J. J. L.	戴闻达	荷兰	外交官/汉学家	荷兰公使馆，莱登大学	北京，莱登	1915－1940	OM
Dykstra, Rev, S. A.	戴希孟	荷兰	牧师	归正基督教会	Jukao 江苏	1927－1929	OM
Dyson, Verne					上海	1924－1929	OM
Dzau, Ponchen L. E.				哈密尔顿饭店	上海	1933－1936	OM
Eastlack, W. C.						1866	RM

续表

英 文 名	中文名	国籍	身份/职业	部 门	居 住 地 点	在会时间	会员类别
Ebbs, W.				泰来洋行	上海	1886–1888	OM
Ecke, Gustav	艾锷风	德国	教授	辅仁大学	北京	1934–1940	OM
Eckfeldt, T. W.		英国				1869–1875	RM
Edgar, Rev. J. H.	叶长清	英国	教士	内地会	打箭炉	1910–1924	OM
Edkins, Rev. J., D. D.	艾约瑟	英国	牧师	亚洲文会记录秘书	上海,北京	1857–1897	CM
Edmondston, David C.				汇丰银行	香港,广州,青岛,哈尔滨	1917–1946	OM
Edmunds, C. K.	晏文士	美国	大学校长	岭南大学	广州	1916–1929	OM
Edwards, Mrs. Martin					上海	1912–1916	OM
Eggleton, W. G.				雷氏德研究院		1937–1940	OM
Ehlers, Aug.			商人		上海	1886–1888	OM
Eisler, Capt. W. L.				美敦洋行	上海	1935–1936	OM
Eitaki, H.	永泷久吉	日本	外交官	日本领事馆	上海	1908–1913	OM
Eitel, E. J., PHD.	艾德	德国			阿得雷德	1869–1907	NRM/OM/HM
Elahi, M. Fazal				英国皇家地理学会	上海	1933–1935	OM
Elias, Ney	爱连斯	英国				1869–1877	RM/NRM
Eliot, Sir Charles, K. C. M. G.	爱理鹗	英国	语言学家	香港大学	香港	1913–1924	OM
Elliot, Dr.						1864	RM
Elliston, H. B.	亚力斯顿	英国	记者		北京	1925–1929	OM
Elwin, Rev. Arthur		美国	牧师	圣公会	上海,汉口,杭州	1890–1901	OM
Ely, Mrs. J. A.	伊理夫人	美国		圣约翰大学,圣公会		1917–1939	OM
Ely, Prof. John A.	伊理	美国	教授/牧师	圣约翰大学	上海	1917–1939	OM

续表

英文名	中文名	国籍	身份/职业	部门	居住地点	在会时间	会员类别
Elzear, T. M.				东方汇理银行	上海	1936-1940	OM
Emanoff, N. N.	叶美诺夫		建筑师	新瑞和洋行	上海	1933-1936	OM
Emens, W. S.	易孟士	美国	外交官		上海	1886-1888	OM
Emms, A.		英国		雷氏德研究院	上海	1935-1936	OM
Enders, Mrs. Gordon B.					上海	1922-1936	RM
Endicott, C. E.						1870-1876	OM
Engel, Max. M.	恩赍曹			公司	上海、北京	1911-1936	OM
Englaender, A. L.	延兴阿				上海	1928-1933	OM
Enright, J. A.		英国	海关人员	帝国邮局	上海	1901	OM
Ensinger, H.		德国	外交官	德国领事馆	上海	1901	OM
Eriksen, A. H.	伊立生	丹麦		中国电报处	北京	1915-1940	LM
Ermiloff, P.	阿美路	俄国	海关人员	海关	上海	1935-1936	OM
Erslev, E.				亚细亚火油公司	上海	1915-1917	OM
Eskelum, A. H.				立基洋行	上海	1931-1936	OM
Essex Institute, Librarian	图书馆	美国	图书馆	艾塞克斯学院图书馆	麻萨诺塞州	1906-1940	OM
Eudicott, C. E.						1877	RM
Evan-Jones, Dr. E.					上海	1932-1936	OM
Evans, Edward	伊文思	英国	教士	教士公所	上海	1917-1922	OM
Evans, H.	埃凡	英国	商人			1870-1876	RM
Evans, J.	伊珍尼(女)		教士	美国公理会		1869-1870	NRM
Evans, Joseph J.	伊约瑟	英国	书商	伊文思图书有限公司	上海	1916-1936	OM

续表

英 文 名	中文名	国 籍	身份/职业	部 门	居 住 地 点	在会时间	会员类别
Exter, Bertus van				荷兰银行、荷兰冶港公司	上海、烟台	1916－1924	OM
Ezekiel, M. D.	爱资拉		商人	沙逊洋行	上海	1894－1895	OM
Ezra, Edward				洋行	上海	1899－1901	OM
Ezra, Moise				花旗银行	上海	1935－1940	OM
Faber Rev. Ernst	花之安	德国	教士/汉学家		上海	1886－1897	OM
Fairbrother, Capt.						1864	RM
Fairburn, H. J.		英国			南京、上海	1933－1940	OM
Fairchild, Mrs. F. A.	费巧尔	英国	商人		上海	1917	OM
Fairfax, Lieut. B. C.					威海卫	1901	OM
Falck, Miss Elizabeth H.	福尔格（女）	美国	教士	广慈医院、圣公会	上海	1935－1940	OM
Falck, Prof. M. F.			教授	圣约翰大学	上海	1935－1946	OM
Falconer, Dr.	霍近拿		商人			1865	OM
Fan Gilbert T. B.				福公司	上海	1933－1936	OM
Farago, E., Esq.	法朱格	匈牙利	海关专员	海关	宜昌、北京、福州、广州	1877－1897	OM
Farby, Prof. M. F.			教授	福建协和大学	福州	1924－1940	LM
Fardel, H. L.				市属幼稚园	上海	1918－1923	OM
Farnswarth, L. L.				柯达公司	上海	1939－1940	OM
Faulkner, Dr.						1866	NRM
Fautereau-Vassel, Mms. P. de				法国学堂	上海	1921－1923	OM
Fauvel, A. A., Esq.	福威勒	法国	海关人员		上海	1870－1883	NRM
Faxon, H. C.	法克生	美国	商人		北京	1924－1929	OM

续表

英 文 名	中文名	国 籍	身份/职业	部 门	居 住 地 点	在会时间	会员类别
Fearn, Dr. Anne Walter	斐尧臣夫人	美国	医师	美国领事馆	上海	1911－1938	OM/LM
Fearn, Dr. Mrs. J. B.	斐佰夫人	美国	教士	监理会	上海	1911－1933	OM/LM
Fearon, R. I.	费隆	美国	商人			1866－1874	RM
Fedrow, Capt. E.					上海	1914－1916	OM
Feetham, Hon. Mr. Justice, C. M. G.				工部局	上海	1930－1936	OM
Feldman, M M.				济业银行	上海	1935－1940	OM
Fell, Walter				和记洋行	威海卫	1900－1901	OM
Fenton, A. E.					上海	1938－1940	OM
Fenton, A. H.				工部局	上海	1911－1913	OM
Ferguson, Capt. D.				领江公司	上海	1932－1936	OM
Ferguson, Dr. J. W. H.	费克森	荷兰	海关人员	海关	上海,汉口,哈尔滨	1910－1932	OM
Ferguson, His Ex. , J. H.	费果荪	荷兰	外交官		北京,烟台	1878－1884	OM
Ferguson, John C. ,PHD.	福开森	美国	政府顾问	南洋公学校长	北京,上海,南京	1896－1940	OM/LM
Ferguson, T. T. H.	费妥玛	荷兰	海关人员	海关	北京,天津,上海	1900－1923	OM
Ferguson, W.N. , F. R. G. S.			教士	大英圣书公会	成都	1916－1929	OM
Fergusson, T. T.	法格圣	英国	商人	滋大洋行	烟台	1873－1888	NRM/OM
Ferrajolo, R.	费费乐	意大利	外交官	意大利领事馆	上海,汉口,南京,沈阳	1920－1936	OM
Ferro, G. Vigna del		意大利	外交官	意大利领事馆	上海	1903－1908	OM
Fesenmeyer, F. R. , R. N.			海关人员	海关	上海	1860	RM
Fetherstonhaugh, J.	斐敦好	英国			上海	1912－1913	OM
Filsinger, E.				公司	上海	1935－1936	OM

续表

英 文 名	中文名	国 籍	身份/职业	部 门	居 住 地 点	在会时间	会员类别
Finch, A. B.			报人	上海泰晤士报、字林西报	上海	1922-1934	OM
Finch, B.			报人	会德丰洋行	上海	1926-1933	OM
Fink, C.	芬克	德国		大德国新闻纸馆	上海	1899-1907	OM
Finzi, Vito	费尹济	意大利	外交官	意大利领事馆	上海	1885-1888	OM
Firth, B.				维乐士有限公司	上海	1926-1929	OM
Firth, Miss M.			教师	文化公学	上海	1920-1923	OM
Fischer, Emil. S.	斐士	奥地利	商人	游艺津会	天津	1894-1940	OM/LM
Fisher, A.					九江、上海	1864-1866	RM
Fisher, H. J.	费世	英国	海关人员	海关	天津、秦皇岛、唐山	1877-1885	OM
Fisk, G. W.		英国		开滦矿务局	天津、秦皇岛、唐山	1919-1929	OM
Fitch, Rev. George A.	费吴生	美国	牧师	基督教育年会	南京、上海、重庆	1921-1940	OM
Fitch, Robert F., D.D	费佩德	美国	教士	北长老会	杭州	1918-1922	OM
Fittock, W. H.					上海	1859-1877	RM/NRM
Fitzgerald, M. O.						1875-1877	RM
FitzRoy, G. H.	费士来					1866	RM
Fleischer, B. W.	费莱煦			大陆报馆	上海	1912-1915	OM
Fleischer, Walter				圣约翰大学	上海	1946-?	OM
Flemons, Sidney				上海电话公司	上海	1917-1940	OM
Fletcher, W. J. B.	佛来遮	英国	领事人员	英国领事馆	福州	1916-1924	OM
Flint, Hugh				怡和洋行	上海	1924-1932	OM
Flothow, Carl				禅臣洋行	上海	1886-1888	OM

续表

英 文 名	中文名	国 籍	身份/职业	部 门	居 住 地 点	在会时间	会员类别
Flothow, Hugo				顺全隆洋行	上海	1886–1888	OM
Fly, H. E.				工部局	上海	1910–1911	OM
Focke, J. H., DR. JUR.	佛客			德国领事馆	上海	1882–1888	OM
Follett, Miss Matilda				上海疗养所	上海	1940–?	OM
Fong, F. Sec.					上海	1930–1933	OM
Fontanel, E.	方达理	瑞士	外交官	瑞士领事馆	上海	1939–1940	OM
Foo, Ping-sheug, LL. D.				中华民国外交部	重庆	1939–1940	OM
Forbe, F. H.				怡泰代理行	上海	1935–1936	OM
Forbes, A. H.	福贝士	英国	海关人员	中国海关	上海	1941–?	OM
Forbes, F. B.	福勃士	英国	商人			1864–1884	RM
Forbes, H. de Courcey						1873–?	RM
Forbes, Miss M.				美大航空公司	上海	1934–1940	OM
Forbes, Rev. Carl.						1874–?	RM
Forke, Prof. Dr. A.	伏尔克	德国	外交官	德国领事馆 汉堡大学	上海,汉堡	1894–1946	CM/OM/HM
Forrest, R. J.	富礼赐	英国	领事人员		伦敦	1866–1877	NRM
Forsyth, J. S. Esq.						1865	OM
Fowler, Dr. Henry		英国	医师	伦敦会	伦敦	1927–1929	OM
Fowler, J. A.					上海	1913–1919	OM
Fox, Harry H., G. M. G.	傅乐仁	英国	外交官	英国领事馆	北京,上海,成都	1907–1933	OM
Francis, Frank	傅夏礼			工部局	上海	1910–1912	OM
Francis, R.					上海	1888–1893	OM

续表

英 文 名	中文名	国籍	身份/职业	部 门	居 住 地 点	在会时间	会员类别
Franck, Rev. G. M.	傅文博	英国	牧师	大英圣书公会	成都	1922－1939	OM
Franke, Otto, PH. D.	福兰阁	德国	外交官	德国领事馆	上海,北京,厦门	1890－1897 1900－1901	OM
Franklin, C. S.	樊克令	美国	律师	樊克令哈灵敦律师公馆	上海	1935－1946	OM
Franks			军人			1857	RM
Fraser, D.	傅瑞丞	英国		上海总会	上海	1931－1934	OM
Fraser, E. D. H., C. M. G.	法磊斯	英国	领事人员	英国领事馆	汉口	1907－1919	OM
Fraser, Munro, J. P.						1873	NRM
Fraser, John						1870－?	RM
Fraser, M. F. A.	富美基	英国	外交官	英国领事馆	上海	1888－1912 1924－1934	OM
Fraser, Miss Jean				圣约翰大学,尚贤堂	上海	1912－1919	OM
Fraser, Munro, J. P.						1873	NRM
Fraser,Sir Everard,K. C. M. G.				英国领事馆	上海	1907－1921	OM
Frater, Alex.	费里德	英国	外交官	英国领事馆	上海,琼州,汕头	1869－1893	NRM/OM
Fredet, J.				旅华法国商务总会	上海	1922－1940	OM
Freeman, Mrs. Z. S.			工商界	中美商业银行、中华懋业银行	北京,上海	1922－1924	OM
Freemen, F. R.				道门郎联合公司	上海	1932－1936	OM
Freemen, Mansfield	费孟福	美国	工商界	友邦人寿保险公司	上海	1925－1946	OM
Freer, Charles L.		美国			底特律,密西根州	1910－1913	OM
Freise, Ignaz A. C. J.					上海	1932－1936	OM
Fretwell, V. V. W.				英商亚细亚火油公司	上海	1941－1946	OM

续表

英 文 名	中文名	国 籍	身份/职业	部 门	居 住 地 点	在会时间	会员类别
Freyn, H. J.				美国总会	上海	1937－1946	OM
Fries, L. Litter von	费理司	奥地利	海关专员	海关	上海	1886－?	OM
Fries, S. Ritter von	费习孟	奥地利	海关助理员	海关	上海,台南	1885－1892	OM
Frieswyk, G. A.	费理威	荷兰	海关人员	利华公司	上海	1905－1908	OM
Fritsche, H. PH. D.	费理饬	德国	天文学家	北京天文台	北京	1877－1897	CM
Fritz, Chester	吉士德			新丰洋行	上海	1937－1940	OM
Fritz, Mrs. Bording S.				新丰洋行	上海	1933－1936	OM
Froomkin, Joseph					上海	1946－?	OM
Fryer, C. H.				泰隆洋行	上海	1935－1936	OM
Fryer, E. C.		英国			上海	1912－1918	OM
Fryer, George B.	傅步兰	英国		太古洋行、美华书馆、东吴大学	烟台,苏州	1901－1946	OM
Fryer, Prof. John	傅兰雅	英国	编辑	江南制造总局翻译室	上海	1868－1928	CM/HM
Fulford, H. E.	椂福礼	英国	外交官	英国领事馆	天津,上海,牛庄	1885－1913	OM
Fung, Yee					上海	1900－1908	OM
Furnas, W. J.				公和洋行		1940－1946	OM
Gabbott, F. R.		德国	教授		上海	1929－1946	CM
Gabelentz, Prof. Georg von der	嘎伯冷茨	德国	外交官	德国领事馆	柏林,莱比锡	1884－1894	OM
Gabriel, Hermann, DR. JUR.	嘉比烈		教士	雅礼会	厦门	1884－1897	OM
Gage, Rev. Brownell	盖葆赖	美国		新丰洋行	长沙	1915－1932	OM
Gain, P. D. G.					上海	1941－1946	OM

续表

英 文 名	中文名	国籍	身份/职业	部 门	居 住 地 点	在会时间	会员类别
Gale, Esson M., M. A., PH. D.	盖乐	美国	领事人员	盐务稽核所	汉口,长春	1911–1940	OM
Gale, S. R.					上海	1898–1901	OM
Galle, P. E., Dr., M. D.						1869–1878	RM
Galmburg, F. H.				泰和洋行		1910–1913	OM
Galt, Rev. E. W.	高厚儒	美国	牧师	公理会	保定,汾州	1924–1940	OM
Galvin, J. W.	盖尔芬	英国	海关人员	海关	上海	1940–1946	OM
Gamble, Sidney D.	甘博	美国	学人		纽约	1922–1946	LM
Gamble, Wm	姜别利	美国	教士			1866–1870	RM
Gande, W. J.	盛特	英国	商人	源和有限公司	上海	1938–1940	OM
Gande, W. M.		英国		源和洋行	上海	1938–1940	OM
Gardien, H. G.		英国	银行	汇丰银行	汉口,上海,天津	1906–1934	OM
Gardner, C. T., C. M. G.	嘉托玛	英国	领事人员	英国领事馆	广州,烟台,厦门,汉口	1877–1921	OM/CM
Garhaz, J. F.		美国		海关	上海	1929–1933	OM
Garner, Dr. Emily	贾医生(女)	美国	医师	妇孺医院	武昌	1911–1924	OM
Garrett, N.				华中大学	南京	1937–1946	OM
Garritt, Rev. J. C.	甘路德	美国	牧师	北长老会		1907–1936	OM/LM
Garrod, S. H.		美国		昌兴火轮船公司	上海	1931–1946	OM
Gates, Miss J.		美国	图书馆管理员	美国国会图书馆东方学部	华盛顿	1931–1946	LM
Gatti, Carlo			纺丝厂经理	怡和洋行	上海	1886–1894	OM
Gaunt, Percy		英国		工部局卫生处	上海	1921–1940	OM

续表

英 文 名	中文名	国 籍	身份/职业	部 门	居 住 地 点	在会时间	会员类别
Gaunt, Rev. T., M. A.	恭多马		牧师	工部局,南京神学院,昆明圣教医院	上海,南京,昆明,宁波	1921－1940	OM
Gauss, C. E.	高思	美国	外交官	美国领事馆	上海	1936－1940	OM
Gawler, G. N.	戈略尔	英国	海关人员	海关	上海,香港,汕头	1925－1940	OM
Gearey, F. H.				天祥洋行	上海	1938－1940	OM
Gearey, Miss G.				亚细亚火油公司	杭州	1923	OM
Gebhardt, F.			商人	地亚士洋行,广泰洋行,地亚士洋行	上海	1886－1888	OM
Gedrath, O.					上海	1892－1893	OM
Genechten, Rev. Ed. Van			牧师	天主教堂	北京	1936－1940	OM
Gerecke, E.				德华银行	上海	1891－1892	OM
Gerharz, J. W. F.	葛哈芝	荷兰	海关人员	海关	上海,厦门,海口	1921－1936	OM
Gerhaz, J. E.				海关	上海	1929－1932	OM
Gerhevitch, Joseph					上海	1946－?	LM
Gerken, Chas.	哲尔满			天祥洋行	香港	1922－1940	LM
Germain, T. C.		英国	海关人员	海关	上海九龙	1934－1946	OM
Gest Chinese Research Library	图书馆	加拿大	图书馆	麦吉尔大学	蒙特利尔	1922－1936	OM
Getty, Miss Alice					巴黎	1921－1929	OM
Ghiselin, Rev. C.		美国	牧师	美国长老会	台州	1918－1919	OM
Ghisi, E	计细	意大利	商人	义丰洋行	上海	1893－1923	OM
Gibb, Mrs. J. Mcgregor	翟博	美国	学人		上海	1934－1940	OM
Gibson, H. E.	裘毕胜	美国	商人	大来洋行	上海	1915－1946	OM

续表

英 文 名	中文名	国籍	身份/职业	部门	居住地点	在会时间	会员类别
Gibson, J.	郭乐升	英国	海关人员		上海	1859	RM
Gibson, Mrs. H. E.	裴毕胜夫人				上海	1939	OM
Gicher, M. E.						1946	OM
Gieter, Prof. Leon de			教授	帝国邮局	北京	1899–1901	OM
Gil de Urbarri, Ramiro, Esq.						1882–1884	OM
Gilby, J. H.				汇中饭店	上海	1916–1918	OM
Gilchrist, Edward	克立基	美国	海关人员	海关	宁波,福州	1908–1924	OM
Giles, Bertram	翟比南	英国	外交官	英国领事馆	福州,长沙	1902–1911	OM
Giles, Mrs. L.					上海	1939–1940	OM
Giles, Prof. Herbert Allen	翟理思	英国	外交官	英国领事馆	上海,宁波,天津,福州	1880–1934	CM/HM
Giles, Lancelot	翟兰思	英国	外交官	英国领事馆	天津,厦门	1902–1911	OM
Giles, W. R.	纪乐士	英国	记者	京津报馆	北京	1920–1924	OM
Gilfillan, Jas.						1865–1877	RM
Gillet, T. H.		英国		上海自来水公司	上海	1941–1946	OM
Gilliam, J.	吉勒德			英商大英烟公司	上海,天津,汉口,哈尔滨	1915–1938	OM
Gillis, Capt. J. H.		美国	外交官	美国领事馆	北京	1911–1940	OM
Gimbel, C., M. Sc.				联合法院	镇江	1914–1919	OM
Giolma, A. de Bretton				福公司	Ja-Mei-Sen 河南	1909–1913	OM
Gipperich, H.	吉溥利	德国	商人		天津	1909–1918	OM
Giquel, P. M.	日意格	法国	军人			1865–1885	NRM
Gish, Rev. E. P.			牧师		南京	1919–1924	OM

续表

英 文 名	中文名	国 籍	身份/职业	部 门	居 住 地 点	在会时间	会员类别
Givens, T. P.				工部局警署	上海	1935—1936	OM
Gladki, P. M.				中东铁路	哈尔滨	1915—1920	OM
Glathe, A.	吉罗福			雅利洋行	上海	1929—1935	OM
Glover, G. B., Esq.		美国	海关人员		上海,九江	1875—1885	RM/LM
Gockson, William	郭顺	中国		永安有限公司	上海	1937—1940	OM
Goddard, W. G.		澳大利亚			墨尔本	1911 1929—1936	OM
Godfrey, C. H.				工部局	上海	1909—1922	OM
Goebel, Max				比利时领事馆	上海	1890—1893	OM
Goetz, A.						1875—1877	RM
Goffe, H.	葛福	英国	外交官	英国领事馆	南京,成都,汉口,云南	1905—1915	OM
Göhring, A.				瑞记洋行	汉口	1913—1917	OM
Goldring, Mrs. P. W.				汇中饭店	上海	1920—1928	OM
Goldring, P. W.					上海	1919—1927	OM
Goldsmith, B.				中商公司	上海	1881—1885	OM
Golovatsky, Miss T.					上海	1946—?	OM
Gomersall, W. C.	高默朔	英国	商人	信昌机器工程股份有限公司	上海	1941—1946	OM
Goodeell, Roseoe A.				陕西学堂	西安	1905—1910	OM
Gooding, Miss L.		美国	教士	燕京女校	北京,南昌	1925—1929	OM
Goodnow, Dr. Frank J.	古德诺	美国	法学家		巴尔底摩	1914—1917	OM
Goodnow, Hon. J.	古纳	美国	外交官	美国领事馆	上海	1901	OM

续表

英 文 名	中文名	国籍	身份/职业	部门	居住地点	在会时间	会员类别
Goodrich, Dr. L. C.	傅路德	美国	学者	哥伦比亚大学汉语系图书馆	纽约	1933 – 1946	LM
Goodwin, C. W.						1866 – 1874	RM/CM
Goodwin, Dr. Theodore S.				广济医院	杭州、成都	1939 – 1940	OM
Gordon, A. Howard	高登	英国	工程师		上海	1924 – 1931	OM
Gordon, Col. C. G.	戈登	英国	军人			1866 – 1894	CM
Gordon, J. M.				太子洋行	上海、香港	1924 – 1925	OM
Gordon, Mrs. E. A.				东京饭店	东京	1923 – 1924	OM
Gordon, O. K.						1864	RM
Gottburg, W.						1870 – 1881	RM
Goucher, Rev. J. F., D.D., LL. D.		美国	牧师	巴尔底摩	马里兰州	1915 – 1918	OM
Gould, R. F.						1864	RM
Gould, Rev. R. J.	库茂枝	英国	牧师	大英圣书公会	汉口	1931 – 1932	OM
Goullart, P.				美国运通公司	上海	1930 – 1940	OM
Gowing, Lionel F.		英国	记者	北华捷报	伦敦	1885 – 1888	OM
Gowland, G. H.				渣打银行	上海	1907 – 1913	OM
Gracie, W. H.						1866 – 1868	RM
Graffenried, E. de				瑞士领事馆	上海	1935 – 1936	OM
Graham, David C., M. A., PH. D.	葛维汉	美国	教士	大美浸礼会	成都	1924 – 1940	OM
Gran, E. M.				建兴建筑事务所	上海	1930 – 1940	OM
Grandgerard, C. P.					上海	1939 – 1940	OM

续表

英 文 名	中文名	国籍	身份/职业	部 门	居 住 地 点	在会时间	会员类别
Grant, Charles				别发洋行	上海	1901-1907	OM
Grant, Dr. J.				洛克菲勒基金会	上海	1935-1936	OM
Grant, G. P.						1868	RM
Grant, G. V.						1866	RM
Grant, J. B.	兰安生	美国	医师		上海	1916-1924	OM
Grant, P. V.	格兰特	英国	工商界	和记洋行	上海	1869-1892	RM/OM
Gratton, F. M., F. R. I. B. A.				洋行	上海	1889-1901	OM
Graves, Bp. F. R., D. D.	郭斐蔚	美国	教士	圣约翰大学	上海	1918-1939	OM
Graves, Miss Lucy J.	郭路珊(女)	中国	教士	圣玛利亚教堂	上海	1929-1940	OM
Graves, R. C.				海关	天津	1918-1931	OM
Gray, C. Norman					上海	1919-1924	OM
Gray, Walter				罗柏洋行	上海	1925-1929	OM
Greaves, J. R.				太古洋行	上海	1913-1917	OM
Green, A.	格令	英国		鹰立球钢厂	上海	1926-1929	OM
Green, G. H. Jr.				花旗银行	上海	1941-1946	OM
Green, I. R.				晋隆洋行	上海	1918-1920	OM
Green, Mrs. D. Lyman				字林西报	上海	1935-1936	OM
Green, O. M.	葛林	英国	记者	字林西报	上海	1909-1913	OM
Green, Paymaster Commr				上海英国海军事务所	上海	1922-1929	OM
Greenfield, J. N.	格连维	英国	邮政人员	邮局	上海	1941-?	OM
Gregg, Miss Alice	郭爱理(女)	美国	教士		纽约	1927-1929	OM

续表

英 文 名	中文名	国 籍	身份/职业	部 门	居 住 地 点	在会时间	会员类别
Gribble, H. Esq.	记里布	英国				1865	OM
Griebenow, M. G.	季维菴	美国	教士	宣道会	甘肃 Labrang(Hsiaho)	1937－1940	OM
Grierson, R. C.	纪尔森	英国	海关人员	海关	上海	1918－1929	OM
Grimani, E. H.	纪默理	英国	海关人员			1873－1877	NRM
Grimmo, A. E. P.				工部局卫生处	上海	1924－1936	OM
Grodtman, Johans		德国		亨利洋行，谦信洋行	上海	1898－1946	OM/LM
Groeneveldt, W. P.						1874－1877	NRM
Groenman, F. E. H.	赫龙门	荷兰	外交官	荷兰领事馆	上海	1929－1946	LM
Groff, G. W.	高老甫	美国	大学教师	岭南大学	广州	1923－1929	OM
Gröne, H. Dawson	克勒纳	英国	海关人员		九龙,香港,杭州	1908－1913 1934－1940	OM/LM
Gronert, M.					上海	1896－1901	OM
Groom, E. A.						1864－1877	RM
Groote, Dr. J. J. M. De	高延	荷兰	汉学家		厦门,海口,来登	1887－1922	OM/CM/HM
Grosbois, Ch., M. A.	高博爱	法国	教育界	法董局,法文书馆	上海	1922－1946	OM
Grosse, V.	格罗思	俄国	外交官	俄国领事馆	上海	1912－1931	OM
Grossmann, Dr. A.					上海	1939－1946	OM
Grove, F.				南京－湖南铁路	伦敦	1915－1919	OM
Gruman, G.					上海	1923－1929	OM
Gubbay, R. A., Esq.						1878－1883	RM
Gubby, D. S.				新沙逊洋行	香港	1924－1929	OM
Guernier, R. C.	葛尔尼	法国		海关	汉口,上海	1901－1909	OM

附录：皇家亚洲文会北华支会研究

续表

英 文 名	中文名	国 籍	身份/职业	部 门	居 住 地 点	在会时间	会员类别
Guillien, F.	祁理恒	法国	外交官	法国领事馆	龙州	1894－1901	OM
Gulick, L. H., Rev., M. D.	古烈		牧师	教务杂志编辑，上海福音会	上海	1885－1888	OM
Gulik, Dr. R. H. Van	高佩罗	荷兰	外交官	荷兰领事馆	东京	1939－1940	OM
Gull, E. Manico	葛罗	英国	海关人员	英商公会	上海	1915－1935	OM
Gundlach, J. F. von		英国			上海	1886－1888	OM
Gundry, R. S.	盖德润	英国	记者/报人			1864	RM
Gunsberg, Baron G. de					上海	1892－1901 1908－1946	OM/LM
Guppy, H. B., Esq	古庇	英国	医生		伦敦	1880－1888	OM
Gutmann, B. E.					上海	1947－?	OM
Gutt, C. J.	顾德	德国	海关人员	先灵洋行	上海	1928－1936	OM
Gwynne, T. H.	葛泾	英国	海关人员	邮政局	上海,北京,杭州,南昌	1913－1940	OM/LM
Gwynne, G. L.			海关人员	海关	万县	1913	OM
Gwyther, J. H.						1864	RM
Gyles, Paymaster Rear-Admiral					汉普郡	1919－1936	OM
Gyles, H. A. D. J., Commer.		英国			上海	1919－1932	OM
Ha, Harris					上海	1935－1936	OM
Haas, J. Ritter von	夏士	奥匈帝国	外交官	奥匈帝国领事馆	上海	1869－1894	RM/OM
Hackmann, H.		荷兰			阿姆斯特丹	1903－1946	LM
Hackmann, Pastor		英国			上海	1894－1901	OM
Haden, G. W.	海单					1878	RM
Hague, E. P.			记者/报人			1875－1883	RM/OM

续表

英 文 名	中文名	国 籍	身份/职业	部　门	居 住 地 点	在会时间	会员类别
Hague, W. A.						1868	RM
Hail, Rev. W. J., PH. D.	解维廉	美国	牧师	雅礼大学	长沙	1922－1936	OM
Halbritter, R. H.				礼和洋行	上海	1901－1908	OM
Hall, Commander, W. R.		美国		美国海军		1928－1929	OM
Hall, J. C.	贺若贤	英国	牧师	英国领事馆	横滨	1888－1923	LM
Hall, Rev. W. S.						1878	NRM
Hallifax, T. E.					汉城	1889－1897	OM
Hamano, Makoto				上海日本居留民团	上海	1935－1936	OM
Hambleton, Roscoe L.					上海	1933－1934	OM
Hamburger, M.						1939－1940	OM
Hamill, Alfred E.		美国			伊利诺州	1934－1940	OM
Hamill, V. S.	韩密尔	英国	海关人员	海关	上海	1939－1940	OM
Hamill, W. Orr				黄浦运输公司	上海	1939－1940	OM
Hamilton, Dr. A. Isabel				金陵大学哲学系	南京,上海	1930－1934	OM
Hamilton, E.			牧师			1875－1877	RM
Hamilton, Rev. R.					上海	1859－1864	RM
Hamition, A. de C.				慎昌洋行	上海	1918－1924	OM
Hammond, J. L.	哈门德	美国	海关人员			1870－1878	RM
Hammond,Miss Louis S.				美国圣公会	无锡,南京	1917－1934	OM
Hamp, Mrs. M.				上海语言学校	上海	1940－?	OM
Hampson, Cyril W.				航业周报	上海	1920－1924	OM
Han, Dr. Y. S.				圣约翰大学	上海	1935－1936	OM

续表

英 文 名	中文名	国 籍	身份/职业	部 门	居 住 地 点	在会时间	会员类别
Hanbury, Sir Thomas	汉璧礼	英国	商人	公平洋行	上海	1857—1906	OM
Hance, H. F., PHD.	韩士	英国	外交官	英国领事馆	黄埔、广州	1865—1885	CM
Hancock, H. T.		英国	外交官	美孚公司	上海	1914—1929	OM
Hancox, Lieut. H. R., R. N.		英国	外交官	英国领事馆	北京	1922—1924	OM
Handell, T.				海河运输公司	天津	1930—1932	OM
Handley-Derry, H. F.	韩垒德	英国	外交官	英国领事馆	天津、宁波、重庆、宜昌	1903—1933	OM
Handley-Derry, L.				开滦矿务局办事处	上海	1935—1940	OM
Hangchow Christian College Library	图书馆	中国	图书馆	之江大学图书馆	杭州	1924—1946	LM
Hanke, Miss Ch.				德孚洋行	上海	1938—1940	OM
Hannen, N. J.	韩能	英国	外交官/法官	大英按察使	上海	1869—1897	OM
Hansen, Arthur J.	韩卫道	美国		信义公所	汉口、香港	1937—1940	OM
Hanson, George C.	韩森	美国	外交官	美国领事馆	莫斯科	1933—1934	OM
Hanson, Mrs. Victor	韩森	美国	教士	沪江大学、浸礼会	上海	1933—1946	OM
Hanssen, H. P.	晏生	英国	商人			1864—1877	RM
Hansteen, J. W.				挪威副领事	上海	1915—1916	OM
Happer, Andrew P., Jr.	哈巴安	美国	海关人员	海关	牛庄、上海、广州	1885—1897	OM
Happer, Rev. A. P., D. D.	哈巴安德	美国	医师	北长老会		1864—1897	CM
Harbison, Charles W., Jr.		美国		美国圣公会	苏州	1940—1946	OM
Hard, Dr. W. M.		英国			巴塘	1912—1924	OM
Harding, H. I.	哈尔定	英国	外交官	英国领事馆	北京、喀什、长沙、广州	1904—1946	OM/LM

续表

英文名	中文名	国籍	身份/职业	部门	居住地点	在会时间	会员类别
Harding, J. R.	哈尔定	英国	工程师	海关	厦门	1885－1893	OM
Hardoon, S. A.	哈同	英国	商人		上海	1928－1930	OM
Hardstaff, Dr. R. J.					波士顿,伦敦	1907－1920	OM
Hardy, Dr. W. M.	哈德	美国	医师	基督教堂	巴塘	1912－1936	OM
Hargens, G.				禅臣洋行,沙逊洋行	上海	1885－1887	OM
Harper, Rev. A. P., D. D.			牧师			1873－1878	CM
Harpur, C.				工部局	上海	1901 1908－1946	OM
Harrassowitz, Otto					莱比锡	1896－1901	OM
Harris, A. H.	夏立士	英国	海关人员		上海,滨海维斯顿	1902－1908	OM
Harris, Frank A.	哈利士	英国		沪宁铁路	南京,上海	1932－1934	OM
Harris, Mrs. H. E.					上海	1941－?	OM
Harris, Townsend	虾厘士	美国	外交官	美国驻日本领事馆		1858	CM
Harrison, Miss E. L.				太古洋行	上海	1925－1926	OM
Harruchecorne, A.				法国领事馆	重庆	1898－1908	OM
Hart, Dr. Henry H., A. B.				加利福尼亚大学东方艺术文化演讲师	洛杉矶	1924－1940	RM
Hart, G. M.						1875－1877	OM/LM
Hart, J. H.	赫政	英国	海关人员	海关	上海	1885－1901	OM/LM
Hart, Joseph	赫德		工程师	爱礼司洋行	福州	1934－1936	OM
Hart, Rev. V. C., M. A.	赫斐秋	美国	牧师		上海,成都,汉口	1887－1901	OM
Hart, Sir Robert, K. C. M. G.	赫德	英国	海关人员	海关	北京	1858－1910	CM/HM

续表

英 文 名	中文名	国 籍	身份/职业	部 门	居 住 地 点	在会时间	会员类别
Hartman, B.A.	贺德铭	美国	商人	公利洋行	上海	1931-1940	OM
Hartopp, E.L					上海	1931-1936	OM
Harvey, C.W.	贺嘉立	美国	教士	基督教青年会	上海	1922-1929	OM
Harvey, J.E.	哈惠		工程师	哈惠氏造船厂	上海	1939-1940	OM
Harvey, Rev. E.D.		美国	牧师	雅礼大学	长沙	1924-1936	OM
Harwood, W.						1869-1870	RM
Hasbund, A.H.				英上平安电影有限公司	哈尔滨,上海	1927-1934	OM
Hatano, Yoshihiro	波多野善大	日本	学人	日本商业学校	上海	1935-1940	OM
Haughwout, F.G.						1935-1940	OM
Haughwout, Mrs. F.G.				美国总会	上海	1935-1940	OM
Haward, Edwin	何立德			字林西报	上海	1931-1946	LM
Hawes, J.A.						1868-1874	RM
Hawkings, W.J.					上海	1920-1924	OM
Hawtrey, M						1869-1970	RM
Hay, Rev. A., B.A.		英国	牧师		中塞克斯郡	1937-1940	OM
Hayes, A.A., Jr						1869-1877	RM
Hayes, G.						1866	RM
Hayes, L. Newton	海士	美国	教士	基督教青年会	上海	1924-1941	OM
Hayim, A.J.				利安洋行	上海	1928-1946	LM
Hayim, Ellis				利安洋行	上海	1930-1940	OM/LM
Hays, Miss Florence C.	海史(女)	美国	教士	圣约翰大学	上海	1923-1925	OM
Hays, Mrs. John					上海	1911-1919	OM

411

续表

英文名	中文名	国籍	身份/职业	部门	居住地点	在会时间	会员类别
Hayter, H. W. G.				法新汇报馆	上海	1912–1915	OM
Haytor, L.				大北电报公司	上海	1908–1909	OM
Haywartd, Capt. J. L.				养生公司	上海	1933–1936	OM
Hazelton, Mrs. E. J.				内地会	上海	1947–?	OM
Heacock, Mrs. H. E.				亚美洋行	上海	1921–1935	OM
Healey, G.				英商会	上海	1947–?	OM
Healey, Leonard C.				工部局立格致书院	上海	1913–1940	OM
Heaney, R. S.		英国		英国领事馆	上海	1933–1935	OM
Heard, A. F.	夏尔德	美国	商人	俄国驻上海领事馆（兼任该国领事）	上海	1866–1874	NRM
Heard, Augustine, Jr.	欧德	美国	商人			1868–1877	NRM
Heaton-Smith, E. B.				仁记洋行	上海	1922–1933	OM
Hedin, Dr. Sven	斯文赫定	瑞典	探险家		斯德哥尔摩	1935–1940	HM
Heeren, Rev. J. J. PH. D.	奚尔恩	美国	大学教师	齐鲁大学	济南	1915–1940	OM
Heffer, G. S.					上海	1911–1913	OM
Heiberg, A.						1874–1877	NRM
Heidal, Rev. Abraham	海道尔	美国	牧师		高易	1931	OM
Heidenstam, H. von	海德生	瑞典	工程师	黄浦运输公司	上海	1916–1936	OM
Heine, Miss A. de J.		美国			纽约	1931–1936	OM
Heinemann, Heinz-Egon				西方文艺社	上海	1939–1946	OM
Helde, G. G.	赫立德	美国	教士	基督教青年会	成都	1922–1928	OM
Helmick, Judge Milton J.	希尔米克	美国	法官	美国在华法院	上海	1934–1940	OM

续表

英 文 名	中文名	国籍	身份/职业	部门	居住地点	在会时间	会员类别
Hemeiling, Dr. K.	赫墨龄	美国	海关人员	海关	北京,芜湖,天津	1902-1917	OM
Hemingway, B.				英商亚细亚火油公司	牛庄,杭州,沈阳,温州,上海	1922-1940	OM
Henchman, A. S.				汇丰银行	上海	1929-1940	OM
Henderson, D. M.	韩得善	英国	海关人员	海关	上海	1870-1897	OM
Henderson, Dr. James	韩德森	英国	传教医师		上海	1860	RM
Henderson, Ed., M. D.		英国	医生	工部局卫生处	上海	1876-1897	OM
Henderson, J., Esq.	海德迹	英国	矿师兼商人		天津	1878-1884	NRM
Henke, Frederick G., PH. D.		美国	教士	金陵大学	南京	1912-1936	OM
Henningsen, J.	佰宁生	丹麦	电信企业家	大北电报公司	上海	1885-1888	OM
Henry Lester Institute of Medical Research			机构	雷氏德医学研究院	上海	1933-1940	LM
Henry, Augustine	韩尔礼	英国	海关人员	海关	宜昌,台湾,蒙自	1881-1906	OM
Henry, J. M	香雅各	美国	教士	岭南大学	广州	1922-1940	OM
Hepburn, J. C., LL. D.	合文	美国	医师		横滨	1864-1901	CM
Hepner, Rev. C. W. PH. D.			牧师	沪美学堂	东京	1931-1940	LM
Herman, T.	艾勒思	比利时	商人		上海	1937-1940	OM
Hers, Joseph				陇海铁路	北京,上海,郑州	1907-1940	OM
Hertz, H.				矮克发洋行		1874-1877	RM
Herz, Rudolf				渣华邮船公司	上海	1936-1940	OM
Heusden, W. Van					上海	1940-1946	OM
Hewlett, A. R.	有雅芝	英国	外交官			1866-1873	NRM

续表

英 文 名	中文名	国籍	身份/职业	部 门	居 住 地 点	在会时间	会员类别
Hey, E.	海文		商人		上海	1886–1901	OM
Hickling, N. W.				工部局	上海	1922–1936	OM
Hicks, E. P.				工部局卫生处	上海	1923–1927	OM
Hildebrandt, Adolf		德国		壁恒公司	上海	1907–1940	LM
Hill, Dr. R. A. P.		英国		麦加利银行	上海	1921–1929	OM
Hill, F. J.					上海	1946–?	OM
Hill, M. Stow		美国			纽约	1908–1913	OM
Hillburn, Samuel M.				关西学院	神户	1940–?	OM
Hille, Miss Bessie M.	海佩息		教士	北长老会	上海	1937–1946	OM
Hiltner, Dr. W. G.		美国			上海	1920–1929	OM
Hilton-Johnson, Capt. A. H.				工部局、警察局	上海	1908–1913	OM
Himly, K.		普鲁士	领事人员			1869–1877	RM
Himus, Godfrey W.				甬江电厂	上海	1920–1921	OM
Hinckley, F. E., PHD.					上海	1907–1923	OM
Hinckling, N. W.				丹凤保险公司	上海	1922–1929	OM
Hind, H. M.				工部局实业处	上海	1928–1936	OM
Hinder, Miss E. M.				工部局卫生处	上海	1930–1946	OM
Hindson, A. E. C.	罕声	英国	商人		上海	1914–1919	OM
Hindson, C. K.				海关	上海	1934–1935	OM
Hippisley, A. E.	贺璧理	英国	海关人员		广州、上海、北京	1876–1938	OM/LM
Hirom, C. J.				公裕太阳火险公司	上海	1930–1934	OM

续表

英 文 名	中文名	国 籍	身份/职业	部 门	居 住 地 点	在会时间	会员类别
Hirsch, Emil Edler von	许乙诗	奥匈帝国		奥匈帝国领事馆	上海	1887–1888	OM
Hirsch, Rabbi W.					上海	1923	OM
Hirth, F., PH.D.	夏德	德国	海关人员		上海,重庆,镇江	1877–1926	OM/HM
Hiscock, F. H.			领航员	英商哈非公司	汉口,上海	1905–1913	OM
Hjousbery, E.				晋隆洋行	上海	1880–1887	OM
Ho, Sie Sice					上海	1941–?	OM
Ho, T. K., M.B.A.				工部局秘书处	上海	1935–1940	OM
Hobart, Mrs. A. T.				美孚公司	南京	1927–1929 1935–1940	OM
Hobden, H.					上海	1932–1934	OM
Hobson, B., M.B.	合信	英国	医师		上海	1866–1873	CM
Hobson, Benjamin					上海	1858	RM
Hobson, H.					上海,重庆,厦门,格拉斯顿伯里	1866–1877	NRM
Hobson, H. E.	好博迹	英国	海关人员		上海	1868–1922	OM
Hobson, Rev. John	好不生	英国	牧师		上海	1858	RM
Hocking, Samuel	侯金	英国	海关人员		代顿(俄亥俄州)	1926–1929	OM
Hockly, J. M.						1864	RM
Hodges, Mrs F. E.			牧师		上海	1915–1930	OM
Hodges, Rev. H. C., M. A.					上海	1887–1901	OM
Hodgson, C. P.					涵管	1859	CM
Hodgson, Miss D				工部局教育处	上海	1939–1940	OM

续表

英 文 名	中文名	国 籍	身份/职业	部 门	居 住 地 点	在会时间	会员类别
Hodous, Rev. L.	何乐益	美国	教士		福州	1913－1946	LM
Hoehnke, F.				上海啤酒公司	上海	1913 1932－1939	OM
Hoetinck, B.				荷兰领事馆	汕头	1880－1901	OM
Hoetter, A.				德孚洋行	上海	1910－1929	OM
Hogg, E. Jenner					上海	1864－1877 1908－1919	OM
Hogg, J. D.		英国		英国领事馆	曼谷	1917－1920	OM
Holdsworth, E.						1868－1874	RM
Hollingworth, H. G.	荷魏尔	英国				1865－1870	NRM
Holm, F. W.				光裕机器油行	上海	1903－1908	OM
Holmstrom, J. E.				京奉铁路	奉天	1922－1929	OM
Holst, J. M.				大北电报公司	上海	1886－1888	OM
Holt, Bishop Dr. Ivan Lee		美国	牧师		达拉斯	1935－1940	OM
Holt, Rev. W. S.						1882－1883	OM
Holwill, E. T.	侯立威					1873－1877	NRM
Hommel, RP.		美国		远东探险队、哥伦比亚博物馆	北京、青岛	1927－1940	OM
Hone, Dr. Harman				矮克发洋行	上海	1933－1946	OM/LM
Hookham, F. J.				颐中烟草股份有限公司	上海	1939－1940	OM
Hoover, Lyman		美国		基督教青年会	纽约	1939－1940	OM
Hope, Admiral Sir James	何伯	英国	军人			1866－1870	LM
Hopkins, Paul S.					上海	1933－1946	OM

续表

英 文 名	中文名	国籍	身份/职业	部　门	居住地点	在会时间	会员类别
Hoppisley, A. E.					伦敦	1876－1946	LM
Hornby, Lieut-Colone J. W.				万国商团	上海	1939－1940	OM
Hornby, Sir Ed.	洪卑	英国	法官			1865－1874	OM
Horne, A.		美国			洛杉矶	1924－1929	OM
Hosie, Alex., M. A.	谢立山	英国	外交官	英国领事馆	温州,广州,牛庄,成都	1877－1906	OM
Hosken, Mrs. Wm H.				美商赫思根公司	上海	1935－1936	OM
Hosli, H				信昌机器工程股份有限公司	上海	1947－？	OM
Hou, Dr. Hsiang-ch'uan				雷氏德研究院	上海	1935－1946	LM
Hough, Frank L.					上海	1935	OM
Hough, Mrs. F. L.					上海	1935	OM
Houghton, Charles				工部局卫生处	上海	1908－1926	OM
House, I. E.				平和洋行	上海	1946－？	OM
Houston, J. H. W.	瑚斯敦	英国	海关人员	海关	杭州	1900－1908	OM
Houston, Miss. Alice M.				基督教青年会	上海	1937－1938	OM
How, A. J.	赫福理		商人		上海	1876－1887	OM
How, Mrs. Bang				警卫报	上海	1933	OM
Howard, A. E. Neville				京奉铁路,平沈铁路	天津	1924－1929	OM
Howard, Mrs. A. E. N.				大信古玩行	上海	1932－1946	OM
Howard, William					上海	1861	RM
Howell, A.						1857－1874	NRM

续表

英 文 名	中文名	国 籍	身份/职业	部 门	居 住 地 点	在会时间	会员类别
Howell, E. B.	好威乐	英国	海关人员	海关	天津、上海、北京、腾越	1909－1929	OM
Howell, W. G.				亚洲文会理事会	上海	1859	RM
Howells, R. M.				工部局卫生处	上海	1928－1940	OM
Howells, W.				中央警署	上海	1917－1919	OM
Howes, Mrs. J. M.				沪美学堂	上海	1924－1929	OM
Hoyt, Mrs. Lansing		美国			上海	1935－1940	OM
Hsia, Anson					上海	1941－？	OM
Hsia, Dr. Ching-Ling					上海	1925－1936	OM
Hsia, S. C.					上海	1941－？	OM
Hsu Chia-Kuang		中国			上海	1888－？	OM
Hsu Ch'iu－I		中国		花旗银行	上海	1887－1888	OM
Hsu, Sing－loh				工部局翻译处	上海	1932－1936	LM
Hsu, Wellington Sewson					上海	1936	OM
Hu Chao Chin					上海、北京	1937－1946	OM
Hu Shih B. A., PH. D.	胡适	中国			上海、北京	1928－1940	OM
Hu, Stephen M. H.	胡梅基	中国		雷氏德研究院	上海	1935－1946	OM
Huang I-Pao		美国			密尔瓦基	1946－？	OM
Hubbard, G. E.	赫播德	英国	银行家/外交官	汇丰银行	伦敦	1932－1936	OM
Hubbard, Rev. H. W.	胡本德	美国	牧师	公理会	保定、上海	1924－1940	OM
Hubbe, P. G., Esq.			商人	禅臣洋行	上海	1877－1885	OM
Hubert, Mrs. Elizabeth B.					上海	1939－1940	OM

续表

英文名	中文名	国籍	身份/职业	部门	居住地点	在会时间	会员类别
Hubert, Mrs. R. S. R.				昌兴火轮船公司	上海	1938-1940	OM
Hubert, R. S. Richard.				昌兴火轮船公司	上海	1938-1940	OM
Hudson, Mrs. Alferd J.					宁波	1909-1933	OM
Hudspeth, Rev. W. H.	王树德	英国	牧师	循道会	上海	1940-1946	OM
Huebsch, Geo, H.					上海	1947-?	OM
Hugall, T. N.				工部局	上海	1911-1913	OM
Huges, T. F.			海关专员	海关	芜湖	1885-1886	OM
Hughes, A. J.	郁赐	英国	保险商	中国保险协会	上海	1909-1940	OM
Hughes, O.						1865	OM
Hughes, P. J.	许士	英国	外交官	英国领事馆	上海	1864-1901	OM/HM
Hughes, Rev. E. R.	修中诚	英国	教士	基督教青年会	厦门,上海	1929-1940	OM
Hughes, T. F.	许妥玛	英国	海关人员	海关	上海,芜湖	1885-1888	OM
Hughes, W. E.				亚细亚火油公司	杭州,苏州,济南	1921-1940	OM
Huldermann, P.				大德国新闻纸馆	上海	1936-1938	OM
Hume, Edward, H., M.D.	胡美	美国	医师	雅礼会,中国红十字医院,雅礼大学	上海,长沙	1922-1946	OM/LM
Hummel, A. W., PH. D	恒慕义	美国	牧师	华北协和华语学校	北京,汾州	1919-1946	OM/LM
Hummel, R. Ure				长利洋行	上海	1911-1919	OM
Hunter, Miss				西童女书院	上海	1920-1925	OM
Hunter, Rev. James A.	亨德	美国	牧师	公理会	北京	1924-1929	OM
Hunter, W. Dulaney				美国领事馆	上海	1894-1897	OM
Huntington, E. R.				海明洋行	上海	1933-1946	LM
Husk, William S.				沪美学堂	上海	1939-1940	OM

续表

英 文 名	中文名	国籍	身份/职业	部门	居住地点	在会时间	会员类别
Hussey-Freke, F.	斐礼格	英国	海关人员	海关	上海,天津,九江	1899－1908	OM
Huston, J. C.	胡思敦	美国	外交官	美国领事馆	汉口	1917－1925	OM
Huston, Rev. J.			牧师	内地会	成都	1914－1928	OM
Hutchison, D. C.				和记洋行	上海	1926－1940	OM
Hutchison, J. C., O. B. E.	胡阶森	英国	外交官	英国大使馆	上海	1941－1946	OM
Hutchison, J. L.				英美烟公司	上海	1916－1919	OM
Hutchison, W., B. SC. (Leeds)				万国运转公司	汉口	1931－1933	OM
Hutter, Rev. S. A., M. A., LL. D.		美国	牧师		弗吉尼亚	1890－1901	OM
Hwang, Prof. K. C.				中央大学	南京	1935－1936	OM
Hwlett, A. R.						1868	NRM
Hyde, James Hazen		法国			巴黎	1908－1910	OM
Hyde, Prof. Ed. Geo.			教授		上海	1937－1940	OM
Hykes, Rev. J. R., D. D.	海格思	美国	牧师	大美圣经会	上海	1897－1901	OM
Hylbert, Mrs. L. C.	赫培德		牧师	教士公所	上海	1928－1932	OM
Hynd, R. R.				汇丰银行	上海	1913－1916	OM
Hyndman, H.			出版商	望益纸馆	上海	1885－1887	OM
Hynes, A. C.				汇丰银行	上海	1919－1922	OM
Ibs, Major, F. W.			海关人员	海关	嵋州	1924－1929	OM
Ibsen, Th.				电报局	上海	1913－1916	OM
Ilyine, Mrs. Catherine					上海	1942－1946	OM
Imada, T.				三井洋行	上海	1912－1915	OM

附录:皇家亚洲文会北华支会研究

续表

英 文 名	中文名	国 籍	身份/职业	部 门	居 住 地 点	在会时间	会员类别
Imbault-Huart C., Esq.	于雅乐	法国	领事人员	法国领事馆	广州,汉口,北京	1880-1897	OM
India Office Library	图书馆	英国	图书馆	印度图书馆	伦敦	1922-1924	OM
India Office,Superintendent	机构	英国		英国外交部印度司	伦敦	1926 1935-1939	OM
India Office, the Librarian	图书馆	英国	图书馆	东印度公司图书馆	伦敦	1927-1929	OM
Indtituta of Chinese Cultural Studies	机构	中国	机构	金陵大学中国文化研究所	南京	1931-1940	OM
Innocent, Rev. J.	英约翰	英国	教士	圣道堂	上海	1860-1874	OM
Institute of Social Science Library	图书馆	中国	图书馆	中央研究院社会科学研究所	昆明	1937-1940	OM
Inui, Kiyo Sue, LL. D.				日本领事馆	上海	1933-1940	OM
Ironside, William				太古洋行	汉口	1919-1920	OM
Irvine, D. A.				亚细亚火油公司	重庆,上海	1913-1933	OM
Irvine,Miss Elizabeth	明义	美国	教士	北长老会	上海	1910-1935 1938-1946	OM
Irwine, H. G.					上海	1920-1924	OM
Isief, J. P.				大北电报公司	上海	1917-1929	OM
Itoi, S.				横滨正金银行		1910-1912	OM
Ivanoff, V. N.					上海	1940-?	OM
Jack, J. B.	查格长	英国	海关人员	海关	汉口,上海	1890-1901	OM
Jackson, Rev. James	霍雅各	美国	牧师	文华大学	武昌	1908-1913	OM
Jacobs, J. E.	雅克博	美国	外交官	美国领事馆	上海,北京	1922-1930	OM
Jacobsen, Axel					上海	1933-1936	OM
Jaffry, Capt. Paul					上海	1934-1940	OM

续表

英文名	中文名	国籍	身份/职业	部门	居住地点	在会时间	会员类别
Jager, A. G. de				飞利浦洋行	上海	1935–1940	OM
Jaieson, C.						1864	RM
Jameson, C. D.					北京	1915–1916	OM
Jameson, J. A.					上海	1908–1910	OM
Jameson, J. N.					上海	1908–1915	OM
Jamieson, D. M.						1874	RM
Jamieson, George, C. M. G.	哲美森	英国	领事人员	英国领事馆、英国在华法院	九江、上海	1868–1920	OM/CM
Jamieson, J., Esq.					烟台	1878–?	NRM
Jamieson, J. W.	杰弥迹	英国	外交官	英国领事馆	广州、上海、天津	1888–1930	OM
Jamieson, R. A.	詹美生	英国	报人	礼查饭店	上海	1864–1893	OM
Jansen, D. C.				大北电报公司	上海	1877–1893	OM
Janssen, O.					上海	1908–1909	OM
Janssen, W. C.					汉口	1873–1877	RM
Jarvis, R. Y.				美国领事馆	上海	1937–1940	OM
Jaspar, M. A.		法国		法国领事馆	上海	1933–1940	OM
Javrotsky, J.	仇洛纪	俄国	海关人员	中国海关	上海、广州	1934–1940	OM
Jefferds, M.					费城	1896–1901	OM
Jefferys, Dr. W. Hamilton					上海	1908–1918	OM
Jeffrey, Sydney					香港	1892–1897	OM
Jeffreys, James						1864–1870	RM
Jemeson, C. D.					北京	1911–1913	OM

续表

英 文 名	中文名	国籍	身份/职业	部 门	居住地点	在会时间	会员类别
Jen, Dr. Yu Wen					上海	1936-1940	OM
Jenkins, B. Dr.	秦镇西	美国				1865-1869	CM
Jenks, Prof. J. W.		美国	政治经济学家	康乃尔大学	纽约	1903-1932	OM
Jensen, C. A.	精琦	美国		大北电报公司	天津,北京	1918-1924	OM
Jernigan, T. R.	佑尼干	美国	外交官/律师		上海	1906-1920	OM
Jessel, W.			教士	宝丰洋行	上海	1912-1919	OM
Jesus, C. Montalto de					上海,澳门	1902-1919	OM
Joffe, Franz						1940-?	OM
John, N. T.		美国		美国领事馆	上海	1912-1919	OM
John, Rev. Griffith	杨格非	英国	牧师		汉口	1864-1911	CM
Johnn Morriss						1864	RM
Johnson, B. C. M.				汇丰银行	上海	1926-1934	OM
Johnson, F. B.	庄纯	英国	商人/外交官	丹麦领事馆	上海	1864-1885	RM/OM
Johnson, Hon. N. T.	詹森	美国	外交官	美国领事馆	北京,重庆	1912-1940	OM
Johnson, Miss Lydia	章秀敏(女)		教士	基督教育年会	杭州,武昌	1935-1940	OM
Johnson, O. S., PH. D.		美国		沃巴什学院	克劳夫茨维尔	1927-1936	OM
Johnston, A. J.	认信					1870-1873	RM
Johnston, J., Dr. M. D.			医生	英国长老会		1864-1884	RM
Johnston, R. F. M. A.	庄士敦	英国	政府顾问		北京,威海卫	1907-1936	OM
Johnstone						1864	RM

续表

英 文 名	中文名	国 籍	身份/职业	部 门	居 住 地 点	在会时间	会员类别
Johnstone, Mrs. K. W.					上海	1935-1939	OM
Jolly, J. Keith				太古洋行	上海	1935-1940	OM
Jolly, P. B.		英国	海关人员	海关	上海、沈阳、琼口	1913-1940	OM
Jones, C. T.				亚洲文会理事会	上海	1858-1860	RM
Jones, Dr.						1865	OM
Jones, Edward P.		英国		英国领事馆	上海	1910-1918	OM
Jones, G. S.				卜内门公司	上海	1920-1922	OM
Jones, H. J. S.				铁道部沪杭宁线	上海	1923-1933	OM
Jones, J. Frank					上海	1916-1920	OM
Jones, J. R., M. A.	钟理思		教士	工部局秘书处	上海	1924-1946	OM
Jones, Loftus E. P.					上海	1908-1915	OM
Jones, W. P.	陈士威廉					1866-1877	NRM
Jong, Th. de J. de	卓思恩	荷兰	外交官	荷兰公使馆	北京	1914-1936	OM
Jordan, Dr. J. H., MC.			医师	工部局卫生处	上海	1922-1940	OM
Jordan, Mrs. F. C.	赵尔丹夫人	美国		颐中烟草股份有限公司	天津	1939-1940	OM
Jorgensen, O.		荷兰		大北电报公司	上海	1913-1932	OM
Josefsen-Bernier, S.				驳船公司行	上海	1935-1936	OM
Joseph, Ellis				乔哲夫兄弟洋行	上海	1935-1940	LM
Joseph, R. M.				乔哲夫兄弟洋行	上海	1935-1946	LM
Joseph, S. M.				汇中饭店	上海	1920-1946	OM/LM
Jost, A		瑞士		达昌洋行	上海	1912-1940	OM/LM

续表

英 文 名	中文名	国 籍	身份/职业	部 门	居 住 地 点	在会时间	会员类别
Julien, Prof. Stanislas	儒莲	法国	教授			1866—1868	HM
Jurgeson, A. J.				万泰有限公司	上海	1926—1929	OM
Justesen, M. L.				大丰洋行	上海	1913—1936	OM
K'ung T'ien-cheng					上海	1912—1913	OM
Ka, H. E.						1864	RM
Kadoorie, Horace				嘉道理父子洋行	上海	1935—1946	LM
Kahn, Gaston	甘司东	法国	外交官	法国领事馆	上海	1913—1919	OM
Kaill, Joseph				奥匈帝国领事馆	天津	1912—1913	OM
Kallberg, Miss E.	高钥佩（女）	瑞典	教士	湖北信义会	长沙	1936—1940	OM
Kann, Edward	耿爱德	奥地利	记者		上海	1929—1946	OM
Kannowski, Mrs. P.						1908—1913	OM
Kano, Dr. Nacki.	狩野直喜	日本	学界	京都大学	京都	1902—1920	OM
Kanzaki, S.				三井洋行	上海	1906—1919	OM
Kao, Perkins					上海	1936—1940	OM
Karlbeck, Orvas		瑞典		铁道部津浦路，瑞典远东文物博物馆	蚌埠，滁州，上海	1914—1936	OM
Karlgren, Dr. B.	高本汉	瑞典	汉学家	哥德堡大学	哥德堡	1922—1936	OM
Karmilof, Mme, Olga					上海	1939—1940	OM
Kashiwada, T.	柏田忠一	日本	学界		上海	1918—1924	OM
Kassatkin, S.						1942—1946	OM
Kau, Dr. L. S.					上海	1936—1940	OM
Kauffman, Rev. M.			牧师			1865—1866	RM

续表

英文名	中文名	国籍	身份/职业	部门	居住地点	在会时间	会员类别
Kay, Miss Michael				汇中饭店	上海	1939-1940	OM
Kaye, W.						1874-1877	NRM
Keaney, Dr. F. P.					上海	1933-1936	OM
Keegan, J. J.				花旗银行	纽约	1927-1929	OM
Keeler, Henry B.		英国		美孚公司	镇江,上海,苏州	1916-1919	OM
Keen, Mrs. E.				纽约时报远东办事处	上海	1935-1940	OM
Keen, R. D.				工部局西童男书院	上海	1935-1940	OM
Keeton, G. W., B A., LL B		英国		香港大学艺术学院	香港	1926-1936	OM
Keir, J.						1866	RM
Keischke, Dr. Ito.		日本	医生		东京	1875-1908	CM
Kelley, Miss A. S.				上海华童公学(工部局设)	上海	1910-1913	OM
Kellner, E. G.					上海	1935-1936	OM
Kellogg, C. R.	克立鹄	美国	教士	私立福建协和大学	福州	1919-1936	OM
Kelsey, H. F.				英商中华机器凿井有限公司	上海	1935-1936	OM
Kemer, P. P. M.				海关	湖口	1901-1908	OM
Kemp, G. S. Foster				上海华童公学(工部局设)	上海	1908-1922	OM
Kendall, H. M.				麦景合氏公司	上海	1928	OM
Kendrew, J. A.					上海	1942-1946	OM
Kenmure, Alexander				大英圣公会	上海	1877-1901	OM
Kennedy, Capt. E. R.				工部局警署	上海	1936	OM
Kennedy, General J. D.				美国领事馆	上海	1888	OM

续表

英　文　名	中文名	国　籍	身份/职业	部　门	居　住　地　点	在会时间	会员类别
Kennedy, George	金守拙	美国	教育界		上海	1929-1934	OM
Kennett, W. B.	开纳脱	英国	律师	英商大英烟公司	上海	1918-1931	OM
Kent, A. S.		加拿大			上海、沈阳	1913-1936	OM
Kern, D. S.					成都	1912-1934	OM/LM
Kerr, J.	寇尔	英国	海关人员	中国海关		1864	RM
Kerr, W. J.				工部局	上海	1939-1940	LM
Keswick						1857	RM
Keswick, J. J.	葛司会	英国	商人	怡和洋行	上海、香港	1885-1901	OM
Khaw, Dr. O. K.			医师/博士	北京协和医院	北京、成都	1935-1940	OM
Ki Chun				济业银行	上海	1935-1940	OM
Kiang, Kang-hu, Prof. Dr.	江亢虎	中国	教授	华西协和大学	成都	1923-1929 1936	OM
Kiborn, Dr. L. G.						1934-1946	OM
Kidner, W. Esq.						1865	OM
Kilner, E.		英国		工部局	上海	1909-1936	OM
Kimura, Dr. K.		英国		上海自然科学研究所	上海	1935-1940	OM
Kimura, Dr. Shigeru				上海自然科学研究所	上海	1935-1938	OM
King Chien Kun					上海	1932-1946	LM
King, C. J.						1864-1877	RM
King, Cheyuen Foon					上海	1935-1936	OM
King, Dr. G. E.	金文宽	英国	教士		兰州	1919-1924	OM
King, Dunt					上海	1938-1940	OM

续表

英文名	中文名	国籍	身份/职业	部门	居住地点	在会时间	会员类别
King, F.						1869-1877	RM
King, G. W. P.					上海	1917-1920	OM
King, Paul H.	庆丕	英国	海关人员	海关	上海、芜湖、厦门、天津	1886-1920	OM
King, Prof. Harrison			教授	圣约翰大学	上海	1927-1940	OM
King, Sohtsu G.					北京、上海	1924-1946	LM
King, W. W.						1864-1866	RM
Kingsmill, G. H. J., Esq.			工程师	建筑工程行	上海	1864-1885	RM
Kingsmill, Gerald					上海	1905-1908	OM
Kingsmill, T. W.	金斯密	英国	建筑师		上海	1864-1909	OM/HM
Kinnear, Henry R.				仁记洋行	上海	1907-1919	OM
Kirton, Mrs. Walter				中国公论西报馆	北京	1911-1915	OM
Klautke, Rektor Paul		德国		同济大学	上海	1924-1946	LM
Klebanoff, N. M.					上海	1936-1939	OM
Klein, Darre'					上海	1917-1919	OM
Kleinwachter, F.	康发达	德国	海关人员		上海、厦门、镇江、宁波	1868-1893	OM
Kleinwächter, G. H. J.	康发逵	德国	海关人员			1881-1884	OM
Kliene, Charles	葛麟瑞	丹麦	海关人员	海关	上海	1916-1946	LM
Kliene, R.	葛麟祥	丹麦	海关人员	美国在华法院	宁波	1890-1893	OM
Klimanek, P. H.				奥匈帝国领事馆、禅臣洋行	上海	1909-1913	OM
Kloevekorn, Dr.				德国学校	上海	1914-1917	OM
Klubien, J.	古禄编	丹麦	海关人员	海关	汕头、北京、广州、南京、九江	1913-1936	OM

续表

英 文 名	中文名	国 籍	身份/职业	部 门	居 住 地 点	在会时间	会员类别
Klubien, S. A.	古禄彬	丹麦	海关人员	海关	汕头、沈阳、上海	1916-1920	OM
Knight, F. P.	鼐德	美国	商人	美、法、瑞等国领事馆	牛庄	1865-1881	NRM
Knight, Sparrow J. Esq.						1865	OM
Knights, A. E.					上海	1896-1901	OM
Knox, Carlos C				上海电力公司	上海	1940-1946	OM
Knudsen, A. F.					上海、香港	1938-1940	OM
Kobelt, A.				达昌洋行		1935-1940	OM
Koch, E.						1864-1868	RM
Koester, Rev. Dr. H.			牧师	天主堂	兖州、北京	1936-1946	LM
Kolobaskin, N.					上海	1908-1909	OM
Komiya, Yoshitaka	小宫义孝	日本	学界	上海自然科学研究所		1935-1938	OM
Kopelmann, R.					上海	1946-?	OM
Kopp, E. C.					上海	1919-1924	OM
Kops, Paul F.	克保罗		律师	阿乐满律师事务所	上海	1935-1946	OM
Kopsch, H.	葛显礼	英国	海关人员	海关	上海、宁波、镇江、九江	1877-1897	OM
Koptiayeff, M.					北京	1897	OM
Korff, Adlbert				美最时洋行	上海	1886-1888	OM
Kotenev, A. M.				工部局	上海	1924-1946	OM/LM
Kozoolin, P. J.				工部局翻译处	上海	1934-1940	OM
Kraetzer, E. D.	恺自迩	法国	外交官	法国领事馆	上海	1886-1887	OM

续表

英 文 名	中文名	国籍	身份/职业	部门	居住地点	在会时间	会员类别
Kranssen, H. P.						1868	RM
Kranz, Rev. Paul	安保罗	德国	牧师	德国同善会	上海	1897–1920	LM
Krapf, Dr.				德医学校	上海	1912–1919	OM
Kratzsech, Dr. K.				德国领事馆	上海	1906–1909	OM
Krauss, A. A.	克尔沃司		商人			1866–1883	NRM/RM
Krebs, E.	夏礼铺	德国	外交官	德国领事馆	北京	1895–1932	OM/LM
Kreitner, Prof. G., Chevalier de		奥地利			横滨	1883–1884	CM
Kreitner, G. Ritter von						1880–1893	CM
Kremer, P. P. M.	克雷摩	法国	海关人员	海关	上海	1901–1907	OM
Kremsir, G.	康铭瑞		商人		上海	1894–1897	OM
Kreulen, R. A.				北美保险公司		1941–1946	OM
Krey, W., Esq.	克黎	德国	海关人员	海关	宜昌	1878–1883	NRM
Kreyer, Rev. C. Ph. D.			教士			1874–1878	RM
Krill, Joseph				奥匈帝国领事馆	天津	1895–1919	OM
Kring, K. G.					厦门	1911–1918	OM
Krisel, A.	柯理瑟	美国	外交官	美国领事馆	上海	1914–1946	OM/LM
Kumling, F.					上海	1912–1913	OM
Kroes, T.	哥老司		商人	荷兰、比利时领事		1865–1870	RM
Kroff, Aug.			商人	最美时洋行	上海	1886	OM
Kroker, Bruno				中国杂志出版公司	上海	1938–1940	OM
Kronenberg, F.					上海	1912–1917	OM

续表

英 文 名	中文名	国 籍	身份/职业	部 门	居 住 地 点	在会时间	会员类别
Kronenberg, Mrs. F.					上海	1912–1917	OM
Kronvall, Erik	克论威	瑞典	外交官	瑞典领事馆	上海	1937–1940	OM
Krueger, Pastor E.					上海	1930–1940	OM
Krumling, Dr. F.					郴州,贵州	1912–1919	OM
Krysinski, Dr. J.	郭雷新斯基	波兰	外交官		上海	1934–1940	OM
Ku Hung Ming	辜鸿铭				上海	1906–1915	OM
Kuang Yu Cheng					上海	1946–?	OM
Kuck, Fritz W.				德孚洋行	上海	1930–1936	OM
Kuhn, Karl					上海	1935–1940	OM
Kuhner, Prof. Nicolas		俄国	教授	东方研究院	海参崴	1901–1907	OM
Kuhu, Mrs. I. C.					上海	1924–1929	OM
Kulp, D. H.	葛学溥	美国	教士	沪江大学社会学系	上海	1915–1924	OM
Kundsen, A. F.					上海	1938	LM
Kunisawa, Shimbei				南满铁路株式会社	东京	1917–1946	OM
Kunze, R.				大德国新闻纸馆	上海	1909–1913	OM
Kuo Ping-wen, Dr.				大华公司	上海	1932–1936	OM
Kuo, C. C.				中华摄影公司,中华广播公司	上海	1932–1936	OM
Kuo, P. K., PH. D. (Harvard)				武汉大学	武昌	1936–1940	OM
Kurokawa, S.				日本油船公司	横滨	1911–1916	OM
Kurz, Dr.				德国医学校	上海	1911–1913	OM

续表

英文名	中文名	国籍	身份/职业	部门	居住地点	在会时间	会员类别
Kwang Hsih, His Lordship				乐德洋行	上海	1934–1936	OM
Kwauk, S. Z.				贫儿教养院	上海	1932–1940	OM
Kwauk, Z. U.				沪宁铁路	上海	1931–1946	LM
Kwei, S. Shun		中国		大上海办公室	上海	1934–1939	OM
Kwok, T. W.					上海	1939–1946	LM
Kwong, Edward Y. K.	邝耀坤	中国	文化界	《评论》杂志社	上海	1932–1936	OM
Kwong, H. K.				警卫报	上海	1933	OM
Lacey, Norman H.					纳塔尔	1941–1946	OM
Lachian, Miss A.		英国		上海外国育婴所,威斯敏斯特银行	上海	1923–1936	OM
Lacy, Rev. Dr. W. H.		美国	教士	沪江大学	上海	1909–1925	OM
Laforest, L.				电车轨道公司	上海、北京	1917–1924	OM
Laird, R.				公裕太阳火险公司	上海	1939–1940	OM
Lake, Capt. P. M. B.				怡和洋行	上海	1916–1923	OM
Lalcaca, Cawas, M.D.					上海	1908	OM
Lamansky, V. V.					上海	1932–1936	OM
Lamarge, F.		美国	教授	柯达公司	华盛顿	1942–1946	OM
Lamb, Prof. W. H.				农业部	上海	1911–1913	OM
Lambelet, A. R. A.					上海	1933–1936	OM
Lambert, Henri	郎培安	比利时	工程师	比国银公司	上海	1932–1940	OM
Lambertz, H.				德国总会	上海	1915–1919	OM

续表

英 文 名	中文名	国籍	身份/职业	部门	居住地点	在会时间	会员类别
Lamprey, Dr.		英国	医生			1864	RM
Lamson, H. D.	兰俊德	美国	教士	沪江大学社会学系	上海,坎伯利奇	1929–1936	OM
Lancaster						1878–?	NRM
Lanciarez, Chevalier E. M.	兰家丽	意大利	外交官	意大利领事馆	上海	1886–1887	OM
Landale, D. F.				怡和洋行	上海	1936	OM
Landesen, Arthur C, von		俄国	外交官	俄国领事馆	哈尔滨,吉林	1909–1920	OM
Landis, Dr. E. B.		美国	教士		木浦(朝鲜)	1894–1911	LM
Lane, W. C.			教育者		上海	1939–1940	OM
Lang, H.	兰一来	英国	商人兼报人			1865–1874	RM
Lange, Robert					上海	1924–1933	OM
Langley, Capt. J.	郎利	美国	海关人员	海关	上海	1909–1916	OM
Lanman, Prof. Charles R.		美国	教授	哈佛大学	坎伯利奇	1908–1940	HM
Lanning, George	蓝宁	英国	教育者	工部局	上海	1908–1919	OM
Lanning, V. H.				怡和洋行	上海	1916–1933	OM
Latham, T.			商人		上海	1886–1888	OM
Latimer, N.	赖德茂					1864	RM
Latourette, Prof. K. S.	赖德烈	美国	史学家	雅礼会 美国丹尼森大学	长沙,耶鲁	1912–1946	OM/LM
Lauderdale, T.				花旗银行	上海	1932–1934	LM
Laufer, Berthold, Dr.	劳费尔	美国	东方学家	芝加哥自然历史博物馆,哥伦比亚大学	芝加哥	1901–1933	OM/LM
Laurell, Y.	劳立尔	瑞典	商人		上海	1940–1946	OM

续表

英 文 名	中文名	国籍	身份/职业	部 门	居 住 地 点	在会时间	会员类别
Laurence, L.			商人	怡和洋行	上海	1923–1928	OM
Laurenz, Mrs. Rudolf.	劳伦司	德国			上海	1932–1934	OM
Laver, Capt. H. E.		英国			上海	1909–1946	OM/LM
Lawford, L. H.	罗福德	英国	海关人员	海关	北京	1913–1946	OM
Lawrance, Edward.						1864–1866	RM
Lay, A. C. Hyde	李赫德	英国	海关人员	海关	上海	1940–?	OM
Lay, W. G.	李蔚良	英国	海关人员	海关	汕头、广州、上海、澳门	1902–1920	OM
Lay, W. T.	李华达	英国	海关人员			1865–1877	NRM
Layton, J. T. J.				太古洋行	上海	1939–1940	OM
Leach, W. A. B.				工部局	上海	1914–1929	OM
Leamer, Dr. Bruce V.		美国			上海	1934–1940	OM
Leavens, D. H.		美国		雅礼大学、美国芝加哥大学	长沙、芝加哥	1914 1917–1946	OM/LM
Leavenworth, Prof. Chas. G.		美国		南洋公学	上海	1901–1940	OM/LM
Lechler, J. H., M. D.	路景荣	英国	医师	海关	锦竹	1929–1940	OM
Lederer, P.					上海	1936–1938	OM
Ledwidge, J. G.	雷达威		化学师		上海	1941–1946	OM
Lee, A. W.				海关	汉口	1910–1916	OM
Lee, A. W. Simms	李爱伦	美国	教士	圣雅各学校	芜湖	1923–1924	OM
Lee, Dr. John Y.	李耀邦	中国			上海	1936–1946	LM
Lee, Dr. Y. Y.		中国		中国地质研究所	南京	1935–1936	OM

续表

英文名	中文名	国籍	身份/职业	部门	居住地点	在会时间	会员类别
Lee, J. M.				汉密敦饭店	上海	1940-?	OM
Lee, Prof. Shao-chang	李绍昌		教授	夏威夷大学	夏威夷	1933-1940	OM
Lee, W. Y., PH. D.	李伟		工商界		上海	1936-1946	OM
Lee, William Yinson	李元信	中国	工商界	中国银行、上海太平洋保险公司	香港、上海	1933-1946	OM
Leete, W. Rockwell	黎金磐	美国	牧师	公理会、怙岭美国学校	天津、汾州、九江、保定	1918-1946	OM
Lefever, Rufus H.	李让礼	美国	外交官	美国圣公会	青岛、北京、沅陵	1924-1940	OM
Legendre, Gen. C. W.		美国				1868-1877	NRM
Legge, Prof. James, D. D.	理雅各	英国	大学教授	牛津大学	上海	1864-1897	HM
Leith, A. C.				汇丰银行	上海	1935-1940	OM
Lemiere, J. E.		法国	报人/编辑	中法新汇报	上海	1897-1901	OM
Lemiere, J. Em		法国			上海	1939-1940	OM
Lemke, F.				公司	上海	1890-1893	OM
Lenhart, Miss L. E.	刘贤德(女)		教士	圣安德鲁医院	无锡	1928-1936	OM
Lenz, Dr. G. Jahn						1934-1936	OM
Lenz, Ph., PH. D.	连择	德国	外交官	德国领事馆	北京、上海、烟台	1885-1893	OM
Leonard, J. K.	林纳	英国	海关人员	宝顺洋行		1869-1870	RM
Lépisser, E.	兰璧茜	法国	海关人员	海关	上海	1885-1894	OM
Leslie, T.		英国			上海	1914-1946	OM
Lester, Miss E. S.	李淑德(女)	美国	教士	中西女塾	上海	1919-1936	OM/LM
Leung, S. C.				基督教青年会	上海	1939-1946	OM

续表

英文名	中文名	国籍	身份/职业	部门	居住地点	在会时间	会员类别
Leveson, W. E.				工部局	上海	1905－1919	OM
Levine, C. O.				岭南大学	广州	1923－1929	OM
Levis, John H.	来维思		会计师		上海	1937－1946	OM
Levi-Schiff de Suvero, Commdr. Vittorio		意大利		天津意大利人居留地管理局	天津	1935－1940	OM
Levisson, W.				上海电话公司	上海	1923－1924	OM
Levy, A.						1866	RM
Levy, E. S.					上海	1935－1940	LM
Lewis, D. J.				美国商会	上海	1920－1924	OM
Lewis, J.	吕意思	英国	海关人员	工部局卫生处	上海	1932－1936	OM
Lewis, Mrs. D. J.				美商总会,德士古火油公司	上海,青岛	1920－1932	OM
Lewis, Robert E.		美国	教士	基督教青年会	上海	1901－1907 1935－1936	OM
Lewis, S. H.				工部局秘书处	上海	1921－1929	OM
Li Kaun-I					上海	1946－?	OM
Li Fu Poi						1946－?	OM
Li Ming	李明	中国	银行业	浙江兴业银行	上海	1932－1946	LM
Li, Dr. Chen-nan		中国		中国银行研究室	上海	1941－?	OM
Li, Dr. Ting An		中国		上海市健康中心	上海	1933－1934	OM
Liang, Dr. Pao-kan					上海	1937－1940	OM
Liang, Dr. Poe				医药研究院	上海	1938－1940	OM

续表

英文名	中文名	国籍	身份/职业	部门	居住地点	在会时间	会员类别
Liao, Joshua W. K., M. A., PH. D.	廖温魁	中国			上海	1940—1946	OM
Liao, Miss Man-his					上海	1946—?	OM
Liddell, C. Oswald	黎德尔	英国	商人		上海	1908—1924	OM
Liddell, Mrs. John	常立达尔太太	英国			上海	1934—1940	OM
Lieder, Ph.				信义洋行	上海	1886—1894	OM
Lieu, Dr. D. K.					上海	1933—1934	OM
Lieu, Dong-tsung, M. A.					上海,香港	1940—?	OM
Lieu, Lindsay				盐务稽核所	上海	1934—1940	OM
Light, S. F.				厦门大学	厦门	1922—1929	OM
Lillico, Stuart				中国科学美术杂志社	上海	1934—1940	OM
Lim Boom Kong, Dr.				厦门大学	厦门	1930—1940	OM
Limprich, Dr. W.		德国		德华普通中学	天津	1911—1917	OM
Lindau, Rudolph, PHD.					柏林	1864—1912	CM
Linde, Mrs. A. M. de				敦明打字学堂	上海	1922—1936	OM
Lindsay, Dr. Ashley W.	林则	加拿大		卫理公会,华西协和大学	成都	1910—1946	OM/LM
Ling, C. P.				商部办事处	上海	1932—1936	OM
Ling, Dr. D. G.	林光荣	中国			上海	1935—1946	OM
Linge, Mrs. A. J.					上海	1925—1929	OM
Lister, Alford					上海,重庆,宜昌	1870—1877	NRM
Little, A. J.	立德	英国	商人	字林西报	上海	1864—1909	OM
Little, Edward S.	李德立	英国	教士/商人	英商华茂洋行	上海	1900—1940	LM

续表

英 文 名	中文名	国 籍	身份/职业	部 门	居 住 地 点	在会时间	会员类别
Little, L. K.	李度	美国	海关人员	海关	上海、广州	1931–1946	OM
Little, L. S. Esq., M. D.			医师/博士	上海公济医院、北华捷报	上海	1878–1897	OM
Little, Mrs. Archibald J.	立德夫人	英国	不缠足会成员	不缠足会	上海	1906–1926	CM/HM
Little, R. W.	立德禄	英国	商人/报人	北华捷报	上海	1864–1901	OM
Littledale, A.						1865–1866	OM
Littledals, A. D.						1869–1870	RM
Litton, G. J. L.	烈敦	英国	外交官	英国领事馆	重庆	1896–1901	OM
Liu, Chung-shee H., Editor, Science		中国	编辑	中国科学社		1936	OM
Liu, Dr. Herman C. E.	刘湛恩	中国	大学教师	沪江大学	上海	1932–1934	OM
Liu, H. S.				太古洋行	上海、香港	1935–1946	LM
Liu, Yu-wen		中国		中国基督教青年会太平洋关系研究所	上海	1935–1946	OM
Liversidge, Rev. H.	雷海明		教士	内地会	Kaiting(四川)	1922–1923	OM
Llorente, Conde de	罗德邻	西班牙	领事秘书	西班牙领事馆	上海	1886–1887	OM
Lloyd, J. M.						1864–1866	RM
Lloyd, Mrs. Magdalen					上海、北京	1930–1936	OM
Lo, Hsiu-chi					上海	1946–?	OM
Lobenstine, Rev. E. C.	罗炳生	美国	牧师	美国北长老会	上海	1916–1920 1935–1936	OM
Lobzowsky, Dr. C. E.				太古洋行	上海	1932–1934	OM
Lock, W. H.					香港	1937–1946	OM
Lockhart, Hon. J. H. Stewart, C. M. C.	骆任廷	英国	外交官	香港殖民当局	威海卫、香港	1885–1929	OM/HM

续表

英 文 名	中文名	国 籍	身份/职业	部 门	居 住 地 点	任会时间	会员类别
Lockhart, Mrs. (O. C.) Joana. K.	罗晗脱	美国	盐务	盐务稽核所	上海	1933－1946	OM
Lockhart, Wiliam	雒魏林	英国	医师	伦敦会		1857－1908	RM/CM
Lockwood, W. W.	骆维廉	英国	教士	基督教青年会	上海	1913－1936	OM
Loehr, A. G.				英国领事馆	上海	1916－1922	OM
Loewenberg, Dr. R. D.					上海	1935－1940	OM
Lofting, J. H.				德罗洋行	上海	1922－1926	OM
Logan, Col. M. H., M. C., O. B. E.				巴麻单拿洋行	上海	1931－1933	OM
Lonsain, A. J. R.				荷兰银行	上海	1934－1940	OM
Lord, Rev. R. D.	罗瑞芝	英国	牧师	广仁医院,中华圣公会	济南,兖州,扬州	1918－1940	OM
Lord, Samuel	乐德	英国	商人		上海	1921－1924	OM
Louis, Jacot-Guillarmod				瑞士领事馆	上海	1935－1936	OM
Low, Dr. C. W.				华安和群保寿股份有限公司	上海	1932－1946	OM
Low, E. G., Esq.				协隆洋行	汉口	1881－1893	OM
Low, P. C.				公司	北京,上海	1936－1946	OM
Lowder, E. Gordon	劳达尔	英国	海关人员	海关	上海	1904－1908 1921	OM
Lowder, G. G.	劳德	英国	海关人员	海关	安东	1878－1881	RM
Lowder, H. G.	劳德迩	英国	海关人员	海关	上海	1914－1916	OM
Lowder, Mrs. E. G.	劳达尔夫人				南京	1921	OM
Lowdermilk, Dr. W. C.	罗德民	美国	大学教师	金陵大学	上海	1936－1940	OM
Lowson, A. B.				汇丰银行		1922－1923	OM

续表

英文名	中文名	国籍	身份/职业	部门	居住地点	任会时间	会员类别
Lucas, S. E.			银行	渣打银行、中国银行、麦加利银行	天津、北京、上海	1906-1940	OM
Lueder-Redewisch, C.						1878-?	RM
Lütgens, Alfred.		德国	外交官	德国领事馆	上海	1913-1919	OM
Lumsden, A.						1870-1877	NRM
Lumsden, Miss F. R. G. S.				英国领事馆	大理、上海	1922-1929	OM
Lund, Dr. Hugo		芬兰	大学教师	赫尔辛基大学	赫尔辛基	1901	OM
Lunkley, Mr. R. E.				沃的斯电梯公司	上海	1935-1936	OM
Lunt, Carroll		美国	出版商/报界		上海	1937-1938	OM
Luthy, Charles	尤塔	瑞士		罗德洋行	上海	1910-1940	OM/LM
Luthy, Emil					上海	1917-1946	LM
Lutovinow, Archimandrite				俄国教士团	北京	1895-1901	OM
Luzac, C. G.					伦敦	1901	OM
Ly Dr. J. Usang			大学教师	上海交通大学	上海	1932-1946	LM
Lyall, Leonard A.	赖发洛	英国	海关人员	海关	上海、北京	1892-1939	OM/LM
Lyman, Prof. E. R.			教授	格致书院	上海	1898-1901	OM
Lynch, Dr. J.					镇江	1900-1907	OM
Lynill, J.P.						1864	RM
Lyon, Rev. D. Willard, D. D.	来会理	美国	牧师	基督教青年会	上海	1904-1946	OM/LM
Lyons, Mrs. M.				英商启东烟草股份有限公司	营口	1939-1940	OM
Ma, Dr. Y. C.					上海	1933-1936	OM

续表

英 文 名	中文名	国 籍	身份/职业	部 门	居 住 地 点	在会时间	会员类别
Ma, Man Fai				先施进出口公司	上海	1937–1940	OM
Maas, N.				黄浦运输公司	上海	1937–1940	OM
Mabee, Fred C.		美国	大学教师	南浸信会学校,沪江大学	上海	1912–1936	OM
Macbeth, Miss A.		英国			上海	1915–1935	OM
MacDonald, A. R.						1864–1866	RM
MacDonald, Donald						1941–?	OM
MacDonald, R. C.				教士公所	上海	1930–1931	OM
MacDonald, W.				海关	上海	1912–1919	OM
MacDonell, A. M.				美国邮政代办处	上海	1918–1924	OM
MacGillivray, Rev. Donald	季理斐	加拿大	教士	加拿大长老会	上海	1901–1930	OM
Macgowan, D. J. M. D.	玛高温	美国	传教医师		温州,宁波	1860–1892	CM
MacGregor, D.	麦克利	英国	园林专家	工部局	上海	1913–1917	OM
Macgregor, John				怡和洋行	上海	1888–1893	OM
MacGregor, Miss Gleys					上海	1946–?	OM
Macintyre, Rev. John	马钦泰	英国	教士		牛庄	1880–1892	OM
Mackay, A. C.				英国领事馆	哈尔滨	1925–1929	OM
Mackay, J. A.				花旗银行	上海	1937–1940	OM
Mackenzie, I. C.	麦更孜	英国	外交官	英国领事馆	上海	1936	OM
Mackey, Jas				海关	厦门,台湾	1886–1894	OM
Mackinlay, Miss M. F.	金灿煊(女)		教士	基督教育年会	上海	1921–1923	OM
Mackinnen, Miss F. D.				圣玛利亚书院	上海	1939–1940	OM

续表

英 文 名	中文名	国 籍	身份/职业	部 门	居 住 地 点	在会时间	会员类别
Mackinnon, J. B. A.				工部局	上海	1905—1906	OM
Mackintosh, J. S.		加拿大				1864—1866	RM
Macklin, Dr. W. E.	马林		传教医师		南京	1900—1901	OM
Maclay, R. H., Esq.					天津	1881—1882	OM
Maclean, P.					上海	1860—1866	RM
Maclellan, J. W.		英国		北华捷报	上海	1888—1893	OM
Macleod, Dr. N.			医生/博士		上海	1915—1920	OM
MacLeod, R. A.		美国			圣路易斯	1924—1929	OM
MacNair, Prof. H. F., PHD.	密亨利	美国	教授	圣约翰大学	上海	1920—1940	OM/LM
Macoun, J. H.	麻振	英国	海关人员	海关	上海、南京、厦门、北京	1894—1934	OM
MacRae, J. D.	瑞思培	加拿大	教士	山东齐鲁大学,太古轮船公司	济南、上海、常德	1910—1936	OM
Mactzokin, N. P.		俄国		俄国东方学会	哈尔滨	1917—1919	OM
Madsen, W.					上海	1932—1934	OM
Maginnis, A. F. L.				太古轮船公司	上海	1932—1936	OM
Magle, Rev. Hans	梅恒士	丹麦	牧师	丹麦路德会	欧登赛(丹麦)	1932—1940	OM
MaGrath, C. D.		美国		晋隆洋行	上海	1910—1920	OM
MaGrath, Mrs. C. D.					上海	1910—1919	OM
Maguire, Mrs. C. E.		英国			上海	1921—1924	OM
Maher, Joseph	马依(女)		洋员	太古洋行	上海	1930—1936	OM
Mahnfeldt, R.					上海	1912—1916	OM
Maignan, H.						1875—1883	RM

续表

英 文 名	中文名	国 籍	身份/职业	部 门	居 住 地 点	在会时间	会员类别
Main, Duncean	梅腾更	英国	教士	圣公会	杭州,汉口	1900-1934	OM
Maintz, A. Esq.						1865-1866	RM
Maitland, H.				汇丰银行	上海	1929-1935	OM
Maitland, J. A.						1864-1866	RM
Major, E.	美查	英国	商人兼报人		上海	1887-1897	OM
Major, J. M.				美国总统轮船公司	上海	1940-?	OM
Major, John	美哲	英国	商人			1858-1868	RM
Makarin, N.					上海	1939-1940	OM
MaLean, Winfiejd Augus				公理会		1925-1928	OM
Mamet, O.	满三德	比利时	商人	门头沟煤矿	北京	1922-1946	LM
Man, J. A.		英国	海关人员			1864-1877	NRM
Mangum, W. P.	孟金	美国	外交官			1866-1881	NRM
Mann, J. a.						1866-?	NRM
Mann, James, Esq., M. D.						1882-1883	OM
Manning, G. J.					上海	1939-1940	OM
Mar Dr. Peter	马骊德	中国	生物化学及医学家	雷氏德研究院	上海	1935-1940	OM
Marbon, Charles B.				燕京大学	北京	1911-1924	OM
March, B. F., Jr.	马尔智	美国	学人			1924-1933	OM
Marden, G. E.				会德丰洋行	香港	1940-?	OM
Margerie, Mme. Roland de						1941-?	OM

续表

英 文 名	中文名	国籍	身份/职业	部门	居住地点	在会时间	会员类别
Margliouth, Miss E. R.	马瑞珍			中华圣公会	济南,泰安	1924–1932	OM
Markham, J.	马安	英国	领事人员		上海	1859–1870	NRM
Marques, Jose Martinho	马吉士	葡萄牙	翻译			1866	HM
Marques-Pereira, J. F.		葡萄牙		大太阳报	里斯本	1900–1910	HM
Marsh, B. F., Jr				密西根大学博物馆	密西根	1924–1934	OM
Marsh, E. L.	马许	英国		汇丰银行	上海	1908–1946	OM/LM
Marshall, Miss M. C.					上海	1912–1915	OM
Marshall, Miss M. E.					上海	1946–?	OM
Marshall, R. Calder				祥兴洋行	上海	1908–1946	OM
Marsoulies, A. du P.					上海	1917–1924	OM
Marston, E.						1864–?	RM
Marteau, E. de				洋行	上海	1896–1897	OM
Martillière, Dr.			医师/博士	沙逊大厦	上海	1930–1936	OM
Martin, C. H.				华俄道胜银行	上海,大连,烟台	1918–1925	OM
Martin, G.	马丹	法国	商人		北京	1864	RM
Martin, G. R.				公司		1915–1917	OM
Martin, Hugh	麦丁	英国	商人	瑞和洋行	上海	1932–1936	OM
Martin, J. P.	马丁	英国	商人			1876–1877	OM
Martin, Miss J. M.				工部局卫生处	上海	1924–1932	OM
Martin, Mrs. W. A.	马荣思		教士	惠龙饭店,内地会	上海	1916–1936	OM
Martin, O.						1864	RM

续表

英 文 名	中文名	国籍	身份/职业	部 门	居 住 地 点	在会时间	会员类别
Martin, Rev. W. A. P., D. D., LL.D.	丁韪良	美国	教士	同文馆,长老会	北京	1864–1916	CM/HM
Martin, Thos.						1864	RM
Martinella, A.				意大利租界管理局	天津	1921–1936	OM
Martinoff, G.					天津	1889–1894	OM
Marx, Edwin	马轲	美国		美国基督会	上海	1940–?	OM
Marzal, Y. De Faria J. De				西班牙领事馆	北京	1890–1897	OM
Mason, Isaac	梅益盛	英国	教士	仁济医院,英国公宜会	上海	1916–1938	OM/LM/HM
Mass, N. N.		英国			伦敦	1937	OM
Masson, J. R.				太古洋行	香港	1935–1940	OM
Mateer, J. L.						1875–1877	RM
Mather, B.	马百熙		教士	英国安立会	北京	1918–1924	OM
Mather, Wm. A.	马德	美国	教士	长老会	保定	1926–1940	OM
Mathieson, N.			牧师	太古洋行	上海	1915–1924	OM
Mathieson, Rev. J. C.	陈明新			加拿大联合会	怀庆,常德	1929–1940	OM
Matsumoto, S.	松本三之介	日本	学界	同盟社通讯社	上海	1935–1940	OM
Matzokin, N. P.		俄国		俄国东方学会	哈尔滨	1917–1920	OM
Maughan, J.R., A R I B A				德和洋行	上海	1934–1939	OM
Maxwell, Dr. J. L.	马雅各	英国	教士	雷氏德研究院	上海,汉口	1931–1940	OM
Maxwell, Dr. J. Preston	马士敦	英国	教士	北京协和医科大学	北京	1917–1934	OM
Maybon, Charles B.		法国	教师	法国远东语言学校	上海	1911–1925	OM
Mayell, Eric				二十世纪福斯影片公司	上海	1939–1940	OM

续表

英 文 名	中文名	国籍	身份/职业	部门	居住地点	在会时间	会员类别
Mayers, Frederick J.	梅尔士	英国	海关人员	海关	镇江	1917－1928	LM
Mayers, Sidney F.	梅尔思	英国	外交官	中英银公司	北京	1907－1933	OM
Mayers, W. F.	梅辉立	英国	领事人员			1864－1874	NRM/CM
McBain, E. B.				麦边洋行	上海	1934－1940	OM
McCabe, P. J.					哈尔滨	1922－1934	OM
McCallum, C. A.				海关	福州	1901－1908	OM
McCartee, D. B., A. M.	麦嘉缔	美国	教士			1858－1897	CM
McCarthy, G. J.				大来轮船公司	上海	1935－1946	OM
McClatchie, H. P.	马夏礼	英国	外交官		汉口，烟台	1875－1882	OM
McClatchie, Rev. Canon.			牧师			1869－1877	CM
McClure, Prof. F. A., PH. D.	麦克开拉启	美国	牧师	英国圣公会	上海	1866－1884	CM
McCollop, J.	莫古礼	美国		岭南大学	广州	1935－1940	OM
McDaniel, C. Yates			报人	上海泰晤时报、大美晚报、美联社	上海，南京，香港	1864	RM
McDonald, B. A.				嘉达洋行	上海	1930－1940	OM
McDonald, C. M.				上海总会	上海	1936	OM
McDonald, Ranald					上海	1940－1946	OM
McDonald, Ranald G.	麦克道	英国	律师		上海	1939－1940	OM
McDougal, H., M. B.	玛都嘉	英国	医师		厦门	1930－1936	OM
McEuen, K. J.	麦兑隐	英国	警察	工部局	上海	1885－1893	OM
						1908－1936	OM

续表

英文名	中文名	国籍	身份/职业	部门	居住地点	在会时间	会员类别
McFarlane, Rev. A. J.	马辅仁	英国	牧师	博学书院,伦敦会	上海	1915-1924	OM
McGavin, David	麦兴仁	英国		苏格兰圣书会	上海	1940-?	OM
McGee, Prof. Norman			教授	南洋公学	上海	1901	OM
McGillivray, Mrs. D.	马达命夫人		教士	美国遣使会	上海	1933-1934	OM
McGrew, Dallas		美国		花旗银行	上海	1917	OM
McHugh, Capt. J. M., U.S.M.C.	麦克猷	美国	军人			1935-1940	OM
McInnes, Miss G.				工部局	上海	1913-1924	OM
McInnes, Miss L.				汇丰银行	上海	1913-1918	OM
McIntosh, Miss E. W.		加拿大		中国圣公会	归德	1923-1946	OM
McIntosh, Rev. G.	金多士	英国	教士	美华书馆,美国长老会	上海	1889-1911	OM
McLaughlin, Rev. Wallace H.	马克罗	美国	牧师	汉口信义书局,福音会	汉口	1931-1940	OM
McLean, Winfield Angus		加拿大		美国公理会	汾州	1925-1940	OM
Mclorn, D.	麦伦达	英国	海关人员	大清银行	上海	1935-1940	OM
McMillen, O. W.	睦美灵	美国	教士	培英中学	广州	1923-1946	OM/LM
McMullen, Dr. R. J.	明思德	美国	教士	美国长老会	上海	1938-1946	LM
McNeely, Miss M. V.	李梅红	加拿大	教士	广学书局	上海	1928-1940	OM
McNeill, John	马克尼	英国	海关人员		上海	1937-1940	OM
McNeill, Mrs. Duncan		英国		大美圣公会	汉普郡	1913-1924	OM
McNulty, Rev. Henry A.	梅乃魁	美国	牧师		苏州	1918-1940	OM
Mead, E, W.	密尔德	英国	外交官	英国领事馆	北京,上海,成都	1916-1936	OM
Meade, Richard H. Jr., M.D.		美国		同仁医院	安庆	1925-1929	OM
Meadows, J. A. T.	密妥士	英国	外交官/工商界			1866	NRM

续表

英 文 名	中文名	国 籍	身份/职业	部 门	居 住 地 点	在会时间	会员类别
Meadows, T. T.	密迪乐	英国	外交官	英国领事馆	宁波	1858–1868	CM/HM
Medhurst, Rev. C. Spurgeon			教士	尚贤堂	上海	1888 1911–1915	OM
Medhurst, Sir Walter H., K. C. B.	麦华陀	英国	领事人员		上海	1861–1885	RM/HM
Meerdervoort, J. L. Dr. C. Pompe van, M. D.					长崎	1858–1874	CM
Meinhardt, Mrs. C. D.				美国领事馆	上海	1928–1936	OM
Meister, O., C. E., M. E.	麦士德	瑞士	商人		上海	1922–1936	LM
Melchers, W.				虾厘洋行	上海	1886–1888	OM
Mell, Rudolf				德华普通中学	广州	1911–1924	OM
Meller, H.						1866	RM
Melnikoff, D. M.				新泰洋行	汉口	1919–1946	LM
Melrose, Mrs. M. R.				长老会	海南	1925–1929	OM
Menaies Rev. J. M.			牧师		开封、常德	1914–1923	OM
Mencarini, J.	绵嘉义	西班牙	海关人员	海关	上海、厦门、福州	1884–1936	OM
Mendel, Rev. Brown			牧师	上海犹太人学校	上海	1933	OM
Mendelsen, Major Joseph A., M. C.		美国	军人	美国军事顾问团	天津	1933–1946	LM
Mendows., T. T.						1866	HM
Meng, C. Y. W.		中国	官员	实业部	南京	1925–1936	OM
Meng, Prof. Hsien-chen		中国	教授		苏州	1935–1936	OM
Mengel, E.		丹麦		中国电报局	云南	1913–1928	OM

续表

英文名	中文名	国籍	身份/职业	部门	居住地点	在会时间	会员类别
Mennie, D.				屈臣氏大药房	上海	1916—1940	OM
Menzies, Rev. J. M.	明义士	加拿大	牧师	齐鲁大学中国研究院	济南、承德、开封	1914—1940	OM
Merian, Hans		瑞士			巴塞尔	1921—1946	LM
Merian, J.		瑞士			上海	1921—1933	LM
Merian, J. R. A.					上海	1921—1924	OM/LM
Merins, Dr. E. M.				圣约翰大学	上海	1916—1924	OM
Meritt, C. J.					上海	1941—?	OM
Merklinghaus, Dr. P.	麦令毫	德国	领事人员	德国领事馆	济南、长沙	1906—1913	OM
Merrill, H. F.	墨贤理	美国	海关人员	海关	广州、上海	1910—1918	OM
Merriman, Mrs. W. L.					上海	1910—1926	OM
Merrins, Dr. E. M.				圣约翰大学	上海	1916/1925	OM
Merz, C., PH. D.	梅泽	德国	外交官	德国领事馆	厦门、台湾、上海	1882—1897	OM
Mesny, General W.	麦士尼	英国			汉口	1890—1901 1914—1919	OM
Mesny, H. P.				英商驻华邓禄普有限公司	上海	1911—1946	OM/LM
Messing, Otto		德国		德华银行	柏林	1901—1906	OM
Metzger, E.		德国			斯图加特	1887—1888	OM
Meyer, A.						1866—1870	NRM
Meyer, H. Fugel		丹麦		黄埔运输公司	上海	1920—1946	OM/LM
Meyer, Mrs. B. L.					上海	1938—1940	OM
Meyer, Paul W.	麦迹	美国	外交官	美国领事馆	北京、青岛	1936—1946	OM
Meyer, R.					上海	1887—1888	OM

续表

英 文 名	中文名	国籍	身份/职业	部门	居住地点	在会时间	会员类别
Meyer, Th.	梅业	法国	外交官		上海	1886－1888	OM
Meyers W. S. F.						1866	NRM
Miau Way-kaung, M. D.		中国		工部局病理实验室	上海	1935－1936	OM
Michener, C. K.		英国	海关人员			1913－1915	OM
Michie, A.	宓吉				上海	1861－1877	RM
Middleton, Herbert E.				工部局秘书处	上海	1909－1913	OM
Middleton, James S.					上海	1861	RM
Middleton, John						1870－1877	RM
Milhorat, W. B. O.				志大洋行	上海	1930－1936	OM
Milhorat, A. T.		美国			新泽西	1919－1920	OM
Millard, T. F.	密勒	美国	报人	大陆报	上海	1911－1919	OM
Miller Dr.						1864	RM
Miller, H. B.	梅拉	美国	外交官	美国领事馆	牛庄	1901	OM
Miller, Rev. G. D. B.			牧师			1875－1878	NRM
Milles, W. J. , F. R. C. S.					上海	1885－1909	OM
Millican, Rev. F. R.	梅立德	美国	牧师	广学会,循道会	上海	1935－1946	OM
Millington, F. C.	美灵登	英国	商人	美灵登广告有限公司	上海	1932－1933	OM
Mills, E. W. P.	弥勒斯	英国	外交官	英国领事馆	上海,汉口,宜昌,北京	1920－1946	OM
Mills, Major D. A. , R. E.		英国			德文部	1888－1901	OM
Milne, H.						1873－1874	RM
Milne, W. C.	美魏茶	英国	教士	伦敦会	福州	1860	CM

续表

英 文 名	中文名	国籍	身份/职业	部门	居住地点	在会时间	会员类别
Milsom, A.						1869-1877	RM
Milsom, E.						1865-1868	RM
Mirams, D. G.				工部局实业处	上海	1939-1940	OM
Mironnff, Prof. N. D.			教授		上海	1924-1936	OM
Miskin, Stanely C.				亚细亚火油公司	汉口	1913-1934	OM
Mitchell, Miss E. E.				基督教青年会	上海	1915-1917 1921-1922	OM
Mitchell, Rev. F. K.			牧师			1864	RM
Mitchell, T. E.	宓吉尔	英国	商人	保众保险公司	上海	1926-1933	OM
Mitchell, W. A.	宓齐尔		商人	慎昌洋行	上海	1916-1918	OM
Mitchell, W. H.						1866	RM
Mittag, M.				兴隆洋行	上海	1887-1888	OM
Moffett, Rev. L. J.			牧师		江阴	1910-1912	OM
Mogabgab, A.				瑞达洋行	上海	1932-1946	OM
Mohr, Wolfgang					上海	1937-1939	OM
Mohrbacher, Rev. Father C. M.			牧师	天主教	兖州	1930-1936	OM
Molgaard, V. B.				大英圣书公会	昆明	1936-1940	OM
Molines, Edouard				义品放款银行	汉口	1920-1929	OM
Möllendorff, O. F. Von	穆林德	德国	领事人员	德国领事馆	广州,天津	1877-1894	OM
Möllendorff, P. G. Von	穆麟德	德国	海关人员	海关	上海,天津,北京	1877-1892	OM
Möller, O.		德国		帝国电报局	上海	1894-1901	OM
Molojatoff, Mrs. M. T.					上海	1946-?	OM

续表

英 文 名	中文名	国籍	身份/职业	部门	居住地点	在会时间	会员类别
Moncreiff, J.E.	孟克明	美国	教士	华西协和大学,浸礼会	成都	1927–1946	OM/LM
Moncreiff, T.						1857	RM
Mongan, J.	孟甘	英国	外交官		上海,天津	1859–1878	NRM
Moninger, Miss M. M.	孟言嘉	美国	教士	北长老会	海口	1916–1934	OM
Montmorand, Vt. Brenier de						1865–1866	RM
Mooallen, Mrs. A. A.					上海	1933	OM
Moorad, George	慕大辟	美国		上海泰晤时报	上海	1934–1936	OM
Moore, Bishop, D. H.	穆信诚	英国	教士	工部局,内地会	上海	1901–1917	OM
Moore, Dr. A.				笃志女校	扬州	1913–1946	LM
Moore, Miss Florence E.				横滨正金银行	天津	1937–1940	OM
Moorhead, Dr. H. B.						1901–1911	OM
Morakuma, Y.						1913	OM
Morel, E.	莫汝		商人兼领事	比利时领事馆		1869–1874	RM
Morgan, Rev. Evan	莫安仁	英国	教士	广学会	上海	1901–1939	LM/HM
Morley, A.		日本		上海泰晤时报	上海	1935–1938	OM
Morocma, Y.				横滨正金银行	横滨	1912–1917	OM
Morris, Herbert S.		英国			上海	1878–1882	OM
Morrison, A. R. G.	莫礼迹		律师	中英银公司	上海	1940–?	OM
Morrison, Dr. G. E.	莫理循	英国	记者	英国领事馆	北京	1897–1919	OM
Morrison, G.J., Esq.	毛里迹	英国	工程师	玛礼孙洋行	上海	1880–1901	OM
Morrison, M. C.	马理生	英国	外交官	英国领事馆		1865–1870	NRM
Morriss, Dr. H. H.	马立师	美国	教士	同仁医院	上海	1909 1914–1946	OM

续表

英 文 名	中文名	国籍	身份/职业	部门	居住地点	在会时间	会员类别
Morriss, Gordon				德和洋行	上海	1933－1946	OM
Morriss, H. E.					上海	1919－1924	OM
Morriss, Harry					上海	1932－1940	LM
Morriss, Mrs. Hayley					上海	1914－1918	OM
Morrow, E. K.		美国	教士	美以美会	上海	1915－1916	OM
Morse, C.J.					上海	1901－1946	LM
Morse, H. B.	马士	美国	海关人员	海关	上海	1888－1933	OM/HM
Morse, W. R.	穆尔思	加拿大	教师	华西协和大学	成都	1930－1939	LM
Mörsel, F. H.					仁川	1889－1894	OM
Mortensen, Mrs. T., PH. D.					上海	1946－?	OM
Mortensen, Rev. Ralph	慕天恩	美国	牧师	圣经公会	汉口、上海、河南	1920－1946	OM
Mortensen, W.				大北电报公司	烟台	1913－1917	OM
Mortimore, Mrs. W., M.D.			牧师	英美会	成都	1922－1927	OM
Mortimore, R. H.	麦迪莫	英国	外交官	英国领事馆	上海	1885－1892	OM
Moses, M.			商人	沙逊洋行	上海	1885－1887	OM
Moses, Mrs. A. E.			报人		上海	1931－1935	OM
Mossman, Samuel	马诗门	英国			上海	1861	OM
Mossop, A. G.	莫恕伯	英国	律师	英国在华医院	上海	1922－1946	OM/LM
Mostaert, E.				陇海铁路	郑州	1922－1924	OM
Moule, A. E.	慕雅德	英国	牧师	大英圣公会	上海	1888－1892	OM

续表

英 文 名	中文名	国籍	身份/职业	部 门	居 住 地 点	在会时间	会员类别
Moule, Rev. A. C.	慕阿德	英国	牧师		泰安	1902－1933	OM
Moule, Right Rev. G. E., D. D.	慕稼谷	英国	教士	教士公所	杭州,汉口	1864－1911	OM/HM
Moule, Ven. Archdeacon A. E.				大英圣公会	上海	1888－1892	OM
Mowat, A. R. D.				英国领事馆	上海	1870－1873	RM
Mowjee, A. M. J.				八巴厘洋行	上海	1888	OM
Münter, L. S.		荷兰		大北电报公司	北京	1913－1918	OM
Muirhead, R. B.						1910－1936	OM
Muirhead, Rev. W.	慕维廉	英国	教士	伦敦会	上海	1942－?	OM
Muller, C. E.				旗昌洋行	上海	1864－1897	CM
Muller, Charles					上海	1886－1887	OM
Muller,Dr. C.					上海	1916－1918	OM
Muller-Beeck, Geo		德国	参赞	德国领事馆	横浜	1938－1939	OM
Mullett,Dr. H. J.	吉士道	加拿大	教士		成都	1886－1901	OM
Mulliner, La Mar				美国运通银行	上海	1921－1924	OM
Mulock, Capt. G., R. N.				大美长老会	上海	1939－1940	OM
Munday,Miss M. C.					上海	1922－1928	OM
Munn, Rev. Wm			牧师	工部局	上海	1941－?	OM
Munro-Faure, P. H.			教士	北长老会,亚细亚火油公司	杭州,上海,九江	1910 1921－1946	OM
Munson, E. H.	尚爱物	美国		基督教青年会	上海	1938－1939	OM

续表

英 文 名	中文名	国 籍	身份/职业	部 门	居 住 地 点	在会时间	会员类别
Munthe, Mrs. Alexander E.	曼德夫人		文学家		北京	1921–1946	OM/LM
Murphine, Shepley					上海	1921–1929	OM
Murphy, H. K., A. I. A.	茂非	美国	建筑师		上海	1921–1924 1932–1946	OM/LM
Murphy, Mrs. Henry K.	茂非夫人				上海	1921–1925	OM
Murray, C. P.				美国领事馆	上海	1930–1936	OM
Murray, D. S.				大英圣书公会	上海	1887–1894	OM
Murray, J. G.	穆勒思		海关人员			1864–1874	NRM
Murray, W.	麦利	英国				1869–1877	NRM
Musso, G. D.	穆安素	意大利	律师	德华银行	上海	1924–1936	OM
Musson, Rev. Wm.					香港	1896–1897	OM
Myburgh, P. A.						1865–1866	RM
Mylne, H.						1866–1870	RM
Mysore University	迈索尔大学	印度	机构	迈索尔大学	迈索尔	1920–1928	OM
Nakajima, K.		日本		东亚同文书院	上海	1930	OM
Nakayama, M.		日本			奈良	1931	OM
Nakayama, Shozen		日本			奈良	1931–1940	OM
Nance, Prof. W. B.	文乃史	美国	教士	东吴大学	苏州,上海	1922–1940	OM
Nash, E. T.			军人	工部局秘书	上海	1929–1946	OM
Nathan, Major W. S.	那森	英国		福公司	上海	1932–1936	OM
Nathorst, Miss Ruth G.	罗育德(女)		教士	湘北瑞华信义会/	长沙	1934–1940	OM
Navarra, B. R. A.				北华捷报	上海	1890–1897	OM

续表

英 文 名	中文名	国籍	身份/职业	部 门	居住地点	在会时间	会员类别
Neale, Richard E.				英国政府当局高级法院	上海	1918	OM
Neil, T.						1869–1874	RM
Neild, Dr. F. M.	倪迹	英国			上海	1916–1933	OM
Nelson, T.						1857–1858	RM
Nemazee, M.					香港	1939–1940	OM
Nethery, Dr. Wm. M.			海关人员	安息浸礼会	沈阳	1933–1936	OM
Newbery, J. Esq.	牛百里	英国				1865	OM
Newbery, Miss E. E.				天主教学校	上海	1918–1919	OM
Newcomb, Capt. Frank		英国		太古洋行	上海	1917–1929	OM
Newel, Fritz				《日日新闻》	汉口	1913–1916	OM
Newell, Dr. Mary F.				妇孺医院	上海	1914–1916	OM
Newell, Mrs. Isaac.	牛维乐夫人	美国	外交官		北京	1935–1936	OM
Newman, A. L.	钮曼	英国	海关人员	海关	上海	1933–1936	OM
Newman, Kenneth				美国领事馆	上海	1920–1940	OM
Nicholson, J. B.	倪克森	美国	外交官	太古洋行	长沙	1919	OM
Nicholson, William			船长		香港	1919–1925	OM
Nicolson, Sir Frederick W.		英国	海关人员			1857	RM
Nielsen, Albert	倪额森	挪威		中国海关	厦门	1894–1946	OM/LM
Nimitz, Capt. C. W.				海军部	华盛顿	1934–1936	OM
Nishiyama, T.	西山勉	日本	金融界	横滨正金银行	上海	1910–1918	OM
Niskanen, V.	倪斯嘉南	芬兰	外交官	法国外事处	上海	1936–1940	OM
Nixon, F. A.				邮局	北京	1913–1916	OM

续表

英文名	中文名	国籍	身份/职业	部门	居住地点	在会时间	会员类别
Noble, W. E.				安康保险公司	上海	1939—1940	OM
Nocentini, L.		意大利	汉语秘书	意大利领事馆	上海	1884—1909	OM
Noetzli, H.	那礼士	瑞士	海关人员		汉口	1864—1866	RM
Nord, Dr. H.				德国领事馆	南京,北京	1904—1918	OM
Nordquist, O.				邮局		1920—1929 1937—1940	OM
Norman, B. B.				华俄道胜银行		1912—1913	OM
Norman, G. K.				太古洋行	上海	1912—1913	OM
Norman, H. C.		英国	商人	大陆报	上海	1912—1936	OM
Norman, W. von	福哪门	瑞典		维昌洋行	上海	1932—1934	RM
Normann, Prof. W. de						1859	OM
Norton, Prof. J. R.	那敦		教士	圣约翰大学,美国圣公会	镇江,温州	1914—1916 1928—1940	OM
Novion, A.	那威勇	法国	海关专员	海关	上海,镇江,厦门	1885—1901	OM
Nully, R. de	德努理	法国		海关		1884—1909	RM
Nutt, J.						1864—1866	OM
Nutter, Mrs. Florence				诚信洋行	上海	1934—1936	OM
Nye, Gideon. Jr.	奈益	美国	副领事	美国领事馆	广州	1882—1887	OM
Nye, Mrs. A. H.					上海	1927—1929	OM
Nyholm, F.					上海	1935—1940	OM
Nyström, Dr. E. T.	新常富	瑞典	工程师	山西大学	太原,北京	1920—1940	OM
Oakes, Rev. W. Longden		英国	牧师	循道会	长沙	1919—1946	OM/LM

续表

英文名	中文名	国籍	身份/职业	部门	居住地点	在会时间	会员类别
Oakeshott, R. E.	吴贵福（女）	英国	教士	内地会	上海	1946–?	OM
O'Beien, M. H.		美国		美国在华法院	上海	1908–1911	OM
O'Brien-Butler, P. E.	领必廉	英国	外交官	英国领事馆	沈阳、上海、烟台、云南	1886–1946	OM/LM
O'Bolger, R. E.				柯达公司	上海	1935–1940	OM
Odaki, F.			编辑	东亚同文书院	上海	1930–1936	OM
O'Dod, J. H.	俄地	英国	医生		上海	1895–1901	OM
O'Driscoll, Dr. J. A.		英国	外交官	英国领事馆	上海	1928–1929	OM
Ogden, A. G. N., C. M. G., O. B. E.	鄂克登				上海	1947–?	OM
Ogilvie, Rev. C. L.	欧格非		牧师	爱美印刷所、美国北长老会	上海	1913–1919	OM
Ohlinger, Rev. F.	武林吉	美国	牧师	华美书局、美以美会	上海	1905–1909	OM
Ohlmer, E.	阿理文	德国	海关人员	海关	北京、上海	1885–1929	OM/LM
Okamatsu, Dr. Samtaro	冈松参太郎	日本	学界	南满铁路	大连	1910–1917	LM
Olcott, Col. H. S.					马德拉斯	1902–1909	LM
Oldroyd, Miss Gertrude N.	翁素兰（女）	美国	教士	美以美会	上海	1935–1936	OM
Olesen, O. F.		英国	记者	大北电报公司	北京	1924–1929	OM
Oliphant, L.	俄理范	英国				1864	RM
Oliver, A. W. L.	欧利巴	英国	海关人员	海关	上海、九龙	1924–1940	OM
Oliver, Andrew				美孚公司	上海	1939–1940	OM
Oliver, Dr. A. E.	阿礼华	英国	海关人员		汉口	1910–1917	OM
Ollerdessen, F. C. H.				美商恒丰机器厂	上海	1939	OM

续表

英 文 名	中文名	国 籍	身份/职业	部 门	居 住 地 点	在会时间	会员类别
Ollerton, Joseph E.					上海	1916－1924	OM
Olsen, F. A.				合众人寿保险公司	上海	1932－1936	OM
Olyphant, A.						1866	RM
O'Naill-Lane, Mrs.					上海	1920 1924－1929	OM
Onley, Rev. F. G.	文励益	英国	牧师	中国基督教圣书会	汉口	1934－1946	OM/LM
Oppe, H. S.					上海	1908－1915	OM
Oppenheim, Dr.		德国			慕尼黑	1925－1928	OM
Oppert, E.				泰和洋行		1864－1866	RM
Orchardson, T. H.						1910－1913	OM
Oriental Study Expedition		美国	机构	波莫纳学院	加利福尼亚	1930－1934	LM
Orme, Peter						1878－？	RM
Ortmans, A.						1866	NRM
Osborn, Rev. G. R.	欧卓志	英国	牧师	武昌博文中学、循道会	武昌	1936－1940	OM
Osborne, Mrs. Katherine		美国			波士顿	1934－1940	OM
Osgood, A. J.				谦信洋行	上海	1901－1902	OM
O'Shea, H.				北华捷报	上海	1897－1901	OM
O'Shea, J.	和若望	美国	教士	上海泰晤时报、遣使会		1910－1913	OM
Oss, John	史约翰	美国	教士		上海	1942－？	OM
Othmer, Prof. Dr. W.	欧特曼	德国	教授	同济大学	上海	1924－1933	LM
Ottewill, H. A.	奥泰蔚	英国	外交官	英国领事馆	镇江、上海、云南	1913－1929	OM
Otto, Earl, PH. D.					上海	1939－1940	OM

续表

英 文 名	中文名	国 籍	身份/职业	部 门	居 住 地 点	在会时间	会员类别
Ottomeier, P. A. W.			商人	裨臣洋行	上海	1886—1897	OM
Ouskouli, M. H. A.					上海	1917—1936	OM
Ovesen, H. E.				中国电报局	烟台	1910—1917	OM
Owen, Rev. G. S.	文书田	英国	教士	伦敦会	北京	1869—1887	OM
Owens, A. C.	武文	美国		威海卫男子学校	蓬莱	1929—1940	OM
Oxenham, E. L.	欧森南	英国	外交官	英国领事馆	镇江	1887—1894	OM
Ozorio, C. E. L.			商人	花旗银行		1911—1913	OM
Paasch, C. , Esq.	巴许	德国			北京	1882	NRM
Paddock, Rev. B. H.		美国	牧师		延平	1916—1946	OM/LM
Pade, K. F.				大北电报公司	上海	1920—1933	OM
Pagh, E. K.				大北电报公司	上海	1908—1933	OM
Pai, Dr. Sitsan				浙江大学	杭州	1935—1936	OM
Pain, J. C.				亚细亚火油公司	汉口	1933—1939	OM
Pak, Dr. Chunbyung					上海	1936—1940	OM
Palamountain, B.	拨拉茂旦	英国	海关人员	海关	上海	1886—1893	OM
Palevoi, S. A.				俄国邮政局	天津	1917—1923	OM
Palm, J. M.					上海	1907—1913	OM
Palmer, Capt. A. B.					上海	1936—1940	OM
Palmer, Rev. E. R.			教士			1878	RM
Palmer, W. M.	巴尔穆	美国		盐务稽核所	北京、上海、长春	1914—1929	LM

续表

英文名	中文名	国籍	身份/职业	部门	居住地点	在会时间	会员类别
Palun, L. M.					上海	1907-1910	OM
Paping, E.				法新汇报馆	上海	1916-1922	OM
Pardon, W.						1864-1866	RM
Parker, C. E.						1864	RM
Parker, E. H.	庄延龄	英国	外交官	英国领事馆	上海,镇江,广州	1877-1924	OM/HM
Parker, Rev. Dr. A. P.	潘慎文	美国	牧师	中西书院	上海	1901-1924	OM
Parkes, Harry Smith	巴夏礼	英国	外交官		上海,北京	1858-1884	HM
Parkinson, F. B.					汉口	1890-1897	OM
Parlane, L. J.				远东时报馆	上海	1912-1913	OM
Parrott, Dr. H. T.					上海	1901	OM
Parrott, E. A.					上海	1909-1911	OM
Parson, Desmond				汇丰银行	北京	1934-1946	OM/LM
Parsons, E. C.					上海	1916-1918	OM
Parsons, E. E.				大礼拜堂	上海	1916-1940	OM
Partington, T. Bowen				私立英华书院	汕头,香港	1917-1919	OM
Pasquier, G. A.				字林西报	上海	1922-1926	OM
Passikides, C. J.				工部局财务处	上海	1921-1922	OM
Paterson, A.				怡和洋行	上海,香港	1873-1874	RM
Paterson, J. J.					上海,香港	1922-1946	LM
Patersson, J. W.	巴得胜	瑞典	海关人员	海关	上海,汉口,广州	1882-1907	OM

续表

英文名	中文名	国籍	身份/职业	部门	居住地点	在会时间	会员类别
Patra, John					上海	1939-1940	OM
Patrick, Dr. H. C.					上海	1912-1940	OM
Patton, Rev. C. E.	毕嘉罗	美国	牧师	美国北长老会	上海	1924-1946	LM
Paturel, C.				笔剌洋行	上海	1894-1897	OM
Paulun, Dr. E. H.	宝隆	德国	商人/医生	宝隆洋行/宝隆医院	上海	1893-1908	OM
Payn, T.						1870-1874	RM
Payne, Mrs. Harry F.				美国钞票公司	上海	1933-1939	OM
Peake, Cyrus H., PH. D.	毕格	美国	学人	哥伦比亚大学	纽约	1940-1946	OM
Pearce, H. L.				字林西报	上海	1923-1924	OM
Pearce, Sir Ed.	庞亚士	英国	商人	老公茂洋行	上海	1923-1927	OM
Pearson, C. Dearne				上海自来水公司	上海	1908-1936	OM
Pearson, G. W.	毕尔逊	英国	外交官	英国领事馆	芜湖、上海	1908-1915	OM
Peck, Mrs. Willys R.	裴克	美国	外交官	美国领事馆	南京、重庆	1933-1940	OM
Pecorini, D.		意大利	海关人员	海关	上海	1909-1913	OM
Peek, S. H.				英商四海保险公司	上海	1933-1936	OM
Peet, Alice L.					上海	1918-1921	OM
Peet, Gilbert E.					上海	1918-1929	OM
Peffer, Nathaniel	裴斐	美国	学者	美国运通银行,大陆报	北京	1918-1946	OM
Peiyang University Liberian	图书馆	中国	图书馆	北洋大学图书馆	天津	1911-1946	LM
Pelliot, Prof. Paul	伯希和	法国	汉学家		巴黎	1901-1946	OM/HM
Penfold, F. G.				祥兴洋行	上海	1916-1946	OM

续表

英 文 名	中文名	国籍	身份/职业	部 门	居住地点	在会时间	会员类别
Penfold, Miss J. A.					上海	1914	OM
Penfold, Miss W. M.				天主教女校	上海	1939－1946	OM
Pennett, C. W.				怡和机器有限公司		1932－1940	OM
Pereira, Marques, A. F.			牙医		上海	1865－1882	HM
Perkins, H. M., D. D. S.	博金式	美国	外交官	美国领事馆	上海	1884－1893	OM
Perkins, Mahlon F.				泰隆洋行	上海	1914－1946	OM
Perkins, N. G.			学者		上海	1905－1908	OM
Perleberg, M. X.	白珠山	德国		德国领事馆	上海	1941－1946	OM
Pernazsch, Dr. Gerhard					上海	1910－1919	OM
Perrins, Mrs. K. M.				圣约翰大学	上海	1922－1924	OM
Perry, Charles E.					上海	1936－1940	OM
Perry, Dorothy R. (Mrs. L. C.)					杭州	1946－?	OM
Perry, E. W.				美国长老会	宁波	1919－1920	OM
Perry, Edgar, B, SC				美孚公司	上海	1925－1929	OM
Perry, Harold G.				南星颜料厂	上海	1932－1946	OM
Perry, L. C.			商人		上海	1946－?	OM
Perry, S. M.	潘利		海关人员			1937－1940	OM
Perry, W. W., Esq.	爱司格	英国			塞克斯郡	1883－1884	OM
Perry-Ayscough, H. G. C.				联合人寿保险公司	上海	1913－1916	OM
Persen, K. A.			教授	同济大学	上海	1935－1936	OM
Perterman, Dr. B.						1928－1934	OM

续表

英文名	中文名	国籍	身份/职业	部门	居住地点	在会时间	会员类别
Peters, H.				德国领事馆	上海	1906–1910	OM
Petersen, Julius V.				大北电报公司	上海	1894	OM
Petersen, Rev. John		丹麦		荆州神道学院	荆州	1937–1940	OM
Petersen, V.	毕特生	丹麦	电报工程师	中国电报总局	上海	1906–1936	OM
Peterson, A.	贝得胜	美国	海关人员	宝隆洋行	汉口	1913–1919	OM
Peterson, Dr. Denton E.					香港、上海、天津	1887–1901	OM
Peterson, R. A.	毕德生	美国	教士		俄亥俄州	1924–1946	OM/LM
Peterson, V. A.				大北电报公司	上海	1915–1919	OM
Petrement, A.		玻利维亚		比利时领事馆	天津	1908–1913	OM
Pettgrew, Hon. R. F.					华盛顿	1900–1908	OM
Pettus, Prof. W. B.	裴德士	美国	教士	华北协和华语学校、青年会	北京	1915–1946	LM
Pfanner, Pierre		德国		达昌洋行	上海	1935–1946	OM
Pfisher, Dr. M.	费士达	德国		北京协和医院	北京	1922–1929	OM
Phelps, Dryden L., PH. D.	费尔璞	美国	教师	华西协和大学	成都	1929–1946	LM
Phillips, E. S. J.	费笠子			美国总会	上海	1941–?	OM
Phillips, Geo.	费理伯	英国	领事人员	英国领事馆	福州	1888–1894	OM
Phillips, H.		英国	外交官	英国领事馆	哈尔滨、上海、福州、广州	1912–1929 1938–1939	OM
Phillips, Rev. L. Gordon	力戈登	英国	牧师	伦敦会	厦门	1917–1919	OM
Pichon, L., Esq., M. D.	毕顺	法国	海关人员		上海	1876–1907	OM
Pickens, Rev. C. L.	毕敬士	美国	牧师	美国圣公会	汉口	1931–1946	OM
Pickering, G.	碧格龄	英国	海关人员	雷士理船会社	北京、上海	1939–1940	OM

续表

英 文 名	中文名	国籍	身份/职业	部门	居住地点	在会时间	会员类别
Pickwoad, Edwin					上海	1860	RM
Picozzi, R.				同茂丰蛋厂公司	上海	1937-1939	OM
Piffaretti, J.				瑞士领事馆	上海	1938-1939	OM
Piry, Théophile	帛黎	法国	海关人员	海关	北京,上海,宁波	1884-1908	OM
Pitman, John.			商人		东京	1879-1885	OM
Place, Monseigneur de la					北京	1866-1878	CM
Plancy, V. Colin de		法国				1877-1923	OM/LM
Platt,Dr. B. S.		英国		雷氏德研究院	上海	1935-1940	OM
Platt, Robert		美国	教授	芝加哥大学	芝加哥	1917-1924	OM
Playfair, G. M. H.	白挨底	英国	领事人员	英国领事馆	上海	1885-1918	OM/LM/CM
Plews,Mrs. J. C.		美国	牧师		上海	1929-1936	OM
Plopper,Dr. C. H.	罗金声	美国	教士	金陵神学院,美国基督会		1940-?	OM
Plumer, James M.	濮聚玛	美国	海关人员	海关	天津,上海	1931-1946	LM
Poate, F. W.		意大利	海关人员	隆茂洋行	上海	1928-1940	OM
Poletti, P.	布列地	俄国	海关人员	海关	北京,天津	1912-1913	LM
Polevoy, S. A.	包利伟	意大利	海关人员			1917-1936	OM
Poli, G. D., Esq.	博利					1883	OM
Polk,Dr. Margaret H.	博明慧(女)	美国	教士	监理会	上海	1915-1924	OM
Pollard						1864	RM
Pollard, Robert T., M. A.	浦纳德	美国	教授	圣约翰大学	上海	1924-1936	OM
Pollock, F. A.				怡和洋行	上海	1936-1940	OM

续表

英 文 名	中文名	国籍	身份/职业	部 门	居住地点	在会时间	会员类别
Pollock, John	波乐	美国	海关人员	海关	汕头	1881－1887	OM
Pomeroy, E. C.					上海	1923－1929	OM
Porter, A. R.				联合人寿保险公司	上海	1935－1936	OM
Porter, Harold, C. M. G.	柏达	英国	外交官	汇丰银行	上海	1930－1936	OM
Porter, J. V.	巴尔特	英国	海关人员	海关	上海	1935－1946	LM
Porter, Prof. Lucius C.	博晨光	美国	教士	燕京大学,监理会	北京	1933－1946	OM
Porter, Mrs. C. W.	鲍德	英国	会计师	上海电话公司	上海	1934－1940	OM
Porterfield, W. M.	包达甫	美国	教士	圣约翰大学	上海	1920－1940	OM
Post, Nicolas				奥匈帝国领事馆	香港,上海	1897－1909	OM
Poston, D. G.				圣约翰大学	上海	1938－1940	OM
Pott, James H.	卜其吉	美国	教士	圣约翰大学,圣公会	上海	1935－1936	OM
Pott, Rev. Dr. F. L. Hawks	卜舫济	美国	教士	圣约翰大学,圣公会	上海	1894－1940	OM/HM
Pott, W. S. A.	卜惠廉	美国	教士	圣约翰大学,圣公会	上海	1914－1929	OM
Potter, J. S.				美商上海地产公司	上海	1941－1946	OM
Pottinger, T. P.				公裕太阳火险公司	上海	1938－1948	OM
Poullain, H. V.				邮政总局	上海	1933－1934	OM
Poulsen, H. S.				大北电话公司	上海	1935－1946	OM
Pousty, F. E.					宁波	1915－1933	OM
Powell, J. B.	鲍维尔	美国	报人	密勒氏评论报	上海	1918－1940	OM
Pratt, F. L.	波兰脱	澳大利亚	报人	公论报有限公司	上海	1935－1940	OM
Pratt, J. T.	布辣德	英国	外交官	英国领事馆	南京,济南	1909－1936	OM

续表

英 文 名	中文名	国籍	身份/职业	部门	居住地点	在会时间	会员类别
Pratt, R. S.	布理嘉	英国	外交官	英国领事馆	厦门,天津	1921-1924	OM
Prejevalsky, Col. N.		俄国	军人		圣彼得堡	1880-1888	HM
Prentice, John	普恩济士	英国	工程师	和记洋行	上海	1885-1924	OM
Preuss, Dr. J.					上海	1939-1946	OM
Price, Dr. M. T.		美国	教授	芝加哥大学	芝加哥	1925-1936	OM
Price, G. U.					厦门	1886-1894	OM
Price, Mrs. Maurice			教授	大正洋行	上海	1919-1924	OM
Price, W. D. M.				芝加哥大学	上海	1931-1933	OM
Prideaux-Brune, H. I.	樟德本	英国	外交官	英国领事馆	北京,南京,昆明,上海	1914-1940	OM
Primrose, J. A.		丹麦	学界			1866	RM
Prip-MÖller, J., F. I. A	艾术华			教士公所	上海	1929-1946	OM
Pripp, J. H.				外交部	斯德哥尔摩	1946-?	OM
Probst, W.	普罗斯德	德国	董事	工部局董事会		1864-1870	RM
Provand, A.						1870-1873	RM
Pryer, W. B.	朴贲懿			亚洲文会博物馆	上海	1868-1877	RM
Public Library of Newark, The	图书馆		机构	纽瓦克公共图书馆	新泽西	1924-1946	OM
Puckle, Mrs. B.					上海	1938-1939	OM
Puckle, Raymond D. A.					上海	1932-1940	OM
Pugh, Ellis.					上海	1911-1913	OM
Pumpelly, Raphael	彭北莱	美国				1866-1875	CM
Purdon, J. G.	白敦	美国	董事	工部局董事会		1869-1877	RM

续表

英 文 名	中文名	国籍	身份/职业	部 门	居 住 地 点	在会时间	会员类别
Pure, Alfred				马来亚政府		1946-?	OM
Pure, Jacob					上海	1939-1940	OM
Putnam, Dr. Herbert				美国国会图书馆	华盛顿	1908-1946	HM
Pye, Rev. Watts, O.	裴太太(女)	美国	牧师	监理会	汾州	1917-1924	LM
Pyke, Rev. Frederick M	白辅德	美国	牧师	美以美会	泰安	1924-1929	OM
Pym, E. T.	斌尔钦	英国	海关人员	海关	台南、烟台	1885-1892	OM
Quien, F. C.					北京、上海	1913-1924	OM
Quigley, Prof. H. S.	桂克礼	美国	教授	明尼苏达大学政治学系	明尼苏达	1923-1928	OM
Quin, Mrs. J.					上海	1916-1924	OM
Quong, Miss Rose	邝如丝(女)				伦敦	1936-1940	OM
Qwen, Rev. G. S.		英国		伦敦会	北京	1872-1888	OM
Raasch, C., Esq.						1882	OM
Raaschou, T.	乐斯考	丹麦	外交官	丹麦领事馆	上海	1912-1924	OM
Radowitz, M. le Baron von						1864-1866	RM
Raeburn, D. J.			海关人员	海关	上海	1916-1946	OM
Rakusen, Dr. C. P.				晶光眼镜公司	上海	1935-1940	OM
Ramsay, H. F.	拉木塞	英国	商人/外交官	瑞典驻汉口领事馆(兼任领事)	汉口	1881-1888	OM
Ramondino, F.	蓝梦亭	意大利	外交官	意大利大使馆	上海、北京	1922-1936	OM
Rankin, C. W.	兰金	美国	教士	监理会	上海	1915-1924	OM
Rappenecker, Dr. K.					上海	1914-1916	OM
Rasschon, T.				丹麦领事馆		1912-1913	OM

续表

英 文 名	中文名	国籍	身份/职业	部门	居住地点	在会时间	会员类别
Rathsam, Th.	蓝德山	德国	外交官	德国领事馆	广州,上海	1887—1894	OM
Rathvon, N. Peter					上海	1916—1917	OM
Raven, F. J.				普益银公司	上海	1933—1935	OM
Raven, Mrs. F. J.				普益银公司	上海	1933—1936	OM
Ravens, T. Bu"low von				海关	上海	1903—1917	OM
Rayner, Charles			商人	礼和洋行,致富栈房	上海	1886—1908	OM
Rayner, S.				华童公学		1912—1917	LM
Rea, Geo. Bronson	李亚	美国	工程师兼报人	远东时报馆	上海	1931—1936	OM
Read, Dr. Bernard E.	伊博恩	英国		雷氏德研究院	上海	1933—1946	OM
Read, H. H.				上海总会	上海	1933—1940	OM
Reding, J. E.	聂鼎	俄国	外交官			1869—1878	RM
Reeks, A. J.	李格斯	英国	海关人员			1882	OM
Rees, Alwyn H. H.				亚细亚火油公司	上海	1917—1920	OM
Rees, C. A.						1870—1877	RM
Rees, Claude A.				公和洋行	上海	1889—1892	OM
Rees, Rev. Dr. W. Hopkyn	瑞思义	英国	教士	广学会	上海,伦敦	1914—1924	OM
Reeves, Capt. J. H.	黎富思	美国	外交官	美国领事馆	北京	1910—1916	OM
Reichelt Rev. K. L.	艾香德	挪威	牧师	东亚基督教道友会	上海	1928—1930	OM
Reid, A. G., M. D.	立德	英国	医生	海关		1857—1877	NRM
Reid, David	李大卫	英国	工部局董事	履泰洋行,工部局	上海	1868—1882	OM

续表

英 文 名	中文名	国 籍	身份/职业	部 门	居 住 地 点	在会时间	会员类别
Reid, M. C.				柯达公司	上海	1939—1946	OM
Reid, Miss S. H.	魏撒拉(女)		教士	圣约翰大学、圣公会	上海	1925—1936	OM
Reid, Rev, Dr. Giblbert	李佳白	美国	教士	尚贤堂	上海	1907—1919	OM
Reid, Robt.						1866	NRM
Reifler, Dr. E.			医师/博士	震旦大学	上海	1939—1946	OM
Reifsnyder, Dr. Elizaeth	罗医生(女)	美国	教士	妇孺医院 美以美会	上海	1913—1917	OM
Reinsch, Dr. Paul	芮恩施	美国	外交官	美国公使馆	北京	1914—1922	OM
Reinsdorf, F.	赉恩斯德	德国	外交官	德国领事馆	北京、广州、台湾	1883—1908	OM
Reiss, E. O.	艾瑞时	德国		海关	北京	1906—1936	OM
Reiss, Dr. F.		美国			上海	1923—1946	OM
Reiss, Mrs. A.					上海	1921—1924	OM
Reme, W.	雷美	英国	工部局	工部局董事会		1864—1875	RM
Remer, C. F.	林茂	美国	教授	圣约翰大学	上海、广州	1913—1916	OM
Remusat, J. L.	勒慕萨	法国	海关人员	海关	广州	1885—1912	OM
Rennell, T. B.	连勒	美国	海关人员			1864—1877	NRM
Rennie, Sir Richard T.		英国	法官	高等法院	上海	1885—1887	OM
Reynolds, F. A.	连那士	英国	商人			1865—1877	RM
Rhein, J.	来因	荷兰	领事人员	荷兰领事馆	北京	1877—1888	OM
Rich, Capt. W. W.			军人		上海	1900—1901	OM
Richard, Rev. Timothy	李提摩太	英国	教士	广学会	上海	1894—1918	CM/HM
Richardson, J. W.	李家森	英国	海关人员	海关	北京、上海九江、镇江	1889—1913	OM
Richert, G.		瑞典		黄埔运输公司	上海	1919—1924	OM

续表

英 文 名	中文名	国籍	身份/职业	部 门	居 住 地 点	在会时间	会员类别
Richthofen, Baron Ferdinand von	李希霍芬	德国	地质学家	莱比锡大学	莱比锡	1880－1897	HM
Ridge, W. Sheldon		英国	报人	中国公论西报馆	上海	1904－1908 1912－1918	OM
Rietveld,Miss H.	李洽		教士	中华基督教育年会	烟台	1925－1928	OM
Ringer, B.S., M.D.	花夏莲(女)	英国	医师		厦门	1885－1886	OM
Rinkel, Ferd	凌尔	英国		德华银行	纽约	1890－1894	OM
Ripley, Mrs. Geo.				艺术博物馆	上海	1910	OM
Rispaud,Capt. J.H.J.			海关/邮政	邮政	南京,上海,哈尔滨,成都	1933－1934	OM
Ritchie, W. W.	李齐	英国	经理	里虹口旗昌缫丝局	上海	1907－1936	OM
Riva, Achille			商人兼报人			1885－1888	OM
Rivington, C.	李闻登	英国				1873－1883	OM
Roberson, J. Barr			商人	比国银公司	上海	1868－1870	RM
Robert, A.	罗伯		教士	圣约翰大学,圣公会	上海	1930－1946	OM
Roberts,Prof. Donald	罗道纳	美国		洋行	上海	1916－1946	OM/LM
Roberts, I. E.			教师	圣约翰大学	上海	1932	LM
Roberts,Mrs. F. M.			牧师	圣约翰大学	上海	1935－1946	LM
Roberts, Rt. Rev. W. P.	罗德培	美国		工部局	上海	1939－1946	OM
Roberts, W. J.			领事人员	英国领事馆		1924	CM
Robertson, Barr J.				纽约时报办事处	上海	1873－1875	HM
Robertson, D. B.	罗伯孙	英国		雷氏德研究院,香港大学	上海	1859－1880	OM
Robertson, Douglas					上海	1933－1935	OM
Robertson,Dr. R. C.					上海,香港	1933－1940	OM

续表

英文名	中文名	国籍	身份/职业	部门	居住地点	在会时间	会员类别
Robertson, E. S.		英国			萨里郡	1932－1936	OM
Robertson, J.				纽约时报办事处	上海	1933	OM
Robinson, A.						1865－1873	RM
Robinson, E., Esq.						1883	OM
Robinson, F. Alan	罗宾生			大英按察使司衙门	上海	1914－1919	OM
Robinson, Mrs. F. A.	罗宾生夫人					1918－1919	OM
Robinson, Prof. Henry H.			教授		武昌	1890－1897	OM
Robson, G.						1864	RM
Roche, Mr. E.						1858	CM
Rocher, Emile	弥乐石	法国	领事人员		上海、厦门	1877－1894	OM
Rocher, Louis	雷乐石	法国	海关人员	海关	广州、上海、汉口	1884－1910	OM/LM
Rochlin, Miss Cecillia			博物学家		上海	1941－？	OM
Rock, Dr. Joseph F.	洛克	美国			昆明	1933－1940	OM
Rockhill, Hon. W. W.	柔克义	美国	外交官	美国领事馆	北京	1885－1913	OM/HM
Rodert, M. N.					上海	1866－1874	CM
Rodgers, J. M.				浸信会联合会	上海	1918 1924－1936	OM
Roe, F. H.				亚广有限公司	上海	1935－1936	OM
Roecheisen, Dr. H.				矮克发洋行	上海	1935－1936	OM
Rohl, E.						1873－1874	RM
Röhreke, H.					上海	1935－1936	OM

续表

英 文 名	中文名	国 籍	身份/职业	部 门	居 住 地 点	在会时间	会员类别
Rondot, M.						1858	CM
Rondot, Natalis		法国		里昂商会	里昂	1864–1908	CM
Roots, Bishop L. H.	吴德施	美国	教士	大美圣公会	汉口	1916–1940	OM
Ross, Cav. G.	罗斯	意大利		意大利领事馆	广州,上海,汉口	1908–1924 1931–1946	OM/LM
Rose, Archibald, C. I. E.	娄斯	英国	外交官	英国领事馆	上海,北京,腾越	1901 1908–1920	OM
Rosenbaum, S.	罗心本	奥地利	海关人员	海关	镇江	1896–1901	OM
Rosenberg, Paul				欧美旅行社	上海	1946–?	OM
Rosenthal, A. E.					伦敦	1869–1873	RM
Ross, A.	罗辛甫	英国	海关人员	汇丰银行	上海	1910–1913	OM
Rossi, Comm. G. de		意大利	外交官	意大利领事馆	上海	1920–1924	OM
Rössler, Dr. W.	乐斯喇	德国	外交官	德国领事馆	广州,上海	1904–1913	OM
Rost, S.					上海	1913–1916	OM
Rosthorn, A. Edler von	罗士恒	奥地利	海关人员/领事	海关,奥匈帝国领事馆	上海,北京	1888–1909	OM
Rosthorn, De Arthur von						1888–? 1940–1946	HM
Rotours, Robert des	戴侯社	法国	汉学家		塞纳	1933–1946	OM/LM
Roulston, Rev. W. A.	任鸿道	加拿大		加拿大联合会	卫辉	1931–1940	OM
Roundy, Prof.						1865–1866	RM
Rouse, Rollar C. P.	劳士诗	英国	海关人员	海关	昆明	1939–1940	OM
Rowbotham, A. H.	罗博登	美国	教授	清华大学	北京	1920–1924	OM
Rowe, E. S. B.		英国		工部局	上海	1907–1940	OM/LM

473

续表

英 文 名	中文名	国籍	身份/职业	部门	居住地点	在会时间	会员类别
Rowe, H. B.				工部局	上海	1907－1908	OM
Rowe, O. S. Benbow				上海总会，上海股票交易所	上海	1933－1940	LM
Roy, M.				义品放款银行	汉口	1925－1929	OM
Ruberg, Waldemar			商人	大北电报公司	上海	1884－1885	OM
Rucker, H. von.				兴华公司	上海	1886－1887	OM
Ruegg, E., Esq.						1878－1883	OM
Ruffé, M. D'Auxion de					上海	1930－1939	OM
Ruhstrat, Ernst				海关	镇江，上海	1886－1893	OM
Rummel, J. K.				上海电力公司	上海	1940－1946	OM
Russell, Miss Maud	陆慕德(女)	美国		基督教青年会	上海	1935－1946	LM
Russell, Robert R.				上海电力公司	上海	1939－1940	OM
Russell, Sir Jas., C. M. G.	陆思尔	英国	海关人员		香港	1870－1892	OM
Russell, The Hon. James.			法官		香港	1870－1885	OM
Russell, W. B.	劳德	英国	海关人员	海关	福州	1886－1888	OM
Russell, W. M.						1936－1940	OM
Ruxton, Lt. Col. R. M. C.				盐务稽核所	上海	1934－1940	OM
Rydberg, A. G.	吏克圣	瑞典		瑞典行道会	汉口	1939－1940	OM
Ryrie, The Hon. Phineas.					香港	1878－1882	NRM
Sabelstrom, G. B.				上海啤酒公司	上海	1932－1936	OM
Sadoine, Baron A.		英国		海关	汉口	1922－1929	OM
Sadwin, Mrs. A.					上海	1935－1940	OM

续表

英 文 名	中文名	国籍	身份/职业	部　门	居 住 地 点	在会时间	会员类别
Saedon, E. W.					伯明翰	1916/1935	OM
Saeki, Dr. P. Y.		日本			东京	1931-1946	LM
Sahara, T.	佐原笃介	日本	报人	文汇报、盛京时报	上海、沈阳	1908-1932	OM/LM
Saint-Hubert, G. de Capt.				义品放款银行、陇海铁路	天津、郑州	1922-1929	OM
Sakamoto, Prof. Y.		日本	教授	东亚同文书院	上海	1927-1936	OM
Salter, G. H. C. Esq.	索乐德	美国	外交官			1865	OM
Sammons, Hon. T.	萨门司	美国	外交官	美国领事馆	上海	1915-1924	OM
Sampaio, Lieut. M. C.					巴洛达	1866-1877	CM
Sampatrao, H. H. the Prince		印度	王子			1893-1940	HM
Sampson, T.	三顺	英国	校长	粤省同文馆	广州、上海	1864-1897	OM
Samson, J.			商人	履泰洋行	上海	1877-1901	OM
Samwer, Ernst				德国领事馆	天津	1886-1888	OM
Sander, H.				普益地产公司	上海	1922-1938	OM
Sanders, Arthur H.				普爱会	荼陵	1917-1924	OM
Sanger, F. J.				雷氏德研究院	上海	1936-1940	OM
Santelli, Dr. R.		加拿大		齐鲁大学	济南、成都	1934-1946	LM
Sargent, Clyde B.						1936-1940	OM
Sargent, G. T.				慎昌洋行	上海	1917-1924	OM
Sarkar, Prof. B. K.			教授		加尔各答	1915-1929	LM
Sassoon, Chaeles						1869-1877	RM
Sassoon, E. A.						1878	RM
Sassoon, Jacob.						1869-1877	RM

续表

英 文 名	中文名	国籍	身份/职业	部 门	居住地点	在会时间	会员类别
Sassoon, Sir Victor				沙逊洋行	上海	1935-1946	LM
Sator, G.					上海	1935-1940	OM
Satow, Sir Ernest	萨道义	英国	外交官		德文郡	1906-1929	HM
Saunders, W.			摄影师		上海	1865-1888	OM
Saunders, W. A.			教士	内地会	清水	1936-1940	OM
Sawdon, E. W.				广益书院、华西协和大学	重庆、成都	1916-1936	OM
Sayer, G. Button.			记者	字林西报	上海	1908-1917	OM
Scanlon, T. R.				美国葡萄公司	上海	1937-1940	OM
Schab, Dr. von	福沙伯	德国	海关人员		上海	1901-1920	OM
Schaeffer, S.				大北电报公司	上海	1913-1918	OM
Schendel, G. van				比利时领事馆	上海	1910-1911	OM
Schereschewsky, Right Rev. S. I. J.	施约瑟	美国	牧师	美国圣公会	上海、纽约	1860-1906	OM/HM
Scherzer, F.	师克勤	法国	领事人员		上海	1881-1885	OM
Schilling, E. J.				大通银行	天津	1936-1940	OM
Schindler, Dr. A. K.	师谋	德国	外交官	德国领事馆	上海	1907-1910	OM
Schirmer, Kurt				海关	上海	1903-1918	OM
Schjøth, Fr.	奈德	挪威	海关人员	德国领事馆	镇江、宁波、重庆	1885-1910	OM
Schlettwein, Ulrich	施利克	奥匈帝国	外交官		上海	1911-1915	OM
Schlik, R.				礼和洋行		1873-1877	RM
Schmacker, B.					上海	1887-1894	OM
Schmidt, C., Esq.			教士			1878-1883	OM

续表

英 文 名	中文名	国籍	身份/职业	部门	居住地点	在会时间	会员类别
Schmidt, E.					天津	1859－1864	RM
Schmidt, Ernest J.				大通银行	上海、青岛	1941－1946	OM
Schmidt, K.				礼和洋行	上海	1888－1919	OM
Schmitz, G. H.		美国		有利洋行	上海	1936－1940	OM
Schneider, Sister M.					上海	1930－1936	OM
Schoch, J. E.		瑞士		达昌洋行	唐山	1924－1946	LM
Schoder, H.				启新水泥厂	马尼拉	1916/1920	OM
Scholey, Mrs. G. A. Jr.					海口	1935－1946	LM
Schomburg, A.	森宝		商人		柏林	1894－1897	OM
Schott, Prof. Wilhelm	许德	德国	东方学家		青岛	1887－1888	HM
Schraimer, Dr.				德国领事馆		1895－1910	OM
Schregardus, N. H.	崔楷德	荷兰	海关人员	海关	上海、蒙自	1900－1909	OM
Schroder, A.			药商/药剂师	咸同贞药房	上海	1885－1888	OM
Schröder, H.				启新水泥厂	唐山	1916－1919	OM
Schubert, Paul von				爱礼司洋行	上海	1939－1940	OM
Schüler, Pastor W.				德国教堂	上海	1911－1913	OM
Schultz, Capt. C. A.			领航员	大北电报公司	上海、天津	1877－1885	OM
Schulze, F. W.				海关	烟台、上海	1879－1888	OM
Schuurman, T. E.				荷兰领事馆	上海	1930－1933	OM
Schwabe, E.				泰和洋行	上海	1909－1916	OM
Schwarz, Kurt L.					加利福尼亚	1946－?	OM

续表

英文名	中文名	国籍	身份/职业	部门	居住地点	在会时间	会员类别
Schwarzl, M. G.				颐中烟草股份有限公司会计部	上海	1929－1946	OM/LM
Schwemann, D. W.			商人	禅臣洋行	上海	1885	OM
Schwerz, Ernest J.						1940－?	OM
Schwyzer, F.	施惠瑞		副总董	法董局	上海	1932－1936	OM
Scott, Archibald	萨允格	英国	领事人员	工部局	上海	1908－1909	OM
Scott, James				英国领事馆	广州、上海	1893－1909	OM
Scott, W.				波莫纳学院	加利福尼亚	1930－1946	LM
Scranton, W. B.					大连	1916－1917	OM
Seaman, John F.	希孟	美国	商人		上海	1908－1913	OM
Seckendorff, Baron Edm. von		德国	外交官	德国领事馆	天津、汕头、上海	1880－1901	OM
Secker, F.				爱礼司洋行	上海、北京	1930－1946	LM
Seco, R.	色固	西班牙	外交官	西班牙领事馆	上海	1906－1910	OM
Segalen, Dr. Victor		法国			上海	1917－1922	LM
Segalen, Y. V.				东方汇理银行	上海	1939－1940	OM
Seguela, R.	萨桂乐		盐务	盐务稽核所	宜昌	1937－1940	OM
Seigne, J. W.					上海	1913－1916	OM
Selke, O.				璧恒公司	上海	1910－1913	OM
Sell, Rev. Ralph. PH.D				私立信义初级中学	即墨	1940－?	OM
Senger,Miss Nettie M.	宋恩乐(女)	美国		美国友爱会	忻口、天津、北京	1923－1946	OM/LM
Service, John S.	谢伟思	美国	外交官	美国领事馆	上海	1939－1940	OM

续表

英 文 名	中文名	国籍	身份/职业	部门	居住地点	任会时间	会员类别
Service, R. Roy	谢安道	美国	教士	基督教青年会	上海	1924–1935	OM
Seward, G. F.	西华	美国	外交官			1864–1888	RM/HM
Shackleton, Rev. A.			牧师	崇祯堂	汉阳	1939–1940	OM
Shadwell, C.B., R. N.		英国	船长			1858–1884	HM
Shahmoon, A. E.					上海	1935–1936	OM
Shahmoon, Erza					上海	1931–1946	OM
Shang, S. Y.						1937	OM
Shanghai American School, Princial	学校	中国	机构	沪美学堂	上海	1929–1933	OM
Shangtung Christian University	大学	中国	机构	山东齐鲁大学	济南	1922–1932	OM
Shao, Dr. C. L.	邵家麟	中国		光华大学	上海	1939–1940	OM
Shaw, Norman	奈瑞瑞	英国	海关人员	中国海关	北京,上海,广州,香港	1912–1946	OM/LM
Shearer, G.						1873–1876	NRM
Shearstone, T. W.	薛士冕	英国	商人		上海	1918–1924	OM
Shelton, Dr. A. L.	史德文	美国	教士	美国基督会	巴塘	1918–1922	LM
Shen, C. P.				柯达公司	上海	1939–1946	OM
Shen, Wesley				基督教青年会	上海	1930–1934	OM
Sheng, E. Y. E.	盛恩颐	中国	工商界	汉冶萍公司	上海	1937–1946	OM
Sheng, S. Y.						1937–1940	OM
Shengle, J. C.	沈格理	英国	商人	江苏麻药厂	上海	1905–1929	OM
Sheppard, Rev. G. W.	牧作霖	英国	牧师	大英圣书公会	上海	1923–1936	OM

续表

英文名	中文名	国籍	身份/职业	部门	居住地点	在会时间	会员类别
Sherriff, Dr. Florence Mrs. A. W.			学者	沪江大学	上海	1936–1940	OM
Sheveleff, M. G.					海参崴	1891–1901	OM
Shields, E. T.			教士	美国圣公会	雅口（四川）	1913–1916	OM
Shields, Leighton				大美国按察使衙门	上海	1940–?	OM
Shimoda, U.				南满铁路株式会社	上海	1936	OM
Shin, K. K., M. A.						1933–1934	OM
Shinagawa, E., Esq.			领事人员		上海	1879–1885	OM
Shinjo, Dr. Shinzo		日本	研究员	上海自然科学研究所	上海	1935–1936	OM
Shioya, T.		日本		日本朝鲜银行	上海、青岛	1922–1946	OM
Shipley, J. A. G.		美国			上海	1911–1924	OM
Shipway, G. W.					上海	1924–1929	OM
Shirokogoroff, S. M.	史禄国	俄国	人类学家	清华大学、厦门大学	北京、厦门、广州	1923–1939	OM
Shneider, A.					上海	1936–1940	OM
Shrimpton, E. R. G.					上海	1936	OM
Shriro, J. A.				石利洛洋行	上海	1935–1946	OM
Shu, Dr. H. J.				海关	汉口、九龙	1921–1940	RM
Sibbald, F. C.	席福	英国	海关人员			1857–1870	NRM
Sidford, H. E.						1864–1875	OM
Siebold, L.	喜博德	德国	海关人员	海关	北京	1903–1908	OM
Siegel, H. W.				孔士洋行	汉口	1932–1940	OM
Silloway, Miss M. E.				上海语言学校	上海	1940–?	OM

续表

英 文 名	中文名	国 籍	身份/职业	部 门	居 住 地 点	在会时间	会员类别
Silsby, Rev. J. A.	薛思培	美国	牧师	南长老会	上海	1911–1933	OM
Silveira, A. da						1866–1875	RM
Sim, Alexander, Lieut. F. d					英格兰	1866–1880	CM
Sim, Alexander, Esq.			领事人员		英格兰	1878–1882	RM
Simon, G. E.	西蒙	法国	领事人员			1860–1873	CM
Simpson, Cecil					伦敦	1907–1912	OM
Simpson, B. Lenox	辛博森	英国	海关人员		北京	1907–1930	OM
Sinclair, Gregg, M.		瑞典		夏威夷大学	火奴鲁鲁	1937–1940	OM
Siren, Prof. O.	喜仁龙	瑞典	美术史家	国家博物馆	斯德哥尔摩	1922–1940	OM/LM
Sites, F. R.				美国钢铁公司	上海	1916–1924	OM
Sites, Prof. C. M L, PH. D.		美国	教授	南洋公学	上海	1899–1908	OM
Six, Rev. Ray L.	陆睿		牧师		庐州	1924–1934	OM
Sjoholm, Rev. Gunnas A.			牧师	湘北瑞华信义会	益阳	1936–1940	OM
Skatschkoff, his Ex. C. A.	孔琪庭	俄国	外交官		圣彼得堡	1878	NRM
Skatschkoff, J. E.						1876–1877	RM
Skinner, Dr. A. H.		美国	教士	晋隆洋行	汉口	1919–1936	OM
Skinner, T. V. S.	徐君礼(女)				上海	1935–1940	OM
Skold, Sam	韩德霖	瑞典	教士	瑞典行道会	汉口、上海	1939–1940	OM
Skottowe, A. B.				大东电报公司	上海	1912–1915	OM
Skvortzov, B. W.		俄国		海关	哈尔滨	1918–1936	OM
Skyrme, Commdr. F. H. E.				怡和洋行	上海	1936–1940	OM

续表

英 文 名	中文名	国 籍	身份/职业	部 门	居 住 地 点	在会时间	会员类别
Slevogt, M.			商人		上海	1879－1885	OM
Sly, H. E.	斯来	英国	外交官	英国领事馆	上海	1900－1915	OM
Smallbones, J. A.				工部局电力处	上海	1913－1929	OM
Smart, J. D.				汇丰银行	马尼拉	1910－1913	OM
Smit, A. H.	施美德	美国	教士	归正基督教会	如皋	1939－1940	LM
Smith, A. E.				大英医院药房有限公司	上海	1913－1918	OM
Smith, D. H.	施扶华	英国	教士	圣道公会	天津	1935－1936	OM
Smith, Dr. A. Guy					上海	1910－1912	OM
Smith, Dr. H.	司美福	美国			万县	1922－1924	OM
Smith, Ernest K	施美士	美国	教授	燕京大学英语系	北京	1933－1940	OM
Smith, J. Langford	施密士	英国	外交官	英国领事馆	杭州、宜昌	1908－1934	OM
Smith, Miss Viola				美国领事馆	上海	1935－1936	OM
Smith, R. G.					上海	1910－1911	OM
Smith, T. G.						1873－1878	RM
Smith, The Hon Cecil C.					新加坡	1870－1883	OM
Smothers, Frank					上海	1934－1936	OM
Smyth, Rev. Geo. B.	施美志	美国	牧师	美以美会	伯克利	1907－1911	OM
Snethlage, H.			商人	海关	上海	1885－1901	OM
Snuggs, Harold H.	时俊光	美国	教士	美国南浸信会		1941－?	OM
Sokobin, Samuel	索克斌	美国	外交官	美国领事馆	青岛	1934－1940	OM
Sokoisky, Geo. E.		美国			上海	1924－1936	OM

附录:皇家亚洲文会北华支会研究

续表

英 文 名	中文名	国 籍	身份/职业	部　门	居 住 地 点	在会时间	会员类别
Solbe, E.						1865	OM
Solie, E.						1866	NRM
Solly, W. J.				英国邮局		1912–1913	OM
Sommarström, Rev. J.	夏定川	瑞典	教士	瑞华会	武昌	1939–1940	OM
Soong, Dr. T. F.				上海商业储蓄银行	上海	1935–1936	OM
Soothill, Prof. W. E.	苏慧廉	英国	教士		牛津	1911–1913 1927–1934	OM
Sophokloff, G. A.				中东铁路公司	哈尔滨	1915–1920	OM
Sorensen, J. Ibsen				大北电报公司	上海	1908–1912	OM
Sorge, Dr. Richard					上海	1930–1934	OM
Soul, G. S.					上海	1860	RM
Souter, Wm. E.	苏育德	英国	教士	华洋义赈会、圣经会	上海	1925–1932	OM
South Manchuria Railway Library	图书馆	中国	机构	南满铁路图书馆	大连	1910–1940	LM
Southcott, Mrs. V. C.				汇丰银行	北京、上海、威海卫	1919–1940	OM
Southey, Major R.		英国	海关人员	海关	上海	1900–1901	OM
Southey, T. S.	邵提	英国	博物学家	中国科学美术杂志社	上海、厦门	1880–1909	OM
Sowerby, A. de C.	苏阿德	英国			上海、天津	1893 1916–1946	OM/HM
Sowerby, Mrs. Clarice S.					上海	1939–1940	OM
Sparke, C. E.	司派克	英国	商人	司派克保险公司	上海	1932–1940	OM
Speelmen, M.	施佩仁	荷兰	商人	万国储蓄会	上海	1935–1940	LM

续表

英 文 名	中文名	国籍	身份/职业	部门	居住地点	在会时间	会员类别
Speicher, Rev. Dr. J.	施雅各	美国	教士		广州	1916	OM
Spencer, Joseph E.		美国		盐务稽核所	汉口	1932–1940	OM
Speyer, C. S.				公司	上海	1933–1935	OM
Spiegler, M.					上海	1936–1946	OM
Spiker, Clarence, J.	思派克	美国	外交官	美国领事馆	北京、上海、汕头、汉口	1918–1940	OM
Spillwanek, Ivan	司皮礼瓦尼克	苏联	外交官	苏联领事馆	上海	1936–1940	OM
Spinney, W. F.	司必立	美国	海关人员	海关	广州、上海	1885–1897	OM
Squires, R. W.	施贵亚	英国	商人	时评洋行	上海	1935–1936	OM
Sprouse, Phillp. D.	石博思	美国		美国领事馆	汉口	1941–?	OM
St. Croix, F. A. de		英国		保顺洋行	上海	1893–1920	OM
Staheyeff, Miss T.					上海	1921–1924	OM
Standford University Library	图书馆	美国	机构	斯坦福大学图书馆	加利福尼亚	1922–1946	OM/LM/HM
Stanley, Dr. A.	史笪来	英国		工部局	上海	1905–1930	OM
Stanton, Edwin F.	司丹敦	美国	外交官	美国领事馆	上海	1939–1940	OM
Stanton, Mrs. E. F.	司丹敦太太				上海	1939–1940	OM
Stapleton-Cotton, W. V.				邮政董事会	北京	1906–1929	OM
Starkey, E.	星灵	英国	教士	长老会	香港、上海	1906–1910	OM
Starkey, Reg. D., Esq.			牧师		上海	1877–1885	OM
Starling, S. B.	司波伦	英国		隆茂洋行	重庆	1923–1929	OM
Startseff, A. D.	四达柞福	俄国	商人	顺丰洋行	天津	1889–1897	OM
Stedeford, E. T. A., Dr.	施福德	英国		白累德医院	温州	1919–1946	OM/LM

续表

英 文 名	中文名	国 籍	身份/职业	部 门	居 住 地 点	在会时间	会员类别
Steen, O. G.	司坦	美国	商人	大来洋行	上海	1936—1946	OM
Stein, E.	师德音	俄国	外交官	俄国领事馆	天津	1894—1901	OM
Stent, G. C. , Esq.	司登得	英国	海关人员		上海	1875—1883	OM
Stepanov, Simeon T.	施德乐	俄国	海关人员	海关	厦门	1897—1913	OM
Stepharius, C.	史滴法	德国	商人		上海	1885—1888	OM
Stephen, Alex. G.				汇丰银行	上海	1911—1919	OM
Stephenson, K. G.	司蒂文	美国	商人	老公茂洋行	上海	1938—1939	OM
Stephenson, Lieut. Chas. , U. S. A.				美国妇婴医院	汉口	1922—1924	OM
Stephenson-Jellie, J. W.	泽礼	英国	海关人员	海关	天津,九龙	1909—1913	OM
Steptoe, H. N.	司特图	英国	外交官	英国领事馆	北京,上海	1920—1929	OM
Stevens, Jno. , D. D. , D. LIT.	史梯文	美国	商人		上海	1885—1897	OM
Stevenson, Spencer B.				洋行	上海	1917—1920	OM
Stewart, K. D.				元芳洋行	上海	1911—1920	OM/LM
Stewart, Rev. J. L.	杜荣昌	加拿大	教士	华西协和大学	成都	1916—1946	OM
Stewart, Rev. H. B.			牧师	伦敦会		1911—1913	OM
Stewart, Wm. H.				汇丰银行	上海	1936—1939	OM
Stiner, S. Ch.				瑞士领事馆	上海	1939—1940	OM
Stocker, E. C.					上海	1921—1924	OM
Stockton, G. C.				美国学堂	上海	1914—1934	OM
Stockwell, R. K.				通用电器有限公司	上海	1935—1940	OM
Stone,Mrs. E. S.		美国			上海	1928—1933	OM

续表

英 文 名	中文名	国籍	身份/职业	部 门	居 住 地 点	在会时间	会员类别
Stonehouse, Rev. John	石牧师		牧师	伦敦会	北京	1886－1888	OM
Stops, Miss L.				美敦洋行	上海	1925－1929	OM
Storfer, A. J.					上海	1939－1940	OM
Stout, A.						1864	RM
Stranack, M. W.				晋隆洋行	上海	1935－1936	OM
Strauss, Samuel W.					上海	1923－1924	OM
Strehlneck, E. A.	史德匿	俄国	海关/古玩	史德匿古玩行	上海	1909 1912－1940	OM/LM
Strehlneek, M. W.					上海	1935－1936	Ljgm
Streib, U.				裕兴洋行	上海	1914－1920	OM
Streich, K. A., Esq.					北京	1881	NRM
Streich, K. L.			翻译	德国领事馆	上海,汕头	1880－1901	OM
Strewe, M. Y.				大德国新闻纸馆	上海	1913－1916	OM
Stripling, A. B.			海关专员		仁川	1877－1901	OM
Struthers, John				华英饭店	上海	1930－1934	OM
Stuart, Geo. A., M.D.	师图尔	美国		美以美会	南京,上海	1897－1910	OM
Stuebel, Dr. Med. H.				同济大学	昆明	1937－1940	OM
Stuhlmann, C. C.	施德明	德国	海关人员		福州	1873－1881	NRM
Sturdevant, Mrs. E. W.					上海	1934	OM
Stursberg, W. A.	司达柏	英国	海关人员		南京,开封	1919－1939	OM
Styan, F. W.			商人	安达生洋行	上海	1884－1901	OM
Suga,Capt. T.		日本			上海	1919－1946	LM

续表

英 文 名	中文名	国籍	身份/职业	部 门	居 住 地 点	在会时间	会员类别
Sullivan, W. T.		美国		美亚保险公司	上海	1939–1940	OM
Sultz, Miss F.					上海	1930	OM
Summerfield, J. A.		美国	商人	美华地产公司	上海	1935–1936	OM
Summerskill, Miss E. R.				上海外国育婴所	上海	1921–1927	OM
Sun, Mrs. J. H.	沈怀仁	中国	工商界		上海	1930–1936	OM
Sung, Prof. William Z. L.	沈嗣良	中国	教授	圣约翰大学	上海	1933–1940	OM
Suter, Hugo	许德			德华银行	上海	1909–1913	OM
Sutherland, H.	沙道兰	英国	海关人员	公昌洋行	福州	1876–1901	OM
Sutherland, T.						1865–1870	NRM
Swain, R.					上海	1914–1915	OM
Swallow, R. W.	燕瑞博	英国		福公司	上海,开封	1933–1936	OM
Swan, J. E.	师煌	美国	商人	新丰洋行	上海	1934–1936	OM
Swan, Mrs. A. H.	史温夫人	美国	教士	基督教青年会	上海	1928–1936	OM
Swann, R. N.					上海	1926–1940	LM
Swenson, Rev. Herman	宋益谦	美国	牧师	内地会	固原,西安	1931–1946	CM
Swinhoe, Robert	郇和	英国	领事人员	英国领事馆	厦门	1858–1876	CM
Syburg, F. von		德国	副领事	德国领事馆	上海	1886–1892	OM
Sykes, E. A.				泰和洋行	上海	1909–1924	OM
Syle, Rev. E. W.	帅福守	美国	教士		汉城	1857–1875	RM/CM
Symatinkoff, N.				俄国领事馆	上海	1900–1901	OM
Symons, C.J.F., Dean						1921–1927	OM
Sze, S. C. Thomas					上海	1939–1940	OM

续表

英 文 名	中文名	国籍	身份/职业	部 门	居 住 地 点	在会时间	会员类别
Széchényi, Count Bela		匈牙利			Zinkendorf 匈牙利	1880－1918	CM
T'ang Leang-li			编辑	民众论坛	上海	1933－1940	OM
Tachibana, M.	立华政树	日本	海关人员	海关	上海,大连,青岛	1881 1900－1936	OM
Tai, Dr. T. C.		中国	银行	中国银行	上海	1935－1946	OM
Taintor, E. C.	廷得尔	美国	海关人员			1868－1877	NRM
Takaiwa, K.					上海	1928－1929	OM
Talbot, F. A. W.						1866	NRM
Talbot, G. W.						1864	RM
Talbot, R. M.	铎博贵	美国	海关人员	海关	上海,汕头,南京	1915－1940	OM
Tan, Miss Pai-Men					上海	1946－?	OM
Tan, Mrs. W. H.				上海电力公司	上海	1935－1940	OM
Tangeraas, Anders	汤格柔	挪威	教士	中华信义会湘中总会	益阳	1937－1940	OM
Tanner, H.	田纳	芬兰	外交官			1942－?	OM
Tanner, Paul von	单尔	俄国	海关助理员		福州,汉口,九江,上海	1881－1927	OM
Tapp, W. H.						1865	OM
Tarby, H.				太古洋行	上海	1931－1940	OM
Tarby, Mrs. H.				太古洋行	上海	1931－1939	OM
Tarrant, Wm.	达伦	英国	报人			1864－1868	RM
Tata, D. B., Esq.	泰泰	印度	商人	庚兴洋行	上海	1874－1888	OM
Tata, J. P.						1858－1874	RM
Tate, G.				上海电力公司	上海	1937－1940	OM

续表

英 文 名	中文名	国籍	身份/职业	部 门	居 住 地 点	在会时间	会员类别
Tatz, Prof. L.			教授	美艺有限公司	上海	1937—1940	OM
Tayler, A. Ll.					上海	1885—1927	OM
Tayler, W. H.				圣约翰大学	上海、镇江、九龙	1922—1924	OM
Taylor, F. E.	戴乐安	英国	海关人员	海关		1885—1917	OM
Taylor, G. E.	戴德华	美国	学人	燕京大学	北京	1935—1940	OM
Taylor, George	太罗	英国	海关人员	海关	上海	1891—1901	OM
Taylor, Harry A.				文华大学	武昌	1927—1929	OM
Taylor, Hedley				泰和洋行	上海	1933—1936	OM
Taylor, J. W.	泰罗		商人			1865—1866	RM
Taylor, W. H.		英国	教授	圣约翰大学	上海	1922—1940	OM
Tazaki, Dr. Jinge				商贸高中	长崎	1926—1929	OM
Tchang Si, Dr.				北平动物研究所	北京	1935—1936	OM
Tebbs, J. A.				天主教学堂	上海	1935—1940	OM
Teesadale, J. H.	天赐德	英国	律师	哈华托律师事务所	上海	1908—1936	OM
Teevan, T. Foster				圣约翰大学	上海	1939—1940	OM
Tejldor, Manuel		古巴		外交部	哈瓦那	1910—1911	OM
Telberg, V. G.				北平书局	青岛	1935—1936	OM
Temasi, Dr. G. de					上海	1929—1934	OM
Tenney, Dr. C. D.	丁嘉立	美国	外交官	美国公使馆	北京	1913—1924	OM
Tenney, Dr. T. C.				美国领事馆	南京	1911—1913	OM
Tettenborn, A.	德登赉	德国	外交官			1865—1866	RM

续表

英 文 名	中文名	国籍	身份/职业	部 门	居住地点	在会时间	会员类别
Thackeray, Brigadier.		英国	军人	英军司令部	上海	1935-1940	OM
Thackeray, Mrs. F. S.				英军司令部	上海	1935-1940	OM
Thayer, Judge R. H.				大美国按察使衙门	上海	1909-1915	OM
Thellefsen, E. S.				大北电报公司	上海	1935-1940	OM
Thin, Dr.						1865-1866	RM
Thin, G., M. D.						1868-1877	RM
Thomas, Ivor		加拿大		美孚公司	上海	1924-1934	OM
Thomas, J. A.	唐默思	美国	商人		纽约	1930-1939	OM
Thomas, J. A. T.				晋隆洋行		1890	OM
Thomas, Rev. J.					上海	1913-1936	RM
Thomason, A. B.				利利洋行	上海	1864-1878	RM
Thomason, Miss Lilian	汤默生（女）	美国	大学教师	沪江大学、南长老会	上海	1928-1933	OM
Thompson, Miss A. M.						1942-?	OM
Thomson, Miss A. P.				华懋公司	上海	1940-1946	OM
Thomson, R. L.				泰晤时报	伦敦	1896-1909	OM
Thorbecke, Mme. Ellen				天主教堂	上海	1939-1940	NM
Thorne, C.	唐嘉敦					1864-1877	OM
Thornton, A. E.				雷氏德研究院	上海	1936-1939	OM
Throop, M. H.	都孟高	美国	教士	圣约翰大学、美国圣公会	上海	1912-1946	OM
Thwing, Prof. E. P., M. D.		美国	教授		纽约	1890-?	OM
Thwing, Rev. E. W.	丁义华	美国	牧师	教士公所、美国北长老会	上海	1912-1913	OM

续表

英 文 名	中文名	国 籍	身份/职业	部 门	居 住 地 点	在会时间	会员类别
Thyen, Joh.	提恩	德国	商人		汉口	1894–1908	OM
Tilby, A. R.						1864–1866	RM
Timm, J.				大北电报公司	上海	1891–1894	OM
Timm, J. M.				大北电报公司	上海	1908–1913	OM
Timperley, H. J.	田伯烈	澳大利亚	记者		北京、上海	1931–1933 1936–1940	OM
Ting I-hsien			海关人员	海关统计局	上海	1890–1940	OM
Ting Yen-po					上海	1939–1940	OM
Ting, K. T.				海关总署	上海	1935–1946	OM
Tipton, Rev. W. H.	帕威林	美国	牧师	南长老会	上海	1933–1936	OM
Tirzon, Pablo				工部局新闻处	上海	1922–1924	OM
Tochterman, Karl	德克曼	德国	海关人员	海关	北京	1900–1946	OM/LM
Toda, E., Esq.	多达	西班牙	领事人员			1881–1884	OM
Toeg, I. A.					上海	1935–1946	OM
Toeg, Mrs. S. E.					上海	1935–1946	LM
Tollenaere, Th. de				比利时领事馆	上海	1910–1912	OM
Toller, W. Stark				英国领事馆	上海、宁波、重庆	1907 1912–1934	OM
Tolly, Lieut.					上海	1935–1940	OM
Tomita, Dr. Gunji				上海自然科学研究所	上海	1935–1936	OM
Tong, Pao-shu					上海	1935–1940	LM
Tong, T. E.				天福洋行	上海	1928	OM

续表

英 文 名	中文名	国籍	身份/职业	部门	居住地点	在会时间	会员类别
Torckler, F.						1868	RM
Torrance, Rev. Thos	陶然士	美国	教士	美国圣公会	成都	1909–1910 1922–1940	OM/LM
Touche, J. D. la	德拉图什	英国	海关人员	海关	镇江,秦皇岛,蒙自	1907–1922	OM
Toussaint, G. C.		法国		法国领事馆	上海	1917–1921	OM
Touty, M. H.				拈竹洽洋行	上海	1935–1946	OM
Traver, Miss Edith G.	萘福恩(女)		教士	大英浸礼会	汕头	1926–1929	OM
Tribe, Dr. Ethel N.				伦敦会	上海	1910–1911	OM
Triggs, A. S.						1874–1877	RM
Trivett, Very Rev. Dean, M. A., D. D.			牧师		上海	1932–1936	OM
Trollope, Rt. Rev. Bishop, M. N.			牧师		汉城	1900–1932	LM
Trubner, N.						1865–1866	M
Truebner, Joerg, PH. D.			学者		柏林	1930–1931	OM
Tsai Yuen-Pei	蔡元培	中国				1921–1938	OM
Tsao, Y. H. M. A., ED. D.				基督教青年会第二学校	上海	1935	OM
Tsen, Dr. D. C.				圣约翰大学	上海	1932–1936	OM
Tseng, T. K.				债务委员会	上海	1935–1940	OM
Tseu, Yun-tsing					上海	1940	OM
Tsu, Dr. P. N.				诸圣堂	上海	1935–1940	OM
Tsu, Dr. Y. Y.			教师	圣约翰大学	上海	1935–1936	OM
Tsu, Mrs. Lan-Taung					上海	1935–1946	OM/LM

续表

英 文 名	中文名	国 籍	身份/职业	部 门	居 住 地 点	在会时间	会员类别
Tucker, E. A.				基督教青年会	汉口,杭州	1915－1918	OM
Tucker, G. E.					上海	1911－1936	OM
Tucker, Luther				寰球中国学生会	上海	1938－1940	OM
Tucker,Mrs. G. E.					上海	1911－1936	OM
Tung, Yuh Mou				西湖博物馆	杭州	1935－1940	RM
Turnbull, W. A.						1875－1877	RM
Turner, D.						1864－1866	RM
Turner, J. H. L.	端纳	英国	海关人员	中国海关	上海	1936－1940	OM
Turner, R. C.		英国		工部局	上海	1915－1919	OM
Turner, Skinner, Judge	汤纳	英国	法官	大英按察使司衙门	上海	1916－1927	OM
Turral, G. R.	刁茹乐	英国	外交官	英国领事馆	上海	1941－?	OM
Twentyman, J. R.				韩森洋行,高昌船坞	上海	1890 1894－1928	OM
Twinem, J.	屠迈伦	英国	海关人员	琼州海关	琼州	1885－?	OM
Twyman, B.	德为门	英国	外交官	英国领事馆	上海,镇江	1907－1913	OM
Tyers, R. R.						1866	NRM
Tyler, W. F.	戴理尔	英国	海关人员	海关	上海,北京	1915－1929	OM
Tylor F. E.				海关		1885 1918－1919	OM
Tyson, G.					上海	1865－1866	RM
Uchida, Naosaku	内田直作	日本	学人	东亚同文书院		1933－1940	RM
Underwood, G. R., M. B.	安德威	英国			九江	1888－1894	OM
Ungern-Sternberg, Baroness L. Von				西门子电气公司	上海	1924－1938	OM

续表

英 文 名	中文名	国籍	身份/职业	部门	居住地点	在会时间	会员类别
University Library, The	图书馆	中国	机构	汇文书院图书馆	南京	1923—1930	OM
University of Rangoon, Librarian	图书馆	缅甸	机构	仰光大学图书馆	仰光	1934—1940	OM
University of Shanghai	大学	中国	机构	沪江大学	上海	1936—1938	OM
Unwin F. S.		英国	海关人员	海关	上海	1914—1936	OM
Upersft, Rev. W.	安文		牧师		重庆	1900—1901	OM
Upham, F. S.				工部局	上海	1919—1920	OM
Valdez, J. M. T.	华德师	葡萄牙	外交官	葡萄牙领事馆	上海	1888—1908	OM
Valentin, Prof. Jules		法国	教授	南洋公学	上海	1901—1913	OM
Valk, M. H. van der		荷兰	外交官	荷兰领事馆	广州	1934—1940	OM
Van Corbach, T. B.				爱尔德建筑事务所	上海	1913—1936	OM
Van der Woude, R.					上海	1915—1924	OM
Van Norden, Warner M		美国			纽约	1910—1919	OM
Van Os, A. P.				美华地产公司	上海	1935—1940	OM
Vanderburgh, R. M.				Melo Junior College	上海	1927—1940	OM
Vandervort, Charles T.					加利福尼亚	1930—1936	OM
Vargas, Dr. Phillip de	王克私	瑞士	大学教师	燕京大学、基督教青年会	北京	1933—1946	OM
Vassallo, Capt.						1870—1874	RM
Vauthier, Georges					上海	1921—1924	OM
Verbert, L.					上海	1913—1924	OM
Verea, M. Ancira					上海	1926—1929	OM

续表

英 文 名	中文名	国 籍	身份/职业	部 门	居住地点	在会时间	会员类别
Vereinigung der Freunde des China-Institutes, Frankfurt A./M.			机构		上海	1935–1940	OM
Veryard, Robert K.	费雅	中国		佛郎府中国学院友谊会	长沙	1917–1936	OM
Viguers, R. T.				基督教青年会	武昌	1937–1940	OM
Viguier, S. A.	威基调	法国	海关人员	华中大学	上海	1864–1879	RM
Villard, R. A. de	费拉尔	德国	海关人员	海关	上海	1895–1901	OM
Vincent, A. R.			翻译	海关	上海	1908–1909	OM
Vischer, A.				英国在华领事馆	上海	1864	RM
Visiere, A.			外交官	法国领事馆	北京	1880–1901	OM
Vitale, G.	威达雷	意大利	商人	法国领事馆	北京	1894–1909	OM
Vizenzinovitch, Mrs. V.	魏生取夫人		药商/药剂师	意大利领事馆	上海	1914–1946	OM/LM
Voelkel, S.				咸同贞药房	上海	1885–1910	OM
Vogel, Dr. jur. Werner					上海	1930–1936	LM
Voigt, M.				华懋公寓	上海	1933–1946	LM
Voillemont, E. C.					上马恩省	1888/1915	LM
Volpicelli, Comdr. Z.	武尔披齐	意大利	领事人员	意大利领事馆	香港	1886–1936	OM/CM/LM
Vosy-Bourbon, A.				良济药房	上海	1892–1901	OM
Vouillemont, E. G		法国	银行	华俄道胜银行	上海	1888–1913	LM
Wade, H. T.				上海总会	上海	1886–1901	OM
Wade, R. H. R.	威厚澜	英国	海关人员	海关	上海、天津	1918–1940	OM
Wade, Sir Thomas F.	威妥玛	英国	外交官		北京	1859–1893	HM
Waeber, C.	韦贝	俄国	外交官	同文馆	北京、里加	1894–1913	LM

续表

英 文 名	中文名	国籍	身份/职业	部门	居住地点	在会时间	会员类别
Wagstaff, W. W.				美艺有限公司	上海	1922－1940	OM
Wahl, Capt. D. R.						1937－1940	OM
Wainer, M. S.					上海	1946－?	OM
Wainer, S. A.					上海	1946－?	OM
Wakefield, C. E. S.	伟克非	英国	海关人员	中国海关	长沙	1912－1917	OM
Wakefield, Samuel					上海	1910	OM
Walcott, R. D.				盐务稽核所	Wutingchiao(Via Kiating)四川	1939－1940	OM
Walker, Brigade-Major						1874	NRM
Walker, Dr. Anton				盐务稽核所	上海	1933	OM
Walker, Miss R.			大学教师	圣玛利亚教堂	上海	1929－1940	OM
Walker, Mrs. M. P.	华克大大		大学教师	圣约翰大学	上海	1931－1940	OM
Walker, Dr. W. J. D.		美国		华盛顿大学物理系	纽约	1930－1940	OM/LM
Wall, A. J.				汇丰银行	上海	1937－1938	OM
Wallace, B. K.	武烈士	英国	海关人员	海关	上海	1939－1946	OM
Wallace, D.					福州	1906－1909	OM
Wallberg, R.				顺利洋行	上海	1887－1888	OM
Waller, A. J.				别发洋行	上海	1916－1938	OM
Walline, Rev. Edwin E.	华连	美国	牧师	北长老会	上海	1936－1940	OM
Wallwork, E. E.				模拿印铸机器制造厂	上海	1939－1946	OM
Walsh, T.				亚洲文会会计	上海	1858	OM
Walshe, Rev. W. Gilbert	华立熙	英国	教士		上海	1901	OM

续表

英 文 名	中文名	国籍	身份/职业	部门	居住地点	在会时间	会员类别
Wang, Chi-han					上海	1939-1940	OM
Wang, Chi-yung	王志远	中国	留美博士	上海美术学校	上海	1935-1936	OM
Wang, Chung-hui	王宠惠	中国	政客		上海、北京	1913-1924	OM
Wang, Chung-Yu					汉口	1924-1934	OM
Wang, H. E. Dr. C. T.					上海	1933-1946	LM
Wang, Hsien-Ting				开滦矿务局办事处	上海	1940-?	OM
Wang, Hua Min				海关	天津	1937-1940	OM
Wang, Mrs. T. C.					上海	1935-1936	OM
Wang, S. L., L. L. B.				上海银行大楼	上海	1941-?	OM
Warburg, C. G., Esq.					上海	1882	OM
Ward, Bishop Ralph A.				卫理公会	上海	1946-?	OM
Ward, F. Kingdon				嘉泰洋行	上海	1910-1920	OM
Ward, H. Lipson	华特	英国	律师	哈贷托律师事务所	上海	1928-1936	OM
Ward, Mrs. H. Lipsom	华特夫人				上海	1920-1921	OM
Ward, Mrs. Robert S.	华瑞德	美国	外交官	美国领事馆	福州、天津	1937-1940	OM
Warden, H. H.		美国				1870-1877	NRM
Ware, Miss Alice					上海	1918-1925	OM
Warner, Mrs. C. B.		美国		俄列冈大学艺术博物馆	俄列冈	1925-1946	LM
Warner, Mrs. Murray					芝加哥、旧金山	1909-1917	OM
Warren, R. L.	霍李家	英国	海关人员	海关	上海	1906-1911	OM
Warren, Rev. G. G.	任修本	英国	牧师	循道会	长沙	1909-1926	OM

续表

英文名	中文名	国籍	身份/职业	部门	居住地点	在会时间	会员类别
Warren, Sir Pelham, K. C. M. G.	霍必澜	英国	外交官	英国领事馆	上海	1904–1926	OM/HM/CM
Washbrook, H. G.		英国		福赐德工程事务所	北京、天津	1908–1940	OM/LM
Washbrook, W. A.	倭卜士	英国	海关人员		镇江	1881–1909	OM
Waston, R. A. C.					上海	1930–1934	OM
Watkins, Miss J.					苏州	1914–1920	OM
Watkins, Miss J. H.				金陵大学	南京	1922–1929	OM
Watmore, R.						1865–1866	OM
Watson, Dr. P. T.	万德生	美国	教士	美国公理会	汾州	1920–1946	LM
Watters, T. M. A.	瓦特斯	英国	外交官	英国领事馆	广州、琼州、宜昌	1865–1897	OM
Way, Mrs. W. H.				怡和机器有限公司	上海	1931–1946	OM
Weatherall, M. E.					北京	1919–1924	OM
Webb, Dr. H. W.				工部局卫生处	上海	1928–1936	OM
Webb, Edward	韦伯	英国	外交官	任葡萄牙领事	上海	1858–1866	RM
Webb, Mrs. C. H.					上海	1919–1924	OM
Webster, J.	魏雅各	英国	教士	苏格兰长老会		1866	NRM
Webster, J. A.			领事人员	英国领事馆	上海	1858	RM
Webster, Rev. James			牧师	循道会、协和神学院	宝庆、长沙、武昌	1911–1933 1935–1946	OM
Wei, H.	韦文起	中国	留美博士		上海	1936–1940	OM
Wei, Lott H. T.	韦宪章	中国	留美博士	财政界	上海	1931–1934	OM
Weiss, J.				德国领事馆	上海	1901–1909	OM

附录：皇家亚洲文会北华支会研究

续表

英 文 名	中文名	国籍	身份/职业	部　　门	居 住 地 点	在会时间	会员类别
Welch, A.J.	惠而司	英国	商人	通济洋行	上海	1933-1940	OM
Welch, Bishop Herbert					上海	1929	OM
Welch, W. A.				通济洋行	上海	1933-1935	OM
Well, T. Eliot				美国领事馆	重庆	1937-1940	OM
Wellesley, Gerald E.	魏思勒	英国	商人			1940-?	RM
Wells, Miss Laura	魏懿德(女)	美国	教士	广仁医院,美国圣公会	上海	1878	OM
Wen Yuan-ning	温源宁	中国	编辑	Hsia Monthly	上海	1940-?	OM
Weng, Kochai C., B. A.				开滦煤矿办事处	天津	1935-1940	OM/LM
Wenyon, Rev. Chas		英国	牧师	卫理斯教书局	广州	1929-1946	OM
Wernay, Mrs. Luchia					上海	1892-1901	OM
Werner, E. T. C.	倭讷	英国	领事人员	英国领事馆	北京	1929-1934	OM
West China Union University Library	图书馆	中国	机构	华西协和大学	成都	1915-1940	OM
West, John				别发洋行	上海	1924	OM
Westall, R. R.						1901-1913	RM
Westbrook, Dr. C. H., M. A., PH. D.		美国	教授	沪江大学	上海	1864	OM
Westbrook, E. J.				亚细亚火油公司	上海	1930-1940	OM
Wetmore, W. Shepard	华地玛	美国	商人		上海	1916-1927	RM
Wheeler, G. H.					上海	1860-1884	RM
Wheeler, W. R.		美国	牧师/教师	长老会,金陵大学	杭州,南京	1870-1877	RM
Wheelock, T. R.				会德丰洋行	上海	1919-1936	OM
						1914-1919	OM

499

续表

英文名	中文名	国籍	身份/职业	部门	居住地点	在会时间	会员类别
White, A H.	卫德	英国		老中庸洋行	上海	1915–1918	LM
White, Dr. Hugh H.					上海	1928–1933	OM
White, F. W.	惠达	英国	海关人员		牛庄,汉口,上海	1873–1885	OM
White, head, Miss Edith		美国		美国公理会	上海	1921–1924	OM
White, Miss Laura M.	亮乐月(女)	美国	教士	广学会,美以美会	上海	1916–1938	OM
White, Mrs. T. C.					北京	1912–1913	OM
White, Ralph M.	白本立	美国	教士	长老会	上海	1933–1946	OM
White, Rev. F.J., D.D.	魏馥兰	美国	牧师	沪江大学	上海	1933–1940	OM
White, Rev. H. W.	白秀生	美国	牧师	南长老会	盐城	1915–1923	OM
White, Rt. Rev. Wm. C.	怀履光	加拿大	牧师	英国圣公会	开封	1913–1946	OM/LM
White, T. W.						1876–1877	NRM
White, W. V. D.					济南	1939–1940	OM
Whitearight, A. R.						1913–1915	OM
Whitfield, G.						1864–1870	NRM
Whitgob, E. J.				工部局卫生处	上海	1935–1936	OM
Whitmore, F.						1865–1866	OM
Whittaker, E.					上海	1947–?	OM
Whittall, E.						1865–1877	NRM
Whittall, Jas.					上海	1858	RM
Whittemore, Norman Clark					汉城	1936–1940	OM

续表

英 文 名	中文名	国籍	身份/职业	部 门	居住地点	在会时间	会员类别
Whittick, Prof. F. G.			教授	山东省立大学堂（Imperial College）	济南	1908–1913	OM
Whitty, A. G.						1880	RM
Whyte, Lady		英国		大华饭店	上海	1930–1940	OM
Whyte, Frederick	怀德	英国	外交官	大华饭店	上海	1930–1940	OM
Wickes, Dean R.	卫克思	美国	教士	公理会	临清	1924–1940	OM
Wicking, H.			商人		香港	1877–1888	NRM
Widler, Emile	维勒		商人	锦隆洋行	上海	1923–1936	OM
Wilbur, Mrs. H. A.	韦尔佩		教士	基督教青年会		1920–1946	OM/LM
Wilcox, R. C.			编辑	孖剌报	香港	1877–1901	OM
Wild, Capt.						1866–1875	CM
Wilde, Mrs. H. R.					上海,哈尔滨	1915–1923	OM
Wilden, H. A.	韦礼德	法国	外交官	法国领事馆	上海	1917–1934	OM
Wilder, Amos P.	维礼德	美国	外交官	美国领事馆	上海	1909–1913	OM
Wilder, Dr. Geo. D.	万卓志	美国		公理会	北京,德州	1924–1940	OM
Wildt, R. E.						1939–1940	OM
Wiley, J. Hundley, M. A., PH. D.	怀埃莱	美国	大学教师	沪江大学	上海	1933–1934	OM
Wilfley, L. R.	威尔拂雷		法官			1908–1910	OM
Wilhelm, P.			汉学家	福家洋行	上海	1924–1936	LM
Wilhelm, Pastor Richard	卫礼贤	德国			青岛	1910–1924	OM
Wilkinson, F. E.	伟晋颂	英国	外交官	英国领事馆	福州,沈阳,南京,牛庄	1909–1924	OM
Wilkinson, F. S.				佰丰泰洋行	上海	1911–1946	OM

续表

英 文 名	中文名	国 籍	身份/职业	部 门	居 住 地 点	在会时间	会员类别
Wilkinson, H. P.	威金生	英国	律师	大英按察使司衙门	上海	1909–1934	OM
Wilkinson, Rev. A. H.		英国	牧师		曼彻斯特	1922–1923	OM
Wilkinson, W. H.	务谨顺	英国	外交官	英国领事馆	汕头,宁波	1893–1897	OM
Willbur, Mrs. H. A.					上海	1920 1925–1926	OM
Williams, C. A. S.	威立师	英国	汉学家	海关	北京,温州,镇江	1919–1946	OM/LM
Williams, Capt. C. C.		英国		太古洋行	上海	1918–1935	OM
Williams, H., F. R. G. S.				南德克萨斯大学		1927–1929	OM
Williams, H. D.	威涵励		海关人员			1866–1877	NRM
Williams, Dr. J. T.	威林士	美国	教士	美国浸信会	上海	1925–1946	OM
Williams, P. Watkins					上海	1939–1940	OM
Williams, Prof. E. T., LL. D.	卫理	美国	外交官	美国领事馆,美以美会	上海	1889–1946	CM/OM/HM
Williams, Prof. F. W.	卫斐列	美国	教授	加利福尼亚大学	纽黑文	1895–1927	OM
Williams, S. J.	魏荣华	英国	海关人员	工部局财务处	上海	1920–1921	OM
Williams, S. Wells, L. L. D.	卫三畏	美国	领事人员			1857–1883	RM/HM
Williamson, Rev. A., LL. D.	韦廉臣	英国	教士			1864–1888	CM
Willis, Miss. L.	卫廉美(女)		教士	基督教青年会	上海	1930–1931	OM
Wilson, A. R. D.				扬子保险公司	上海	1921–1929	OM
Wilson, A. Sidney				哈利福托律师事务所	上海	1908–1917	OM
Wilson, D. A.				祥泰木行有限公司	上海	1935–1936	OM
Wilson, G. L., F. S. I.				公和洋行地产部	上海	1921–1940	OM
Wilson, J. H., Esq.	魏素安	美国	海关人员			1883	OM

续表

英文名	中文名	国籍	身份/职业	部门	居住地点	在会时间	会员类别
Wilson, Mrs. Geo. N.				大美长老会	上海	1921-1923	OM
Wilson, R.					上海	1860	RM
Wilson, R. E.	惠理生(女)	美国	教士	南长老会	上海	1912 1918-1929	OM
Wilson, Rev. J. Wallace		英国	牧师	伦敦会	长沙,汉口	1901-1918	OM
Wilton, E. C.	韦礼敦	英国	外交官	英国领事馆	北京,宜昌	1900-1919	OM
Winchester, Dr. C. A.	文极司聪	英国	外交官			1865-1870	NRM
Winford, W.				康记洋行	上海	1907-1909	OM
Wingate, J. D.						1866	NRM
Wingate, Major A. W. S.		英国	军人	英国领事馆	北京	1900-1913	OM
Winter, F. B.				汇丰银行	上海	1931-1940	OM
Winter, R. S.				工部局秘书处	上海	1930-1936	OM
Winterfeldt, Dr. Victoria von	文德斐	德国	外交官	中国银行	上海	1935-1940	OM
Wise, Edgar S.				美国总统轮船公司	上海	1946-?	OM
Wissmann, Prof. Dr. von		德国	教授	中央大学	南京	1932-1936	OM
Witschiebe, C. E.				汇丰银行	上海	1940-?	OM
Witt, Miss E. N.					北京	1912-1924	OM
Wodehouse, H. E.						1870-1877	NRM
Woets, J.				义品放款银行	北京	1919-1924	OM
Wogack, Col.	沃嘎克	俄国	军官	俄国领事馆	天津	1893-1901	OM
Wolcott, R. D.	华克勒	美国	盐务	盐务稽核所	上海	1939-1940	OM
Wolf, Hermann	何忞夫		商人		上海	1901	OM

续表

英 文 名	中文名	国籍	身份/职业	部门	居住地点	在会时间	会员类别
Wong Yun Wu	王云五	中国	出版商	商务印书馆	上海	1927－1940	OM
Wong, Dr. K. C.	黄继祥	中国			上海	1939－1940	OM
Wong, Thompson	王文秀	中国	工商界	柯达公司	上海	1939－1940	OM
Woo, B. Y.					上海	1946－?	OM
Woo, Yao-tchi				海关	上海	1934－1946	OM
Wood, A. G.	羌得	英国	商人	仁记洋行	上海	1875－1934	OM
Wood, Dr. Julia N.				妇孺医院	上海	1914－1919	OM
Wood, J. W.					上海	1859	RM
Wood, Lieut.						1864	RM
Wood, Mrs. E. A. P.				上海自来水公司	上海	1940－?	OM
Wood, Mrs. Edwin					上海	1879	OM
Woodhead, H. G. W.	伍德海	英国	记者	字林西报、东方时务月报	上海	1906－1916 1935－1940	OM
Woodward, A. M. T.	何道华	法国	商人		上海	1921－1936	LM
Worcester, G. R. G.	夏士德	英国	海关人员	海关	上海	1939－1946	OM
Worden, W. L.		美国	军人	德士古火油公司	上海	1940－1946	OM
Worton, Major W. A.	吴尔敦		教士	美国对华军事访问团	重庆	1936－1940	OM
Wright, Miss Elizabeth	文理明（女）	美国	牧师	妇孺医院、内地会	上海	1927－1929	OM
Wright, Rev. H. K.	励德厚			北长老会		1919－1923	OM
Wright, S. F.	魏尔特	英国	海关人员	海关	北京、上海、九江	1916－1946	OM/LM
Wright, T. W.	魏来德	英国	海关人员	海关	上海	1896－1897	OM
Wu Ting-fang, Dr.	伍廷芳	中国	政客		上海	1913－1922	OM

续表

英 文 名	中文名	国 籍	身份/职业	部 门	居 住 地 点	在会时间	会员类别
Wu, Chenfu F.	胡经甫	中国	大学教师	燕京大学	上海	1935-1936	OM
Wu, General Te-Chen	吴铁诚	中国	政客		上海	1935-1946	LM
Wu, John C. H., J. D.	吴经熊	中国			上海	1930-1946	OM/LM
Wu, Lien-teh, Dr.	伍连德	中国	防疫学家	国家检疫所	上海、北京、哈尔滨	1913-1946	OM/LM
Wu, Stephen				印刷厂	上海	1935-1936	OM
Wunsch, Dr. H.					上海	1936	OM
Wurmb, Baron, O. G. von		英国		皇家自由公会	伦敦	1911-1915	OM
Wylie, Alex, Esq.	伟烈亚力	英国	教士	大英圣书公会	上海	1858-1885	CM/HM
Yada, S.				英国领事馆	上海	1924-1928	OM
Yamada, Kenkichi	山田谦吉	日本	学人	东亚同文书院	上海	1921 1932-1934	OM
Yankotsky, George					朝鲜	1932-1936	OM
Yao, S. Y.	姚善友			沪江大学	上海	1947-?	OM
Yard, Rev. J. M.	雅尔德		牧师	美以美会	成都	1920-1921	OM
Yaron, A.				协隆洋行	上海	1941-?	OM
Yates, Smith					上海	1920-1924 1934	OM
Yen, Teng-chien	严敦建	中国	留美博士		苏州、上海	1934-1940 1946-?	OM
Yeo, Yuson	颜慈			佰业地产有限公司	上海	1935-1940	OM
Yetts, Dr. W. Perceval		英国	军官	英国驻华海军部	上海	1909-1946	OM/LM/HM
Ying Wing		中国	上海道台			1869-1870	RM
Ying, H. E.	应宝时					1864	RM

续表

英 文 名	中文名	国籍	身份/职业	部门	居住地点	在会时间	会员类别
Yokoyama, R.	横四赖三	日本		东京商务办	上海	1918－1923	OM
Yonde, F.						1868	NRM
York Club, The	俱乐部	加拿大	机构	纽约总会	多伦多	1920－1924	OM
Youde, F.						1865－1884	OM
Young, C. E.				亚德洋行	上海	1935－1936	OM
Young, Dr. W. Perceval				工部局	上海	1912－1913	OM
Young, Miss M. L.				女子学校	上海	1935－1936	OM
Young, R. C.				工部局	上海	1912－1936	OM
Young, Rev. R.			牧师	教会(美国)	忻口	1913－1918	OM
Young, Reverend R.				内地会		1913	OM
Young, S. C.				警察局	上海	1928－1940	OM
Yui, O. K.					上海	1935－1940	OM
Yule, Col. H., C. B.	裕尔	英国	汉学家		伦敦	1874－1885	HM
Yung Wing	容闳	中国				1868－1870	RM
Zacharice, D. M, M. D.						1870－1877	RM
Zau, F. D.				万国诊所	上海	1928－1932	OM
Zedelius, C., M. D.	新部部	德国	医师	德国领事馆	上海	1885－1894	OM
Zee Zaixiang				卜内硷公司	上海	1935－1936	OM
Zia, Rev. Z. K.				广学会	上海	1931－1933	OM
Zih Dzu Sing			银行	渣打银行	上海	1932－1946	LM
Zimmermann, E. C.	崔美满	美国	教士	路德会	沙市	1938－1946	OM/LM
Zindel, W. A.				瑞记洋行	上海	1937－1940	OM

续表

英 文 名	中文名	国 籍	身份/职业	部 门	居 住 地 点	在会时间	会员类别
Zooyef, Dr.		俄国		俄国领事馆	上海	1890-1897	OM
Zottoli, Père Angelot S. J.	晁德莅	意大利		耶稣会徐家汇	上海	1886-1901	HM
Zwemer, Rev. Samuel M.		美国	牧师	普林斯顿神学院	普林斯顿,开罗	1917-1946	OM/LM

参 考 文 献

一、论　　文

王毅:《皇家亚洲文会北中国支会述论》,《复旦学报》2003年第5期。

胡道静:《历史上以上海为研究对象的学术团体》,《档案与历史》1998年第2期。

张海林:《上海亚洲文会述论》,《南京大学学报》1996年第1期。

赖特(C. H. Wright)著、李国鼎译:《西洋杂志之沿革》,《图书馆学季刊》第四卷第一期。

陈潜:《西人译中国书籍及在中国发行之报章》,《东方杂志》第五卷第九期。

傅振伦:《中国博物馆史略》,《东方杂志》十一卷十五号。

Perceval Yetts 著、汪家正译:《不列颠的中国研究》,《东方杂志》第四十一卷二十二号。

(日)石田干之助:《欧人之汉学研究》,《中法大学月刊》第五卷第一号。

姚从吾:《欧洲学者对于匈奴的研究》,《国学季刊》第二卷第三期。

芮逸夫:《僚(獠)为仡佬(犵狫)试证》,《历史语言研究所集刊》第二十册(上册),民国三十七年。

聂斯克著、张玛丽译:《西夏语研究小史》,《国立北平图书馆馆刊》第四卷第三期。

陈受颐:《鲁滨孙的中国文化观》,《岭南学报》,第一卷第三期。

谭卓垣:《广州的定期刊物调查》,《岭南学报》第四卷第三期。

柯老斯(F. A. Krauze)著、姚从吾译:《蒙古史发凡》,《辅仁学志》第一卷第二期。

袁同礼:《中国音乐书举要》,《图书馆季刊》第四卷第三期。

吴元涤:《植物学分类发达史》,《博物学杂志》第一卷第四期。

经利彬:《谭微道在中国生物学上之贡献》,《真理杂志》第一卷第四期(1944年)。

胡隽吟:《中德学会与中德文化》,《中德学志》,第五卷第一、二期合订本(1943年)。

《史禄国博士逝世》,《科学》第二十四卷第三期。

《西洋汉学论文提要》,《史学消息》,第一卷第一期。

《亚细亚协会图书馆将停办》,《中华图书馆协会会报》第六卷第二期。

《亚洲文会图书馆兴工重建》,《中华图书馆协会会报》第六卷第五期。

《上海文化的现状》,《中华图书馆协会会报》第十三卷第一期(1938年7—9月)。

《倡设公共图书馆之商榷》,《申报》1922年4月14日。

《上海应该设美术科学博物院谈》,《申报》1922年7月7日。

《主设美术博物院之继起》,《申报》1922年7月10日。

《江亢虎当选亚洲文会会员》,《申报》1923年11月2日。

《亚洲文会正式落成》,《申报》1933年2月25日。

《亚洲文会经济极感困乏》,《申报》1937年6月26日。

谭维理:《1830—1920年美国人之汉学研究》,《清华学报》(台湾)新二卷第二期(1961年)。

王萍:《西方算学之输入》,《中研院近代史研究所专刊》第17辑(1966年)。

胡光麃:《百余年来影响我国的六十名洋客》,《传记文学》第三十五卷第三期。

黄汲青:《中国地质科学的主要成就》,《中国科技史料》1983年第3期。

中国历史第一档案馆:《第一次鸦片战争后福州问题史料》,《历史档案》1990年第2期。

张寄谦:《哈佛燕京学社》,《近代史研究》1990年第3期。

吴凤鸣:《1840年至1911年外国地质学家在华调查与研究工作》,《中国科技史料》1992年第1期。

茅海建:《关于广州反入城斗争的几个问题》,《近代史研究》,1992年第6期。

张洪顺:《马戛尔尼和阿美士德对华评价与态度的比较》,《近代史研究》1992年第3期。

戚文娟:《上海文物整理仓库的历史功绩》,《上海文化史志通讯》1994年第33期。

周振鹤:《〈六合丛谈〉综论》,《中华文史论丛》第61辑。

王开玺:《鸦片战争前后清政府制夷思路探论》,《近代史研究》1995年第6期。

王世伟:《上海公共图书馆发展史略》,《图书馆杂志》1998年第1期。

(法)高第著、马军译:《对英国汉学家伟烈亚力的回忆》,《中国史研究动态》1998年第5期。

《晚清欧人在华游历历史资料》,《历史档案》2002年第2期。

马军:《博物院路与中西文化交流》,《读书》2002年第1期。

杨志刚:《博物馆与中国近代以来公共意识的拓展》,《复旦学报》1999年第3期。

耿昇:《西方汉学界对开封犹太人调查研究的历史与现状》,《西北第二民族学院学报》2000年第4期。

马军:《上海社科院西文汉学旧籍简介》(四),《史林》2003年第4期。

王树槐:《卫三畏与〈中国丛刊〉》,见林治平编《近代中国与基督教论文集》,宇宙光出版社1981年版。

丁建弘、李霞:《中德学会与中德文化交流》,见黄时鉴主编《东西交流论谭》,上海文艺出版社1998年版。

(德)傅吾康(Wolfgang Franke)著,陈燕、袁媛译:《十九世纪的欧洲汉学》,《国际汉学》第七辑,大象出版社2002年版。

阎纯德:《汉学和西方的汉学研究》,《汉学研究》(第三集),中国和平出版社1998年版。

李学勤:《〈法国汉学〉序》第一辑,清华大学出版社1996年版。

柳存仁:《从利玛窦到李约瑟:汉学研究的过去与未来》,转引自林徐典《汉学研究之回顾与前瞻》(文学语言卷),中华书局1995年版。

二、专　　著

1. 中文

《上海指南》卷四《公益团体》,商务印书馆,宣统元年。

贝德士编:《西方东方学报论文举要》,金陵大学中国文化研究所印行,民国二十二年。
李璜译述:《古中国的跳舞与神秘故事》,中华书局1933年版。
冯陈祖怡编:《上海各国图书馆概揽》,中国国际图书公司1934年版。
杨遵仪编:《中国地质文献目录》,国立北平研究院总办事处出版课印行,民国二十四年。
胡道静:《上海图书馆史》,上海通志馆期刊抽印本,1935年。
苏阿德著、戚铭远译:《中国博物学:上海博物院指南》,亚洲文会北华支会,1937年。
岑德彰编译:《上海租界略史》,劝业书局,民国二十六年。
(美)霍塞著、越裔译:《出卖上海滩》,大地出版社1941年版。
丁则良译:《东方学》,人民出版社1954年版。
上海图书馆编:《前亚洲文会图书馆图书目录》,1955年打印稿。
马士:《中华帝国对外关系史》第一卷,生活·读书·新知三联书店1957年版。
(美)泰勒·丹涅特著、姚广译:《美国人在东亚》,商务印书馆1959年版。
中国科学院地理研究所编:《中国地貌学文献目录1855—1958》,科学出版社1960年版。
黄苇:《上海开埠初期对外贸易研究》,上海人民出版社1961年版。
陶振誉等著:《世界各国汉学研究论文集》(第一辑),台湾"国防研究院"印行,1968年。
(英)李约瑟著《中国科学技术史》第一卷第一分册,科学出版社1975年版。
中国社科院新闻研究所"新闻研究资料"编辑室编辑:《新闻资料研究》,第三辑,新华出版社1981年版。
李希泌、张淑华编:《中国古代藏书与近代图书馆史料(春秋至五四前后)》,中华书局1982年版。
杜石然等编:《中国科学技术史稿》(下),科学出版社1983年版。
广东文史研究馆译:《鸦片战争史料选译》,中华书局1983年版。
(英)亨利·莱昂斯著、陈先贵译:《英国皇家学会史》,云南省机械工程学会、云南省学会研究会,1985年。
(美)R. K. 默顿著,范岱年、吴忠、蒋效东译:《十七世纪英国的科学技术与社会》,四川人民出版社1986年版。
孙越生:《俄国的中国学家》,见中国社会科学文献情报中心编《俄苏中国学手册》,中国社会科学出版社1986年版。
莫东寅:《汉学发达史》,上海书店1989年版。
李志刚:《基督教与近代中国文化论文集》,宇宙光出版社,1989年版。
张孟闻:《中国科学史举隅》,《民国丛书》第一编第90册,上海书店1989年版。
岑家梧:《中国艺术论集》,《民国丛书》第二编第66册,上海书店1989年版。
福开森著、毛一心译:《中国建筑史概论》,《民国丛书》第五编第87辑,上海书店1989年版。
章鸿钊:《中国地质学发展小史》,《民国丛书》第二编第88册,上海书店1989年版。
戈公振:《中国报学史》,《民国丛书》第二编49册,上海书店1990年版。
胡道静:《上海博物院史略》,见《上海研究资料续集》,《民国丛书》第四编第81册,上海书店1993年版。

郭卫东主编:《近代外国在华文化机构综录》,上海人民出版社1993年版。

中国植物学会编:《中国植物学史》,科学出版社1994年版。

张国刚:《德国的汉学研究》,中华书局1994年版。

高平叔主编:《蔡元培文集——卷八·语言文字》,锦绣出版事业公司1995年版。

《上海文物博物馆志》,上海社科院出版社1997年版。

李天纲:《中国礼仪之争:历史·文献和意义》,上海古籍出版社1998年版。

黄时鉴:《东西文化交流史论稿》,上海古籍出版社1998年版。

(法)戴仁主编,耿昇译:《法国当代中国学》,中国社会科学出版社1998年版。

中国地名委员会编:《外国地名译名手册》(中型本),商务印书馆1998年版。

薛理勇主编:《上海掌故辞典》,上海辞书出版社1999年版。

熊月之主编:《上海通史》第六卷(晚清文化卷),上海人民出版社1999年版。

熊月之主编:《上海通史》第十五卷(附录),上海人民出版社1999年版。

(英)约·罗伯茨编著,蒋重跃、刘林海译:《十九世纪西方人眼中的中国》,时事出版社1999年版。

方汉奇:《中国新闻事业编年史》(上),福建人民出版社2000年版。

汪晓勤:《中西科学交流的功臣——伟烈亚力》,科学出版社2000年版。

上海档案馆编:《工部局董事会会议录》(第五册),上海古籍出版社2001年版。

黄光域编:《中国近代专名翻译词典》,四川人民出版社2001年版。

陈伯海主编:《上海文化通史》,上海文艺出版社2001年版。

曹伯言整理:《胡适日记全编》(五),安徽教育出版社2001年版。

顾犇:《中国国家图书馆外文善本书目》,北京国书馆出版社2001年版。

叶再生:《中国近现代出版通史》,华文出版社2002年版。

陈以爱:《中国现代学术研究机构的兴起——以北大研究所国学门为中心的探讨》,江西教育出版社2002年版。

葛兆光:《域外中国学十论》,复旦大学出版社2002年版。

戈公振:《中国报学史》,上海古籍出版社2003年版。

梁元生著,陈同译:《上海道台研究——转变社会中之联系人物,1843—1890》,上海古籍出版社2003年版。

2. 英文

Wylie, A. , *The Jewish Roll from Kai-Fung-Foo*, Notes and Queries on China and Japan, 1868, Vol. II, Oct.

A Catalogue of the Library of the China Branch of the Royal Asiatic Society Includeing the Library of Alex Wylie, Shanghai, Printed at the "Ching-Foong" General Printing office, 1872.

A Catalogue of the Library of the China Branch of the Royal Asiatic Society, Shanghai, Printed at the "Shanghai Mercury" office, 1881.

A Catalogue of the Library of the China Branch of the Royal Asiatic Society, Shanghai, Kelly and Walsh limited, 1894.

Ayscough, Florence Wheelock, "Preface to the Fouth Edition" in the Catalogue of the North China Branch of the Royal Asiatic Society, Shanghai, 1909, ppvi-ix.

Otness, Harold M: The one bright spot in shanghai: A history of the Library of the North China Branch of the Royal Asiatic Society, Journal of the Hong Kong Branch of the Asiatic Society (Hong Kong), Vol. 28, 1988.

Municipal Council, Shanghai: Report for the year ended 31st Dec 1885, Kelly & Walsh, Limited., 1886.

George Lanning & Samuel Couling: The History of Shanghai, Shanghai, Kelly & Walsh, Ltd., 1921.

Frederick Eden Pargiter Compiled, Centenary Volume of the Royal Asiatic Society of the Great Britain and Ireland 1823 −1923, Published by the Royal Asiatic Society, London, 1923.

Kennth Scott Latourette, A History of Christian Mission in China, New York, 1929.

W. Y. Chyen Compiled and Edited, Handbook of Cultural Institutions in China, Chinese National Committee on Intellectual Co-operation, Shanghai, 1936.

Stuart Simmons and Simon Digby, The Royal Asiatic Society: its history and treasures, Leiden: Published for the Royal Asiatic Society by E. T. Brill, 1979.

Borton M. Scwartz, Robert H. Eward, Culture and Society, Taibei, 1972.

Lodwick, Kathleen L., The Chinese recorder index: a guide to Christian missions in Asia, 1867 −1941, Scholarly Resources Inc., c1986.

3. 法文

LEP. JERôME TOBAR. S. J., Inscriptions Juives de K'Ai-Fong-Fou, Chang-Hai Imprimerie de La Mission Catholoque Orphelinat de T'ou-SÈ-Wè, 1900.

4. 日文

小竹文夫:《上海の英国亚细亚学会北支那支会图书馆》,见东亚同文书院支那研究部:《支那研究》第十九号(昭和四年(1930年)五月发行)。

山口昇编:《欧米人の支那に于けろ文化事业》,佐原研究室出版,上海日本堂发行,大正十年(1921年)。

石田干之助:《欧米人に於けろ支那学の现况》,见东亚同文会调查编辑部编:《支那》,1929年7−9月号。

石田干之助:《欧米人に於けろ支那研究》,东京创元社昭和十七年(1942年)刊行,第105−112页。

满铁上海事务所编:《上海アヅア学会北支那支部の杂志编纂主任 Galeの记事》,《满铁调查资料》,第十一所揭,昭和七年十二月。

姊崎正治:《欧米人の东洋学现况》,东亚同文会发行《支那》,昭和八年十二月号。

满铁调查部:《英国王立亚细亚学会北支支部志索引》,昭和十五年十二月。

上海市政研究会编:《上海の文化》,华中铁道刊,昭和十九年三月。

三、报　　刊

1. 西文

《皇家亚洲文会北华支会会刊》(Journal of the North China Branch of the Royal Asiatic Society)，1858—1948年。

《北华捷报》(North China Herald)，1851—1910年。

《字林西报》(North China Daily News)，1935—1951年。

《皇家亚洲学会中国支会纪要》(Transactions of the China Branch of the Royal Asiatic Society)，1847年。

《工部局年报》(Municipal Council Shanghai：Report for the year from 1864—1941年)。

《中国丛报》(Chinese Repository)，1831—1851年。

《通报》(T'oung Pao)，1890—1951年。

《华裔学志》(Monumenta Serica)，1933—1948年。

《教务杂志》(The Chinese Recorder)，1861—1941年。

《中国评论》(China Review)，1872—1901年。

《新中国评论》(The New China Review)，1920—1924年。

《哈佛亚洲研究》(Journal of Asiatic Studies)，1936—1952年。

《远东博物院集刊》(Bulletin of the Museum of Far Eastern Antiquities) 1929—1951年。

《远东季刊》(The Far Eastern Quarterly)，1934—1948年。

《华西边疆研究会会报》(Journal of the West China Border Research)，1922—1946年。

《中国科学与美术杂志》(The China Journal of Science & Arts)，1923—1943年。

《美国东方学会会报》(Journal of the American Oriental Society)，1899—1940年。

《大不列颠及爱尔兰皇家亚细亚学会会报》(Journal of the Royal Asiatic Society of Great Britain & Ireland)，1875—1952年。

《亚洲学报》(Journal Asiatique)，1922—1938年。

《东亚杂志》(Ostasiatische Zeitschrift)，1938年。

《法兰西远东语言学校校刊》(Bulletin de L'ecole Francaise D'Extréme-Orient Hanoi) 1918—1938年。

《汉学杂志》(Sinica)、1925—1936年。

《东方学院学报》(Bulletin of the School of Oriental Studies)，1917—1939年。

《东洋文库研究纪要》(Memoirs of the Research Department of the Toyo Bunko)，1926—1938年。

《亚洲艺术评论》(Revue Des Arts Asiatiques)，1932年。

《中国社会及政治学报》(The Chinese Social and Political Science Review)，1928—1941年。

2. 中文

《东方杂志》，1904—1948年。

《科学》,1915—1920 年,1928—1941 年。
《国立中央研究院史语所集刊》,1928—1949 年。
《国学季刊》,1923—1951 年。
《史学消息》,1936—1937 年。
《燕京学报》,1927—1951 年。
《辅仁学志》,1928—1947 年。
《清华学报》,1924—1947 年。
《国闻周报》,1922—1937 年。
《图书季刊》,1939—1946 年。
《国立北平图书馆馆刊》,1928—1937 年。
《中法大学月刊》,1931—1937 年。
《中华图书馆协会会报》,1925—1946 年。
《国立中山大学语言历史研究所集刊》,1929—1937 年。
《地学杂志》,1910—1919 年。
《北平图书馆月刊》,1928—1929 年。
《社会科学》(北大),1922—1936 年。
《史地学报》,1921—1926 年。
《国立武汉大学社会科学季刊》,1930—1938 年。
《国立武汉大学文哲季刊》,1930—1942 年。

3. 日文

《东方学报》(日文),1929—1933 年。

四、档　案

《自然博物馆情况报告(1956 年 3 月 3 日)》、《上海市文化局·社文:文化部关于召开全国博物馆工作会议的通知及我局汇报上海各博物馆的工作报告》,上海市档案馆档案号:B172-1-220。